Simple

Intuitive, bite-sized lessons look and feel like games, to keep students engaged. Finely tuned algorithms evaluate learner responses and tailor the content through spaced repetition. In addition, the app lets instructors track student progress toward specific milestones.

Mobile

Duolingo lets students learn and practice on their mobile devices whenever they find the time and wherever inspiration strikes. This mobility, together with push notifications to remind students to practice, encourages consistent daily practice.

Fun

Duolingo uses elements of gamification—point scoring and social competition with others—to keep students engaged and moving forward as they acquire new language skills.

Dedicado a Manuel Eduardo Zayas-Bazán Recio (1912–1991)

Y a Mabel J. Cameron (1914–2004)

Y a Dorothy Marcella Kronk Nibert (1914–1994)

"Y aunque la vida murió, nos dejó harto consuelo su memoria"
—JORGE MANRIQUE

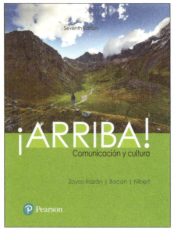

Every year thousands of adventurous travelers walk the Inca Trail to reach Machu Picchu, one of the Seven Wonders of the World. Some stretches of the trip are easier than others. The trail is unpredictable and ever-changing, but there is always something new to discover: a different vista, another stream, a new mountain to cross. Embarking on the discovery of a new language is a similar experience. As you develop your cross-cultural and language competence, you will discover, step after step, new products, practices, and perspectives that define the fascinating cultures of the Spanish-speaking world. We hope that by the end of this program, you will look back and realize how far you have traveled!

¡ARRIBA!

Comunicación y cultura

SEVENTH EDITION

Eduardo Zayas-Bazán
Emeritus, East Tennessee State University

Susan M. Bacon
Emerita, University of Cincinnati

Holly J. Nibert
The Ohio State University

Pearson

330 Hudson Street, New York, NY 10013

Executive Editor of Courseware Portfolio Management: Amber Chow
Editor in Chief: Carolyn Merrill
Director of Market Development: Helen Richardson Greenlea
Senior Field Marketing Manager: Mellissa Yokell
World Languages Consultants: Yesha Brill, Doug Brauer, Raúl J. Vázquez López
Product Development Manager: Bridget Funiciello
Managing Editor: Harold Swearingen
Program Manager: Ana Piquinela
Senior Development Editor: Sarah Link
Senior Digital Media Manager: Amy Gibbons
Producer, Production & Digital Studio for MyLab Spanish: Amanda Albert Podeszedlik
Project Coordination, Text Design, and Electronic Page Makeup: Lumina Datamatics
Cover Designer: Jill Ort
Cover Illustration/Photo: Anna Gorin
Manufacturing Buyer: Roy Pickering
Printer/Binder: LSC Communications
Cover Printer: Phoenix Color/Edwards Brothers

Library of Congress Cataloging-in-Publication Data
Names: Zayas-Bazán, Eduardo. | Bacon, Susan M. | Nibert, Holly J.
Title: ¡Arriba! : comunicación y cultura / Eduardo Zayas-Bazán, Susan M. Bacon, Holly J. Nibert.
Description: Seventh edition. | New York : Pearson, 2017.
Identifiers: LCCN 2017045981 | ISBN 9780134813738
Subjects: LCSH: Spanish language—Textbooks for foreign speakers—English.
Classification: LCC PC4112 .Z38 2017 | DDC 468.2/421—dc23
LC record available at https://lccn.loc.gov/2017045981

2 18

 Pearson

Student Edition
ISBN-10: 0-13-481373-1
ISBN-13: 978-0-13-481373-8

Annotated Instructor Edition:
ISBN-10: 0-13-489257-7
ISBN-13: 978-0-13-489257-3

A la Carte Edition:
ISBN-10: 0-13-487756-X
ISBN-13: 978-0-13-487756-3

Brief Contents

Scope and Sequence

STRUCTURES	CULTURE	READING / WRITING

Preface

Let ¡Arriba! guide you on your journey to learning Spanish

Welcome to the adventure of learning Spanish, and to *¡Arriba!, 7ᵗʰ edition*, your introduction to Spanish language and its rich and vibrant cultures. We offer the features that have made *¡Arriba!* a top-selling introductory college program, while remaining faithful to our promise to make it dynamic, flexible, and current.

For *¡Arriba!, 7ᵗʰ edition*, we have reenvisioned our content to perform more effectively in **MyLab Spanish** and we have partnered with **Duolingo**, an exciting language learning tool that makes language practice mobile, simple, and fun. We continue to offer the printed Student Edition, as well as the Annotated Instructor's Edition. Our goal is to deliver a flexible and highly personalized approach that will meet the varied needs of instructors and students, whether instruction is face-to-face, hybrid, or online. Moreover, with help from a core panel of reviewers, we have made many important and exciting changes to the Student program. Finally, you will see that the list of online supplements provides a simple, straightforward teaching and learning experience.

Make language practice fun with Duolingo!

More than 150 million people have used **Duolingo**'s simple, game-like interface to help them learn a language.

Now Pearson has partnered with **Duolingo** to bring our market-leading content to their award-winning and fun mobile language learning app.

Pair **Duolingo** with *¡Arriba!* and your students will have access to exclusive digital content that is aligned to the program and designed to help higher education language learners succeed in the classroom and beyond.

What's new with MyLab Spanish?

Part of the world's leading collection of online homework, tutorial, and assessment products, Pearson **MyLab Languages** is designed with a single purpose in mind: to improve the results for all higher education students, one student at a time.

Revolutionary and evolutionary.   Created by and for language instructors and learners, and based on years of research and data collection from over one million users, **MyLab Spanish** brings together a wide array of language-learning tools and resources in one convenient, easily navigable site. The *¡Arriba!* **MyLab Spanish** course includes an interactive version of the student text, an online student activities manual, and all audio and video materials. Additional tools, including Vocabulary and Grammar tutorials, English Grammar Readiness checks, and practice tests personalize instruction to meet the unique needs of individual students. Instructors can use the system to create assignments, set grading parameters, review and create student synchronous video and asynchronous audio activities, and provide feedback on student work. For more information, visit us at www.pearson.com/mylab/languages.

NEW! Updated fresh look.   The overall look and feel of **MyLab Spanish** was refreshed to give students and instructors a modern, clean, and user-friendly experience. No new course download is needed—simply log in and experience the new look and feel.

NEW! Enhanced course organization and delivery of materials.   For *¡Arriba!*, *7th edition*, we have thoroughly revised and organized the student component list to offer a more streamlined, straightforward learning experience. The supplement list includes:

- eText activities, including all audio and video content
- Integrated Performance Assessments and Can-Do Surveys. This brand new supplement appears at point of use, every two or three chapters.
- Student Activities with robust functionality to include audio, video, **MediaShare**, **LiveChat**, **WeSpeke**, and a variety of highly interactive activities. Using guided activities available in **MyLab Spanish**, students practice language, share cultures, and explore interests within **WeSpeke**, a social network for online practice and cultural exchange. Afterwards, they summarize their interactions.
- Flashcards and Tutorials
- Practice Tests
- Audio program
- *Club cultura* video program—both the select edited versions featured in the Student edition and the unabridged versions
- *Entrevistas* video program

Featuring Integrated Performance Assessments (IPAs) and *Can-Do Statements* in MyLab Spanish!

Driven by market research and with the help of experts from the field, we have incorporated **Integrated Performance Assessments (IPAs)** and *NCSSFL-ACTFL Can-Do Statements* into our program to help instructors guide and assess learner progress. As students progress through the course, instructors can assign IPA tasks to complete online every two or three chapters. The IPA tasks use authentic sources and focus on real-life contexts that students will find both engaging and meaningful. The ample activities, variety of comprehension and production strategies, and authentic text formats in the Student Edition direct students toward the communicative goals set out by the IPA tasks. To assist instructors with planning, the AIE indicates the activities in the Student Edition that target each of the three modes of communication: Interpretive, Interpersonal, and Presentational.

After each IPA task, students will complete a self-assessment based on the Can-Do Statements. This self-assessment is designed to help students track their own progress towards specific levels of proficiency. Both features will be available online in **MyLab Spanish** at specific points in the course.

LiveChat is the synchronous audio and video recording tool that provides students with the opportunity to speak with their classmates online in pairs or in groups.

With a fresh journalistic approach, the *Club cultura* video program brings the Spanish-speaking world to life through vibrant video episodes shot on location in 22 Spanish-speaking countries, including the United States.

What's new to the Student Program?

An exciting new design. The newly designed *¡Arriba!, 7ᵗʰ edition*, gives students and instructors a modern, clean, and user-friendly experience.

Vibrant new chapter openers. Each chapter opens up with a fine art image and a *Club cultura* video shot on location in the region of focus. Students can explore online details of the art piece and reflect on how the images relate to cultural products, practices, and perspectives.

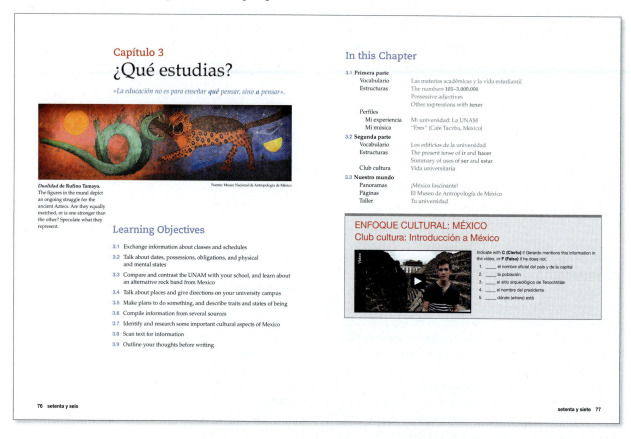

Logical sequence of activities. Activities in both *Vocabulario* and *Estructuras* move consistently from meaningful, form-focused reception to communicative self-expression.

Simplified, easy to implement info-gap activities. *¡Necesito información!* activities have straightforward directions that quickly get students on task to problem-solve or role-play situations related to the chapter's cultural and thematic focus.

Improved vocabulary presentations. Based on thoughtful feedback from instructors, the revised *Vocabulario* sections purposefully integrate and highlight key vocabulary into the introductory contextualized dialogues. In addition, the revised *Vocabulario* lists provide a more cohesive presentation of high-frequency expressions.

Revised grammar presentations. While keeping the same thoroughness of the previous edition, the streamlined and visually appealing grammar explanations in *Estructuras* help students grasp concepts more easily as they study on their own.

New self-assessment in presentations. *¿Comprendes?*, a quick self-check activity in each vocabulary and grammar presentation, helps students confirm that they are ready to move forward, or that they should review the presentation again. *¿Recuerdas?* activities, placed before appropriate grammar presentations, help students connect previous knowledge to what they are about to learn.

¿Comprendes? Complete the sentences with **por** or **para**.

Teníamos pasajes (1) _____ Nueva York. (2) _____ eso, caminamos (3) _____ la terminal y buscamos el mostrador de Avianca. Compramos un sándwich (4) _____ comer en el avión.

Respuestas: 1. para; 2. Por; 3. por; 4. para

Updated cultural topics with a personal and authentic glimpse into the cultures of the Spanish-speaking world. While keeping our approach of weaving culture throughout the chapter, we have updated the following features:

- *Perfiles*: Updated *Mi experiencia* readings reflect current cultural practices in the Spanish-speaking world. *Mi música* artists represent diverse musical genres, and appeal to students' musical interests with award-winning artists, such as Calle 13 (Puerto Rico), Ana Tijoux (Chile), and Bebe (Spain).

- *Cultura en vivo* and *Presencia hispana*: These short cultural notes in English have been updated to present relevant information about related cultural topics, and Hispanics in the United States.

- *Club cultura* **video integrated into the Student Edition:** Based on your feedback, we now feature select short clips of the engaging, journalistic-style *Club cultura* video series. They appear first in the chapter opener as a cultural advance organizer, and later in the new *Club cultura* video section. The carefully designed activity sequence, including listening/viewing strategies, helps students access key points of the videos. These thematic videos explore contemporary cultural practices and aspects of daily life, such as university life at the UNAM, foods from Chile, and African influence in Cuban music.

- *Panoramas*: The cultural spread features new images, topics, and insights to both engage and inform students.

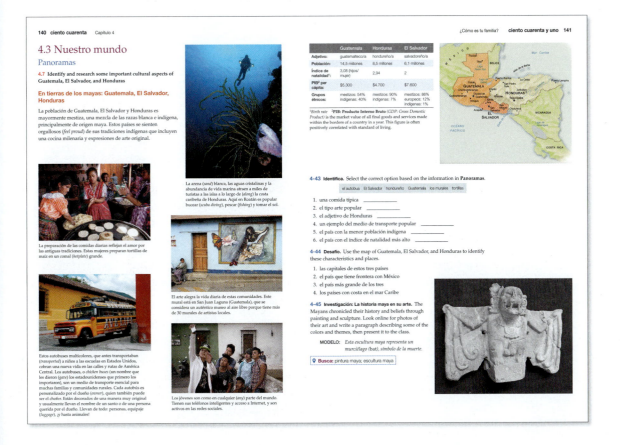

Revised *Páginas* section to develop reading skills. The revised *Páginas* section includes several new readings, and now features a reading strategy and an activity sequence to put it into practice.

Revised *Taller* section to develop writing with confidence. The revised *Taller* section includes several new writing tasks, and now features a writing strategy and an activity sequence designed to put it into practice.

What's new to the Instructor Resources?

Annotated Instructor Edition (AIE). Teacher annotations have been completely updated and continue to offer robust instructional support to instructors in a variety of categories, including the ACTFL standards and IPA preparation, pedagogy, culture, and additional activities.

The **Instructor Resources (IR)** provide additional teaching materials, available for download within **MyLab Spanish** and on our **Instructor Resource Center (IRC)**. The materials have been revised to ensure a straightforward presentation. The site also includes the *¡Arriba!* teaching philosophy, sample syllabi, full lesson plans, audio and video scripts, Testing Program, PowerPoint Presentations, and much more!

Testing Program. The fully online *¡Arriba!* **Testing Program** has been carefully edited to ensure close coordination with the main text and the **Student Activities**. Available within **MyLab Spanish** is a user-friendly test-generating program known as **MyTest** that allows instructors to select, arrange, and customize testing modules to meet the needs of their courses. Once created, tests can be printed on paper or administered online. The recordings in the **Audio Testing Program** that accompany the listening comprehension activities are also available within **MyLab Spanish**.

PowerPoint Presentations. These visual aids have been updated to reflect changes to the scope and sequence. They include visual materials from the textbook, together with dynamic presentations on each grammar point covered in the text.

Acknowledgments

The *¡Arriba!* program is the result of careful planning between ourselves and Pearson, and ongoing collaboration with students and you—our colleagues—who have been using each of our editions. We look forward to continuing this dialogue and sincerely appreciate your input. We owe special thanks to the many members of the Spanish teaching community whose comments and suggestions helped shape the pages of every chapter.

We gratefully acknowledge and thank our reviewers for the Seventh Edition:

Maria G. Akrabova, *Metropolitan State University of Denver*
Ana E. Almonte, *Hudson Valley Community College*
Frances Alpren, *Vanderbilt University*
Luz María Álvarez, *Johnson County Community College*
Stephanie M. Álvarez, *University of Texas-Pan American*
Raysa Amador, *Adelphi University*
Stacy Amling, *Des Moines Area Community College, Boone Campus*
Debra Andrist, *Sam Houston State University*
José Badillo, *Metropolitan Community College in Omaha, Nebraska*
Dimaris Barrios-Beltrán, *Amherst College*
Sonia Barrios Tinoco, *Seattle University*
Yasmine Beale-Rivaya, *Texas State University*
Mara-Lee Bierman, *Rockland Community College*
Marie Blair, *University of Nebraska-Lincoln*
Miryan Boles, *Texas Southern University*
Laura H. Bradford, *Salt Lake Community College*
Lillie Busby, *Sam Houston State University*
Julia Bussade, *University of Mississippi*
Alicia T. Casals, *Texas Southern University*
Zoila Castro, *University of Rhode Island*
Lina L. Cofresí, *North Carolina Central University*
Christine Coleman Núñez, *Kutztown University of Pennsylvania*
Heather Colburn, *Northwestern University*
Debra Currere, *Northern Illinois University*
John B. Davis, *Indiana University South Bend*
William Deaver, *Armstrong Atlantic State University*
Héctor Enríquez, *University of Texas at El Paso*
Bruce K. Fox, *St. Johns River State College*
David F. Hanson, *University of Puget Sound*
Kimberly Harris, *Boise State University*
Brent Hart, *College of Western Idaho*
Catherine Hebert, *Indiana University South Bend*
Qiu Y. Jiménez, *Bakersfield College*
Assen Kokalov, *Purdue University North Central*
Suzanne LaVenture, *Davidson County Community College*
Jeanine LeMieux, *Mott Community College*
Allison Libbey Titus, *University of Wisconsin-Milwaukee*
Maria Lipson, *Community College of Baltimore County*
Victoria Maillo, *Amherst College*
Sandra Mulryan, *Community College of Baltimore County*
Jamilet Ortiz, *Housatonic Community College*
Jodie Parys, *University of Wisconsin-Whitewater*
Nilsa O. Pérez-Cabrera, *Blinn College*
Renato Rodríguez, *Parkland College*
David C. Rubi, *Paradise Valley Community College*
Linda Saborío, *Northern Illinois University*
Jonathan Stowers, *Salt Lake Community College*
John P. Sullivan, *Prairie View A&M University*
Gabriel Valenzuela, *Spokane Falls Community College*
Caroleena Vargas, *University of Rhode Island*

Titania Vargas, *Illinois Central College*
Julio Verdi, *Texas State University*
María Villalobos-Buehner, *Rider University*
Rebecca White, *Indiana University Southeast*
Carolina Wilson, *Texas State University*
Annette Zapata, *Arkansas State University*

Reviewers for Seventh Student Edition

Maria Akrabova, *Metropolitan State University of Denver*
Ana E. Almonte, *Hudson Valley Community College*
Raysa Amador, *Adelphi University*
Dimaris Barrios-Beltrán, *Amherst College*
Mara-Lee Bierman, *Rockland Community College*
Laura H. Bradford, *Salt Lake Community College*
Julia Bussade, *University of Mississippi*
Heather Colburn, *Northwestern University*
John Davis, *Indiana University South Bend*
Héctor Enríquez, *University of Texas at El Paso*
Bruce Fox, *St. Johns River State College*
David Hanson, *University of Puget Sound*
Assen Kokalov, *Purdue University North Central*
Kimberly Harris, *Boise State University*
Brent Hart, *College of Western Idaho*
Catherine Hebert, *Indiana University South Bend*
Qiu Y. Jiménez, *Bakersfield College*
Suzanne LaVenture, *Davidson County Community College*
Allison Libbey Titus, *University of Wisconsin-Milwaukee*
Dr. Sandra Mulryan, *Community College of Baltimore County*
Jamilet Ortiz, *Housatonic Community College*
Nilsa Pérez-Cabrera, *Blinn College*
David C. Rubi, *Paradise Valley Community College*
Linda Saborio, *Northern Illinois University*
John P. Sullivan, *Prairie View A&M University*
Caroleena Vargas, *University of Rhode Island*

Duolingo Educator Summit

Aurora Castillo-Scott, *Georgia College and State University*
Wendy Gallagher, *Metropolitan State University of Denver*
Karen Jones, *Santa Fe College*
Kelly Kinsbury-Brunetto, *University of Nebraska-Lincoln*
Raúl Llorente, *Georgia State University*
María Manni, *University of Maryland Baltimore County*
Kelley Melvin, *University of Missouri-Kansas City*
Carla Oñate, *University of Maryland College Park*
Danielle Richardson, *Davidson County Community College*
Kacie Tartt, *University of Central Florida*
Lisa Volle, *Central Texas College*

Duolingo Beta Testers

Tim Altanero, *Austin Community College*
Joelle Bonamy, *Columbus State University*
An Chung Cheng, *University of Toledo*
Dulce de Castro, *Collin College*
Cindy Doutrich, *York College of Pennsylvania*
Dina A. Fabery, *University of Central Florida*
Lloyd Frías, *Loyola University Maryland*
Marie Guiribitey, *Florida International University*
Anne Hlas, *University of Wisconsin-Eau Claire*
Becky Jaimes, *Austin Community College*
Caridad Jiménez, *University of Florida and Santa Fe College*
Roberto Jiménez-Arroyo, *University of South Florida Sarasota-Manatee*
Karen Jones, *Santa Fe College*
Marga Kelly, *Sierra College*
Ryan LaBrozzi, *Bridgewater State University*
Suzanne LaVenture, *Davidson County Community College*
Roxana Levin, *St. Petersburg College*
Raúl Llorente, *Georgia State University*
Nuria López-Ortega, *University of Cincinnati*
Laura Manzo, *Modesto Junior College*
Marco Mena, *Massachusetts Bay Community College*
Charles Molano, *Lehigh Carbon Community College*
Cheryl Moody, *Pulaski Technical College*
Carla Oñate, *University of Maryland College Park*
Lynn Pearson, *Bowling Green State University*
Danielle Richardson, *Davidson County Community College*
Kate Risse, *Tufts University*
Judy Rodríguez, *California State University, Sacramento*
Aaron Roggia, *Oklahoma State University*
Nohelia Rojas-Miesse, *Miami University*
Dora Romero, *Broward College*
John Rosenberger, *Davidson County Community College*
Daniela Schuvaks Katz, *Indiana University-Purdue University Indianapolis*
Kacie Tartt, *University of Central Florida*
Gregory Thompson, *Brigham Young University*
Encarna Turner, *Wake Forest University*

Student Participants

Yunus Asian, *Edmonds Community College*
Morgan Leighton, *Edmonds Community College*
Jacob Anderson, *Greenville Technical College*
Nassir Canada, *Greenville Technical College*
Daniel Roberts, *Greenville Technical College*
Alyiah Robinson, *Greenville Technical College*
Anais Rockman, *Greenville Technical College*
Zachery Roles, *Greenville Technical College*
Mary Smoak, *Greenville Technical College*
Benjamin Taylor, *Greenville Technical College*
Jean Anselmi, *Red Rocks Community College*
Hannah Eggers, *Red Rocks Community College*
Karen Jaramillo, *Red Rocks Community College*
Rebecca Larson, *Red Rocks Community College*
Christian Prather, *Red Rocks Community College*
Sean Rogers, *Red Rocks Community College*
Polina Sarana, *Red Rocks Community College*
Gary Swartz, *Red Rocks Community College*

Chandra Moss, *Santa Fe College*
Danielle Buys, *Sierra College*
Ekta Chauhan, *Sierra College*
Hailey Craig, *Sierra College*
Cianna García, *Sierra College*
Zoe Gibson, *Sierra College*
Rachel Hanley, *Sierra College*
Michelle Hayward, *Sierra College*
Sally Loeza, *Sierra College*
Dale McGaughy, *Sierra College*
Donna Phan, *Sierra College*
Kristen Shugart, *Sierra College*
Megan Sinclair, *Sierra College*
Mariah Steinmetz, *Sierra College*
Sarah Tileston, *Sierra College*
Maya Wistos, *Sierra College*
Kaitlyn Coyne, *University of Florida*
Emma Ascensao, *University of Rhode Island*
Jillian Bernier, *University of Rhode Island*
Skylar Betzold, *University of Rhode Island*
Miya Brophy-Baermann, *University of Rhode Island*
Rebecca Dickinson, *University of Rhode Island*
Kaylin Drumm, *University of Rhode Island*
Amalia Duckworth, *University of Rhode Island*
Samantha Falkowski, *University of Rhode Island*
Chris Gambacorto, *University of Rhode Island*
Chase Hall, *University of Rhode Island*
Hannah Marie Ilagan, *University of Rhode Island*
Mary Kate Lewis, *University of Rhode Island*
Sydney Morris, *University of Rhode Island*
Jessica Newbury, *University of Rhode Island*
Victor Ochoa, *University of Rhode Island*
Connor Perry, *University of Rhode Island*
Aaron Purington, *University of Rhode Island*
Casey Rockwood, *University of Rhode Island*
Sabrina Rodríguez-Gervais, *University of Rhode Island*
Alex Rosa, *University of Rhode Island*
Michael Rose, *University of Rhode Island*
Hannah Sorlien, *University of Rhode Island*
Brooke Taylor, *University of Rhode Island*
Victor Akuffo, *University of Rhode Island*
Winifer Ali, *University of Rhode Island*
Molly Beluk, *University of Rhode Island*
Stephanie Blot, *University of Rhode Island*
Shannon Costello, *University of Rhode Island*
Sarah De La Cerda, *University of Rhode Island*
Veronica Dinneen, *University of Rhode Island*
Mateo Efstathopoulos, *University of Rhode Island*
Garrett Elderkin, *University of Rhode Island*
Betzy Escobar, *University of Rhode Island*
Crispin Ferris, *University of Rhode Island*
Robert Leniart, *University of Rhode Island*
Alexander Ling, *University of Rhode Island*
Michelle Macdonald, *University of Rhode Island*
Bastian Madsen, *University of Rhode Island*
Rory Martyn, *University of Rhode Island*
Justyce Morris, *University of Rhode Island*
Lauren Mulvey, *University of Rhode Island*
Katie Nehring, *University of Rhode Island*
Natalie Pérez, *University of Rhode Island*
Nichole Raia, *University of Rhode Island*

Katherine Remavich, *University of Rhode Island*
Connor Rogers, *University of Rhode Island*
Jesika Salisbury, *University of Rhode Island*
Haleigh Staradumsky, *University of Rhode Island*
Esteban Tamayo, *University of Rhode Island*
Stephanie Teran, *University of Rhode Island*
Ryan Tracy, *University of Rhode Island*
Austin Yeung, *University of Rhode Island*
Penelope Bremner, *University of Wisconsin-Eau Claire*
Kate Forner, *University of Wisconsin-Eau Claire*
Brenna Lindsey, *University of Wisconsin-Eau Claire*
Mariah Meyers, *University of Wisconsin-Eau Claire*
Kathryn Rhutasel, *University of Wisconsin-Eau Claire*
Hannah Sisto, *University of Wisconsin-Eau Claire*
Kayla Wruk, *University of Wisconsin-Eau Claire*
Nathan Kane, *University of Wisconsin-Eau Claire*

Webinar Activities

Mariana Bahtchevanova, *Arizona State University*
Patrick Brugh, *Loyola University of Maryland*
Rosa Chávez, *Tarrant County College*
María Elena Crickette, *University of California, Santa Barbara*
Dina A. Fabery, *University of Central Florida*
Camilla Fiorina, *University of California, Santa Barbara*
Lloyd Frías, *Loyola University of Maryland*
Sarah Gordon, *Utah State University*
Sue Guillaud, *Ball State University*
Xavier Gutiérrez, *University of Alberta*
Monika Holzschuh, *Queen's University*
Pia Köstner, *University of New Orleans*
Penny Lovett, *Wake Technical Community College*
Laure Mauffray, *Winthrop University*
Silvia Choi, *Georgia Gwinnett College*
Markus Muller, *California State University, Long Beach*
Benjamin Nelson, *University of South Carolina Beaufort*
Brian Olovson, *University of Iowa*
Maricelle Pinto-Tomas, *University of Iowa*
John Riley, *Greenville Technical Community College*
Alyse Schoenfeldt, *Palm Beach State College*
Svetlana Singer, *Texas A&M University-Kingsville*
Sabrina Spannagel, *University of Washington*
Tamesia Sosa, *Madison College*

Reviewers

Karen Acosta, *Valdosta State University*
Johanna Alberich, *Troy University*
Tyler Anderson, *Colorado Mesa University*
Bruno Arzola, *Tacoma Community College*
Yuly Asención Delaney, *Northern Arizona University*
Barbara Ávila-Shah, *University at Buffalo, State University of New York*
María Brucato, *Northeastern University*
Julia Bussade, *The University of Mississippi*
Eduardo Cabrera, *Millikin University*
Sara Casler, *Sierra College*
Tami Cavitt, *New Mexico Junior College*
Karina Clarke, *Metropolitan Community College*
Blake Crossley, *Colorado Mesa University*
Debra Currere, *Northern Illinois University*
Rita De Luca Guerriero, *University of Central Florida*

Mary Ann Dellinger, *Virginia Military Institute*
Héctor Enríquez, *University of Texas, El Paso*
Dina A. Fabery, *University of Central Florida*
Lisa Fraguada-Pileggi, *Delaware County Community College*
Margarita García-Notario, *SUNY Plattsburgh*
Amy George-Hirons, *Tulane University*
Scott Gibby, *Austin Community College*
Alicia Gignouz, *University of Montana*
James Griesse, *University of South Carolina Beaufort*
Ana Hansen, *Pellissippi State Community College*
Patricia Harrigan, *Community College of Baltimore County*
Michael Harrison, *San Diego Mesa College*
Douglas A. Jackson, *University of South Carolina Upstate*
Tatiana Johnston, *Colorado State University-Pueblo*
Ryan LaBrozzi, *Bridgewater State University*
Stephanie Langston, *Georgia State University Perimeter College*
Courtney Lanute, *Florida Southwestern State College*
Kajsa Larson, *Northern Kentucky University*
Jeff Longwell, *New Mexico State University*
Frances Matos-Schultz, *University of Minnesota*
Teresa McCann, *Prairie State College*
Eva Mendieta, *Indiana University Northwest*
Cheryl Moody, *Pulaski Technical College*
Bridget Morgan, *Indiana University South Bend*
Jeanne Mullaney, *Community College of Rhode Island*
Benjamin J. Nelson, *University of South Carolina Beaufort*
Carmel O'Kane, *Northeastern Illinois University*
Michelle Orecchio, *University of Michigan*
Marilyn Palatinus, *Pellissippi State Community College*
Carlos Pedroza, *Palomar College*
Luis Peralta, *Millikin University*
Nilsa Pérez-Cabrera, *Blinn College, Bryan Texas*
Dolores Rangel, *Georgia Southern University*
Sandra L. Reynolds, *Raritan Valley Community College*
Alegría Ribadeneira, *Colorado State University–Pueblo*
Mary Rice, *Concordia College*
Marcos Romero, *Aquinas College*
Anita Saalfeld, *Metropolitan Community College*
Virginia Sánchez-Bernardy, *San Diego Mesa College*
Christine Stanley, *Roanoke College*
Kelly Suero, *Troy University*
Cristina Szterensus, *Rock Valley College*
María Tajes, *William Paterson University*
Kacie Tartt, *University of Central Florida*
Linda Tracy, *Santa Rosa Junior College*
Jennifer Valko, *East Carolina University*
Mayela Vallejos Ramírez, *Colorado Mesa University*
Amy Vassar, *College of Western Idaho*
Lisa Volle, *Central Texas College*
Richard Williams, *Benedict College*
Olivia Yánez, *College of Lake County*

ACTFL Focus Group Participants

Javier Aliegro, *Elgin Community College*
Tim Altanero, *Austin Community College*
Jorge Arteta, *Brandeis University*
Carlos Baez, *North Hennepin Community College*
Dikka Berven, *Oakland University*
Kathleen Bizzarro, *Colorado College*
Susana Blanco-Iglesias, *Macalester College*

Matt Borden, *Carthage College*
Flor María Buitrago, *Muhlenberg College*
Yolanda Burgos-Olinger, *Sinclair Community College*
Beatriz Calvo-Peña, *Barry University*
Elsa Castillo, *California State University Fresno*
Aurora Castillo-Scott, *Georgia College*
Krista Chambless, *University of Alabama at Birmingham*
An Chung Cheng, *University of Toledo*
Becky Cottrell, *Metropolitan State University of Denver*
Jorge Cubillos, *University of Delaware*
Dulce de Castro, *Collin College*
Mary Ann Dellinger, *Virginia Military Institute*
David Detwiler, *Mira Costa College*
Aurea Diab, *Dillard University*
Michael Dillon, *Morehouse College*
Cindy Doutrich, *York College of Pennsylvania*
Cindy Ducar, *Bowling Green State University*
Dina A. Fabery, *University of Central Florida*
Silvana Falconi, *Boston College*
Rachel Fournier, *Troy University*
Margarita García-Notario, *SUNY Plattsburgh*
Kevin Gaugler, *Marist College*
Yolanda González, *Valencia College*
Marie Guiribitey, *Florida International University*
Andrew Healey, *Bloomsburg University*
Sarah Hirsch, *University of New Hampshire*
Anne Hlas, *University of Wisconsin-Eau Claire*
Elizabeth Inman, *College of the Holy Cross*
Carmen Jany, *California State University, San Bernardino*
Amos Kasperek, *Bob Jones University*
Nieves Knapp, *Brigham Young University*
Kris Knisely, *University of South Dakota*
Ryan LaBrozzi, *Bridgewater State University*
Lina Lee, *University of New Hampshire*
Raúl Llorente, *Georgia State University*
Maria Manni, *University of Maryland Baltimore County*

Frances Matos-Schultz, *University of Minnesota*
Maria Matz, *University of Massachusetts*
Mercedes Meier, *Miami Dade College*
Marco Mena, *Massachusetts Bay Community College*
Lisa Merschel, *Duke University*
Christiane Metral, *Smith College*
Nicole Mills, *Harvard University*
Charles H. Molano, *Lehigh Carbon Community College*
Monica Montalvo, *University of Central Florida*
Francisco Montaño, *Lehman College*
Giuditta Monterosso, *Massasoit Community College*
Tania Muino-Loureiro, *Northeastern University*
Marie Noussi, *Linfield College*
Cornelia Okraski, *Queens University of Charlotte*
Michelle Orecchio, *University of Michigan*
Lucía Osa-Melero, *Duquesne University*
Lynn Pearson, *Bowling Green State University*
Florencia Pecile, *Kirkwood Community College*
Marina Peters-Newell, *University of New Mexico*
Ángela Pinilla, *Georgia Southern University*
Kem Pinto, *John A. Logan College*
Isabel Rivero, *Carthage College*
Nohelia Rojas-Miesse, *Miami University*
Fanny Roncal, *Concordia College*
Christian Rubio, *Bentley University*
María Salomé-Chavarría, *University of Houston-Victoria*
Daniela Schuvaks Katz, *Indiana University-Purdue University Indianapolis*
Gina Sherriff, *Norwich University*
Patricia Smith, *Tufts University*
Kelly Suero, *Troy University*
Kacie Tartt, *University of Central Florida*
Sandra Trapani, *University of Missouri-St. Louis*
Helga Winkler, *Moorpark College*
Nancy Zimmerman, *Kutztown University*

We are grateful to the many individuals and organizations who granted permission to use photos and literary selections (see Text and Photo Credits).

We wish to express our gratitude to the countless people at Ohlinger Publishing Services and at Pearson who contributed their ideas, tireless efforts, and publishing experience to the publication of the seventh edition of *¡Arriba!* We are especially grateful for the guidance of Gisela Aragón-Velthaus and Sarah Link, Development Editors, for all their work, suggestions, attention to detail, and dedication to the text. They, along with Ana Piquinela, Program Manager, provided support and encouragement needed to achieve final products, both print and digital. The collaboration of Amy Gibbons, Senior Digital Media Manager, and Amanda Albert Podeszedlik (**MyLab Spanish**), was instrumental in coordinating digital components.

We thank Lumina Datamatics for providing services in text design, electronic page composition, and page review: Katy, Project Coordinator; Keith, Illustrator; Pedro, Proofreader; and Elizabeth, Cold Reader.

We are indebted to our market development and marketing teams, Helen Richardson Greenlea, Mellissa Yokell, and World Languages Consultants Yesha Brill, Doug Brauer, and Raúl J. Vázquez López, who kept us informed of instructor and student needs in the field.

Our phenomenal and talented supplement authors managed to coordinate their efforts with ours, always keeping an eye on both deadlines and accuracy. They include Andrew Bowen (managing and editing of **Testing Program** and **Student Activities**), Gabriela Ferland (**Testing Program**), Katie Wade and Gregg Courtad (**Student Activities**), and Debbie Coniglio (OPS Audio Project Manager).

We express our sincere thanks to Amber Chow, Executive Editor of Courseware Management for Pearson, and Carolyn Merrill, Editor in Chief for Ohlinger Publishing Services, for their guidance and support through every aspect of the *¡Arriba!* program.

Lastly, we give our love and deepest appreciation to our families: Lourdes, Cindy, Eddy, and Lindsey, Elena, Ed, Lauren, Luis, and Will; Wayne, Alexis, Sandro, Ignacio and Isla; Camille, Chris, Eleanor, Teresa, Toby, and Bernadette; and Pete; Valayda and Jesse (1945–2008); Roger and Britt; Dave, Nancy, Wesley, and Megan; Leisa and David; and Tammy.

Eduardo Zayas-Bazán
Susan M. Bacon
Holly J. Nibert

Capítulo 1
Hola, ¿qué tal?

«Si vives alegre, rico eres».

Inca Princess, early 1800s.
The conquest of the Americas caused a clash between two very different worlds and civilizations. Although the indigenous peoples already had highly structured beliefs, the Spaniards encouraged or forced them to convert to Christianity. This painting depicts an Inca princess, claimed by her descendants to be the first Christian Inca woman.

Inca Noblewoman, Cuzco, Peru, Early 1800s. Denver Art Museum Collection: Gift of Dr. Belinda Straight by exchange and New World Department Acquisition Funds. 1996.18. Photography courtesy Denver Art Museum.

Learning Objectives

1.1 Meet and greet others

1.2 Talk about yourself and others

1.3 Discuss the advantages of being bilingual, and learn about an alternative hip-hop group from Puerto Rico

1.4 Describe your classroom, and respond to classroom instructions

1.5 Identify and describe people, places, and things, including dates

1.6 Use visuals to aid comprehension

1.7 Recognize the expanse of the Hispanic world

1.8 Identify cognates to understand text

1.9 Move from phrases to sentences

In this Chapter

ENFOQUE CULTURAL: LA DIVERSIDAD DEL MUNDO HISPANO
Club cultura: Bienvenidos a Club cultura

Video

Indicate with **C (Cierto)** if these items will be included in the video series, or **F (Falso)** if they will not be included.

1. _____ the Caribbean

2. _____ Africa

3. _____ Asia

4. _____ the Complutense Film Festival

5. _____ indigenous cultures

6. _____ music and dance

1.1 Primera parte

Vocabulario

1.1 Meet and greet others

Saludos y despedidas

 En la universidad.

¿Comprendes? Indicate if each statement is **Cierto** (*true*) or **Falso** (*false*). Correct the false statements. If you need help, check the vocabulary list.

1. Jorge y María Luisa son amigos (*friends*).   C / F

2. La señora López es estudiante.   C / F

3. María Luisa está muy mal.   C / F

Answers: 1. C; 2. F: Es profesora.; 3. F: Está muy bien.

Vocabulario

Saludos	Greetings
Buenos días.	*Good morning.*
Buenas noches.	*Good evening.*
Buenas tardes.	*Good afternoon.*
¿Cómo está usted?	*How are you?* (for.)[1]
¿Cómo estás?	*How are you?* (inf.)
Hola.	*Hello, Hi.*
¿Qué pasa?	*What's happening? What's up?* (inf.)
¿Qué tal?	*What's up?* (inf.)

Respuestas	Responses
De nada.	*You're welcome.*
¿De verdad?	*Really?*
Encantado/a.	*Pleased to meet you.*
Gracias.	*Thank you.*
Igualmente.	*Likewise.*
Lo siento.	*I'm sorry.*
Más o menos.	*So-so.* (lit. *More or less.*)
Mucho gusto.	*Nice to meet you.*
(Muy) Bien.	*(Very) Well.*
(Muy) Mal.	*(Very) Bad.*
Todo bien.	*All's well.*

Presentaciones	Introductions
¿Cómo se llama usted?	*What's your name?* (for.)
¿Cómo te llamas (tú)?	*What's your name?* (inf.)
Me llamo...	*My name is...* (lit. *I call myself...*)
Mi nombre es...	*My name is...*
Soy... (ser)	*I am... (to be)*
¿Y tú?	*And you?*

Despedidas	Farewells
Adiós.	*Good-bye.*
Hasta luego.	*See you later.*
Hasta mañana.	*See you tomorrow.*
Hasta pronto.	*See you soon.*
Nos vemos.	*See you.*

Títulos	Titles
el señor (Sr.)	*Mr.*
la señora (Sra.)	*Mrs., Ms.*
la señorita (Srta.)	*Miss*

En la clase	In class
la clase	*class*
el/la estudiante	*student (male/female)*
el/la profesor/a	*professor (male/female)*
la tarea	*homework*
la universidad	*university*

Expresiones para la clase	Expressions for class
¿Cómo se dice...?	*How do you say...?*
¿Cómo se escribe...?	*How do you write...?*
¿Qué significa...?	*What does... mean?*
Otra vez, por favor.	*Again, please.*

Variaciones

Numerous greetings and farewells are used in the Spanish-speaking world and variations are common. The expression **¿Qué onda?** (*What's up?*) is popular in Mexico. A brief **Buenas** for *Good afternoon/evening* is typical in Spain. Speakers from many Latin American countries commonly use the expression **¡Chau!** (also spelled **¡Chao!**) to say *Good-bye!*

---

[1]Abbreviations: for. (formal); inf. (informal); lit. (literally)

))) Letras y sonidos

Spanish vowels

In Spanish, each of the five letters **a**, **e**, **i**, **o**, **u** corresponds to one and only one vowel *sound*. In English, these same five letters correspond to many different vowel sounds, which tend to be long and glided. For example, the letter *a* creates five different vowel sounds in the following words: f*a*ther, c*a*t, *a*pproach, bl*a*me, *a*we.

What vowel sound in English corresponds to each of the letters **a**, **e**, **i**, **o**, **u** in Spanish?

- The letter **a** is pronounced like the *a* in f*a*ther, but is shorter.

    más   pasa   nada   mañana   encantada

- The letter **e** is pronounced like the *e* in th*e*y, but is shorter with no final glide.

    es   tres   mesa   deporte   interesante

- The letter **i** is pronounced like the *i* in mach*i*ne, but is shorter.[1]

    mi   niño   libro   tímido   inteligente

- The letter **o** is pronounced like the *o* in al*o*ne, but is shorter with no final glide.

    o   hola   color   exótico   nosotros

- The letter **u** is pronounced like the *u* in fl*u*te, but is shorter.

    tú   azul   lunes   gusto   música

Aplicación

1-1 ¿Qué tal? Select a logical response for each statement or question.

> MODELO: Adiós.
> *Hasta luego.*

1. _____ Soy el doctor Gómez.
2. _____ Gracias.
3. _____ ¿Cómo se llama usted?
4. _____ Mucho gusto.
5. _____ Buenas tardes, Tomás.

a. Me llamo Pedro Guillén.
b. Buenos días, doctor.
c. De nada.
d. Buenas tardes, profesora.
e. Igualmente.

))) **1-2 ¿Quiénes son? (*Who are they?*)** Listen to the short conversations and indicate the number of each conversation next to the corresponding situation.

_____ two friends saying good-bye

_____ a teacher and student introducing themselves

_____ a young person greeting an older person

_____ two friends greeting each other

_____ two students introducing themselves

---

[1]Be careful to avoid the *i* sound in s*i*t in the following words, since this sound does not exist in Spanish: **inteligente, interesante, introvertido, impaciente, tímido, simpático, misterioso.**

1-3 **Presentaciones.** The following people are meeting for the first time. Act out what they might say to each other. Practice using different ways to introduce yourself.

MODELO:

el profesor Solar
y Ester Muñoz

PROFESOR SOLAR:	*Buenas tardes. Soy el profesor Solar.*
ESTER:	*Buenas tardes, profesor Solar.* *Mi nombre es Ester Muñoz.*
PROFESOR SOLAR:	*Mucho gusto.*
ESTER:	*Igualmente.*

la Sra. Aldo y la
Sra. García

Patricia y Marcos

Eduardo y Manuel

1-4 **Saludos.** How do you greet friends and relatives? People you meet for the first time? Does the age of the person make a difference?

Paso 1 Read the following to compare your experience with many Spanish speakers.

> Many Spanish speakers use nonverbal signs when interacting with each other. These signs vary, depending on the social situation and on the relationship between the speakers. In a friendly setting, two people will often kiss each other lightly on one (Latin America) or both (Spain) cheeks. In a more formal setting, people who meet each other for the first time shake hands, both when greeting and when saying good-bye to each other. In many places, men who know each other well often greet each other with an **abrazo** (*hug*) and pats on the back. Women tend to greet each other and their male friends with one (or two) light kisses on the cheeks.

Paso 2 Introduce yourself to five of your classmates. Shake hands or kiss lightly on the cheek as you ask them their names and how they are. Then say good-bye.

1-5 **¿Cómo está usted?** In pairs, take turns assuming the roles of instructor and student. Act out the following situation.

MODELO: ESTUDIANTE 1: *Buenos días...*
          ESTUDIANTE 2: *Hola...*

Profesor/a	Estudiante
It's morning. Greet the student, introduce yourself, and ask his/her name.	Answer your instructor. Then ask him/her how he/she feels.
Respond to the student, and ask the same.	Respond logically. Then say good-bye.
Respond logically.	Respond logically.

Cultura en vivo

You will find that comfortable physical distance differs between cultures. For example, when holding a conversation, Hispanics tend to stand closer to each other than in many other cultures. As a test, stand at arm's distance from a classmate; then take one step closer. Which distance feels more comfortable for holding a conversation with a friend?

Estructuras

1.2 Talk about yourself and others

The Spanish alphabet

The Spanish alphabet contains twenty-seven letters, including one that does not appear in the English alphabet: ñ.

Letra (*Letter*)	Nombre (*Name*)	Ejemplos (*Examples*)	Pronunciación (*Pronunciation*)
a	a	Ana	
b	be	Bárbara	The letters **b** and **v** are pronounced exactly alike, as a **b**.
c	ce	Carlos, Cuba, Cecilia	In all varieties of Spanish, the letter **c** before **a**, **o**, or **u** sounds like the English *k*. In Latin America, the letter **c** before **e** or **i** is pronounced like the English *s*. In most of Spain, **c** before **e** or **i**, and the letter **z**, are pronounced like the *th* in *thanks*.
d	de	Dios, Pedro	
e	e	Ernesto	
f	efe	Fernando	
g	ge	gato, gusto, gitano	The letter **g** before **a**, **o**, or **u** is pronounced like the English *g* in *gate*. Before **e** or **i**, the letter **g** is pronounced the same as Spanish **j** (or a hard English *h*).
h	hache	Hernán, hola, hotel	The letter **h** is always silent.
i	i	Inés	
j	jota	José	The letter **j** is like a hard English *h* sound.
k	ka	kilómetro, karate	The letter **k** is not common and usually appears only in words borrowed from other languages.
l	ele	Luis	
m	eme	María	
n	ene	Nora, nachos	
ñ	eñe	niño	The **ñ** sounds like *ny* as in *canyon*.
o	o	Óscar	
p	pe	Pepe	
q	cu	Quique, química	
r	ere	Laura, Rosa	At the beginning of a word, **r** is always pronounced like a trilled **rr**.
s	ese	Sara	
t	te	Tomás	
u	u	usted, Úrsula	
v	uve *or* ve	Venus, vamos	The letters **b** and **v** are pronounced exactly alike, as a **b**.
w	doble uve *or* doble v	Washington, windsurf	The letter **w** is not common and usually appears only in words borrowed from other languages.
x	equis	excelente, México	The letter **x** is usually pronounced like *ks*, but also occasionally like the Spanish **j**.
y	ye	soy, Yolanda, maya	The letter **y** is pronounced as in *toy* or *yard*.
z	zeta	zorro, lápiz	In Latin America, the letter **z** is pronounced like the English *s*. In most of Spain, it sounds like the *th* in *thanks*.

¿Comprendes? Identify the missing word for each of these place names.

1. *Ene - u - e - uve - o:* _____ México

2. *Pe - a - ese - o:* El _____

3. *Jota - u - a - ene:* San _____

Answers: 1. Nuevo; 2. Paso; 3. Juan

Aplicación

1-6 ¿Qué vocal falta? Complete the names of these famous **hispanos** with the missing vowels. **¡Ojo!** (*Watch out!*): For letters with an accent, say **con acento** after saying the name of the letter: **eme - a - ere - i con acento - a (María)**.

> MODELO: __ v __   M __ nd __ s (actriz)
> *e, a, e, e (Eva Mendes)*

1. J __ nn __ fer   L __ p __ z (actriz y cantante)
2. R __ f __ el   N __ d __ l (tenista)
3. J __ ss __ c __   __ lb __ (actriz)

1-7 ¿Qué consonante falta? What consonants are missing from the names of these countries in the Spanish-speaking world? Complete each name with the missing consonants.

> MODELO: Mé __ i __ o
> *x (equis), c (ce)*

1. Ar __ enti __ a
2. Bo __ i __ ia
3. El Sa __ __ ado __
4. Co __ __ a __ ica
5. Para __ ua __
6. Espa __ a

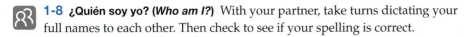

1-8 ¿Quién soy yo? (*Who am I?*) With your partner, take turns dictating your full names to each other. Then check to see if your spelling is correct.

1-9 ¿Qué es? Many Spanish words are the same or similar in English. In pairs, take turns spelling out and writing down two or three random words from the box; then check to see if you have each spelled the words correctly. If you need to hear the spelling again, ask your partner to repeat by saying **Otra vez, por favor**.

> MODELO: ESTUDIANTE 1: (spells out **taco**) *te - a - ce - o*
> ESTUDIANTE 2: (after writing down the word) *¿Taco?*
> ESTUDIANTE 1: *Correcto.*

actor	auto	coco	melón
alcohol	banana	doctor	rodeo
álgebra	café	hotel	solar
animal	chocolate	limón	tomate

Presencia hispana

Hispano, latino, or **español?** These terms are often used interchangeably in the U.S. to describe people with origins in Spanish-speaking countries. However, to be more precise, **hispano** refers to anyone of Spanish-speaking origin; **latino** refers to anyone from Latin America, including Brazil; **español** refers *only* to a person from Spain, or to the Spanish language. Many **hispanos** and **latinos** speak **español**, but are not **españoles**. Do you identify yourself by your nationality, ethnic origin, or the language you speak?

¿Cómo se escribe "cigüeña" (*stork*)?

The numbers *0–100*

Numbers in Spanish are expressed as follows:

0–9	10–19	20–29	30–39
cero	diez	veinte	treinta
uno	once	veintiuno	treinta y uno
dos	doce	veintidós	treinta y dos
tres	trece	veintitrés	treinta y tres
cuatro	catorce	veinticuatro	treinta y cuatro
cinco	quince	veinticinco	treinta y cinco
seis	dieciséis	veintiséis	treinta y seis
siete	diecisiete	veintisiete	treinta y siete
ocho	dieciocho	veintiocho	treinta y ocho
nueve	diecinueve	veintinueve	treinta y nueve

40–49:	cuarenta, cuarenta y uno, cuarenta y dos, cuarenta y tres...
50–59:	cincuenta, cincuenta y uno, cincuenta y dos, cincuenta y tres...
60–69:	sesenta, sesenta y uno, sesenta y dos, sesenta y tres...
70–79:	setenta, setenta y uno, setenta y dos, setenta y tres...
80–89:	ochenta, ochenta y uno, ochenta y dos, ochenta y tres...
90–99:	noventa, noventa y uno, noventa y dos, noventa y tres...
100–109:	cien, ciento uno, ciento dos, ciento tres...

- **Uno** becomes **un** before a masculine singular noun and **una** before a feminine singular noun.

un libro	*one book*
una mesa	*one table*
un profesor	*one professor (male)*
una profesora	*one professor (female)*

- In compound numbers, **-uno** becomes **-ún** before a masculine noun and **-una** before a feminine noun.

veintiún libros	*twenty-one books*
veintiuna profesoras	*twenty-one female professors*

- The numbers **dieciséis** through **diecinueve** (16–19) and **veintiuno** through **veintinueve** (21–29) are generally written as one word. The condensed spelling is not used after 30.

- **Cien** is used when it precedes a noun or when counting the number 100 in sequence.

cien estudiantes	*one hundred students*

- **Ciento** is used in compound numbers from 101 to 199.

ciento uno	*one hundred and one*
ciento cuarenta y cinco	*one hundred and forty-five*

The ancient Maya developed a precise base-20 counting system that included zero (shell), one (dot), and five (bar). Can you find the three vertical bars and the three dots to form the number 18?

¿Comprendes? Provide the correct numeral for each item.

1. Ciento ocho estudiantes: _____

2. Treinta y nueve profesoras: _____

3. Setenta y una clases: _____

Answers: 1. 108; 2. 39; 3. 71

Aplicación

1-10 ¿Qué número falta? Figure out the patterns of numbers below and complete them with the logical numbers in Spanish.

> **MODELO:** uno, _tres_ , cinco, _siete_, nueve, _once_

1. dos, _____, seis, ocho, _____, doce, _____

2. uno, cinco, nueve, _____, diecisiete, veintiuno, _____

3. cinco, diez, _____, veinte, veinticinco, _____, _____

4. treinta, cuarenta, _____, _____, setenta, _____, _____

5. once, veintidós, _____, cuarenta y cuatro, cincuenta y cinco, _____, setenta y siete, _____

1-11 Te toca a ti (_It's your turn_). In pairs, take turns challenging each other with an original sequence of numbers. See the previous activity for models.

1-12 ¿Qué se hace en Madrid (_What do people do..._)? Read the tourist guide to find information about what to do in Madrid. Write the page numbers for each category and say them in Spanish.

> **MODELO:** _52_ música
> _en la página cincuenta y dos_

1. _____ puntos de interés

2. _____ niños

3. _____ conciertos

4. _____ ballet

5. _____ arte público

6. _____ deportes

7. _____ fiestas

8. _____ ópera

Cultura en vivo

The lottery is an important means of generating funds in many countries and draws players from all income levels. In Spain, _el sorteo de Navidad_, held on December 22, is the most popular, attracting an average expenditure of 73 euros per Spaniard. Although a full ticket sells for 200 euros, they are sold in **décimos** (_tenths_) for 20 euros each. The payout for _el Gordo_ (the big one) can be over 700 million euros.

Puesto (_Stand_) de lotería en Sevilla, España. ¿Cuál es tu número favorito?

1-13 ¿Cuál (*What*) es tu número de teléfono? Work with three or four classmates to give and take down each other's numbers. Notice that telephone numbers in Spanish can be stated in groups of two digits rather than in single digits.

> MODELO: ESTUDIANTE 1: *¿Cuál es tu número de teléfono?*
> ESTUDIANTE 2: *(331) 555-2240: tres, tres, uno, cinco, cincuenta y cinco, veintidós, cuarenta*

1-14A ¡Necesito información! In pairs, take turns telling each other how many people are in different places to see if you agree. **Estudiante B**: see **Appendix 1**, page A-1.

> MODELO: ESTUDIANTE A: *(15 estudiantes en clase)*
> *Hay* (There are) *15 estudiantes en clase.*
> ESTUDIANTE B: *(14 estudiantes en clase) No es cierto. Hay catorce.*

Estudiante A:

55 estudiantes en la cafetería	77 profesoras en la universidad
21 universidades en Miami	91 profesores en la universidad
100 clases en la lista	

1-15 ¿Cuántos son? Individually follow the model to create four simple math problems. Then, in pairs, challenge each other to solve them in Spanish. Useful expressions: **+ más** and **– menos**.

> MODELO: $25 + 15 = 40$
> ESTUDIANTE 1: *¿Cuántos son veinticinco más quince?*
> ESTUDIANTE 2: *Cuarenta.*
> ESTUDIANTE 1: *Correcto.*

Subject pronouns and the present tense of *ser*

Subject pronouns refer to people (*I, you, he,* etc.).

Subject pronouns			
SINGULAR		**PLURAL**	
yo	*I*	**nosotros/nosotras**	*we (m/f)*
tú	*you* (inf.)	**vosotros/vosotras**	*you* (m/f; inf., Spain)
usted (Ud.)	*you* (for.)	**ustedes (Uds.)**	*you* (for.)
él, ella	*he, she*	**ellos, ellas**	*they* (m./f.)

You have already used some forms of the verb **ser**. Here are all of the forms of the present, along with the subject pronouns.

ser (*to be*)					
SINGULAR			**PLURAL**		
yo	**soy**	*I am*	nosotros/as	**somos**	*we are*
tú	**eres**	*you are* (inf.)	vosotros/as	**sois**	*you are* (inf.)
usted (Ud.)	**es**	*you are* (for.)	ustedes (Uds.)	**son**	*you are* (for.)
él/ella	**es**	*he/she is*	ellos/ellas	**son**	*they are*

- Because the verb form shows the subject of a sentence, you can omit subject pronouns unless they are needed for clarification or emphasis.

¿**Eres** de Puerto Rico?	*Are you from Puerto Rico?*
Sí, **soy** de Puerto Rico.	*Yes, I'm from Puerto Rico.*
Yo no, pero **ellos** son de Puerto Rico.	*I'm not, but they're from Puerto Rico.*

¿Quién es usted?

¿Yo?

- Use **tú** to address a friend, a family member, or a pet. Use **usted** for an acquaintance or a person in a position of authority (a supervisor, teacher, or older person) to show formality or respect.

  | Pablito, **tú eres** mi mejor amigo. | *Pablito, you are my best friend.* |
  | Perdone, **¿es usted** la profesora? | *Excuse me, are you the professor?* |

- **Vosotros/as** and **ustedes** are the plural of **tú** and **usted**, respectively, but in all of Latin America, **ustedes** is used for both the informal and formal plural *you*. **Vosotros/as** is commonly used in Spain.[1]

  | Amigos, **ustedes son / vosotros sois** muy pacientes. | *Friends, you are very patient.* |

- The verb **ser** expresses origin, occupation, inherent qualities, or identity.

¿De dónde **eres**?	*Where are you from?*
Soy de Toronto.	*I am from Toronto.*
¿Cómo **es** la profesora?	*What is the teacher like?*
Es muy inteligente.	*She is very intelligent.*
¿Qué **es** esto?	*What is this?*
Es la Casa Rosada.	*It's the Pink House.*

La Casa Rosada es la sede (*seat*) del Poder Ejecutivo de la República Argentina.

¿Comprendes? Identify the correct verb for each subject: **soy**, **eres**, **es**, **somos**, or **son**.

1. ustedes _____

2. tú y yo _____

3. Guillermo _____

4. tú _____

5. yo _____

Answers: 1. son; 2. somos; 3. es; 4. eres; 5. soy

Aplicación

1-16 En la clase de la profesora Gómez. Select the correct form of the verb **ser** according to the context.

Hoy hay (*there is*) examen en la clase de la profesora Gómez. Los estudiantes (1) somos/son inteligentes, pero la profesora (2) eres/es muy exigente (*demanding*) y la clase (3) es/sois muy difícil (*difficult*). Roberto dice: "Profesora, nosotros (4) somos/son buenos estudiantes, y el examen (5) son/es mañana, ¿no? La profesora responde: "¡Ay, Roberto! ¡Yo (6) son/soy la profesora! ¡El examen (7) es/son hoy y ya (8) es/soy tarde!"

---

[1]*¡Arriba!* uses **ustedes** as the plural of **tú**, except where cultural context would require otherwise.

1-17 Salvador Dalí y Diego Rivera. Read about these two artists whose artwork is very different, yet revered world over.

Paso 1 Read the descriptions and complete the text with the correct forms of **ser**.

Salvador Dalí y Diego Rivera (1) _____ dos de los artistas más famosos del mundo (*world*). Los dos artistas (2) _____ del siglo XX, pero sus experiencias y sus estilos (3) _____ muy diferentes. Salvador Dalí (4) _____ español. (5) _____ de Figueras, un pueblo (*town*) cerca de Barcelona. Dalí (6) _____ famoso no solo por su arte surrealista, sino también por su apariencia extravagante. La muerte de Dalí (7) _____ en 1989 a la edad de ochenta y cuatro años.

Diego Rivera (8) _____ mexicano. (9) _____ de Guanajuato, una ciudad (*city*) colonial al norte de la Ciudad de México. El año de su nacimiento (10) _____ 1886 y el año de su muerte (11) _____ 1957. Rivera (12) _____ famoso por sus murales que describen (*depict*) la historia de México, especialmente la conquista de México por los españoles. Su estilo (13) _____ realista.

Paso 2 Answer these questions in Spanish, based on the reading in **Paso 1** about Salvador Dalí and Diego Rivera.

1. Where is Dalí from? Where is Rivera from?
2. What do Rivera and Dalí have in common?
3. How do they differ?
4. What painting, sculpture, or mural by either of these artists have you seen? What is its theme?

1-18 Ramón y Rosario. Two students meet in the student center before class.

Paso 1 Write the correct forms of the verb **ser** to complete their conversation.

RAMÓN: Hola, yo (1) _____ Ramón Larrea Arias.

ROSARIO: Encantada, Ramón. (2) _____ Rosario Vélez Cuadra.

RAMÓN: ¿De dónde (3) _____?

ROSARIO: (4) _____ de Puerto Rico, ¿y tú?

RAMÓN: (5) _____ de Panamá, pero mis padres (*parents*) (6) _____ de Colombia.

ROSARIO: ¿Cómo (7) _____ tu clase de inglés?

RAMÓN: Mi clase (8) _____ muy interesante y mis compañeros de clase (9) _____ muy simpáticos (*nice*).

ROSARIO: ¿Cómo (10) _____ la profesora?

RAMÓN: (11) _____ muy inteligente. Ella (12) _____ de Canadá.

ROSARIO: ¡Ay, lo siento! Tengo clase ahora (*now*). Hasta luego, Ramón.

RAMÓN: Nos vemos, Rosario.

Paso 2 In pairs, create a similar conversation to exchange information about yourselves or a personality you create.

1-19 Tus preferencias. Work individually to complete these questions with the correct form of **ser**. Then, in pairs, take turns asking and responding to each other's questions.

> MODELO: ESTUDIANTE 1: ¿Cuál _es_ tu número de teléfono?
>   ESTUDIANTE 2: *Es el 361-555-1234.*

1. ¿Quién _____ tu actor favorito?
2. ¿Cómo _____ él/ella?
3. ¿ _____ él/ella mexicano/a?
4. ¿_____ (tú) aficionado/a al cine español?
5. ¿_____ actores también tú y tus amigos?

¡Conversemos!

First, ask yourself whether you can perform the following communicative functions in Spanish. Then act out the scenarios with two or three classmates. Ask and respond to at least three questions in each situation.

✓ CAN YOU	WITH YOUR CLASSMATE(S) . . .
☐ meet and greet others?	**Situación: En clase.**
	This is your first day of class. Take turns introducing yourselves as a professor or student and ask others their names.
	Para empezar (*Getting started*): *¿Cómo te llamas? ¿Cómo se llama usted?*
☐ spell your name?	**Situación: En el centro de estudiantes internacionales.**
	You and your partner welcome students to a reception for international students and must write everyone's name on name tags. Take turns asking their names and how to spell them.
	Para empezar: *¿Cómo te llamas? ¿Cómo se escribe...?*
☐ perform simple math problems in Spanish?	**Situación: Planes para una fiesta.**
	Challenge each other to calculate how many soft drinks (*refrescos*) and pizzas you need if you invite 5, 10, or another number of friends.
	Para empezar: *Con cinco amigos, necesitamos diez refrescos y... pizzas. Con... amigos, necesitamos...*
☐ talk about yourself and others?	**Situación: En clase.**
	Ask your classmates and your professor who they are and where they are from. How many are from the same city or town? Is anyone from another country?
	Para empezar: *¿Quién eres tú / es usted? ¿De dónde…?*

Perfiles

1.3 Discuss the advantages of being bilingual, and learn about an alternative hip-hop group from Puerto Rico

Mi experiencia

SOY BILINGÜE

1-20 Para ti (*For you*). Do you have friends or family members who speak more than one language? Did they grow up speaking two languages, learn a second language in school, or live in a place where English was not the primary language? What are the economic, political, and social advantages to being bilingual and bicultural in today's world? Read the excerpt from Ramón García Torres's blog below about growing up bilingual.

¡Hola! ¿Qué pasa? My name is Ramón García Torres and I live in New York City. My family is originally from Puerto Rico; my parents moved to New York when I was just a kid. Growing up, I spoke Spanish at home and learned English in school, like most of my friends in the neighborhood. I'm very proud of my Puerto Rican heritage and of being both bicultural and bilingual. Currently, I study international business at New York University, and in the future I hope to work with a company with locations here and abroad. It's true that knowing two languages offers many professional and social opportunities, but for me, speaking Spanish and English with family and friends is what I know; it's my experience. My friends and I love to watch the Latin Grammys and are especially proud when Calle 13 wins an award, like Record of the Year and Song of the Year for their hit "Latinoamérica."

1-21 En su opinión. With a partner, explore your experiences and ideas about bilingualism by discussing these questions.

1. What are your reasons for studying Spanish?
2. Do you plan to use Spanish in a particular career or in another facet of your life? How so?
3. Have you studied or do you speak other languages besides English and Spanish? What about your friends and family?
4. What other people in the media or public eye can you name who are bilingual? How has it helped them?
5. What can you do outside of class to improve your Spanish language and cultural understanding?

Presencia hispana

Although Puerto Ricans are U.S. citizens, they have no representation in the U.S. Congress, nor are they allowed to vote in U.S. presidential elections unless they reside in one of the 50 states. They are subject to the military draft, and pay into Social Security, but do not pay federal income taxes on income earned in P.R. However, the high cost of living and unemployment on the island have caused many to immigrate to the U.S. mainland, especially to New York and Florida. What event in 1898 led to the cession of Puerto Rico from Spain to the U.S.?

Mi música

"LATINOAMÉRICA" (CALLE 13, PUERTO RICO)

The alternative hip-hop group **Calle 13** has become popular for songs that highlight underlying social and political issues in Latin America. "Latinoamérica" has been heralded for its sound, content, and impactful images in the music video. The song features stepbrothers René Pérez Joglar and Eduardo José Cabra, as well as several guest artists. As you watch the video, notice both the stunning images and the possible social commentary the artists make.

ANTES DE VER Y ESCUCHAR (*PRE-VIEWING AND -LISTENING*)

1-22 Tú no puedes comprar... You will hear lyrics and view scenes extolling things no one can buy. Guess the meaning of these words in English and select the appropriate word for each concept.

the heat   my happiness   the colors   my sorrows   the wind   the rain   the clouds   the sun

Tú no puedes comprar...

1. el viento _____
2. el sol _____
3. el calor _____
4. mis dolores _____

5. los colores _____
6. mi alegría _____
7. las nubes _____
8. la lluvia _____

PARA VER Y ESCUCHAR (*WHILE-VIEWING AND -LISTENING*)

1-23 Vistas. Search online to find a video and lyrics (*la letra*) of "Latinoamérica." Then, indicate with **C** (**Cierto**) or **F** (**Falso**) if the image appears in the video. Finally, choose one image that strikes you as impactful or meaningful and explain why.

1. _____ agricultores y pescadores (*fishermen*)
2. _____ aviones (*planes*)
3. _____ bebés
4. _____ comida y bebida (*food and drink*)
5. _____ rascacielos (*skyscrapers*)

6. _____ dinero (*money*)
7. _____ montañas
8. _____ viejos y jóvenes (*old and young people*)
9. _____ un corazón (*heart*)

> 📍 **Busca:** video Calle 13 Latinoamérica; Calle 13 Latinoamérica letra

DESPUÉS DE VER Y ESCUCHAR (*POST-VIEWING AND -LISTENING*)

1-24 Opinión. The speech at the beginning of "Latinoamérica" is Quechua, an indigenous language dating from long before the conquest of Peru. How does the language fit into the message of the song? How does the image of the beating heart connect the music to the land?

1.2 Segunda parte

Vocabulario

1.4 **Describe your classroom, and respond to classroom instructions**

En la clase

))) **¿Qué pasa hoy en la clase de la profesora García?**

PROFESORA GARCÍA:	Buenos días. Por favor, **saquen la tarea** para hoy. Miguel, **lee** el número uno, por favor.
MIGUEL:	**Perdone**, profesora, no **tengo** la tarea.
PROFESORA GARCÍA:	¿Paulina?
PAULINA:	Un momento, profesora. **Necesito** mi **tableta**.
PROFESORA GARCÍA:	¿Ramón?
RAMÓN:	Perdone, profesora. **Repita, por favor.**
PROFESORA GARCÍA:	Todos, **saquen un papel** y **escriban** su nombre. **Hoy hay prueba.**

¿Comprendes? Indicate if each statement is **Cierto** (*true*) or **Falso** (*false*). Correct the false statements. If you need help, check the vocabulary list.

1. _____ La clase es hoy.
2. _____ Miguel tiene la tarea.
3. _____ Hay tarea en la clase de la profesora García.
4. _____ Paulina necesita su computadora portátil.

Answers: 1. C; 2. F: No tiene la tarea; 3. C; 4. F: Necesita su tableta.

))) Vocabulario

¿De qué color es?	What color is it?
amarillo/a	yellow
anaranjado/a	orange
azul	blue
blanco/a	white
gris	gray
marrón / color café	brown
morado/a	purple
negro/a	black
rojo/a	red
rosado/a	pink
verde	green

Objetos en el salón de clase	Objects in the classroom
el bolígrafo	pen
la calculadora	calculator
la computadora (portátil)	(laptop) computer
el cuaderno	notebook
el diccionario (en línea)	(online) dictionary
el lápiz	pencil
el libro	book
el mapa	map
el marcador	marker
la mesa	table
la mochila	backpack
el papel	paper
la pizarra (interactiva)	chalkboard (interactive whiteboard)
la prueba	quiz
la puerta	door
el reloj	clock, watch
la silla	chair
la tableta	tablet
el teléfono (celular/inteligente)	(cell) phone / smartphone

Personas	People
el hombre	man
la mujer	woman

Descripciones	Descriptions
barato/a	cheap, inexpensive
caro/a	expensive
grande	big
pequeño/a	small

Adverbios	Adverbs
aquí	here
hoy	today
mañana	tomorrow

Verbos	Verbs
hay	there is, there are
necesito, necesita (necesitar)	I need, s/he needs (to need)
tengo (tener)	I have (to have)

Expresiones para los estudiantes	Expressions for students
No comprendo.	I don't understand.
No sé.	I don't know.
Repita[1], por favor.	Repeat, please.
Perdone.	Excuse me.

Expresiones para la clase (tú/Uds.)	Expressions for the class (inf./for.)
Abre (Abran) el libro.	Open your book(s).
Cierra (Cierren) el libro.	Close your book(s).
Contesta (Contesten) en español.	Answer in Spanish.
Escribe (Escriban) en la pizarra.	Write on the board.
Escucha. (Escuchen.)	Listen.
Estudia. (Estudien.)	Study.
Lee (Lean) el diálogo.	Read the dialogue.
Repite. (Repitan.)	Repeat.
Saca (Saquen) la tarea.	Take out your homework.
Ve (Vayan) a la pizarra.	Go to the board.

Variaciones

- A few words for colors vary in the Spanish-speaking world. **Marrón** is also **color café** or **pardo**. **Rosado** may be **(el color) rosa**, and **morado** may be **púrpura** or **(el color) violeta**. Also, **anaranjado** may be simply **naranja**.
- Names for technology also vary: *laptop* is **la (computadora) portátil** in Latin America and **el (ordenador) portátil** in Spain. *Cell phone* is generally **el (teléfono) celular** in Latin America and **el (teléfono) móvil** in Spain.

Aplicación

1-25 ¿Cuántos/as hay en la clase? Take inventory of your classroom. Indicate how many of each item there are.

MODELO: <u>20</u> estudiantes

_____ pizarras   _____ mapas   _____ sillas

_____ bolígrafos   _____ teléfonos inteligentes   _____ tabletas

_____ mesas   _____ cuadernos   _____ libros de español

_____

[1]**Repita** is a formal command, appropriate to use with your professor.

1-26 ¿Qué haces cuando...? (*What do you do when...?*) Listen to a Spanish teacher make various requests in the classroom, and indicate the number of each request next to what you would do.

_____ I answer in Spanish.　_____ I write the sentence.　_____ I repeat the alphabet.

_____ I open my book.　_____ I close the book.　_____ I go to the board.

_____ I read the dialogue.　_____ I listen to the music.

1-27 Los colores y la percepción. How do you perceive colors?

Paso 1 Select the appropriate association for each color, according to long-held notions in Western culture.

1. _____ el azul
2. _____ el marrón
3. _____ el verde
4. _____ el anaranjado
5. _____ el rojo
6. _____ el morado
7. _____ el amarillo

a. el sol, el oro

b. la competición, la actividad, el fuego (*fire*)

c. la tranquilidad

d. la magia, el romance, la imaginación, la realeza (*royalty*)

e. la sensualidad, el color de la Madre Tierra

f. la energía, la pasión

g. la regeneración, el futuro, la conservación

Paso 2 As a group, take a survey to find out the following information.

1. ¿Cuál es el color favorito de la clase?
2. ¿Qué significa ese color, según la información en el **Paso 1**?
3. ¿Hay una diferencia en preferencia entre los hombres y las mujeres de la clase?

1-28 ¡Escucha bien! In pairs, take turns giving and acting out commands in Spanish. Choose from these options.

MODELO: ESTUDIANTE 1: *Abre el libro.*
ESTUDIANTE 2: (opens his/her book)
ESTUDIANTE 1: *Correcto.*

Cierra el libro.	Ve a la pizarra.	Saca la tarea.
Repite tu nombre.	Saca el lápiz.	Escribe tu nombre.
Ve a la puerta.	Lee el diálogo.	Abre el cuaderno.

1-29A ¡Necesito información! You are a student departmental worker. Below is a list of items you need for your department. Call the bookstore and give the clerk your supply order. Mark the items your clerk can supply, as he/she may have a lesser quantity. When you finish, compare your lists. **Estudiante B**: see **Appendix 1**, page A-1.

MODELO: ESTUDIANTE A: *¿Hay cinco calculadoras?*
ESTUDIANTE B: *Sí, tengo diez. / No, solo (only) hay cuatro.*

Estudiante A:

_____ 1 reloj	_____ 14 tabletas	_____ 20 diccionarios
_____ 10 sillas	_____ 80 bolígrafos	_____ 75 cajas (*boxes*) de marcadores
_____ 5 mapas	_____ 90 lápices	_____ 100 cajas de papel
_____ 33 libros	_____ 11 mesas	

1-30 Veo algo... (*I see something...*) In pairs, take turns describing an object to see whether your classmate can guess what it is. Use colors and adjectives from **Vocabulario**.

MODELO: ESTUDIANTE 1: *Veo algo verde y grande.*
ESTUDIANTE 2: *¿Es la pizarra?*

Estructuras

1.5 **Identify and describe people, places, and things, including dates**

Days of the week; months of the year; seasons

LOS DÍAS DE LA SEMANA (*DAYS OF THE WEEK*)

2018
JUNIO

Playa Girón, Cuba

LUNES	MARTES	MIÉRCOLES	JUEVES	VIERNES	SÁBADO	DOMINGO
				1	2	3
4	5	6	7	8	9	10
11	12	13	14	15	16	17
18	19	20	21	22	23	24
25	26	27	28	29	30	

¿Qué día es el cinco de junio?

- Use the expression **¿Qué día es…?** to ask the day of the week.

  | **¿Qué día es** hoy? | *What day is today?* |
  | **¿Qué día es** mañana? | *What day is tomorrow?* |

- The days of the week are all masculine: **el** lunes, **el** martes, **el** miércoles, **el** jueves, **el** viernes, **el** sábado, **el** domingo.

- Do not use the definite article after **es** when telling what day of the week it is.

  Hoy **es jueves**.   *Today is Thursday.*

- *On Monday… , on Tuesday…* , etc., is expressed by using the definite article **el**.

  El examen es **el lunes**.   *The exam is on Monday.*

- In the plural, the days of the week express the idea of doing something regularly.

  Voy al gimnasio **los sábados**.   *I go to the gym on Saturdays.*

- Days that end in **-s** have the same form in the singular and the plural. **El lunes → los lunes**.

> La clase de filosofía es **los lunes**, **los miércoles** y **los viernes**.
>
> *Philosophy class is on Mondays, Wednesdays, and Fridays.*

- Calendars usually begin the week with **lunes** (Monday), not **domingo** (Sunday). The days of the week are written in lowercase.

¿Comprendes? Select the most logical letter to complete each sentence.

1. El primer día de la semana es ____.
2. El quinto (*fifth*) día es ____.
3. El fin de semana es ____.

a. el sábado y el domingo
b. el lunes
c. el viernes

Answers: 1. b; 2. c; 3. a

LOS MESES Y LAS ESTACIONES DEL AÑO (*MONTHS AND SEASONS OF THE YEAR*)

Las estaciones en Nueva York

el invierno
- diciembre
- enero
- febrero

la primavera
- marzo
- abril
- mayo

el verano
- junio
- julio
- agosto

el otoño
- septiembre
- octubre
- noviembre

- To ask the date:

> **¿Cuál es la fecha de hoy?**
> **¿Qué fecha es hoy?**
>
> *What's today's date?*

- To answer:

> **Hoy es (el)** dos de febrero.
>
> *Today is February 2nd.*

- Use **el primero** for the first day of the month. All the other days use cardinal numbers (**el cuatro**, **el once**).

  el primero de enero   *January 1st*
  el cinco de mayo   *May 5th*

- The definite article is used to talk about the seasons but is omitted to say what season it is.

  ¿Cómo es **la primavera** aquí?   *What is spring like here?*
  Es **verano** ahora en Argentina. *It's summer now in Argentina.*

- As with days of the week, write the names of months and seasons in lowercase.

- Write the date with the day first and then the month.

  11-05 el once de mayo   **12-06** el doce de junio

¿Comprendes? Identify these dates in Spanish.

MODELO: 13-02: *el trece de febrero*

1. 03-12 _____   2. 01-08 _____   3. 27-04 _____

Answers: 1. el tres de diciembre; 2. el primero de agosto; 3. el veintisiete de abril

Aplicación

1-31 **Fiestas importantes en el mundo hispano.** Select the appropriate date for each of these holidays celebrated in the Spanish-speaking world.

1. _____ En EE. UU. es una fiesta para celebrar la cultura mexicana.
2. _____ El Día de la Raza (o el Día de Cristóbal Colón) es en el otoño.
3. _____ La fiesta de la Virgen de Guadalupe es en el invierno.
4. _____ El día festivo (*holiday*) para los trabajadores (*workers*) es en la primavera.
5. _____ En Costa Rica, el Día de la Madre es en el verano.
6. _____ El Día de los Muertos (*Dead*) es el día después de la Noche de Brujas (*Halloween*).

a. el 12 de diciembre
b. el primero de noviembre
c. el 5 de mayo
d. el 15 de agosto
e. el 12 de octubre
f. el primero de mayo

Un altar para celebrar el Día de los Muertos en México

1-32 **Fechas importantes en EE. UU. y Canadá.** Indicate the dates of the following celebrations.

MODELO: *el diecisiete de marzo*

el Día de San Patricio

1.   2.   3.   4.

la Noche de Brujas   la Nochevieja   el Día de la Independencia   el Día de San Valentín

Es junio y Miguel esquía en Bariloche, Argentina.

1-33 Las estaciones del año. Remember that the seasons in the Northern and Southern Hemispheres are inverted. Write the season in which each month falls in the Northern Hemisphere. Then do the same with the Southern Hemisphere.

	Hemisferio Norte	**Hemisferio Sur**
1. agosto	_____	_____
2. diciembre	_____	_____
3. marzo	_____	_____
4. octubre	_____	_____

1-34A ¡Necesito información! Take turns asking each other questions to fill in the missing days, dates, and months on each of your grids. **Estudiante B**: see **Appendix 1**, page A-2.

> MODELO: ESTUDIANTE A: (You need) *¿Un mes de otoño?*
> ESTUDIANTE B: (Your partner needs) *octubre*

Estudiante A:

You need...	My partner gives me...	Your partner needs...
¿Un mes de otoño?	*octubre*	
1. el Día de la Independencia		el 14 de febrero
2. un día con nueve letras		enero
3. un mes con treinta días		mayo
4. un día que no hay clases		febrero
5. un mes de verano		el lunes

1-35 ¿Cuándo es tu cumpleaños? In groups of six or seven students, take turns reporting your birthdays. Have one person fill in the dates for each month reported. Present your findings to the class to compile a chart for the entire group. Use the following questions as a guide.

> MODELO: *Mi cumpleaños es el 17 de enero.*

1. ¿Cuál (*Which*) es el mes más común de la clase?
2. ¿Cuál es el mes menos común de la clase?
3. ¿Hay dos personas con el mismo (*same*) día de cumpleaños?

Nombre del / de la estudiante	Fecha de cumpleaños

Nouns and articles

Nouns identify persons, places, or objects. Spanish nouns—even those denoting nonliving things—are either masculine or feminine in gender, and singular or plural. The definite article (*the*) must agree with the noun. In Spanish, there are four forms of the definite article (*the* in English):

	Masculine	Feminine
Singular	el	la
Plural	los	las

TALKING ABOUT PEOPLE

- Any noun denoting a masculine person is masculine; many of these end in **-o**. Any noun denoting a feminine person is feminine; many of these end in **-a**.

el muchacho	*boy*	**la** muchach**a**	*girl*
el hombre	*man*	**la** mujer	*woman*

- Most masculine person nouns ending in a consonant simply add **-a** to form the feminine.

el profesor / **la** profesor**a**	*male/female professor*
el señor / **la** señor**a**	*Mr./Mrs.*

- Some person nouns use the same form for masculine and feminine; the article indicates the gender.

el artista / **la** artista	**el** estudiante / **la** estudiante

- Use the definite article with titles when talking **about** someone (even yourself), but not when addressing someone directly.

La profesora Gómez es española.	*Professor Gómez is Spanish.*
Soy **la** profesora Gómez.	*I'm Professor Gómez.*
¡Buenos días, profesora Gómez!	*Good morning, Professor Gómez!*

TALKING ABOUT THINGS

- Most nouns ending in **-o** are masculine. Most nouns end in **-a** are feminine. (Some common exceptions are: **el día** and **el mapa**, which are masculine.)

el cuadern**o**	*the notebook*	**la** puert**a**	*the door*

- Most nouns ending in **-ad** and **-ión** are feminine.

la universi**dad**	*university*	**la** nac**ión**	*nation*

- Most nouns ending in **-ma** are masculine.

el proble**ma**	*problem*	**el** dra**ma**	*drama*

- Nouns ending in **-e** or a consonant can be masculine or feminine. The article indicates what the gender of the noun is.

la clase	*class*	**el** lápiz	*pencil*

¿Comprendes? Provide the correct definite article for each word.

1. _____ señor

2. _____ profesora

3. _____ verdad

4. _____ problema

Answers: 1. el; 2. la; 3. la; 4. el

EL PLURAL DE LOS SUSTANTIVOS (*PLURAL FORMS OF NOUNS*)

Masculine		Feminine	
los muchachos	*the boys*	**las muchachas**	*the girls*
los libros	*the books*	**las mesas**	*the tables*
los hombres	*the men*	**las mujeres**	*the women*

- Add **-s** to nouns ending in a vowel, or **-es** to nouns ending in a consonant.

  Add *-s*   **Add** *-es*

  el libro → los libros   la mujer → las mujeres

  la clase → las clases   la universidad → las universidades

- For nouns that end in **-z**, change the **z** to **c** in the plural. When the last syllable of a word that ends in a consonant has an accent mark, the plural no longer needs an accent.

  z → c   **ón → ones**

  el lápiz → los lápices   la lección → las lecciones

¿Comprendes? Provide the plural form of each word.

1. el lápiz _____   2. la mochila _____   3. el mapa _____

Answers: 1. los lápices; 2. las mochilas; 3. los mapas

LOS ARTÍCULOS INDEFINIDOS (*INDEFINITE ARTICLES*)

In Spanish, there are four forms of the indefinite article.

	Masculine		Feminine	
Singular	**un** bolígrafo	*a pen*	**una** silla	*a chair*
Plural	**unos** bolígrafos	*some pens*	**unas** sillas	*some chairs*

- Indefinite articles (*a, an, some, a few*) also agree with the noun they modify.

  un diccionario   *a dictionary*

  unas computadoras   *some (a few) computers*

- Omit the indefinite article when telling someone's profession, unless you qualify the person (good, bad, hardworking, etc.).

  Lorena es profesora de arte.   *Lorena is an art professor.*

  Lorena es **una** buena profesora.   *Lorena is a good professor.*

¿Comprendes? Provide the indefinite article for each word.

1. _____ pizarra   2. _____ cuaderno   3. _____ papeles

Answers: 1. una; 2. un; 3. unos

Aplicación

1-36 ¿Qué pasa en la clase de español? Select the correct article or X, if none is required.

En (1) <u>el/la</u> clase de español hay (2) <u>una/unas</u> profesora y veinte estudiantes.

(3) <u>Los/Las</u> estudiantes son norteamericanos. (4) <u>La/Una</u> profesora es argentina.

(5) <u>El/La</u> señora Sosa es muy exigente. Ella dice: "¡Buenas tardes, estudiantes!

¡Saquen (6) <u>la/una</u> tarea, por favor, y abran (7) <u>el/X</u> libro!" Entonces ella dice,

"María, lee (8) <u>el/los</u> número uno, por favor". María responde: "Perdone,

(9) <u>X/la</u> profesora. No tengo (10) <u>el/la</u> cuaderno".

1-37 Desafío. Working with a partner, take turns challenging each other to provide the correct definite and indefinite article. Confirm by saying **correcto** or **incorrecto**.

MODELO: ESTUDIANTE 1: libro
           ESTUDIANTE 2: *el libro / un libro*
           ESTUDIANTE 1: *Correcto.*

puerta	universidades	mapa	problema
calculadoras	mesa	bolígrafos	lápiz
libros	muchachos	estudiante	silla
hombre	mujer	relojes	poema

Hay unos estudiantes en la Pontificia Universidad Católica en Buenos Aires.

1-38 ¿Qué hay? Describe where the following items can be found, using the correct definite and indefinite articles.

MODELO: *Hay una profesora en la clase.*

¿Qué hay?	¿Dónde? (*Where?*)
cuaderno(s)	silla(s)
estudiante(s)	clase
teléfono(s) inteligente(s)	mesa(s)
computadora portátil	pizarra
mochilas	mochila
ejemplos de gramática	universidad

1-39 ¿Qué hay en tu mochila? In pairs, ask each other what you have in your backpacks. What do you have in common?

MODELO: ESTUDIANTE 1: *¿Hay un lápiz en tu mochila?*
ESTUDIANTE 2: *Sí. / No.*

Adjective forms, position, and agreement

- Descriptive adjectives describe and give additional information about objects and people. They agree in gender and number with the nouns they modify; they generally follow the nouns.

una profesora **buena**	*a good professor*	las señoras **simpáticas**	*the nice ladies*
un cuaderno **rosado**	*a pink notebook*	los bolígrafos **rojos**	*the red pens*

- Adjectives ending in **-e** or a consonant have the same masculine and feminine forms.

un libro **grande**	*a big book*	una computadora **grande**	*a big computer*
un bolígrafo **azul**	*a blue pen*	una silla **azul**	*a blue chair*

- Add **-a** to form the feminine of adjectives of nationality ending in a consonant, and adjectives that end in **-dor**.

el profesor **español**	*the Spanish professor*
la estudiante **española**	*the Spanish student*
un libro **francés**	*a French book*
una mujer **francesa**	*a French woman*
un hombre **trabajador**	*a hardworking man*
una mujer **trabajadora**	*a hardworking woman*

- The adjectives **bueno** and **malo** may be placed before or after nouns. Drop the final **-o** before a masculine singular noun.

un **buen** estudiante	*a good student*
un **mal** día	*a bad day*

- The adjective **grande** changes to **gran** before any singular noun to mean *great*.

una universidad **grande**	*a big university*
una **gran** universidad	*a great university*

- Here are some adjectives to help you talk about yourself and others.

aburrido/a	*boring*	perezoso/a	*lazy*
bueno/a	*good*	simpático/a	*nice*
malo/a	*bad*	trabajador/a	*hardworking*

- This list of adjectives is made up of cognates, words that are similar in Spanish and English. Can you guess their meanings?

exótico/a	**ideal**	**inteligente**
introvertido/a	**paciente**	**romántico/a**
extrovertido/a	**idealista**	**interesante**
misterioso/a	**pesimista**	**tímido/a**
fascinante	**impaciente**	
optimista	**realista**	

¿Comprendes? Select the most appropriate adjective for each noun.

1. _____ una pizarra…
2. _____ una estudiante…
3. _____ unos teléfonos…

a. tímida
b. interactiva
c. inteligentes

Answers: 1. b; 2. a; 3. c

Aplicación

1-40 Parejas. Select the logical adjectives to describe the nouns listed. Pay close attention to the gender and number of the nouns.

anaranjadas   caros   extrovertidas   morado   rosada   simpática   tímido   trabajadores

1. las sillas _____
2. el bolígrafo _____
3. los relojes _____
4. la mochila _____

5. la estudiante _____
6. el muchacho _____
7. los profesores _____
8. las amigas _____

1-41 ¿De qué color? Provide the color for each item in your classroom.

MODELO: la pizarra
La pizarra es negra (blanca/verde).

1. el mapa
2. los lápices
3. el libro de español
4. los cuadernos
5. las sillas

6. la puerta
7. los papeles del profesor / de la profesora
8. la mochila de… (John, etc.)

1-42 Pingüinos de Magallanes, Argentina. Answer these questions based on the photo.

1. ¿De qué colores son los pingüinos de Magallanes?
2. ¿De qué color es el mar?
3. ¿Cómo son los pingüinos (*What are they like*)?

1-43 ¿Cómo es? ¿Cómo son? Combine nouns and adjectives to make logical sentences in Spanish. Remember to use the correct forms of **ser** and make articles, nouns, and adjectives agree in gender and number.

> MODELO: los estudiantes
> *Los estudiantes son buenos.*

el libro de español		barato/caro
los profesores		interesante/simpático
mis amigos y yo	**soy/es/son**	inteligente/trabajador
yo		bueno/malo
la universidad		grande/pequeño
mis clases		estadounidense/español/...
		rojo/anaranjado/amarillo/negro/...

1-44 En su opinión. In pairs, take turns asking and responding to questions about people and things you know. Be sure that articles and adjectives agree with the noun they modify.

> MODELO: ESTUDIANTE 1: ¿Cómo son los profesores de esta universidad?
> ESTUDIANTE 2: *Son muy buenos.*

1. ¿Cómo es el/la profesor/a?
2. ¿Cómo son los futbolistas de la liga NFL?
3. ¿De qué color es tu mochila?
4. ¿De qué color son los libros de español?
5. ¿Cómo es la universidad?
6. ¿Cómo es tu carro?
7. ¿De qué color es tu teléfono celular?
8. ¿Cómo son tus amigos?

¡Conversemos!

First, ask yourself whether you can perform the follow functions in Spanish. Then act out the scenarios with two or three classmates. Ask and respond to at least three questions in each situation.

✓ CAN YOU . . .	WITH YOUR CLASSMATE(S) . . .
☐ describe your classroom?	**Situación: En la universidad.**
	You each have a different Spanish class. Describe them to each other, including the professors, students, and classroom objects. Include descriptive adjectives with colors when appropriate.
	Para empezar (*Getting started*): *¿Cómo es tu clase de español? ¿Cómo son...?*
☐ respond to classroom instructions?	**Situación: En la clase de español.**
	Take turns using classroom expressions to tell the group what to do. They will either perform the function, ask you to repeat it, or say that they do not understand or don't know.
	Para empezar: *Abre...*
☐ talk about days and dates?	**Situación: En casa.**
	Ask each other when some events take place, for example, **el examen, la fiesta, el partido de fútbol, el cumpleaños del / de la profesor/a, el Día de los Muertos, el Año Nuevo...**
	Para empezar: *¿Cuándo es/son...?*
☐ talk about yourself and others?	**Situación: Yo soy...**
	You and your classmates are running for office in your university's student government. Introduce yourselves, say where you are from, and describe the kind of people you are.
	Para empezar: *Me llamo/Soy... Soy de... y soy...*

Club cultura

1.6 Use visuals to aid comprehension

Explora el mundo hispano

Estrategia para ver

Use visuals to aid comprehension. As you watch a video, focus your attention on the visuals to help you understand what you hear. For example, if the visual is a place, the narrator is most likely talking about a place. Also, when the video features people, pay close attention to the actions, body language, facial expressions, and intonation of the speaker(s).

ANTES DE VER EL VIDEO

1-45 La diversidad del mundo hispano. You will watch a video about the diversity of the Hispanic world. Name five points or images you expect the video to discuss or show.

AL VER EL VIDEO

1-46 El mundo hispano. Watch a segment of **Club cultura** and use the visuals to help you indicate with **C** (**Cierto**) or **F** (**Falso**) which of these items are featured in the video. What features from this list did you predict in Activity **1-45**?

	Cierto	Falso
1. las montañas de los Andes	____	____
2. el mar Caribe	____	____
3. los bosques de la Amazonía	____	____
4. una corrida de toros (*bullfight*)	____	____
5. el surf en El Salvador	____	____
6. una fiesta de independencia	____	____
7. un mercado en Guatemala	____	____
8. un partido (*match*) de vóleibol	____	____
9. una academia de béisbol	____	____

DESPUÉS DE VER EL VIDEO

1-47 El mundo hispano. Write three adjectives to describe what you have observed in the video.

   MODELO: *Las montañas son… Las playas son… La ciudad de… es…*

1.3 Nuestro mundo

Panoramas

1.7 Recognize the expanse of the Hispanic world

La diversidad del mundo hispano

En el Nuevo Mundo, los españoles encontraron (*found*) civilizaciones avanzadas como la de los aztecas, los mayas y los incas. Hoy los sitios arqueológicos contrastan con las grandes ciudades.

Estrategia para **Panoramas**

Throughout *¡Arriba!* we encourage you to discover the diversity of Hispanic cultures across five continents. You will see a diversity of peoples and cultures, great cities and vast, open regions, antiquity and modernity. Use these images and other strategies you learn throughout this program to understand the text. Look for words that are similar to English words (cognates) to help you derive their meaning.

España presenta contrastes entre lo antiguo y lo moderno. Por ejemplo, es un modelo para la energía renovable.

Las mujeres mayas de Guatemala son famosas por sus textiles que son una tradición milenaria.

Santiago, Chile, una metrópolis cosmopolita y sofisticada

Todos los años hay desfiles puertorriqueños que celebran la herencia puertorriqueña en Estados Unidos.

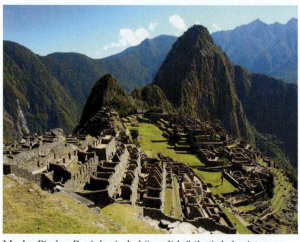

Machu Picchu, Perú, la ciudad "perdida" (*lost*) de los incas

Mundo hispano

Número de hispanohablantes en el mundo: 495 millones

Número de estudiantes de español: 21 millones

Número de países donde es lengua oficial: 20

Número de hispanohablantes en EE. UU.: 45 millones (14%)

Importancia del español en *Twitter*: Segundo (después del inglés)

1-48 Identifica. Select the correct option based on the information in **Panoramas**.

> 14%   20   495 million   desfiles   the Incas

1. the number of countries where Spanish is an official language

2. one important pre-Columbian culture in the Americas in the sixteenth century

3. the number of Spanish speakers in the world

4. the percentage of the U.S. population that speaks Spanish

5. a way to celebrate Puerto Rican heritage in the U.S.

1-49 Desafío. In pairs, work together to see how many Spanish-speaking countries you can name without looking at the map. After checking your answers, compare your results with those of other groups in the class.

1-50 Proyecto: El Viejo Mundo y el Nuevo Mundo. The cultural and physical diversity of the Hispanic world offers a wealth of opportunities for travel. Choose from **Barcelona, Cartagena de Indias, la Patagonia, Machu Picchu, Santiago de Chile, Puerto Rico,** or another place that interests you, to investigate more about its characteristics. Write a summary of what you find. Follow the **Modelo**.

Para empezar: *[Nombre] está en... Es un sitio muy [adjetivo]. Tiene (It has)... Es importante ver (see)... La foto es de...*

> 📍 **Busca:** Barcelona, Cartagena de Indias, Patagonia, Machu Picchu, Santiago de Chile, Puerto Rico

MODELO: *El sitio arqueológico de Copán está en Honduras. Es un sitio muy importante de la antigua civilización maya. Es importante ver las pirámides y las estelas de Copán. La foto es de Waxakajuun Ub'aah K'awiil.*

Páginas

1.8 **Identify cognates to understand text**

Versos sencillos, "XXXIX" (José Martí, Cuba)

José Martí (1853–1895) was a prolific writer, intellectual, and patriot. Besides being known for his struggle to gain Cuba's independence from Spain, he is famous for his poetry, some of which has been popularized through song ("Guantanamera"). This selection comes from a series of short poems entitled *Versos sencillos* and discusses how the poet treats both his friends and his enemies.

Estrategia para leer

Identify cognates to understand text. Cognates are words or expressions that are identical or similar in two languages. Spanish and English share many cognates. For example, **profesor**/*professor* and **universidad**/*university*. When you read Spanish, use cognates to help you understand the text.

ANTES DE LEER (*PRE-READING*)

1-51 **Los cognados.** Read the poem quickly and try to identify words that look similar in English. Then, check the meaning of those words in a bilingual dictionary.

AL LEER (*WHILE-READING*)

1-52 **El poema.** Read the poem more carefully. When you feel confident of its meaning, read it aloud. Remember to use cognates to support your understanding of the text.

El Mausoleo de José Martí, Santiago de Cuba

¡OJO!

Remember that you do not have to know every word to understand a passage and glean essential information. Featured reading strategies and related practice activities will help you augment your reading comprehension skills in Spanish.

"XXXIX"

Cultivo una rosa blanca,

En julio como en enero,

Para el amigo sincero

Que me da[1] su mano[2] franca.

Y para el cruel que me arranca[3]

El corazón[4] con que vivo,

Cardo[5] ni ortiga[6] cultivo:

Cultivo una rosa blanca.

---

[1]*gives* [2]*hand*

[3]*yanks out*

[4]*heart*

[5]*thistle* [6]*nettle, a prickly plant*

DESPUÉS DE LEER (*POST-READING*)

1-53 El poeta. Which of the following seem to describe the poet from what he writes? Indicate **Sí** or **No** for each statement. Which of these words are cognates?

1. _____ Es blanco.
2. _____ Es optimista.
3. _____ Tiene amigos.
4. _____ Tiene enemigos.
5. _____ Es generoso.
6. _____ Su mes favorito es julio.

1-54 Los símbolos. The poet uses colors and objects as symbols or metaphors. Select the symbol or metaphor that best corresponds to each element from the poem. What else do these colors and objects symbolize for you?

1. _____ la rosa blanca
2. _____ en julio y en enero
3. _____ la mano franca
4. _____ me arranca el corazón
5. _____ cardo ni ortiga

a. siempre (*always*)
b. el amor, la paz
c. me causa dolor (*pain*)
d. el castigo (*retribution*)
e. la sinceridad

¿De qué color son las rosas en el Mausoleo de José Martí?

1-55 Guantanamera. The song based on *Versos sencillos* has been performed and recorded countless times. Search the Internet for a version of the song. Write a short paragraph to answer the questions that follow.

📍 **Busca:** Guantanamera video

- ¿Cómo se llama el/la cantante (*singer*) o el grupo?
- ¿De dónde es/son?
- ¿Cómo es/son?
- ¿Cómo es la canción (*song*)?

1-56 Tu "Guantanamera". This song was written in the 1920s and popularized on a local Cuban radio program where the host closed each show by commenting in song on a current (often controversial or tragic) news event. The verse structure with eight syllables lent itself to fresh content any time the singer wished to improvise. In pairs, compose a verse in English for "Guantanamera," and then share it with the class.

MODELO: *We have an app for directions*
and one for restaurants around
We have an app for directions
and one for restaurants around
and when it comes to learning Spanish
there are many to be found...
Guantanamera, guajira guantanamera...

Taller

1.9 **Move from phrases to sentences**

Tu perfil

Estrategia para escribir

Move from phrases to sentences. Use these basic rules to create sentences in Spanish. You will learn more about these throughout *¡Arriba!*

1. Follow the standard word order: *subject + verb + rest of the sentence*
2. Place adjectives after nouns.
3. Use adverbs in the same way as in English. Ex: **Necesito un libro mañana**.
4. Add **no** before a verb to make a sentence negative.
5. Use the connectors **y** (*and*), **o** (*or*) to connect ideas. Ex: **Soy buena y trabajadora**.

1-57 **Un perfil para una red social.** When you write a social network profile, how do you describe yourself to people you have not met?

ANTES DE ESCRIBIR (*PRE-WRITING*)

Brainstorm information you would like to include. First, write a list of adjectives that describe you. Then, write a list of adjectives to describe your university, classes, and professors.

AL ESCRIBIR (*WHILE-WRITING*)

Follow these steps to create a social network profile:

- Introduce yourself.
- Using adjectives from your list, describe what you are like.
- Describe your university, classes, and your professors.
- Say what your favorite color is (**Mi color favorito es el...**).
- Add any other personal details about yourself (your birthday, favorite day of the week, etc.).

DESPUÉS DE ESCRIBIR (*POST-WRITING*)

- **Revisar (*Review*).** Review the following elements in your profile:
  - ☐ Make sure all sentences have a clear subject and verb.
  - ☐ Check that all of your adjectives agree with the nouns they modify.
  - ☐ Check your use of the verb **ser**.
- **Intercambiar (*Exchange*).** Exchange your profile with a classmate's. Then make suggestions and corrections, and add a comment about the profile.
- **Entregar (*Turn in*).** Rewrite your profile, incorporating your classmate's suggestions. Then turn in the profile to your instructor.

En este capítulo...

🔊 Vocabulario

Primera parte

Saludos	Greetings
Buenos días.	*Good morning.*
Buenas noches.	*Good evening.*
Buenas tardes.	*Good afternoon.*
¿Cómo está usted?	*How are you? (for.)*
¿Cómo estás?	*How are you? (inf.)*
Hola.	*Hello, Hi.*
¿Qué pasa?	*What's happening? What's up? (inf.)*
¿Qué tal?	*What's up? (inf.)*

Respuestas	Responses
De nada.	*You're welcome.*
¿De verdad?	*Really?*
Encantado/a.	*Pleased to meet you.*
Gracias.	*Thank you.*
Igualmente.	*Likewise.*
Lo siento.	*I'm sorry.*
Más o menos.	*So-so. (lit. More or less.)*
Mucho gusto.	*Nice to meet you.*
(Muy) Bien.	*(Very) Well.*
(Muy) Mal.	*(Very) Bad.*
Todo bien.	*All's well.*

Presentaciones	Introductions
¿Cómo se llama usted?	*What's your name? (for.)*
¿Cómo te llamas (tú)?	*What's your name? (inf.)*
Me llamo...	*My name is... (lit. I call myself...)*
Mi nombre es...	*My name is...*
Soy... (ser)	*I am... (to be)*
¿Y tú?	*And you?*

Despedidas	Farewells
Adiós.	*Good-bye.*
Hasta luego.	*See you later.*
Hasta mañana.	*See you tomorrow.*
Hasta pronto.	*See you soon.*
Nos vemos.	*See you.*

Títulos	Titles
el señor (Sr.)	*Mr.*
la señora (Sra.)	*Mrs., Ms.*
la señorita (Srta.)	*Miss*

En la clase	In class
la clase	*class*
el/la estudiante	*student (male/female)*
el/la profesor/a	*professor (male/female)*
la tarea	*homework*
la universidad	*university*

Expresiones para la clase	Expressions for class
¿Cómo se dice...?	*How do you say...?*
¿Cómo se escribe...?	*How do you write...?*
¿Qué significa...?	*What does... mean?*
Otra vez, por favor.	*Again, please.*

Segunda parte

¿De qué color es?	What color is it?
amarillo/a	*yellow*
anaranjado/a	*orange*
azul	*blue*
blanco/a	*white*
gris	*gray*
marrón / color café	*brown*
morado/a	*purple*
negro/a	*black*
rojo/a	*red*
rosado/a	*pink*
verde	*green*

Objetos en el salón de clase	Objects in the classroom
el bolígrafo	*pen*
la calculadora	*calculator*
la computadora (portátil)	*(laptop)computer*
el cuaderno	*notebook*
el diccionario (en línea)	*(online) dictionary*
el lápiz	*pencil*
el libro	*book*
el mapa	*map*
el marcador	*marker*
la mesa	*table*
la mochila	*backpack*
el papel	*paper*
la pizarra (interactiva)	*chalkboard (interactive whiteboard)*
la prueba	*quiz*
la puerta	*door*
el reloj	*clock, watch*
la silla	*chair*
la tableta	*tablet*
el teléfono (celular/inteligente)	*(cell) phone / smartphone*

Personas	People
el hombre	*man*
la mujer	*woman*

Descripciones	Descriptions
barato/a	*cheap, inexpensive*
caro/a	*expensive*
grande	*big*
pequeño/a	*small*

Adverbios	Adverbs
aquí	*here*
hoy	*today*
mañana	*tomorrow*

Verbos	Verbs
hay	*there is, there are*
necesito, necesita (necesitar)	*I need, s/he needs (to need)*
tengo (tener)	*I have (to have)*

Los números 0–100   See page 10.
Expresiones para los estudiantes   See page 19.
Days of the week; months; seasons   See page 21.

Subject pronouns and *ser*   See page 12.
Expresiones para la clase (*tú/Uds.***)**   See page 19.
Descriptive adjectives   See page 28.

Capítulo 2
¿De dónde eres?

«Dime con quién andas y te diré quién eres».

Don Quijote de Pablo Picasso.
In this iconic drawing, Picasso has captured the futile struggle between reality (the windmills) and imagination (what he sees as terrifying giants). What other cultural icons occur to you in relation to Spain?

Learning Objectives

2.1 Describe yourself and others

2.2 Ask and respond to questions about people, places, and things

2.3 Identify how names reflect a person's heritage, and learn about an alternative rock musician from Spain

2.4 Discuss activities you do and like to do

2.5 Talk about your activities and obligations

ENFOQUE CULTURAL: ESPAÑA
Club cultura: Introducción a España

Indicate the correct option for each question, based on the video.

1. ¿Está (*Is*) Horacio ahora en Madrid, Barcelona o Sevilla?
2. ¿Está en un bar, una universidad o una plaza?
3. ¿Es el clima en el sur seco, lluvioso (*rainy*) o frío?
4. ¿Es la gente española muy morena, amable o vieja?

2.1 Primera parte

Vocabulario

2.1 **Describe yourself and others**

Las descripciones y las nacionalidades

Paco   Chema   Isabel   Clara

Carlos   la profesora   Ángeles   Ramón
          Vargas

¿Quiénes son? El Bar Campus es **un lugar** muy popular entre los estudiantes de la Universidad Complutense de Madrid.

PACO:	¿Quién es **la muchacha morena** con la computadora portátil?
CHEMA:	Es Isabel, una estudiante **española**, de Sevilla. Y la otra (*other*) muchacha, con el suéter negro, es Clara, es **estadounidense**.
ISABEL:	¿Quién es **el muchacho joven** con la mochila?
CLARA:	Es Carlos, un estudiante **canadiense**. Y la mujer con él es la profesora Vargas. Es **venezolana** y es una muy buena profesora de filosofía.
ÁNGELES:	¡Pero (*But*), hombre! ¿De quién recibes tantos (*so many*) mensajes de texto?
RAMÓN:	¡Es que tengo **muchos** amigos! Y todos son muy **activos** en sus celulares.
LA PROFESORA VARGAS:	¿**A qué hora es** tu clase de historia? Es ahora mismo (*right now*), ¿no?
CARLOS:	No, ¡**es a las tres y media en punto**!

¿Comprendes? Select the appropriate description for each character. If you need help, check the vocabulary list.

1. _____ Isabel
2. _____ la profesora Vargas
3. _____ Ramón

a. Es moreno y muy popular.
b. Es de España.
c. Es venezolana.

Answers: 1. b; 2. c; 3. a

Vocabulario

Características físicas	Physical characteristics
alto/a	tall
bajo/a	short
bonito/a	pretty, cute
delgado/a	slender
feo/a	ugly
fuerte	strong
gordo/a	fat
guapo/a	good-looking
joven	young
moreno/a	dark (skin, hair)
rubio/a	blond (fair)
viejo/a	old

Otras características	Other characteristics
activo/a	active
nuevo/a	new
pobre	poor
rico/a	rich

Nacionalidades de habla española[1]	Spanish-speaking nationalities
argentino/a	Argentine
chileno/a	Chilean
colombiano/a	Colombian
cubano/a	Cuban
dominicano/a	Dominican
ecuatoriano/a	Ecuadorian
español/a	Spanish
estadounidense	American
mexicano/a	Mexican
panameño/a	Panamanian
peruano/a	Peruvian
puertorriqueño/a	Puerto Rican
salvadoreño/a	Salvadoran
venezolano/a	Venezuelan

Otras nacionalidades (País)	Other nationalities (Country)
alemán[2], alemana (Alemania)	German (Germany)
brasileño/a (Brasil)	Brazilian (Brazil)
canadiense (Canadá)	Canadian (Canada)
chino/a (China)	Chinese (China)
coreano/a (Corea)	Korean (Korea)
francés, francesa (Francia)	French (France)
inglés, inglesa (Inglaterra)	English (England)
italiano/a (Italia)	Italian (Italy)
japonés, japonesa (Japón)	Japanese (Japan)
portugués, portuguesa (Portugal)	Portuguese (Portugal)

Los lugares	Places
la capital	capital city
la ciudad	city
el país	country

Las personas	People
el/la amigo/a	friend
el/la muchacho/a	boy/girl
los padres	parents

Variaciones

- In the Spanish-speaking world, many terms describe an attractive physical appearance. You hear **guapo/a** in Spain to describe both males and females. In Mexico, you hear **linda** to refer to a female. The terms **bonita** and **hermosa** are common in many countries, but again, only for a female. In addition to **guapo**, a man can be **atractivo**, **apuesto**, or **bien parecido**.
- In addition to **estadounidense**, you may hear the terms **norteamericano/a** and **americano/a** to refer to people from the U.S. However, most native Spanish speakers from Latin America prefer **estadounidense**, since North America also includes Canada and Mexico, and the U.S. is only one country of many in the Americas.

---

[1]Do not capitalize adjectives of nationality in Spanish.
[2]In Spanish, the masculine singular form of the nationality often corresponds to the language spoken in the country.

Aplicación

2-1 ¿Quién eres tú? Listen to Carlos and his friends talk about themselves. Based on the information in **Vocabulario**, identify with a number the speaker who makes each statement.

_____ Carlos _____ Isabel _____ Chema _____ Ramón _____ la profesora Vargas

2-2 En la Plaza Mayor, Madrid. Complete the following steps.

Paso 1 Complete the conversation between two people who meet for a drink at the Plaza Mayor.

Un café en la Plaza Mayor, Madrid

amiga	ciudad	Me llamo
buenos	eres	país
capital	española	panameño

JUAN: ¡Hola! Soy Juan Luis Ruiz. ¿Cómo te llamas?

MARISOL: (1) _____ Marisol. ¿De dónde (2) _____, Juan?

JUAN: Soy (3) _____.

MARISOL: ¡Ah! Mi (4) _____ Ana es de Colón, en la costa caribeña.

JUAN: Yo soy de la Ciudad de Panamá, la (5) _____. ¿Y tú, Marisol? ¿De dónde eres?

MARISOL: Ay, yo soy (6) _____, de Madrid.

JUAN: ¡Qué bueno! Tu (7) _____ es muy bonita y España es un (8) _____ fascinante. ¡Y los cafés son muy (9) _____, también!

Paso 2 With a partner, take turns introducing yourselves. Give your name, nationality, an adjective that describes you, and one that does not.

MODELO: ESTUDIANTE 1: *Hola, soy Isabel. Soy mexicana. Soy una chica extrovertida. No soy muy alta.*

ESTUDIANTE 2: *Buenos días. Me llamo…*

Cultura en vivo

In Spain, students often meet for **un café**, **un refresco**, or **una caña** (small beer) at **un bar estudiantil**. The bar may be on or off campus or in a student residence, **un colegio mayor**. How does this compare with your university?

2-3 ¿Cuál es su (*his/her*) nacionalidad? In pairs, take turns giving the names of the countries where the following people are from, and their nationalities.

MODELO:　Felipe de Borbón / España
　　　　　Es de España. Es español.

1. Shakira / Colombia
2. Penélope Cruz y Pedro Almodóvar / España
3. Miguel Cabrera / Venezuela
4. Ricardo Darín / Argentina
5. Nosotros...

Pedro Almodóvar, director, con Penélope Cruz, actriz

Shakira, cantautora y roquera

Miguel Cabrera, beisbolista

2-4 ¿Qué es? ¿Quién es? (*What is it? Who is it?*) In pairs, challenge each other to identify and describe the people and places, using words from the list. If you agree, say **Sí, es cierto**. If you don't, say **No es cierto** and offer your own opinion. Be sure that adjectives agree with the nouns they modify.

MODELO:　ESTUDIANTE 1: *¿Qué es Madrid?*
　　　　　ESTUDIANTE 2: *Es la capital de España. Es una ciudad grande.*
　　　　　ESTUDIANTE 1: *Sí, es cierto.*

La Habana	Eva Longoria	El Salvador
Lima	Rafael Nadal	Javier Bardem
Óscar de la Hoya	Bogotá	Pau Gasol

la capital	cubano/a	activo/a	grande
una ciudad	español/a	alto/a	joven
un país	mexicano/a	bonito/a	moreno/a
un hombre	peruano/a	delgado/a	rico/a
una mujer	puertorriqueño/a	fuerte	rubio/a

Presencia hispana

Many immigrants from the Basque region (**el País Vasco**) of Spain settled in the western regions of North America, beginning as early as 1840. Then, during World War II, the U.S. government recruited Basque workers to help alleviate labor shortages. There are people of Basque heritage in every state, but the greatest presence is in Idaho, where many important community and political leaders are of Basque descent. Both **eusquera** and **español** are official languages of the Basque region of Spain. What ethnic groups predominate in your area? Do any preserve their heritage language?

 2-5 ¿Su país, su nacionalidad y su lengua? These people are famous worldwide. In pairs, take turns identifying their country, nationality, and language.

MODELO: Horacio (presentador de **Club cultura**)
Horacio es de España. Es español. Habla español.

Alemania	China	Francia	Japón
Canadá	Corea	Inglaterra	Rusia

1. Yoko Ono (artista, cantautora)
2. Vladimir Putin (presidente)
3. Justin Trudeau (hombre de Estado [*statesman*])
4. Jackie Chan (experto en artes marciales)
5. Benedict Cumberbatch (actor)
6. Ban Ki-moon (hombre de Estado)
7. Audrey Tautou (actriz)
8. Angela Merkel (mujer de Estado)
9. Ronaldinho (futbolista)

 2-6 ¿Quién soy? In pairs, take turns challenging each other to guess what famous person you are. Use adjectives from **Vocabulario**.

MODELO: ESTUDIANTE 1: *Soy alta, morena, bonita y estadounidense. Vivo (I live) en Nueva York con Jay-Z.*
ESTUDIANTE 2: *¿Eres Beyoncé?*
ESTUDIANTE 1: *Sí, es cierto.*

Estructuras

2.2 Ask and respond to questions about people, places, and things

The present tense of *estar*

The English verb *to be* has two equivalents in Spanish, **ser** and **estar**. You have already used the verb **ser** in **Capítulo 1** to identify, describe, and give origin.

¿Recuerdas? Complete the sentences with the correct form of **ser**.

1. Nosotros _____ venezolanos.

2. Yo _____ puertorriqueña, y mis padres _____ cubanos.

Answers: 1. somos; 2. soy; son

The chart shows the present tense forms of **estar**.

Estoy muy enferma.

¿Cómo está Ud. hoy, señora?

estar (*to be*)			
SINGULAR		**PLURAL**	
yo	est**oy**	nosotros/as	est**amos**
tú	est**ás**	vosotros/as	est**áis**
Ud.	est**á**	Uds.	est**án**
él/ella	est**á**	ellos/as	est**án**

- Use **estar** to indicate the location of specific objects, people, and places.

    Barcelona **está** en España. *Barcelona is in Spain.*
    Los profesores **están** en la universidad. *The professors are in the university.*

- Use these phrases with **estar** to indicate location:

    cerca (de) *close (to)*   **en** *in*   **lejos (de)** *far (from)*

- Use **estar** with adjectives to express a condition or state, such as how a person is feeling, or his/her current situation.

    Estoy enamorada de Javier Bardem. *I'm in love with Javier Bardem.*
    Pero él **está casado** con Penélope Cruz. *But he is married to Penélope Cruz.*

- Use **estar** with adjectives to describe physical, mental, and emotional states or conditions.

aburrido/a	*bored*	**enojado/a**	*angry*
cansado/a	*tired*	**listo/a**	*ready*
casado/a (con)	*married (to)*	**nervioso/a**	*nervous*
contento/a	*happy*	**ocupado/a**	*busy*
divorciado/a	*divorced*	**preocupado/a**	*worried*
enamorado/a (de)	*in love (with)*	**seguro/a**	*sure*
enfermo/a	*sick*	**triste**	*sad*

¿Comprendes? Complete the conversation with the appropriate form of **estar**.

—¿Dónde (1) _____ Uds.?

— (Nosotros) (2) _____ en un café, pero José (3) _____ en clase. ¿Dónde (4) _____ tú?

Answers: 1. están; 2. estamos; 3. está; 4. estás

Aplicación

2-7 Alejandro y Raquel. Alejandro Sanz is one of Spain's most important contemporary artists. In 2012, he married his long-time girlfriend, Raquel Perera. Read the account of the wedding and select the correct form of **estar** to complete the story.

Hoy, en Cáceres, España, los amigos de Alejandro Sanz (1) estás/están muy contentos. Es la boda (*wedding*) de Alejandro y Raquel Perera. Ellos (2) están/estáis muy enamorados y (3) estás/están listos para comenzar su vida de casados. Alejandro (4) está/estás muy guapo y Raquel (5) están/está muy bonita. Dice (*Says*) Sanz: "Gracias a vosotros que (6) estamos/estáis aquí hoy con nosotros. Raquel y yo (7) estoy/estamos muy enamorados y (8) estoy/estás seguro de nuestro (*our*) futuro juntos (*together*)".

Alejandro Sanz

2-8 Planes para una visita a Cáceres. Julia and Celia are planning to visit Cáceres. Complete their telephone conversation with the correct form of **estar**.

Cáceres es una bonita ciudad medieval española.

JULIA: ¿Diga?

CELIA: Julia, soy Celia. ¡Oye!, ¿dónde (1) _____ (tú) ahora?

JULIA: (2) _____ en mi oficina. (3) _____ muy ocupada.

CELIA: ¡Pero, Julia! ¡Hoy vamos (*we're going*) con Carlos y Juan a hablar con el agente para planear el viaje (*trip*) a Cáceres!

JULIA: ¡Es verdad! ¿Qué hora es? ¿Dónde (4) _____ Carlos y Juan?

CELIA: Ellos (5) _____ en la agencia. ¿(6) _____ (tú) lista para salir (*to leave*) ahora?

JULIA: Sí. Mi oficina (7) _____ cerca de la agencia. Nos vemos en quince minutos.

2-9 ¿Cómo estás? Imagine that you are in the following situations. Describe how you feel, using the verb **estar** and an appropriate adjective from the list.

aburrido/a	enamorado/a (de)	listo/a	preocupado/a
cansado/a	enfermo/a	nervioso/a	seguro/a
contento/a	enojado/a	ocupado/a	triste

MODELO: en una fiesta
            Estoy contento/a cuando estoy con mis amigos.

1. a la medianoche (12 a.m.)
2. con una persona especial
3. en clase
4. con Alejandro Sanz

5. cuando hay mucho trabajo
6. en una ciudad grande
7. en el hospital
8. lejos de la familia

2-10 Lo siento, no está aquí. Imagine that you are trying to avoid talking to someone on the telephone. In pairs, take turns inventing excuses for each other when the person calls. Use these possibilities as as guide.

MODELO: ESTUDIANTE 1: *Hola, ¿está Carlos?*
ESTUDIANTE 2: *Lo siento, Carlos está en el gimnasio. Está con Luis.*
ESTUDIANTE 1: *¿De verdad? ¡Yo estoy en el gimnasio y ellos no están aquí!*

Lugares		Excusas	
biblioteca (*library*)	museo	enfermo/a	hay un partido (*game*)
hospital	restaurante	hay examen	en una clase de arte
estadio	centro estudiantil	hay un proyecto importante	en una fiesta

Telling time

¿QUÉ HORA ES?

¿Recuerdas? Provide the numbers in Spanish.

1. 25 _____   2. 30 _____   3. 15 _____

Answers: 1. veinticinco; 2. treinta; 3. quince

¿Qué hora es?

Es la una.

- Use the verb **ser** to express the time in Spanish. Use **es** for *one o'clock, noon* (**mediodía**), and *midnight* (**medianoche**); use **son** for all other times.

Es la una.

Es mediodía.

Son las dos de la tarde.

- Use **y** for minutes *past* or *after* the hour; use **menos**[1] for minutes *before* or *till* an hour.

Son las tres **y** veinte.

Son las siete **menos** diez.

- The terms **cuarto** and **media** are equivalent to the English expressions *quarter* (fifteen minutes) and *half* (thirty minutes). You can also say **quince** and **treinta**.

Son las cinco menos **cuarto (quince).**

4:30

Son las cuatro y **media (treinta).**

---

[1]This is the traditional way to tell time. It is now common to use **y** for :01 to :59. **7:50 = Son las siete y cincuenta.**

- To ask at what time an event takes place, use **¿A qué hora es...?** To answer, use **es a la/las** + *time*.

  ¿A qué hora es la clase?   *(At) What time is the class?*
  Es a las ocho y media.   *It is at half past eight.*

- Use the expressions **de la mañana**, **de la tarde**, or **de la noche** to tell specific times, and **en punto** for *on the dot* or *sharp*.

  La fiesta es a las ocho **de la noche**.   *The party is at eight o'clock in the evening.*

  El partido de fútbol es a las seis **en punto de la tarde**.   *The soccer game is at six sharp in the afternoon.*

- Use the expressions **por la mañana**, **por la tarde**, and **por la noche** as a general reference to *in the morning*, *in the afternoon*, and *in the evening*.

  No tengo clases **por la mañana**.   *I don't have classes in the morning.*

- Many Spanish-speaking countries use the 24-hour clock for schedules and official timekeeping. The zero hour is equivalent to midnight, and 12:00 is noon. The p.m. hours are 13:00–24:00.

  21:00 = **las nueve de la noche**   16:30 = **las cuatro y media de la tarde**

Expansión   Learning to tell time in Spanish

1. To become proficient in telling time in Spanish, you'll need to make sure you have learned Spanish numbers well. Practice counting by fives to 30: **cinco**, **diez**, **quince**, **veinte**, **veinticinco**, **treinta**.

2. Think about and say aloud times that are important to you: **Tengo clases a las nueve, a las diez...**, **Hay una fiesta a las...**, etc.

3. Every time you look at your watch, say the time in Spanish.

¿Comprendes? Provide the times in Spanish.

1. 1:30 a.m. _____   2. 4:15 p.m. _____   3. 12 a.m. _____

Answers: 1. Es la una y media/treinta de la mañana. 2. Son las cuatro y cuarto/quince de la tarde. 3. Es (la) medianoche.

Aplicación

2-11 La vida diaria de Horacio. Horacio is one of the narrators for **Club cultura**. Read about his schedule, and then select the time that corresponds to each of his activities.

Horacio trabaja (*works*) en la universidad; es investigador. A las siete de la mañana, está en el laboratorio. Trabaja en su investigación hasta (*until*) el mediodía. A las doce y media, está en un restaurante de la universidad con sus amigos. A la una y cuarto de la tarde, está en el gimnasio. A las tres menos diez, está en su oficina. Trabaja hasta las ocho y media en punto. A las nueve de la noche, está otra vez en casa con sus amigos. Ahora son las once y media y Horacio habla por teléfono con su amigo.

1. _____ Está en casa.	a. 7:00 a.m.
2. _____ Está en el gimnasio.	b. 12:00 p.m.
3. _____ Llega (*He arrives*) al laboratorio.	c. 12:30 p.m.
4. _____ Está en el restaurante.	d. 1:15 p.m.
5. _____ Habla por teléfono.	e. 2:50 p.m.
6. _____ Está en su oficina.	f. 9:00 p.m.
7. _____ Sale (*He leaves*) del laboratorio.	g. 11:30 p.m.

2-12 Mi día. What is a typical day for you? How does your schedule compare to those of your classmates?

Paso 1 Complete these statements as they relate to you.

MODELO: Estoy en la universidad *a las ocho de la mañana*.

1. Estoy en casa _____.
2. Estoy en el trabajo (*work*) _____.
3. Estoy en un café _____.
4. Estoy en clase _____.
5. Estoy en la cafetería _____.
6. Estoy en la cama (*bed*) _____.

Paso 2 Compare your responses with those of a classmate.

MODELO: *Yo estoy en la universidad a las ocho de la mañana. ¿Y tú?*

Cultura en vivo

In the Spanish-speaking world, you may discover that time is flexible in some social occasions; in fact, often guests arrive late for a party or event. However, you can expect trains and buses will leave and arrive on schedule. In business and academic contexts, practices vary, but it is most common for meetings and classes to begin on time. When is punctuality important for you, and when is it acceptable to be late?

2-13A ¡Necesito información! Complete your calendar by asking your partner when the events with missing times take place. To ask your partner to repeat something, remember to say: **Repite, por favor. Estudiante B**: see **Appendix 1**, page A-2.

MODELO: la clase de inglés (09:30)

ESTUDIANTE A: *¿A qué hora es la clase de inglés?*
ESTUDIANTE B: *Es a las nueve y media de la mañana.*

Estudiante A:

Hora	Actividad
(09:30)	la clase de inglés
08:00	la clase de historia
_____	la clase de arte
11:45	la clase de español
_____	el examen
17:40	el partido[1] de fútbol
_____	el programa de televisión *Juego de tronos*
21:15	el programa de noticias en la televisión
_____	el concierto

[1]*match*

2-14 El AVE. *El AVE (Tren de Alta Velocidad)* is Spain's popular high-speed train. Search for the *AVE* web page to find information about schedules and train service from Madrid to Barcelona, Málaga, and Sevilla. Select a destination city and route and write a short paragraph to provide the following information.

📍 **Busca:** renfe horarios y precios; renfe ave

- un destino desde (*from*) Madrid
- el número del tren
- la hora de salida (*departure*)
- la hora de llegada (*arrival*)
- los días y fechas sin (*without*) servicio
- el costo para ir en la clase turista; el costo total en dólares

La hora de salida a Barcelona es a las 10:30; la llegada a Barcelona es a la una de la tarde.

Formation of *yes/no* questions and negation

LA FORMACIÓN DE PREGUNTAS *SÍ/NO*

When speaking, use a rising intonation for a *yes/no* question. When writing, use an inverted question mark (¿) at the beginning of the question, and the standard question mark (?) at the close. There are three ways to ask a *yes/no* question.

Statement: Picasso es de Málaga.

Questions: You can ask questions in three ways.

1. Add question marks to a declarative sentence:

   ¿Picasso es de Málaga?   *Picasso is from Málaga?*

2. Invert the order of the subject (S) and verb (V).

   ¿Es Picasso de Málaga?   *Is Picasso from Málaga?*

3. Add a tag word or phrase, such as **¿no?** or **¿verdad?** with rising intonation.

   Picasso es de Málaga, ¿no?
   Penélope Cruz es de Madrid, **¿verdad?**

NEGACIÓN

- Negate a statement by placing **no** before the verb.

Juan **no** es de Portugal.	*Juan is not from Portugal.*
Nosotros **no** somos canadienses.	*We're not Canadian.*

- Answer a *yes/no* question either with **Sí,...** or **No, no....**

¿Es Warren Buffet rico?	**Sí,** Warren Buffet es rico.
¿Es Shakira de España?	**No, no** es de España.

¿Comprendes? Provide three *yes/no* questions that would be answered by:

Sí, Salma Hayek es mexicana.

1. _____   2. _____   3. _____

Now, negate the response above:

4. _____

Answers in any order: 1. ¿Es mexicana Salma Hayek? 2. ¿Salma Hayek es mexicana? 3. Salma Hayek es mexicana, ¿verdad? (¿no?) 4. No, (Salma Hayek) no es mexicana.

Aplicación

  2-15 ¿Es verdad? In pairs, take turns asking *yes/no* questions.

> **MODELO:** Málaga es una ciudad española.
> *¿Málaga es una ciudad española?*
> *¿Es Málaga una ciudad española?*
> *Málaga es una ciudad española, ¿no? (¿verdad?)*

1. El Real Madrid es un club de fútbol español.

2. Salvador Dalí es un artista importante.

3. Bebe es una cantante popular.

4. Las playas (*beaches*) en España son muy bonitas.

5. Los ciclistas españoles son muy fuertes.

2-16 ¿Verdad? In pairs, ask each other questions based on the following statements by inverting the subject and the verb, or using a tag question. Respond to your partner's questions in a truthful manner.

> MODELO: La novela *Don Quijote* es famosa.
> ESTUDIANTE 1: *¿Es famosa la novela* Don Quijote? (*La novela* Don Quijote *es famosa, ¿verdad?*)
> ESTUDIANTE 2: *Sí, la novela* Don Quijote *es famosa.*

1. La actriz Eva Mendes es fea.
2. Pau Gasol de los Spurs es bajo.
3. Denzel Washington es un actor francés.
4. Lionel Messi es de Argentina.
5. Marta Domínguez es mexicana.

Marta Domínguez, política española y excorredora

Interrogative words

¿Recuerdas? Complete each question with the correct interrogative word.

1. ¿_____ te llamas?
2. ¿_____ pasa?
3. ¿A _____ hora es la fiesta?
4. ¿_____ estás? ¿Bien?

Answers: 1. Cómo; 2. Qué; 3. qué; 4. Cómo

We use interrogative words at the beginning of a sentence to form questions. Here are the most frequently used interrogative words:

¿Quién eres tú?

Palabras interrogativas		Ejemplos	
¿Cómo...?	*How...?*	**¿Cómo** estás?	*How are you?*
	What...?	**¿Cómo** eres?	*What are you like?*
¿Cuál(es)...?	*Which (one/ones)...?*	**¿Cuál** es tu libro?	*Which one is your book?*
¿Cuándo...?	*When...?*	**¿Cuándo** es tu clase de español?	*When is your Spanish class?*
¿Cuánto/a(s)?	*How much (many)...?*	**¿Cuántos** estudiantes hay?	*How many students are there?*
¿Dónde...?	*Where...?*	**¿Dónde** hay una silla?	*Where is there a chair?*
¿De dónde...?	*From where...?*	**¿De dónde** es Almodóvar?	*Where is Almodóvar from?*
¿Adónde...?	*(To) Where...?*	**¿Adónde** vas?	*Where are you going?*
¿Por qué...?	*Why...?*	**¿Por qué** no hay clase mañana?	*Why is there no class tomorrow?*
¿Qué...?	*What...?*	**¿Qué** estudias?	*What are you studying?*
¿Quién(es)...?	*Who...?*	**¿Quién** es ella?	*Who is she?*
¿De quién(es)...?	*Whose...?*	**¿De quién** es el bolígrafo?	*Whose is the pen?*

¡OJO!

The adjective **cuánto** agrees with the noun it modifies.
¿Cuánto dinero (*money*)?
¿Cuánta publicidad (*publicity*)? ¿Cuántos libros?
¿Cuántas personas?

- When you ask a question using an interrogative word, your intonation usually will fall.

¿Cómo se llama el profesor?   *What is the professor's name?*

- Both **qué** and **cuál** may be translated as *what* or *which*, but they are not interchangeable. Generally, **qué** is used to request a definition or explanation. It can also be followed by a noun to mean *which*. **Cuál** implies a choice or selection and generally is not followed by a noun.

¿Comprendes? Select the correct interrogative for each question.

1. ¿_____ es el profesor? El Sr. Vargas.

2. ¿_____ es esto? Un libro.

3. ¿_____ no hay fiesta? Porque (*Because*) hay clase.

a. Por qué

b. Qué

c. Quién

Answers: 1. c; 2. b; 3. a

Aplicación

2-17 Los sanfermines. People from around the world flock to Pamplona for **la fiesta de San Fermín**, one of Spain's most famous festivals.

Paso 1 Select the logical question for each answer.

1. _____ La fiesta de San Fermín es muy famosa.

2. _____ Es en Pamplona, en el norte de España.

3. _____ El primer día es el 6 de julio y el último (*last*) día es el 14 de julio.

4. _____ Las personas y los toros corren (*run*) por las calles (*streets*).

5. _____ Ernest Hemingway es el autor de la novela *The Sun Also Rises*, que describe la fiesta.

a. ¿Quiénes corren por las calles?

b. ¿Cómo se llama el novelista?

c. ¿Cómo es la fiesta de San Fermín?

d. ¿Dónde es la fiesta?

e. ¿Cuándo es la fiesta?

Paso 2 Two people meet in Pamplona and are planning to run with the bulls. Complete their conversation using interrogative words or phrases.

JESÚS: Hola. Soy Jesús, un estudiante de Salamanca. Y tú, (1) ¿_____ eres?

CARMEN: Hola. Soy Carmen, de Bilbao. (2) ¿_____ estás aquí en Pamplona?

JESÚS: Porque la fiesta es emocionante (*exciting*). (3) ¿A _____ hora es el encierro (*running of the bulls*)?

CARMEN: A las ocho en punto.

JESÚS: ¿(4) _____ son los toros? ¿Son muy grandes?

CARMEN: Son grandes y rápidos, pero es una experiencia muy emocionante. ¿(5) _____ estudias?

JESÚS: En la Universidad de Salamanca... Ay, son las ocho menos cinco. Estoy un poco nervioso. (6) ¿_____ estás tú?

CARMEN: ¡Lista! (*Ready!*)

Cultura en vivo

With a population under 200,000, many of the residents of Pamplona leave the city during **los sanfermines**, as more than 200,000 tourists descend on the town for that week. These inexperienced runners often take risks that cause unnecessary injuries. What kind of event or festival would make you want to leave town for a few days?

2-18 ¿Qué? o ¿Cuál? Complete the questions with **qué** or **cuál(es)**, depending on the context. Then answer the questions.

> MODELO: ¿_Cuál_ de las mujeres es tu profesora?
> *Es la mujer morena.*

1. ¿_____ hora es?
2. ¿_____ es tu clase favorita?
3. ¿_____ estudias?
4. ¿_____ son tus libros?
5. ¿_____ hay en tu mochila?

2-19A ¡Necesito información! Each of you will assume a new identity, and then ask your partner questions to learn what you have in common.

Paso 1   Choose the identity of one of the people outlined below and read the information.

Estudiante A:

Identidad masculina	Identidad femenina

Ramón Santos Gómez	Luisa Pérez Fernández
España	Colombia
alto, delgado y muy activo	baja, bonita y muy activa
Universidad de Salamanca	Universidad Complutense de Madrid
biología	sociología
fantástica	muy interesante
el profesor Sánchez	la profesora Alvarado
50 estudiantes en la clase	25 estudiantes en la clase

Paso 2   Use the prompts below to find out what you have in common. **Estudiante B**: see **Appendix 1**, page A-3.

> MODELO: ESTUDIANTE A: (Where studying?) ¿*Dónde* estudias?
> ESTUDIANTE B: *Estudio en la Universidad Complutense. ¿Y tú?*
> *¿Dónde estudias?*

1. (Name?) ¿_____ te llamas?
2. (From?) ¿De _____ eres?
3. (Description?) ¿_____ eres?
4. (Favorite class?) ¿_____ es tu clase favorita?
5. (What is class like?) ¿_____ es la clase?
6. (How many students?) ¿_____ estudiantes hay en la clase?

2-20 Profesor/a... Ask your professor several questions. He/she will respond truthfully to some, but not to all, of the questions. See if you can guess which answers are true and react with **¿Es cierto? ¿De verdad?** or **¡No es verdad!**

MODELO: ESTUDIANTE: *Profesor/a, ¿de dónde es usted?*
 PROFESOR/A: *Soy de Bolivia.*
 ESTUDIANTE: *¿De verdad?*
 PROFESOR/A: *Sí, es cierto, de la ciudad de La Paz.*

¡Conversemos!

First, ask yourself if you can perform the following functions in Spanish. Then act out the scenarios with two or three classmates. Ask and respond to at least three questions in each situation.

✓ CAN YOU...	WITH YOUR CLASSMATE(S)...
☐ describe yourself and other people?	**Situación: Gente bonita.**
	You're looking at a magazine with popular personalities. Choose one celebrity and take turns describing him or her. Agree or disagree with each other, according to your opinion. Use descriptive adjectives such as **alto/a**, **guapo/a**, **joven**, etc.
	Para empezar: *Para mí, Penélope Cruz es...*
☐ locate people, places, and things; express feelings and conditions?	**Situación: Una conversación por teléfono.**
	Try to find out as much as you can about each other at this moment: where you are, how you feel, and why. Use expressions such as **en**, **lejos de**, **cerca de** and adjectives, such as **cansado/a**, **listo/a**, etc.
	Para empezar: *¡Hola, Juan! ¿Dónde estás en este momento? ¿Estás...?*
☐ ask and respond to questions?	**Situación: En un café.**
	You meet each other for the first time when you share a table in the coffee shop. Ask each other questions to find out what you have in common. Use interrogatives such as **cómo, (de) dónde, qué, cuál**, etc.
	Para empezar: *Hola, ¿cómo te llamas? ¿Cuál es tu...?*

Perfiles

2.3 **Identify how names reflect a person's heritage, and learn about an alternative rock musician from Spain**

Mi experiencia

NOMBRES Y APELLIDOS

2-21 **Para ti.** Do you know the origin of your last name? Do you plan to change your last name if you marry? Read about Chelsea's experiences in Spain learning about names, and think about what your complete name would be if you followed the same custom.

¡Saludos de Chelsea Cooper! ¡Estoy aquí en Madrid, España! This is my first year abroad studying film at the Universidad Complutense, and I'm writing this blog to keep my friends up to date with my experiences.

This week the department is doing a film series of one of my favorite actors, Penélope Cruz Sánchez, although you probably know her best as Penélope Cruz. People's names here fascinate me: people use both their paternal surnames (**el apellido paterno**) and their maternal surnames (**el apellido materno**), so in Penélope's case, you can guess that her father's last name is **Cruz** and her mother's is **Sánchez**. Even after marrying Javier Bardem, she still keeps **Cruz** as her surname. I think there are advantages to these naming practices; for example, if a woman gets married (or divorced, for that matter), her name never changes, as she keeps her paternal surname throughout her life. By the same token, her children will keep her family name alive. It's curious though, that some people are known by their **apellido materno**, as is the case Penélope's husband, the famous actor **Javier** Ángel Encinas **Bardem**. What is important for me is that with this custom, a person's name becomes his/her identification for life and reflects family heritage.

One of my favorite Spanish musicians is María Nieves Rebolledo Vila, better known as Bebe. What versatility! I'm hoping to attend one of her concerts while I'm here! Have you seen the music video "K.I.E.R.E.M.E."? ¡Es divertido[1]!

[1]*fun*

2-22 **En su opinión.** In pairs, take turns asking and answering these questions.

1. ¿Cuál es el apellido paterno de Penélope? ¿Cuál es el apellido paterno de su esposo, Javier?

2. ¿Cuál es su nacionalidad?

3. ¿Cuál es tu apellido paterno? ¿Y tu apellido materno?

Mi música

"K.I.E.R.E.M.E." (BEBE, ESPAÑA)

Bebe was born into a musical family and spent her youth surrounded by musical instruments and harmony. In addition to singing, she is an accomplished guitarist and actor. Always experimenting, her musical style ranges from ballad to rock and rap. She was nominated for five Latin Grammy Awards in 2005 and won Best New Artist.

ANTES DE VER Y ESCUCHAR

2-23 La letra. The title of the song, "K.I.E.R.E.M.E." appears to be the first initials of a string of words; however, when read aloud, it sounds like **quiéreme**, or *love me* in Spanish. The verb **querer** means *to love* or *to want*, and throughout the song, the artist plays on this phrase with variations, such as, *I want*, *you want*, *whatever*, and *however*, all of which use a form of the verb **querer**. What results is a kind of **trabalenguas**, or tongue twister. Practice reading the letters aloud in Spanish: **K–I–E–R–E–M–E**. Then, try to anticipate the refrain.

PARA VER Y ESCUCHAR

2-24 La canción. This song communicates the singer's wish that she and her lover stop quarrelling and just love each other. Search online to find the video and lyrics (*la letra*) of "K.I.E.R.E.M.E." As you listen or watch, answer the questions.

1. ¿Cuál es el título de la canción?
2. ¿Qué elementos, visuales o auditivos, se repiten en la canción?
3. En tu opinión, ¿cómo es la canción? ¿Te gusta? ¿Por qué?

DESPUÉS DE VER Y ESCUCHAR

2-25 Descripciones. Use adjectives from **Vocabulario** to describe Bebe in Spanish. Refer to her photo and to images from the video.

   MODELO: *Bebe es...*

2.2 Segunda parte

Vocabulario

2.4 Discuss activities you do and like to do

¿Qué haces? ¿Qué te gusta hacer?

))) **Busco un tutor.** En la Facultad de Lenguas en la Universidad Complutense de Madrid, Celia busca un tutor.

[1]*exchange*

¿Comprendes? Identify the correct speaker of each statement: **Cecilia**, **Rogelio**, or **la ayudante**.

1. _____ Busco trabajo.

2. _____ Trabajo en una oficina.

3. _____ Soy estudiante de intercambio.

Answers: 1. Rogelio; 2. la ayudante; 3. Cecilia

Vocabulario

¿Qué haces?	What do you do (are you doing)?
abrir	to open
asistir a	to attend
aprender (a + *infinitive*)	to learn (to do something)
ayudar	to help
bailar	to dance
buscar	to look (for)
caminar	to walk
comer	to eat
comprar	to buy
comprender	to understand
creer	to believe
deber (+ *infinitive*)	to owe (to ought to do something)
decidir	to decide
descansar	to rest
desear	to wish
enseñar	to teach
escribir	to write
escuchar	to listen
estudiar (lenguas)	to study (languages)
hablar	to speak, to talk
leer	to read
llegar	to arrive
mandar (mensajes de texto)	to send (text messages)
mirar	to look at, to watch
practicar (un deporte)	to practice, to play (a sport)
preparar	to prepare

¿Qué haces?	What do you do (are you doing)?
recibir	to receive
regresar	to return
tomar	to drink, to take
trabajar	to work
vender	to sell
ver	to see, to watch
viajar	to travel
visitar	to visit
vivir	to live
Adjetivos	**Adjectives**
difícil	difficult
fácil	easy
Otras palabras y expresiones	**Other words and expressions**
¿Qué te gusta hacer?	What do you like to do?
Me gusta[1] (+ *infinitive*)	I like (+ infinitive)
Te gusta (+ *infinitive*)	You (inf.) like (+ infinitive)
¡Qué suerte!	How lucky!

Variaciones

In Mexico, speakers commonly use **platicar** in place of **hablar** to express *to talk* or *to have a conversation*. **Hablar**, in contrast, usually means *to call (by phone)* in Mexico, whereas in other countries, **llamar** is more typical.

))) Letras y sonidos

More on vowels in Spanish

In addition to the vowel sounds for **i** and **u** (**li-bro, lu-nes**), these letters also may represent *glides*, which are brief, weak sounds that combine with a vowel to form a single syllable. The letter **y** also represents a glide in some words.

| a-d**i**ós | s**i**e-te | ve**i**n-te | so**y** | ha**y** |
| n**u**e-vo | g**u**a-po | E**u**-ro-pa | es-tu-d**i**áis | U-ru-g**u**ay |

The letters **i** and **u** are not always glides when next to other vowels in Spanish, however. When they are vowels and not glides, a written accent mark is used.

| d**í**-a | r**í**-o | pa-**í**s | Ra-**ú**l |

---

[1]You will learn more about **gustar** and similar verbs in **Capítulo 6**.

Aplicación

2-26 ¿Es cierto? Which of these statements refer to you? If true, write **Sí,...** If not true, write **No, no....**

> MODELO: _____ vivo en Texas.
> *Sí,* vivo en Texas. (*No, no* vivo en Texas.)

1. _____ busco trabajo.
2. _____ necesito tutor.
3. _____ trabajo en una oficina.
4. _____ soy estudiante de intercambio.
5. _____ llego tarde a clase.
6. _____ leo Facebook™ todos los días.
7. _____ recibo muchos mensajes de texto.
8. _____ tomo café por la mañana.

2-27 ¿Qué pasa? Listen to descriptions of what is happening and indicate the number of the statement that corresponds to each drawing.

_____

_____

_____

_____

_____

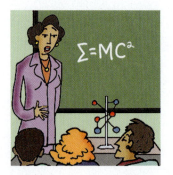

_____

2-28 ¿Qué te gusta hacer? Tell a classmate three activities that you like, and three that you don't like to do. Do you have any interests in common?

MODELO: *Me gusta practicar fútbol, pero no me gusta leer novelas.*

(No) Me gusta...

comer chocolate	trabajar por la noche
escuchar música	leer novelas
comprar por Internet	llegar temprano a clase
tomar café	caminar en el parque
escribir poesía	vivir en la residencia
aprender lenguas	asistir a conciertos
practicar los verbos	viajar
mirar la televisión	bailar en la Feria de Abril de Sevilla

Cultura en vivo

The **Feria de Abril de Sevilla** takes place two weeks after **Semana Santa** (*Holy Week*). Each day the **fiesta** begins with the parade of carriages and riders at midday, carrying Seville's leading citizens to the bullring. From around nine at night until six or seven the following morning, at first in the streets and later within the decorated tents along the river, you will find crowds partying and dancing, drinking the fine sherry from Jerez, and eating **tapas**. How does this celebration compare to fairs that you know?

Me gusta asistir a la Feria de Abril de Sevilla.

2-29 ¿Debo o no? There are some things you should do and others you should not do.

Paso 1 Identify the things, which in your opinion, you should and should not do.

Debo... No debo...

☐	☐	aprender los verbos en español
☐	☐	bailar hip-hop
☐	☐	tomar café descafeinado
☐	☐	ayudar a los amigos
☐	☐	caminar 30 minutos por día
☐	☐	escribir un mensaje de texto en clase
☐	☐	escuchar música clásica
☐	☐	leer novelas románticas
☐	☐	vender mi carro
☐	☐	comprar una bicicleta

 Paso 2 Compare your lists with those of a partner to see what you have in common and how you differ.

MODELO: ESTUDIANTE 1: *Debo asistir a la clase de español.*
ESTUDIANTE 2: *Yo también debo asistir a la clase de español.*

Estructuras

2.5 Talk about your activities and obligations

The present tense of regular *-ar* verbs

Spanish verbs are classified into three groups according to their infinitive ending (**-ar**, **-er**, or **-ir**). Each of the three groups uses different endings to produce verb forms (conjugations) in the various tenses. Here are the present tense endings of **-ar** verbs:

hablar (*to speak*)			
yo	habl + o	→	habl**o**
tú	habl + as	→	habl**as**
Ud.	habl + a	→	habl**a**
él/ella	habl + a	→	habl**a**
nosotros/as	habl + amos	→	habl**amos**
vosotros/as	habl + áis	→	habl**áis**
Uds.	habl + an	→	habl**an**
ellos/as	habl + an	→	habl**an**

- The present tense has several equivalents in English: (1) the simple present; (2) an ongoing action; (3) an action in the near future.

Estudio ingeniería. { *I study engineering.*
I am studying engineering.
I will study engineering.

LEARNING REGULAR VERB CONJUGATIONS

1. The first step is being able to recognize the infinitive stem: the part of the verb before the ending.

Infinitive			Stem
hablar	habl**ar**	→	habl
estudiar	estudi**ar**	→	estudi
trabajar	trabaj**ar**	→	trabaj

2. Refer back to the **Vocabulario** to practice the forms of several **-ar** verbs. Identify the stem; then write the various verb forms by adding the present-tense endings.

3. Next, practice **-ar** verb conjugations orally. Create two sets of index cards. Write a subject pronoun on each card for one set. For the other, write a regular **-ar** verb. Select one card from each set and form the verb with the selected pronoun.

4. Think about how each verb action relates to your own experience by putting verbs into a meaningful context. For example: **Estudio matemáticas. Juan estudia ingeniería.**

¿Comprendes? Select the correct form of the logical verb for each sentence: **escuchan**, **tomo**, and **deseamos**.

1. Mis amigos _____ música de Bebe.

2. Nosotros _____ tomar una clase de arte.

3. Yo _____ café en el bar.

Answers: 1. escuchan; 2. deseamos; 3. tomo

Aplicación

2-30 Preguntas y respuestas. Select the logical response for each question.

1. _____ ¿Qué compras en la librería?
2. _____ ¿Quién enseña literatura española?
3. _____ ¿Qué necesitas para la clase de matemáticas?
4. _____ ¿Con quiénes estudias?
5. _____ ¿Qué instrumento musical practicas?
6. _____ ¿Dónde trabajas?

a. con mis amigos de la residencia
b. una calculadora
c. la profesora Rodríguez
d. libros y lápices
e. en una oficina
f. el trombón

2-31 ¿Qué hacen? What is everyone doing today?

Paso 1 Select the most logical activity that corresponds to each of these images.

a. Jacinto

b. Arturo

c. Víctor / Catalina

d. Leonor

e. Luis / Memo

f. Sonia

1. _____ bailar en una fiesta
2. _____ buscar trabajo
3. _____ hablar por teléfono
4. _____ viajar a España
5. _____ escuchar música
6. _____ trabajar en el laboratorio

Paso 2 Create a sentence for each situation, based on the information you have.

MODELO: practicar tenis
Eugenia practica tenis.

Eugenia

Paso 3 Use the drawings in **Paso 1** to ask a classmate whether he/she does these activities and when.

MODELO: ESTUDIANTE 1: *¿Y tú? ¿Practicas tenis como (like) Eugenia?*
ESTUDIANTE 2: *Sí, practico tenis.*
ESTUDIANTE 1: *¿Cuándo?*
ESTUDIANTE 2: *Por la mañana. ¿Y tú?*

The present tense of regular -er and -ir verbs

You have just learned the present tense forms of regular **-ar** verbs. The following chart shows the forms for regular **-er** and **-ir** verbs. Refer back to **Vocabulario** (page 59) to see more verbs with these endings.

	comer (*to eat*)	vivir (*to live*)
yo	com**o**	viv**o**
tú	com**es**	viv**es**
Ud.	com**e**	viv**e**
él/ella	com**e**	viv**e**
nosotros/as	com**emos**	viv**imos**
vosotros/as	com**éis**	viv**ís**
Uds.	com**en**	viv**en**
ellos/as	com**en**	viv**en**

¿Viven Uds. en la capital?

No, vivimos en la costa.

- The present tense endings of **-er** and **-ir** verbs are identical except for the **nosotros** and **vosotros** forms.

    Aprend**o** español.   *I learn Spanish.*   Aprend**emos** español   *We learn Spanish.*
    Viv**o** en casa.   *I live at home.*   Viv**imos** en casa.   *We live at home.*

- **Ver** (*to see, to watch*) is an **-er** verb with an irregular **yo** form. Also note that the **vosotros/as** form has no accent because it is only one syllable.

    Veo la televisión.   *I'm watching television.*
    Veis la televisión también.   *You're watching television, too.*

ver (*to see, to watch*)			
yo	**veo**	nosotros/as	vemos
tú	ves	vosotros/as	veis
Ud.	ve	Uds.	ven
él/ella	ve	ellos/as	ven

¿Comprendes? Select the logical verb for each sentence.

1. Tú _____ el libro en clase.   a. asiste
2. Mis amigos _____ la tarea.   b. abres
3. Isabel _____ a clase al mediodía.   c. escriben

Answers: 1. b; 2. c; 3. a

Aplicación

2-32 Paco Álvarez. Paco is a student at a Spanish university.

Paso 1   Read about Paco and his plans, and select the logical verb in parentheses to complete the paragraph.

> MODELO: Todos los días *escribe*/aprende un mensaje a sus padres.

Hola, soy Paco Álvarez y (1) vendo/vivo en Madrid, España. (2) Asisto/
Escribo a la Universidad Complutense donde estudio relaciones internacionales.
(3) Debo/Creo que es importante (4) aprender/recibir otras lenguas y
(5) comprender/creer otras culturas, por eso (*that's why*) también estudio francés e
inglés. (6) Abro / Asisto a clase a las nueve de la mañana y a las dos de
la tarde. Los viernes, después de las clases, mis amigos y yo estamos en
un bar cerca de la universidad donde tomamos una caña y unas tapas y
(7) comprendemos/decidimos qué hacer por la noche. Normalmente vamos
(*we go*) a la discoteca Danzoo y allí (8) recibimos/vemos a amigos de otras
universidades. Después de bailar toda la noche, tomamos chocolate y
(9) vendemos/comemos churros en un café que (10) abre/vive a las 6:00 de la
mañana. ¿Y el resto del fin de semana? ¡(11) Abrimos/Vivimos en la biblioteca!

Presencia hispana

Spanish cuisine has become increasingly popular in the U.S. Go to any large city to find a **tapas** bar where you can sample some of the popular small plates found in Spanish bars, such as **chorizo** (*sausage*), **pinchos de tortilla** (*slices of Spanish omelet*), and **calamares** (*squid*), to name a few. You can eat **tapas** any time, usually accompanied by a glass of wine or a **caña**. How do **tapas** compare with the appetizers that you usually have?

Paso 2   Answer questions based on what you have just read.

1. ¿Dónde vive Paco?
2. ¿Por qué estudia otras lenguas?
3. ¿Qué hace (*does he do*) a las nueve y a las dos?
4. ¿Dónde están Paco y sus amigos los viernes después de clase?
5. ¿A quiénes ven en la discoteca?
6. ¿Qué toma y come Paco y sus amigos por la mañana?

2-33 ¿A qué hora? Compare your routine with that of a classmate.

Compramos chocolate y churros en la
Chocolatería San Ginés.

Paso 1   Take turns asking each other at what time you do the following activities.Be sure to write the correct form of the verbs in your questions and responses.

> MODELO: **mirar** la televisión
> ESTUDIANTE 1: *¿A qué hora miras la televisión?*
> ESTUDIANTE 2: *Miro la televisión a las nueve de la noche.*

1. **leer** las noticias
2. **asistir** a clase
3. **escribir** correos electrónicos
4. **deber** trabajar
5. **recibir** mensajes de texto
6. **abrir** tu libro de español para estudiar

Paso 2   Summarize what you have in common and how you differ.

> MODELO: *Nosotros miramos la televisión a las nueve de la noche. Él/ella también mira la televisión por la tarde, pero yo no.*

2-34 **Actividades típicas.** Complete the sentences by forming the verb in parentheses and adding a logical ending.

> **MODELO:** Mis compañeros y yo (asistir a)...
> *asistimos a la clase de español a las diez.*

1. Mi familia y yo (vivir)...

2. En clase, los profesores (escribir)...

3. Normalmente tú (recibir)...

4. En el mercado, el comerciante (vender)...

5. En el café, tú y yo (comer)...

6. Yo siempre (leer)...

2-35 **¿Qué pasa?** In pairs, take turns using the verbs to describe the scene in the photograph: what there is, who the people are, what they are like, and what they are (not) doing. Use your imagination.

abrir	caminar	escribir	hablar	mirar	visitar
asistir a	descansar	escuchar	hay	ser	vivir

> **MODELO:** (hay) *Hay muchas personas. Una mujer...*

En Barcelona, muchas personas visitan el Parc Güell diseñado por el arquitecto Antoni Gaudí.

2-36A **¡Necesito información!** In pairs, ask each other questions to share information about these daily activities. Add one original question. Do you have any responses in common? **Estudiante B**: see **Appendix 1**, page A-3.

> **MODELO:** ESTUDIANTE A: *¿A qué hora llegas a clase?*
> ESTUDIANTE B: *Llego a la una y media de la tarde.*
> ESTUDIANTE A: *Pues, yo llego a la una.*

Estudiante A:

1. ¿Cuándo estudias?

2. ¿Qué lenguas hablas bien?

3. ¿Lees las noticias en Internet?

4. ¿Asistes a clase por la noche?

5. ¿Qué deporte practicas?

6. ¿...?

2-37 **¿Y tú?** Write a short paragraph in which you discuss some of your daily activities using verbs that end in **-ar**, **-er**, and **-ir** (refer back to **Vocabulario** for a list). Connect your thoughts by using the expressions **pero** (*but*), **y** (*and*), and **también** (*also*).

> **MODELO:** *Estudio dos lenguas: inglés y español. También estudio ciencias y administración de empresas. Trabajo en la cafetería. Me gusta escribir poesía y asistir a conciertos de música rock. Veo* The Walking Dead *en la televisión.*

The present tense of *tener*

- As in English, **tener** (*to have*) is used to show possession. The forms are irregular.

  ¿**Tienes** clase a las ocho? *Do you class at 8?*
  No, **tengo** clase a las nueve. *No, I have class at 9.*

- **Tener que** + *infinitive* is used to express obligation (*to have to*).

  Mañana **tengo que** asistir   *Tomorrow I have to attend class.*
  a clase.
  ¿**Tienes que** leer una   *Do you have to read a biography*
  biografía de Picasso?   *about Picasso?*

Tengo que terminar esta pintura para las cinco de la tarde.

tener (*to have*)			
yo	**tengo**	nosotros/as	tenemos
tú	tienes	vosotros/as	tenéis
Ud.	tiene	Uds.	tienen
él/ella	tiene	ellos/as	tienen

¿Comprendes? Select the logical verb for each sentence.

1. ¿Tú ___ estudiar esta noche? a. tienes
2. Nosotros ___ clase en cinco minutos. b. tienes que
3. Tú ___ un cuaderno rojo. c. tenemos

Answers: 1. b; 2. c; 3. a

Aplicación

2-38 Mis obligaciones. There is often not enough time in the day to do all you must.

Paso 1 Individually, indicate which activities you need to do tomorrow.

Tengo que...

☐ asistir a clase.
☐ ver un video.
☐ llegar temprano a clase.
☐ practicar un instrumento musical.
☐ estudiar la lección.

☐ mandar un mensaje de texto a un amigo.
☐ comprar comida (*food*).
☐ ayudar a un/a amigo/a.
☐ escribir una composición.
☐ trabajar por la tarde.

Paso 2 In pairs, refer back to your responses to compare what you each have to do and not do tomorrow. Which of you has more obligations?

MODELO: ESTUDIANTE 1: *¿Qué tienes que hacer mañana?*
ESTUDIANTE 2: *Mañana tengo que practicar piano y escribir una composición. No tengo que estudiar la lección. ¿Y tú?*
ESTUDIANTE 1: *Pues, creo que tengo más obligaciones...*

2-39 ¿Qué tienen en común? Write eight sentences in Spanish, saying what various people have in common. Use the verbs **ser** and **tener**, as well as other verbs from the chapter.

MODELO: *Sofía Vergara y Shakira son colombianas. Tienen muchos amigos. Trabajan mucho.*

Christina Aguilera	el beisbolista Miguel Cabrera	el rapero Pitbull
Paz Vega	Alejandro Sanz	Bill Gates
yo	el futbolista Lionel Messi	el tenista Rafael Nadal
tú	Venus Williams	Warren Buffett

2-40 ¿Tienes? Take turns asking each other if you have the items on the list. Then, summarize what you have in common.

MODELO: un libro de historia

ESTUDIANTE 1: *¿Tienes un libro de historia?*

ESTUDIANTE 2: *Sí, tengo. (No, no tengo libro de historia, pero tengo un libro de física.)*

☐ un diccionario bilingüe	☐ un reloj digital	☐ un libro grande
☐ un teléfono inteligente	☐ una profesora española	☐ una foto de Bebe
☐ un examen difícil	☐ un radio japonés	☐ un cuaderno viejo
☐ una mochila negra	☐ un lápiz rojo	☐ un buen amigo

¡Conversemos!

First, ask yourself if you can perform the following functions in Spanish. Then act out the scenarios with two or three classmates. Ask and respond to at least three questions in each situation.

✓ CAN YOU...

☐ talk about what you do and what you like to do?

☐ talk about what you have, and what you have to do or should do?

WITH YOUR CLASSMATE(S)...

Situación: En un café.

You've just been introduced to each other. Discuss what you like to do, and what you do on a daily basis, to find out what you have in common. Use **(no) me gusta** and a variety of **-ar**, **-er**, and **-ir** verbs using conjugated and infinitive forms, as needed.

Para empezar: *Me gusta estudiar… Siempre estudio… También…*

Situación: ¿Qué tienes que hacer?

Which of you is busier? Take turns comparing your busy lives, each trying to outdo the other in order to get some sympathy. Be sure to use **tener que** and **deber**, and appropriate responses, such as **Lo siento** and **¿De verdad?**

Para empezar: *Tengo que preparar... Debo estudiar...*

Club cultura

2.6 **Anticipate content**

En la Universidad Complutense

Estrategia para ver

Anticipate content. Before you watch a video, gather as much information as possible. Look at the title, visuals, and captions, as well as the activities. If there are contextual notes, read them in advance. Then, take all this information to predict what the video will be about. Be sure to verify your predictions after viewing.

ANTES DE VER EL VIDEO

2-41 **Predicciones.** You will watch a video about a prestigious Spanish university. Look at all the evidence available (title, culture note, activities, etc.) and come up with three ideas that could be discussed in the video you will watch.

> **Nota cultural:** La Universidad Complutense de Madrid, fundada en 1293, es una de las universidades más antiguas y prestigiosas del mundo. Sus exalumnos incluyen pensadores (*thinkers*) y artistas famosos y ganadores del Premio Nobel. Entre sus 83.000 estudiantes, hay miles de estudiantes internacionales. Tiene 80 carreras académicas (*degree courses*) y el costo de la matrícula (*tuition*) es solo 26€ por crédito en el primer año. Los estudiantes internacionales pagan 126€ por crédito.

AL VER EL VIDEO

2-42 **La Universidad Complutense de Madrid.** Indicate with **C** (**Cierto**) if these topics are discussed or shown in the video, or **F** (**Falso**) if they are not. Which items did you predict?

1. _____ the number of students
2. _____ number of degrees offered (*carreras*)
3. _____ where international students come from
4. _____ the cost of tuition (*la matrícula*)
5. _____ sports that can be practiced
6. _____ a communications student
7. _____ an art student
8. _____ a business student

DESPUÉS DE VER EL VIDEO

2-43 **Tu experiencia.** Compare your university with the Universidad Complutense by selecting the statements that you agree with. Then, answer this question in Spanish: Which of the characteristics of the Complutense would make you want to study there for a semester?

Mi universidad...

☐ es muy grande también (*also*).
☐ tiene clases de negocios (*business*).
☐ tiene muchos estudiantes.
☐ es muy vieja.

☐ es más (*more*) económica.
☐ tiene estudiantes extranjeros.
☐ tiene muchas carreras.
☐ tiene muchos deportes.

2.3 Nuestro mundo

Panoramas

2.7 Identify and research some important cultural aspects of Spain

Descubre España

Millones de turistas visitan España todos los años para experimentar sus bellas vistas, su rica historia, sus tradiciones, su innovador presente y su fabulosa comida.

Cada región de España tiene una versión especial de paella, un plato a base de arroz (*rice*). La paella valenciana contiene mariscos (*seafood*), chorizo (*sausage*), pollo (*chicken*) y otros ingredientes.

Hay muchas rutas, pero un solo destino para los miles de peregrinos (*pilgrims*) que siguen el Camino de Santiago para llegar a Santiago de Compostela en Galicia. Algunos empiezan (*begin*) en Francia, otros en Alemania y otros en España.

Bilbao, antes (*before*) una ciudad industrial y contaminada, hoy es un monumento a la fusión de lo antiguo y lo moderno. El Museo Guggenheim es solo un ejemplo de la transformación de esta ciudad.

El flamenco es un estilo de música y baile originario de Andalucía, el sur de España. Es una fusión de influencias judías, moras, gitanas y cristianas.

Si deseas probar (*try*) algo excepcional, debes visitar una jamonería, una tienda auténtica española, donde venden todo tipo de jamón (*ham*), salchichas (*sausages*) y otros productos de cerdo (*pork*). Aquí puedes comer tapas o una bocata (tipo de sándwich) de jamón, y tomar una copa con tus amigos.

España

Población: 40,5 millones

Lengua nacional: castellano (español)

Lenguas regionales: gallego, eusquera (vasco), aranés, catalán, valenciano

Turistas cada año: 65 millones

Estudiantes universitarios: 1,8 millones

Edad mínima para tomar alcohol: 16 años

Edad mínima para conducir (*minimum driving age*): 18 años

2-44 Datos. Select the correct option based on the information presented in **Panoramas**.

65 millones	Bilbao	una jamonería
la paella	Madrid	Santiago de Compostela

1. dónde llegan muchos peregrinos: _____

2. dónde está el Museo Guggenheim: _____

3. dónde comer un buen jamón: _____

4. un plato con base de arroz: _____

5. el número de turistas que visitan España cada año: _____

6. la capital de España: _____

2-45 Investigación: España. Of the many tourists to Spain, about 35 percent visit Madrid, Barcelona, Andalucía, and/or Valencia. Choose one of these destinations and complete the form with the information you discover. Illustrate your presentation with a photo.

📍 **Busca:** Spain info

MODELO: *La ciudad de _____ está en _____. Tiene _____ habitantes. Es una ciudad _____ con _____. Los turistas visitan también _____. Un producto importante es _____. La foto es de _____.*

Páginas

2.8 Identify opinions

La corrida de toros: ¿Cultura o tortura?

Estrategia para leer

Identify opinions. Facts are statements supported and proven by evidence, such as data and statistics. Opinions, in contrast, reflect the views of a group or an individual regarding those facts. To identify opinions, look for key words that indicate perspective, such as **creo** (*I think*), **pienso/opino** (*I believe*), **en mi opinión**, **desde mi punto de vista** (*from my point of view*), **para mí** (*to me*), (**no**) **me gusta(n)**.

ANTES DE LEER

2-46 **¿Qué sabes?** (*What do you know?*) Write three statements regarding what you already know about bullfighting. Classify them as facts or opinions.

> **MODELO:** *I believe the color red angers or incites the bull.* (Opinion)

AL LEER

2-47 **¿A favor o en contra?** Read comments from a private social media group where one of the members asks the group about their opinions **a favor** or **en contra**. As you read the messages, identify which members are in favor of bullfighting and which are against. Also, indicate which clues help you identify those opinions.

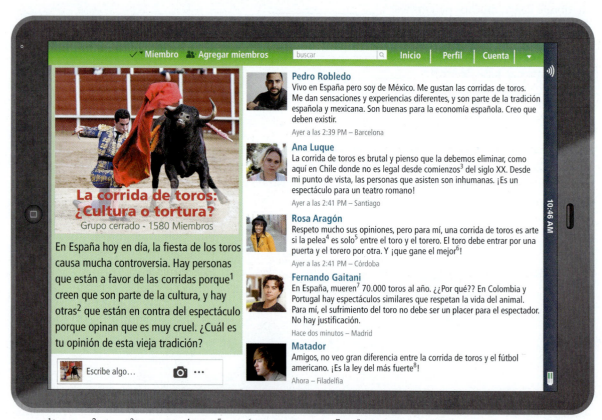

Pedro Robledo
Vivo en España pero soy de México. Me gustan las corridas de toros. Me dan sensaciones y experiencias diferentes, y son parte de la tradición española y mexicana. Son buenas para la economía española. Creo que deben existir.
Ayer a las 2:39 PM – Barcelona

Ana Luque
La corrida de toros es brutal y pienso que la debemos eliminar, como aquí en Chile donde no es legal desde comienzos[3] del siglo XX. Desde mi punto de vista, las personas que asisten son inhumanas. ¡Es un espectáculo para un teatro romano!
Ayer a las 2:41 PM – Santiago

Rosa Aragón
Respeto mucho sus opiniones, pero para mí, una corrida de toros es arte si la pelea[4] es solo[5] entre el toro y el torero. El toro debe entrar por una puerta y el torero por otra. Y ¡que gane el mejor[6]!
Ayer a las 2:41 PM – Córdoba

Fernando Gaitani
En España, mueren[7] 70.000 toros al año. ¿¿Por qué?? En Colombia y Portugal hay espectáculos similares que respetan la vida del animal. Para mí, el sufrimiento del toro no debe ser un placer para el espectador. No hay justificación.
Hace dos minutos – Madrid

Matador
Amigos, no veo gran diferencia entre la corrida de toros y el fútbol americano. ¡Es la ley del más fuerte[8]!
Ahora – Filadelfia

La corrida de toros: ¿Cultura o tortura?
Grupo cerrado · 1580 Miembros

En España hoy en día, la fiesta de los toros causa mucha controversia. Hay personas que están a favor de las corridas porque[1] creen que son parte de la cultura, y hay otras[2] que están en contra del espectáculo porque opinan que es muy cruel. ¿Cuál es tu opinión de esta vieja tradición?

[Escribe algo…]

---

[1]*because* [2]*others* [3]*beginning* [4]*fight* [5]*only* [6]*may the best win* [7]*die* [8]*survival of the fittest*

DESPUÉS DE LEER

2-48 Haz las preguntas. Complete the questions with the most appropriate interrogative words. Then answer the questions.

1. ¿_____ se llama el grupo?

2. ¿_____ es la persona que compara (*compares*) la corrida de toros con el fútbol americano?

3. ¿_____ vive?

4. ¿En _____ países es tradición la corrida de toros?

5. ¿_____ es la corrida como un partido (*game*) de fútbol americano?

2-49 ¿A favor o en contra? Describe the position each group member has about the topic of bullfighting. Also, explain what reason each member gives to support their opinions.

Participante	A favor	En contra
Pedro R.		
Ana L.		
Fernando G.		
Rosa A.		
Matador		

2-50 Manolete. Since his tragic death, this **torero** has become a legend in the tradition of Spanish bullfighting. Search the Internet to complete the following information about him.

1. Nombre completo

2. Nacionalidad

3. Año de nacimiento

4. Edad cuando murió (*Age at death*)

5. Una descripción de Manolete (dos adjetivos)

📍 **Busca:** Manolete torero

Manolete fue (*was*) uno de los toreros más populares de todos los tiempos.

Los niños reciben a la Reina Letizia en Almería.

Taller

2.9 **Plan for an interview**

Una entrevista

Estrategia para escribir

Plan for an interview. In order to conduct a good interview, you should know your subject, and prepare questions that will elicit good responses. Research your candidate online and jot down anything that sparks your interest. Try to come up with possible questions for those topics.

2-51 **Una entrevista con un famoso.** *¡Ellos!* is a blog that follows the lives of the rich and famous. You work for that blog and you are are being asked to prepare to interview a famous Spaniard.

ANTES DE ESCRIBIR

Choose a famous Spaniard you'd like to interview; for example, la Reina Letizia, Alberto Contador, Penélope Cruz, Javier Bardem, Marta Domínguez, Pablo Picasso, Rafael Nadal, Alejandro Amenábar, Alejandro Sanz, Bebe, or another. Research your person online and note four to five interesting facts about the person, in Spanish.

AL ESCRIBIR

Follow these steps:

- Research your candidate online. Write a couple of facts about the person to help guide your questions.
- Write a couple of lines greeting the person and introducing yourself.
- Use the **Ud.** form of verbs to write four to five questions based on what you have learned from your research. Include both **sí/no** questions and others to elicit information (**¿Cúando...? ¿Dónde...? ¿Por qué...?**).
- Write one question asking for the person's opinion about an issue. (**¿Qué opina Ud. de...? / ¿Qué piensa de...?**)
- Write a couple of lines thanking the person for their time.

DESPUÉS DE ESCRIBIR

- **Revisar.** Review your interview to assure the following:
  - ☐ agreement of nouns, articles, and adjectives
  - ☐ agreement of subjects and verbs
  - ☐ correct spelling, including accents
- **Intercambiar.** Exchange your interview with a classmate's. Then make suggestions and corrections, and add a comment about the interview.
- **Entregar.** With your classmate's suggestions in mind, make any necessary corrections, and then turn in the interview to your instructor.

En este capítulo...

)) Vocabulario

Primera parte

Características físicas	Physical characteristics
alto/a	tall
bajo/a	short
bonito/a	pretty, cute
delgado/a	slender
feo/a	ugly
fuerte	strong
gordo/a	fat
guapo/a	good-looking
joven	young
moreno/a	dark (skin, hair)
rubio/a	blond (fair)
viejo/a	old

Otras características	Other characteristics
activo/a	active
nuevo/a	new
pobre	poor
rico/a	rich

Nacionalidades de habla española	Spanish-speaking nationalities
argentino/a	Argentine
chileno/a	Chilean
colombiano/a	Colombian
cubano/a	Cuban
dominicano/a	Dominican
ecuatoriano/a	Ecuadorian
español/a	Spanish
estadounidense	American
mexicano/a	Mexican
panameño/a	Panamanian
peruano/a	Peruvian
puertorriqueño/a	Puerto Rican
salvadoreño/a	Salvadoran
venezolano/a	Venezuelan

Otras nacionalidades (País)	Other nationalities (Country)
alemán, alemana (Alemania)	German (Germany)
brasileño/a (Brasil)	Brazilian (Brazil)
canadiense (Canadá)	Canadian (Canada)
chino/a (China)	Chinese (China)
coreano/a (Corea)	Korean (Korea)
francés, francesa (Francia)	French (France)
inglés, inglesa (Inglaterra)	English (England)
italiano/a (Italia)	Italian (Italy)
japonés, japonesa (Japón)	Japanese (Japan)
portugués, portuguesa (Portugal)	Portuguese (Portugal)

Los lugares	Places
la capital	capital city
la ciudad	city
el país	country

Las personas	People
el/la amigo/a	friend
el/la muchacho/a	boy/girl
los padres	parents

Segunda parte

¿Qué haces?	What do you do (are you doing)?
abrir	to open
asistir a	to attend
aprender (a + *infinitive*)	to learn (to do something)
ayudar	to help
bailar	to dance
buscar	to look (for)
caminar	to walk
comer	to eat
comprar	to buy
comprender	to understand
creer	to believe
deber (+ *infinitive*)	to owe (to ought to do something)
decidir	to decide
descansar	to rest
desear	to wish
enseñar	to teach
escribir	to write
escuchar	to listen
estudiar (lenguas)	to study (languages)
hablar	to speak, to talk
leer	to read
llegar	to arrive
mandar (mensajes de texto)	to send (text messages)
mirar	to look at, to watch
practicar (un deporte)	to practice, to play (a sport)
preparar	to prepare
recibir	to receive
regresar	to return
tomar	to drink, to take
trabajar	to work
vender	to sell
ver	to see, to watch
viajar	to travel
visitar	to visit
vivir	to live

Adjetivos	Adjectives
difícil	difficult
fácil	easy

Otras palabras y expresiones	Other words and expressions
¿Qué te gusta hacer?	What do you like to do?
Me gusta (+ *infinitive*)	I like (+ infinitive)
Te gusta (+ *infinitive*)	You (inf.) like (+ infinitive)
¡Qué suerte!	How lucky!

Adjectives with *estar* See page 45.	**Telling time** See page 47.	**Interrogative words** See page 52.

Capítulo 3
¿Qué estudias?

*«La educación no es para enseñar **qué** pensar, sino **a** pensar».*

Fuente: Museo Nacional de Antropología de México

***Dualidad* de Rufino Tamayo.**
The figures in the mural depict an ongoing struggle for the ancient Aztecs. Are they equally matched, or is one stronger than the other? Speculate what they represent.

Learning Objectives

3.1 Exchange information about classes and schedules

3.2 Talk about dates, possessions, obligations, and physical and mental states

3.3 Compare and contrast the UNAM with your school, and learn about an alternative rock band from Mexico

3.4 Talk about places and give directions on your university campus

3.5 Make plans to do something, and describe traits and states of being

3.6 Compile information from several sources

3.7 Identify and research some important cultural aspects of Mexico

3.8 Scan text for information

3.9 Outline your thoughts before writing

In this Chapter

ENFOQUE CULTURAL: MÉXICO
Club cultura: Introducción a México

Indicate with **C (Cierto)** if Gerardo mentions this information in the video, or **F (Falso)** if he does not.

1. _____ el nombre oficial del país y de la capital
2. _____ la población
3. _____ el sitio arqueológico de Tenochtitlán
4. _____ el nombre del presidente
5. _____ dónde (*where*) está

3.1 Primera parte

Vocabulario

3.1 **Exchange information about classes and schedules**

Las materias académicas y la vida estudiantil

))) **Un horario complicado.**

MARCELA: Oye, Pedro, ¿qué **materias** tienes este **semestre**?

PEDRO: A ver, tengo siete en total: **historia** económica, **economía** política, teoría económica, investigación, **matemáticas**…

MARCELA: ¡Estás loco! ¡Todas son muy difíciles! Yo solo tengo cuatro clases este semestre.

PEDRO: Sí, pero menos mal (*thank goodness*) que no tengo clase los viernes. ¡Ahora tengo **un fin de semana** largo para descansar!

ANA: ¡Vamos a comer!

BEATRIZ: Ahora mismo no. Tengo que escribir **un correo electrónico** y **después** comemos.

ANA: **¡Apúrate!** Tenemos que comer **antes de** la clase de **geología** a las dos.

¿Comprendes? Identify who is described: **Ana**, **Beatriz**, **Marcela**, or **Pedro**.

1. Tiene muchas materias este semestre.
2. Tiene cuatro materias.
3. Desea comer.
4. Tiene que escribir un correo electrónico.

Answers: 1. Pedro; 2. Marcela; 3. Ana; 4. Beatriz

Vocabulario

Las materias	(Academic) Subjects
la administración de empresas	business administration
la arquitectura	architecture
el arte	art
la biología	biology
el cálculo	calculus
las ciencias políticas/sociales	political/social science
las comunicaciones	communications
la contabilidad	accounting
el derecho	law
la educación física	physical education
la economía	economics
la filosofía	philosophy
la física	physics
la geografía	geography
la geología	geology
la historia	history
la informática / la computación	computer science
la ingeniería (eléctrica)	(electrical) engineering
las matemáticas	mathematics
la medicina	medicine
la pedagogía	teaching, education
la psicología	psychology
la química	chemistry

Otros sustantivos	Other nouns
la carrera	career, field, major
el/la chico/a	boy/girl
el correo electrónico	e-mail
el fin de semana	weekend
el horario (de clases)	(class) schedule
el semestre	semester

Adjetivos	Adjectives
complicado/a	complicated
exigente	challenging, demanding
obligatorio/a	obligatory, required

¿Cuándo es?	When is it?
antes (de)	before
después (de)	after

Variaciones

- In Spain, **la administración de empresas** is more often **las empresariales**.
- In Mexico and other Latin American countries, the noun **chico/a** is used as an adjective synonymous with **pequeño/a** or *small*, for example, **un país chico** (or even **chiquito**, **chiquitito**). The term **chavo/a** is a common alternative for *boy/girl* in Mexico.

Aplicación

3-1 ¿Qué estudias? Follow the steps to complete the activity.

Paso 1 Indicate which of the following classes you take.

MODELO: *Estudio…*
☑ biología, ☑ historia, ☑ lenguas y ☑ química.

☐ administración de empresas
☐ álgebra
☐ antropología
☐ arquitectura
☐ arte
☐ biología
☐ ciencias políticas

☐ ciencias sociales
☐ comunicaciones
☐ educación física
☐ filosofía y letras
☐ física
☐ geografía

☐ geología
☐ historia
☐ informática
☐ ingeniería
☐ lenguas
☐ literatura
☐ matemáticas
☐ música

☐ pedagogía
☐ psicología
☐ química
☐ relaciones internacionales
☐ sociología
☐ ¿otra?

Paso 2 Create a schedule in Spanish with the days and times of your courses.

Paso 3 Share your schedule with a classmate and then answer the questions based on your conversation.

MODELO: ESTUDIANTE 1: *¿Qué estudias este semestre?*
ESTUDIANTE 2: *Administración de empresas.*
ESTUDIANTE 1: *¿Cuándo?*
ESTUDIANTE 2: *Los lunes y los miércoles a las ocho y media.*

1. ¿Quién tiene el horario más conveniente? ¿Por qué?
2. ¿Quién tiene el horario más complicado? ¿Por qué?
3. ¿Quién tiene las materias más difíciles? ¿Por qué?
4. ¿Qué clases tienen en común?

Cultura en vivo

Students in Mexico, as in many parts of the world, begin their specializations very early in their university career. The curriculum is usually fixed and the number of courses students must take varies by **facultad** (*school*). During their final semesters students have more choice, but still mostly within their majors. What is your opinion of a set curriculum in your major? Do you prefer challenging or less demanding classes?

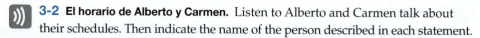

3-2 El horario de Alberto y Carmen. Listen to Alberto and Carmen talk about their schedules. Then indicate the name of the person described in each statement.

1. Tiene clase ahora.	Alberto	Carmen
2. Estudia matemáticas.	Alberto	Carmen
3. Tiene una clase difícil.	Alberto	Carmen
4. Tiene un profesor exigente.	Alberto	Carmen
5. Estudia química.	Alberto	Carmen
6. Tiene examen hoy.	Alberto	Carmen
7. Tiene que hablar con el profesor.	Alberto	Carmen
8. Tiene que trabajar esta noche.	Alberto	Carmen

3-3 ¿Cuándo? In groups of three to four students and using your charts from Activity **3-1**, take turns asking these questions to decide on a time when you are all free to meet outside of class.

1. ¿Qué estudias este semestre (trimestre)?
2. ¿A qué hora es tu clase de…? ¿Qué días de la semana?
3. ¿Cuándo trabajas? ¿Es muy complicado tu horario?
4. ¿Qué clase/s tenemos todos/as? ¿A qué hora estamos todos/as libres (*free*)?

Expansión   More on structure and usage

Todo/a/s (*every, all*) can be an adjective or a pronoun.

Adjective: *all (of), every*

todo el día *all day*

todo el mundo *everyone, everybody* (lit. *all the world*)

todas las noches *every night*

todos los días *every day*

Pronoun: *everything, all, everyone, everybody*

Me gusta todo. *I like it all.*

Todos están aquí. *Everyone is here.*

3-4 El calendario de la universidad. In small groups, discuss your schedules by semester. Use these questions as a guide and summarize what you have in common.

1. ¿Cuál es tu semestre favorito, el del otoño o el de la primavera?
2. ¿Qué haces en el verano? ¿Estudias? ¿Trabajas? ¿Tomas vacaciones?
3. ¿Cuál es tu semestre más difícil? ¿Por qué? ¿Cuál es tu profesor/a más exigente?
4. ¿Tienes muchas clases obligatorias?
5. ¿Tienes que trabajar durante el semestre?
6. ¿Terminas tu carrera en la primavera? ¿Qué haces después de completar tu carrera?

Estructuras

3.2 **Talk about dates, possessions, obligations, and physical and mental states**

The numbers *101–3.000.000*

Express numbers greater than 100 as follows:

101	ciento uno/a	800	ochocientos/as
200	doscientos/as	900	novecientos/as
300	trescientos/as	1.000	mil
400	cuatrocientos/as	4.000	cuatro mil
500	quinientos/as	100.000	cien mil
600	seiscientos/as	1.000.000	un millón (de)
700	setecientos/as	3.000.000	tres millones

- Use **ciento** in compound numbers between 100 and 200.

    ciento diez, **ciento** treinta y cuatro, etcétera

- When the numbers 200 to 900 modify nouns, they agree in gender with the noun.

    doscient**as** universidades

    seiscient**as** veinti**una** alumnas

    cuatrocient**os** cincuenta y **un** profesores

- When counting, **mil** is always singular and never uses **un**.

    mil, dos **mil**, tres **mil**, etcétera

- Express the year in Spanish with thousands.

    mil novecientos cuarenta y cinco   *nineteen forty-five (1945)*

    dos mil dieciséis   *twenty sixteen (2016)*

- The plural of **millón** is **millones**. Add **de** when **millón** or **millones** is followed immediately by a noun.

    dos **millones** trescientas mil personas

    un millón **de** pesos

    dos millones **de** dólares

- In Spain and in most of Latin America, thousands are marked by a period and decimals by a comma.

Spain/Latin America	**United States/Canada**
$10.000	$10,000
$2,50	$2.50
$10.450,35	$10,450.35

¿Comprendes? Indicate the correct numerical representation for each number.

1. quinientos treinta y siete: 56 – 536 – 537

2. mil novecientos uno: 191 – 1.901 – 1.910

3. dos millones trescientos cuarenta: 2.340 – 2.000.340 – 2.340.000

Answers: 1. 537; 2. 1.901; 3. 2.000.340

Aplicación

3-5 ¿Qué número es? Write the numerals that correspond to each number.

> MODELO: doscientos cuarenta y nueve
> *249*

1. quinientos noventa y dos   _____
2. diez mil setecientos once   _____
3. un millón seiscientos treinta y tres mil doscientos nueve   _____
4. novecientos mil ciento veintiuno   _____
5. ciento cuarenta y cinco   _____

3-6 ¿En qué año? When did or will these events take place?

Paso 1 Select the correct historical event for each year.

> MODELO: 1776
> *mil setecientos setenta y seis; la independencia de Estados Unidos*

1. _____ 2020   a. la Copa Mundial de Fútbol en Catar
2. _____ 2000   b. la primera elección del presidente Obama
3. _____ 2008   c. el nuevo milenio
4. _____ 1810   d. la conquista de México por Hernán Cortés
5. _____ 1521   e. la Guerra de Independencia de México
6. _____ 2022   f. los Juegos Olímpicos en Japón

Paso 2 Write out each year mentioned in **Paso 1**.

Paso 3 Write out two other important years and have classmates say what other events took place.

3-7A ¡Necesito información! You and your classmate are compiling end-of-year inventory figures in a bookstore. Each of you has missing data. Take turns asking each other questions to fill in the missing information on your grids. Then check all your figures by calling out each item and quantity. **¡Ojo!** (*Watch out!*) Make sure you use the correct form of **un/a**, when necessary. **Estudiante B**: see **Appendix 1**, page A-4.

> MODELO: ESTUDIANTE A: *Necesito escritorios. ¿Cuántos tienes?*
> ESTUDIANTE B: *Tengo cinco mil dos (5.002) escritorios.*

Estudiante A:

_5.002_ escritorios	525 calculadoras
816 pizarras	_____ computadoras
111.000 cuadernos	1.526 diccionarios
_____ mapas	2.400 libros de texto
_____ sillas	_____ bolígrafos

3-8 La lotería del Tec de Monterrey. The Instituto Tecnológico de Monterrey has a yearly lottery in which they give away houses, furniture, cars, and shopping sprees. You have just won the 2-million-peso (about $100,000) shopping spree. In pairs, decide how you will spend your prize money without going over budget.

MODELO: ESTUDIANTE 1: *Compramos dos escritorios ejecutivos por cuarenta mil pesos.*
ESTUDIANTE 2: *No, mejor* (better) *compramos un escritorio ejecutivo y una silla ejecutiva por treinta mil pesos.*

Presupuesto (*Budget*) $2.000.000 (PESOS)

escritorio ejecutivo	$20.000	reloj de oro	$250.000
bicicleta de fibra de carbono	$670.000	carro híbrido	$500.000
silla ejecutiva	$10.000	motocicleta Vespa	$20.000
computadora portátil	$15.000	teléfono inteligente	$12.000
televisor plasma	$20.000	tableta	$11.500
videojuego	$960	robot personal	$6.000
semana en Cancún	$19.000	jeans de diseñador	$5.000

Possessive adjectives

¿Recuerdas? You have already used **mi(s)** and **tu(s)** to express possession. Complete the statements with the correct forms.

Tengo mi libro y (1) _____ lápices. Tienes (2) _____ cuaderno y tu mochila.

Answers: 1. mis; 2. tu

Here are all the forms of possessive adjectives in Spanish.

Subject pronoun	With singular nouns	With plural nouns	
yo	mi	mis	*my*
tú	tu	tus	*your (inform.)*
Ud.	su	sus	*your (form.)*
él/ella	su	sus	*his, her*
nosotros/as	nuestro/a	nuestros/as	*our*
vosotros/as	vuestro/a	vuestros/as	*your (inform.)*
Uds.	su	sus	*your (form.)*
ellos/as	su	sus	*their*

• Possessive adjectives agree in number with the nouns they modify, not the possessor. **Nuestro/a** and **vuestro/a** also agree in gender.

mi libro	*my book*	**mis** libros	*my books*
nuestra clase	*our class*	**nuestras** clases	*our classes*

- Possessive adjectives go before the nouns they modify.

  Nuestros amigos llegan a las ocho.   *Our friends arrive at eight o'clock.*

- The construction **de** + *noun* can also indicate possession. It is equivalent to the English apostrophe.

  La hermana **de** Marcela estudia ingeniería.   *Marcela's sister studies engineering.*

- The preposition **de** followed by the definite article **el** contracts to **del**: **de** + **el** = **del**.[1]

  Los exámenes **del** profesor son difíciles.   *The professor's exams are difficult.*

  No es mi cuaderno, es **de** él.   *It's not my notebook, it's his.*

- Although **su** and **sus** can have different meanings (*your, his, her, their*), the context usually indicates who the possessor is.

  María y José leen **su** libro.   *María and José read their book.*

  Ramón habla con **sus** amigos.   *Ramón speaks with his friends.*

¿Comprendes? Complete each sentence with the logical possessive adjectives.

1. Tenemos _____ libros y _____ horario de clases.

2. El profesor de matemáticas tiene _____ calculadora.

3. ¿Tienes _____ tableta y _____ celular?

Answers: 1. nuestros, nuestro; 2. su; 3. tu, tu

Aplicación

3-9 Pedro. Pedro is a student at the UNAM in Mexico City.

Paso 1 Read about Pedro and select the logical possessive adjective to complete each sentence.

Hola, soy Pedro, estudiante de la UNAM. (1) Su/Mi carrera es ingeniería eléctrica.

Tengo clases por la mañana y trabajo por la tarde. Vivo en un apartamento cerca de (*close to*) la universidad, pero voy (*I go*) a (2) mi/tu casa los fines de semana. (3) Mi/Vuestra familia vive en Guanajuato. (4) Mis/Tus clases más difíciles son informática y cálculo. El profesor de cálculo tiene (5) su/mi doctorado de una universidad norteamericana. Este año voy a ser estudiante de intercambio (*exchange student*) en Canadá, donde estudio francés también. (6) Mi/Su novia (*girlfriend*) es de Quebec. Voy a conocer (*meet*) a (7) su/nuestra familia y a (8) mis/sus amigos.

Paso 2 Write as many questions as you can about Pedro to ask a classmate. Use interrogatives, such as **cuándo, dónde, cuál/es, quién/es, de dónde**, etc.

MODELO: ESTUDIANTE 1: *¿Cuándo son sus clases?*
ESTUDIANTE 2: *Sus clases son por la mañana.*

---

[1]The preposition **de** does not contract with the subject pronoun **él**.

3-10 ¿De quién/es es/son? Combine elements from each column to write to whom or what the following things belong.

    MODELO: *La clase de arquitectura es del profesor Vázquez. Es su clase.*

el celular	el departamento de ingeniería
el reloj inteligente	los profesores de química
los diccionarios	el profesor joven
el mensaje de texto	mi amigo
la mochila vieja	la universidad
el horario de clases	la profesora de matemáticas
el correo electrónico	el estudiante de geología
el videojuego	la estudiante de arte

3-11 Tu experiencia en la universidad. Think about your university experience.

Paso 1 Complete the sentences with appropriate possessive adjectives and consider if the statement is **C (cierto)** or **F (falso)** for you. Then add two to three statements of your own.

    MODELO: Tengo cinco materias. Todas *mis* materias son interesantes.
              (¿Cierto o falso?) __C / F__

1. Nosotros tenemos un gimnasio impresionante. _____ gimnasio es nuevo y conveniente. (¿Cierto o falso?) _____

2. La librería tiene muchos libros, y _____ precios (*prices*) son bastante buenos. (¿Cierto o falso?) _____

3. Tengo un apartamento cerca de la universidad. _____ apartamento es grande y moderno. (¿Cierto o falso?) _____

4. Tienes una computadora portátil. _____ computadora es nueva y rápida. (¿Cierto o falso?) _____

5. Mis amigas tienen buenos horarios de clase. Todas _____ clases son después de las 10:00 de la mañana. (¿Cierto o falso?) _____

Paso 2 Compare your opinions with those of a classmate. Do you agree?

    MODELO: ESTUDIANTE 1: *Yo tengo cinco materias. Todas mis materias son*
                       interesantes.
             ESTUDIANTE 2: *Yo tengo cuatro materias. Todas mis materias son*
                       interesantes también.

3-12 ¿Cómo es? In pairs, take turns telling each other what the following things and people are like. Ask at least two follow-up questions about each topic.

    MODELO: clase
             ESTUDIANTE 1: *¿Cómo es tu clase de inglés?*
             ESTUDIANTE 2: *Mi clase es difícil.*
             ESTUDIANTE 1: *¿Sí? ¿Por qué?*
             ESTUDIANTE 2: *Porque el profesor es muy exigente.*

1. amigos	3. profesor/a de…	5. trabajo
2. apartamento	4. universidad	6. horario

3-13 Una universidad excepcional. In groups of three, write a description of your university or college using the list below as a guide. Be sure that all adjectives agree with the nouns they modify. Then share your description with the class.

la universidad	la carrera de negocios	los equipos deportivos (*sports teams*)
los salones de clase	los estudiantes	los profesores
la cafetería	el horario de clases	los exámenes
las computadoras	los amigos	los clubes sociales

MODELO: *Nuestra universidad es pequeña pero bonita. Tiene…*

Other expressions with *tener*

¿Cúantos años tienes?

Tengo cinco.

¿Recuerdas? You have used **tener** to show possession and **tener que** to say you have to (do something). Complete each sentence with the correct option: **tienen, tengo, tenemos que**.

Yo (1) _____ muchos amigos. Mis amigos y yo (2) _____ asistir a clase todos los días. Hoy la profesora dice: "Lo siento, clase, pero hoy Uds. (3) _____ examen".

Answers: 1. tengo; 2. tenemos que; 3. tienen

- Use **tener** to express age.

  tener… años   *to be… years old*
  ¿Cuántos años **tienes**?   *How old are you?*

- There are other common expressions that use **tener** where English uses the verb *to be*. Note that many of these refer to things we might feel (hunger, thirst, cold, etc.).

  ¿**Tienes** hambre?   *Are you hungry?*
  No, pero **tengo** frío.   *No, but I'm cold.*
  Mis amigos **tienen** ganas de visitar   *My friends feel like visiting (are eager to*
  México.   *visit) Mexico.*

tener calor

tener frío

tener hambre

tener sed

tener miedo

tener sueño

tener cuidado

tener prisa

Uno y uno son dos. (1+1=2)

tener razón

tener ganas de

¿Comprendes? Complete the sentences with a logical expression with **tener**.

1. Tomo agua porque tengo _____.

2. Buscamos un suéter porque tenemos _____.

3. Es la una de la mañana y tienes _____.

Answers: 1. sed; 2. frío; 3. sueño

Aplicación

3-14 Tengo... Select a logical response to each question or statement.

1. _____ ¿Tienes que estudiar ahora?	a. Es su cumpleaños. Tiene cinco años.
2. _____ ¿Qué comen Uds.?	b. Seguramente tienen mucho calor.
3. _____ No, uno y uno no son tres.	c. Sí. ¡Tengo mucha prisa!
4. _____ ¿El concierto es en cinco minutos?	d. Sí. Tengo examen mañana.
5. _____ Mis padres están en Arizona en julio.	e. Tienes razón. Son dos.
6. _____ Hoy es un día especial para Juanito.	f. Un sándwich. Tenemos hambre.

3-15 Un concierto. Silvia and Patricio are going to a Café Tacvba concert.

Paso 1 Read the conversation between Silvia and Patricio before the concert. Select the correct form of the verb **tener** and indicate the full expression it uses.

PATRICIO: El concierto es en media hora, ¿tienes sed?

SILVIA: Sí, agua fría, por favor porque (1) tengo/tienes mucho calor.

PATRICIO: Pues, (2) tienen/tengo ganas de tomar café porque (3) tengo/tienes un poco de sueño. Con siete materias, siempre (4) tengo/tienes que estudiar hasta muy tarde.

SILVIA: Como tú y yo (5) tenemos/tienen prisa, debemos comer un sándwich en el bar aquí cerca.

PATRICIO: (6) Tenemos/Tienes razón, (7) tengo/tienen hambre también. Y los sándwiches aquí son muy buenos.

Paso 2 Answer the questions using expressions with **tener**.

1. ¿Por qué quiere agua fría Silvia?

2. ¿De qué tiene ganas Patricio y por qué?

3. ¿Por qué tiene sueño Patricio?

4. ¿Por qué tienen prisa Silvia y Patricio?

5. ¿Qué deben hacer (do) antes del concierto? ¿Por qué?

3-16 **¿Y tú...?** In pairs, take turns completing each statement truthfully. Use complete sentences and add necessary information.

MODELO: Tengo ganas de visitar... *México. Allí hablan español.*

1. Tengo frío...

2. Tengo calor...

3. Tengo ganas de comer...

4. Tengo prisa...

5. Tengo cuidado...

6. Tengo miedo...

7. Tengo hambre...

8. Tengo sed...

3-17 **¿Cuántos años tienen?** You may be familiar with these famous Mexicans.

 Paso 1   Take turns saying how old they are.

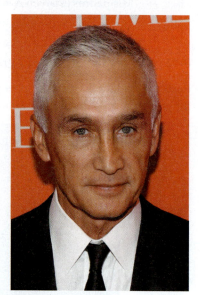

MODELO: Jorge Ramos (1958), presentador de Univisión
Tiene... años.

1. Gael García Bernal (1978), actor: *Diarios de motocicleta, Y tu mamá también, Babel, Mozart in the Jungle*

2. Sara Ramírez (1975), cantante y actriz: *Grey's Anatomy*

3. César Ramos (1983) y Gustavo Egelhaaf (1984), actores: *Cuatro lunas*

4. Salma Hayek (1966), actriz: *Fools Rush In, Once Upon a Time in Mexico, Bandidas, Tale of Tales*

5. Carlos Contreras (1970), deportista de NASCAR

Paso 2   Search online for information about one of the figures mentioned above and write a paragraph about him/her. Include answers to these questions.

- ¿Cuál es su nombre completo?

- ¿Cuál es su nacionalidad?

- ¿Cómo es?

- ¿Dónde vive ahora?

- ¿Por qué es famoso/a?

- ¿Tienes ganas de conocer (*meet*) a la persona? ¿Por qué?

Presencia hispana

You may hear the term *Chicano* to refer to U.S. residents who trace their ancestry to Mexico. The term originally referred to people who lived in areas once belonging to Mexico: Texas, New Mexico, California, Nevada, Arizona, and parts of Colorado and Wyoming. Later, it became associated with a political movement aimed to improve civil rights for people of Mexican heritage. The Chicano movement in the 1960s and 70s was key in bringing to the fore not only political and social issues, but also art forms that are still relevant. However, when referring to identity, many people with Mexican heritage prefer the term *Mexican* over *Mexican American* or *Chicano*. Do you identify yourself by your ethnicity, heritage, or nationality?

¡Conversemos!

First, ask yourself if you can perform the following communicative functions in Spanish. Then act out the scenarios with two or three classmates. Ask and respond to at least three questions in each situation. When responding, you may wish to react with expressions such as **¿De verdad?**, **¡Yo también!** or **¡No es verdad…!**

✓ CAN YOU …	WITH YOUR CLASSMATE(S) …
☐ exchange information about classes and schedules?	**Situación: En el centro estudiantil.** Talk about your classes, say what you are studying, and ask the others about their schedules and what their classes are like. **Para empezar:** *¿Qué estudias? ¿Cuándo es tu clase de…?*
☐ talk about dates when events occurred?	**Situación: Desafío.** Take turns quizzing each other on dates of events that are important to you. **Para empezar:** *la muerte de Prince (dos mil dieciséis)*
☐ talk about possessions?	**Situación: En clase.** Use possessive adjectives to discuss who owns the things you have in front of you. **Para empezar:** *¿De quién es…?*
☐ talk about physical and mental states?	**Situación: En un café.** Talk about how you feel by using expressions with **tener**, such as **tener hambre**, **sueño**, **ganas de**, etc. and then explain why you feel that way. **Para empezar:** *Tengo ganas de… porque…*

Perfiles

3.3 Compare and contrast the UNAM with your school, and learn about an alternative rock band from Mexico

Mi experiencia

MI UNIVERSIDAD: LA UNAM

3-18 Para ti. How many students are in your university? Which college or department is the largest? Is there an entrance exam for your university? Read about Susana Buendía and her experiences at the UNAM (Universidad Nacional Autónoma de México).

[1]*awaits me*

[2]*to encourage them to think about*

[3]*almost*

[4]*Wow! (Mex.)*

[5]*lecture-based*
[6]*workshops* [7]*about*

[8]*I have just received*
[9]*bachelor's degree*
[10]*That's why*

¡Hola y muchos saludos desde San Cristóbal de las Casas, Chiapas! Estoy aquí para empezar mi año de servicio social en una escuela rural de Chiapas.

¡Qué día me espera[1] mañana! Tengo que preparar una presentación sobre la UNAM para un grupo de estudiantes. El objetivo es animarles a pensar en[2] ir a estudiar a México algún día. Menos mal que solo es sobre la Facultad de Filosofía y Letras y no de toda la universidad. En mi presentación, tengo que explicar que en el sistema de la UNAM hay más de 330.000 estudiantes y casi[3] 38.000 profesores. Además de los estudios, cada año hay más de 10.000 actividades culturales, como conciertos, exhibiciones y obras de teatro. ¡Órale![4] ¡La UNAM es enorme!

Mi experiencia en la UNAM es fantástica. Tengo clases de tipo conferencia[5] y también talleres[6] más pequeños donde conversamos sobre[7] la materia y le hacemos preguntas al profesor. El examen de admisión es bastante caro y difícil, pero como es una universidad pública, la matrícula es muy baja. Acabo de recibir[8] mi licenciatura[9], pero como muchos estudiantes en mi carrera, tengo que hacer un año de servicio social. Por eso[10] estoy aquí en Chiapas este año.

Para mi presentación, voy a ponerles también música de uno de mis grupos favoritos, Café Tacvba, que es muy popular entre mis amigos en la UNAM.

3-19 En su opinión. What similarities and differences can you perceive between the UNAM and your own university? Working in small groups, discuss your opinions and record your group's responses. Be prepared to share with the class.

Semejanzas:	Diferencias:

Mi música

"ERES" (CAFÉ TACVBA, MÉXICO)

Café Tacvba (or **Tacuba**) is a Mexican alternative rock band that has enjoyed steady success for over two decades, winning several Grammy and Latin Grammy awards, including one each for "Best Rock Song" and "Best Alternative Song." Known for their versatility, their music combines modern rhythms from rock to hip-hop, along with Latin folk (**mariachi**, **ranchero**, **tejano**, and **samba**) styles. "Eres" is on the album *Cuatro caminos*.

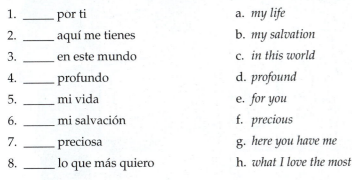

ANTES DE VER Y ESCUCHAR

3-20 El tema de la canción. Select the English equivalent for these words or phrases in "Eres." Then, hypothesize what the song is about.

1. _____ por ti
2. _____ aquí me tienes
3. _____ en este mundo
4. _____ profundo
5. _____ mi vida
6. _____ mi salvación
7. _____ preciosa
8. _____ lo que más quiero

a. *my life*
b. *my salvation*
c. *in this world*
d. *profound*
e. *for you*
f. *precious*
g. *here you have me*
h. *what I love the most*

PARA VER Y ESCUCHAR

3-21 La canción. Search online for the song or video of "Eres" by Café Tacvba. As you listen or watch, write three complete sentences in Spanish to describe what you hear or see.

MODELO: Los artistas… *son muy activos.*

1. La canción… 2. El ritmo… 3. Los artistas…

> ⚲ **Busca:** Cafe Tacvba Eres video; Tacvba Eres letra

DESPUÉS DE VER Y ESCUCHAR

3-22 ¿Y tú? Create your own funny or serious version of "Eres." Use the theme and expressions listed in **3-20** to write five or six lines about someone or something important in your life. Present it to the class and include a dedication.

MODELO: *"Eres" por…, dedicada a… (mi universidad, mi madre, mi compañero/a de cuarto…)*

3.2 Segunda parte

Vocabulario

3.4 **Talk about places and give directions on your university campus**

Los edificios de la universidad

Beto   Rosa   Tomás

)) **¿Dónde está la biblioteca?** El campus de la Universidad Nacional Autónoma de México (UNAM) es enorme y tiene muchos **edificios**. Los estudiantes nuevos en la universidad buscan diferentes lugares en el mapa.

BETO: Oye, Tomás, ¿sabes dónde está **la biblioteca**?

TOMÁS: Pues, mira (*Well, look*), está cerquita[1], **al lado de la librería**.

ROSA: ¿Y **la cancha de tenis**? ¿Y **el observatorio**?

TOMÁS: La cancha está **detrás del estadio**. Y el observatorio está **enfrente del** estadio. Vamos (*Let's go*), te acompaño (*I'll go with you*).

¿Comprendes? Complete each sentence with the correct option: **enfrente**, **al lado**, and **detrás**.

1. La biblioteca está _____ de la librería.

2. El observatorio está _____ del estadio.

3. La cancha de tenis está _____ del estadio.

Answers: 1. al lado; 2. enfrente; 3. detrás

_____

[1]*cerquita = cerca*. In the Hispanic world, it is common to use diminutives, in this case meaning "really close."

))) Vocabulario

Los edificios	Buildings
el auditorio	auditorium
la biblioteca	library
la cafetería	cafeteria
la cancha de tenis	tennis court
el centro estudiantil	student union
el estadio	stadium
la Facultad de Arte	School of Art
la Facultad de Ciencias	School of Science
la Facultad de Derecho	School of Law
la Facultad de Filosofía y Letras	School of Humanities
la Facultad de Ingeniería	School of Engineering
la Facultad de Medicina	School of Medicine
la Facultad de Pedagogía	School of Education
el gimnasio	gymnasium
el laboratorio	(language/computer) laboratory
la librería	bookstore
el museo	museum
el observatorio	observatory
la rectoría	president's office
el teatro	theater

¿Dónde está?	Where is it?
al lado (de)	beside, next to
a la derecha (de)	to the right (of)
a la izquierda (de)	to the left (of)
cerca (de)	close (to)
delante (de)	in front (of) (as in a row or line)
detrás (de)	behind
en	in, on
enfrente (de)	facing, across (from)
entre	between
lejos (de)	far (from)
Verbos	**Verbs**
hacer	to do; to make
ir (a)	to go

Variaciones

In Spain, **la cancha de tenis** is more commonly **la pista de tenis**. In Spain, Argentina, Chile, and other countries, **la cafetería** is also **el comedor (universitario)** in the university context.

))) Letras y sonidos

Syllabification

In Spanish, every syllable contains one vowel, which may be accompanied by glides and/or consonants. Consonants combine with vowels to form syllables as follows.

- A single consonant (including **ch**, **ll**, **rr**) attaches to the following vowel.

  se-ño-ri-ta   mu-cha-cho   bo-ca-di-llo   pi-za-rra

- Two consonants attach to the following vowel when they consist of a strong consonant (**p, b, t, d, c, g, f**) followed by **r** or **l**.

  a-brir   pro-ble-ma   no-so-tros   bo-lí-gra-fo

  When two consonants do not form this combination, they are separated.

  tar-de   de-por-te   blan-co   es-tu-dian-te

- With combinations of three consonants that include **p, b, t, d, c, g, f** plus **r** or **l**, in positions two and three, the last two consonants attach to the following vowel.

  com-pli-ca-do   hom-bre   es-cri-to-rio   in-glés

  Without this sequence of sounds, only the last consonant attaches to the following vowel.

  pers-pec-ti-va   ins-ta-lar   cons-tan-te   sols-ti-cio

- With four consonants, the last two always attach to the following vowel.

  ins-truc-tor   abs-trac-to

Aplicación

3-23 ¿Qué asocias con...? Select the logical place for each activity.

1. _____ Aquí trabaja el rector de la universidad.
2. _____ Observamos las estrellas y los planetas.
3. _____ Compramos libros, cuadernos, lápices y más.
4. _____ Miramos obras de arte y artefactos bonitos.
5. _____ Vemos un partido de fútbol.
6. _____ Practicamos tenis.

a. en el estadio
b. en la librería
c. en la cancha
d. en el museo
e. en el observatorio
f. en la rectoría

))) **3-24 En la cola (*Standing in line*).** Listen to a description of people standing in line. Place the number of the description in front of the name of each person.

el hombre de la taquilla   Marcela   Pepe   Paula   Mercedes   Adrián

_____ Marcela   _____ Mercedes   _____ Pepe
_____ Adrián   _____ Paula   _____ el hombre de la taquilla

3-25 Nuestra universidad. In pairs, write five sentences about where buildings are located on your campus; some sentences should be true and some should be false. Then switch partners and take turns reading your sentences, saying if they are true or false and correcting false ones. Share two sentences with the class.

MODELO: ESTUDIANTE 1: *La biblioteca está al lado del laboratorio de química.*
             ESTUDIANTE 2: *¡No es cierto! La biblioteca está entre la rectoría y la librería.*

3-26A ¡Necesito información! In pairs, take turns asking and answering questions in order to complete the missing information on your class schedules. Use the verb **ser** in all of your questions and responses. **Estudiante B**: see **Appendix 1**, page A-4.

MODELO: ESTUDIANTE A: *¿A qué hora es la clase de cálculo?*
             ESTUDIANTE B: *Es a las 8:30. ¿Dónde es la clase de cálculo?*

Estudiante A:

Hora	Clase	Lugar	Profesor/a
8:30	cálculo	Facultad de Informática	María Gómez García
9:00	psicología	Facultad de Ciencias	
	biología		Julia Gómez Salazar
12:00		gimnasio	Héctor Camacho
	física		Carlos Santos Pérez

Estructuras

3.5 **Make plans to do something, and describe traits and states of being**

The present tense of *ir* and *hacer*

The Spanish verbs **ir** and **hacer** are irregular.

ir (*to go*)			
SINGULAR		**PLURAL**	
yo	**voy**	nosotros/as	**vamos**
tú	**vas**	vosotros/as	**vais**
Ud.	**va**	Uds.	**van**
él/ella	**va**	ellos/as	**van**

hacer (*to do; to make*)			
SINGULAR		**PLURAL**	
yo	**hago**	nosotros/as	**hacemos**
tú	**haces**	vosotros/as	**hacéis**
Ud.	**hace**	Uds.	**hacen**
él/ella	**hace**	ellos/as	**hacen**

¡Hola, Susana! ¿Adónde vas?

Voy a hacer mi tarea en la biblioteca.

- **Hacer** is irregular only in the **yo** form.

  Hago la tarea por las noches.   *I do homework at night.*

- When you are asked a question using **hacer,** you usually respond with another verb.

  Ricardo, ¿qué **haces** aquí?   *Ricardo, what are you doing here?*
  Busco un libro para mi clase.   *I'm looking for a book for my class.*

- **Hacer** is also used in idiomatic expressions such as: **hacer un viaje** (*to take a trip*) and **hacer preguntas** (*to ask questions*).

  Tengo que **hacer una pregunta.**   *I have to ask a question.*
  Susana va a **hacer un viaje** a San   *Susana is going to take a trip to San*
    Miguel.   *Miguel.*

- **Ir** is generally followed by the preposition **a**. When the definite article **el** follows the preposition **a**, they contract to **al: a** + **el** = **al**.

  Luis y Ernesto van **al** centro   *Luis and Ernesto are going to the student*
    estudiantil.   *center.*

- The construction **ir a** + *infinitive* is used in Spanish to express future action. It is equivalent to the English construction *to be going to + infinitive*.

  ¿Qué **vas a hacer** esta noche?   *What are you going to do tonight?*
  Voy a estudiar en la biblioteca.   *I'm going to study in the library.*

¿Comprendes? Complete each sentence with the correct verb: **vamos**, **hago**, **van**, **hacemos**.

Mis amigos y yo (1) _____ muchas actividades. Mis amigos (2) _____ a museos.
Nosotros (3) _____ al teatro. Yo (4) _____ ejercicio todos los días.

Answers: 1. hacemos; 2. van; 3. vamos; 4. hago

Aplicación

3-27 ¿Qué asocias con...? Select the logical activity for each place.

1. _____ Estamos en la biblioteca.
2. _____ Estás en el laboratorio de física.
3. _____ Son las 9:05 y no estás en clase.
4. _____ Estamos en el estadio.
5. _____ Carlos está en el Museo de Antropología.
6. _____ Mi profesora está en su oficina.

a. Hace su trabajo para la clase.
b. Vamos a practicar fútbol.
c. Haces un experimento.
d. Va a ver el mural de Rufino Tamayo.
e. Vas a llegar tarde.
f. Hacemos la tarea.

3-28 Gael García Bernal. This film star, producer, and director (*Amores perros, Y tu mamá también, Babel, Diarios de motocicleta, Mozart in the Jungle*) is considered one of Mexico's finest actors. Complete the sentences with the correct form of **ir (a)** or **hacer** to find out what is happening in his life.

Gael García Bernal está en su apartamento en Nueva York. Tiene hambre; por eso, (1) _____ preparar los sándwiches. Sus hijos (*children*) son pequeños, pero (2) _____ ayudar a hacer los sándwiches también. Gael dice (*says*): "Mañana nosotros (3) _____ un viaje a Guadalajara a visitar a mis padres. Después, (4) _____ Buenos Aires donde vive Dolores, la mamá de mis hijos". En este momento, ella (5) _____ una película (*movie*) nueva. Todos nosotros (6) _____ Punta del Este a pasar tiempo en la playa (*beach*).

3-29 ¿Qué hacen? Guess what the following people are doing, according to where they are. Complete each sentence with the correct form of **hacer** and a logical option from the list below.

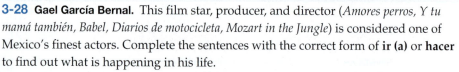

| amigos | ejercicio | la pasta | preguntas | la tarea | el trabajo |

MODELO: sándwiches
En la cafetería, la señora *hace sándwiches*.

1. En la biblioteca, yo _____.
2. En clase, nosotros _____.
3. En el gimnasio, tú _____.
4. En la oficina, los secretarios _____.
5. En el restaurante, el chef _____.
6. En una fiesta, todos nosotros _____.

3-30 Planes para un viaje. In groups of three, make plans to attend a soccer game at a rival university. Use the following questions to guide you.

MODELO: ¿Adónde van?
Vamos a San Antonio para asistir al partido de fútbol.

1. ¿Con quiénes van?
2. ¿Adónde van?
3. ¿Por cuánto tiempo van?
4. ¿Qué van a comprar?
5. ¿Cuándo van a regresar (*return*)?
6. ¿A qué hora van?
7. ¿Qué van a hacer?
8. ¿Qué no van a hacer?

Presencia hispana

Over the decades, the language of many Mexican Americans, as well as that of other Spanish-speaking immigrants, has been so heavily influenced by English that many refer to it as *Spanglish*. However, Spanish-language newspapers such as *La Opinión* in Los Angeles and *La Raza* in Chicago help promote Spanish language literacy among their readers. What are the benefits of being literate in two languages?

Summary of uses of *ser* and *estar*

¿Recuerdas? Complete each sentence with the correct form of **ser** or **estar**.

1. (Nosotros) _____ estudiantes.
2. La rectoría _____ al lado del museo.

Answers: 1. somos; 2. está

USE *SER* TO EXPRESS...

- **characteristics** (an adjective of appearance, size, color, or nationality).

  Tomás **es** alto y delgado.   *Tomás is tall and thin.*
  Somos mexicanos.   *We are Mexican.*

- **profession or identity** (a noun or noun phrase that restates the subject).

  Mi hermana **es** artista.   *My sister is an artist.*
  Leo y Ligia **son** mis padres.   *Leo and Ligia are my parents.*

- **time, dates, and seasons.**

  Son las cinco de la tarde.   *It's five o'clock in the afternoon.*
  Es primavera.   *It's spring.*
  Es martes.   *It's Tuesday.*

- **the location or time of specific events.**

  La fiesta **es** en mi casa.   *The party is at my house.*
  El concierto **es** a las ocho.   *The concert is at eight o'clock.*

- **impersonal expressions.**

  Es obligatorio asistir a clase.   *It's required to attend class.*
  Es fascinante estudiar la cultura   *It's fascinating to study Hispanic culture.*
  hispana.

- **origin or possession** (with the preposition **de**).

  Gael **es de** México.   *Gael is from Mexico.*
  Los murales **son de** Juan   *The murals are Juan O'Gorman's.*
  O'Gorman.

USE *ESTAR* TO EXPRESS...

- **a state, mood, or changeable condition** (adjective).

  Pedro **está** casado.   *Pedro is married.*
  Las chicas **están** contentas.   *The girls are happy.*

- **an exceptional or unusual condition, or a compliment** (adjective).

  Sarita, tienes ocho años; ¡**estás** muy   *Sarita, you're eight years old;*
  grande!   *you are (look) so big!*
  Carlos, no hay examen hoy. ¡**Estás**   *Carlos, there isn't an exam today.*
  loco!   *You're crazy!*

- **the location of specific persons, places, or things.**

  La librería **está** cerca.   *The bookstore is nearby.*
  Guadalajara **está** lejos de Cancún.   *Guadalajara is far from Cancún.*

Some adjectives have different meanings when used with **ser** or **estar**.

Adjective	With *ser* (traits)	With *estar* (states)
aburrido/a	*to be boring*	*to be bored*
feliz	*to be happy, fortunate*	*to feel happy*
malo/a	*to be bad, evil*	*to be ill*
rico/a	*to be rich*	*to taste good (food)*
verde	*to be green (color)*	*to be green (not ripe)*

¡OJO!

Remember to use **hay** to say *there is/are*, usually with indefinite things, numbers, or countable nouns.

Esta noche **hay una fiesta** en mi casa.	*There's a party at my house tonight.*
Hay más de 55 millones de hispanos en EE. UU.	*There are more than 55 million Hispanics in the U.S.*

¿Comprendes? Complete the sentences with **es** or **está**.

Pablo (1) _____ de Veracruz. Veracruz (2) _____ en el Golfo de México. Pablo (3) _____ contento de vivir en un lugar bonito.

Answers: 1. es; 2. está; 3. está

Aplicación

3-31 ¿Cómo respondes? Select the most logical response to each question.

1. _____ ¿Por qué estás en el laboratorio?
2. _____ ¿Eres canadiense?
3. _____ ¿Dónde es el concierto de Café Tacvba?
4. _____ ¿De quién es el horario de clases?
5. _____ ¿Dónde está la Facultad de Medicina?
6. _____ ¿Cómo es tu libro de biología?
7. _____ ¿Quién es la mujer que está cerca de Juan?

a. Es en el estadio.
b. Está detrás de la Facultad de Ciencias.
c. Es Alejandra, su amiga.
d. Es digital y tiene muchas fotos interesantes.
e. Porque necesito terminar la tarea de química.
f. Es de la estudiante de geografía.
g. No, soy mexicana.

3-32 Una boda (*wedding*) mexicana. Mariachi musicians are a festive and typical part of Mexican weddings.

Paso 1 Complete Ana's description of a wedding in San Miguel de Allende, using the correct form of **ser** or **estar**.

Esta noche (1) _____ la boda de mi mejor amiga, Consuelo. Ella y su novio, Miguel, (2) _____ estudiantes de medicina. La boda (3) _____ a las siete de la noche. La ceremonia religiosa (4) _____ en la Parroquia (*name of church*), y en la puerta hay un grupo de mariachis que tocan (*play*) música. La Parroquia (5) _____ grande y muy elegante; (6) _____ en la plaza principal de San Miguel de Allende. El novio (7) _____ alto y guapo. La novia (8) _____ baja y morena y (9) _____ bellísima (*gorgeous*), como todas las novias. Las flores de la novia (10) _____ rosas amarillas y blancas. ¡Todos (11) _____ muy contentos! ¡Que vivan los novios! (*Long live the bride and groom!*)

Paso 2　Write a short paragraph about an event you know using these questions as a guide.

- ¿Qué es?
- ¿Dónde es?
- ¿A qué hora es?
- ¿Quiénes están?
- ¿Cómo es el evento?
- ¿Cómo están todos en este momento?

 3-33 ¿Quién es? In pairs, take turns using **ser** and **estar** to describe people you know about, or others, and guessing who the person is.

MODELO:　ESTUDIANTE 1: *Es una mujer. Es alta, activa y bonita. Es morena. Es famosa.*
Es estadounidense. Está en Nueva York. Está casada con...
ESTUDIANTE 2: *¡Es Beyoncé!*
ESTUDIANTE 1: *¡Tienes razón! (¡No, no tienes razón!)*

Gael García Bernal, actor	Lionel Messi, futbolista	Lady Gaga, cantante
Sofía Vergara, actriz	Mariano Rivera, beisbolista	Rafael Nadal, tenista
Pitbull, rapero	El Hijo del Santo, luchador (*wrestler*)	Carlos Santana, roquero

El Hijo del Santo es luchador mexicano.

Cultura en vivo

La lucha libre (*wrestling*) is a popular spectator sport in Mexico. One of the most famous wrestlers was **El Santo**, who became a folk hero and a symbol of justice for the common man through his appearances in comic books and movies. The anniversary of his death in 1984 is still commemorated by pilgrimages to his mausoleum in Mexico City. Known for his emblematic silver mask, his youngest son, **el Hijo del Santo**, continues the tradition today. Is there someone like **El Santo** in the U.S. or Canada? Is he or she a folk hero for you?

3-34 ¿Cómo es el Tec de Monterrey? Search online to find out more about this important Mexican university. Write a summary of your findings in Spanish, using these questions as a guide.

- ¿Cuál es su nombre oficial?
- ¿Cuántos campus hay? ¿Cuántos estudiantes hay en total?
- ¿Dónde está uno de sus campus?
- ¿Cuáles son algunas de las carreras del campus?
- ¿Está lejos de o cerca de una playa (*beach*)? ¿de una ciudad grande?
- ¿Deseas visitar el campus? ¿Por qué?

📍 **Busca:** Tec de Monterrey

¡Conversemos!

First, ask yourself if you can perform the following communicative functions in Spanish. Then act out the scenarios with two or three classmates. Ask and respond to at least three questions in each situation.

✓ CAN YOU . . .

☐ identify places and give directions on your university campus?

☐ make plans to do something?

☐ describe traits and states of being?

WITH YOUR CLASSMATE(S) . . .

Situación: Estudiantes nuevos.

You're acting as an orientation leader for new students. Describe your university and give instructions on how to find different buildings. Use expressions such as **está entre**, **enfrente de**, etc. to say where things are.

Para empezar: *La univerdidad es grande. Tiene muchas facultades, por ejemplo… La Facultad de Música está….*

Situación: En la biblioteca.

Ask and answer questions about where you are going later and what you are going to do. Make plans to do something tonight.

Para empezar: *¿Qué vas a hacer?*

Situación: En una fiesta universitaria.

Introduce yourself and talk about yourself using the verb **ser** to say where you are from, your profession, what you are like, and the verb **estar** to say how you feel with adjectives such as **cansado/a**, **enojado/a**, **ocupado/a**, etc.. Ask questions to find out about the other person, as well.

Para empezar: *Hola, yo soy… y soy de…*

Club cultura

3.6 Compile information from several sources

Vida universitaria

Estrategia para ver

Compile information from several sources. You can find information about a culture from various sources: reading a text, researching online, listening to music, watching a video, talking to people, among many. Use several sources to improve your understanding.

ANTES DE VER EL VIDEO

3-35 La UNAM. Simply stated, the UNAM is enormous! More than that, **la Ciudad Universitaria** boasts one of the most eye-catching and diverse campuses in the world. Read the highlights in **Sobre la UNAM**.

AL VER EL VIDEO

Sobre la UNAM

☐ La UNAM es la universidad más grande de Latinoamérica.
☐ En los edificios hay murales de algunos de los artistas más famosos del mundo: David Alfaro Siqueiros, Diego Rivera y Juan O'Gorman.
☐ La Ciudad Universitaria tiene 15 facultades, 135 bibliotecas, 26 museos, un estadio olímpico, un observatorio, muchas cafeterías y una reserva ecológica.
☐ Entre sus exalumnos, hay presidentes, diplomáticos, artistas, escritores, científicos, atletas, empresarios (*businesspeople*) y ganadores (*winners*) del Premio Nobel.

3-36 La vida universitaria. Watch Gerardo describe life at the UNAM; then, indicate the correct option to complete each statement logically.

1. En la UNAM hay más de… (a) 6.000 (b) 16.000 (c) 60.000 estudiantes extranjeros (*international*).
2. Gerardo estudia… (a) biología. (b) derecho. (c) arte.
3. Él asiste a clase… (a) los sábados. (b) por la mañana. (c) por la tarde.
4. Él busca información en… (a) la Facultad de Matemáticas. (b) la rectoría. (c) la biblioteca.
5. Los murales representan… (a) la historia de México. (b) la conquista española. (c) los Juegos Olímpicos de 1968.
6. Más tarde, Gerardo espera ir a… (a) tomar un café con sus amigos. (b) la Facultad de Ciencias. (c) una fiesta.

DESPUÉS DE VER EL VIDEO

3-37 Investigar la UNAM. Go online to find more images of the UNAM. Choose a building or installation to describe, giving its location, purpose, and appearance, as well as any other information of interest.

> **MODELO:** *La Facultad de Derecho es bonita y grande. Está entre la Facultad de Filosofía y la Facultad de Economía. Es para estudiar derecho. Los estudiantes de derecho son…*

📍 **Busca:** imágenes ciudad universitaria UNAM

3.3 Nuestro mundo

Panoramas

3.7 Identify and research some important cultural aspects of Mexico

¡México fascinante!

El México de hoy es una síntesis de influencias indígenas, coloniales, modernas y naturales.

Los antiguos mayas sabían mucho de matemáticas, astronomía y arquitectura. Hoy, el sitio arqueológico de Chichén Itzá es parte del Patrimonio de la Humanidad (*World Heritage Site*) de la UNESCO y una de las "nuevas séptimas maravillas del mundo" (*New 7 Wonders of the World*). Esta pirámide se llama El Castillo (*Castle*).

La Ciudad de México exhibe notables contrastes entre lo viejo y lo nuevo. El Museo Soumaya, concebido por el multimillonario Carlos Slim, es en honor de su esposa y contiene colecciones de arte antiguo y moderno.

México es famoso por su artesanía. Estas figuras talladas (*carved*) de madera fusionan las culturas indígenas y la española.

La Quebrada está en el puerto de Acapulco. Es un acantilado (*cliff*) de 45 metros de altura, de donde algunos jóvenes valientes practican clavadismo (*diving*) en el momento exacto cuando alcanza (*reaches*) el mar la mayor profundidad por la cresta de las olas (*waves*).

El tianguis es un mercado tradicional que data de la época prehispánica. Por lo general, es al aire libre y durante un solo día a la semana, por ejemplo, el tianguis del domingo, o el tianguis del martes. Aquí venden de todo: comida, ropa (*clothing*), teléfonos celulares, electrodomésticos... Hay también puestos donde preparan comida típica, como tacos y tortas (*sándwiches*), y algunas veces hay músicos que tocan música tradicional.

México

Población: 122.000.000

Alfabetismo: 94.5%

Expectativa de educación formal[1]: 13 años

Número de universidades: 155

Usuarios de los medios sociales en Internet: 71%

Usuarios de teléfonos inteligentes: 60%

[1]*Average level of formal education*

3-38 Identifica. Select the correct option based on the information in **Panoramas**.

| Carlos Slim   Chichén Itzá   el clavadismo   figuras talladas de madera   los mayas   Soumaya |

1. un sitio arqueológico _____

2. un museo notable _____

3. una antigua civilización _____

4. un multimillonario mexicano _____

5. un deporte extremo _____

6. una artesanía (*handicraft*) popular _____

3-39 ¿Qué saben de México? Without looking at the map, see how many of these places you can identify.

1. la capital de México

2. el nombre de un golfo

3. una ciudad con una playa (*beach*) famosa

4. una ciudad en la frontera con EE. UU.

3-40 Investigación: Metro de la Ciudad de México. First, go online to investigate a place to visit in Mexico City. For example, **el Palacio de Bellas Artes**, **el parque Chapultepec**, **el Zócalo**, **la Plaza Garibaldi**, **el Museo Nacional de Antropología**, **la Zona Rosa**, **la Basílica de la Virgen de Guadalupe**, **el Museo de Arte Popular**. Then, create an itinerary, listing all the steps to get there on the Metro. Use the UNAM's Universidad station as your starting point. Include the following information for each place you want to visit. Then present your work to the class.

- su nombre y dónde está
- qué tiene de interés
- la línea de Metro que tienes que tomar
- una foto representativa

⚲ Busca: Ciudad México metro

MODELO: *Voy a visitar el zoológico en el Parque Chapultepec. Para ir, tengo que tomar la Línea 3 y… Allí voy a ver… El costo del boleto (ticket) es…*

Páginas

3.8 Scan text for information

El Museo de Antropología de México

Estrategia para leer

Scan text for information. You can scan a document to find specific information—a name, date, statistic, fact, price—without reading the whole article. Keep in mind what you are searching for and the format in which it will likely appear. It may be helpful to use your finger to run down the page until you find what you need.

ANTES DE LEER

3-41 Información importante. Scan the document to answer these questions before reading in more detail.

1. ¿Dónde está?

2. ¿Qué día está cerrado (*closed*)?

3. ¿Cuánto cuesta la admisión?

AL LEER

3-42 El museo. Read the text again in more detail to answer this question in English: **¿Qué colecciones tiene el museo?**

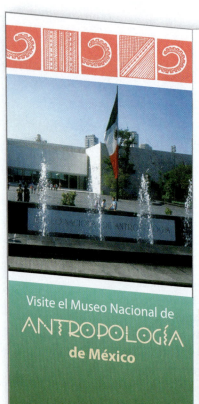

Visite el Museo Nacional de ANTROPOLOGÍA de México

El Museo Nacional de Antropología del Distrito Federal de México fue inaugurado en 1964 para albergar[1] lo más representativo de los avances de la época en la investigación antropológica sobre el mundo prehispánico y sus descendientes, los pueblos indígenas de México.

La Sala de los mayas en el museo contiene una importante colección de piezas[2] de las ancestrales comunidades mayas, que nos permiten apreciar diferentes etapas[3] y escenarios de su historia y su visión del mundo. En la sala hay testimonios de la vida diaria[4], de sus costumbres y tradiciones en torno a[5] la guerra[6], al comercio y a su pensamiento[7] religioso con prácticas rituales.

Los mayas desarrollaron una brillante cultura, construyendo grandes centros cívico-ceremoniales con pirámides y bellas obras[8] de arte.

De martes a domingo de 9:00 a 19:00 hrs. El lunes permanece cerrado.

ADMISIÓN:

$57,00 m.n. (domingo entrada gratuita al público nacional y a los extranjeros residentes en México.)

Entrada gratuita a:
- Niños menores de trece años
- Estudiantes y maestros con credencial vigente[9]
- Adultos mayores de 60 años, jubilados[10] y pensionados
- Pasantes[11] e investigadores del INAH[12]

[1]*house* [2]*pieces, items* [3]*stages* [4]*daily* [5]*pertaining to* [6]*war* [7]*thought* [8]*works* [9]*current* [10]*retired persons*
[11]*interns* [12]*researchers from INAH (Instituto Nacional de Antropología e Historia)*

DESPUÉS DE LEER

3-43 ¿Cómo es el museo? Indicate the correct option to complete each statement logically.

1. El museo está en...
   a. Teotihuacán.
   b. Ciudad de México.
   c. Cancún.

2. La colección maya incluye...
   a. pinturas de los años 1950.
   b. figuras de guerreros (*warriors*).
   c. animales prehistóricos.

3. La colección refleja...
   a. la vida diaria.
   b. las fiestas del pueblo.
   c. el uso de animales.

4. No tienen que pagar los...
   a. adultos.
   b. turistas.
   c. estudiantes.

5. La entrada es gratis (*free*)...
   a. los domingos.
   b. los lunes.
   c. los días festivos.

3-44 Investigación. Search online to find this information about the renowned Museo Nacional de Antropología and write a report of your findings.

1. tres salas permanentes

2. una exposición temporal

3. una pieza interesante

> ⚲ **Busca:** Museo Nacional Antropología México

3-45 Su investigación. In pairs, compare what you learned in your research. Decide whether or not you will visit this museum during a trip to Mexico City, and state your reasons. Here are some possibilities:

Tengo/No tengo ganas de visitar el Museo porque…

(no) me gustan los murales.

(no) me gusta la antropología.

(no) me gusta aprender sobre las antiguas civilizaciones.

(no) me gusta la cultura mexicana.

la entrada es gratis para estudiantes.

¿otra razón?

Tallados en piedra en Chichén Itzá

Taller

Tu universidad

Estrategia para escribir

Outline your thoughts before writing. Having an outline will help you organize your ideas in a clear, coherent manner. Try these steps:

1. Write a statement to announce the overall content or intent (thesis).
2. Write at least three ideas or statements to support your thesis.
3. Write a summary statement to reiterate your thesis.

3-46 Una descripción de tu universidad. How would you describe your university and college experience to a prospective Spanish-speaking student?

ANTES DE ESCRIBIR

Organize your thoughts by creating an outline about your student experience.

- Complete the following opening statement.

  ¡Saludos! Me llamo… y estudio… Debes considerar la Universidad de… porque…

- Write three ideas that support your opening statement. Each of these will form the basis of a paragraph.

  Los profesores son…   *Las clases son…*

  Los compañeros son…   *El campus tiene/es/está…*

  Las facilidades tienen/son/están…, por ejemplo, (la biblioteca, las canchas de tenis, la Facultad de Música, etc.)… Aquí vas a…

- Reiterate your opening statement and summarize your argument.

  En resumen…

AL ESCRIBIR

Follow your outline to develop your description. Write a paragraph about each idea in **Antes de escribir** by providing additional details and examples. Connect your ideas with words such as **y**, **pero**, and **porque**.

DESPUÉS DE ESCRIBIR

- **Revisar.** Review the following elements of your description:
  - ☐ use of **ser** and **estar**, **ir**, **hacer**, and other **-er** and **-ir** verbs
  - ☐ forms of verbs (**yo voy; tú vas…**)
  - ☐ forms of nouns and adjectives (**materias difíciles; una profesora buena…**)
  - ☐ correct spelling, including accents
- **Intercambiar.** Exchange your description with a classmate's; make grammatical corrections and content suggestions. Pay special attention to the organization of the argument. Did you find it clear and convincing?
- **Entregar.** Revise your original description, incorporating your classmate's suggestions. Then, turn in your revised description and the response from your classmate to your instructor.

En este capítulo...

 Vocabulario

Primera parte

Las materias	(Academic) Subjects
la administración de empresas	business administration
la arquitectura	architecture
el arte	art
la biología	biology
el cálculo	calculus
las ciencias políticas/sociales	political/social science
las comunicaciones	communications
la contabilidad	accounting
el derecho	law
la educación física	physical education
la economía	economics
la filosofía	philosophy
la física	physics
la geografía	geography
la geología	geology
la historia	history
la informática / la computación	computer science
la ingeniería (eléctrica)	(electrical) engineering
las matemáticas	mathematics
la medicina	medicine
la pedagogía	teaching, education
la psicología	psychology
la química	chemistry

Otros sustantivos	Other nouns
la carrera	career, field, major
el/la chico/a	boy/girl
el correo electrónico	e-mail
el fin de semana	weekend
el horario (de clases)	(class) schedule
el semestre	semester

Adjetivos	Adjectives
complicado/a	complicated
exigente	challenging, demanding
obligatorio/a	obligatory, required

¿Cuándo es?	When is it?
antes (de)	before
después (de)	after

Segunda parte

Los edificios	Buildings
el auditorio	auditorium
la biblioteca	library
la cafetería	cafeteria
la cancha de tenis	tennis court
el centro estudiantil	student union
el estadio	stadium
la Facultad de Arte	School of Art
la Facultad de Ciencias	School of Science
la Facultad de Derecho	School of Law
la Facultad de Filosofía y Letras	School of Humanities
la Facultad de Ingeniería	School of Engineering
la Facultad de Medicina	School of Medicine
la Facultad de Pedagogía	School of Education
el gimnasio	gymnasium
el laboratorio	(language/computer) laboratory
la librería	bookstore
el museo	museum
el observatorio	observatory
la rectoría	president's office
el teatro	theater

¿Dónde está?	Where is it?
al lado (de)	beside, next to
a la derecha (de)	to the right (of)
a la izquierda (de)	to the left (of)
cerca (de)	close (to)
delante (de)	in front (of) (as in a row or line)
detrás (de)	behind
en	in, on
enfrente (de)	facing, across (from)
entre	between
lejos (de)	far (from)

Verbos	Verbs
hacer	to do; to make
ir (a)	to go (to)

Expressions with *todos/a/os/as* *See page 6.* **The numbers *101–3.000.000*** *See page 7.* **Possessive adjectives** *See page 9.*
Other expressions with *tener* *See page 12.* **Expressions with *hacer*** *See page 21.* **Adjectives with *ser* and *estar*** *See page 23.*

Capítulo 4
¿Cómo es tu familia?

«Al hombre mayor, dale honor».

***Domingo en la Palma*, Fernando Llort, El Salvador.** Considered the National Artist of El Salvador, Llort founded a school to teach local people artwork containing symbols representing El Salvador. What does this painting say about the communities and culture of El Salvador?

Fuente: Fernando Llort

Learning Objectives

4.1 Talk about family

4.2 Express preferences and plan family activities

4.3 Compare families, and learn about a pop fusion musician from Honduras

4.4 Extend and respond to invitations

4.5 Point out people and things, make plans, and discuss what and whom you know

4.6 Watch for the main idea

4.7 Identify and research some important cultural aspects of Guatemala, El Salvador, and Honduras

4.8 Skim for the main idea

4.9 Use appropriate conventions in informal writing

In this Chapter

ENFOQUE CULTURAL: GUATEMALA, EL SALVADOR, HONDURAS
Club cultura: Introducción a El Salvador

Indicate with **C** (**Cierto**) if Gerardo mentions this information in the video, or **F** (**Falso**) if he does not.

1. _____ El Salvador tiene fronteras con Guatemala y Honduras.

2. _____ Tiene una población de 16 millones.

3. _____ Una actividad popular es escalar un volcán.

4. _____ La capital es Chichicastenango.

5. _____ Un edificio (*building*) importante es la Catedral Metropolitana.

6. _____ Un pueblo indígena son los lencas.

4.1 Primera parte

Vocabulario

4.1 Talk about family

Miembros de la familia

)) **Una tamalada en familia. La familia** Suárez es muy **unida**. Están en casa de Joaquín y Chela para celebrar el cumpleaños (*birthday*) del **abuelo** con una tamalada.

Suegra, ¿qué servimos con los tamales? — Chela

Tomás

El guacamole que prepara el abuelo.

Anita

doña Marina

Tomasito

Mami, ¿cuándo vamos a almorzar? ¡Tengo hambre!

Clara

Gracias, hijo. ¡Pasar tiempo en familia es maravilloso! — don Ramón

¡Feliz cumpleaños, padre!

Joaquín

¿Comprendes? Identify who does each action: **don Ramón**, **Chela**, or **Tomasito**.

1. _____ Prepara tamales en su casa.

2. _____ Celebra su cumpleaños.

3. _____ Tiene hambre.

Answers: 1. Chela; 2. don Ramón; 3. Tomasito

))) Vocabulario

Miembros de la familia	Family members
el/la abuelo/a	*grandfather/grandmother*
el/la cuñado/a	*brother-in-law/sister-in-law*
el/la esposo/a	*husband/wife*
el/la hermanastro/a	*stepbrother/stepsister*
el/la hermano/a (mayor/menor)	*(older/younger) brother/sister*
el/la hijo/a	*son/daughter*
la madrastra	*stepmother*
la madre	*mother*
el/la nieto/a	*grandson/granddaughter*
el/la niño/a	*child*
el/la novio/a	*boyfriend/girlfriend, groom/bride*
la nuera	*daughter-in-law*
el padrastro	*stepfather*
el padre	*father*
el/la perro/a	*dog*
el/la primo/a	*cousin*
el/la sobrino/a	*nephew/niece*
el/la suegro/a	*father-in-law/mother-in-law*
el/la tío/a	*uncle/aunt*
el yerno	*son-in-law*

Verbos	Verbs
almorzar (ue) (conmigo/contigo)	*to have lunch (with me / with you)*
costar (ue)	*to cost*
dormir (ue)	*to sleep*
empezar (ie)	*to begin*
encontrar (ue)	*to find*
entender (ie)	*to understand*
ganar	*to earn*
jugar (ue) a	*to play*
pasar	*to spend (time)*
pedir (i)	*to ask for, to request*

Verbos	Verbs
pensar (ie) (en)	*to think (about)*
pensar (ie) (+ infinitive)	*to plan (to do something)*
perder (ie)	*to lose*
poder (ue)	*to be able, can*
preferir (ie)	*to prefer*
querer (ie)	*to want, to love*
recordar (ue)	*to remember*
repetir (i)	*to repeat, to have a second helping*
seguir (i)	*to follow*
servir (i) (la comida; un refresco)	*to serve (the meal; a soft drink)*
soñar (ue) (con)	*to dream (about)*
venir (ie)	*to come*
volver (ue)	*to return*

Adjetivos	Adjectives
casado/a	*married*
soltero/a	*single, unmarried*
unido/a	*close, close-knit*

Variaciones

- The term **niño/a** has many local variants meaning *kid*; for example, **chamaco/a** (Mexico, Central America), **chamo/a** (Venezuela), **nene/a** (Argentina), **crío/a**, **chaval/a** (Spain).
- In Mexico, **padre** is used as an adjective to mean *awesome*, as in **¡Qué padre!**, **Está muy padre**, or **¡Padrísimo!** The term **madre** is used in a lot of Mexican slang, so much so that it often is avoided in favor of **mamá** when speaking about someone's mother.
- In Spain, the term **tío/a** has a colloquial meaning roughly equivalent to American English *guy/gal, dude, buddy.*

Aplicación

4-1 ¿Quién es quién en la familia de don Ramón? Don Ramón explains his relationship to members of his family. Select the family member that corresponds to each description.

1. _____ Es el hijo de mi hijo.
2. _____ Son los padres de mi madre.
3. _____ Es la esposa de mi hijo.
4. _____ Son los hijos de mi hermano.
5. _____ Es la hija de mis tíos.

a. sus sobrinos
b. su nieto
c. su nuera
d. sus abuelos
e. su prima

4-2 La familia de Tomasito. Look at Tomasito's family tree and describe the relationships between these members.

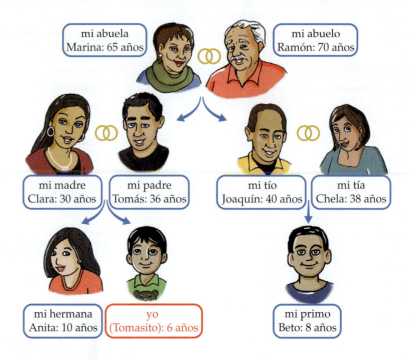

mi abuela
Marina: 65 años

mi abuelo
Ramón: 70 años

mi madre
Clara: 30 años

mi padre
Tomás: 36 años

mi tío
Joaquín: 40 años

mi tía
Chela: 38 años

mi hermana
Anita: 10 años

yo
(Tomasito): 6 años

mi primo
Beto: 8 años

MODELO: Tomasito y Anita
          Son hermanos.

1. don Ramón y doña Marina
2. Chela y don Ramón
3. Anita y Beto
4. Beto y Tomás
5. don Ramón y Anita
6. Joaquín y Clara

4-3 La boda (*wedding*) de Celia y Roberto. Answer the questions based on the invitation to the wedding of Celia Sosa Sánchez and Roberto Suárez Ferrero.

1. ¿Quiénes son los novios?
2. ¿Cómo se llaman los padres de la novia?
3. ¿Dónde es la ceremonia? ¿Y la recepción?
4. ¿En qué fecha y a qué hora es la ceremonia?

JOSÉ SOSA BELÉNDEZ
Elena Sánchez de Sosa

&

RAMÓN SUÁREZ BUENAHORA
Marina Ferrero Bravo

tienen el honor de invitarle al matrimonio de sus hijos
Celia Teresa y Roberto Ramón. El sábado diecinueve
de mayo de dos mil dieciocho a las tres de la tarde.

Misa Nupcial en Iglesia San Jorge

San Salvador, El Salvador

Recepción y cena Salón Real, Hotel Princesa

4-4 Entre familia. Learn about Clara Ana's family.

 Paso 1 Listen as Clara Ana describes her family and complete her family tree by writing the names of each family member.

Clara Ana

1. _____   5. _____
2. _____   6. _____
3. _____   7. _____
4. _____

Paso 2 Take another look at the family tree you completed in **Paso 1** and describe how the people are related to each other.

MODELO: *Clara Ana es la hija de...* (etc.)

4-5 Tu árbol genealógico. Individually, draw a family tree, in which some are real family members and some are fictitious. In pairs, take turns describing your family and deciding if each is telling the truth.

MODELO: ESTUDIANTE 1: *Mi abuelo se llama Juan. Es moreno, inteligente y trabajador. Vive en Madrid.*
ESTUDIANTE 2: *No es verdad. No es posible. / ¿De verdad? Cuéntame más.* (Tell me more.)

Estructuras

4.2 Express preferences and plan family activities

The present tense of stem-changing verbs: *e → ie, o → ue, e → i*

¿Quiere un sándwich de pollo?

No, señor, prefiero una hamburguesa.

¿Recuerdas? You've used regular **-ar**, **-er**, and **-ir** verbs and a few irregular verbs. Complete each sentence with the correct form of a logical verb: **asistir, hacer, ir.**

1. En el gimnasio, mi familia y yo _____ ejercicio.
2. Mi hermana _____ a clases de tenis.
3. Mis padres _____ a tomar clases de yoga.

Answers: 1. hacemos; 2. asiste; 3. van

- Some verbs require a change in the stem vowel[1] of the present forms, except in **nosotros/as** and **vosotros/as**. There are three main stem changes: **e → ie; e → i; o → ue**.

e → ie

querer (*to want, to love*)			
yo	qu**ie**ro	nosotros/as	queremos
tú	qu**ie**res	vosotros/as	queréis
Ud.	qu**ie**re	Uds.	qu**ie**ren
él/ella	qu**ie**re	ellos/as	qu**ie**ren

- Other common **e → ie** verbs:

empezar	pensar (+ *infinitive*)
entender	perder
pensar (en)	preferir

¿A qué hora **empieza** la función?	*At what time does the show start?*
En mi familia, **preferimos** cenar en casa.	*In my family, we prefer to have dinner at home.*

- Note that both **tener** and **venir** also have an irregular **yo** form.

Tengo tres hermanas. ¿Cuántas **tienes** tú?	*I have three sisters. How many do you have?*
Vengo a casa a cenar esta noche, pero no **viene** mi hermana Laura.	*I'm coming home for dinner tonight, but my sister Laura isn't coming.*

Ella siempre sueña que está en la playa.

o → ue

volver (*to return, to come back*)			
yo	**vue**lvo	nosotros/as	volvemos
tú	**vue**lves	vosotros/as	volvéis
Ud.	**vue**lve	Uds.	**vue**lven
él/ella	**vue**lve	ellos/as	**vue**lven

- Other common **o → ue** verbs:

almorzar	jugar a
costar	poder
dormir	recordar
encontrar	soñar (con)

---

[1]In these forms, the stem contains the stressed syllable.

Almorzamos con mis abuelos todos los domingos.	*We have lunch with my grandparents every Sunday.*
¿**Sueñas con** tener hijos algún día (*some day*)?	*Do you dream about having children someday?*
¿Cuánto **cuestan** los refrescos?[1]	*How much do the soft drinks cost?*

- Note that **jugar** changes **u → ue**. The preposition **a** + **el** contracts to form **al**.

  Mañana **juego al** tenis con mi tía.   *Tomorrow I'm playing tennis with my aunt.*

e → i

pedir (*to ask for, to request*)			
yo	pido	nosotros/as	pedimos
tú	pides	vosotros/as	pedís
Ud.	pide	Uds.	piden
él/ella	pide	ellos/as	piden

- Other common **e → i** verbs:

  repetir   servir

¿**Servimos** la sopa primero?	*Do we serve the soup first?*
Si tengo mucha hambre, **repito** la sopa.	*If I'm very hungry, I have a second helping of the soup.*

- Note that all **e → i** stem-changing verbs have the **-ir** ending.

¡Repito! ¡No estoy enojada contigo!

¿Comprendes? Complete each sentence with the correct form of a logical verb: **costar**, **perder**, **servir**.

1. ¿Cuánto _____ las pizzas que pedimos?

2. Mi mamá siempre _____ agua con la comida.

3. Cuando mi tía juega al tenis, ella no _____.

Answers: 1. cuestan; 2. sirve; 3. pierde

Aplicación

4-6 Una entrevista con Rigoberta Menchú. Rigoberta Menchú won the Nobel Peace Prize for her work with the indigenous peoples of Guatemala.

Paso 1 Read the interview and select the logical verb to complete each sentence.

REPORTERA: Señora Menchú, usted es famosa por su trabajo con los indígenas de Guatemala. También (1) juega/tiene un Premio Nobel por su labor. ¿Qué (2) piensa/recuerda hacer ahora?

RIGOBERTA: (3) Encuentro/Quiero trabajar por los derechos humanos (*human rights*) para las personas oprimidas (*oppressed*) del mundo.

REPORTERA: ¿(4) Pierde/Viene a Washington este año?

RIGOBERTA: No, este año no (5) puedo/recuerdo ir porque debo estar en Nueva York. (6) Quiero/Sirvo en un comité de las Naciones Unidas.

REPORTERA: Ud. está casada, ¿no? ¿Cuántos hijos (7) pide/tiene?

RIGOBERTA: (8) Pido/Tengo un hijo. Se llama Mash Nahual J'a (*Spirit of Water*). Mi hijo, mi esposo y mis hermanos (9) juegan/pierden un papel (*role*) muy importante en mi vida.

---

[1]Use only the third-person singular or plural of **costar**: **cuesta(n)**.

Rigoberta Menchú, activista guatemalteca con dos de sus hermanos

Presencia hispana

Although not as large a presence as Mexican Americans, U.S. citizens with ties to Central America have been gaining stature in local politics, especially in regions where they have a sizeable community, for example, in Long Island, where Salvadoran Americans hold office on local school boards and town councils. Why is it important for minority groups to exercise their right to vote? Are there efforts to register new citizens in your community?

Paso 2 Answer the following questions based on the interview.

1. ¿Por qué es famosa Rigoberta Menchú?
2. ¿Qué piensa hacer este año?
3. ¿Qué hace en Nueva York?
4. ¿Está casada o soltera? ¿Tiene hijos?
5. ¿Qué piensa Rigoberta de su familia?

4-7 Ana María y Antonio hacen planes. Ana María was invited by her cousin Antonio to visit him in Ciudad de Guatemala. Complete her narrative with the correct forms of logical verbs.

| costar | entender | pensar | preferir |
| empezar | jugar | perder | querer |

Podemos asistir a un concierto en el Palacio de la Cultura.

Mi primo Antonio y yo hacemos planes para el viernes. (1) Nosotros _____ ir al cine. Antonio (2) _____ ver una película (*movie*) de El Salvador que se llama *Sobreviviendo Guazapa*[1]. Yo (3) _____ las películas francesas, pero Antonio no (4) _____ francés. Su madre piensa que debemos jugar al tenis. Antonio juega bien, pero yo (5) _____ mal y siempre (6) _____. También hay un concierto de música hondureña el viernes; los boletos (*tickets*) (7) _____ 200 quetzales y el concierto (8) _____ a las ocho.

---

[1]See **Páginas** for a review of this movie.

4-8 En casa. Every household is different.

Paso 1 Write complete sentences as they are true for your household. Make sure the verbs agree with their subjects.

> MODELO: En mi casa, nosotros (**servir**) (refrescos; café; agua; cerveza...) con la cena (*dinner*).
> *En mi casa, servimos refrescos con la cena.*

En mi casa...

1. Yo (**almorzar**) (solo/a; con mi novio/a; con mi familia; con mis amigos/as...).
2. Durante la cena, mi familia (**preferir**) (ver la televisión; hablar de política; escuchar la radio; hablar de fútbol...).
3. Nosotros (**jugar**) al (tenis; fútbol; béisbol; tenis de mesa...).
4. Mis (amigos; hermanos) (no) (**poder**) (comer conmigo; ver la televisión conmigo; estudiar conmigo; trabajar conmigo...).
5. Mañana nosotros (**pensar**) preparar comida (mexicana; italiana; francesa; estadounidense...).
6. Cuando hay una comida especial, mis (padres; hermanos; amigos) (**volver**) (tarde; temprano; a tiempo).

 Paso 2 In pairs, compare your households to see what you have in common.

> MODELO: ESTUDIANTE 1: *En mi casa, servimos refrescos con la cena. ¿Y en tu casa?*
> ESTUDIANTE 2: *Bueno, en mi casa servimos agua o café.*

En mi casa servimos tamales en la Navidad.

Cultura en vivo

Tamales are a popular food throughout Central America and Mexico. They are made with corn **masa** (*dough*) stuffed with a **relleno** (*filling*) of meat or vegetables, then wrapped in corn husks or plantain leaves and steamed. **Tamales** are a favorite dish at Christmas and other special occasions when friends and family get together for a **tamalada**, a **tamal**-making party. The **tamalada** is a special time for everyone to share news and events while they work. What food traditions bring your family together?

4-9 Una fiesta sorpresa. In pairs, plan a surprise party for a relative. Take turns responding to these questions to make your plans.

> MODELO: ESTUDIANTE 1: *¿Para quién es la fiesta de cumpleaños?*
> ESTUDIANTE 2: *Es para mi abuelo.*

1. ¿Cuántos años tiene?
2. ¿A quiénes piensas invitar a la fiesta?
3. ¿A qué hora empieza la fiesta?
4. ¿Cuánto cuestan las bebidas (*drinks*) y la comida que piensas servir?
5. ¿Qué música prefieres para la fiesta?

4-10 ¡Tengo! Form a group of four or five. Then, work individually to write meaningful sentences in Spanish. Each sentence must include family members and have a different subject, verb, and additional information. The first person who believes he/she has **five** correct sentences calls out: **¡TENGO!** The rest of the group will assess if the sentences are correct and have all the required elements.

MODELO: *(Yo) Almuerzo con mis primos en la universidad.* (correcto)

costar	entender	pensar (en)	repetir
empezar	jugar (a)	perder	servir
encontrar	pedir	recordar	venir

4-11 Festival de cine latino. Take a look at the announcement below to see the movies for the festival. Then, in small groups, discuss which movies you prefer to see and why. Which is the most popular among your group? Use the different types of movies listed to help in your discussion.

películas...		
sentimentales	de acción	en 3ʳᵃ dimensión
humorísticas	políticas	de suspenso
de misterio	trágicas	argentinas/chilenas/españolas/mexicanas

MODELO: *Quiero ver* Relatos salvajes *porque prefiero…*

FESTIVAL DE CINE HISPANO

No — Chile

Director: Pablo Laraín

Interpretación: Gael García Bernal

Drama histórico: Es la época del dictador Augusto Pinochet, un hombre organiza la "campaña del No" para acabar con la dictadura.

2013 – Primera cinta chilena candidata al Óscar a la Mejor película de habla no inglesa

Julieta España

Director: Pedro Almodóvar

Interpretación: Emma Suárez y Adriana Ugarte

Drama: Julieta vive en Madrid y acaba de perder a su esposo Xoan. Su hija, Antía, acaba de cumplir 18 años y decide huir sin ninguna explicación. La película está inspirada en tres relatos de Alice Munro.

2016

Relatos salvajes Argentina

Director: Damián Szifron

Interpretación: Ricardo Darín, otros

Comedia: Esta comedia negra consiste en seis cortos. Se convirtió en la película más exitosa de la historia del cine argentino. Según el director, la conexión temática se refiere a "la difusa frontera que separa a la civilización de la barbarie".

2014 – Nominada al Óscar: Mejor película de habla no inglesa

La jaula de oro México

Director: Diego Quemada-Díez

Interpretación: Brandón López, Karen Noemí Martínez Pineda, otros

Drama: Narra la historia de unos jóvenes migrantes guatemaltecos y un joven indígena tzotzil en su viaje a Estados Unidos.

2013 – *Un Certain Regard*, Festival de Cannes y 80 premios internacionales

4-12A ¡Necesito información! Each of you has a separate set of questions for a pair of newlyweds. First, form the verbs according to their subject. Then, ask each other your questions and respond logically. **Estudiante B:** see **Appendix 1**, page A-4.

MODELO:　ESTUDIANTE A: ¿Quién _quiere_ (querer) ir a una fiesta?
　　　　　 ESTUDIANTE B:　Mi primo Juan siempre quiere ir. Le gusta mucho bailar.

Estudiante A:

Mis preguntas	Mis respuestas
1. ¿Cuándo _____ (almorzar) ustedes en casa?	Empezamos la luna de miel (*honeymoon*) en marzo.
2. ¿Por qué _____ (dormir) tu esposo al mediodía?	Mi papá prepara la comida y mis hermanos sirven la comida.
3. ¿Quiénes en tu familia _____ (recordar) la fecha de tu aniversario de bodas?	Sí, pensamos vivir aquí cerca de la familia.
4. ¿Con qué _____ (soñar) tú?	Todos jugamos al tenis.

Direct objects, the personal *a*, and direct object pronouns

LOS COMPLEMENTOS DIRECTOS

¿Quieres invitar a Jorge?

¡Sí, vamos a invitarlo!

- A direct object is the noun that generally follows and receives the action of the verb. The direct object is identified by asking *what* or *whom* about the verb. It can either be a person or an inanimate object.

　　Anita llama **a su primo Luis**.　　*Anita calls her cousin Luis. (Answers the question: She calls whom?)*

　　Pablo compra **un teléfono celular**.　　*Pablo is buying a cell phone. (Answers the question: He's buying what?)*

LA *A* PERSONAL

- When the direct object is a definite person or persons, **a** precedes the noun in Spanish. This is known as the personal **a**.

　　Quiero mucho **a** mi papá.　　*I love my father a lot.*

- The personal **a** is required before every specific human direct object in a series.

　　Visito **a** Emilio y **a** Lola.　　*I visit Emilio and Lola.*

- When the interrogative **quién(es)** requests information about the direct object, the personal **a** precedes it.

　　¿**A** quién llama Elisa?　　*Whom is Elisa calling?*

- The personal **a** is usually omitted after the verb **tener**.

　　Julia y Ricardo tienen un hijo.　　*Julia and Ricardo have a son.*

- The personal **a** is not used with a direct object that is an unspecified person.

　　Ana quiere un novio extrovertido.　　*Ana wants an outgoing boyfriend.*

¡OJO!

Remember that the preposition **a** + **el** = **al**.

　　Mi hermano tiene que visitar **al** médico.　　*My brother has to visit the doctor.*

Te quiero mucho.

LOS PRONOMBRES DE COMPLEMENTO DIRECTO

- A direct object **noun** is often replaced by a direct object **pronoun**.
  I see **José**. → I see **him**.

Singular		Plural	
me	*me*	nos	*us*
te	*you* (inf.)	os	*you* (inf.)
lo/la	*you* (for.) (masc./fem.)	los/las	*you* (for.) (masc./fem.)
lo/la	*him/her, it* (masc./fem.)	los/las	*them* (masc./fem.)

- Use direct object pronouns in conversation when the object is established or known.

  Hijo, ¿cuándo ves **a tu primo**? *Son, when will you see your cousin?*
  Lo veo esta noche, padre. *I'll see him tonight, father.*

- When the conversation alternates between first and second persons (*me, us, you*), remember to make the appropriate changes.

  Querida, ¿**me** quieres de verdad? *Dear, do you really love me?*

  Sí, **te** quiero con todo el corazón. *Yes, I love you with all my heart.*

- Place the direct object pronoun directly before the conjugated verb **or** attach it to the infinitive.

  Te voy a llamar esta tarde. ⎱ *I am going to call you this afternoon.*
  Voy a llamar**te** esta tarde. ⎰

- In negative sentences, place the direct object pronoun between **no** and the verb.

  —¿Ves a José? *Do you see José?*
  —No, no **lo** veo. *No, I don't see him.*

¿Comprendes? Complete each dialogue with the logical direct object pronoun or **a** personal.

1. —¿Cuándo vas a visitar a María Elena? —_____ voy a ver esta noche.

2. —¿Puedes llamarme más tarde? —¡Sí, _____ llamo a las tres!

3. —¿Llamas _____ José y _____ Ana también? —¡Sí, los llamo ahora mismo!

Answers: 1. La; 2. te; 3. a/a

Aplicación

4-13 De luna de miel en Guatemala. Celia and Roberto are going to Guatemala for their honeymoon.

Paso 1 Select the response that corresponds to each question.

1. _____ Celia, ¿quieres escalar (*climb*) el volcán Acatenango?

2. _____ Roberto, ¿tienes tu cámara?

3. _____ Celia, ¿quieres visitar el mercado de artesanías (*handicraft*)?

4. _____ Roberto, ¿por qué no llamamos a los padres esta tarde?

5. _____ Celia, ¿me ayudas a buscar la mochila?

6. _____ Roberto, debes tomar muchas fotos de las artesanías en el mercado.

a. Buena idea, vamos a llamarlos a las cinco.

b. Sí, la tengo en mi mochila.

c. Está bien. Las tomo con mi cámara nueva.

d. Claro, te ayudo enseguida, mi amor.

e. Sí, vamos a escalarlo mañana.

f. Sí, lo debemos visitar en Chichicastenango.

Paso 2   Una visita a Chichicastenango. Search online for information about this town that Celia and Roberto will visit. Answer the questions in complete sentences, using direct object pronouns.

◉ Busca: Chichicastenango

1. ¿Qué días puedes visitar el mercado?
2. ¿Venden comida en el mercado?
3. ¿Puedes visitar la iglesia de Santo Tomás?
4. ¿Puedes ver muchas artesanías bonitas en el mercado?
5. ¿Puedes hablar español en Chichicastenango?

En Guatemala puedes subir al volcán activo Acatenango.

4-14 En la Universidad Francisco Marroquín. Antonio is a student at the Universidad Francisco Marroquín in Ciudad de Guatemala. Read the conversation between him and his cousin Rosario; write the personal **a** (or **al**) wherever necessary, or **X** if neither is needed.

ROSARIO: Oye, Antonio, ¿(1) _____ quién ves todos los días?

ANTONIO: Yo siempre veo (2) _____ Tomás en la universidad. Tomamos (3) _____ café todas las tardes.

ROSARIO: ¿Ven ustedes (4) _____ muchos amigos allí?

ANTONIO: Sí, claro. Siempre vemos (5) _____ Mercedes y (6) _____ Gustavo. A veces (*Sometimes*) sus hermanos toman (7) _____ un refresco con nosotros también.

ROSARIO: ¿Pasas mucho tiempo con ellos?

ANTONIO: Sí, esta noche todos, menos Gustavo, vamos a ver (8) _____ una película muy buena. Gustavo no puede ir porque tiene que visitar (9) _____ padre de su novia. Vamos a invitar (10) _____ tu amigo, Héctor, también.

4-15 Servicio en una escuela rural hondureña. Students from several North American universities often perform service in rural Honduras. Complete the exchanges between Ester, her brother, Jairo, and the director of this school in Concepción.

MODELO: DIRECTOR: Ester, ¿tienes la cámara para tomar fotos de los niños?
 ESTER: *Sí, la tengo. / No, no la tengo.*

DIRECTOR: Ester, ¿tienes las medicinas para los niños?
 ESTER: 1. _____

DIRECTOR: ¿Quieren Uds. ver la biblioteca de la escuela?
 ESTER: 2. _____

DIRECTOR: Jairo, ¿tienes tu cuaderno para escribir tus observaciones?
 JAIRO: 3. _____

DIRECTOR: ¿Encuentras a los niños enfrente de la escuela?
 JAIRO: 4. _____

DIRECTOR: ¿Desean Uds. visitar la clínica ahora?
 ESTER: 5. _____

DIRECTOR: Jairo, ¿mañana quieres comprar los refrescos para los estudiantes?
 JAIRO: 6. _____

Los estudiantes en Concepción posan para la cámara.

4-16A ¡Necesito información! *Diario Latino* is an independent newspaper in El Salvador. You are reporters who are preparing to interview Fernando Llort, the famous Salvadoran artist who designed the renovated façade for the Catedral Metropolitana. Ask each other questions and respond logically. **Estudiante B**: see **Appendix 1**, page A-5.

MODELO: ESTUDIANTE A: *¿Tienes tu cuaderno para escribir apuntes (notes)?*
 ESTUDIANTE B: *Sí, lo tengo.*

Estudiante A:

Mis preguntas	Mis respuestas a las preguntas de mi compañero/a
1. ¿Tienes la dirección de la Catedral Metropolitana?	Claro, quiere verlo.
2. ¿Tiene el señor Llort la lista de preguntas?	Sí, pero no lo juega muy bien.
3. ¿Habla inglés el artista?	No, no tiene tiempo para leerla.
4. ¿Van a visitar Honduras el artista y su familia?	Sí, voy a llamarlo ahora.

Fachada de Llort de la Catedral Metropolitana de San Salvador

4-17 En tu familia. Ask each other who does these activities in your family. Use the correct form of each verb and object pronoun in your responses.

MODELO: **leer** novelas románticas

ESTUDIANTE 1: *En tu familia, ¿quién lee novelas románticas?*

ESTUDIANTE 2: *Mi hermana las lee.*

1. **ver** mucho la televisión
2. **llamarte** por teléfono constantemente
3. **perder** su teléfono celular
4. **querer** ver videos de acción
5. **pedir** café en un restaurante
6. **preferir** música de *rock*

¡Conversemos!

With two or three classmates, act out the following scenarios. Ask and respond to at least four questions in each situation.

✓ CAN YOU...	WITH YOUR CLASSMATE(S)...
☐ talk about family?	**Situación: En el centro estudiantil.**
	Ask about each other's families, what they do, and what they're like.
	Para empezar: *¿Cómo es tu...? ¿Qué hace tu...?*
☐ express preferences?	**Situación: Por teléfono.**
	Call a family member on the phone to make plans to do something tomorrow. Use stem-changing verbs like **preferir, querer, costar, jugar, perder, poder,** etc.
	Para empezar: *¿Aló...? Habla... ¿Quieres ver una película o prefieres...?*
☐ plan family activities?	**Situación: Una fiesta.**
	Make plans for a family party. Discuss several options, stating what you are going to serve and do for the party. Ask and respond to questions, using direct objects and direct object pronouns (**lo, la, los, las**).
	Para empezar: *¿Vamos a servir tamales o pizza? ¡Tamales y pizza! Vamos a comprarlos en la pizzería...*

Perfiles

4.3 Compare families, and learn about a pop fusion musician from Honduras

Mi experiencia

LA FAMILIA HISPANA ¿TÍPICA?

4-18 Para ti. Which family members do you consider to be part of your immediate family? How many of them live at home? Have any of your family members considered moving away for economic reasons? Here, a Honduran woman responds to an online post asking about the typical Hispanic family. Do you think there is such a thing as a typical Hispanic, U.S., or Canadian family?

**[1]*so much*
[2]*In addition*

[3]*recent***

[4]*leave behind*

[5]*support*

[6]*birthrate*   [7]*has decreased*

Chicacuriosa **pregunta:** ¿Hay una familia típica hispana?

Mejor respuesta:

Maríahondureña **responde:** Desde mi punto de vista, hay tanta[1] variedad que es imposible generalizar el concepto de "familia hispana". Además[2], con la globalización, la movilidad y los cambios culturales durante los últimos[3] años, la palabra *familia* es muy dinámica. Primero, tenemos que pensar en la migración, especialmente en los países centroamericanos, por razones económicas y políticas. En mi país, Honduras, es común que los padres y los hijos mayores tienen que dejar[4] a sus familias y buscar trabajo para poder mandarles dinero. Las mujeres, como mi mamá y yo, tenemos que trabajar para mantener a los niños más pequeños. Pero tenemos el apoyo[5] familiar de mis tíos y de mis abuelos para mantener la unidad familiar. Segundo, hoy día hay más oportunidades para la mujer de recibir una buena educación y por eso el índice de natalidad[6] ha disminuido[7] de más de cuatro hijos por mujer a solo tres. Así que la idea del núcleo familiar con madre, padre e hijos no es universal y es imposible decir que hay un solo modelo.

Un cantautor popular hondureño que habla del tema de la globalización es Guillermo Anderson. Vas a ver que sus canciones siempre combinan el humor con la realidad.

4-19 En su opinión. In pairs, take turns reacting to each of these statements, according to the reading.

MODELO: La familia típica consiste en los padres y muchos hijos.
          Estoy de acuerdo (I agree), *porque... / No estoy de acuerdo, porque…*

1. Para la familia hispana, el núcleo familiar consiste en los padres, los hijos, los abuelos y toda la familia política (*in-laws*).
2. Para la familia hispana, es común vivir cerca de su familia.
3. La madre hispana no tiene que trabajar fuera de la casa.
4. El índice de natalidad es muy alto entre las familias hispanas.
5. La mujer, casada o soltera, tiene que ser económicamente independiente.

Mi música

"EL ENCARGUITO" (GUILLERMO ANDERSON, HONDURAS)

Guillermo Anderson was born in the port town of La Ceiba, where all Caribbean cultures of Honduras come together: descendants of Mayans and other indigenous people, the **garífuna** slaves from West Africa, European settlers, and **mestizos**, which are all reflected in his music. Honduras has recognized his contributions with numerous honors, including naming him **Embajador Cultural de Honduras**. His unexpected death in 2016 put the entire country in mourning. "El encarguito" is a humorous piece about a "care package" (literally, *a little request*) that a person sends to a family member abroad.

ANTES DE VER Y ESCUCHAR

4-20 Comida hondureña. Using context and cognates, select the description that best corresponds to the food mentioned. Have you ever seen or tasted any of them?

1. _____ un chicharrón con yuca	a. two pounds of cheese curd
2. _____ una sopa de capirotadas	b. donkey milk
3. _____ los nacatamales	c. type of **tamal**
4. _____ dos libras de cuajada	d. egg bread and rose bread
5. _____ pan de yema y pan de rosa	e. cracklings (fried pig skin) with yucca
6. _____ leche de burra	f. a soup made with broth and corn fritters with eggs and cheese

PARA VER Y ESCUCHAR

4-21 La canción. Look online for a video of Guillermo Anderson performing this song. He expresses concerns about getting his **encarguito** safely through customs (**la aduana**). Which of the following may represent his dilemma? Indicate the correct answer.

1. _____ El encarguito es muy grande.
2. _____ No se permite entrar con comida ni bebidas (*drinks*) en otro país.
3. _____ La persona que lleva el encarguito lo va a comer en el viaje.
4. _____ El encarguito tiene la dirección equivocada (*wrong address*).

> **Busca:** Guillermo Anderson video Encarguito; Guillermo Anderson letra Encarguito

DESPUÉS DE VER Y ESCUCHAR

4-22 Un encarguito tuyo. Imagine that you are spending a year in Honduras and miss your family and the things that remind you of home. Write a paragraph stating the foods or other items that several family members send to you, and why they are important.

MODELO: *De mi hermano recibo… porque…*

4.2 Segunda parte

Vocabulario

4.4 Extend and respond to invitations

El ocio

))) **Una invitación.** Raúl **invita** a Laura a ver **una película.**

RAÚL: Laura, soy Raúl. Te llamo para ver si quieres ir al **cine** esta noche.

LAURA: **Me gustaría...** ¿**Sabes** qué película **ponen**?

RAÚL: Sí, hay una película de El Salvador en el Rialto. No sé si la **conoces.** Se llama *Sobreviviendo Guazapa.* Es a las siete. ¡**Te invito!**

LAURA: Un momento, me llama mi madre. Te llamo en unos minutos.

Pasan unos minutos y Laura llama a Raúl.

LAURA: Hola, Raúl, **lo siento, pero no puedo salir** esta noche. ¿**Qué tal si** vamos mañana?

RAÚL: **Sí, claro.** Nos vemos mañana.

¿Comprendes? Indicate which person is described, based on the dialogue: **Raúl (R)** or **Laura (L).**

1. _____ Está en un café al aire libre.

2. _____ Quiere ir al cine esta noche.

3. _____ Sabe a qué hora es la película.

Answers: 1. L; 2. R; 3. R

Vocabulario

El ocio	Leisure time
el café (al aire libre)	*(outdoor) cafe*
el centro	*downtown*
el cine	*movie theater*
el concierto	*concert*
la entrada	*admission ticket*
la función	*show*
la invitación	*invitation*
la orquesta	*orchestra*
el parque	*park*
el partido	*sports game*
la película	*movie*

Verbos	Verbs
conocer (conozco, conoces…)	*to know (someone), to be familiar with (something) (I know, you know . . .)*
invitar	*to invite*
pasear	*to take a walk*
poner (pongo, pones…)	*to put, to place (I put, you put . . .)*
poner una película	*to show a movie*
saber (sé, sabes…)	*to know something (I know, you know . . .)*
saber + *infinitive*	*to know how to do something*
salir (salgo, sales…)	*to leave, to go out (I leave, you leave . . .)*
tocar	*to play (an instrument, music)*
traer (traigo, traes…)	*to bring (I bring, you bring . . .)*

Para hacer una invitación	To extend an invitation
¿Qué tal si...?	*How about . . .?*
¿Quieres ir a...?	*Do you want to go to . . .?*
¿Te gustaría (+ *infinitive*)...?	*Would you like (+ infinitive) . . .?*
¡Te invito!	*(It's) My treat!*
¿Vamos a...?	*Should we go . . .?*

Para aceptar una invitación	To accept an invitation
De acuerdo.	*Fine with me, Okay.*
Me encantaría.	*I would love to.*
Paso por ti.	*I'll come by for you, I'll pick you up.*
Sí, claro.	*Yes, of course.*

Para rechazar una invitación	To reject an invitation
Estoy muy ocupado/a.	*I'm very busy.*
Gracias, pero no puedo...	*Thanks, but I can't . . .*
Lo siento, tengo que...	*I'm sorry, I have to . . .*

Variaciones

- Although **entrada** (from **entrar**, *to enter*) is understood in most countries, in Mexico and areas of South America, **boleto** is more common and generally refers to occupying a seat.
- The adjective phrase **de película** colloquially means *fantastic, awesome*, as in **un carro de película** (*an awesome car*). Also, in Spain, you'll hear **peli** for **película.**
- When you answer the phone in many Spanish-speaking countries, you'll use **¿Aló?** However, in Mexico, you'll likely use **¿Bueno?**, and in Spain, **¿Diga?** or **¿Dígame?**

))) Letras y sonidos

Word stress and written accent marks in Spanish

Most words in Spanish (for example, all nouns, verbs, adjectives, and adverbs) carry word stress, where one syllable in the word is given special emphasis. In Spanish, word stress always falls on one of the last three syllables of the word: **tra-ba-ja-dor**, **in-te-li-gen-te**, **sim-pá-ti-co**. In some cases, word stress is indicated in writing with an accent mark, or **acento (ortográfico)**, according to the following rules:

- Usually, words ending in a consonant (except **n** or **s**) are stressed on the *last syllable*.

  a-**brir**　ins-truc-**tor**　es-pa-**ñol**　re-**loj**　us-**ted**　ac-**triz**

  Exceptions to this rule require a written accent mark.

  Víc-tor　**ú**-til　di-**fí**-cil　**fút**-bol　**lá**-piz　**sánd**-wich

- Usually, words ending in a vowel or the consonant **n** or **s** are stressed on the *second-to-last syllable*.

  bo-**ni**-ta　tra-**ba**-jo　tra-**ba**-jan　jo-**ven**　tra-**ba**-jas　no-**so**-tros

  Exceptions to this rule require a written accent mark.

  es-**tá**　a-**quí**　es-**tán**　lec-**ción**　es-**tás**　in-**glés**

- Words with stress on the *third-to-last syllable* always require a written accent mark.

  nú-me-ro　**mú**-si-ca　bo-**lí**-gra-fo　**jó**-ve-nes　**miér**-co-les

- Some words seem identical but are different in emphasis and meaning. A written accent mark differentiates them from each other.

  él = *he*　**tú** = *you*　**mí** = *(to) me*　**¿Qué?** = *What?*　**¿Có-mo?** = *How?*
  el = *the*　**tu** = *your*　**mi** = *my*　**que** = *that*　**co-mo** = *how, as, like*

- A written accent mark also is used with an **i** or **u** to indicate hiatus (that is, when one of these letters, adjacent to another vowel, represents a separate syllable).

  dí-a　**grú**-a　pa-**ís**　Ra-**úl**

Aplicación

4-23 Asociaciones. Select the activity that best corresponds to each place.

1. _____ el cine　　　　　　　a.　ir de compras
2. _____ el parque　　　　　　b.　tomar un refresco
3. _____ el café　　　　　　　c.　jugar al frisbi
4. _____ el teatro　　　　　　d.　ver un partido
5. _____ el centro　　　　　　e.　asistir a una función
6. _____ el estadio　　　　　　f.　ver una película

4-24 Otras actividades. Complete this paragraph about Raúl and Laura's day together, with logical words or expressions from **Vocabulario**.

Raúl y Laura van al (1) _____ para ver una película. Llegan unos minutos antes para comprar (2) _____. Después de la película, caminan por (3) _____ y toman refrescos en un café (4) _____, donde hay música jazz. La música que toca la (5) _____ es maravillosa. El día siguiente, Laura invita a Raúl a ir a un (6) _____ de béisbol.

4-25 Marilú invita a José. Marilú and José are making plans to hang out together.

 Paso 1   Listen as Marilú and José talk on the telephone. Then indicate the correct option to complete each statement based on their conversation.

1. Marilú invita a José a…

    a. comer.   b. bailar.   c. pasear por el parque.

2. José acepta la invitación para…

    a. esta noche.   b. mañana.   c. las tres de la tarde.

3. Los chicos también van a ver…

    a. un partido.   b. una película.   c. un programa de televisión.

4. Es evidente que los chicos son…

    a. hermanos.   b. amigos.   c. novios.

5. Marilú y José no tienen que estudiar porque…

    a. mañana no hay clases.   b. su clase es fácil.   c. no hay tarea para mañana.

 Paso 2   Take turns inviting each other to one of the places mentioned in **Paso 1**. Ask what day, where, what time, and so on. The model will give you some ideas of questions you can ask in your conversation.

> **MODELO:**   ESTUDIANTE 1: *Oye, … ¿Quieres ir…? ¡Te invito!*
>
>   ESTUDIANTE 2: *No sé. (¿Cuándo? / ¿Dónde? / ¿A qué hora? /*
>   *¿Por qué? / ¿Con quiénes?)*
>
>   ESTUDIANTE 1: …

4-26A ¡Necesito información! You are friends who would like to make plans to hang out together. Talk about what you would like to do, following the guide. **Estudiante B**: see **Appendix 1**, page A-5.

Estudiante A: 1. Complain to your friend that you are bored so that he/she will invite you to do something. 2. Decline at least three of the invitations, making excuses. 3. Accept one or more you like, and then arrange the details together.

> **MODELO:**   ESTUDIANTE A: *Estoy aburrido/a.*
>   ESTUDIANTE B: *¿Quieres ir a bailar? (¿Te gustaría…?; ¿Prefieres…?)*
>   ESTUDIANTE A: *Me encantaría. ¡Vamos! / Gracias, pero no puedo. No tengo dinero.*

Algunas excusas:

estar cansado/a	no tener carro	no tener dinero/tiempo
no tener ganas	tener que…	tener mucho trabajo

4-27 El fin de semana. In groups of three or four, use the questions as a guide to make plans for this weekend. Then, summarize your conversation for the class.

¿Adónde quieren ir?	¿Qué necesitan?	¿Con quiénes van?
¿Qué quieren hacer?	¿Qué día?	¿Quién paga (*pays*)?
¿Cómo es?	¿A qué hora empieza?	¿A qué hora vuelven a casa?

> **MODELO:**   *Queremos ver un partido de fútbol el sábado a la una de la tarde. Después, vamos a pasear por el centro y ver a nuestros amigos. Los invitamos a tomar un refresco en el Café Luna. Luego, volvemos a casa en autobús. Llegamos a casa a las siete y media.*

Cultura en vivo

In Spanish-speaking countries, when you say **¡Te invito!**, it implies that you are paying for the other person. On a birthday, it is usual for the person celebrating to invite everyone else, rather than be invited. Do you invite or get invited on your birthday?

> Chela, ¿tienes planes para esta noche?
>
> Pues, debo estudiar para el examen de sociología…
>
> Yo también, pero hay una fiesta en mi casa, y…
>
> ¿A qué hora?
>
> ¿Quiénes van? ¿Van a tener música?
>
> ¡Todos van! ¿Te animas?[1]

[1]*Are you in?*

Estructuras

4.5 **Point out people and things, make plans, and discuss what and whom you know**

Demonstrative adjectives and pronouns

Demonstrative adjectives and pronouns point out people and objects and the relative position and distance between the speaker and the person or object modified.

	SINGULAR	PLURAL		RELATED ADVERBS
masc. / fem.	**este / esta**	**estos /estas**	*this/these (close to me)*	**aquí** *(here)*
masc. / fem.	**ese / esa**	**esos / esas**	*that/those (close to you)*	**allí** *(there)*
masc. / fem.	**aquel / aquella**	**aquellos / aquellas**	*that/those (over there, distant from both of us)*	**allá** *(over there)*

ADJETIVOS DEMOSTRATIVOS

Este chico es muy guapo.

Sí, pero aquel es muy rico.

- Like other adjectives, demonstrative adjectives agree in number and gender with the noun they modify. They usually go before a noun.

  ¿De quién son **esos** refrescos?   *Whose soft drinks are those?*

- Demonstrative adjectives are usually repeated before each noun in a series.

  Esta película y **estos** actores son mis favoritos.   *This movie and these actors are my favorites.*

- In everyday usage, **ese/aquel**, **esa/aquella** (*that*), and **esos/aquellos**, **esas/aquellas** (*those*) are interchangeable. However, the **aquel** forms are preferred to point out objects and people that are relatively farther away than others.

  ¿Cuánto cuestan **esas** rosas y **aquellas** violetas?   *How much are those roses and those violets (further away, over there)?*

PRONOMBRES DEMOSTRATIVOS

- When you omit the noun, the demonstrative adjective becomes a demonstrative pronoun.

  (**Adjective**) ¿Ves a **ese** hombre alto?   *Do you see that tall man?*
  (**Pronoun**) ¿Cuál? ¿**Ese** o **aquel**?   *Which one? That one (closer) or that one (farther away)?*

- The neuter forms **esto**, **eso**, and **aquello** are invariable pronouns. They refer to ideas, actions, concepts, or to unspecified objects or things.

  Aquello no me gusta.   *I don't like that.*
  No comprendo **eso**.   *I don't understand that.*
  Esto está mal.   *This is wrong.*
  ¿Qué es **esto** / **eso** / **aquello**?   *What's this/that?*

¿Comprendes? Select the logical demonstrative.

1. Quiero (este/estos) libros y (ese/esos) bolígrafos.

2. No entiendo (ese/eso).

3. ¿Qué película prefieres? ¿(Esta/Ese) o (aquella/aquel)?

Answers: 1. estos/esos; 2. eso; 3. Esta/aquella

Aplicación

4-28 Información: San Salvador. Laura is visiting San Salvador for the first time and is asking for information.

Paso 1 Read the conversation between Laura and a tourist information agent who explains some of the most popular points of interest. Select the appropriate demonstrative adjectives and pronouns to complete the conversation.

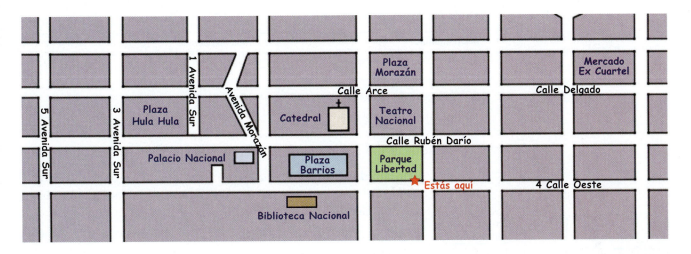

AGENTE: (1) Esta/Este es un mapa del centro de la ciudad y algunos puntos de interés.

LAURA: Ah, verdad. ¿Qué es (2) esto/esta enfrente de la Plaza Barrios?

AGENTE: Bueno, hay tres edificios enfrente de la Plaza. (3) Eso/Ese, cerca de usted, es la Biblioteca Nacional. (4) Este/Aquel, cerca de mí, es el Palacio Nacional.

LAURA: ¿Y (5) aquella/este iglesia?

AGENTE: (6) Aquella/Aquel es la Catedral. Usted debe visitarla.

LAURA: ¿Y el mercado?

AGENTE: Es (7) aquello/aquel edificio en la Calle Delgado. Si quiere, puede ir en taxi o caminar. En ruta, puede comprar entradas para un concierto en (8) este/aquel edificio, el Teatro Nacional.

Paso 2 Look at the map again and discuss with your partner what places you would like to visit. Your location is indicated with the star.

MODELO: ESTUDIANTE 1: *¿Quieres visitar esa catedral?*
ESTUDIANTE 2: *No, prefiero visitar este parque.*

4-29 ¿Qué es esto? Take turns asking each other to identify at least three classroom objects.

MODELO: ESTUDIANTE 1: (point to table close to both of you) *¿Qué es esto?*
ESTUDIANTE 2: *Es una mesa. ¿Y aquello (distant from both of you)?*
ESTUDIANTE 1: *Es...*

4-30 Mi familia. Bring in a photo of your family or make a drawing of an imaginary family. Hold up your photo/drawing for others in your small group to see and take turns asking and telling about family members.

MODELO: ESTUDIANTE 1: *¿Quién es aquel señor?*
ESTUDIANTE 2: *Este es mi hermano. Es alto y moreno. Tiene... años.*
ESTUDIANTE 3: *¿Cómo se llama esa chica?*

Presencia hispana

El Salvador has a population of six million people. Due to political, social, and economic strife, it is estimated that some two million have emigrated to the U.S. or Canada. This means that thousands of families left behind in El Salvador have been affected, as well. Many fear that the massive migration has led to the deterioration of those families. How can families maintain cohesion when members are forced to be separated?

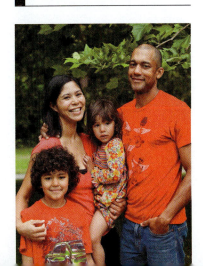

4-31A ¡Necesito información! Each of you has a separate set of questions with demonstratives. First, choose the correct form of the demonstrative for your questions. Then, ask each other your questions and respond logically. **Estudiante B**: see **Appendix 1**, page A-5.

MODELO: ¿De quién es (esto/este) lápiz?

      ESTUDIANTE A: *¿De quién es este lápiz?*

      ESTUDIANTE B: *Ese lápiz es de la profesora.*

Estudiante A:

Mis preguntas	Mis respuestas
1. ¿De quiénes son (estos/estas) mochilas?	¿Esto? ¡Es un tamal!
2. ¿Cómo es (este/esta) clase?	Estas son de mis padres.
3. ¿Cómo son (aquello/aquellos) estudiantes?	Aquella es muy exigente.
4. ¿Quiénes son (esos/esas) chicas?	Aquel es del profesor.

The present tense of *poner, salir,* and *traer*

¿Recuerdas? You've learned some verbs that are irregular only in the **yo** form of the present tense. Write the correct form of the logical verb, **ver** or **hacer**.

(Yo) (1) _____ la tarea por la tarde y (2) _____ la televisión por la noche.

Answers: 1. Hago; 2. veo

¿Traes la comida ahora?

Sí, la pongo en la mesa en un momento.

Here are some other verbs that are only irregular in the first person.

	poner (*to put, to place*)	salir (*to leave, to go out*)	traer (*to bring*)
yo	pongo	salgo	traigo
tú	pones	sales	traes
Ud.	pone	sale	trae
él/ella	pone	sale	trae
nosotros	ponemos	salimos	traemos
vosotros	ponéis	salís	traéis
Uds.	ponen	salen	traen
ellos/ellas	ponen	salen	traen

Si **traes** tu libro, **traigo** mi portátil.   *If you bring your book, I'll bring my laptop.*

Ustedes **ponen** libros en su mochila.   *You put books in your backpack.*

Expansión **More on *salir*.** Each of the following expressions with **salir** has its own meaning.

salir a (+ *infinitive*): *to go out (to do something)*

    Salen a cenar los sábados.   *They go out to dinner on Saturdays.*

salir con: *to go out with, to date*

    Diana **sale con** Lorenzo.   *Diana goes out with Lorenzo.*

salir de: *to leave a place, to leave on a trip*

    Salgo de casa a las siete.   *I leave home at seven.*

salir para: *to leave for (a place), to depart*

    Mañana **salen para** Tegucigalpa.   *Tomorrow they leave for Tegucigalpa.*

¿Comprendes? Complete with the correct form of a logical verb: **poner**, **salir**, or **traer.**

Esta tarde, (1: yo) _____ una película en mi casa. Mis hermanos vienen a verla y (2) _____ refrescos. Ellos (3) _____ para su casa a las once de la noche.

Answers: 1. pongo; 2. traen; 3. salen

Aplicación

4-32 Un correo electrónico de mamá. Clara's mom writes an e-mail about their plans for the day.

Paso 1   Read the e-mail and select the logical verb to complete it.

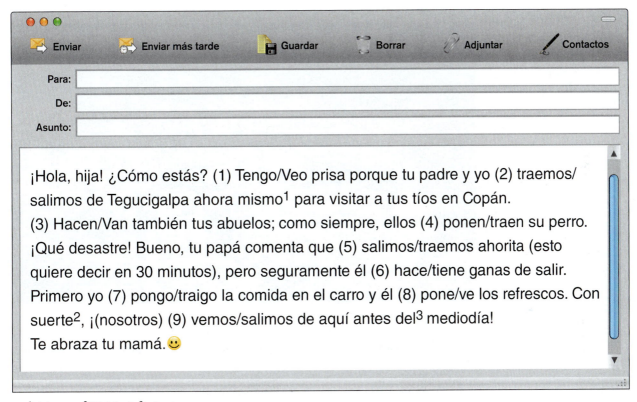

¡Hola, hija! ¿Cómo estás? (1) Tengo/Veo prisa porque tu padre y yo (2) traemos/salimos de Tegucigalpa ahora mismo[1] para visitar a tus tíos en Copán.
(3) Hacen/Van también tus abuelos; como siempre, ellos (4) ponen/traen su perro. ¡Qué desastre! Bueno, tu papá comenta que (5) salimos/traemos ahorita (esto quiere decir en 30 minutos), pero seguramente él (6) hace/tiene ganas de salir. Primero yo (7) pongo/traigo la comida en el carro y él (8) pone/ve los refrescos. Con suerte[2], ¡(nosotros) (9) vemos/salimos de aquí antes del[3] mediodía!
Te abraza tu mamá. 😊

[1]*right now* [2]*With luck* [3]*before*

Paso 2   Answer the following questions based on the e-mail.

1. ¿Dónde viven los padres de Clara?
2. ¿Qué hacen los padres de Clara hoy?
3. ¿Qué traen los abuelos?
4. ¿Qué ponen sus padres en el carro?
5. ¿A qué hora piensan salir finalmente?

Si estás en Copán, debes salir a ver las ruinas mayas.

4-33 Clara y Tomás hacen un viaje. Clara's husband is going along on her business trip. Complete the paragraph with the correct forms of logical verbs from the list. You will use each verb only once.

hacer	poner	salir	traer	ver

Mi esposo Tomás y yo (1) _____ planes para ir a El Salvador. (2) _____ para la capital, San Salvador, a las 9 de la mañana. Antes de salir, (yo) (3) _____ la guía turística en mi maleta (*suitcase*). Después, (4) _____ las noticias en la televisión para escuchar el pronóstico (*forecast*) meteorológico para la capital. En mi oficina, mi secretaria me (5) _____ el itinerario con la información del hotel.

Hay muchos volcanes cerca de San Salvador.

4-34 Planes. Take turns finding out about each other's plans for the weekend.

MODELO: ¿A qué hora **salir** (tú) para...?
ESTUDIANTE 1: *¿A qué hora sales para la casa de tu familia?*
ESTUDIANTE 2: *Salgo para la casa a las diez de la mañana.*

1. ¿Adónde **salir** (tú)...?
2. ¿A qué hora **salir** (tú) para...?
3. ¿Quién **hacer** la comida?

4. ¿Qué música **poner** (tú)?
5. ¿Quién **traer** los refrescos?
6. ¿Qué **ver** (tú) allí?

4-35 En una fiesta familiar. You and your partner are getting ready for a family gathering. Separately, write four questions about who is responsible for each task. Use a different subject, verb, and additional information in each question. Then, ask each other your questions, being careful to respond with an appropriate subject.

MODELO: ESTUDIANTE 1: *¿Quién pone las flores (flowers) en la mesa?*
ESTUDIANTE 2: *Mi padre las pone en la mesa.*

Tareas necesarias:
salir a comprar los refrescos
hacer los sándwiches
poner la comida en la mesa
salir a buscar más sillas
traer la música
tener las sillas y las mesas

Persona(s) responsable(s):
los invitados (*guests*)
tú
mi hermana (padre, madre, etc.)
todos nosotros
yo
el abuelo (la abuela, etc.)

4-36 ¿Quiénes? Walk around the classroom and ask some of your classmates questions, using the information in the chart. Try to ask all of your questions, each one to a different person. Write the name and response in the box.

MODELO:　**poner** sus libros en la mochila

ESTUDIANTE 1: *Becky, ¿pones tus libros en la mochila?*

ESTUDIANTE 2: *Sí, los pongo en la mochila. (No, no los pongo en la mochila.)*

YOU WRITE: *Becky (no) los pone en la mochila.*

salir los sábados con los amigos _____	**traer** su libro a clase _____	**ver** películas en español _____
traer dinero hoy _____	**ver** a su familia este fin de semana _____	**traer** su teléfono celular _____
ver el fútbol en la televisión _____	**poner** azúcar (*sugar*) en su café _____	**salir** para su casa este fin de semana _____

Saber and *conocer*

The verbs **saber** and **conocer** can both mean *to know*, however, they are not interchangeable. Both verbs have irregular **yo** forms.

	saber (*to know*)	conocer (*to know*)
yo	sé	conozco
tú	sabes	conoces
Ud.	sabe	conoce
él/ella	sabe	conoce
nosotros	sabemos	conocemos
vosotros	sabéis	conocéis
Uds.	saben	conocen
ellos/ellas	saben	conocen

- **Saber** means *to know a fact* or to have *knowledge or information* about someone or something.

  ¿**Sabes** dónde está el cine?　　　　*Do you know where the movie theater is?*

  No, no **sé**.　　　　*No, I don't know.*

- With an infinitive, **saber** means *to know how to do something.*

  La tía Berta **sabe** bailar tango.　　　　*Aunt Berta knows how to dance the tango.*

- **Saber** may be followed with an interrogative word or **si** (*if*).

  ¿**Sabes dónde** es la fiesta?　　　　*Do you know where the party is?*

  No **sé si** mis padres quieren salir esta noche.　　　　*I don't know if my parents want to go out tonight.*

¡Ellos saben bailar muy bien!

María, conoces a Pablo, ¿verdad?

- **Conocer** means *to be acquainted* or *to be familiar* with a person, place, or thing.

  Tina **conoce** a mis abuelos.   *Tina knows (is acquainted with) my grandparents.*

  Conozco San Salvador.   *I know (am acquainted with) San Salvador.*

- Remember to use the personal **a** with **conocer** to express that *you know a specific person.*

  La profesora **conoce a** mis tíos.   *The professor knows my aunt and uncle.*

STUDY TIPS FOR *SABER* AND *CONOCER*

saber	conocer
knowing a fact or information	knowing people
knowing a skill (how to do something)	knowing a place
may be followed by an infinitive, an interrogative word, or **si**	*never* followed by an infinitive or **si**

¿Comprendes? Complete with the correct form of **conocer** or **saber**.

—(1) ¿_____ (tú) a Gerard Piqué, el esposo de Shakira?

—No, no lo (2) _____, pero (3) _____ quién es.

Answers: 1. Conoces; 2. conozco; 3. sé

Aplicación

4-37 Una chica extraordinaria. Julia Catalina Flores has an extraordinary talent for a girl her age.

Paso 1 Read the article about Julia and select the forms of **saber** and **conocer**.

Julia Catalina Flores: la charanguista más joven de El Progreso

Julia Catalina Flores Ramírez sabe tocar la guitarra y desde la edad de 6 años toca en la banda de su papá. (Foto por Suyapa Carias)

¿Conoces a Julia? Pues si la ves en el grupo de su padre, vas a saber que es una chica extraordinaria. Aunque es pequeña y tímida, es una experta con el *charango*, un instrumento similar a la guitarra. Es de una madera hondureña muy especial y rara. Ella dice que conoce su charango como a un miembro de su familia.

Julia vive en el pueblo de El Progreso en el norte de Honduras. Cuando las personas la escuchan tocar, están maravilladas por su talento. Ella dice que le gusta tocar con su familia y hacer feliz a la gente. Ya sabe tocar más de 200 canciones. Si la quieres escuchar, el grupo cobra (*charges*) unos 25 lempiras por canción. Pero tienes que viajar a Honduras, porque ella es muy joven para salir de viaje como música profesional.

Paso 2   Answer the questions based on the reading.

1. ¿Dónde vive Julia?
2. ¿Cómo es?
3. ¿La conoces?
4. ¿Qué sabe hacer?
5. ¿Cuántas canciones sabe?
6. ¿Quieres conocerla algún día? ¿Por qué?

Paso 3   Complete the conversation between Marcela and Carmiña, who would like to meet Julia. Use the correct forms of **saber** and **conocer**.

MARCELA: ¿(Tú) (1) _____ a Julia Catalina Flores?

CARMIÑA: No, yo no la (2) _____ personalmente, pero (3) _____ que es hondureña.

MARCELA: Todos (4) _____ que ella toca muy bien el charango, ese instrumento musical similar a la guitarra.

CARMIÑA: Marcela, ¿(5) _____ si Julia vive en El Progreso?

MARCELA: Sí, vive allí. Su familia es muy famosa. Mi novio y yo (6) _____ la ciudad, pero no (7) _____ dónde vive la familia exactamente.

CARMIÑA: Quiero invitarla a tocar en una fiesta, pero no (8) _____ si puede ir. Vamos a buscar información en Internet.

Cultura en vivo

Instruments used in Salvadoran popular music include marimba, flutes, drums, scrapers, and gourds, as well as more recently imported guitars and other instruments. Political chaos tore El Salvador apart in the late 20th century, and music was often suppressed, especially that with strong indigenous influences. Why is music censored? When has music been censored in the U.S. or Canada?

4-38 A jugar.   Form small groups, and then work individually to write three sentences in Spanish with **conocer** and three with **saber**, some true and some false. Each sentence must have a different subject and complement. The first person who thinks he/she has six grammatically correct sentences calls out: **¡TENGO!** and reads aloud the sentences to the others. The rest of the group will try to determine if the sentences are true or false.

MODELO: *Mi hermano sabe tocar la guitarra.*
Yo conozco a Fernando Llort. (etc.)

4-39 ¿Quién? Ask as many classmates as possible questions regarding the topic in each box in the chart. Write the name of each person on the chart, noting his/her answer (as **sí** or **no**). **¡OJO!** Be sure to use the correct verbs (**sabes/sé** or **conoces/conozco**) and the personal **a** as needed in your questions and responses.

MODELO: la fecha de hoy
ESTUDIANTE 1: *¿Sabes la fecha de hoy?*
ESTUDIANTE 2: *Sí, la sé. Es 15 de noviembre.*

qué hora es	mi número de teléfono	si hay un restaurante salvadoreño cerca de aquí	un rapero hispano
un restaurante salvadoreño	Jennifer López	cuándo hay examen	la capital de Honduras
el presidente de Guatemala	dónde está Copán	bien esta ciudad	mis padres

¡Conversemos!

With two or three classmates, act out the following scenarios. Ask and respond to at least four questions in each situation.

✓ CAN YOU...

☐ extend and respond to invitations and make plans to do something?

☐ point out people and things?

☐ discuss what and whom you know?

WITH YOUR CLASSMATE(S)...

Situación: Por teléfono.

Call a friend and invite him or her to do something with you. Decide between you what you want to do, when, and who else you should invite.

Para empezar: *¿Aló...? ¿Te gustaría...?*

Situación: Actores y músicos.

You are at a party with celebrities. Use demonstrative adjectives and pronouns (**este**, **ese**, **aquel**, and their various forms) to talk about some of the people you see close by, further away, and far away from you. Be sure to use gestures to illustrate the demonstratives.

Para empezar: *Esta fiesta es muy buena, pero no me gusta ese actor. Aquella señorita que está allá es muy bonita...*

Situación: Chismes (Gossip).

Try to one-up each other by saying what and whom you know and what you know how to do, using **conocer** and **saber**.

Para empezar: *Conozco a Lionel Messi...*

Club cultura

4.6 Watch for the main idea

Guatemala: Los mayas

Estrategia para ver

Watch for the main idea. During a video, you will see and hear details that support one main idea. Take note of the characters, location, activities, and events. These will help you identify the main idea.

ANTES DE VER EL VIDEO

4-40 Los mayas de Centroamérica. Read the facts about Mayan civilization in **Sobre los mayas**. Then write a sentence about a possible main idea of this video.

Posible idea principal: _____

_____

> **Sobre los mayas**
> ☐ La civilización maya reinó (*reigned*) durante 3.000 años.
> ☐ Los mayas ocuparon (*occupied*) el territorio hoy conocido como Guatemala, Belice, El Salvador, Honduras y una gran parte del sur de México.
> ☐ Los españoles tardaron (*took*) 170 años para conquistarlos.

AL VER EL VIDEO

4-41 Los mayas. Watch the segment about the Mayas and indicate the sentence that best represents the main idea. How does your answer compare to the one you wrote in Activity **4-40**?

1. Los mayas tenían (*had*) un calendario muy preciso.
2. Sus descendientes conservan sus tradiciones, su cultura y algunos de los idiomas mayas.
3. Los mayas observaban (*observed*) los astros y predecían (*predicted*) las estaciones.
4. Los mayas tenían un sistema de jeroglíficos (*hieroglyphics*) muy sofisticado.

DESPUÉS DE VER EL VIDEO

4-42 Los detalles. Indicate the most logical option to complete each statement.

1. Los antiguos mayas eran muy (altos / valientes / ricos).
2. Guatemala tiene el mayor número de (depósitos de petróleo / tumbas de conquistadores españoles / sitios arqueológicos).
3. Muchos de los descendientes mayas (viven en la capital / hablan un idioma (lengua) maya / viajan al extranjero [*abroad*]).
4. En una ceremonia maya, una ofrenda importante es (el chocolate / el oro / la sangre [*blood*]).
5. Para los mayas, el color amarillo simboliza (el valor / la victoria / el agua).

4.3 Nuestro mundo

Panoramas

4.7 Identify and research some important cultural aspects of Guatemala, El Salvador, and Honduras

En tierras de los mayas: Guatemala, El Salvador, Honduras

La población de Guatemala, El Salvador y Honduras es mayormente mestiza, una mezcla de las razas blanca e indígena, principalmente de origen maya. Estos países se sienten orgullosos (*feel proud*) de sus tradiciones indígenas que incluyen una cocina milenaria y expresiones de arte original.

La arena (*sand*) blanca, las aguas cristalinas y la abundancia de vida marina atraen a miles de turistas a las islas a lo largo de (*along*) la costa caribeña de Honduras. Aquí en Roatán es popular bucear (*scuba diving*), pescar (*fishing*) y tomar el sol.

La preparación de las comidas diarias reflejan el amor por las antiguas tradiciones. Estas mujeres preparan tortillas de maíz en un comal (*hotplate*) grande.

El arte alegra la vida diaria de estas comunidades. Este mural está en San Juan Laguna (Guatemala), que se considera un auténtico museo al aire libre porque tiene más de 30 murales de artistas locales.

Estos autobuses multicolores, que antes transportaban (*transported*) a niños a las escuelas en Estados Unidos, cobran una nueva vida en las calles y rutas de América Central. Los autobuses, o *chicken buses* (un nombre que les dieron (*gave*) los estadounidenses que primero los importaron), son un medio de transporte esencial para muchas familias y comunidades rurales. Cada autobús es personalizado por el dueño (*owner*), quien también puede ser el chofer. Están decorados de una manera muy original y usualmente llevan el nombre de un santo o de una persona querida por el dueño. Llevan de todo: personas, equipaje (*luggage*), ¡y hasta animales!

Los jóvenes son como en cualquier (*any*) parte del mundo. Tienen sus teléfonos inteligentes y acceso a Internet, y son activos en las redes sociales.

	Guatemala	Honduras	El Salvador
Adjetivo:	guatemalteco/a	hondureño/a	salvadoreño/a
Población:	14,5 millones	8,5 millones	6,1 millones
Índice de natalidad[1]:	3,08 (hijos/mujer)	2,94	2
PIB[2] per cápita:	$5.300	$4.700	$7.600
Grupos étnicos:	mestizos: 54% indígenas: 40%	mestizos: 90% indígenas: 7%	mestizos: 86% europeos: 12% indígenas: 1%

[1]*Birth rate* [2]**PIB: Producto Interno Bruto** (*GDP: Gross Domestic Product*) is the market value of all final goods and services made within the borders of a country in a year. This figure is often positively correlated with standard of living.

4-43 Identifica. Select the correct option based on the information in **Panoramas**.

el autobus   El Salvador   hondureño   Guatemala   los murales   tortillas

1. una comida típica _____
2. el tipo arte popular _____
3. el adjetivo de Honduras _____
4. un ejemplo del medio de transporte popular _____
5. el país con la menor población indígena _____
6. el país con el índice de natalidad más alto _____

4-44 Desafío. Use the map of Guatemala, El Salvador, and Honduras to identify these characteristics and places.

1. las capitales de estos tres países
2. el país que tiene frontera con México
3. el país más grande de los tres
4. los países con costa en el mar Caribe

4-45 Investigación: La historia maya en su arte. The Mayans chronicled their history and beliefs through painting and sculpture. Look online for photos of their art and write a paragraph describing some of the colors and themes, then present it to the class.

MODELO: *Esta escultura maya representa un murciélago* (bat)*, símbolo de la muerte.*

📍 **Busca:** pintura maya; escultura maya

Páginas

4.8 Skim for the main idea

Sobreviviendo Guazapa, CineNuevo

Contexto de la película: From 1980–1992 in El Salvador, the right-wing military forces and the left-wing guerilla coalition FMLN engaged in a bloody civil war. The most outrageous act was in 1980: the assassination of Archbishop Óscar Romero while he was celebrating Mass. *Sobreviviendo Guazapa* is the first feature-length film written and produced in El Salvador with a full cast of Salvadoran, primarily novice actors.

Estrategia para leer

Skim for the main idea. Skimming is to read quickly to get the main idea of the passage. It involves identifying topic sentences and key words. After you know what the passage is about, you will usually go back to read for specific information.

ANTES DE LEER

4-46 Las secciones. This reading has a title box and three sections. First, say what the title box tells you about the main idea; then select the description that best describes the content of each heading.

1. _____ Sinopsis
2. _____ Sobre la película
3. _____ Premios

   a. algunos detalles sobre la filmación
   b. el reconocimiento de los méritos de la película
   c. un resumen del argumento (*plot*)

AL LEER

4-47 CineNuevo. Take a look at the review that appears on the site CineNuevo. Skim it quickly to get the main idea. Which of these is most probable?

☐ Salvadoran films are known for winning important film festival awards.
☐ The brutal civil war in El Salvador lasted three years.
☐ This is a film about humanity, even in times of war.

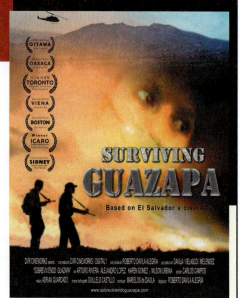

GÉNERO: Aventura/Drama
DIRECTOR/PRODUCTOR: Roberto Dávila
DURACIÓN: 1 hora, 53 minutos
AUDIO: Español, Digital Surround

Sinopsis

Dos combatientes enemigos entre sí[1], atrapados en el caos de los ataques al volcán de Guazapa, se unen para salvar sus vidas. En el camino se encuentran con una niña perdida[2] y deciden ayudarla a volver con su familia. A partir de ese momento, enfrentan juntos múltiples pruebas de sobrevivencia[3].

Sobre la película

Es la primera película salvadoreña de ficción sobre la guerra civil realizada por salvadoreños. El inicio del rodaje[4], se vio retrasado por los huracanes *Wilma*, *Stan* y *Katrina*. Para el *casting*, hubo convocatoria abierta a través de periódicos locales. Varios de los actores seleccionados no tenían experiencia, pero se destacaron[5] en la prueba. Actores y extras recibieron entrenamiento militar previo al rodaje. Hubo dos accidentes durante el rodaje en que resultaron lastimados[6] los actores principales. La realización de la película tomó tres años.

Premios

Sobreviviendo Guazapa ha sido Selección Oficial en más de seis festivales internacionales de cine, galardonada con un Premio Especial en el Festival de Cine Hispano de Toronto, honrada como Premio de Apertura del Festival de Cine de Viena, Austria y ganadora de Premio a Mejor Actor en el Festival Ícaro.

Según el crítico Héctor Ismael Sermeño (*Trazos culturales*): Su gran logro[7] es ver la guerra a la distancia, sin pasiones personales, ideologías partidarias o sentimentales… Dávila no quiere reflejar la historia, la utiliza como marco[8] para contar su argumento y lo hace con dignidad.

---

[1]*themselves* [2]*lost* [3]*survival* [4]*filming* [5]*they stood out* [6]*injured* [7]*achievement* [8]*backdrop*

DESPUÉS DE LEER

4-48 La película. Complete the statements according to what you have read.

> los huracanes   militar   positiva   premios   tres años

1. La realización de la película duró (*lasted*)…
2. Hubo (*There were*) retrasos por…
3. Los actores recibieron entrenamiento (*training*)…
4. La película recibió varios…
5. La opinión del crítico Héctor Ismael Sermeño es muy…

4-49 En su opinión. Work in pairs to place the following movie features in order of importance. Which of these categories would make you want to see the film *Sobreviviendo Guazapa*? In what ways do you agree or differ in opinion? Finally, do you agree or disagree on seeing the film?

Orden de importancia	Estamos de acuerdo
_____ el argumento	
_____ el director	
_____ el género (aventura, acción, sentimental)	
_____ la lengua	
_____ los actores	
_____ los premios	

4-50 Un héroe salvadoreño. Archbishop Óscar Romero was assassinated in 1980 by the right-wing Salvadoran government because he denounced the military violence against the people. Use the questions to describe what you see in his memorial monument in San Salvador, shown below.

1. ¿Quién es la figura en blanco y negro?
2. ¿Qué relaciones familiares crees que hay entre las personas en el mural?
3. ¿Quién puede ser la persona en la prisión?
4. ¿Quiénes crees que son las personas en el fondo (*background*) del mural?

El arzobispo Óscar Romero denunció la violencia militar de los años 70 en El Salvador. Este monumento a la Memoria y la Verdad en el parque Cuscatlán, San Salvador, conmemora su vida y su obra.

Taller

4.9 **Use appropriate conventions in informal writing**

Una invitación

Estrategia para escribir

Use appropriate conventions in informal writing. The writing style you use with friends and family is very different from what you use with your professors, boss, or in a professional setting. Here are some tips:

1. Use the **tú** form of verbs.
2. Use informal salutations, such **¡Hola!**, **¿Qué tal?**, **¿Qué onda?** (*What's up?*) or **Querido/a**.
3. Include informal expressions, such as **pues, …** or **bueno, …**.
4. Write a little about what's new in your life; then, state the reason why you're writing.
5. Use an informal closing, such as: **Nos vemos**, **Hasta pronto**, **Un (fuerte) abrazo** (*a [big] hug*), **Un beso** (*A kiss*), **Con cariño** (*With affection*), **Saludos de** (*Best wishes from*).

4-51 **Una invitación por correo electrónico.** You will write a short e-mail to invite a friend to spend the weekend with you. Follow the steps and use the model and questions to guide you.

> **MODELO:**   *¿Qué tal, Pilar? Aquí estamos toda la familia en…, para pasar… Aquí hay una foto de…*

ANTES DE ESCRIBIR

Use these questions to guide you:

¿Dónde estás ahora?	¿Con quiénes?	¿Por cuánto tiempo?
¿Cuál es la invitación?	¿Cuándo?	¿Cosas que debe traer?
¿Qué actividades pueden hacer?	¿Una foto del lugar?	¿Más información?

AL ESCRIBIR

Follow these steps to write your e-mail:

- **Saludo.** Choose an appropriate informal greeting.
- **El mensaje.** Incorporate the information you listed above. Use words such as **y**, **pero**, and **porque**, **bueno**, or **pues** to link your ideas.
- **Respuesta.** Ask for a reply to your letter: **Responde pronto**.
- **Despedida.** Close the letter with an informal farewell.

DESPUÉS DE ESCRIBIR

- **Revisar.** Review the following elements in your letter:
  - ☐ use of stem-changing verbs
  - ☐ use of **saber** and **conocer** and the personal **a**
  - ☐ use of direct objects and direct object pronouns
  - ☐ use of demonstratives (**este**, **ese**, **aquel**, etc.)
  - ☐ correct spelling, including accents
- **Intercambiar.** Exchange your invitation with a classmate's; make grammatical corrections and content suggestions. Then respond to the invitation.
- **Entregar.** Rewrite your original invitation, incorporating your classmate's suggestions. Then turn in your original invitation and the response from your classmate to your instructor.

En este capítulo...

))) Vocabulario

Primera parte

Miembros de la familia	Family members
el/la abuelo/a	grandfather/grandmother
el/la cuñado/a	brother-in-law/sister-in-law
el/la esposo/a	husband/wife
el/la hermanastro/a	stepbrother/stepsister
el/la hermano/a (mayor/menor)	(older/younger) brother/sister
el/la hijo/a	son/daughter
la madrastra	stepmother
la madre	mother
el/la nieto/a	grandson/granddaughter
el/la niño/a	child
el/la novio/a	boyfriend/girlfriend, groom/bride
la nuera	daughter-in-law
el padrastro	stepfather
el padre	father
el/la perro/a	dog
el/la primo/a	cousin
el/la sobrino/a	nephew/niece
el/la suegro/a	father-in-law/mother-in-law
el/la tío/a	uncle/aunt
el yerno	son-in-law
Verbos	**Verbs**
almorzar (ue) (conmigo/contigo)	to have lunch (with me / with you)
costar (ue)	to cost
dormir (ue)	to sleep
empezar (ie)	to begin
encontrar (ue)	to find
entender (ie)	to understand
ganar	to earn
jugar (ue) a	to play
pasar	to spend (time)
pedir (i)	to ask for, to request
pensar (ie) en	to think (about)
pensar (ie) (+ infinitive)	to plan (to do something)
perder (ie)	to lose
poder (ue)	to be able, can
preferir (ie)	to prefer
querer (ie)	to want, to love
recordar (ue)	to remember
repetir (i)	to repeat, to have a second helping
seguir (i)	to follow
servir (i) (la comida; un refresco)	to serve (the meal; a soft drink)
soñar (ue) (con)	to dream (about)
venir (ie)	to come
volver (ue)	to return
Adjetivos	**Adjectives**
casado/a	married
soltero/a	single, unmarried
unido/a	close, close-knit

Segunda parte

El ocio	Leisure time
el café (al aire libre)	(outdoor) cafe
el centro	downtown
el cine	movie theater
el concierto	concert
la entrada	admission ticket
la función	show
la invitación	invitation
la orquesta	orchestra
el parque	park
el partido	sports game
la película	movie
Verbos	**Verbs**
conocer (conozco, conoces...)	to know (someone), to be familiar with (something) (I know, you know . . .)
invitar	to invite
pasear	to take a walk
poner (pongo, pones...)	to put, to place (I put, you put . . .)
poner una película	to show a movie
saber (sé, sabes...)	to know something (I know, you know . . .)
saber + infinitive	to know how to do something
salir (salgo, sales...)	to leave, to go out (I leave, you leave . . .)
tocar	to play (an instrument, music)
traer (traigo, traes...)	to bring (I bring, you bring . . .)
Para hacer una invitación	**To extend an invitation**
¿Qué tal si...?	How about . . .?
¿Quieres ir a...?	Do you want to go to . . .?
¿Te gustaría (+ infinitive)...?	Would you like (+ infinitive) . . .?
¡Te invito!	(It's) My treat!
¿Vamos a...?	Should we go . . .?
Para aceptar una invitación	**To accept an invitation**
De acuerdo.	Fine with me, Okay.
Me encantaría.	I would love to.
Paso por ti.	I'll come by for you, I'll pick you up.
Sí, claro.	Yes, of course.
Para rechazar una invitación	**To reject an invitation**
Estoy muy ocupado/a.	I'm very busy.
Gracias, pero no puedo...	Thanks, but I can't . . .
Lo siento, tengo que...	I'm sorry, I have to . . .

Direct object pronouns   *See page 120.*
Demonstratives adjectives and pronouns   *See page 130.*
Expressions with *salir*   *See page 132.*

Capítulo 5
¿Cómo pasas el día?

«Un lugar para cada cosa y cada cosa en su lugar».

Mola de un búho, **mujer guna anónima.** For many Guna women in Panama, making **molas**, a handcrafted traditional design made with fabric, is a daily activity. **Molas** commonly represent the flora and fauna of Central America. What does this subject matter say about the Guna people?

Learning Objectives

5.1 Talk about personal care items and routines

5.2 Describe your daily routine and feelings, and make comparisons

5.3 Compare opinions about ecotourism, and learn about a ska-rock fusion band from Panama

5.4 Talk about the home and household chores

5.5 Describe superlative qualities and actions in progress

5.6 Ask and answer questions to clarify information

5.7 Identify and research some important cultural aspects of Costa Rica, Nicaragua, and Panama

5.8 Trigger background knowledge to understand text

5.9 Know your audience

In this Chapter

ENFOQUE CULTURAL: COSTA RICA, NICARAGUA, PANAMÁ
Club cultura: Introducción a Costa Rica

Indica con **C (Cierto)** si esta información se menciona en el video o **F (Falso)** si no se menciona.

1. _____ la población

2. _____ su apodo (*nickname*): los costarricenses

3. _____ sus fronteras con Guatemala y Panamá

4. _____ el color de la arena (*sand*)

5. _____ la distancia entre los mares (*seas*)

6. _____ un deporte popular

5.1 Primera parte

Vocabulario

5.1 Talk about personal care items and routines

Las actividades diarias

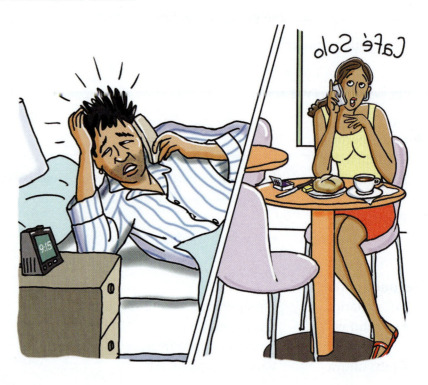

Fabián llega tarde. Rosario está en el café desde las nueve de la mañana. Ahora son las nueve y quince.

FABIÁN:	¿Sí?
ROSARIO:	¡Hola, Fabián!
FABIÁN:	¿Sí? ¿Quién es?
ROSARIO:	¡Yo! ¡Rosario! Estoy aquí en el Café Solo. ¿Dónde estás tú?
FABIÁN:	¡Ay! En la cama (*bed*). Llego en cinco minutos. Solo tengo que **levantarme, ducharme, afeitarme, peinarme, vestirme**...
ROSARIO:	¡Fabián! ¡Eres un caso!

Rosario toma su café y piensa...

ROSARIO:	A veces (*Sometimes*) **me pongo furiosa** con Fabián. No **se despierta** a tiempo. Bueno, también es un buen amigo y siempre **nos divertimos** juntos.

¿Comprendes? Complete the statements with a logical expression: **amigos, la cama, molesta, un café**.

1. Rosario está en _____.
2. Fabián está en _____.
3. Rosario está _____.
4. Ellos son _____.

Respuestas: 1. un café; 2. la cama; 3. molesta; 4. amigos

)) Vocabulario

Las actividades diarias	Daily activities
acostarse (ue)	to go to bed
afeitarse	to shave
bañarse	to take a bath
cepillarse (los dientes, el pelo)	to brush (your teeth, your hair)
despertarse (ie)	to wake up
dormirse (ue, u)	to fall asleep
ducharse	to take a shower
lavarse (las manos)	to wash (your hands)
levantarse	to get up, to stand up
maquillarse (la cara, los ojos)	to put makeup on (your face, your eyes)
peinarse	to comb your hair
quitarse (la camisa)	to take off (your shirt)
secarse	to dry yourself off
sentarse (ie)	to sit down
vestirse (i, i)	to get dressed
Las emociones	Some emotions
ponerse contento/a	to become happy
furioso/a	angry
molesto/a	annoyed
sentirse (ie, i)	to feel

Los artículos de uso personal	Personal care items
el acondicionador	conditioner
el brillo de labios	lip gloss
el cepillo (de dientes)	(tooth)brush
el champú	shampoo
la crema (de afeitar)	(shaving) cream
el espejo	mirror
el jabón	soap
el maquillaje	makeup
la máquina de afeitar	electric shaver
la navaja de afeitar	razor
el peine	comb
el secador	hair dryer

Variaciones

Levantarse can mean *to get up (in the morning)* or *to stand up (from a sitting position)*. In parts of Latin America, however, *to stand up* is often expressed with **pararse**.

Aplicación

5-1 ¿Qué asocias con estas actividades? Selecciona el objeto que mejor corresponde a cada actividad.

1. _____ quitarse
2. _____ afeitarse
3. _____ peinarse
4. _____ secarse el pelo
5. _____ lavarse el pelo
6. _____ lavarse la cara
7. _____ acostarse
8. _____ sentarse

a. en la cama
b. con champú
c. con crema y navaja
d. con jabón
e. con un peine
f. con un secador
g. en una silla
h. el maquillaje

)) 5-2 Los señores Rodríguez. Escucha la descripción de la rutina diaria de la familia Rodríguez. Indica a quién(es) se refiere cada oración a continuación: al Sr. Rodríguez, a la Sra. Rodríguez o a los dos.

La actividad	El señor	La señora	Los dos
1. Debe levantarse temprano todos los días.	_____	_____	_____
2. Trabaja en una oficina.	_____	_____	_____
3. Tiene que bañarse por la mañana.	_____	_____	_____
4. Tiene que afeitarse.	_____	_____	_____
5. Toma café por la mañana.	_____	_____	_____
6. Almuerza con otras personas.	_____	_____	_____
7. Hace ejercicio (*exercise*) después de comer.	_____	_____	_____
8. Prepara la cena.	_____	_____	_____

5-3 ¿Qué asocian con...? En grupos de tres o cuatro, formen asociaciones de las palabras o expresiones de **Vocabulario** con estas actividades o emociones.

MODELO: afeitarse
la cara, la crema de afeitar, la navaja de afeitar, ...

bañarse	mirarse	ponerse molesto/a
ponerse contento/a	dormirse	cepillarse
ponerse impaciente	ponerse nervioso/a	sentirse cansado/a

5-4 ¿Qué tienen que hacer? Identifica qué tienen que hacer estas personas cada día. Añade (*Add*) más información sobre cada dibujo (*drawing*).

MODELO: *Pancho tiene que acostarse temprano porque mañana tiene que ir a la escuela.*

Pancho

1.

Juanito

2.

Maribel

3.

Alonso

4.

Tomás

5.

Carlos

6.

Sara

7.

doña María

8.

tía Luisa

5-5 **El arreglo personal.** Hay muchos productos de maquillaje y de arreglo personal.

Paso 1   Busca un producto de arreglo personal en Internet. Descríbelo: ¿Cuánto cuesta? ¿Es para hombres o para mujeres? ¿Es un producto bueno en tu opinión? ¿Quieres comprarlo? ¿Por qué?

   MODELO: *Toja Sensible es una crema de afeitar para hombres. La quiero comprar porque...*

> 📍 **Busca:** productos belleza; maquillaje; secadores pelo; jabones; máquinas afeitar

Paso 2   Diseña un anuncio (*ad*) para vender un producto original. Sigue el modelo.

   MODELO:

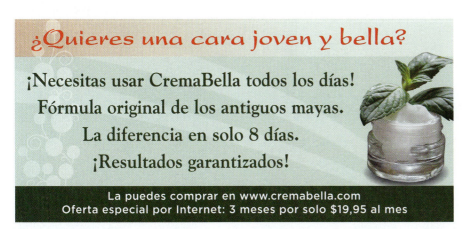

¿Quieres una cara joven y bella?

¡Necesitas usar CremaBella todos los días!
Fórmula original de los antiguos mayas.
La diferencia en solo 8 días.
¡Resultados garantizados!

La puedes comprar en www.cremabella.com
Oferta especial por Internet: 3 meses por solo $19,95 al mes

5-6 **¿Qué tienen que hacer para arreglarse todos los días?** En parejas, túrnense para contarse (*tell each other*) su rutina personal. ¿Qué hacen en común y en qué se diferencian? ¿Por qué? Usen verbos del **Vocabulario** y las expresiones de la lista.

primero	entonces	cuando es necesario	si hay tiempo
después	muchas veces	siempre	finalmente

   MODELO: ESTUDIANTE 1: *Primero, tengo que levantarme a las siete y media de la mañana.*
   ESTUDIANTE 2: *Primero, debo levantarme a las siete porque tengo clase a las ocho en punto. Si hay tiempo, …*

Después de bañarme, tengo que...

Estructuras

5.2 **Describe your daily routine and feelings, and make comparisons**

Reflexive constructions: Pronouns and verbs

¿Recuerdas? You learned about direct objects and direct object pronouns in **Capítulo 4**. Provide the appropriate direct object pronoun to complete the response.

—¿Me llamas esta tarde?   —Sí, _____ voy a llamar a las tres.

Respuesta: te

When the subject of the verb also receives the action of the verb, it is called *reflexive*. In English, the object sometimes includes *self* or *selves: I see myself. We wash ourselves.*

Isabel **se peina**.
Isabel combs her hair.

Isabel **peina a su hermana**.
Isabel combs her sister's hair.

The drawing on the left depicts a reflexive action (it is her hair); the drawing on the right depicts a non-reflexive action (it is her sister's hair).

LOS PRONOMBRES REFLEXIVOS

- Reflexive pronouns are identical to direct object pronouns, except for the third-person **se** for both singular and plural.

Subject pronoun	Reflexive pronoun	Verb (*lavarse*)
yo	**me** (*myself*)	**lavo**
tú	**te** (*yourself*)	**lavas**
Ud.	**se** (*yourself*)	**lava**
él/ella	**se** (*himself, herself*)	**lava**
nosotros/as	**nos** (*ourselves*)	**lavamos**
vosotros/as	**os** (*yourselves*)	**laváis**
Uds.	**se** (*yourselves*)	**lavan**
ellos/as	**se** (*themselves*)	**lavan**

- Place reflexive pronouns before the conjugated verb or attach to the infinitive, as with direct object pronouns.

Sofía, ¿vas a maquillar**te** ahora?   } *Sofía, are you going to put on your*
Sofía, ¿**te** vas a maquillar ahora?   *makeup now?*

- Use the definite article, not the possessive adjective, to refer to parts of the body and articles of clothing.

Pedro se pone **el** sombrero.   *Pedro puts on his hat.*
Me lavo **las** manos.   *I wash my hands.*

- You must use reflexive pronouns in all reflexive constructions, even when they can be omitted in English.

Pepe **se afeita** antes de acostarse.   *Pepe shaves before going to bed.*
Marina siempre **se baña** a las ocho.   *Marina always bathes at eight.*

LOS VERBOS REFLEXIVOS

- Use reflexives with actions describing personal care and daily habits when the same person performs and receives the action.

Voy a acostarme temprano.	*I'm going to bed early.*
Mis hermanos se despiertan tarde todas las mañanas.	*My brothers wake up late every morning.*

- You can also use these verbs non-reflexively when someone other than the subject receives the action.

Elena **acuesta** a su hija menor.	*Elena puts her youngest daughter to bed.*
¿**Despiertas** a tu compañero de cuarto?	*Do you wake up your roommate?*

- Verbs that express feelings, moods, and conditions are often used reflexively. In English, these are expressed as *to get* or *to become*, or similar.

alegrarse (de)	*to become happy*	**enojarse (con)**	*to get angry (with)*
divertirse (ie, i)	*to have fun*	**olvidarse (de)**	*to forget*
enamorarse (de)	*to fall in love (with)*	**ponerse + adj.**	*to get/become + adj.*
enfermarse	*to become sick*	**sentirse (ie, i) + *adj.***	*to feel + adj.*

Me alegro de ganar.	*I am happy to win.*
Jorge va a **ponerse** furioso si pierde.	*Jorge is going to get furious if he loses.*

- Some verbs have different meanings when used with reflexive pronouns.

Nonreflexive		Reflexive	
acostar (ue)	*to put to bed*	acostarse (ue)	*to go to bed*
dormir (ue, u)	*to sleep*	dormirse (ue, u)	*to fall asleep*
encontrar (ue)	*to find*	encontrarse (ue) (con)	*to meet up with someone*
enfermar	*to make sick*	enfermarse	*to become sick*
ir	*to go*	irse	*to go away, to leave*
levantar	*to lift*	levantarse	*to get up*
llamar	*to call*	llamarse	*to be called (as when giving your name)*
llevar	*to carry*	llevarse (bien/mal)	*to get along (well/badly)*
poner	*to put, to place*	ponerse	*to put on (clothing), to become*
quitar	*to remove*	quitarse	*to take off (clothing)*
vestir (i, i)	*to dress*	vestirse (i, i)	*to get dressed*

LAS CONSTRUCCIONES RECÍPROCAS

- Use the plural verb and the plural reflexive pronouns **nos**, **os**, and **se** when an action is **reciprocal**, that is, when expressing to *each other* or *one another*.

Nos queremos mucho.	*We love each other a lot.*
Los novios **se ven** todos los días.	*The sweethearts see one another every day.*

- Usually the context will indicate a reciprocal action. However, for clarity, you can also add the phrase **el uno al otro / la una a la otra**.

Los niños se despiertan **el uno al otro.**	*The children wake each other up.*

¿Comprendes? Provide the logical reflexive pronouns.

Yo siempre (1) _____ alegro de estar contigo. No (2) _____ enojas conmigo cuando (3) _____ levanto tarde.

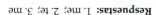
Respuestas: 1. me; 2. te; 3. me

¡Ay! Parece que se quieren mucho.

Aplicación

5-7 ¿Son compatibles? Selecciona la respuesta lógica para cada pregunta para saber si un/a amigo/a nuevo/a es compatible como posible compañero/a de casa.

Preguntas	Respuestas
1. _____ ¿A qué hora te levantas por la mañana?	a. No, generalmente me llevo bien con los demás (*others*).
2. _____ ¿Te duermes enfrente de la televisión?	b. Generalmente a las siete, si no me acuesto muy tarde.
3. _____ ¿Dejas tu computadora portátil en la cama por la noche?	c. No, generalmente me ducho rápidamente. Uso muy poca agua.
4 _____ ¿Te diviertes con amigos los sábados por la noche?	d. No, nunca me olvido de ponerla en el escritorio.
5. _____ Cuando te duchas, ¿usas toda el agua caliente?	e. Bueno, me duermo si es un programa aburrido.
6. _____ ¿Te enojas fácilmente con las personas?	f. Pues sí. Siempre nos llamamos para salir los sábados porque nos gusta divertirnos.

5-8 Irving Saladino. En los Juegos Olímpicos de Beijing, Irving Saladino ganó la medalla de oro (*gold*) en el salto de longitud (*long jump*). Es el primer panameño en ganar una medalla.

Paso 1 Lee sobre la vida diaria de Irving Saladino y selecciona el verbo más apropiado para completar el párrafo.

> **MODELO:** Los amigos de Irving Saladino *se alegran* / se duermen cuando él gana una competencia.

Desde (*Since*) 2014, Irving Saladino representa a Panamá en el salto de longitud. Su vida es muy activa. Tiene que (1) divertirse / levantarse temprano porque tiene que hacer ejercicio para estar en buenas condiciones físicas. Después de hacer ejercicio, va al club y (2) se quita / se sienta a ver su video de entrenamiento (*training*). Por la tarde, (3) se divierte / se enferma con sus amigos en un café y (4) se acuesta / se pone muy contento cuando tocan música latina, especialmente la de sus compatriotas panameños Los Rabanes. Por la noche, después de levantar pesas (*weights*), (5) se baña / se enoja y (6) se acuesta / se levanta temprano, pues al día siguiente (7) se despierta / se olvida a las seis de la mañana porque tiene un entrenamiento riguroso.

Paso 2 En parejas (*in pairs*), preparen cuatro preguntas sobre el párrafo del **Paso 1** para hacerle a otra pareja de la clase y contesten las de ellos.

> **MODELO:** PAREJA 1: *¿De dónde es Irving Saladino?*
> PAREJA 2: *Es de Panamá. ¿A qué hora…?*

Presencia hispana

Many American athletes have roots in Spanish-speaking countries, the greatest number being Major League Baseball players. The Dominican Republic alone has accounted for 600; next is Cuba (180), and then Panama (50). The island of Puerto Rico has accounted for 240. How many Hispanic athletes are you familiar with? Do you know their country of origin?

5-9 ¿En qué orden lo hacen? Sigue los pasos para completar esta actividad.

Paso 1 Pon (*Put*) estas actividades en orden lógico según (*according to*) tu rutina diaria.

_____ me duermo	_____ me afeito
_____ me peino	_____ me despierto
_____ me ducho	_____ me acuesto
_____ me cepillo los dientes	_____ me lavo la cara

 Paso 2 Ahora, en parejas, comparen sus rutinas. ¿Qué tienen en común y en qué se diferencian?

Expansión **The noun *vez*.** Use the noun **vez** to express the following:

a veces *sometimes, at times*

de vez en cuando *once in a while*

una vez *one time, once*

Tomás se afeita **dos veces** a la semana. *Tomás shaves two times a week.*

Me duermo en la biblioteca **de vez en cuando**. *I fall asleep in the library once in a while.*

5-10 Una relación especial. En parejas, túrnense para hacerse preguntas sobre una relación especial que tienen con alguna persona: un/a novio/a, un/a amigo/a o un familiar.

MODELO: ESTUDIANTE 1: *¿Se conocen bien?*
ESTUDIANTE 2: *Sí, nos conocemos muy bien.*

1. ¿Con qué frecuencia se ven?
2. ¿Se quieren mucho?
3. ¿Dónde se encuentran generalmente?
4. ¿Cuándo se mandan mensajes de texto?
5. ¿Cuántas veces al día se llaman por teléfono?
6. ¿Se entienden bien?
7. ¿Qué hacen cuando se ven?
8. ¿Se respetan mucho?

5-11 ¿Lógico o ilógico? Individualmente, escriban cinco oraciones completas con verbos reflexivos, algunas lógicas y otras ilógicas. Después, formen grupos de tres o cuatro y túrnense para leer en voz alta (*aloud*) sus oraciones y decir si son lógicas o ilógicas. Corrijan (*Correct*) las ilógicas.

MODELO: ESTUDIANTE 1: *Me afeito con el cepillo de dientes.*
ESTUDIANTE 2: *¡Ilógico! Te afeitas con la máquina de afeitar.*

Comparisons of equality and inequality

COMPARACIONES DE IGUALDAD

- In English, we compare characteristics of people, places, things and actions that are **equal** with the expression *as . . . as: I'm* **as** *smart* **as** *you. You run* **as** *fast* **as** *your sister*. In Spanish, we use:

> **tan** + *adjective/adverb* + **como**

Joaquín es **tan** amable **como** Roberto.	*Joaquín is as nice as Roberto.*
María habla **tan** rápidamente **como** su hermana.	*María speaks as fast as her sister.*

- In English, we compare nouns with *as much* or *as many*: **as much** *money*; **as many** *apples*. In Spanish, remember that **tanto/a** is an adjective, and must agree in gender and number with the noun or pronoun it modifies.

> **tanto/a(s)** + *noun* + **como**

Tengo tantos peines como cepillos.

Tienes **tanta** paciencia **como** Eugenio.	*You have as much patience as Eugenio.*
Tengo **tantos** hermanos **como** ustedes.	*I have as many siblings as you.*

- To compare equal **actions** in Spanish, use:

> *verb* + **tanto como**

Mis hermanos se divierten **tanto como** tú.	*My brothers have as much fun as you.*

¿Comprendes? Provide logical equal comparisons to complete the statements.

Tengo (1) _____ cremas (2) _____ perfumes. No tengo (3) _____ champú (4) _____ tú. Yo me maquillo (5) _____ rápidamente (6) _____ tú. Tú te cepillas los dientes (7) _____ (8) _____ yo.

Respuestas: 1. tantas; 2. como; 3. tanto; 4. como 5. tan; 6. como 7. tanto; 8. como

COMPARACIONES DE DESIGUALDAD

- In English, we compare people, places, things, and actions that are **unequal** with the expressions *more . . . than* or *less . . . than*.

  - Make unequal comparisons in Spanish with:

> **más/menos** + *adjective/adverb/noun* + **que**

¡Ahora, tengo menos pelo que tú!

Adjective: Memo es **menos** responsable **que** Claudio.	*Memo is less responsible than Claudio.*
Adverb: Yo me visto **más** rápidamente **que** tú.	*I get dressed faster than you.*
Noun: Tienes **menos** maquillaje **que** yo.	*You have less makeup than I (do).*

- When comparing numbers of things, use:

más/menos de + *number*

Tengo **más de** cinco botellas de champú.

I have more than five bottles of shampoo.

Panamá tiene **menos de** cuatro millones de habitantes.

Panama has fewer than four million inhabitants.

- To compare unequal **actions**, use:

verb + **más/menos** + **que**

Estudio **más que** tú.

I study more than you (do).

LOS ADJETIVOS COMPARATIVOS IRREGULARES

Some Spanish adjectives have both regular and irregular comparative forms. The irregular forms do not require *más/menos*:

Adjective	Regular form	Irregular form	
bueno/a	más bueno/a	**mejor**	*better*
malo/a	más malo/a	**peor**	*worse*
viejo/a	más viejo/a	**mayor**	*older*
joven	más joven	**menor**	*younger*

- The irregular forms **mejor** and **peor** are more common than the regular forms.

Esta máquina de afeitar es **peor** que una navaja.

This electric shaver is worse than a razor.

Dormimos **mejor** cuando hace frío.

We sleep better when it is cold.

- **Mayor**, **menor**, and **más joven** are commonly used with people; **más viejo/a** may be used with inanimate objects.

Manuel es **menor** que Berta y yo soy **mayor** que Manuel.

Manuel is younger than Berta, and I am older than Manuel.

Mi teléfono celular es **más viejo** que el de mi hermano.

My cell phone is older than my brother's.

RESUMEN (*SUMMARY*) DE LAS COMPARACIONES DE IGUALDAD Y DE DESIGUALDAD

Equal comparisons	Unequal comparisons
nouns: **tanto/a(s)** + *noun* + **como** + *noun* or *pronoun*	nouns/adjs./advs.: **más/menos** + *adj./adv./noun* + **que** + *noun* or *pronoun*
adjectives/adverbs: **tan** + *adj./adv.* + **como** + *noun* or *pronoun*	with numbers: **más/menos** + **de** + *number*
verbs: *verb* + **tanto como** + *noun* or *pronoun*	verbs: *verb* + **más/menos** + **que** + *noun* or *pronoun*

¿Comprendes? Provide unequal comparisons to complete the statements.

1. Mi jabón cuesta $2 y es de muy buena calidad (*quality*). Tu jabón cuesta $4 y es de baja calidad. Mi jabón cuesta _____ _____ tu jabón y es _____ _____ tu jabón.

2. Pablito tiene diez años. Juan tiene nueve. Pablito es _____ _____ Juan. Juan es _____ _____ Pablito.

Respuestas: 1. menos que; mejor que; 2. mayor que; menor que

Los cantantes (*singers*) Edén Muñoz y Armando Ramos son dos de los jueces de *Va Por Ti* en Univisión.

Aplicación

5-12 *Va Por Ti*. Este programa de Univisión busca el próximo talento musical. Los jueces (*judges*) comparan a los participantes en el concurso.

Paso 1 Selecciona la opción correcta para completar la conversación.

MODELO: Ramón es muy bueno. Canta _*mejor que*_ Luis.

más de cien	mejor que	más atractivo que
menos brillante que	menos talento que	tan imparciales como

EDÉN: ¡Qué guapo es ese joven costarricense! Es mucho (1) _____ los otros.

ARMANDO: Es guapo, pero ¿tiene talento? ¿Canta (2) _____ la chica mexicana?

EDÉN: En mi opinión, la chica mexicana tiene (3) _____ la panameña.

ARMANDO: Pero la panameña tiene (4) _____ canciones en su repertorio.

EDÉN: Sin embargo (*However*), es (5) _____ los cantantes de México.

ARMANDO: ¡Hay que decidir quién canta mejor! Tenemos que ser (6) _____ cualquier (*any*) juez.

Paso 2 Túrnense para hacer y contestar preguntas sobre la conversación e inventar más detalles.

MODELO: ESTUDIANTE 1: *¿Cómo es el chico costarricense?*
ESTUDIANTE 2: *Es más bajo que la chica argentina, pero es tan alto como yo.*

5-13 ¿Cómo son? Completa las oraciones con comparaciones lógicas según la información de estos tres países.

	Costa Rica	Nicaragua	Panamá
Habitantes	4.695.942	5.788.531	3.559.408
Economía (PIB)*	59,79 mil millones (*billion*)	27,1 mil millones	58,02 mil millones
Área (kilómetros²)	51.100	130.370	75.420
Área con parques nacionales	27%	17,3%	25%

1. Nicaragua tiene _____ habitantes _____ Panamá. Panamá tiene _____ habitantes _____ Costa Rica.

2. Nicaragua es _____ grande _____ Panamá. Costa Rica es _____ grande _____ Panamá.

3. La economía de Costa Rica es _____ fuerte _____ la de Nicaragua.

4. Costa Rica tiene _____ territorio dedicado a parques nacionales _____ Panamá. Nicaragua tiene _____ terreno dedicado a parques nacionales _____ Panamá.

*Producto Interno Bruto.

5-14 Los Grammy Latinos. Ustedes son reporteros/as de la ceremonia de los Grammy Latinos y tienen que hacer comentarios sobre los artistas.

Paso 1   Completa estas comparaciones según los datos de las personas.

> **MODELO:**   Draco Rosa es __*más*__ alto __*que*__ Juanes.

1. Juanes es _____ bajo _____ Draco Rosa.
2. Draco es _____ _____ Juanes.
3. Juanes tiene _____ álbumes vendidos _____ Draco.
4. Draco se afeita _____ _____ Juanes.
5. Natalia Lafourcade es _____ _____ Gaby Moreno.
6. Natalia tiene _____ premios Grammy _____ Draco.
7. Gaby es _____ alta _____ Juanes.
8. Juanes tiene _____ _____ 14 millones de álbumes vendidos.

Draco Rosa
Año de nacimiento: 1969
Estatura: 1,91 m
Número de premios Grammy: 4
Número de álbumes vendidos: 4 millones

Natalia Lafourcade
Año de nacimiento: 1984
Estatura: 1,42 m
Número de premios Grammy: 9
Número de álbumes vendidos: 5 millones

Juanes
Año de nacimiento: 1972
Estatura: 1,72 m
Número de premios Grammy: 22
Número de álbumes vendidos: 16 millones

Gaby Moreno
Año de nacimiento: 1981
Estatura: 1,56 m
Número de premios Grammy: 1
Número de álbumes vendidos: 3 millones

Paso 2   Busca más información en Internet sobre dos de estos cantantes y escucha una canción de cada uno/a. Luego, escribe sobre cuál te gusta más y por qué. Haz por lo menos tres comparaciones entre ellos/as.

> **MODELO:**   *Me gusta mucho la música de Juanes porque comprendo mejor la letra…*

📍 **Busca:** Juanes video; Draco Rosa video; etc.

5-15 Sus preferencias. Sigan estos pasos.

Paso 1 En grupos pequeños, elijan (*choose*) un tema y conversen sobre sus preferencias y expliquen por qué. Usen comparaciones para expresar sus opiniones.

- los cepillos de dientes eléctricos o los tradicionales
- vivir en una casa o en un apartamento
- los correos electrónicos o los mensajes de texto
- ir al cine o ver la televisión
- acostarse tarde o temprano

MODELO: ESTUDIANTE 1: *Yo creo que es mejor vivir en un apartamento porque una casa cuesta más que un apartamento.*
ESTUDIANTE 2: *Sí, pero una casa es más grande que un apartamento.*
ESTUDIANTE 3: *Pues yo prefiero mi apartamento porque está más cerca de la universidad que tu casa.*

Paso 2 Escribe un resumen de las preferencias de tu grupo. Incluye por lo menos cuatro comparaciones.

MODELO: *En mi grupo estamos de acuerdo: creemos que es mejor vivir en…*

Cultura en vivo

Traditionally, people in Latin America have preferred living in the city where they have easy access to public transportation, schools, and shopping. But even so, customs are changing with the growth of gated communities for the middle and upper-middle class. Do you see living preferences changing in your city or town? Why or why not?

¡Conversemos!

Primero, pregúntate si puedes llevar a cabo (*carry out*) las siguientes funciones comunicativas en español. Después, júntate (*get together*) con dos o tres compañeros/as de clase para presentar las situaciones. Hagan y respondan a por lo menos cuatro preguntas en cada situación.

✓ CAN YOU . . .

☐ talk about personal care items?

☐ describe your daily routine?

☐ express feelings?

☐ make comparisons?

WITH YOUR CLASSMATE(S) . . .

Situación: Un producto nuevo.

Son un/a vendedor/a y un/a cliente interesado/a en una línea nueva de productos para uso personal. Uno/a presenta los productos (**acondicionador, un secador, una máquina de afeitar**, etc.) y explica por qué son buenos. El/La otro/a hace preguntas sobre los productos.

Para empezar: *Usted debe comprar esta máquina de afeitar. Cuesta solo cien dólares y es muy rápida...*

Situación: Un apartamento.

Entrevista a otro/a estudiante para ver si son compatibles como compañeros/as de apartamento. Usen verbos reflexivos como **levantarse**, **acostarse** y **dormirse** para describir sus rutinas diarias y hábitos. Al final, decidan si son o no son compatibles.

Para empezar: *Prefiero levantarme... Siempre me despierto...*

Situación: Confesiones.

Conversen sobre cómo reaccionan en diferentes situaciones. Usen verbos como **sentirse, alegrarse** y **ponerse**.

Para empezar: *Siempre me pongo nervioso/a cuando la profesora me hace una pregunta en clase. ¿Y tú?...*

Situación: En una fiesta.

Conversen sobre las personas que observan en una fiesta y sus acciones. Usen comparaciones de adjetivos, adverbios, sustantivos y verbos.

Para empezar: *En esta fiesta hay tantos chicos como chicas. Creo que Ramón baila mejor que Luis, pero Luis es mucho más inteligente...*

Perfiles

5.3 **Compare opinions about ecotourism, and learn about a ska-rock fusion band from Panama**

Mi experiencia

ECO VOLUNTARIADO EN COSTA RICA

5-16 Para ti. ¿Hay parques nacionales en tu país que se dedican a conservar especies en peligro (*danger*) de extinción? ¿En qué lugares es popular hacer ecoturismo o eco voluntariado? Lee el estado (*status*) de Ramón Vázquez en su página de Facebook sobre el eco voluntariado.

[1]*I've just*

[2]*turtles*

[3]*hatchery*
[4]*arrivals*
[5]*dig up*
[6]*eggs*
[7]*hatchlings*
[8]*shore*

[9]*run*

[10]*We enjoy* [11]*beach*

Acabo de[1] tener otra experiencia súper emocionante aquí en Tortuguero, Costa Rica, uno de los parques nacionales más importantes del mundo para la protección de las tortugas[2] marinas. Cada año viajo desde Panamá hasta Tortuguero como voluntario para ayudar en la protección de esta especie de tortugas que está en peligro de extinción. Participo con mis amigos en los programas de criadero[3] dirigidos por un grupo de naturalistas. Durante las masivas arribadas[4], nosotros los voluntarios desenterramos[5] los huevos[6] y los llevamos a un lugar seguro hasta que nacen las crías[7]. Después, recogemos las crías y vamos hasta la orilla[8] del mar donde, con mucho cuidado, las depositamos. ¡Tienes que ver cómo corren[9] las pequeñas tortugas hacia el mar! Es una experiencia agradable con los compañeros: todos los días nos despertamos temprano, pero no hay tiempo para afeitarse ni maquillarse. Trabajamos mucho todo el día. Cuando regresamos, nos duchamos en duchas al aire libre porque el clima es agradable, y nos acostamos temprano. Disfrutamos de[10] la playa[11], de la música que escuchamos (como Los Rabanes por ejemplo), y más que nada, de los amigos. ¿Nos acompañas?

5-17 En su opinión. En parejas, túrnense para expresar y anotar sus opiniones. ¿En qué puntos están de acuerdo y en cuáles no? Den (*Give*) detalles.

1. Me gusta el ecoturismo.   Sí   No
2. Es bueno proteger (*protect*) las especies en peligro de extinción.   Sí   No
3. Me gustaría hacer eco voluntariado algún día.   Sí   No
4. Me gusta dormirme en la playa.   Sí   No
5. No es importante ducharme todos los días cuando estoy de vacaciones.   Sí   No

5-18 Una visita a Tortuguero. Busca imágenes o videos de Tortuguero en Internet y escribe un estado de Facebook sobre el lugar. Incluye tres observaciones usando (*using*) comparaciones.

MODELO: *Hay menos personas en esta playa que en las de California.*

◉ Busca: video Tortuguero

Mi música

"EVERYBODY" (LOS RABANES, PANAMÁ)

El grupo panameño Los Rabanes es ganador de un Grammy Latino al mejor álbum de rock. Su estilo es una fusión de reggaetón, ska y rock; las letras (*lyrics*) son una mezcla de español e inglés, pero muchas veces las palabras en inglés son irónicas o sarcásticas. Los miembros son Christian Torres, Emilio Regueira Pérez, Javier Saavedra y Randy Cuevas.

ANTES DE VER Y ESCUCHAR

5-19 Comparaciones. Crea oraciones para comparar estas actividades o conceptos. Usa comparaciones de igualdad y de desigualdad.

> **MODELO:** bailar / cantar (fácil)
> *Es más fácil bailar bien que cantar bien.*

1. tocar guitarra / cantar (interesante)
2. ir en carro / ir en autobús (emocionante)
3. las vacaciones en la playa / las vacaciones en la ciudad (agradable)
4. bailar en una fiesta / observar a la gente en una fiesta (divertido)

PARA VER Y ESCUCHAR

5-20 La canción. Busca en Internet el video "Everybody" de Los Rabanes. Escribe una descripción de los cantantes y sus acciones en el video. ¿Cómo son físicamente? ¿Cuántos años tienen? ¿Cómo es la canción? ¿Cómo es el ritmo? ¿Qué hacen los cantantes en el video? ¿Se divierten?

> ⚲ **Busca:** Everybody Rabanes video; Everybody Rabanes letra

DESPUÉS DE VER Y ESCUCHAR

5-21 ¿Cómo se comparan? Escribe un mínimo de cinco comparaciones de igualdad o de desigualdad basadas en el video. Puedes incluir algunos de estos temas.

- la música
- los músicos
- el medio de transporte
- las personas que bailan
- el baile
- los animales

> **MODELO:** *En el video hay tantas mujeres como hombres...*

5.2 Segunda parte

Vocabulario

5.4 Talk about the home and household chores

Los quehaceres domésticos

Vamos a limpiar. Vera quiere invitar a algunos amigos esta noche para una fiesta en el apartamento donde vive con sus tres amigos. Desgraciadamente, **la casa** está muy **desordenada**. Vera se enoja y les manda un mensaje de texto a sus compañeros de apartamento.

¿Comprendes? Provide the correct option for each case: **basura, desordenada, enojada, ropa.**

Vera está (1) _____. La casa está (2) _____. Hay (3) _____ en el piso. Es necesario sacar la (4) _____.

Respuestas: 1. enojada; 2. desordenada; 3. ropa; 4. basura

Vocabulario

Los aparatos domésticos	Household appliances
la aspiradora	*vacuum cleaner*
la lavadora	*washing machine*
el lavaplatos	*dishwasher*
la secadora	*clothes dryer*

Los muebles y accesorios	Furniture and accessories
el basurero	*trash can*
la cama	*bed*
la cómoda	*dresser*
el cuadro	*painting*
el estante	*bookcase*
la lámpara	*lamp*
la mesa de noche	*nightstand*
el sillón	*armchair, overstuffed chair*
el sofá	*sofa, couch*

Las partes de una casa	Parts of a house
el baño	*bathroom*
la casa	*house, home*
la cocina	*kitchen*
el comedor	*dining room*
el cuarto	*room, bedroom*
el dormitorio	*bedroom*
el garaje	*garage*
el jardín	*garden*
el pasillo	*hallway*
el patio	*patio, backyard*
el piso	*floor*
la sala	*living room*

Los quehaceres domésticos	Household chores
hacer la cama	*to make the bed*
hacer las compras	*to go grocery shopping*
lavar (el piso / los platos)	*to wash (the floor / the dishes)*
limpiar/ordenar la casa	*to clean / to straighten up the house*
llenar/vaciar el lavaplatos	*to fill / to empty the dishwasher*
pasar la aspiradora	*to vacuum*
planchar	*to iron*
poner/quitar la mesa	*to set / to clear the table*
recoger la ropa (del piso / de la secadora)	*to pick up / to collect clothes (from the floor / from the dryer)*
sacar la basura	*to take out the garbage*

El dormitorio / La casa está...	The bedroom / The house is . . .
desordenado/a	*messy*
limpio/a	*clean*
sucio/a	*dirty*

Variaciones

Expressing *apartment* varies from country to country. Use **departamento** in Mexico and Argentina, **piso** in Spain, and **apartamento** in Colombia and other places.

Letras y sonidos

The consonant *h* and the sequence *ch* in Spanish

- In Spanish, the letter **h** is silent.

  ho-la   **h**a-cer   **h**om-bre   **h**er-mo-sa   que-**h**a-ce-res

- In the sequence **ch**, however, the letters **c** and **h** combine to create one single sound **ch**, which is pronounced the same as in English *church*.

  mu-**ch**o   no-**ch**e   plan-**ch**a   cu-**ch**i-lla   mu-**ch**a-**ch**o

Aplicación

5-22 En el apartamento de Vera. Selecciona la opción apropiada para completar las frases, según las instrucciones de Vera.

1. _____ Vera escribe una lista de...
2. _____ Enrique necesita vaciar...
3. _____ Enrique tiene que sacar...
4. _____ Es necesario pasar...
5. _____ Rogelio necesita recoger la ropa...
6. _____ Estela tiene que poner...

a. la aspiradora.
b. la basura.
c. del piso.
d. la mesa.
e. los quehaceres.
f. el lavaplatos.

5-23 ¡Emparejar! ¿Dónde encuentras las siguientes cosas? Selecciona el lugar apropiado para cada objeto.

1. _____ la bicicleta   a. el baño
2. _____ el sofá   b. la cocina
3. _____ la ropa   c. la cómoda
4. _____ la cama   d. el dormitorio
5. _____ el lavaplatos   e. el garaje
6. _____ el jabón y el champú f. la sala

5-24 ¿Quién lo hace en su casa? En parejas, túrnense para decir quién hace los quehaceres en su casa y decidan cuál de ustedes es más trabajador/a. Usen pronombres de objeto directo cuando sea posible.

MODELO: lavar los platos
      ESTUDIANTE 1: *Mi hermano los lava.*
      ESTUDIANTE 2: *Pues, en mi casa yo los lavo. Creo que soy más trabajador/a que tú.*

1. pasar la aspiradora   4. poner la mesa   7. lavar la ropa
2. hacer las compras   5. sacar la basura   8. ordenar la casa
3. vaciar el lavaplatos   6. hacer las camas   9. limpiar el baño

5-25 ¡Todo lo que necesita para la casa! Escucha el siguiente anuncio de radio sobre los productos para la casa. Completa el nombre y el precio de cada producto del dibujo correspondiente.

MODELO: *una silla: $19*

1.

_____

2.

_____

3.

_____

4.

_____

5.

_____

6.

_____

Cultura en vivo

Due to the high cost of energy in Central America, people tend to be careful consumers of electricity. For example, household appliances are often smaller, and people commonly hang clothes on a line, rather than use a clothes dryer. However, these countries also have huge potential to generate cheap alternative energies from geothermal, hydro, and solar sources. In fact, renewables supplied over 98 percent of Costa Rica's electricity in 2016, and Nicaragua set their target at 75 percent renewable sources for 2017. These figures compare to 15 percent in the U.S. and 63 percent in Canada. Are you an energy-conscious consumer?

5-26A ¡Necesito información! Se acaban de mudar (*You have just moved*) a una nueva casa y todo está muy desordenado. Ustedes tienen que encontrar los muebles y ponerlos en su lugar. Trabajen juntos/as para encontrarlos y decir dónde deben ponerlos. Al final, comparen los planos (*floor plans*) de la casa. **Estudiante B**: ve al **Apéndice 1**, página A-6.

MODELO: ESTUDIANTE A: *¿Dónde está la bicicleta?*
              ESTUDIANTE B: *Está en el dormitorio. Debemos ponerla en el garaje.*

Estudiante A busca: el sofá, la aspiradora, la cómoda, el cuadro, la lámpara

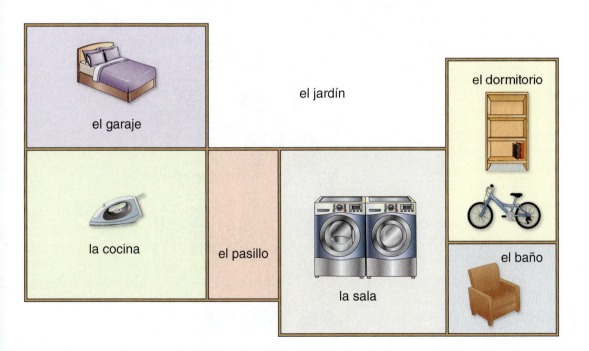

5-27 El plano de mi casa. Individualmente, dibujen (*draw*) el plano de su casa o apartamento (real o imaginario). Incluyan los cuartos, los pasillos y los muebles. Luego, en parejas, túrnense para describirse sus casas y reproducirlas en su papel. Comparen los resultados.

MODELO: *Mi apartamento es pequeño. Tiene...*

Estructuras

5.5 Describe superlative qualities and actions in progress

The superlative

We use superlatives to express the greatest or least quality: *the most, the best, the worst, the least, the biggest, smallest,* etc.

- In English, the superlative is followed by *in* or *of*:

  The bathroom is the **smallest room in** the house.

- In Spanish, the preposition **de** is the equivalent of *in* or *of*:

  > **el/la/los/las + más/menos + *adjective* + de...**

Esta aspiradora es **la más cara de** la tienda.	*This vacuum cleaner is the most expensive in the store.*
El jabón blanco es **el menos caro de** todos.	*The white soap is the least expensive of all.*

- With a superlative noun, the definite article precedes the noun.

  > **el/la/los/las + *noun* + más/menos + *adjective* + de...**

Este es **el** brillo de labios **más** bonito **de** los que venden aquí.	*This is the most beautiful lip gloss of those they sell here.*
Carlos vive en **la** casa **más** pequeña **del** barrio.	*Carlos lives in the smallest house in the neighborhood.*

- Adjectives and adverbs that have irregular comparative forms use the same irregular superlative forms.

Juan es **el mejor de** mis amigos.	*Juan is the best of my friends.*
La tía Isabel es **la mayor de** mis tías.	*Aunt Isabel is the oldest of my aunts.*

¿Comprendes? Select the logical response to each question.

1. _____ ¿Cómo es tu casa?
2. _____ ¿Cómo es el patio?
3. _____ ¿Cómo son los muebles de la sala?

a. Son los más viejos de la casa.
b. Es el mejor del barrio.
c. Es la más pequeña de todas.

Respuestas: 1. c; 2. b; 3. a

Aplicación

5-28 El Canal de Panamá. La nación de Panamá controla el canal desde el 31 de diciembre de 1999.

Paso 1   Lee el párrafo e identifica los superlativos.

> **MODELO:** ¿Cuál es el canal *más grande del mundo*?

El Canal de Panamá no es el más largo, ni (*nor*) el más ancho (*widest*), ni el más profundo (*deepest*), ni el más antiguo del mundo. Pero sí es el único que conecta dos océanos: el Atlántico y el Pacífico, y aún (*even*) hoy es la vía de agua (*waterway*) navegable más importante del mundo. Al principio, enfermedades como la malaria, la fiebre (*fever*) amarilla y el cólera causan los problemas más graves de la construcción del canal. George Goethals es el ingeniero que tiene el mejor resultado de todos para terminar el proyecto. Cuando completa el canal en 1914, es el peor momento de esa época: el comienzo de la Primera Guerra Mundial. Hoy en día, el canal todavía (*still*) es una de las obras de ingeniería más impactantes del mundo.

Más de 14.000 naves (*ships*) pasan por el canal cada año.

Paso 2   Contesta las preguntas sobre el artículo. Después, escribe un breve resumen (*summary*) de la importancia que tiene el Canal de Panamá.

1. ¿Por qué es importante el canal?
2. ¿En qué año se completa?
3. ¿Cuáles son los problemas más graves al principio?
4. ¿Quién es el ingeniero que tiene el mejor resultado de todos?
5. ¿Qué otro evento importante también comienza en 1914?

5-29 Otros superlativos de América Central. Observa el mapa de América Central en **Nuestro mundo** (página 175) para identificar estos lugares superlativos.

> **MODELO:**   el país más sureño (*southern*) de América Central
> *Panamá es el país más sureño de América Central.*

1. el país más grande de América Central
2. el lago más grande de Nicaragua
3. el país con la frontera más larga de América Central
4. el país más estrecho (*narrow*)
5. el país que tiene la más larga extensión de costas de América Central

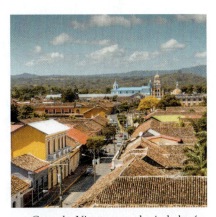

Granada, Nicaragua, es la ciudad más antigua de América Central. Se fundó en 1524.

Presencia hispana

Waves of immigration from Central American countries to the U.S. and Canada have been largely due to political upheaval in the home countries of immigrants, with the notable exceptions of those from Costa Rica and Panama, who are often university-educated scholars coming for post-graduate education or research opportunities. In addition to political stability, what other factors would encourage a person to stay in his or her home country?

5-30 Los mejores lugares de la casa. En parejas, conversen sobre diferentes lugares de la casa: cuáles son los mejores (los más agradables, cómodos, útiles [*useful*], etc.) o los peores para cada actividad.

MODELO: para dormir

ESTUDIANTE 1: *En mi opinión, _____ es el mejor lugar para dormir.*

ESTUDIANTE 2: *No es cierto. Para mí, es el peor. Yo siempre duermo en…*

1. para cocinar
2. para pasar tiempo con amigos
3. para comer
4. para ver la televisión
5. para estudiar
6. para guardar (*keep*) la bicicleta
7. para leer un buen libro
8. para gozar de (*enjoy*) la naturaleza

5-31 Entre todos. En grupos de tres, comparen las personas, cosas o lugares en cada serie. Después, expresen su opinión usando el superlativo. Pueden usar adjetivos de la lista.

bonita/guapo – feo/a	grande – pequeño/a
caro/a – económico/a	mayor – menor
divertido/a – aburrido/a	mejor – peor
generoso/a – tacaño/a (*stingy*)	moderno – antiguo
gordo/a – delgado/a	rápido/a – lento/a

MODELO: Bill Gates – Jeff Bezos – Cameron Díaz

ESTUDIANTE 1: *Creo que Jeff Bezos es más rico que Cameron Díaz.*

ESTUDIANTE 2: *Y Bill Gates es el más rico de los tres.*

ESTUDIANTE 3: *Sí, pero Cameron Díaz es la más bonita de los tres…*

1. Queen Latifah – Oprah – Beyoncé
2. Penélope Cruz – Daisy Fuentes – Mariah Carey
3. Café Tacvba – Bebe – Los Rabanes
4. los carros japoneses – los alemanes – los estadounidenses
5. el béisbol – el fútbol – el básquetbol
6. la ciudad de Miami – la de Chicago – la de San Francisco

The present progressive

In Spanish, the present progressive describes an action going on *at the moment of speaking*. You show *who* is acting with the present tense of the verb **estar**. The present participle (**-ando/-iendo**) form of a verb shows the action and is invariable.

Están hablándose por teléfono.

¿Qué **estás haciendo**?   *What are you doing?*

Estoy lavando los platos.   *I'm washing the dishes.*

- To form the present participle, add **-ando** or **-iendo** to the stem:

habla~~r~~ + **ando** → **hablando**

come~~r~~ + **iendo** → **comiendo**

escribi~~r~~ + **iendo** → **escribiendo**

- Stem-changing **-ir** verbs also have a change in the present participle. In *¡Arriba!*, this change is indicated in parentheses after an infinitive.

dormir (ue, u)	*to sleep*	→	**du**rmiendo	*sleeping*
pedir (i, i)	*to ask for*	→	**pi**diendo	*asking for*
servir (i, i)	*to serve*	→	**si**rviendo	*serving*

- You can either place reflexive and object pronouns before **estar**, or attach them to the end of the present participle. Be sure to add an accent when the pronoun is attached to the participle.

> Nieves está maquill**á**ndo**se**. } *Nieves is putting on makeup.*
> Nieves **se** está maquillando. }
>
> **Te** están mirando. } *They're looking at you.*
> Están mir**á**nd**o**t**e**. }

- To express habitual or future actions, use the simple present.

> **Estudio** para ser científico.   *I'm studying to be a scientist.*
> **¿Vienes** a clase mañana?   *Are you coming to class tomorrow?*

¡OJO!

Leer has an irregular present participle. The **i** from **-iendo** changes to **y**.

Estás **leyendo** el periódico, ¿no?
You're reading the newspaper, aren't you?

¿Comprendes? Complete the sentences with the logical present participle: **durmiendo**, **lavándose**, **poniendo**.

Consuelo está en el baño; está (1) _____ la cara. Ricardo está en la cama; está (2) _____. Yo estoy en el comedor; estoy (3) _____ la mesa.

Respuestas: 1. lavándose; 2. durmiendo; 3. poniendo

Aplicación

5-32 ¿Qué estamos haciendo? Selecciona la actividad más lógica para cada lugar.

> **MODELO:**   Estamos en el laboratorio de ciencias.
> *Estamos estudiando para un examen de biología.*

1. _____ Estamos en el sofá. Hay un partido de fútbol.
2. _____ Estamos en el parque. Hay comida y refrescos.
3. _____ Estamos en un concierto de música rock.
4. _____ Estamos en una cancha.
5. _____ Estamos en la biblioteca porque tenemos que escribir un informe (*report*).
6. _____ Tenemos sueño y estamos en la cama.

a. Estamos escuchando la banda y bailando.
b. Estamos jugando al tenis.
c. Estamos leyendo un libro y haciendo investigación.
d. Estamos durmiéndonos.
e. Estamos haciendo un picnic.
f. Estamos viendo la televisión.

5-33 ¡Imagínate! Escribe dónde están estas personas y qué están haciendo en este momento. Usa tu imaginación. Puedes usar las actividades de la lista.

asistir	dormir	jugar	pasar
cantar	escribir	lavarse	ponerse
cepillarse	hablar	limpiar	preparar
despertarse	hacer	maquillarse	vestirse

> **MODELO:**   el presidente de Costa Rica
> *El presidente de Costa Rica está en Washington. Está visitando a congresistas de Estados Unidos.*

1. Albert Pujols
2. Jimmy Fallon y Chris Rock
3. Mariah Carey

4. Benicio del Toro
5. Lionel Messi y Cristiano Ronaldo
6. Shakira y Gerard Piqué

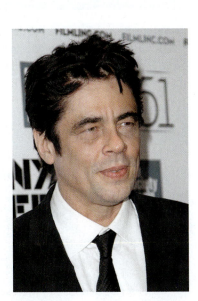

Benicio del Toro, actor y productor puertorriqueño

5-34 Lo siento, no está disponible (*available*). En parejas, imaginen que ustedes son dos recepcionistas en un hotel elegante en la Ciudad de Panamá. Túrnense para inventar excusas para explicar por qué algunos de los clientes importantes no pueden atender las llamadas.

MODELO: ESTUDIANTE 1: *Buenos días. ¿Me permite hablar con el secretario de estado?*
          ESTUDIANTE 2: *Lo siento; el secretario de estado no está disponible ahora. Está hablando con el presidente de Panamá.*

Los Rabanes	Ivanka Trump	LeBron James
Venus y Serena Williams	Eminem y Kanye West	Stephen Colbert
la chef Rachael Ray	América Ferrera (*Superstore*)	Homer y Marge Simpson

Expansión   When making excuses while speaking, there are several expressions you can use to stall for time and come up with a reasonable response:

bueno... *well...*

este... *uhhh...*

el problema es que... *the problem is that...*

lo siento, pero... *I'm sorry, but...*

5-35 ¿Qué estoy haciendo? En grupos pequeños, túrnense para representar algunas de estas acciones y para adivinar (*guess*) qué están haciendo.

MODELO: afeitarse
          ESTUDIANTE 1: (act out shaving) *¿Qué estoy haciendo?*
          GRUPO: *Estás afeitándote.*

acostarse	lavarse las manos	ponerse impaciente
bañarse	levantarse de la cama	ponerse nervioso/a
cepillarse los dientes	maquillarse	sacar la basura
dormirse	ponerse desodorante	secarse el pelo

¡Conversemos!

Primero, pregúntate si puedes llevar a cabo (*carry out*) las siguientes funciones comunicativas en español. Después, júntate (*get together*) con dos o tres compañeros/as de clase para presentar las situaciones. Hagan y respondan a por lo menos cuatro preguntas en cada situación.

✓ CAN YOU ...

☐ talk about the home and household chores?

☐ describe superlative qualities?

☐ describe actions in progress?

WITH YOUR CLASSMATE(S) ...

Situación: En casa.

Decidan entre ustedes quién hace los quehaceres de la casa.

Para empezar: *Paco tiene que...*

Situación: Alquilo apartamento.

Uno/a de ustedes quiere alquilar (*to rent*) su apartamento. Túrnense para describirlo y hacer preguntas sobre dónde está el apartamento, sus cuartos y los muebles. Usen superlativos en su descripción.

Para empezar: *Mi apartamento es el más grande del barrio y también es el más económico...*

Situación: ¿Qué están haciendo?

Observen a sus compañeros/as de clase y describan lo que cada uno está haciendo en este momento.

Para empezar: *Ana está escribiendo en su computadora portátil...*

Club cultura

5.6 Ask and answer questions to clarify information

Panamá: Los emberá

Estrategia para ver

Ask and answer questions to clarify information. As you watch a video, it can be helpful to test your understanding by pausing it to ask and answer questions about what you have seen and heard. Ask yourself, for example, *¿Quién(es)…?* **¿Qué…? ¿Dónde…? ¿Cómo…? ¿Cuándo…? ¿Por qué…?**

ANTES DE VER EL VIDEO

5-36 Los emberá. En este video, vas a conocer a un grupo étnico panameño y algunas de sus costumbres diarias. Escribe una lista de cinco preguntas que tienes sobre este grupo.

> **MODELO:** *¿Qué quehaceres domésticos hacen?*

AL VER EL VIDEO

5-37 Un modo tradicional de vivir. Mira el segmento sobre los emberá de Panamá y trata de (*try to*) contestar tus preguntas. Pausa el video para confirmar tu comprensión y vuelve a verlo otra vez para hacer preguntas adicionales.

DESPUÉS DE VER EL VIDEO

5-38 Los detalles. Selecciona la opción que mejor completa cada oración, según el video.

1. _____ El nombre **emberá** significa…
2. _____ El techo (*roof*) de su casa tiene forma…
3. _____ Usan el cocobolo para sus…
4. _____ Las pinturas representan…
5. _____ Sus modos de vivir son…

a. animales y plantas.
b. artesanías.
c. cónica (de cono).
d. *hombre bueno* o *buen amigo*.
e. tradicionales.

5-39 La vida diaria de los emberá. Escribe un párrafo sobre cómo te imaginas la vida diaria de los emberá, según la información del video. Incluye los quehaceres de la casa y las rutinas diarias.

5.3 Nuestro mundo

Panoramas

5.7 Identify and research some important cultural aspects of Costa Rica, Nicaragua, and Panama

Costa Rica, Nicaragua y Panamá: Destinos emergentes de América Central

Costa Rica, Nicargua y Panamá ofrecen un futuro de sostenibilidad, estabilidad política y buena calidad de vida. Todos gozan de riquezas naturales y biodiversidad única: selvas (*jungles*), bosques nublados (*cloud forests*) y costas con miles de especies de animales y plantas. Costa Rica tiene una larga historia de respeto a los derechos (*rights*) humanos. El hermoso paisaje (*landscape*) de Nicaragua atrae a turistas que exploran sus lagos, volcanes y playas lo que contribuye mucho a su economía. Y Panamá, con su banca internacional y la reciente expansión de su canal, atrae inversiones (*investments*) de todo el mundo.

La playa Ostional, en la costa del Pacífico de Costa Rica, es el único lugar del mundo donde se permite recolectar (*harvest*) algunos de los millones de huevos que ponen las tortugas marinas.

El parque nacional Volcán Tenorio en Costa Rica es uno de muchos donde puedes conocer un bosque tropical, un volcán, un río, una cascada, y además, bañarte en aguas térmicas en un solo día.

El pueblo indígena de los gunas habita el archipiélago caribeño de San Blas. Los gunas creen en el trabajo comunitario como forma de ayudarse para preparar comida y construir sus casas.

Fundada en 1519, hoy la Ciudad de Panamá es la capital y un centro bancario internacional. Su calidad de vida es entre las mejores de Latinoamérica, con su clima tropical, espacios verdes, actividades culturales y gastronomía. Desde 2003, es Capital Americana de la Cultura.

El Lago de Nicaragua está salpicado de (*dotted with*) pequeñas islas volcánicas donde viven comunidades que dependen de la pesca. A pesar de la gran actividad volcánica, llevan una vida tranquila y ofrecen servicios a turistas que desean visitar los volcanes.

	Costa Rica	Nicaragua	Panamá
Población:	4,9 millones	6 millones	3,7 millones
Población urbana:	77%	59%	67%
¿Casas en la playa?	No	No	No
Apartamento de tres dormitorios:	$960 USD/mes	$500 USD/mes	$1.700 USD/mes

5-40 Desafío. Selecciona la opción correcta según la información de **Panoramas**. Algunas opciones se repiten.

del norte al sur	el Caribe y el Pacífico	Nicaragua	Panamá	San José

1. la capital de Costa Rica _____

2. las costas _____

3. el país con frontera con Colombia _____

4. el país con frontera con Honduras _____

5. la ruta del Canal de Panamá _____

6. el país más barato para vivir _____

7. el país con la menor población _____

5-41 Más información. Contesta las preguntas.

1. ¿Cómo es el gobierno de Costa Rica?

2. ¿Qué puedes hacer en el parque nacional Volcán Tenorio?

3. ¿Cómo es la vida diaria de los gunas?

4. ¿Cómo es la Ciudad de Panamá?

5. ¿Qué formación geológica tiene el Lago de Nicaragua?

6. ¿Qué se puede hacer en la playa Ostional?

5-42 Investigación: Una nueva casa. Imagínate que quieres pasar seis meses en Nicaragua, Costa Rica o Panamá. Busca una casa amueblada (*furnished*) en uno de estos tres países y escribe un párrafo describiéndola: dónde está, los cuartos y los muebles y el costo por mes. Incluye una foto. Luego preséntale tu trabajo a la clase.

MODELO: *Voy a alquilar una casa en San Juan del Río, Nicaragua. Tiene dos dormitorios y dos baños, un garaje para dos carros, una sala y un patio. Está completamente amueblada: camas, sofá…*

Páginas

5.8 **Trigger background knowledge to understand text**

Costa Rica: Más feliz que Estados Unidos

Estrategia para leer

Trigger background knowledge to understand text. When you see a text, look at the title, subtitles, photos, captions, and context, and then ask yourself what you know about the subject. This will help you anticipate and connect with what you are about to read.

ANTES DE LEER

5-43 **Tu opinión.** Ordena la lista según tu experiencia de **1: más importante** a **8: menos importante**.

Para mí, la felicidad personal depende de...

_____ la cantidad de dinero (tener mucho es mejor).

_____ la independencia personal.

_____ un buen estado de salud (*health*).

_____ una buena educación.

_____ el sentido de seguridad (*feeling safe*).

_____ una buena comunidad.

_____ un buen gobierno.

_____ otro factor: _____.

AL LEER

5-44 **La felicidad.** Mientras lees el artículo, compara tu lista de condiciones que traen la felicidad con la que informa el estudio. ¿Hay alguna condición que te sorprenda (*surprises you*)?

Costa Rica: Más feliz que Estados Unidos

Condiciones para la felicidad

¿Lo crees? ¿Son más felices las personas que viven en Costa Rica que los estadounidenses*? ¡Es verdad! ¿Por qué será[1]? Pues, según un estudio por el Earth Institute de la Universidad de Columbia en Nueva York, la felicidad no depende completamente de la prosperidad económica de un pueblo, sino que[2] hay ciertas condiciones básicas que hay que tener también. Estas son:

- la confianza[3] del pueblo en su sociedad
- la salud física y mental
- la calidad[4] de gobierno y sus leyes

[1]*How can this be?*

[2]*rather*

[3]*confidence*

[4]*quality*

Cuatro pilares básicos

Es importante que el desarrollo[5] de un país incorpore los cuatro pilares básicos que contribuyen a la sostenibilidad y la felicidad de su gente. Estos son:

- la eliminación de la extrema pobreza
- un plan de desarrollo sostenible
- la inclusión de todos, hombres y mujeres
- un gobierno democrático, justo y sin corrupción

Un modelo para la felicidad

Piénsalo[6]. Costa Rica es un modelo por sus esfuerzos para mejorar el nivel de la educación, promover el desarrollo sostenible, proteger el medio ambiente[7], tener un bajo nivel de crimen, proteger la salud de su gente y fomentar una democracia representativa. No es una labor fácil, pero según el informe del Earth Institute y del comité del Secretario General de la Organización de las Naciones Unidas, es indispensable para llegar a la felicidad.

*Los canadienses son los más felices de las Américas.

[5]*development*

[6]*Think about it.*

[7]*environment*

DESPUÉS DE LEER

5-45 Comprensión. Selecciona la opción correcta para completar las oraciones.

1. Según el artículo, los estadounidenses son menos felices que…
   a. los costarricenses.
   b. los uruguayos.
   c. los europeos.

2. La prosperidad económica…
   a. no se menciona en el artículo.
   b. es el factor más importante para la felicidad de un pueblo.
   c. no es el único (*only*) factor en la felicidad de un pueblo.

3. La felicidad depende de tres condiciones básicas. Una de ellas es…
   a. tener una familia grande.
   b. la salud de las personas.
   c. el estilo de casa en que viven.

4. Para la felicidad de la gente, un país debe eliminar…
   a. la discriminación.
   b. el analfabetismo (*illiteracy*).
   c. la adicción a las drogas.

5. Costa Rica tiene como prioridad…
   a. el acceso a Internet para todos.
   b. la protección del medio ambiente.
   c. la expansión de sus centros urbanos.

5-46 Tu lista y su lista. Compara tu lista de condiciones para la felicidad con las del artículo. ¿Qué tienen en común y en qué difieren? ¿Hay otra condición importante para ti que no se menciona? ¿Estás de acuerdo con las condiciones de la felicidad según el estudio? Explica.

5-47 Buscar la felicidad. En parejas, escojan (*choose*) la condición para la felicidad más importante para ustedes personalmente, para su comunidad y para su país. ¿Es la misma condición para todos?

Taller

Un anuncio de venta (*sales ad*)

Estrategia para escribir

Know your audience. First, decide who your audience is: What is their age range, gender, educational background, economic status? What are their tastes, interests, spending patterns? Think of ideas that will appeal to this group. Do they want the latest styles, the least expensive, the smallest, the most practical, the most fun? Then choose the appropriate details and language to convince your audience that you are offering what it needs and wants.

5-48 **Anuncio para vender una casa.** Vas a diseñar un anuncio digital o una página web para vender una casa o un apartamento.

ANTES DE ESCRIBIR

¿Qué características son las más importantes para tu grupo meta (*target group*)?

- ☐ su ubicación (ciudad, campo, cerca de...)
- ☐ el número de dormitorios
- ☐ los muebles incluidos
- ☐ las actividades en el barrio
- ☐ los "extra": patio, piscina (*pool*), vista, etc.
- ☐ el precio
- ☐ fotos para ilustrar la casa
- ☐ otras características

AL ESCRIBIR

Escribe dos párrafos para describir la casa usando la información del paso anterior. Incluye una foto o un dibujo si es posible. Recuerda: deseas venderla.

DESPUÉS DE ESCRIBIR

- **Revisar.** Revisa la descripción para verificar estos puntos:
  - ☐ el uso correcto de los verbos reflexivos
  - ☐ el uso de comparativos y superlativos
  - ☐ la ortografía, incluidos los acentos
- **Intercambiar.** Intercambia tu anuncio con el de un/a compañero/a y comenten si el diseño es efectivo.
- **Entregar.** Revisa tu anuncio e incorpora las sugerencias de tu compañero/a. Después, dale el anuncio y las respuestas de tu compañero/a a tu profesor/a.

MODELO:

Tu casita en la playa

Costa Rica, ¡el país más feliz del mundo! ¿Estás pensando en vivir en Costa Rica? En esta sencilla casa te levantas todos los días con el canto de las aves. Aquí encuentras la pura felicidad por un precio económico. Un dormitorio, baño, cocina, dos camas, servicio de limpieza, …

En este capítulo...

))) Vocabulario

Primera parte

Las actividades diarias	Daily activities
acostarse (ue)	to go to bed
afeitarse	to shave
bañarse	to take a bath
cepillarse (los dientes, el pelo)	to brush (your teeth, your hair)
despertarse (ie)	to wake up
dormirse (ue, u)	to fall asleep
ducharse	to take a shower
lavarse (las manos)	to wash (your hands)
levantarse	to get up, to stand up
maquillarse (la cara, los ojos)	to put makeup on (your face, your eyes)
peinarse	to comb your hair
quitarse (la camisa)	to take off (your shirt)
secarse	to dry yourself off
sentarse (ie)	to sit down
vestirse (i, i)	to get dressed
Las emociones	**Some emotions**
ponerse contento/a	to become happy
furioso/a	angry
molesto/a	annoyed
sentirse (ie, i)	to feel
Los artículos de uso personal	**Personal care items**
el acondicionador	conditioner
el brillo de labios	lip gloss
el cepillo (de dientes)	(tooth)brush
el champú	shampoo
la crema (de afeitar)	(shaving) cream
el espejo	mirror
el jabón	soap
el maquillaje	makeup
la máquina de afeitar	electric shaver
la navaja de afeitar	razor
el peine	comb
el secador	hair dryer

Segunda parte

Los aparatos domésticos	Household appliances
la aspiradora	vacuum cleaner
la lavadora	washing machine
el lavaplatos	dishwasher
la secadora	clothes dryer
Los muebles y accesorios	**Furniture and accessories**
el basurero	trash can
la cama	bed
la cómoda	dresser
el cuadro	painting
el estante	bookcase
la lámpara	lamp
la mesa de noche	nightstand
el sillón	armchair, overstuffed chair
el sofá	sofa, couch
Las partes de una casa	**Parts of a house**
el baño	bathroom
la casa	house, home
la cocina	kitchen
el comedor	dining room
el cuarto	room, bedroom
el dormitorio	bedroom
el garaje	garage
el jardín	garden
el pasillo	hallway
el patio	patio, backyard
el piso	floor
la sala	living room
Los quehaceres domésticos	**Household chores**
hacer la cama	to make the bed
hacer las compras	to go grocery shopping
lavar (el piso / los platos)	to wash (the floor/the dishes)
limpiar/ordenar la casa	to clean / to straighten up the house
llenar/vaciar el lavaplatos	to fill / to empty the dishwasher
pasar la aspiradora	to vacuum
planchar	to iron
poner/quitar la mesa	to set / to clear the table
recoger la ropa (del piso / de la secadora)	to pick up / to collect clothes (from the floor/ from the dryer)
sacar la basura	to take out the garbage
El dormitorio / La casa está...	**The bedroom / The house is . . .**
desordenado/a	messy
limpio/a	clean
sucio/a	dirty

Reflexive pronouns   *See page 152.*
Comparisons of equality and inequality   *See page 156.*
Fillers to use in conversation   *See page 172.*

Expressions with the noun *vez*   *See page 155.*
The superlative   *See page 168.*

Capítulo 6
¡Buen provecho!

«Disfruta, come y bebe… que la vida es breve».

Palafitos de Chiloé **de Jorge Gonzalo Fernández.** The **archipiélago de Chiloé** lies off the southern part of Chile's 6,435-kilometer coast. People here enjoy the abundant seafood and numerous varieties of potatoes native to Chile.

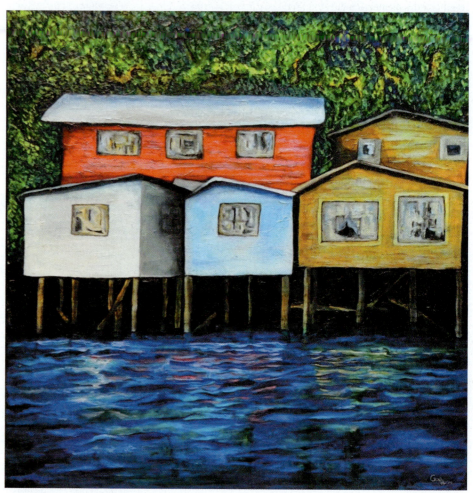

Fuente: Jorge Gonzalo Fernández

Learning Objectives

6.1 Discuss foods and order meals

6.2 Convey who benefits from an action, and express preferences

6.3 Learn about sustainable desert agriculture and a popular Chilean hip-hop artist

6.4 Discuss cooking and recipes

6.5 Talk about events in the past, and how long ago an event happened

6.6 Watch and listen for specific information

6.7 Identify and research some important cultural aspects of Chile

6.8 Use genre and format to anticipate content

6.9 Add supporting details

In this Chapter

ENFOQUE CULTURAL: CHILE
Club cultura: Introducción a Chile

Indica con **C (Cierto)** o **F (Falso)** si escuchas/ves o no esta información en el video.

1. _____ la población de Chile

2. _____ la distancia del norte al sur y del este al oeste

3. _____ sus fronteras con Argentina, Bolivia y Perú

4. _____ sus paisajes (*landscapes*) diversos

5. _____ sus productos agrícolas

6. _____ sus artistas famosos

6.1 Primera parte

Vocabulario

6.1 Discuss foods and order meals

Las comidas y las bebidas

))) ¡**Buen provecho!** El Café del Mar es **un restaurante** popular en Viña del Mar, Chile.

MANOLO: **Mesero, la cuenta**, por favor.

MESERO: Sí, señor.

JORGE: Oye, Manolo, ¿cuánto **dejamos de propina**?

ELÍAS: ¿Qué **te apetece**, querida?

ESME: A ver... **un bistec**, **una ensalada**, **el pastel** de limón y un **vino tinto**.

MATILDE: ¡No me gustan **los mariscos**!

GRACIELA: Pero, Matilde, ¡son **la especialidad de la casa**!

¿Comprendes? Indicate who is described: **el mesero**, **Esme**, **Matilde**, or **Manolo**.

1. _____ Detesta los mariscos.

2. _____ Pide la cuenta.

3. _____ Pide mucha comida.

4. _____ Trae la cuenta.

Respuestas: 1. Matilde; 2. Manolo; 3. Esme; 4. el mesero

))) Vocabulario

Las comidas	Meals
el almuerzo (almorzar [ue])	*lunch (to eat lunch)*
la cena (cenar)	*dinner (to eat dinner)*
el desayuno (desayunar)	*breakfast (to eat breakfast)*
la merienda (merendar [ie])	*afternoon snack (to eat a snack)*

Las carnes y los mariscos	Meats and seafood
el bistec	*steak*
los camarones	*shrimp*
la carne	*meat*
el jamón	*ham*
los mariscos	*shellfish*
el pavo	*turkey*
el pescado	*fish*
el pollo	*chicken*

Las frutas y las verduras	Fruits and vegetables
el ajo	*garlic*
la banana	*banana*
la cebolla	*onion*
la fresa	*strawberry*
las judías verdes	*green beans, string beans*
la lechuga	*lettuce*
el maíz	*corn*
la manzana	*apple*
la naranja	*orange*
la papa	*potato*
el tomate	*tomato*
la toronja	*grapefruit*
las uvas	*grapes*
la zanahoria	*carrot*

Otras comidas	Other foods
el arroz	*rice*
el sándwich	*sandwich*
los frijoles	*beans, legumes*
el huevo	*egg*
el pan	*bread*
el queso	*cheese*
la sopa	*soup*

Los condimentos	Condiments
el aceite (de oliva) y el vinagre	*(olive) oil and vinegar*
el azúcar	*sugar*
la mantequilla	*butter*
la sal y la pimienta	*salt and pepper*
la salsa (picante)	*(hot/spicy) sauce*

Las bebidas	Beverages
el agua (mineral)	*(mineral) water*
el café con leche	*coffee with (hot) milk*
la cerveza	*beer*
el jugo	*juice*
la leche	*milk*
el té (caliente)	*(hot) tea*
el vino (tinto, blanco)	*(red, white) wine*

Los postres	Desserts
el flan	*custard dessert*
las galletas	*cookies*
el helado (de vainilla)	*(vanilla) ice cream*
el pastel (de manzana)	*(apple) pie*
la torta	*cake*
el yogur	*yogurt*

Variaciones

- Names for foods and eating customs vary considerably. In many places, a sandwich is **un emparedado**, and in Chile, it can be **un sánguche**. In Mexico and Spain, **un sándwich** is on sliced white bread. Most people in Mexico prefer **una torta** on a roll, whereas most in Spain prefer **un bocadillo** on a baguette.
- **La banana** has many variations: **el plátano** (Chile, Peru, Mexico, Cuba, Spain), **el banano** (Colombia, Costa Rica, Nicaragua), **el cambur** (Venezuela), **el guineo** (Dominican Republic, Puerto Rico).
- **Mesero/a** varies by country or region: **garzón** (Chile), **mozo/a** (Argentina, Uruguay, Peru), **camarero/a** (Spain).

Expansión   En un restaurante

la cuenta	*bill*
dejar (de) propina	*to leave (as) a tip*
la especialidad de la casa	*house specialty*
el menú	*menu*
el/la mesero/a	*waiter/waitress*

Expresiones

¡Buen provecho!	*Enjoy!*
¿Desea(n) algo de tomar/comer?	*Would you like something to drink/eat?*
Deseo tomar… un refresco.	*I'd like to drink . . . a soda.*
¿Qué te apetece (comer)?	*What do you feel like (eating)?*

Aplicación

6-1 ¿Qué es? Selecciona la opción que mejor corresponde a cada descripción.

MODELO: Es verde. Forma parte de una ensalada.
la lechuga

1. _____ Es una fruta amarilla y larga (*long*).
2. _____ Es un grano (*grain*) blanco que acompaña los frijoles.
3. _____ Es una carne rosada.
4. _____ Es un postre con muchas calorías.
5. _____ Es rojo y se usa en la salsa picante.
6. _____ Es una fruta de la que se hace el vino.

a. el jamón
b. el tomate
c. la banana
d. la torta de chocolate
e. la uva
f. el arroz

6-2 ¡Buen provecho! Identifica la comida y la bebida que piden Marta y Arturo en el Café El Náufrago.

6-3 Ahora ustedes. En parejas, seleccionen un restaurante o café que conocen y luego túrnense para preguntarse qué piden para cada comida.

MODELO: la cena
ESTUDIANTE 1: *¿Qué pides para la cena en Don Pancho?*
ESTUDIANTE 2: *Pido una ensalada de pollo.*
ESTUDIANTE 1: *¿Es todo?...*

1. la cena
2. el desayuno
3. la merienda
4. el almuerzo / la comida

6-4 Sus preferencias. En grupos de tres, conversen sobre sus preferencias de comidas y anoten los resultados.

MODELO: **desayunar** todos los días

ESTUDIANTE 1: *¿Desayunas todos los días? Yo, sí.*
ESTUDIANTE 2: *No, solo cuando tengo tiempo.*
ESTUDIANTE 3: *Sí, siempre* (always) *desayuno.*

desayunar todos los días   **ser** alérgico/a a los mariscos

ser vegetariano/a   **almorzar** en la universidad

comer más pescado que carne   **preferir** la leche a los refrescos

 6-5 ¿Qué compramos para la cena? En parejas, decidan qué van a comprar para la cena en cada una de estas situaciones. Mencionen por lo menos cinco alimentos.

MODELO: Tienen invitados en casa y les gusta preparar platos tradicionales.
           Vamos a comprar un pollo grande, papas, lechuga y tomates para hacer una ensalada. Para el postre...

1. Uno/a de ustedes es vegetariano/a.

2. Uno/a de ustedes se entrena (*is training*) para un maratón.

3. Ustedes están muy ocupados/as y no tienen mucho tiempo.

 6-6A ¡ Necesito información! Hagan el papel de mesero/a (estudiante A) y cliente/a (estudiante B) en un restaurante de buena calidad. Utilicen expresiones del **Vocabulario** y otras para representar la situación. **Estudiante B**: por favor, ve al **Apéndice 1**, página A-6.

MODELO: MESERO/A: *Buenas tardes y bienvenido/a al restaurante...*
                     ¿Qué desea comer?
           CLIENTE/A: *¿Cuál es la especialidad de la casa?*

Estudiante A: Mesero/a

1. Debes saludar al / a la cliente/a y preguntarle qué desea comer.

3. Debes recomendar la especialidad de la casa.

5. Debes preguntar si todo está bien.

7. Debes dar excusas si el/la cliente/a no está contento/a. (Una buena comida toma tiempo en preparar; muchas personas quieren ese plato; etc.)

9. Debes traer la cuenta.

Cultura en vivo

In Chile, **el desayuno** is a light meal: bread with coffee or tea. **El almuerzo** is the main meal with typical dishes, such as **una cazuela** (*stew*), **pescado o carne**, **una ensalada a la chilena (lechuga, tomates y cebolla)**, and **un postre**. In the afternoon, **la merienda** is called **la once**, and consists of bread, a sandwich or **empanada**, and **café o té**. **La cena** is a lighter version of **el almuerzo** and is served at 8 p.m. or later. How do these customs compare with your experience? When do you eat your main meal?

Presencia hispana

The diverse Hispanic population in the U.S. affords a wealth of food choices. Check out a Hispanic market to find ingredients and packaged foods from all over the Hispanic world. Whether you need **plátanos verdes** and **yuca** for a Caribbean meal, **tortillas** and **chiles poblanos** for a Mexican meal, or **empanadas** for a Chilean meal, many specialty foods are available. And don't forget the universally popular **dulce de leche**, a sweet caramel to spread on your **galletas María** (*Marie biscuits*). What Latin American dishes have you tried?

Estructuras

6.2 Convey who benefits from an action, and express preferences

Indirect objects, indirect object pronouns, and the verbs *decir* and *dar*

LOS PRONOMBRES DE COMPLEMENTO INDIRECTO

¿Me puede mostrar los modelos más económicos?

¿Recuerdas? Complete each dialogue with the appropriate direct object pronoun (**Capítulo 4**) or reflexive pronoun (**Capítulo 5**).

1. —¿Se mandan mensajes de texto tú y tu mejor amiga?   —Sí, _____ mandamos mensajes todos los días.

2. —¿Vas a ver a tu amiga hoy?   —Sí, voy a ver_____ esta tarde.

Respuestas: 1. nos; 2. la

- An indirect object indicates *to* or *for whom* an action is carried out.

  I give <u>you</u> the book. You tell <u>me</u> a story.

- In Spanish, the indirect object pronoun can also indicate *from whom* something is bought, borrowed, or taken away. The forms are identical to the direct object and reflexive pronouns, *except* in the third person (**le/les**).

Indirect object pronouns			
SINGULAR		**PLURAL**	
me	*(to) me*	**nos**	*(to) us*
te	*(to) you*	**os**	*(to) you* (fam. Sp.)
le	*(to) you* (for.)	**les**	*(to) you*
le	*(to) him, her*	**les**	*(to) them*

- Indirect object pronouns agree only in number with their noun referent. There is no gender agreement.

  Le lavo los platos.   *I'll wash the dishes (for her/him/you).*

- As with other object pronouns, place the indirect object pronoun between **no** and the conjugated verb.

  No **te** recomiendo ese restaurante.   *I don't recommend that restaurant to you.*

- As with other object pronouns, you can place the indirect object pronoun before the conjugated verb, or attach it to the infinitive or present participle.

  El mesero **nos** tiene que traer la cuenta.
  El mesero tiene que traer**nos** la cuenta.   *The waiter has to bring us the check.*

  El mesero **me** está sirviendo la sopa.
  El mesero está sirviéndo**me** la sopa.   *The waiter is serving me the soup.*

- Add a prepositional phrase to clarify **le** or **les** if the referent is ambiguous.

  le: a él / a ella /a Ud. / a Juan / a María, etc.

  les: a ellos / a ellas / a Uds. / a mis padres, etc.

  Le preparamos la cena **a María**.   *We prepare dinner **for María**.*
  Les traigo un refresco **a Uds**.   *I bring **you** (pl.) a drink.*

- You may also use a prepositional phrase for emphasis. In these examples, the indirect object pronouns **te** and **nos** *are* required, but the phrases **a ti** and **a nosotros** are optional.

Te invito a un café **a ti**, no a ellos.	*I'll invite **you** for coffee, not them.*
¡Juan **nos** va a hacer un pastel especial **a nosotros**!	*Juan is going to make a special cake for **us**!*

¿Comprendes? Complete the mini-dialogue with the appropriate pronouns.

1. —Mesero, ¿_____ trae (a mí) la sopa, por favor?

   —Sí, señora. _____ traigo la sopa ahora mismo.

2. —Paloma, debes servir_____ la sopa a los señores en la mesa número tres.

Respuestas: 1. me; le; 2. les

DECIR Y DAR

The verbs **decir** and **dar** are irregular, and often take indirect object pronouns.

- **Decir** (**i, i**) is an **e → i** stem-changing verb with an irregular first-person singular form (like **tener** and **venir**).

decir (*to say*)			
yo	**digo**	nosotros/as	decimos
tú	dices	vosotros/as	decís
Ud.	dice	Uds.	dicen
él/ella	dice	ellos/as	dicen

Siempre le **decimos** "buenos días" a nuestra mesera favorita.	*We always say "hello" to our favorite waitress.*

¡OJO!

The present participle of **decir** is **diciendo**.

¿Está **diciéndo**te su receta secreta?	*Is she telling you her secret recipe?*

- **Dar** has an irregular first-person singular form, like **ser** and **estar**.

dar (*to give*)			
yo	**doy**	nosotros/as	damos
tú	das	vosotros/as	dais
Ud.	da	Uds.	dan
él/ella	da	ellos/as	dan

La mesera siempre nos **da** un buen servicio.	*The waitress always gives us good service.*

¿Comprendes? Complete the statement with the correct form of **decir** or **dar**.

La mesera me (1) _____ una ensalada de tomate y cebolla, y yo le (2) _____: "¡gracias!"

Respuestas: 1. da; 2. digo

Aplicación

6-7 En la cocina de la abuela. La abuela María está muy ocupada preparando comida para todos sus nietos que la visitan en su casa. Selecciona la respuesta que corresponde a cada situación.

1. _____ Silvia, voy a prepararte una ensalada de verduras.

2. _____ José tiene que ir a trabajar y quiere comer temprano.

3. _____ ¡Les preparo a todos una deliciosa torta de chocolate!

4. _____ Por favor, Ana, ¿me pasas la sal para los frijoles?

5. _____ Felipe, sé que tienes hambre; te doy una banana para tu merienda.

a. ¡Gracias, abuela! Usted siempre nos prepara los postres más ricos.

b. Aquí la tiene, abuela. ¿Le doy también el vinagre?

c. Le voy a preparar a él una sopa de pescado.

d. Gracias, abuela. Me gusta mucho esa fruta.

e. Está bien. Aquí le traigo los tomates y la cebolla.

6-8 Cómo ser el peor mesero. Germán Garmendia, el YouTuber más famoso de Chile y uno de los más famosos del mundo, te da consejos (*advice*) sobre cómo ser el peor mesero del mundo.

Paso 1 Lee los consejos de Germán y selecciona el pronombre de complemento indirecto (o verbo + pronombre) correcto para completar lo que dice.

Hola, soy Germán, y esta semana te voy a hablar de cómo ser el peor mesero en un restaurante elegante. Primero, cuando los clientes llegan al restaurante, (1) les/nos dices que tienen que comer rápido para desocupar (*vacate*) la mesa porque tú necesitas recibir muchas propinas. Segundo, recuerda siempre (2) quitarle/quitarte la chaqueta a la mujer y (3) decirles/decirle a ella: ¡qué fea está, señora! Tercero: Toma el pedido (*the order*) de sus comidas y tómate tu tiempo para volver. No tienes que (4) decirte/decirles nada. Y nunca (5) les/nos des (*give*) pan. ¡Van a pedir menos comida! Cuando son maleducados (*rude*), está bien (6) responderme/responderles con sarcasmo. Por ejemplo: Cuando un cliente (7) te/les dice: "¡Mesero! Este pescado sabe a gato (*tastes like cat*)". Tú dices: "No, ese es el pollo, señor. Nuestro pescado sabe a ratón (*mouse*)". Y si realmente son insoportables (*unbearable*): "Mesero, hay pelos en nuestras sopas. Usted debe (8) darles/darnos otras rápidamente o nos vamos del restaurante". Tú (9) les/te dices: "¿Y qué quieren? Las sopas sin (*without*) pelos son más caras". Finalmente, debes (10) darme/darles una mirada (*look*) fea y seguramente (11) te/me dejan mucha propina.

Paso 2   Escribe una lista de por lo menos cinco consejos que Germán te da. ¿Cuál de esos consejos te parece el peor y por qué?

MODELO: *Me dice que…*

6-9   Un año en Chile. Te vas a Chile por un año para hacer una pasantía (*internship*) como chef. Contesta las preguntas que te hace un/a amigo/a sobre lo que va a pasar.

MODELO: ¿Cuándo vas a darnos tu nueva dirección?
Voy a darles / Les voy a dar mi nueva dirección ahora.

1. ¿Quién te regala (*gives*) los cuchillos (*knives*) de chef?
2. ¿Quién te va a enseñar a cocinar?
3. ¿Cuándo nos subes (*upload*) fotos de la comida chilena?
4. ¿Qué te debemos preparar para tu cena de despedida?
5. ¿Qué platos chilenos vas a prepararnos cuando vuelvas (*when you return*)?

6-10   Cuando estamos en época de examen. En parejas, conversen sobre quiénes se ocupan de estas tareas (*tasks*) cuando ustedes están en época de examen (*exam time*).

MODELO: **prepararte** la comida
Mi compañero me prepara la comida cuando estoy en época de examen.

1. **hacerles** las compras en el mercado
2. **regalarte** una tarjeta prepaga (*gift card*) para una comida
3. **darle** de comer al perro
4. **prepararte** un buen café
5. **decirte** dónde están las galletas
6. **lavarles** los platos a todos los compañeros

6-11   Las especialidades de la casa. En parejas, túrnense para hacer el papel (*play the role*) de mesero/a y cliente/a en algunos restaurantes. El/La mesero/a le recomienda a su cliente/a algunos platos. El/La cliente/a debe pedir una de las recomendaciones.

MODELO: CLIENTE/A: *Por favor, ¿qué me recomienda Ud. aquí en Casa Roma?*
MESERO/A: *Nuestra especialidad es…. Le recomiendo… o…. También…*
CLIENTE/A: *¿Me trae por favor…?*
MESERO/A: *¡Ahora mismo!*

Casa Roma (comida italiana)

El Unicornio (comida vegetariana)

El Rincón Chileno (pescados y mariscos)

Café del Diablo (café y postres)

Cafetería Universo (sándwiches y ensaladas)

Casa Miguel (comida mexicana)

Cultura en vivo

In many restaurants, the cost of service is included in or added to the check. You may see a note at the bottom of the check stating **Servicio incluido**. In Chile, for example, although you are not obligated to leave an additional tip, many patrons leave about 10%. When in doubt, ask the waiter if service is included: **¿Está incluido el servicio?**

¿Te gusta mi coche?

Sí, me gusta mucho.

Gustar and similar verbs

¿Recuerdas? You have expressed what you like to do with **me gusta** + *inf.* or **te gusta** + *inf.*

Answer this question in Spanish: **¿Dónde te gusta almorzar?**

Respuesta: 1. Me gusta almorzar (en casa / en la cafetería, etc.)

- In English, the verb *like* takes a direct object (I like apples). In Spanish, the thing (apples) is the subject of **gustar** (*something is pleasing to someone*).

    Las manzanas me gustan. / Me gustan **las manzanas**.

- Because something is pleasing *to* someone, we use an indirect object with **gustar**.

    Nos gusta la torta de chocolate. *We like chocolate cake.*
    (Chocolate cake is pleasing to us.)

    No **le** gustan los frijoles a Jorge. *Jorge doesn't like beans.*
    (Beans aren't pleasing to him.)

- As a rule, use just the third-person singular or plural (**gusta/gustan**) to agree with the thing or things that are pleasing.

    ¿Te **gusta el arroz**?   *Do you like rice?*
    ¿Te **gustan las papas**?   *Do you like potatoes?*

- Use the singular **gusta** with one or more infinitives.

    ¿Les gusta a ustedes **cenar** y   *Do you like to eat dinner and go to*
    acostarse temprano?   *bed early?*

- Here are some other verbs like **gustar**. Note that the equivalent expressions in English are not direct translations.

aburrir	*to bore, to tire*
apetecer	*to feel like (to appeal to)*
encantar	*to like very much, to be extremely pleasing to*
fascinar	*to fascinate, to be attractive to*
interesar	*to interest, to be in someone's interest*
molestar	*to bother, to annoy*
parecer	*to seem*
quedar	*to be left (over), to remain*

- Remember, you can use a prepositional phrase beginning with **a** to emphasize, clarify, or contrast the indirect object pronoun.

    A mí me encantan los mariscos,   *I love shellfish, but you don't.*
    pero **a ti** no.
    ¿Les parece caro **a ustedes** este   *Does this wine seem expensive to you?*
    vino?

¿Comprendes? Complete the sentences with the logical option: **le encantan**, **no me gustan**, **nos quedan**.

En la cocina: A mí (1) _____ las cebollas; por eso, no voy a ponerlas en la ensalada. Pero, mira, (2) _____ muchas fresas. Vamos a hacer una mermelada. Y voy a prepararle un jugo de zanahorias a Gustavo porque (3) _____ las verduras.

Respuestas: 1. no me gustan; 2. nos quedan; 3. le encantan

Aplicación

6-12 En el restaurante. Selecciona la respuesta que corresponde a cada pregunta.

1. _____ ¿Prefieres comer aquí o en el Café Sur?

2. _____ ¿Trae el mesero el menú?

3. _____ Señores, ¿quieren ver el partido de fútbol?

4. _____ ¿Te apetece una ensalada?

5. _____ ¿Te interesa pedir un postre?

6. _____ ¿Cuánto dejamos de propina?

a. Cinco dólares. No me quedan más.

b. Mejor aquí. Me molesta la música que tocan allí.

c. No, gracias. No me gustan las verduras.

d. Sí, me encanta el flan que hacen aquí.

e. Sí, me parece que lo trae ahora.

f. No, gracias, nos aburren los deportes.

6-13 Un correo de Chiloé. Isabel recibe un correo electrónico de Eduardo. Completa el párrafo con los pronombres de complemento indirecto y el verbo que corresponde.

Hola, Isabel:

Te escribo para contarte sobre mi viaje a Chiloé. ¿Recuerdas la postal de las casas que te mandé (*I sent*) y que se llaman "palafitos"? ¡A mí (1) _____ (parecer/fascinar)! Y la comida aquí es maravillosa: a todos nosotros (2) _____ (encantar/quedar) los mariscos frescos que sirven en los restaurantes. Generalmente por la mañana (a mí) (3) _____ (apetecer/aburrir) tomar un jugo de naranja y pan tostado. Para el almuerzo, siempre como ensalada a la chilena (tomates, cebolla, aceite y sal) y muchas veces (4) _____ (quedar/molestar) parte para la cena. Por la tarde, (a mí) (5) _____ (parecer/apetecer) las empanadas de pino (*pine nut*). ¡Son exquisitas! Aquí hay un plato muy especial que (a mí) (6) _____ (gustar/quedar) mucho; se llama "curanto". Tiene carne, pescado, mariscos y papas, y se prepara en piedras (*rocks*) calientes. (A mí) (7) ¡_____ (interesar/parecer) fenomenal! Finalmente, ¡tienes que probar (*try*) charqui! Es carne seca de caballo (*horse*). ¿(A ti) (8) _____ (aburrir/interesar) probarla?

Un abrazo,

Eduardo

Curanto para dos

6-14 Productos de Chile. ¿Sabes que, en invierno, Estados Unidos y Canadá importan comida de Chile? En parejas, conversen sobre sus gustos y hábitos con estos productos importados de Chile. Usen por lo menos cinco de los verbos de la lista.

apetecer	fascinar	interesar
encantar	gustar	parecer

MODELO: las papas

   ESTUDIANTE 1: *¿Cuándo te apetecen las papas?*

   ESTUDIANTE 2: *Me apetecen cuando tengo mucha hambre.*

1. las cebollas
2. los espárragos
3. el maíz
4. las manzanas
5. los mariscos

6. las peras
7. el pescado
8. las uvas
9. el vino

6-15 Tus preferencias. ¿Cuáles de tus preferencias tienes en común con tus compañeros/as de clase?

Paso 1 Completa la tabla con cosas y actividades que **te interesan, te encantan** o **(no) te gustan**. Usa esta lista como guía e incluye otras cosas también.

- preparar comida complicada
- el café sin azúcar
- conocer Chile
- tomar refrescos con la cena
- las galletas

- salir a comer
- los restaurantes (indios/mexicanos/ chinos...)
- la comida vegetariana (picante, rápida...)
- trabajar como mesero/a

interesar	encantar	(no) gustar
Me interesa salir a comer.	*Me encanta la comida picante.*	*No me gustan las judías verdes.*

Paso 2 Circula por la clase y pregúntales a otros tres estudiantes qué les interesa, les encanta y (no) les gusta. ¿Qué tienen en común?

MODELO: ESTUDIANTE 1: *¿Qué te interesa?*

   ESTUDIANTE 2: *Me interesa… También me encanta…, pero no me gusta…*

¡Conversemos!

Primero, pregúntate si puedes llevar a cabo (*carry out*) las siguientes funciones comunicativas en español. Después, júntate (*get together*) con dos o tres compañeros/as de clase para presentar las situaciones. Hagan y respondan a por lo menos cuatro preguntas en cada situación.

✓ CAN YOU . . .

☐ discuss foods and order meals?

☐ convey who benefits from an action?

☐ express preferences?

WITH YOUR CLASSMATE(S) . . .

Situación: En un restaurante.

Dos de Uds. son clientes/as y otro/a es el/la mesero/a. Van a preguntar y responder sobre las especialidades de la casa y pedir comida y bebida. Usen el vocabulario y las expresiones en el **Vocabulario**.

Para empezar: *Buenas tardes, ¿desean algo de tomar?*

Situación: Un/a amigo/a enfermo/a.

Uno/a de sus amigos está enfermo/a y no puede asistir a clase. Túrnese para decir qué van a hacer para él/ella.

Para empezar: *Le voy a preparar una sopa de pollo...*

Situación: Después de la clase.

Van a hablar de sus opiniones sobre la universidad, los equipos de fútbol, etc., y otros temas de interés común. Usen verbos como **gustar**, **interesar**, **molestar** y **parecer**.

Para empezar: *A mí me interesa(n)... ¿Y a ti?*

Perfiles

6.3 Learn about sustainable desert agriculture and a popular Chilean hip-hop artist

Mi experiencia

LA AGRICULTURA SOSTENIBLE EN EL DESIERTO

6-16 Para ti. ¿Conoces algún lugar donde casi nunca llueve (*almost never rains*)? Así es el desierto de Atacama en el norte de Chile, ¡donde se registraron (*registered*) hasta 400 años sin lluvias! Imagínate cómo es la dieta diaria de los habitantes de esta región. ¿Incluye frutas y verduras? ¿Carne y pescado? ¿Granos? Lee el mensaje de Mariana Rodríguez, una estudiante canadiense que está en Chile.

¹*irrigation*　²*to waste*
³*used*
⁴*raise*

⁵*land*
⁶*moving*
⁷*they thank*　⁸*earth goddess*
⁹*harvest*　¹⁰*I tried*　¹¹*jerky*
¹²*pumpkin*
¹³*beliefs*

¹⁴*did I mention*

Hola, soy Mariana Rodríguez, una estudiante de agronomía en la Universidad de Guelph, Ontario. Estoy en Caspana, un pueblo en el desierto de Atacama, el lugar más seco del mundo, para aprender sobre sus antiguas formas de cultivar la tierra. La gente que vive aquí usa terrazas y sistemas de riego¹ para no desperdiciar² el agua. Estos son métodos que usaron³ sus antepasados prehispánicos. Así pueden cultivar frutas y vegetales y hasta criar⁴ animales.

La vida aquí es muy tranquila; toda la gente se dedica a la agricultura. No se permite vender ni el terreno⁵ ni el agua, porque son patrimonio del pueblo. Una de sus costumbres más conmovedoras⁶ es la ceremonia del año nuevo el 21 de junio, cuando le agradecen⁷ a la Pachamama⁸ el agua y el fruto de las cosechas⁹. Probé¹⁰ algunos platos típicos, como charqui¹¹ y sopaipillas, o pastelitos de calabaza¹². Así que tengo la suerte de conocer un poco más, no solo sobre la agricultura sostenible, sino también de sus creencias¹³ y costumbres.

Al final del semestre de primavera en diciembre, pienso pasar tiempo en Santiago para conocer la ciudad y ver a mis amigos que estudiaron la producción de vino en el Valle de Colchagua. Ah, ¿y te mencioné¹⁴ que ahora soy fanática de la rapera Ana Tijoux? Me encanta y voy a asistir a uno de sus conciertos en Santiago.

6-17 En su opinión. En parejas, comparen su experiencia con la de los habitantes de Caspana. Usen estas preguntas como guía.

1. ¿Hay un desierto en EE. UU. o Canadá tan seco como el de Atacama?

2. ¿Hay una escasez (*scarcity*) de agua donde viven ustedes? ¿Qué hacen ustedes para no desperdiciar agua?

3. ¿Prefieren ustedes comprar productos agrícolas locales o importados? ¿Por qué?

4. ¿Hay celebraciones durante la época de la cosecha donde ustedes viven? ¿Les gusta participar en ellas?

Mi música

"SACAR LA VOZ" (ANA TIJOUX, CHILE)

Soñadora (*dreamer*), desafiante (*defiant*), llena de energía: así es Ana Tijoux (1977–). Esta cantante chilena-francesa es cantautora y compositora de rap. Se la conoce especialmente por sus posiciones sociales, políticas y feministas. Recibió el premio Grammy Latino por la grabación "Universos paralelos" con Jorge Drexler y ha recibido numerosas nominaciones y muchos otros premios. "Sacar la voz" (*Speak up*) refleja su deseo que todos usen o "saquen" su voz para liberarse de la opresión.

ANTES DE VER Y ESCUCHAR

6-18 Sacar la voz. Indica cuáles de estas condiciones te harían (*would make you*) "sacar la voz", como dice Ana Tijoux.

☐ la opresión

☐ la pobreza (ser pobre)

☐ la discriminación

☐ el desempleo (*unemployment*) o el subempleo (*underemployment*)

☐ el cambio climático

☐ el estar sin hogar (casa)

☐ el hambre

☐ la inmigración ilegal

PARA VER Y ESCUCHAR

6-19 La canción. Busca en Internet el video y la letra de "Sacar la voz". ¿Con cuáles de las condiciones anteriores para "sacar la voz" crees que se puede relacionar la canción?

📍 **Busca:** video Sacar la voz Ana Tijoux; Sacar la voz letra

DESPUÉS DE VER Y ESCUCHAR

6-20 Los colores. El video hace un uso especial de los colores. Contesta las preguntas y da tu opinión sobre el efecto.

1. ¿Qué colores predominan?
2. ¿Qué simbolizan los colores en tu opinión?
3. ¿Qué significa al final cuando todos se quitan el pañuelo (*bandana*)?
4. En el video, ¿es "sacar la voz" un deber (*obligation*) individual o colectivo? ¿Cuál es tu opinión?

6.2 Segunda parte

Vocabulario

6.4 Discuss cooking and recipes

En la cocina

🔊 **¡A cocinar!** Ayer (*Yesterday*) Enrique les preparó una cena **sabrosa** a sus amigos.

MAMÁ: ¡Aló, hijo! ¿Cómo te va? ¿Recibiste **la cazuela** que te compré por Internet?

ENRIQUE: Sí, mamá. Disculpa. La usé ayer para **hornear** un pollo para mis amigos.

MAMÁ: ¿De verdad? ¿Qué más les **cocinaste**?

ENRIQUE: ¡Cosas fáciles! Papas **fritas**, ensalada y arroz con leche.

MAMÁ: Y... ¿cómo sabes tú hacer arroz con leche?

ENRIQUE: Encontré **la receta** en Internet. Solo tiene cinco ingredientes: arroz, leche, azúcar, leche condensada y **una pizca** de canela (*cinnamon*). Se cocina en **la estufa**.

MAMÁ: Ay, hijo. ¡Ya no me necesitas para nada!

¿Comprendes? Indicate the correct option to complete each sentence.

1. Enrique encuentra la receta en…
   a. un libro.   b. Internet.   c. las recetas de su mamá.

2. Para preparar arroz con leche, Enrique necesita…
   a. un microondas.   b. una estufa.   c. una tostadora.

Respuestas: 1. b; 2. b

Vocabulario

En la cocina	In the kitchen
la cafetera	coffee maker
la cazuela	stewpot, casserole dish, saucepan
la estufa	stove
el microondas	microwave
el refrigerador	refrigerator
la receta	recipe
la sartén	skillet
el tazón (de cristal)	(glass) bowl
la tostadora	toaster

En la mesa	On the table
la cuchara	spoon
el cuchillo	knife
el plato	plate
la servilleta	napkin
la taza	cup, mug
el tenedor	fork
el vaso	glass

Actividades en la cocina	Kitchen activities
calentar (ie)	to heat
cocinar	to cook
cortar	to cut
echar	to add, to throw in
freír (i, i)[1]	to fry
guardar	to save, to keep, to put away
hornear	to bake, to roast

Actividades en la cocina	Kitchen activities
mezclar	to mix
medir (i, i)	to measure
pelar	to peel
picar	to chop
tostar (ue)	to toast

La preparación	Preparation
asado/a	roasted
frito/a	fried
al horno	baked
a la parrilla	grilled
la pizca (de sal, pimienta, etc.)	pinch (of salt, pepper, etc.)

Para reaccionar	To react
¡Qué rico/a, sabroso/a!	How delicious!
¡Qué asco!	How revolting!

Variaciones

- You will hear **el refrigerador** in Chile and Perú; also **la heladera** (Argentina, Uruguay, Paraguay), **la nevera** (Colombia, Venezuela), or **el frigorífico** (Spain).
- **La estufa** can also be a heating stove in many places, and a cooking stove may also be **la cocina** in some places.

[1]Present tense: *frío, fríes, fríe, freímos, freís, fríen;* Preterit: *freí, freíste, frió, freímos, freísteis, frieron.*

 Letras y sonidos

The sequences *s, z, ce, ci* in Spanish

Generally in Spanish, the letters **s** and **z**, as well as **c** before the vowels **e** and **i**, all correspond to the same sound: the *s* sound in English *sip*.

sal de-**s**a-yu-no a-**z**ú-car **ce**-na ha-**ce**r de-**ci**r

In most parts of Spain, only the letter **s** sounds like the *s* in English *sip*. The letter **z**, as well as **ce** and **ci**, are pronounced like the *th* sound in English *thanks*. Keep these differences in mind as you refine your listening skills. Follow the pronunciation that is consistent with the variety of Spanish that you want to speak, Latin American or Peninsular (Spain).

Aplicación

6-21 ¿Qué necesitas para...? Selecciona el utensilio o aparato que necesitas para hacer cada una de estas acciones.

> MODELO: preparar el café
> *la cafetera*

1. _____ mezclar la sopa   a. la sartén
2. _____ freír las papas   b. la cuchara
3. _____ pelar la manzana   c. la cafetera
4. _____ medir (*measure*) el azúcar   d. el microondas
5. _____ preparar el café   e. la taza
6. _____ calentar la pizza   f. el cuchillo

Cultura en vivo

Bread is a staple in many cultures. In Hispanic cultures, it also figures in many expressions: *Las penas* (*sorrows*) **con pan son menos**, or when something or someone is really good, **tan bueno/a como el pan**, or **Contigo pan y cebolla**, meaning *with you (my love) we can make do with only bread and onions*. The term **compañero/a** derives from **con** + **pan** + **ero**, a person with whom you would share bread. What is the English equivalent of **compañero/a**?

6-22 ¿Qué hacen? Describe lo que hace la persona en cada dibujo con expresiones del **Vocabulario**.

MODELO:

Mario hornea el pollo.

Mario

1.

Lola

2.

El señor Barroso

3.

Dolores

4.

Diego

5.

Estela

6.

Pilar

6-23 En la cocina con el chef Emilio. Escucha la preparación del flan, un postre muy popular en todo el mundo hispano. Indica los ingredientes, los utensilios y las acciones que el chef Emilio utiliza para preparar esta receta.

Ingredientes	Utensilios	Acciones
_____ agua	_____ estufa	_____ echar
_____ azúcar	_____ cuchara	_____ calentar
_____ huevos	_____ licuadora (*blender*)	_____ cortar
_____ jugo de limón	_____ molde	_____ guardar
_____ leche condensada	_____ sartén	_____ hornear
_____ leche evaporada	_____ tazón	_____ mezclar
_____ vainilla	_____ taza	_____ servir

El flan es un postre popular.

6-24 En la cocina. En parejas, túrnense para hacerse estas preguntas sobre sus preferencias. ¿Qué tienen en común?

1. ¿Cómo prefieres el pescado? ¿Al horno, a la parrilla o frito?
2. ¿Cómo prefieres el pollo? ¿Asado, a la parrilla o frito?
3. ¿Qué comida hay en tu refrigerador en estos momentos?
4. ¿Qué le echas usualmente a la ensalada?
5. ¿Qué comidas preparas en el microondas?
6. ¿Qué frutas pelas antes de comerlas?

6-25A ¡Necesito información! La mesa de tu compañero/a tiene cuatro objetos que tú necesitas. Tú tienes cuatro objetos que necesita tu compañero/a. Túrnense para describir sus mesas y así identificar y colocar (*place*) los objetos que faltan. Usen frases como **a la derecha de**, **al lado de**, **a la izquierda de**, **arriba de (***on top of***)** y **debajo de**. **Estudiante B:** por favor, ve al **Apéndice 1**, página A-7.

MODELO: ESTUDIANTE A: *Hay una ensalada arriba de…*
ESTUDIANTE B: *Correcto. Y hay una cuchara y un tenedor grande al lado…*
ESTUDIANTE A: *¡Ah! Falta...*

Estructuras

6.5 **Talk about events in the past, and how long ago an event happened**

The preterit of regular verbs and *hacer* in time expressions in the past

EL PRETÉRITO DE VERBOS REGULARES

- So far you have used verbs in the present tense:

  Como en Café Solo todos los días.　　*I eat at Café Solo every day.*

- To refer to a completed past action in Spanish, you use the **preterit**:

  Ayer **comí** en Café Esmeralda.　　*Yesterday I ate at Café Esmeralda.*

Preterit of regular -ar, -er, and -ir verbs		
-ar	**-er**	**-ir**
tomar	**comer**	**vivir**
yo tom**é**	com**í**	viv**í**
tú tom**aste**	com**iste**	viv**iste**
Ud. tom**ó**	com**ió**	viv**ió**
él/ella tom**ó**	com**ió**	viv**ió**
nosotros/as tom**amos**	com**imos**	viv**imos**
vosotros/as tom**asteis**	com**isteis**	viv**isteis**
Uds. tom**aron**	com**ieron**	viv**ieron**
ellos/as tom**aron**	com**ieron**	viv**ieron**

- The preterit forms for **nosotros/as** of **-ar** and **-ir** verbs are identical to the corresponding present-tense forms. The situation or context of the sentence will clarify the meaning.

- Use the preterit tense to report actions completed at a given point in the past, and to narrate past events.

  Preparé una sopa de mariscos para la cena.　　*I prepared a seafood soup for dinner.*

  Ayer **nos levantamos**, **nos duchamos**, **nos vestimos** y **salimos** para la universidad.　　*Yesterday we got up, showered, got dressed, and left for the university.*

- Remember to use an accent mark on the final vowel for the first- (**yo**) and third-person singular (**Ud./él/ella**) forms of regular verbs, unless the verb is only one syllable.

  Le **eché** aceite de oliva a la ensalada.　　*I added olive oil to the salad.*

  Vi una receta interesante en ese libro.　　*I saw an interesting recipe in that book.*

- Verbs that end in **-car**, **-gar**, and **-zar** have a spelling change in the first-person singular of the preterit in order to keep the original sound of the infinitive. All other forms are regular.

c → qu	buscar	yo bus**qué**
g → gu	llegar	yo lle**gué**
z → c	almorzar	yo almor**cé**

Bus**qué** la receta en Internet.　　*I looked for the recipe on the Internet.*
Almor**cé** poco hoy.　　*I ate little lunch today.*

- These verbs follow a similar spelling-change pattern: **jugar (jugué)**; **empezar (empecé)**; **picar (piqué)**.
- You will often see these expressions with the preterit:

ayer	*yesterday*
anteayer	*the day before yesterday*
anoche	*last night*
la semana pasada	*last week*
una vez	*once*
el año (mes, lunes...) pasado	*last year (month, Monday. . .)*

¿CUÁNTO TIEMPO HACE QUE...?

- To ask how long ago an action or event occurred, use:

> **¿Cuánto tiempo hace que** + *verb phrase in the preterit*?

¿Cuánto tiempo hace que comiste en Don Pancho?	*How long ago did you eat at Don Pancho? (lit. How much time does it make that you ate . . .)*

- To respond, use:

> **hace** + *time expression* + **que** + *verb phrase in the preterit*
> or
> *verb phrase in the preterit* + **hace** + *time expression*

The order of the phrases is interchangeable; however, omit **que** when the verb phrase introduces the sentence.

Hace dos semanas **que comí** allí.	*I ate there two weeks ago. (lit. It makes two*
Comí allí **hace** dos semanas.	*weeks that I ate there.)*

¿Comprendes? Complete the statements with the correct form of an appropriate verb in the preterit: **abrir**, **echar**, **hornear**.

Anoche Jorge (1) _____ un pollo grande. Yo le (2) _____ sal y pimienta a la sopa. Tú (3) _____ una botella de vino.

Respuestas: 1. horneó; 2. eché; 3. abriste

Aplicación

6-26 En la cocina de Enrique. Selecciona la respuesta que corresponde a cada pregunta.

1. _____ ¿Hay aceite y vinagre para la ensalada?

2. _____ ¿Quién le echó pimienta a la sopa?

3. _____ ¿Está listo el horno para el pollo?

4. _____ ¿Dónde están las verduras?

5. _____ Ramón, debes picar las cebollas.

6. _____ ¿Está tostado el pan?

a. La eché yo. ¿Está muy picante?

b. Las guardamos en el refrigerador. ¿Está bien?

c. No encontré el cuchillo para picarlas.

d. Sí, los compró Antonio en el supermercado.

e. Sí, lo tosté y está caliente.

f. Sí, Tomás lo calentó hace quince minutos.

Tortilla española

6-27 Una tortilla española. La tortilla española es muy fácil de preparar.

Paso 1 Lee el párrafo en el que Camila explica la preparación de la tortilla española y selecciona el verbo apropiado para completar su historia.

Hoy yo (1) me levanté/me senté temprano y (2) comí/salí para el mercado donde (3) compré/piqué seis huevos, dos cebollas y dos papas. Una vez en casa, (4) lavé/guardé bien las papas y las (5) repetí/pelé. Luego, (6) corté/horneé las papas y las cebollas en pedazos (*pieces*) muy pequeños. (7) Eché/Comí un poco de aceite de oliva en una sartén. Lo (8) bebí/calenté y (9) cociné/corté las papas y las cebollas. (10) Mezclé/Tosté seis huevos en un tazón. Les (11) eché/calenté un poco de sal a los huevos y luego los (12) horneé/eché a la sartén. (13) Mezclé/Pelé todos los ingredientes con la espátula. Le di la vuelta (*I turned over*) a la tortilla a los cinco minutos y la (14) cociné/mezclé tres minutos más. (15) Corté/Preparé un plato con un poco de perejil (*parsley*) y les (16) piqué/serví la tortilla a mis invitados.

Paso 2 Contesta las preguntas basadas en el **Paso 1**.

1. ¿Cuándo salió Camila para el mercado?
2. ¿Cuáles son los ingredientes de la tortilla española?
3. ¿Qué cocinó primero?
4. ¿Cuántos huevos usó?
5. ¿Por cuánto tiempo en total cocinó la tortilla?
6. ¿Quiénes la comieron?

6-28 Una cena inolvidable. Ema cuenta una experiencia reciente con amigos en un restaurante. Completa su descripción con la forma correcta del pretérito de estos verbos.

buscar	invitar	salir
comer	llamar	tomar
encontrar	llegar	ver

Hace una semana que (yo) (1) _____ un restaurante que me gustó. Mis amigos y yo (2) _____ un anuncio del restaurante en Internet. Yo (3) _____ por teléfono para hacer una reservación. Nosotros salimos a las siete de la noche y (4) _____ al restaurante a las siete y media. La comida nos pareció excelente. Yo comí un bistec y mis amigos (5) _____ un arroz con pollo. Todos nosotros (6) _____ agua mineral y después, café. A la hora de pagar (*pay*), abrí mi bolso (*bag*) y (7) _____ mi tarjeta de crédito, pero no la encontré. ¡Qué vergüenza (*How embarassing*)! Menos mal que mis amigos son muy generosos y pagaron por mí. (Nosotros) (8) _____ del restaurante a las dos de la mañana. El sábado siguiente, yo (9) _____ a todos a cenar a mi casa.

6-29 **Te creo; no te creo.** Individualmente, escriban tres oraciones ciertas y tres oraciones falsas en el pretérito. Luego, en parejas, rétense (*challenge each other*) para decidir si dicen la verdad o no.

almorzar	comer	conocer (a)	llevar	tomar	visitar
besar (a)	comprar	llegar	salir con	trabajar (en)	vivir

MODELO: ESTUDIANTE 1: *Una vez conocí a un chef muy famoso que aparece en televisión.*
ESTUDIANTE 2: *¿Cuándo lo conociste?*
ESTUDIANTE 1: *En 2016.*
ESTUDIANTE 2: *Te creo. / No te creo.*

6-30 **¿Cuánto tiempo hace que…?** Primero, individualmente contesten estas preguntas. Después, en parejas, túrnense para hacerse las preguntas para ver qué tienen en común.

MODELO: ESTUDIANTE 1: *¿Cuánto tiempo hace que horneaste un pollo?*
ESTUDIANTE 2: *Hace tres semanas que horneé uno. ¿Y tú?*

¿Cuánto tiempo hace que…

1. cocinaste una cena especial para alguien? ¿Qué preparaste?
2. lloraste (*did you cry*) después de picar cebollas?
3. comiste tu postre preferido? ¿Qué postre comiste?
4. preparaste bistec a la parilla? ¿Te gustó?
5. tomaste una bebida exótica? ¿Qué tomaste?
6. comiste en un restaurante elegante? ¿Qué restaurante visitaste?

6-31 **Este fin de semana.** Usa verbos de la lista para escribir cinco oraciones contando lo que hiciste (*what you did*) en la cocina durante el fin de semana. Después, en parejas, compartan (*share*) sus experiencias y háganse más preguntas.

calentar	comer	echar	hornear	pelar	picar
cocinar	cortar	guardar	mezclar	preparar	tostar

MODELO: ESTUDIANTE 1: *El sábado le preparé una comida a mi novio/a.*
ESTUDIANTE 2: *¿De verdad? ¿Le cocinaste algo especial?*
ESTUDIANTE 1: *Calenté sopa en el microondas…*

6-32 **Charadas.** En parejas, túrnense para representar estas y otras acciones en el pasado para ver si su compañero/a puede adivinar (*guess*) la acción.

MODELO: ESTUDIANTE 1: (Act out: *Corté el pan.*)
ESTUDIANTE 2: *Cortaste el pan.*

Comí un chile picante.　　　　　　　Freí un huevo en una sartén.
Preparé un jugo de naranja.　　　　　Le eché sal y pimienta a la sopa.
Pelé una zanahoria.　　　　　　　　Abrí una botella de vino.
Calenté la comida en el microondas.　Pelé una banana.

Preterit verbs with a vowel or consonant change

¿Recuerdas? Some **-ir** verbs have a stem change in the present tense and in the present participle. Complete the sentence with the present tense or present participle forms of the verbs.

La mesera nos está (1) _____ (servir) la sopa, pero (yo) (2) _____ (repetir) que nosotros (3) _____ (preferir) la ensalada.

Respuestas: 1. sirviendo; 2. repito; 3. preferimos

EL PRETÉRITO DE LOS VERBOS CON CAMBIO DE RAÍZ: *E → I, O → U*

Stem-changing **-ir** verbs in the present also change in the preterit, but only in the third-person singular and plural. The changes are **e → i** and **o → u**.

| La mesera **repitió** las especialidades del día. | The waitress repeated the daily specials. |
| Los chicos **durmieron** diez horas anoche. | The kids slept ten hours last night. |

	pedir (*to ask for*)	dormir (*to sleep*)
yo	pedí	dormí
tú	pediste	dormiste
Ud.	p**i**dió	d**u**rmió
él/ella	p**i**dió	d**u**rmió
nosotros/as	pedimos	dormimos
vosotros/as	pedisteis	dormisteis
Uds.	p**i**dieron	d**u**rmieron
ellos/as	p**i**dieron	d**u**rmieron

- These verbs follow the same pattern:

medir (i, i)	to measure	**seguir (i, i)**	to follow, to continue
preferir (ie, i)	to prefer	**sentir (ie, i)**	to feel, to be sorry for
repetir (i, i)	to repeat, to have seconds	**servir (i, i)**	to serve

VERBOS QUE CAMBIAN LA *I* EN *Y* EN LA TERCERA PERSONA DEL SINGULAR Y DEL PLURAL

Verbs that end in **-er** and **-ir** preceded by a vowel (**creer**, **leer**, and **oír**) change the **i → y** in the third-person singular and plural. All forms are accented, except the third-person plural.

Mamá no te **creyó** esta mañana.	Mom didn't believe you this morning.
Leyeron la receta con cuidado.	They read the recipe carefully.
¿Oíste que hay un restaurante chileno en Chicago?	Did you hear that there is a Chilean restaurant in Chicago?

	creer (*to believe*)	oír (*to hear*)
yo	cre**í**	o**í**
tú	cre**í**ste	o**í**ste
Ud.	**creyó**	**oyó**
él/ella	**creyó**	**oyó**
nosotros/as	cre**í**mos	o**í**mos
vosotros/as	cre**í**steis	o**í**steis
Uds.	**creyeron**	**oyeron**
ellos/as	**creyeron**	**oyeron**

¿Comprendes? Provide the correct preterit form of the verbs.

—¿(1) _____ (Oír) (tú) las noticias esta mañana?

—Sí, las (2) _____ (oír), pero no las (3) _____ (creer). Mis padres no las (4) _____ (creer) tampoco (*either*).

Respuestas: 1. Oíste; 2. oí; 3. creí; 4. creyeron

Aplicación

6-33 El Mercado Central de Santiago. Según *National Geographic*, el mercado en Santiago es uno de los mejores del mundo. Es famoso por sus frutas y verduras, pescados y mariscos, y restaurantes.

Paso 1 Lee sobre la visita de Rosario y su esposo al Mercado Central y selecciona el verbo apropiado para completar su historia.

> La semana pasada mi esposo y yo (1) creímos/preferimos hacer las compras en el Mercado Central. Cuando llegamos, (2) oímos/pedimos las voces (*voices*) de los vendedores de mariscos. Llegamos a un puesto donde yo (3) pedí/repetí camarones y mi esposo (4) sirvió/pidió calamares frescos. Después, llegamos al puesto de frutas y verduras. Pedí espárragos, pero el vendedor no me (5) creyó/oyó bien. (6) Seguí/Repetí: "Señor, un kilo de espárragos, por favor". Luego, en uno de los restaurantes del Mercado, el camarero nos (7) pidió/sirvió pescado fresco con salsa de mariscos. Después, en casa, mi esposo (8) se sintió/se durmió inmediatamente en el sillón y yo leí el periódico (*newspaper*).

Paso 2 Completa las oraciones con el pretérito del verbo que mejor corresponde para resumir (*summarize*) lo que pasó la semana pasada.

dormirse	leer	preferir	pedir	repetir	servir

1. Hace una semana que Rosario y su esposo _____ comprar en el Mercado Central.
2. En el puesto de pescados y mariscos, _____ camarones y calamares.
3. En el puesto de verduras, Rosario _____, "Un kilo de espárragos, por favor".
4. En el restaurante, el mesero les _____ pescado fresco.
5. Otra vez en casa, Rosario _____ el periódico y su esposo _____.

Presencia hispana

The growing Hispanic population in the U.S. has had a profound impact on our eating and drinking habits. Whether you eat your tortilla chips with guacamole or salsa (now more popular than ketchup), or drink your tequila with salt and lime, you are participating in a food and drink market valued at $11 billion. What Hispanic foods are part of your diet?

6-34 Ayer en mi cocina. Ayer mis amigos y yo preparamos un arroz con pollo. Completa cada oración con la forma correcta del verbo en el pretérito que mejor corresponde a cada una.

cocinar	medir
echar	picar
freír	repetir
leer	

1. Enrique _____ la receta en voz alta (*aloud*).

2. Yo _____ las cebollas y el ajo con el cuchillo.

3. Carlos _____ el pollo en aceite de oliva en la sartén.

4. Sandra _____ una taza de arroz.

5. Tú _____ el arroz a la sartén.

6. Nosotros _____ el arroz con pollo a fuego lento (*low heat*) en la estufa.

7. Daniel y David comieron mucho, y después _____.

6-35 ¿Cierto o falso? En parejas, túrnense para contar anécdotas personales que pueden ser ciertas o falsas. Usen expresiones útiles de **Vocabulario** en sus respuestas.

> MODELO: pedir
> ESTUDIANTE 1: *Una vez pedí camarones con helado.*
> ESTUDIANTE 2: *¡Qué asco! No te creo. No los pediste.*

Una vez...

1. servir	3. pedir	5. freír
2. oír	4. dormirse	6. leer

¡Conversemos!

Primero, pregúntate si puedes llevar a cabo (*carry out*) las siguientes funciones comunicativas en español. Después, júntate (*get together*) con dos o tres compañeros/as de clase para presentar las situaciones. Hagan y respondan a por lo menos cuatro preguntas en cada situación.

✓ CAN YOU...

☐ discuss cooking and recipes?

☐ talk about events in the past?

☐ talk about how long ago an event happened?

WITH YOUR CLASSMATE(S)...

Situación: En la cocina.

Están preparando una receta sencilla (*simple*) en casa. Conversen sobre los ingredientes y los utensilios que necesitan.

Para empezar: *¿Qué preparamos? ¿Tenemos...?*

Situación: En una fiesta.

Conversen sobre lo que pasó (*what happened*) y qué hicieron (*did*) ustedes ayer en una fiesta. Usen una variedad de verbos en el pretérito.

Para empezar: *Ayer, en la fiesta de Daniel, bailé con...*

Situación: Las comidas.

Háganse preguntas sobre cuánto tiempo hace que pasó algo. Usen una variedad de verbos en el pretérito.

Para empezar: *¿Cuánto tiempo hace que cocinaste en casa?*

Club cultura

6.6 Watch and listen for specific information

Chile: Una tierra muy fértil

Estrategia para ver

Watch and listen for specific information. You often need to hear specific details in order to comprehend a passage fully. Prepare yourself by thinking about the theme and location, and by anticipating the kinds of details you might hear.

ANTES DE VER EL VIDEO

6-36 ¿Cómo es Chile? Escribe cuatro detalles que ya sabes de Chile y de su riqueza natural y agrícola. ¿Cuáles de estos detalles esperas (*do you expect*) ver o oír en el video?

> MODELO: *Su capital es Santiago.*

AL VER EL VIDEO

6-37 ¿Qué detalles? Mira el segmento sobre Chile e indica con **Sí** o **No** si los detalles se mencionan o no en el video. ¿Cuáles de estos detalles pudiste (*could you*) anticipar?

1. _____ Tiene una población de 17,3 millones de personas.
2. _____ Fabrican (*They manufacture*) cemento y plásticos.
3. _____ Exportan mucho vino.
4. _____ Hay un mercado histórico en Santiago donde venden comida fresca.
5. _____ El Republicano es un restaurante famoso en Santiago.
6. _____ El vino chileno es de alta calidad.

DESPUÉS DE VER EL VIDEO

6-38 Una tierra muy fértil. Indica la opción que mejor completa cada oración, según el video.

1. Entre otros productos, Chile exporta (fresas / frijoles / maíz).
2. Un mineral importante que exporta es (el cobre [*copper*] / el oro [*gold*] / el aluminio).
3. El Mercado Central de Santiago tiene (un cine / restaurantes / un supermercado).
4. La bebida más importante que exporta es (la leche / el jugo / el vino).
5. Chile produce casi (diez millones / cien millones / mil millones) de botellas de vino cada año.

6-39 Más detalles. Busca más información en Internet sobre Chile y escribe cinco detalles nuevos. Después, en parejas, conversen sobre lo que aprendieron. ¿Qué detalles tienen en común y cuáles son diferentes?

> MODELO: *El desierto de Atacama es el más seco del mundo. Chile exporta muchos productos a Estados Unidos y Canadá durante el invierno del hemisferio norte.*

6.3 Nuestro mundo

Panoramas

6.7 Identify and research some important cultural aspects of Chile

Chile: Un país de contrastes

Chile es un país de contrastes: como es largo (*long*) y estrecho (*narrow*), tiene diferentes climas. En su frontera con Perú por el norte, comienza el desierto de Atacama, seguido por el fértil Valle Central y llegando por fin a la Región de Magallanes y de la Antártica Chilena en el extremo sur.

Si tienes hambre en casi cualquier (*any*) parte de Chile, puedes ir a una empanadería y comprar una empanada. Seleccionas entre las de fruta y las de carne, ¡o las dos! Son ideales para llevar en un pícnic o comer en la calle.

El desierto de Atacama es el más seco e inhóspito del mundo, y según algunos científicos, el más viejo de la historia del mundo. Sin embargo, es rico en minerales y materiales cruciales como el cobre y el nitrato de sodio, importante en los fertilizantes. Aquí los cielos excepcionalmente claros son perfectos para el observatorio ALMA, la matriz de radiotelescopios más grande del mundo.

El clima templado del Valle Central es ideal para el cultivo de frutas y verduras, muchas de las cuales se exportan a EE. UU. y a Canadá durante el invierno norteamericano. El vino chileno es uno de los más apreciados del mundo. Este huaso (*horseman*) hace rondas por una viña (*vineyard*) chilena.

Por su larga costa, la industria pesquera es sumamente importante en Chile. El país produce una gran variedad de pescados y mariscos que exporta a todo el mundo. El archipiélago de Chiloé también atrae a muchos turistas por sus coloridos palafitos (casas de madera [*wood*] construidas sobre pilotes [*piles, stakes*]).

En la región de la Patagonia al sur, hay hermosos lagos, glaciares y volcanes en los Andes. El parque nacional Torres del Paine se conoce por las distintivas formaciones de picos. Es un lugar popular para hacer trekking y camping.

Chile

Población: 17,3 millones

Gobierno: República democrática estable

Festival importante: Fiesta de la Vendimia[1], marzo

Costas: 6.435 km

Productos de exportación: $62 mil millones/año: cobre[2], frutas, pescado, papel y pulpa[3], productos químicos, vino

PIB per cápita: $23,500

[1]*grape harvest*   [2]*copper*   [3]*wood pulp*

6-40 Identifica. Identifica la información según **Panoramas**.

1. productos agrícolas chilenos que se consumen en Estados Unidos y Canadá

2. una zona natural y turística de Chile

3. la extensión de su costa

4. la importancia del desierto de Atacama

5. razones para conocer Chile

6-41 Desafío. Usa el mapa para identificar estos lugares y sus características.

1. ¿Cuál es la capital de Chile?

2. ¿Qué océano está al oeste del país?

3. ¿Con qué países comparte la frontera Chile?

4. ¿Cómo crees que es el clima en Punta Arenas?

6-42 Investigación: Chile. Selecciona un lugar, una persona o un tema (*topic*) que te interesa, como por ejemplo, **la gastronomía, la viticultura, la minería, Ana Tijoux, un restaurante, un/a artista famoso/a**. Usa el modelo para escribir un resumen de tu investigación. Luego preséntaselo a la clase. Debes incluir:

- su nombre y dónde está
- si quieres conocerlo/la algún día y por qué
- por qué es importante o interesante
- cómo es
- si piensas estudiar más sobre este tema
- una foto representativa

📍 **Busca:** lugar interesante Chile, *etc.*

MODELO: *En Santiago, hay un cerro* (hill) *que puedes subir en funicular. Se llama el Cerro San Cristóbal y tiene una vista magnífica de toda la ciudad…*

Páginas

6.8 Use genre and format to anticipate content

¿Importa lo que comes?

Estrategia para leer

Use genre and format to anticipate content. When you recognize the genre of a passage, it helps you anticipate its content. For example, is it an essay, a survey, a poem, a story, or some other category? Ask yourself where it was published: for example, in a magazine, newspaper, book, or poster. Finally, look at the format. Does it have illustrations that help you anticipate the content?

ANTES DE LEER

6-43 ¿Qué vas a leer? Observa el formato de la lectura (*reading*) e indica la opción que describe su género.

    a. una receta

    b. una reseña (*review*) de un restaurante

    c. un anuncio para un mercado

    d. un artículo para informarte sobre la comida

AL LEER

6-44 ¿Creencia o ciencia? Lee el artículo e indica si cada creencia (*belief*) popular en la columna a la izquierda es cierta (**C**) o falsa (**F**), según tu opinión. Después, verifica tus respuestas en la columna a la derecha. ¿Te sorprende alguna (*Are any surprising to you*)? ¿Por qué?

¿Importa lo que comes?

Aquí tienes algunas creencias alimenticias populares. ¿Son ciertas o falsas?

Creencia		Verdad
1. _____ Las sopas instantáneas son saludables[1].		No son tan buenas porque contienen conservantes, saborizantes, mucha sal y otros aditivos no muy buenos para la salud.
2. _____ Las frutas ácidas (por ejemplo, las toronjas) adelgazan[2].		Ningún alimento tiene la función de adelgazar. Es necesario consumir menos calorías de las que el cuerpo necesita y hacer ejercicio frecuentemente.
3. _____ La naranja contiene más vitamina C que el brócoli.		La naranja tiene solo 50mg/100gr de vitamina C. Las frutas y verduras con mayor cantidad de vitamina C incluyen: el mango (1000mg), la guayaba[3] (300mg), el pimentón[4] rojo (190mg) y el brócoli (80mg).
4. _____ La carne de cerdo es más grasosa[5] que la de vaca[6].		En 100 gramos de lomo[7] de cerdo, hay sólo 1 gramo de grasa, mientras que un asado de res[8] tiene 37 gramos de grasa.

[1]*healthy*

[2]*make (one) thinner*

[3]*guava*
[4]*pepper*

[5]*fatty*
[6]*cow*
[7]*loin*
[8]*beef*

5. ____ El consumo de cafeína alivia la migraña[9].		Hay una fuerte controversia al respecto, pero estudios recientes confirman que la cafeína, combinada con otras sustancias, puede ayudar a aliviar el dolor de cabeza.
6. ____ El chocolate produce acné.		El acné es una enfermedad ligada a cambios hormonales y factores hereditarios, no a la dieta.
7. ____ La manzana limpia los dientes.		No, pero como no tiene mucho azúcar no favorece la formación de caries[10].
8. ____ La cerveza engorda.		El consumo en exceso es malo por otras razones, pero es la bebida alcohólica con menos calorías por onza.

[9]*migraine*

[10]*cavities*

DESPUÉS DE LEER

6-45 Lo que comes. Selecciona la opción que mejor completa cada oración, según el artículo.

1. ____ El acné no se relaciona con…
2. ____ Tomar café puede aliviar…
3. ____ La carne de cerdo es…
4. ____ La cerveza contiene…
5. ____ Las manzanas contienen…
6. ____ Las sopas instantáneas contienen…
7. ____ El brócoli contiene…
8. ____ Las frutas ácidas no te ayudan a…

a. el dolor de cabeza (*headache*).
b. poco azúcar.
c. más vitamina C que la naranja.
d. menos calorías que otras bebidas alcohólicas.
e. bajar de peso (*lose weight*).
f. menos grasosa que la de vaca.
g. el consumo de chocolate.
h. sodio y conservantes.

6-46 En su experiencia. En parejas, conversen sobre los puntos del artículo que son lógicos y los que son nuevos o sorprendentes. Incluyan sus creencias sobre algunas comidas que no están en el artículo, por ejemplo, el valor nutritivo de los frijoles, de las frutas moradas o del vino, etc.

MODELO: ESTUDIANTE 1: *"Las manzanas contienen poco azúcar" es lógico para mí. Como manzanas todos los días y creo que son buenas para la salud.*

ESTUDIANTE 2: *"Las sopas instantáneas no son muy buenas para la salud" me sorprende. No voy a tomarlas.*

6-47 Investigación: Comidas saludables. Busca información en Internet sobre una comida que crees saludable. Escribe un resumen de por qué es un mito (*myth*) o una verdad.

 **Busca:** (comida) saludable

Taller

6.9 **Add supporting details**

Una reseña (*review*)

Estrategia para escribir

Add supporting details. When you write a review, you not only give your opinion, but you also add enough detail to help the reader decide whether or not to visit a place, view a film, or buy an item. What does it offer? Is it attractive? Expensive? Offer good service? Do you recommend it? Why or why not?

6-48 **Una reseña de un restaurante.** Vas a escribir una reseña de un restaurante que conoces bien. Incluye detalles para ayudar a otros a decidir si deben ir a ese restaurante o no.

ANTES DE ESCRIBIR

Incluye detalles para ayudar a otros a decidir si deben ir a ese restaurante o no. Considera:

☐ dónde está, sus horas, su especialidad

☐ el número de estrellas (*stars*) que tiene

☐ el costo de la comida (1 tenedor: económico – 5 tenedores: caro)

☐ la calidad de la comida y del servicio

☐ tu recomendación

AL ESCRIBIR

Organiza tus detalles en un párrafo.

> **MODELO:**   *El café Joe's es un lugar informal en Champaign, cerca de la universidad...*

DESPUÉS DE ESCRIBIR

- **Revisar.** Revisa tu reseña para verificar los siguientes puntos:
  ☐ el uso del pretérito
  ☐ la concordancia de adjetivos y sustantivos
  ☐ alguna frase superlativa (es el restaurante más/menos... de...)
  ☐ la ortografía (*spelling*)
- **Intercambiar.** Intercambia tu reseña con la de un/a compañero/a. Mientras leen las reseñas, hagan comentarios y sugerencias sobre el contenido, la estructura y la gramática.
- **Entregar.** Escribe tu versión final, incorporando las sugerencias de tu compañero/a. Después, entrégasela a tu profesor/a.

En este capítulo...

Vocabulario

Primera parte

Las comidas	Meals
el almuerzo (almorzar [ue])	lunch (to eat lunch)
la cena (cenar)	dinner (to eat dinner)
el desayuno (desayunar)	breakfast (to eat breakfast)
la merienda (merendar [ie])	afternoon snack (to eat a snack)

Las carnes y los mariscos	Meats and seafood
el bistec	steak
los camarones	shrimp
la carne	meat
el jamón	ham
los mariscos	shellfish
el pavo	turkey
el pescado	fish
el pollo	chicken

Las frutas y las verduras	Fruits and vegetables
el ajo	garlic
la banana	banana
la cebolla	onion
la fresa	strawberry
las judías verdes	green beans, string beans
la lechuga	lettuce
el maíz	corn
la manzana	apple
la naranja	orange
la papa	potato
el tomate	tomato
la toronja	grapefruit
las uvas	grapes
la zanahoria	carrot

Otras comidas	Other foods
el arroz	rice
el sándwich	sandwich
los frijoles	beans, legumes
el huevo	egg
el pan	bread
el queso	cheese
la sopa	soup

Los condimentos	Condiments
el aceite (de oliva) y el vinagre	(olive) oil and vinegar
el azúcar	sugar
la mantequilla	butter
la sal y la pimienta	salt and pepper
la salsa (picante)	(hot/spicy) sauce

Las bebidas	Beverages
el agua (mineral)	(mineral) water
el café con leche	coffee with (hot) milk
la cerveza	beer
el jugo	juice
la leche	milk
el té (caliente)	(hot) tea
el vino (tinto, blanco)	(red, white) wine

Los postres	Desserts
el flan	custard dessert
las galletas	cookies
el helado (de vainilla)	(vanilla) ice cream
el pastel (de manzana)	(apple) pie
la torta	cake
el yogur	yogurt

Segunda parte

En la cocina	In the kitchen
la cafetera	coffee maker
la cazuela	stewpot, casserole dish, saucepan
la estufa	stove
el microondas	microwave
el refrigerador	refrigerator
la receta	recipe
la sartén	skillet
el tazón (de cristal)	(glass) bowl
la tostadora	toaster

En la mesa	On the table
la cuchara	spoon
el cuchillo	knife
el plato	plate
la servilleta	napkin
la taza	cup, mug
el tenedor	fork
el vaso	glass

Actividades en la cocina	Kitchen activities
calentar (ie)	to heat
cocinar	to cook
cortar	to cut
echar	to add, to throw in
freír (i, i)	to fry
guardar	to save, to keep, to put away
hornear	to bake, to roast
mezclar	to mix
medir (i, i)	to measure
pelar	to peel
picar	to chop
tostar (ue)	to toast

La preparación	Preparation
asado/a	roasted
frito/a	fried
al horno	baked
a la parrilla	grilled
la pizca (de sal, pimienta, etc.)	pinch (of salt, pepper, etc.)

Para reaccionar	To react
¡Qué rico/a, sabroso/a!	How delicious!
¡Qué asco!	How revolting!

EXPANSIÓN En un restaurante See p. 183.
Indirect object pronouns See p. 186.
Decir and *dar* See p. 187.
Gustar and similar verbs See p. 190.

Adverbial expressions in the past See p. 201.
The expression *hace… que* with the preterit See p. 201.
Preterit verbs with a vowel or consonant change See p. 204.

Capítulo 7
¡A divertirnos!

«Vive duro y a lo loco, que la vida dura muy poco».

Juan, no le hagas cosquillas a Pedro de Ramón Oviedo. With his work like an explosion of colors on the canvas, this Dominican artist is considered one of the finest expressionist painters of the 20ᵗʰ century. What does this one (*Juan, don't tickle Pedro*) say about the Dominican way of life?

Fuente: Fundación Ramón Oviedo

Learning Objectives

7.1 Talk about your free time, and make plans to do something

7.2 Report past activities, indefinite things, and contrasting ideas

7.3 Read about Wi-Fi parks in Cuba and a world-famous Dominican artist

7.4 Discuss sports you watch and those in which you participate

7.5 Talk about other activities in the past, and take shortcuts in conversation

7.6 Listen and watch for purpose

7.7 Identify and research some important cultural aspects of Cuba, Puerto Rico, and the Dominican Republic

7.8 Deal with unknown words

7.9 Use transitional expressions

In this Chapter

ENFOQUE CULTURAL: CUBA, PUERTO RICO Y LA REPÚBLICA DOMINICANA
Club cultura: Introducción a Puerto Rico

Indica con **C (Cierto)** o **F (Falso)** si escuchas/ves o no esta información en el video.

1. _____ Puerto Rico es un Estado Libre Asociado (*Commonwealth*).

2. _____ La moneda es el peso puertorriqueño.

3. _____ Tiene dos idiomas (lenguas) oficiales.

4. _____ Hay una variedad de arquitectura en San Juan.

5. _____ Una actividad popular es ir en bicicleta por el Viejo San Juan.

6. _____ Si tienes calor o sed, puedes tomar una "piragua".

7.1 Primera parte

Vocabulario

7.1 **Talk about your free time, and make plans to do something**

El tiempo libre

¿Te divertiste este fin de semana?

¿Comprendes? Select the person who did each action: **Felipe, Luisa, Manuela, Pedro, Teresa, Verónica.**

1. _____ Fue a bailar.

2. _____ Hizo un pícnic.

3. _____ Dio un paseo.

4. _____ Lo pasó mal.

Respuestas: 1. Verónica; 2. Pedro; 3. Manuela; 4. Felipe

Vocabulario

En la playa	At the beach
la bolsa	bag
la heladera	cooler
el hielo	ice
los lentes de natación/sol	swim goggles / sunglasses
la sombrilla	umbrella
la toalla	towel
el traje de baño	swimsuit

Los pasatiempos	Pastimes
chatear	to chat
dar un paseo	to go out, to take a walk
escuchar música	to listen to music
hacer un pícnic	to have a picnic
hacer yoga	to do yoga
ir a una discoteca / un festival / un concierto	to go to a (night)club / festival / concert
jugar a videojuegos / al tenis, etc.	to play videogames / tennis, etc.
leer una novela / las noticias / una revista	to read a novel / the news / a magazine
nadar en el mar / una piscina	to swim in the ocean / a swimming pool
pasar tiempo con amigos	to spend time with friends
salir a comer	to go out to eat
volar (ue) un papalote	to fly a kite

¿Qué tiempo hace?	What is the weather like?
Está nublado.	It's cloudy.
Hace...	It's . . .
buen/mal tiempo.	good/bad weather.
(mucho) calor.	(very) hot.
fresco.	cool.
(mucho) frío.	(very) cold.
(mucha) humedad.	(very) humid.
(mucho) sol.	(very) sunny.
(mucho) viento.	(very) windy.
llover (ue)	to rain
nevar (ie)	to snow

Hacer planes	To make plans
Es un día perfecto para...	It's a perfect day for . . .
¡Fabuloso!	Fabulous! Great!
Me da igual.	It's all the same to me.
pasarlo bien/mal	to have a good/bad time
¡Qué mala suerte!	What bad luck!
¿Qué tal si...?	What if . . . ?

Variaciones

- **Los lentes de sol** are also **los anteojos de sol** in the Americas and **las gafas de sol** in Spain.
- In addition to **el traje de baño**, you will hear **el bañador** in Spain and **la trusa** in Cuba.
- Many Spanish speakers in the Caribbean use **¡Chévere!** to express excitement over an invitation or event. In Argentina and Uruguay, you will hear **¡Bárbaro!**

Aplicación

7-1 ¿Qué hacer? Selecciona la palabra o expresión que mejor completa cada oración.

1. ¡Oye! ¿Te interesa bailar y escuchar música? ¿Vamos a _____?

2. Hace buen tiempo. ¿Por qué no vamos al parque, llevamos sándwiches y hacemos _____?

3. Hoy hace sol. Vamos a dar _____ por el parque.

4. Los refrescos están en _____.

5. El sábado va a hacer mucho calor. ¿Qué tal si vamos a _____ en el mar?

6. ¡Qué feo! Hace muy mal tiempo; hace frío y está _____.

7. Si hace mal tiempo, es un día perfecto para leer _____ tranquilamente en casa.

a. un paseo
b. nadar
c. una revista
d. una discoteca
e. un pícnic
f. nublado
g. la heladera

7-2 **¿Qué tiempo hace en...?** En parejas, miren el mapa meteorológico e identifiquen el tiempo que hace en estos países: **las Bahamas**, **Cuba**, **Haití**, **Puerto Rico**, **la República Dominicana**. Después conversen sobre una actividad que pueden hacer en cada uno de los países, según el tiempo que hace.

MODELO: ESTUDIANTE 1: *¿Qué tiempo hace en…?*
           ESTUDIANTE 2: *Hace… / Está…*
           ESTUDIANTE 1: *¿Qué tal si… en…?*
           ESTUDIANTE 2: *También podemos…*

Cultura en vivo

The warm climate found in the Caribbean islands lends itself to year-round outdoor activities. In Cuban parks, you will see people playing dominoes and chess, kicking a soccer ball, or simply walking. You will also see musicians performing on street corners and people following Latin rhythms impromptu in the streets or on the sidewalks. On Paseo de la Princesa in San Juan, Puerto Rico, locals gather in the evenings to dance. How do these activities compare to yours, or to those in your community, when the weather is nice?

El tiempo

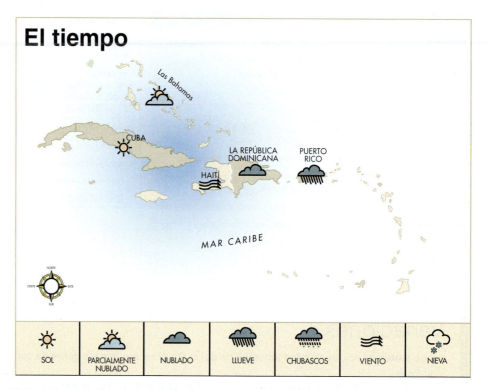

SOL	PARCIALMENTE NUBLADO	NUBLADO	LLUEVE	CHUBASCOS	VIENTO	NIEVA

7-3A **¡Necesito información!** Cada uno/a de ustedes tiene una escena con pequeñas diferencias. Túrnense para describir la escena y descubrir las diferencias. ¿Cuántas diferencias hay? Usen expresiones de la lista de **Vocabulario**. **Estudiante B**: ve al **Apéndice 1**, página A-7.

MODELO: ESTUDIANTE A: *Hay dos mujeres en la playa.*
           ESTUDIANTE B: *Correcto. Las dos mujeres llevan* (are wearing)…

Estudiante A:

7-4 ¿Qué tal si...? Escucha la conversación entre Teresa y Pedro e indica las actividades que deciden hacer juntos (*together*) y las que no.

1. dar un paseo   **Sí   No**

2. hacer un pícnic   **Sí   No**

3. hacer yoga   **Sí   No**

4. jugar a videojuegos   **Sí   No**

5. leer las noticias en línea   **Sí   No**

6. nadar en el mar   **Sí   No**

7. salir a bailar   **Sí   No**

8. salir a comer   **Sí   No**

9. volar un papalote   **Sí   No**

7-5 ¿La tecnología como pasatiempo? Sigan los pasos.

Paso 1 En pequeños grupos, lean la historieta. En su opinión, ¿representa la verdad o exagera? ¿Con cuál(es) de las imágenes se identifican Uds.? ¿Con cuál(es) no se identifican? ¿Alguna vez les dolieron los dedos (*did your fingers hurt*) por usar tantos aparatos tecnológicos?

Paso 2 Individualmente, escriban tres a cuatro actividades que representan para ustedes "un sábado ideal". Después, en grupos, comparen sus actividades. ¿Hay semejanzas? ¿Diferencias? ¿Está el uso de la tecnología entre sus actividades favoritas?

7-6 Mis viejos y yo. En grupos pequeños, conversen sobre sus pasatiempos y los de las personas de la generación de sus padres. ¿Tienen algunos en común? ¿Hacen ustedes actividades con personas mayores?

MODELO: *A mis padres les gusta dar un paseo por la playa, pero yo prefiero chatear con mis amigos. Nos gusta hacer un pícnic juntos.*

Estructuras

7.2 Report past activities, indefinite things, and contrasting ideas

Irregular and strong preterit verbs

¿Recuerdas? Some common verbs are irregular in the preterit. Based on context, can you identify the verbs (**dar**, **ir**, **ser**, **ver**) in this dialogue?

—¿(1) **Viste** la Copa Mundial de Fútbol? (2) **Fue** muy emocionante.

—Sí, mi novia me (3) **dio** entradas para un partido y nosotros (4) **fuimos** juntos.

Respuestas: 1. ver; 2. ser; 3. dar; 4. ir

VERBOS IRREGULARES EN EL PRETÉRITO

- The verbs **ser**, **ir**, **dar**, and **ver** have irregular forms in the preterit. Note that these forms have *no* accents.

Irregular preterit forms			
	ser/ir	**dar**	**ver**
yo	**fui**	di	vi
tú	**fuiste**	**diste**	viste
Ud.	**fue**	**dio**	vio
él/ella	**fue**	dio	vio
nosotros/as	**fuimos**	**dimos**	vimos
vosotros/as	**fuisteis**	**disteis**	visteis
Uds.	**fueron**	**dieron**	vieron
ellos/as	**fueron**	**dieron**	vieron

- The verbs **ser** and **ir** have the same forms in the preterit. The context of the sentence or the situation will clarify the meaning.

¿Qué día **fue** ayer?	*What day was yesterday?*
Fuimos a dar un paseo al centro.	*We went downtown for a walk.*

- **Dar** and **ver** use the same endings as regular **-er** and **-ir** verbs. However, the first and third persons have only one syllable and do not require an accent mark.

Vi a Víctor ayer.	*I saw Víctor yesterday.*
Él me **dio** una novela excelente.	*He gave me an excellent novel.*

VERBOS FUERTES EN EL PRETÉRITO

- Many everyday verbs are said to have "strong" forms in the preterit because their special stem carries the stress or emphasis in the **yo** and **usted/él/ella** forms and do not need an accent. Note also the special set of endings.: **-e, -iste, -o, -imos, -isteis, -ieron**.

Strong preterit forms		
	estar	**tener**
yo	**estuve**	**tuve**
tú	**estuviste**	**tuviste**
Ud.	**estuvo**	**tuvo**
él/ella	**estuvo**	**tuvo**
nosotros/as	**estuvimos**	**tuvimos**
vosotros/as	**estuvisteis**	**tuvisteis**
Uds.	**estuvieron**	**tuvieron**
ellos/as	**estuvieron**	**tuvieron**

Gloria **estuvo** en la playa, pero **tuvo** que irse temprano.	*Gloria was at the beach, but had to leave early.*

- The preterit form of **hay** (from the verb **haber**) is **hubo** for both singular and plural.

Ayer **hubo** un partido de fútbol en el estadio.	*Yesterday there was a soccer game in the stadium.*
Hubo más de 50.000 espectadores.	*There were more than 50,000 spectators.*

¿Comprendes? Complete the dialogue with the correct verbs: **estuve, dio, hubo, viste**.

—¿(1) _____ a Juan Luis Guerra en el concierto?   —¡Sí, y después me (2) _____ su autógrafo!   —¿Cuántas personas (3) _____?   —¡Muchas! Yo (4) _____ en la última fila (*row*).

Respuestas: 1. Viste; 2. dio; 3. hubo; 4. estuve

Aplicación

7-7   Una fiesta en la playa. Selecciona la respuesta que mejor corresponde a cada pregunta para saber qué ocurrió en esta fiesta.

1. _____ ¿Dónde fue la fiesta?
2. _____ ¿Quiénes estuvieron?
3. _____ ¿Tuviste que salir temprano?
4. _____ ¿Vieron Uds. a otras celebridades?
5. _____ ¿Con quién fue Zoe Saldaña?
6. _____ ¿Le diste algo al anfitrión (*host*)?

a. Estuvimos mis amigos y yo.
b. Sí, le di una botella de vino.
c. Sí, vimos a Zoe Saldaña y a Draco Rosa.
d. No, no me fui hasta las dos.
e. Ella fue sola.
f. Fue en la playa Luquillo.

7-8   Un concierto de Pitbull. Ayer por la noche fuiste con varios amigos a un concierto de Pitbull en Santo Domingo.

Paso 1   Completa el párrafo con la forma correcta del pretérito de cada verbo para saber qué ocurrió.

Ayer (1) _____ (haber) un concierto de Pitbull, el famoso rapero cubanoamericano. En el estadio, mis amigos y yo le (2) _____ (dar) las cuatro entradas al agente. (Nosotros) (3) _____ (Ir) hasta los asientos (*seats*), pero (4) _____ (tener) mala suerte. Yo (5) _____ (tener) que sentarme detrás de un chico muy alto y mis amigos (6) _____ (tener) que sentarse detrás de unos altavoces (*speakers*) enormes. La verdad es que yo no (7) _____ (ver) mucho. Pero sí (8) _____ (oír) bien la música. ¡Lo pasamos fenomenal!

Paso 2   En parejas, combinen elementos de cada columna para saber qué pasó en otro concierto al que asistieron. Formen oraciones completas en el pretérito.

MODELO: *Mis amigos y yo… fuimos al concierto en taxi.*

yo	estar allí cinco horas
nuestros amigos	darle la bolsa al agente de seguridad
los músicos	ir al baño
la orquesta	tener que pagar la cuenta
mis amigos y yo	darnos las bebidas
una camarera	ser muy bueno/a

7-9A **¡Necesito información!** Tú y tu compañero/a publicaron en sus páginas de Facebook unos estados (*status updates*) sobre una fiesta que hubo anoche. Cada uno/a tiene parte de la información sobre la fiesta. Háganse preguntas para saber qué pasó. **Estudiante B**: ve al **Apéndice 1**, página A-8.

Estudiante A:

La información que necesito:

1. ¿Para quién fue la fiesta?
2. ¿Cómo reaccionó?
3. ¿Qué le dieron?
4. ¿Por qué salió una persona temprano?
5. ¿Qué música escucharon?

Tu estado con tu versión de la fiesta:

7-10 **¿Quién...?** En grupos de cuatro, túrnense para hacerse preguntas sobre lo que hicieron (*what you did*) la semana pasada. Escriban el nombre de la persona que hizo la actividad en su caja (*box*) correspondiente.

MODELO: jugar al tenis
ESTUDIANTE 1: *Carlos, ¿jugaste al tenis la semana pasada?*
ESTUDIANTE 2: *Sí, jugué el sábado. / No, no jugué (al tenis).*
ESTUDIANTE 1: *¿Con quién? / ¿Por qué no jugaste?*

dar un paseo	estar en un club	pasarlo bien en clase
leer una novela	ir a un partido	tener una fiesta
oír las noticias	nadar en una piscina	chatear
volar su papalote	jugar al tenis	ver una película

Indefinite and negative expressions

¿Recuerdas? Answer these questions in the negative:

1. ¿Nevó ayer?

2. ¿Hubo mucha contaminación?

Respuestas: 1. No, no nevó ayer. 2. No, no hubo mucha contaminación.

In Spanish, you can negate an action by using **no** before the verb, or by using a negative expression. Here is a list of affirmative and corresponding negative expressions.

Afirmativo		Negativo	
algo	something, anything	**nada**	nothing, not anything
alguien	someone, anyone	**nadie**	nobody, no one
algún, alguno/a(s)	any, some	**ningún, ninguno/a(s)**	none, not any
alguna(s) vez/veces	sometime(s)	**ninguna vez**	not once, never
(casi) siempre	(almost) always	**(casi) nunca, jamás**	(almost) never
también	also, too	**tampoco**	neither, not either
o... o	either . . . or	**ni... ni**	neither . . . nor

- Once a sentence is negative, all other indefinite words within the sentence become negative. Sentences that use **no** can have a second negative (**nada, nadie, ningún**), either immediately after the verb, or at the end of the sentence.

  Lucía **no** conoce a **nadie** en la fiesta **tampoco**. — *Lucía doesn't know anybody at the party either.*

  No voy a traer **ni** refrescos **ni** sándwiches para **nadie**. — *I am bringing neither refreshments nor sandwiches for anyone.*

- Omit the **no** when the negative expression precedes the verb.

  Nunca fuimos a la playa con Lourdes. — *We never went to the beach with Lourdes.*

  A **nadie** le dimos las toallas. — *We didn't give the towels to anyone.*

- Use the expressions **nadie** and **alguien** to refer to people. Be sure to add the personal **a** when they appear as direct objects of the verb.

  —¿Viste **a alguien** ayer nadando en el mar? — *Did you see someone yesterday swimming in the ocean?*

  —No, no vi **a nadie** en el agua. — *No, I didn't see anyone in the water.*

- You will almost always use **ninguno/a** in the singular form, except with inherently plural nouns, such as things that come in pairs.

  —¿Te quedan **algunas** entradas? — *Are there any tickets left?*

  —No, no me queda **ninguna** entrada. — *No, there aren't any tickets left.*

  —¿Encontraste mis lentes? — *Did you find my glasses?*

  —No, no encontré **ningunos** lentes. — *No, I didn't find any glasses.*

¡OJO!

Just as the number **uno** shortens to **un** before a masculine singular noun, **alguno** and **ninguno** drop the final **-o**. Be sure to add an accent: **ningún** traje de baño / **algún** tipo de refresco.

¿Comprendes? Complete the dialogues with the correct words: **alguna, ninguna, nunca, siempre**.

—Oye, Juan. ¿Tienes (1) _____ música de Daddy Yankee?

—Lo siento, Paula. No tengo (2) _____.

—No hay comida (3) _____ en las fiestas de Daniel, ¿verdad?

—No, no tienes razón. ¡(4) _____ hay comida!

Respuestas: 1. alguna; 2. ninguna; 3. nunca; 4. Siempre

Aplicación

7-11 Una entrevista con Francisco Lindor. El beisbolista Francisco Lindor nació en Puerto Rico y llegó a jugar para los Indios de Cleveland a la edad de 22 años. Al año siguiente, jugó en la Serie Mundial entre Cleveland y Chicago.

Paso 1   Lee la entrevista con Francisco Lindor y selecciona la expresión más lógica para completarla.

ENTREVISTADORA: Francisco, es un honor conocerte y poder hablar contigo. ¿Deseas (1) algo/alguien de tomar? (2) ¿Algún/Alguien refresco?

FRANCISCO: No, gracias. No quiero (3) nadie/nada por ahora.

ENTREVISTADORA: Bueno. Tienes tanta energía. ¿No te cansas (*get tired*) (4) nunca/nadie?

FRANCISCO: Pues, sí, (5) algunas/ningunas veces, cuando viajo mucho. Pero estoy (6) también/tampoco con mis compañeros del equipo (*team*), y eso ayuda.

ENTREVISTADORA: Francisco, eres una persona muy feliz. (7) Nada/Siempre estás sonriendo (*smiling*).

FRANCISCO: Es verdad. Tengo mucha suerte, y (8) alguien/jamás me siento triste.

Paso 2   Contesta las preguntas, basándote en la entrevista.

1. ¿Qué toma Francisco en la entrevista?
2. ¿Cuándo se cansa?
3. ¿Cuándo está solo en sus viajes?
4. ¿Cuándo se siente triste?
5. ¿Cuándo sonríe (*does he smile*)?

Presencia hispana

Immigrants from the Spanish-speaking islands of the Caribbean have had a profound influence on American culture, including food, entertainment, and sports, especially baseball. Can you identify the sphere of influence of these famous people and things: Albert Pujols and Roberto Clemente; mojitos and daiquiris; Arturo Sandoval and José Feliciano; Benicio del Toro and Daisy Fuentes?

7-12 En el Caribe. Samuel planea hacer un viaje a Puerto Rico para visitar a su prima Verónica. Le hace preguntas en preparación para su viaje. Completa la conversación con la expresión afirmativa o negativa lógica en las respuestas de Verónica.

SAMUEL: Oye, Verónica, ¿cuándo hace frío en Puerto Rico?

VERÓNICA: En el Caribe casi (1) _____ hace frío. Siempre hace sol.

SAMUEL: ¿Y no llueve? ¿No hace viento?

VERÓNICA: Bueno, en caso de un huracán, no va (2) _____ a la playa (3) _____ a nadar en el mar. Si hay (4) _____ huracán, hace mucho viento y llueve mucho.

SAMUEL: Y ¿qué hacen cuando hace buen tiempo?

VERÓNICA: Nos gusta a todos ir a la playa. O vamos a pie (*by foot*) (5) _____ en bicicleta. (6) _____ de nuestros amigos van en carro.

SAMUEL: ¿Llevan bolsa a la playa?

VERÓNICA: Sí, siempre tenemos (7) _____ en la bolsa: un libro, lentes de sol. Hay agua (8) _____. Pero no llevamos (9) _____ de comer.

7-13 ¿Qué pasatiempos prefieren? Sigue los pasos para completar la actividad.

Paso 1 En parejas, túrnense para preguntarse sobre los pasatiempos de la lista. Usen las expresiones **siempre**, **algunas veces**, **casi nunca** y **nunca**, y añadan información personal.

> MODELO: ver películas de ciencia ficción
> ESTUDIANTE 1: *¿Ves películas de ciencia ficción?*
> ESTUDIANTE 2: *¡Siempre! Me gustan mucho las películas de ciencia ficción. El otro día, vi…*

- dar paseos en el invierno
- escuchar música
- ir a un partido los sábados
- hacer un pícnic en el verano
- ir a una discoteca con los amigos
- ir a nadar
- salir con los amigos los viernes
- ¿otra actividad?

Paso 2 Resume (*Summarize*) la información de las actividades del **Paso 1**. Incluye tus opiniones y las de tu compañero/a. ¿Son muy diferentes?

> MODELO: *Mi amigo José casi nunca ve películas de ciencia ficción, pero yo las veo algunas veces.*

Te busqué en Luquillo, pero no te vi.

No fui a Luquillo sino a Playa Azul.

Pero or sino (que)

- In Spanish, you usually use the conjunction **pero** to express *but*.

  Fui a la playa, **pero** llovió.   *I went to the beach, but it rained.*

- However, when *but* means *on the contrary*, *but rather*, or *instead*, use **sino**. **Sino** always corrects or contradicts a negative statement.

  No quiero el periódico **sino** la revista.   *I don't want the newspaper but (rather) the magazine.*

  No pedimos café **sino** té.   *We didn't order coffee, but (rather) tea.*

- Use **sino que** if the correction includes a verb phrase.

  No dimos un paseo, **sino que** nadamos en el mar.   *We didn't take a walk, but (rather) we swam in the ocean.*

  No volaste el papalote, **sino que** jugaste al voleibol.   *You didn't fly the kite, but (instead) played volleyball.*

- Use the expression **no solo... sino (que) también...** to mean *not only . . . but also, ...*

  No solo llovió, **sino que también** hizo viento.   *It not only rained, but it was also windy.*

  Tenemos **no solo** los lentes de sol **sino** la sombrilla **también**.   *We have not only our sunglasses, but the umbrella, too.*

¿Comprendes? Complete each sentence with **pero** or **sino (que)**.

1. No hace mucho sol hoy, _____ llueve.

2. Hay una heladera, _____ no hay refrescos.

Respuestas: 1. sino que; 2. pero

Aplicación

7-14 El meteorólogo. Selecciona la expresión apropiada para completar las oraciones sobre el pronóstico del tiempo.

no solo	pero	sino	sino que	también

1. Aquí en el mapa no hay muchas tormentas _____ sol.

2. Hoy no va a llover mucho, _____ va a hacer sol.

3. Hay humedad por la mañana, _____ va a salir el sol por la tarde.

4. En el norte, está nublado, _____ no hace mucho frío.

5. En la costa, no hace mucho calor _____ fresco.

6. Hace buen tiempo para nadar, _____ cuidado (*careful*) con los tiburones (*sharks*).

7. Por la lluvia en las montañas, no vas a dar un paseo, _____ vas a ver una película en casa.

8. Mañana, _____ voy a ir a la playa, _____ voy a nadar en el mar _____.

7-15 Planes para el fin de semana. En parejas, hagan planes para el fin de semana. Completen lógicamente cada frase con **pero** o **sino (que)** y añadan detalles.

MODELO: Normalmente tenemos que trabajar los sábados…

pero mañana es un día libre porque la jefa (boss) *está en el Caribe.*

1. No tenemos mucho dinero…

2. Vamos a invitar a nuestros amigos…

3. No vamos al cine…

4. Hace buen tiempo…

5. No vamos en carro…

6. Hay un buen concierto en el estadio…

7. Debemos volver temprano…

8. El domingo, no tenemos clase…

¡Conversemos!

Primero, pregúntate si puedes llevar a cabo (*carry out*) las siguientes funciones comunicativas en español. Después, júntate (*get together*) con dos o tres compañeros/as de clase para presentar las situaciones. Hagan y respondan a por lo menos cuatro preguntas en cada situación.

✓ CAN YOU . . .	WITH YOUR CLASSMATE(S) . . .
☐ talk about your free time?	**Situación: Con sus amigos.**
	Conversen sobre actividades que les gusta hacer en su tiempo libre. Expliquen dónde las hacen y por qué.
	Para empezar: *¿Qué prefieres hacer los viernes por la noche?*
☐ make plans to do something?	**Situación: Planes para salir este fin de semana.**
	Uno/a de Uds. tiene entradas para un evento especial. Hagan planes para ir juntos/as. Incluyan información sobre el evento: dónde y cuándo es, y lo que van a hacer después.
	Para empezar: *Tengo entradas para un concierto de Lady Gaga. ¿Qué tal si…?*
☐ talk about some activities in the past?	**Situación: Por teléfono.**
	Uno/a de Uds. llama a su amigo/a para hablar sobre lo que hicieron el fin de semana pasado. Usen verbos como **dar, estar, ir** y **haber** en el pretérito.
	Para empezar: *¿Qué tal fue tu fin de semana?*
☐ talk about indefinite people and things, and things that do not exist, and contrast ideas and descriptions?	**Situación: Solos en casa.**
	Conversen sobre lo que hacen en casa cuando no hay nadie. Usen expresiones negativas como **nadie** y **nunca**, y afirmativas como **alguien** y **siempre**. Usen también las conjunciones **pero** y **sino (que)**.
	Para empezar: *¿Qué haces cuando estás solo/a en casa? ¿Algo especial o nada en particular?*
	Nunca estoy solo/a en mi casa sino que siempre hago planes para salir con…

Perfiles

7.3 Read about Wi-Fi parks in Cuba and a world-famous Dominican artist

Mi experiencia

LOS PARQUES DE WIFI EN CUBA

7-16 **Para ti.** ¿Es importante para ti tener tus aparatos electrónicos a mano para comunicarte con tus amigos y familiares, subir (*upload*) información y fotos a las redes (*networks*) sociales y leer las noticias? ¿Cuál de estas actividades es la más indispensable para ti? Usar Internet en Cuba es posible, pero tiene sus desafíos, como nos explica Chela a continuación.

[1]*foreigners*

[2]*bandwidth*
[3]*slow*

[4]*card*

Hola, soy Chela y vivo en La Habana, Cuba. Muchas veces la gente de afuera[1] nos pregunta por qué no tenemos Internet en nuestras casas. Pues, la razón es porque, por ahora, el gobierno no nos lo permite. Solo tiene Internet un 5% de la población y para ello se necesita un permiso especial del gobierno. Sin embargo, aquí recientemente el gobierno está permitiendo áreas de wifi en algunos parques de la capital, así que por fin podemos conectarnos con amigos y familiares por correo electrónico, mensajes de texto y redes sociales. ¡Pero no creas que es fácil! Para empezar, los parques son muy populares y en las horas en las que van más personas, es casi imposible conectarse. Además, el ancho de nuestra banda[2] es peor que en otras partes del mundo, es decir, ¡es muy, muy lenta[3]! Otro problema es que para la mayoría de la población, cuesta un dineral, ¡dos dólares por hora y el salario promedio de un cubano es de 25 dólares al mes! Para poder tener acceso a Internet, tienes que comprar una tarjeta[4] de ETECSA (Telecomunicaciones de Cuba), la empresa oficial del gobierno; después, tienes que encontrar una zona de wifi, y finalmente, tienes que conectarte. Pero hay beneficios en esta metodología. Muchas veces en los parques de wifi te encuentras con amistades que no ves desde hace tiempo, y aunque no puedas conectarte a Internet, te conectas otra vez con ellas en persona. Esto también es muy lindo.

7-17 **En su opinión.** En parejas, comparen su experiencia usando wifi con la de Chela. ¿Qué tienen en común? ¿En qué se diferencian? Incluyan estos puntos de comparación:

- dónde conectarse
- su conexión en casa
- el costo del servicio
- la velocidad de su conexión
- sus redes sociales
- el contacto personal con otras personas

  MODELO: *Chela no tiene conexión en casa, pero yo sí la tengo...*

Mi música

"FRÍO, FRÍO" (JUAN LUIS GUERRA, LA REPÚBLICA DOMINICANA)

Juan Luis Guerra es uno de los artistas más exitosos del mundo hispano. Cantautor, compositor, productor y músico dominicano, es ganador de dos Grammy, 18 Grammy Latinos y dos Premios Latin Billboard. Estudió guitarra en Santo Domingo y, más tarde, jazz en el Berklee College of Music en Boston. En su música se ve la influencia de ritmos caribeños, especialmente del merengue y de la bachata. Sus letras son muchas veces muy líricas o metafóricas, y a veces políticas.

ANTES DE VER Y ESCUCHAR

7-18 ¿Cómo es su amor? Sigue los pasos para completar la actividad.

Paso 1 En la canción "Frío, frío", el cantautor hace contrastes para saber si su amada lo quiere. ¿Cuáles de estos contrastes son positivos y cuáles son negativos? ¿Cuál indica pasión? ¿Cuál indica desinterés?

- frío, frío
- caliente
- tibio (*lukewarm*)
- se enciende (*sets fire*)

Paso 2 Selecciona la expresión apropiada para completar las oraciones.

no solo	pero	sino	sino que	también

1. Su amor no es frío _____ caliente.

2. Su amor no es muy caliente, _____ es sincero.

3. Un beso tibio _____ lo anima, _____ le da esperanza _____.

PARA VER Y ESCUCHAR

7-19 La canción. Busca en Internet el video de "Frío, frío" en la que participa el neoyorquino Romeo Santos. ¿Cómo caracterizas su estilo? ¿Animado? ¿Romántico? ¿Triste? ¿Alegre? ¿Te gustaría asistir a un concierto de Juan Luis Guerra? Explica.

> 📍 **Busca:** Frío frío feat Romeo Santos; Frío frío letra

DESPUÉS DE VER Y ESCUCHAR

7-20 ¿Frío o caliente? Escribe un mínimo de cinco oraciones basadas en el video con expresiones negativas/afirmativas y **pero, sino (que)**. Puedes incluir algunos de estos elementos.

- los cantantes
- la banda
- la música, el ritmo
- los instrumentos
- el público
- la conexión entre los cantantes y el público

MODELO: *Los cantantes de acompañamiento no solo cantan sino que bailan también.*

7.2 Segunda parte

Vocabulario

7.4 Discuss sports you watch and those in which you participate

Los deportes y las actividades deportivas

Actividades deportivas. En el centro deportivo, los atletas hablan sobre sus actividades.

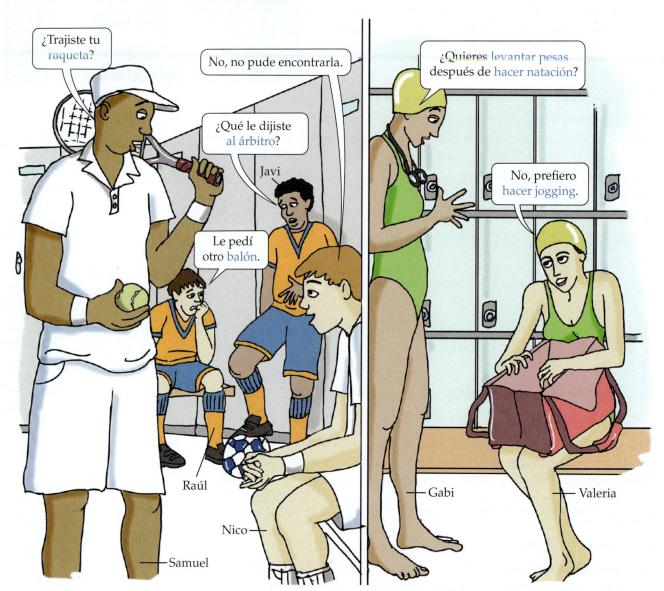

¿Trajiste tu raqueta?

No, no pude encontrarla.

¿Qué le dijiste al árbitro?

Javi

Le pedí otro balón.

¿Quieres levantar pesas después de hacer natación?

No, prefiero hacer jogging.

Raúl

Nico

Samuel

Gabi

Valeria

¿Comprendes? Select the person or people each sentence describes: **Gabi**, **Javi**, **Nico**, **Raúl**, **Samuel**, **Valeria**.

1. Está con traje de baño.

2. Va a jugar al tenis.

3. Va a hacer jogging después de nadar.

4. Habló con el árbitro.

Respuestas: 1. Gabi y Valeria; 2. Samuel; 3. Valeria; 4. Raúl

))) Vocabulario

Actividades deportivas	Sports activities
correr	to run
esquiar (en el agua)	to (water) ski
hacer...	to go/do . . .
alpinismo	mountain climbing
gimnasia deportiva	gymnastics
jogging	jogging
natación	swimming
jugar (ue) al...	to play . . .
básquetbol	basketball
béisbol	baseball
fútbol (americano)	soccer (football)
golf	golf
hockey	hockey
voleibol	volleyball
levantar pesas	to lift weights
montar en bicicleta	to go bike riding
patinar	to skate
practicar atletismo/ciclismo	to do track and field/cycling
surfear	to surf

Personas en los deportes	People in sports
el/la aficionado/a	fan
el/la árbitro/a	referee
el/la atleta	athlete
el/la campeón/campeona	champion, winner
el/la entrenador/a	coach, trainer
el equipo	team
el/la ganador/a	winner

Terminología deportiva	Sporting terminology
la carrera	race
el premio	prize
la temporada	season
el torneo	tournament

El equipo	Equipment
el balón	(soccer, basket) ball
el bate	bat
el guante	glove
el/los patín/patines	skate(s)
la pelota	baseball
la raqueta	racket

En las competencias	In competitions
competir (i, i)	to compete
empatar	to tie (the score)
ganar	to win
perder (ie)	to lose

Variaciones

- You will hear **el baloncesto** in Spain and in some parts of Latin America, instead of **el básquetbol**.
- **Hacer jogging** is used in Latin America, whereas **hacer footing** (from English *foot*) is used in Spain.

))) Letras y sonidos

The sequences *ca, co, cu, que, qui*, and *k* in Spanish

The letter **c** before the vowels **a**, **o**, and **u** sounds like the *c* in English *scan* in all varieties of Spanish. The combinations **que** and **qui** in Spanish, as well as the letter **k**, likewise correspond to the *c* sound in *scan*.

ca-lor   **co**-mi-da   **Cu**-ba   **que**-rer   **qui**-tar-se   **ki**-lo

Be careful not to pronounce the **u** in the sequences **que** and **qui** as a glide. For example, the first syllable in Spanish **qui-tar-se** sounds like English *key*, not *queen*.

Aplicación

7-21 Los deportistas. Selecciona el deporte que mejor corresponde a cada deportista.

¿Cuál de estos deportes haces tú?

1. _____ el/la beisbolista
2. _____ el/la esquiador/a
3. _____ el/la ciclista
4. _____ el/la futbolista
5. _____ el/la alpinista
6. _____ el/la gimnasta

a. montar en bicicleta
b. hacer alpinismo
c. jugar al fútbol
d. hacer gimnasia deportiva
e. jugar al béisbol
f. esquiar

Expansión   More on structure and usage

You can usually identify a person who plays a sport by the suffix **-dor/a** or **-ista**. For example, a person who plays (**jugar**), or practices a sport (**practicar deporte**), is **el/la jugador/a** or **el/la deportista**.

7-22 La mejor golfista mexicana. Aquí vas a saber más sobre una persona extraordinaria.

Paso 1   Selecciona la palabra lógica de la lista para completar el párrafo.

atleta	deporte	ganó	golfista	Premio
competir	Ganadora	golf	jugar	torneos

Según los críticos, Lorena Ochoa no solo es la mejor mujer (1) _____ mexicana de todos los tiempos, sino también la mejor golfista (hombre o mujer) de México. Ella nació y se crió en Guadalajara donde, a la edad de 5, empezó a (2) _____ al golf; a los 6 años empezó a (3) _____ en (4) _____. Ella dice que de niña, le gustaba (*she liked*) seguir a su padre por el campo de golf e imitar su manera de jugar. Los amigos de sus padres siempre le decían que el (5) _____ era un tipo de (6) _____ para los viejos, no para los niños, y especialmente no para las niñas. A la edad de 18, recibió una beca de la Universidad de Arizona y allí aprendió inglés viendo películas y leyendo revistas populares. Durante su estadía en la universidad, recibió el título de (7) _____ del Año de la NCAA por ser la atleta que ganó más torneos en un año. A los 21 años, fue nombrada Novata (*Rookie*) del Año por la LPGA. En México, fue la persona más joven en recibir el (8) _____ Nacional del Deporte, presentado por el presidente Vicente Fox. En su carrera de golfista profesional, (9) _____ el torneo de LPGA dos veces. Lorena Ochoa no es solo una (10) _____ extraordinaria, sino también una persona humanitaria por su fundación que se dedica a jóvenes golfistas mexicanas.

Paso 2   Contesta las preguntas basadas en la lectura.

1. ¿A qué edad empezó a jugar al golf?
2. ¿A qué edad empezó a competir en torneos?
3. ¿Cómo aprendió a hablar inglés?
4. ¿Cuáles son algunos de sus reconocimientos y premios?
5. ¿Por qué la consideran una persona humanitaria además de atleta?

Presencia hispana

There are many important female golfers from the Spanish-speaking world. In the U.S., **Nancy López** was a trailblazer in women's golf in the 1980s, earning 35 tour victories by the age of 30. Two current players are Californian **Lizette Salas**, who graduated from USC, and New Mexican **Gerina Mendoza Piller**, who graduated from UT Austin. Is golf an important women's or men's sport at your university?

7-23 Los deportes. Escucha a Raquel y a Tomás mientras hablan de los deportes que les interesan y que practican. Indica qué descripciones le corresponden a cada uno. Si alguna descripción no le corresponde a ninguno, indica **ninguno**.

	Raquel	Tomás	Ninguno
1. Juega al béisbol.	_____	_____	_____
2. Juega al tenis.	_____	_____	_____
3. Monta en bicicleta.	_____	_____	_____
4. Practica atletismo.	_____	_____	_____
5. Ve el hockey.	_____	_____	_____
6. Es campeón/campeona.	_____	_____	_____
7. Es entrenador/a.	_____	_____	_____
8. Ve la natación en los Juegos Olímpicos.	_____	_____	_____

7-24 ¿Qué hacemos? En parejas, decidan qué deporte quieren hacer, qué necesitan para hacerlo, dónde lo van a hacer y cuándo. Usa las categorías como guía.

MODELO: ESTUDIANTE 1: *¿Quieres hacer alpinismo?*
ESTUDIANTE 2: *¿Qué equipo necesitamos?*
ESTUDIANTE 1: *Necesitamos guantes, botas* (boots) *fuertes y lentes de sol.*
¿Dónde lo hacemos?...

Deporte	Equipo	¿Dónde?	¿Cuándo?
hacer alpinismo	bicicletas	en el campo	ahora mismo
hacer jogging	guantes, botas fuertes	en el gimnasio	el sábado
jugar al tenis	y lentes de sol	en el océano	en diciembre
levantar pesas	pesas	en la cancha	en la primavera
montar en bicicleta	raquetas	en la playa Luquillo	en verano
nadar	trajes de baño	en las montañas	esta tarde
surfear	una tabla (*surfboard*)	por el parque	mañana
	zapatillas de deporte (*athletic shoes*)		

7-25 ¿Cuál es su deporte favorito? En parejas, hablen de los deportes que les gusta ver y los que les gusta practicar. Usen las preguntas como guía y luego preparen un resumen al final.

MODELO: ESTUDIANTE 1: *¿Cuál es tu deporte favorito?*
ESTUDIANTE 2: *Me gusta nadar en verano y…*

- ¿Cuál es tu deporte favorito?
- ¿Dónde y con qué frecuencia lo practicas? ¿O prefieres mirarlo en lugar de practicarlo?
- ¿Con quién lo practicas? ¿Es un deporte individual o de equipo?
- ¿Qué equipo necesitas? (ropa especial, balón etc.)
- ¿Cuál es el nombre del equipo o de tu deportista favorito/a que practica este deporte?

Estructuras

7.5 **Talk about other activities in the past, and take shortcuts in conversation**

More strong preterit verbs

¿Recuerdas? Complete the dialogues with the correct preterit form of **estar**, **ir**, **tener**, **ver**.

—¿Dónde (1) _____ (tú) ayer?

—En casa. (2) _____ que ayudar a mi mamá.

—¿(3) _____ Uds. al concierto de Pitbull?

—No, pero lo (4) _____ en la televisión.

Respuestas: 1. estuviste; 2. Tuve; 3. Fueron; 4. vimos

Like the verbs you practiced in **Primera parte**, several other common verbs have irregular stems and special endings in the preterit.

	poder	poner	saber	venir	hacer	querer	decir	traer
	Strong preterit forms							
yo	**pud**e	**pus**e	**sup**e	**vin**e	**hic**e	**quis**e	**dij**e	**traj**e
tú	**pud**iste	**pus**iste	**sup**iste	**vin**iste	**hic**iste	**quis**iste	**dij**iste	**traj**iste
Ud.	**pud**o	**pus**o	**sup**o	**vin**o	**hiz**o	**quis**o	**dij**o	**traj**o
él/ella	**pud**o	**pus**o	**sup**o	**vin**o	**hiz**o	**quis**o	**dij**o	**traj**o
nosotros/as	**pud**imos	**pus**imos	**sup**imos	**vin**imos	**hic**imos	**quis**imos	**dij**imos	**traj**imos
vosotros/as	**pud**isteis	**pus**isteis	**sup**isteis	**vin**isteis	**hic**isteis	**quis**isteis	**dij**isteis	**traj**isteis
Uds.	**pud**ieron	**pus**ieron	**sup**ieron	**vin**ieron	**hic**ieron	**quis**ieron	**dij**eron	**traj**eron
ellos/as	**pud**ieron	**pus**ieron	**sup**ieron	**vin**ieron	**hic**ieron	**quis**ieron	**dij**eron	**traj**eron

¿Dónde pusiste el balón?

- The preterit forms of **poder**, **poner**, and **saber** have a **u** in the stem.

Pude ir a la piscina.	*I got to go to the pool.*
¿Por qué **pusiste** la toalla allí?	*Why did you put the towel there?*
Supimos quién ganó enseguida.	*We found out (learned about) who won right away.*

- The preterit forms of **venir**, **hacer**, and **querer** have an **i** in the stem.

¿**Vino** Julio al partido ayer?	*Did Julio come to the game yesterday?*
¿Dónde **hicieron** los uniformes?	*Where did they make the uniforms?*
Quise patear el balón, pero no pude.	*I wanted to kick the soccer ball, but I failed.*

- Whenever the stem of a verb in the preterit ends in **j**, as in **decir** and **traer**, the third-person plural ends in **-eron**, not **-ieron**.

Los beisbolistas **dijeron** cosas buenas del entrenador.	*The baseball players said good things about the trainer.*
Trajeron los esquís al comienzo de la temporada.	*They brought their skis at the beginning of the season.*

SIGNIFICADOS ESPECIALES EN EL PRETÉRITO

Certain verbs in Spanish have different connotations when used in the preterit.

	Present	Preterit
conocer	*know someone (be acquainted)*	*met (for the first time; beginning of knowing)*
	Conozco *a Draco Rosa.*	*Lo* **conocí** *después de su concierto.*
	I know Draco Rosa.	*I met him after his concert.*
poder (ue)	*be able (have the ability)*	*managed (to do something)*
	Podemos *ir al partido.*	**Pudimos** *comprar entradas.*
	We can go to the game.	*We managed to buy tickets.*
no poder (ue)	*not be able (without necessarily trying)*	*failed (after trying) (to do something)*
	No **puedes** *salir ahora.*	**No pudiste** *terminar tu tarea.*
	You can't go out now.	*You failed to finish your homework.*
(no) querer (ie)	*(not) want*	*tried (refused)*
	Uds. **(no) quieren** *ir a patinar.*	*Uds.* **quisieron** *encontrar sus patines.* **No quisieron** *ir sin ellos.*
	You (don't) want to go skating.	*You tried to find your skates. You refused to go without them.*
saber	*know (a fact, how to do something)*	*found out, learned*
	Sé *que hay un partido hoy.*	*Lo* **supe** *esta mañana.*
	I know there's a game today.	*I found out this morning.*

¿Comprendes? Complete the sentence with the preterit of **poder** and **traer**.

Ayer Juan (1) _____ jugar al tenis porque (2) _____ su raqueta a la cancha.

Respuestas: 1. pudo; 2. trajo

Aplicación

7-26 Una superestrella está en Puerto Rico. Aquí tienes un artículo publicado en un periódico digital de Puerto Rico.

Paso 1 Lee el artículo y selecciona el verbo más lógico para completarlo.

Paso 2 Contesta las preguntas, basándote en el artículo.

1. ¿Quién estuvo en Puerto Rico? ¿Por qué es famoso?
2. ¿Qué hizo allí?
3. ¿Cuándo supo su tía que estaba (*he was*) allá?
4. ¿A quiénes más vio?
5. ¿Qué le dijo a la tía?
6. ¿Qué le trajo?

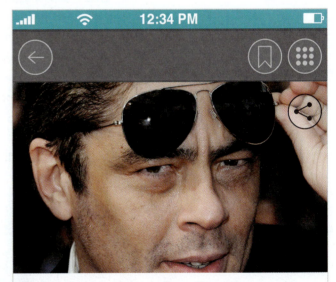

¡Benicio vuelve a San Juan!

Hoy, sábado, llegó el famoso actor y director puertorriqueño Benicio del Toro a la capital. (1) Dijo/Vino a asistir a la fiesta de cumpleaños de su querida tía. Ella no (2) quiso/supo de su presencia hasta la última hora. El actor no (3) quiso/supo revelarle sus planes. (4) Prefirió/Hizo darle la sorpresa. La primera cosa que (5) hizo/puso al llegar fue ir directamente a su casa en Santurce donde (6) dijo/vio a su tía junto con el resto de la familia. Su tía no lo (7) hizo/pudo creer. Benicio le (8) dijo/trajo, "Tía, ¡feliz cumpleaños!" De regalos, le (9) quiso/trajo un bello ramo de flores y un bolso de Carolina Herrera. Según su publicista, Benicio (10) hizo/tuvo que volver a Los Ángeles ayer para trabajar en la película *Avengers: Infinity War.*

7-27 Pero ayer... Completa las oraciones, indicando por qué ayer fue diferente. Usa pronombres de complemento directo cuando sea apropiado.

> MODELO: Siempre hago ejercicio antes de salir para clase, pero ayer...
> *Siempre hago ejercicio antes de salir para clase, pero ayer no lo hice.*

1. Siempre puedo encontrar a la entrenadora en el gimnasio, pero ayer...
2. Todos los días tenemos noticias deportivas en la radio, pero ayer...
3. Todos los días mis padres quieren asistir a los partidos, pero ayer...
4. Todas las tardes los deportistas hacen ejercicio, pero ayer...
5. Generalmente, los aficionados se ponen contentos, pero ayer
6. Casi nunca sé quién gana el partido, pero ayer...
7. Por lo general, los padres traen refrescos para después del partido, pero ayer...
8. Casi siempre podemos ver el partido en la televisión, pero ayer...

7-28 ¿Qué pasó en los Juegos Olímpicos? Lee sobre diferentes atletas que participaron en las últimas Olimpíadas. Completa las oraciones con el verbo más lógico en el pretérito. Usa el pronombre reflexivo si es necesario.

> MODELO: Un beisbolista dominicano ___*trajo*___ su guante favorito al partido.

| conocer | hacer | poder | ponerse | querer | saber | venir |

1. En la competencia de natación, nosotros _____ los nombres de los nadadores, pero no los _____.
2. En gimnasia deportiva, Gabriela _____ un traje de lentejuelas (*sequins*).
3. En patinaje, Carlos no _____ clasificar (*qualify*) y quedó fuera de la competencia.
4. En ciclismo, los españoles _____ lo posible para ganar.
5. Al final del partido de tenis entre la alemana y la rusa, el árbitro _____ a hablar con ellas.
6. Tú _____ pedirle el autógrafo a la ganadora.

Los Juegos Olímpicos de 2016 fueron en Río de Janeiro, Brasil.

7-29 ¿Qué hiciste? En parejas, túrnense para contar lo que hicieron el fin de semana pasado. Usen un mínimo de cinco de estos verbos: **conocer, dar, decir, estar, ir, poder, querer, tener, ver**. Después, resuman sus actividades para la clase.

> MODELO: ESTUDIANTE 1: *¿Qué hiciste el fin de semana pasado?*
> ESTUDIANTE 2: *Fui a... Vi a... (No) pude...*

Double object pronouns

¿Recuerdas? Complete the dialogues with the correct direct or indirect object pronoun.

—¿(1) _____ diste una flor a tu novia?

—No. (2) _____ di una pelota para jugar al béisbol.

—¿Vieron Uds. el partido entre España y Portugal?

—Sí, (3) _____ vimos en la televisión.

Respuestas: 1. Le; 2. Le; 3. lo

You can take shortcuts in conversation and avoid repeating noun objects by using two object pronouns in Spanish as in English.

| ¿Me das la toalla? | *Sí*, **te la** *doy*. |
| *Will you give me the towel?* | *Yes, I'll give* **it to you***. / I'll give* **you it***.* |

Subject pronouns	Indirect object pronouns	Direct object pronouns
yo	me	me
tú	te	te
Ud.	le (*changes to* **se**)	lo/la
él/ella	le (*changes to* **se**)	lo/la
nosotros/as	nos	nos
vosotros/as	os	os
Uds.	les (*changes to* **se**)	los/las
ellos/ellas	les (*changes to* **se**)	los/las

¿Me prestas tu raqueta?

¡Claro! Te la presto.

- When using both pronouns, place the indirect object pronoun before the direct object pronoun.

| Julián, ¿me traes la película? | *Julián, will you bring me the movie?* |
| **Te la** traigo en un momento. | *I'll bring it to you in a moment.* |

- When you attach the pronouns to the infinitive or the present participle, keep the order of the pronouns and add an accent mark to the stressed vowel of the verb.

Carlos, ¿puedes **traerme** la bolsa?	*Carlos, can you bring me the bag?*
Voy a **traértela** enseguida.	*I'll bring it to you right away.*
Estoy **buscándotela** ahora mismo.	*I am looking for it right now for you.*

- Change the indirect object pronoun **le** or **les** to **se** when it precedes a direct object pronoun beginning with **l** (**lo/la/los/las**). Rely on the context of the previous statement to clarify the meaning of **se**.

| ¿Quién **les** trae el balón a los jugadores? | *Who brings the ball to the players?* |
| El entrenador **se lo** trae. | *The coach is bringing it to them.* |

STUDY TIPS – USING DIRECT AND INDIRECT OBJECTS TOGETHER

Here are a few strategies to help you with this structure.

1. Review the use of direct objects and direct object pronouns (see **Capítulo 4**, pages 119–120) and indirect objects and indirect object pronouns (see **Capítulo 6**, pages 186–187).

2. Remember to always combine double object pronouns in the right order: indirect before direct.

3. Become familiar with the sound pronouns make together by repeating out loud phrases such as the following: **(Juan da el libro): me lo da, te lo da, se lo da, nos lo da, os lo da, se lo da.**

¿Comprendes? Restate these sentences using double object pronouns.

1. El árbitro le da el balón al jugador. → _____
2. Mis amigos me compran el refresco. → _____
3. Estoy leyéndoles las biografías de los jugadores a mis amigos. → _____

Respuestas: 1. Se lo da.; 2. Me lo compran.; 3. Estoy leyéndoselas. / Se las estoy leyendo.

Aplicación

7-30 En el gimnasio. Emilia ayuda al entrenador a poner en orden el equipo en el gimnasio. Selecciona la respuesta apropiada que corresponde a cada pregunta de Emilia.

1. _____ ¿Quién tiene las pelotas de béisbol? Tomás, ¿dónde las pusiste?

   a. Claro, vamos a preparársela para las dos de la tarde.

2. _____ ¿Dónde está el balón?

   b. Creo que están aquí. Se los puse en la mesa.

3. _____ El entrenador necesita los guantes.

   c. Sí, se las traemos a Uds. enseguida.

4. _____ Los chicos quieren saber dónde están las raquetas de tenis.

   d. Se las puse en la cancha de tenis esta mañana.

5. _____ ¿Nos traen Uds. las botellas de agua?

   e. Te las puse a ti en la bolsa con los bates.

6. _____ ¿Van Uds. a prepararnos la merienda después del partido?

   f. No sé, pero te lo busco ahora mismo.

7-31 Antes de la carrera. Daniela va a competir en una carrera de ciclismo.

Paso 1 Lee lo que dicen Daniela y su entrenador y selecciona los pronombres directos e indirectos más lógicos según el contexto para completar la conversación. Luego indica cuál es directo y cuál indirecto.

> **MODELO:** Necesito guantes. ¿A quién <u>se los</u>/se las pido?
> *se: indirecto (a quién); los: directo (los guantes)*

DANIELA: Sebastián, ¿me pasas la botella de agua, por favor?

ENTRENADOR: Ahora mismo (1) me la/te la doy, Daniela.

DANIELA: Después, ¿me buscas las barras de proteína? Debes (2) pedírselas/pedírtelas a mi mamá.

ENTRENADOR: ¿Quieres tus lentes ahora?

DANIELA: Sí, por favor, debes (3) traérselos/traérmelos ahora. Y aquí tienes mi teléfono para sacarme muchas fotos en la meta (*finish line*).

ENTRENADOR: Buena idea, Daniela. (4) Se las/Te las saco con mucho gusto. ¡Buena suerte!

Paso 2   Contesta las preguntas, según la conversación anterior. Usa pronombres de complemento directo e indirecto en tus respuestas cuando sea necesario.

1. ¿Quién tiene la botella de agua?

2. ¿A quién se la da?

3. ¿Qué va a comer Daniela?

4. ¿A quién debe pedírselas?

5. ¿Por qué Daniela le da su teléfono al entrenador?

7-32 De viaje en la República Dominicana. Haz el papel de turista en la República Dominicana y responde a las preguntas del guía (*guide*), usando los pronombres de complemento indirecto y directo.

> **MODELO:**   GUÍA: ¿Le doy información sobre el lugar que visitamos?
>
> TÚ: Sí, ¿puede usted dár*mela* ahora?

1. GUÍA: ¿Quiere ver el restaurante donde vamos a cenar?

   TÚ: Sí, ¿_____ enseña ahora?

2. GUÍA: ¿Le traigo las guías turísticas?

   TÚ: No, no es necesario traér_____.

3. GUÍA: ¿Quiere conocer el primer hospital del Nuevo Mundo?

   TÚ: ¡Sí! ¿_____ enseña ahora?

4. GUÍA: ¿Les traigo a ustedes los refrescos?

   TÚ: No, no tenemos sed. No tiene que traér_____.

5. GUÍA: ¿Le doy una propina al mesero?

   TÚ: Buena idea. Debe dár_____ ahora.

6. GUÍA: ¿Les preparo un cóctel a ustedes?

   TÚ: No, gracias. No es necesario preparár_____.

7-33A ¡Necesito información! Ustedes son entrenadores/as que están preparándose para un partido en otra ciudad. Túrnense para preguntarse si tienen los objetos que necesitan y si pueden dárselos, o si no, buscárselos. Luego, hagan una lista de las cosas que tienen que buscar. **Estudiante B**: ve al **Apéndice 1**, página A-8.

> **MODELO:**   ESTUDIANTE A: (la bolsa) *¿Tienes la bolsa?*
>
> ESTUDIANTE B: *Sí, la tengo. Te la doy. / No, no la tengo. Te la busco.*

Estudiante A:

Necesitas	Tienes
el guante	la raqueta
el balón	el bate de aluminio
los lentes de sol	la heladera

Cultura en vivo

It is less common for universities in the Spanish-speaking world to have sports teams like those in the U.S. Instead, young people join clubs or organize informal games with friends. Are sports teams important in your university?

7-34 En el campamento de verano. Ustedes son consejeros/as (*counselors*) en un campamento de verano. En parejas, túrnense para pedir varias cosas y decir si pueden dárselas o no.

> **MODELO:** ESTUDIANTE 1: *¿Me traes los bates?*
>
> ESTUDIANTE 2: *¡Claro! Te los traigo ahora. / Lo siento, no puedo traértelos.*

1. ¿Me das la toalla?
2. ¿Me preparas un café?
3. ¿Nos buscas la pelota?
4. ¿Les das los esquís a los chicos?
5. ¿Te doy la bolsa?
6. ¿Te pido las pesas?

¡Conversemos!

Primero, pregúntate si puedes llevar a cabo (*carry out*) las siguientes funciones comunicativas en español. Después, júntate (*get together*) con dos o tres compañeros/as de clase para presentar las situaciones. Hagan y respondan a por lo menos cuatro preguntas en cada situación.

✓ CAN YOU...

☐ discuss different sports?

☐ talk about activities in the past?

☐ take shortcuts in conversation?

WITH YOUR CLASSMATE(S)...

Situación: Sus gustos.

Conversen sobre los deportes que les gusta ver y jugar, y cuándo los hacen. Hablen también sobre los que no les gustan y por qué.

Para empezar: *¿Qué deportes...? ¿Te gusta hacer/jugar al...? ¿Prefieres... o...?*

Situación: En una gran reunión familiar.

Hablen de personas que conocieron y cosas que supieron en una reunión familiar que tuvieron el año pasado. Usen verbos como **poder, poner, saber, venir, hacer, querer, decir** y **traer** para hablar sobre esta reunión.

Para empezar: *¿Qué tal tu reunión familiar? ¿Qué hiciste?*

Situación: En el gimnasio.

Están haciendo ejercicio en un gimnasio. Pídanse artículos deportivos que necesitan, y contesten usando los dos pronombres indirectos y directos.

Para empezar: *¿Me das la pelota? Sí, te la doy.*

Club cultura

7.6 Listen and watch for purpose

Cuba: La influencia africana

Estrategia para ver

Listen and watch for purpose. When you watch a video, one of your first tasks is to discover what its purpose is: To educate about a topic? To sell something? To report a news item? To entertain? To persuade? What is the presenter's tone of voice like: humorous, serious, formal, or informal? Recognizing the purpose of a video and the speaker's tone will help you understand the message.

ANTES DE VER EL VIDEO

7-35 La herencia africana. En este video vas a ver cómo la herencia africana se manifiesta en algunos aspectos de la cultura cubana. Haz una lista de cinco aspectos de la herencia y de la cultura que esperas ver.

> **MODELO:**   *1. la comida…*

AL VER EL VIDEO

7-36 La cultura africana. Mira el segmento sobre Cuba para ver cuáles de los aspectos culturales que identificaste aparecen en el video.

DESPUÉS DE VER EL VIDEO

7-37 La influencia africana en Cuba. Indica cuáles de estos aspectos se mencionan o se ven en el video. ¿En cuál se ve la mayor influencia, según el video?

1. el arte	**Sí**	**No**
2. la música	**Sí**	**No**
3. el baile	**Sí**	**No**
4. el comunismo	**Sí**	**No**
5. la comida	**Sí**	**No**
6. los deportes	**Sí**	**No**

7-38 El propósito del video. ¿Cuál es el propósito del video: educar, persuadir, vender algo, entretener? ¿Cómo es el tono de voz de la presentadora: alegre, serio, sarcástico, formal, informal? ¿Qué imágenes del video te impresionan más? ¿Por qué?

7-39 Un viaje a Cuba. Imagínate que vas a hacer un viaje cultural a Cuba. ¿Cuáles de los aspectos del video esperas conocer? ¿Hay otros aspectos no mencionados en el video que también te interesan, por ejemplo, la economía, el transporte, la política, los deportes? ¿Por qué?

7.3 Nuestro mundo

Panoramas

7.7 **Identify and research some important cultural aspects of Cuba, Puerto Rico, and the Dominican Republic**

Joyas del Caribe: Cuba, Puerto Rico y la República Dominicana

Hay mucho que disfrutar (*enjoy*) en las islas del Caribe: el clima, las playas, la historia, y sobre todo, la gente.

Las playas de la República Dominicana, con su arena blanca y su agua tibia y cristalina, son ideales para tomar el sol, nadar, bucear (*snorkle*), esquiar sobre el agua y hacer paravelismo (*parasailing*).

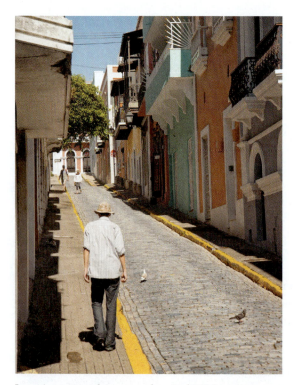

La mejor manera de conocer el centro histórico es a pie (*by foot*). Es agradable dar un paseo y observar las casas multicolores del Viejo San Juan.

El fuerte (*fortress*) San Felipe del Morro (o simplemente, El Morro) fue construido por los españoles en el siglo XVI para proteger la entrada a la bahía. Hoy, es un lugar popular los fines de semana para hacer un pícnic y para volar un papalote (o volar chiringa, como dicen en Puerto Rico).

Los ritmos musicales y el baile tienen un papel importante en la vida diaria de la gente. Es común encontrar músicos en la calle y ver a la gente bailar en los restaurantes y clubes, como en este en La Habana, Cuba.

El amor al béisbol se extiende por las tres islas, donde las academias de béisbol entrenan a los jóvenes que sueñan con jugar algún día en las Grandes Ligas.

	Cuba	Puerto Rico	República Dominicana
Población:	11,2 millones	3,6 millones	10,6 millones
Beisbolistas en las Grandes Ligas:	39	38	183
Medallas olímpicas:	220	9	7
Gobierno:	estado comunista	estado libre asociado[1]	república democrática

[1]*commonwealth*

7-40 Identifica. Identifica la información según **Panoramas**.

1. lo que atrae a muchos turistas a las islas
2. la mejor manera de conocer el centro histórico
3. el país con el mayor número de beisbolistas en las Grandes Ligas
4. un pasatiempo agradable los domingos en Puerto Rico
5. lo que se oye en las calles y en los clubes

7-41 Desafío. Identifica el país o estado que corresponde a cada descripción.

1. el nombre de la isla más grande del Caribe
2. los dos países que ocupan la isla de La Española
3. la península estadounidense cerca de Cuba
4. la isla cuyos (*whose*) habitantes son ciudadanos de Estados Unidos

7-42 Investigación: Las islas hispánicas del Caribe. Investiga en Internet uno de estos temas u otro que te interese: **un deporte popular, un/a deportista famoso/a, la música, el baile**. Usa el modelo para escribir un informe. Luego preséntaselo a la clase. Incluye:

- su nombre y de dónde es
- por qué es importante o interesante
- cómo es
- si quieres conocerlo o practicarlo algún día y por qué
- si piensas estudiar más sobre este tema
- una foto representativa

> **Busca:** deportes populares / deportista famoso / música / baile (Cuba, Puerto Rico, la República Dominicana)

MODELO: *Winifer Fernández es una jugadora de voleibol que participó en los Juegos Olímpicos de 2016. Es dominicana y tiene mucho talento. Muchas personas dicen que es la jugadora más...*

Páginas

7.8 Deal with unknown words

El sueño de las Grandes Ligas

Estrategia para leer

Deal with unknown words. Use these strategies to avoid getting overwhelmed by unknown vocabulary:

1. Look at the word to see if it's familiar in any way. Is it a verb, a noun, or an adjective? Is it a compound word with a part that you recognize?

2. Reread the sentence to see if the context helps you guess the meaning.

3. Say the word aloud. Sometimes hearing the pronunciation will clarify its meaning.

4. Make note of the word, so you can check the meaning later. Then keep reading.

5. If you simply can't go on without knowing a word, look it up, but be sure that you choose the most logical translation (or part of speech) for the context of the reading.

6. Reread the article and summarize it in your own words. Make note of the words you were able to guess by using these strategies.

ANTES DE LEER

7-43 ¿Qué significa? Busca estas palabras en la lectura y usa las estrategias para adivinar (*guess*) su significado.

1. Grandes Ligas

2. pelotero

3. academias

4. cazatalentos

5. lanzador

6. reclutan

AL LEER

7-44 El artículo. Mientras lees el artículo, identifica las palabras que puedes adivinar por el contexto y las que tienes que buscar en un diccionario.

http://deportes.rped.com/el-sueño-de-las-grandes-ligas

Fútbol | NFL | Boxeo | Básquetbol | Lucha Libre | Béisbol   Ver | Audio | Juegos   Entrar

Portada | Resultados | Ligas | Calendario | Clubes | Posiciones | Todos los torneos | Altas y bajas

El sueño de las Grandes Ligas

¿Sueñas con jugar en las Grandes Ligas? ¿Quieres entrenarte para ser pelotero y ganar más de medio millón de dólares el primer año? Entonces, tienes que trasladarte a la República Dominicana, donde hay 30 academias de béisbol para jóvenes de 12 a 20 años, quienes tienen casi todos el sueño de jugar con un equipo profesional estadounidense, canadiense o japonés.

SuperDeportes Digital

Aquí no es raro ver a cazatalentos de los varios equipos observando el entrenamiento de los jóvenes que pasan horas practicando el deporte. De hecho[1], la mayoría de los jugadores dominicanos en las Grandes Ligas fueron descubiertos en una academia dominicana, entre ellos Pedro Martínez, el lanzador de los Red Sox, cinco veces miembro del equipo All-Star y hoy miembro del Salón de la Fama. Todos los años, los equipos reclutan entre 450 a 500 jugadores dominicanos de las academias. Y estas, por los costos de construcción y el empleo de gente local, contribuyen más de 170 millones de dólares a la economía local.

Hay personas que señalan que las academias les dan una ilusión falsa a los jóvenes jugadores, y es verdad que ha habido[2] abusos en el pasado. Pero hoy en día, las academias también son un lugar donde ellos reciben techo[3], comida y una educación, además del entrenamiento. Por eso, especialmente para jóvenes de bajos recursos, esto puede ser una vía para realizar el sueño de su vida.

[1]*In fact*

[2]*there have been*
[3]*place to live* (lit., *roof*)

DESPUÉS DE LEER

7-45 El sueño dominicano. Selecciona la expresión apropiada para completar cada oración.

la economía	el entrenamiento	un equipo	las Grandes Ligas	una ilusión

1. Muchos jóvenes dominicanos sueñan con jugar en _____.

2. En las academias, los cazatalentos observan _____ de los beisbolistas.

3. Algunos de los jugadores dominicanos llegan a ser miembros de _____ estadounidense, canadiense o japonés.

4. Las academias emplean a gente local, lo que contribuye a _____.

5. Algunos dicen que las academias dan _____ falsa.

7-46 Un resumen. Escribe un párrafo para resumir el artículo con tus propias palabras.

MODELO: *Las academias de béisbol en la República Dominicana…*

7-47 Buscar el sueño. En parejas, conversen sobre las ventajas y las desventajas de las academias deportivas (por ejemplo, de natación, de fútbol, de gimnasia deportiva, etc.). ¿Les dan un sueño falso a los jóvenes? ¿Hay algunas mejores que otras?

MODELO: *Creo que las academias de gimnasia deportiva…*

Taller

7.9 Use transitional expressions

Un anuncio publicitario

Estrategia para escribir

Use transitional expressions. Your writing flows more naturally when you use transitional expressions to introduce, connect, and summarize your thoughts, such as: **para empezar** (*to begin*), **aunque** (*although*), **entonces** (*then*), **por ejemplo** (*for example*), **por eso** (*therefore*), **al mismo tiempo** (*at the same time*), **para concluir** (*in conclusion*), and so on.

7-48 **Diseñar un anuncio.** En esta actividad, vas a diseñar un anuncio publicitario para convencer a la gente de que vaya a una de las islas del Caribe que estudiaste en este capítulo para asistir a una academia deportiva.

ANTES DE ESCRIBIR

Anota información sobre el lugar: ¿Qué es? ¿Para quiénes es? ¿Cuándo es? ¿Dónde está? ¿Cómo es el lugar, el clima, etc.? ¿Cuáles son algunos de los atractivos (*attractions*) del sitio? ¿Cuáles son los beneficios personales y profesionales? Luego, agrega una oración final para resumir y convencer por qué uno/a debe ir.

AL ESCRIBIR

El anuncio. Usa las expresiones de **Estrategia para escribir** para presentar, conectar y resumir tus ideas. Incluye una foto, ilustración o video representativo.

MODELO:

¡TRIUNFA EN EL TRIUNFO!

¿Quieres aprender a hacer gimnasia deportiva en la playa?

Debes venir a Puerto Rico, donde hace sol todo el año. Para empezar, aquí en la academia deportiva **El Triunfo** tenemos los mejores entrenadores del deporte; por ejemplo, el entrenador del equipo estadounidense para los Juegos Olímpicos. Además, tenemos excelentes instalaciones para entrenar: un gimnasio, una piscina y una playa… Para concluir, en **El Triunfo**, ¡vas a triunfar!

Llama sin cargo al: 866-555-5555

DESPUÉS DE ESCRIBIR

- **Revisar.** Revisa tu anuncio para ver si fluye bien. Luego, revisa la mecánica.
  - ☐ ¿Incluiste una variedad de vocabulario de este capítulo?
  - ☐ ¿Incluiste expresiones para presentar, conectar y resumir tus ideas?
  - ☐ ¿Verificaste la ortografía y la concordancia?
- **Intercambiar.** Intercambia tu anuncio con el de un/a compañero/a. Mientras leen los anuncios, hagan comentarios y sugerencias sobre el contenido, la estructura y la gramática.
- **Entregar.** Prepara la versión final de tu anuncio publicitario, incorporando las sugerencias de tu compañero/a. Después, entrégaselo a tu profesor/a.

En este capítulo...

))) Vocabulario

Primera parte

En la playa	At the beach
la bolsa	bag
la heladera	cooler
el hielo	ice
los lentes de natación/sol	swim goggles / sunglasses
la sombrilla	umbrella
la toalla	towel
el traje de baño	swimsuit

Los pasatiempos	Pastimes
chatear	to chat
dar un paseo	to go out, to take a walk
escuchar música	to listen to music
hacer un pícnic	to have a picnic
hacer yoga	to do yoga
ir a una discoteca / un festival / un concierto	to go to a (night)club/festival/concert
jugar a videojuegos / al tenis, etc.	to play videogames/tennis, etc.
leer una novela / las noticias / una revista	to read a novel / the news / a magazine
nadar en el mar / una piscina	to swim in the ocean / a swimming pool
pasar tiempo con amigos	to spend time with friends
salir a comer	to go out to eat
volar (ue) un papalote	to fly a kite

¿Qué tiempo hace?	What is the weather like?
Está nublado.	It's cloudy.
Hace...	It's . . .
buen/mal tiempo.	good/bad weather.
(mucho) calor.	(very) hot.
fresco.	cool.
(mucho) frío.	(very) cold.
(mucha) humedad.	(very) humid.
(mucho) sol.	(very) sunny.
(mucho) viento.	(very) windy.
llover (ue)	to rain
nevar (ie)	to snow

Hacer planes	To make plans
Es un día perfecto para...	It's a perfect day for . . .
¡Fabuloso!	Fabulous! Great!
Me da igual.	It's all the same to me.
pasarlo bien/mal	to have a good/bad time
¡Qué mala suerte!	What bad luck!
¿Qué tal si...?	What if . . . ?

Segunda parte

Actividades deportivas	Sports activities
correr	to run
esquiar (en el agua)	to (water) ski
hacer...	to go/do . . .
alpinismo	mountain climbing
gimnasia deportiva	gymnastics
jogging	jogging
natación	swimming
jugar (ue) al...	to play . . .
básquetbol	basketball
béisbol	baseball
fútbol (americano)	soccer (football)
golf	golf
hockey	hockey
voleibol	volleyball
levantar pesas	to lift weights
montar en bicicleta	to go bike riding
patinar	to skate
practicar atletismo/ciclismo	to do track and field / cycling
surfear	to surf

Personas en los deportes	People in sports
el/la aficionado/a	fan
el/la árbitro/a	referee
el/la atleta	athlete
el/la campeón/campeona	champion, winner
el/la entrenador/a	coach, trainer
el equipo	team
el/la ganador/a	winner

Terminología deportiva	Sporting terminology
la carrera	race
el premio	prize
la temporada	season
el torneo	tournament

El equipo	Equipment
el balón	(soccer, basket) ball
el bate	bat
el guante	glove
el/los patín/patines	skate(s)
la pelota	baseball
la raqueta	racket

En las competencias	In competitions
competir (i, i)	to compete
empatar	to tie (the score)
ganar	to win
perder (ie)	to lose

Indefinite and negative expressions *See page 223.*
Pero or *sino (que)* *See page 226.*
Double object pronouns *See page 237.*

Capítulo 8
¿En qué puedo servirle?

«Quien compra ha de tener cien ojos; a quien vende le basta uno solo».

Freddy Toledo, www.freddytoledo.com

Mercado andino **de Freddy Toledo.** The colors and images of this work draw us into a typical market in the Andes of Peru or Ecuador. What items are for sale? How are the people dressed?

Learning Objectives

8.1 Talk about clothes and shopping at a department store

8.2 Describe and narrate in the past, and put things in order

8.3 Learn about shopping in Peru and traditional Andean music

8.4 Shop for personal care products and jewelry

8.5 Narrate in the past, and talk about what people say and believe

8.6 Use images to support narration

8.7 Identify and research some important cultural aspects of Peru and Ecuador

8.8 Step into a character

8.9 Use conventions of storytelling

In this Chapter

ENFOQUE CULTURAL: ECUADOR
Club cultura: Introducción a Ecuador

Indica con **C (Cierto)** o **F (Falso)** si Laura menciona o no esta información en el video.

1. _____ el nombre de la capital

2. _____ un mercado de artesanías

3. _____ un buen modo de transporte

4. _____ las tres regiones del país

5. _____ algunas islas famosas

6. _____ el nombre de un científico famoso

8.1 Primera parte

Vocabulario

8.1 Talk about clothes and shopping at a department store

Las compras y la ropa

Maya
Carlos
Luis
el dependiente
Graciela
la dependienta

De compras. Los clientes del centro comercial El Progreso II en Lima, Perú, desean encontrar descuentos en la ropa.

EL DEPENDIENTE:	Estos trajes están en rebaja.
LUIS:	¿Ah, sí? Entonces, voy a probarme este traje de lana gris.
LA DEPENDIENTA:	Buenos días. ¿En qué puedo servirle?
GRACIELA:	¿Me permite probar estos zapatos? Calzo el número 37.
CARLOS:	Mamá, ¡cómprame esa camiseta roja de Superman!
MAYA:	No, hijo. Todavía no hay una liquidación de fin de temporada.

¿Comprendes? Indicate who each statement describes: **el dependiente**, **Luis**, **la dependienta**, **Graciela**, **Carlos**, **Maya**.

1. _____ Va a probarse los zapatos.

2. _____ Quiere probarse un traje.

3. _____ Vende trajes en rebaja.

4. _____ Lleva dos bolsas grandes.

Respuestas: 1. Graciela; 2. Luis; 3. el dependiente; 4. Carlos

))) Vocabulario

La ropa y los accesorios	Clothing and accessories
el abrigo	*coat*
la billetera	*wallet*
la blusa	*blouse*
las botas	*boots*
los calcetines	*socks*
la camisa	*shirt*
la camiseta (sin mangas)	*t-shirt (tank top)*
las chanclas	*flip-flops*
la chaqueta	*jacket, windbreaker*
la corbata	*tie*
la (mini)falda	*(mini)skirt*
la gorra	*baseball cap*
los pantalones (cortos)	*pants (shorts)*
las sandalias	*sandals*
la sudadera (con capucha)	*(hooded) sweatshirt*
el suéter	*sweater*
el traje	*suit*
los vaqueros	*jeans*
el vestido	*dress*
las zapatillas de deporte	*running shoes, sneakers*
los zapatos (de tacón alto)	*(high-heeled) shoes*

Los materiales	Materials
el algodón	*cotton*
el cuero	*leather*
la lana	*wool*
la seda	*silk*

Descripciones	Descriptions
de cuadros	*plaid*
de manga corta/larga	*short-/long-sleeved*
de moda	*in style*
de rayas	*striped*

Dónde comprar	Where to shop
el almacén	*department store*
el centro comercial	*shopping center, mall*
el mercado (al aire libre)	*(open-air) market*

En la tienda	In the store/shop
la caja	*register*
el/la cliente/a	*customer*
el/la dependiente/a	*sales clerk*
el descuento	*discount*
la ganga	*bargain, good deal*
el precio	*price*
el probador	*fitting room*
el recibo	*receipt*

Verbos	Verbs
calzar	*to wear (shoes)*
estar en rebaja/liquidación	*to be on sale/clearance*
llevar	*to wear*
pagar (en efectivo / con tarjeta de crédito / con celular)	*to pay (with cash / credit card / cell phone)*
probarse (ue)	*to try on*
regatear	*to bargain, to haggle over*

Variaciones

- **La chaqueta** is typically a windbreaker. For suit jacket or blazer, use **el saco** in the Americas, or **la americana** in Spain.
- **Los vaqueros** (lit. *cowboys*), are simply **los yins (jeans)** (Peru), **los bluyines** (El Salvador), **los tejanos** (lit. *Texans*) (Spain), **los pantalones de mezclilla** (*of mixed fibers*) (Mexico), **el (pantalón) pitusa** (Cuba), or **los mahones** (Puerto Rico).
- **Las zapatillas de deporte** can also be **los tenis** in many places.

Expansión

Expresiones para comprar	Shopping expressions
¿En qué puedo servirle(s)?	*How can I help you?*
Quiero / Me gustaría...	*I want/would like . . .*
¿Qué tal le queda(n)?	*How does it / do they fit?*
Me queda(n) bien / estrecho/a(s) / grande(s).	*It fits / They fit fine/small/large.*
¿Qué número calza?	*What size shoe do you wear?*
¿Qué talla usa?	*What (clothing) size do you wear?*

Aplicación

8-1 ¿Dónde están? Selecciona dónde se encuentran estas personas, según la ropa que llevan.

1. _____ Raúl lleva pantalones cortos, una camiseta y unas zapatillas de deporte con calcetines blancos.

2. _____ Maripaz lleva un vestido rosado largo de seda y su amigo lleva un traje formal.

3. _____ Manolito lleva un traje de baño y chanclas.

4. _____ Carmen lleva vaqueros nuevos y un suéter de rayas que quiere comprar, pero no lleva zapatos, solo calcetines.

5. _____ El Sr. Cisneros lleva mucha ropa en los brazos y tiene la tarjeta de crédito en la mano.

a. en el probador de un almacén
b. en una fiesta de quinceañera
c. en la playa
d. en un partido de básquetbol
e. en la caja de una tienda

8-2 En el almacén. Escucha la conversación entre Manuel y una dependienta del almacén Zara. Indica con una **X** los productos que Manuel decide comprar y los que no. Luego, escucha otra vez y escribe el precio de cada artículo que compra Manuel. La moneda de Perú es el sol (S/).

Sí	No	Artículo	Precio
1. _____	_____	calcetines	S/____
2. _____	_____	camisa	S/____
3. _____	_____	billetera	S/____
4. _____	_____	corbata	S/____
5. _____	_____	pantalones	S/____
6. _____	_____	chaqueta	S/____
7. _____	_____	suéter	S/____
8. _____	_____	traje	S/____

Zara, una cadena española de tiendas de última moda, tiene más de 1.800 tiendas por todo el mundo.

8-3A ¡Necesito información! ¿Qué compró Carmen para su viaje a Machu Picchu? Túrnense para completar la información que falta en su recibo. Usen estas preguntas guía: **¿Qué compró por...? ¿De qué talla es/son...? ¿Cuánto costó/costaron…?** Después, confirmen las compras que hizo y cuánto gastó. **Estudiante B**: por favor, ve al **Apéndice 1**, página A-9.

MODELO: ESTUDIANTE A: *¿Qué compró Carmen por veinte soles?*
ESTUDIANTE B: *Compró una camiseta de algodón. ¿De qué talla es?*
ESTUDIANTE A: *Es de la talla cuarenta.*

8-4 ¿Adicto/a a la moda? Contesta las preguntas de la encuesta (*survey*) para saber qué puntuación recibes. Luego, con un/a compañero/a, comparen sus resultados para ver quién es más adicto/a a la moda.

1. Cuando te vistes, ¿combinas todo de acuerdo a los colores y los estilos?
   a. No. Prefiero sentirme cómodo/a.
   b. No combino figuras ni colores en mi ropa.
   c. Me encanta hacer mezclas tanto de colores, ropa y estilos.

2. Las revistas de moda para mí…
   a. las miro en el supermercado, pero raras veces las compro.
   b. no me llaman la atención.
   c. son mi fuente de inspiración; las leo siempre.

3. ¿Cuántas horas pasas en una tienda?
   a. Muchas; tengo que verlo y probármelo todo.
   b. No muchas. Entro, miro, y si me gusta, me lo pruebo y lo compro.
   c. Voy a las tiendas y me pruebo las cosas, pero muy pocas veces compro las costosas.

4. Cuando voy de compras, compro...
   a. solo lo que necesito y cuando lo necesito.
   b. lo que esté a la moda, a veces sin importar si me gusta mucho.
   c. zapatos o una camisa, lo que más me llame la atención.

5. ¿Cuánto dinero gastas al mes en ropa?
   a. No me fijo (*I don't notice*), pero no puede ser mucho.
   b. No sé, pero no importa, ya que estoy a la moda.
   c. No compro ropa cada mes; prefiero comprar cuando la necesite.

6. ¿Sabes qué vas a comprar para cada temporada?
   a. No me fijo en eso; tengo mi propio estilo.
   b. ¡Claro! Siempre conozco las nuevas tendencias.
   c. Posiblemente, pero no salgo corriendo a comprarlo.

Puntos de cada respuesta: 1. a=1, b=2, c=3; 2. a=2, b=1, c=3; 3. a=3, b=1, c=2; 4. a=1, b=3, c=2; 5. a=2, b=3, c=1; 6. a=1, b=3, c=2

Estudiante A:

falabella

DOCUMENTO DE VENTA

OUFDSYEVW9NGOLWI9TOD2OJ

Vendedor	T.T	EmpCent	Operac.	Fecha	Hora	EdPIZN	T
51106219	9	001006	0367886	12/12/2018	19:16	0100000	00

Descripción	Talla	PRECIO (SOLES)
camiseta de algodón	40	S/ 20
blusa de manga corta	36	S/ 50
vaqueros	_____	S/ 75
suéter de lana	38	_____
chaqueta de cuero	_____	S/ 200
_____	39	S/ 39
gorra roja	50	_____

TOTAL COMPRA S/ _____

Gracias por su compra.
Visítenos en www.falabella.com

Puntuación de la encuesta

6–9: Estás lejos de ser adicto/a a la moda, tienes tu propio estilo y esto te hace sentir cómodo/a. Sin embargo (*However*), cuidas tu apariencia.

10–14: Te gusta lucir (*look*) bien e intentas reciclar la ropa para combinarlas según las tendencias.

15–18: Eres adicto/a a la moda; te encanta gastar dinero en ropa. Por esta razón, es posible que tengas más ropa que amigos.

Estructuras

> Antes, mi madre siempre compraba en un almacén. Ahora compra en Internet.

8.2 Describe and narrate in the past, and put things in order

The imperfect of regular and irregular verbs

You've used the preterit in **Capítulos 6** and **7** to express **completed** events in the past (**llovió** = *it rained*). In this chapter, you learn the imperfect, which expresses **incomplete** or **repeated** events in the past (**llovía** = *it was raining; it used to rain*).

There are three common English equivalents of the Spanish imperfect: simple past (with no explicit beginning or end), past progressive, and *used to* + infinitive construction.

Rosario **trabajaba** en la tienda.
{
Rosario worked at the store.
Rosario was working at the store.
Rosario used to work at the store.

EL IMPERFECTO DE VERBOS REGULARES

	hablar	comer	escribir
yo	habl**aba**	com**ía**	escrib**ía**
tú	habl**abas**	com**ías**	escrib**ías**
Ud.	habl**aba**	com**ía**	escrib**ía**
él/ella	habl**aba**	com**ía**	escrib**ía**
nosotros/as	habl**ábamos**	com**íamos**	escrib**íamos**
vosotros/as	habl**abais**	com**íais**	escrib**íais**
Uds.	habl**aban**	com**ían**	escrib**ían**
ellos/as	habl**aban**	com**ían**	escrib**ían**

¡OJO!

With **-ar** verbs, only the first-person plural form has a written accent mark. The imperfect endings for **-er** and **-ir** verbs are identical, and all forms have a written accent mark.

- Use the imperfect for repeated, habitual, or continuous actions in the past with no reference to the beginning or ending.

  Cuando yo **trabajaba** en el almacén, **recibía** un descuento en todo lo que **compraba.**
  When I worked at the department store, I received a discount on everything I bought.

- Use the imperfect to describe an action in progress when another action took place (in the preterit) or was occurring (in the imperfect).

  Estábamos en la tienda cuando **llegaron** nuestras amigas.
  We were in the store when our friends arrived.

  Mientras Rosario **compraba** zapatillas de deporte, Mauricio **miraba** los suéteres.
  While Rosario was buying sneakers, Mauricio was looking at the sweaters.

- Use the imperfect to describe characteristics or states of being (health, emotions, etc.) in the past with no particular beginning or end.

  A mi abuela le **gustaba** comprar en las tiendas.
  My grandmother liked to shop in the stores.

  Tenía muchos amigos entre los dependientes.
  She had a lot of friends among the clerks.

- As a general rule, use the imperfect with time and age in the past.

  ¿Qué hora **era** cuando llegaste?
  What time was it when you arrived?

  Cuando **tenía** diecisiete años, visité Ecuador.
  When I was seventeen, I visited Ecuador.

VERBOS IRREGULARES EN EL IMPERFECTO

Cuando yo era joven, veía a mis abuelos todas las semanas. Vivían cerca y yo iba en bicicleta a visitarlos.

There are only three irregular verbs in the imperfect.

	ir	ser	ver
yo	iba	era	veía
tú	ibas	eras	veías
Ud.	iba	era	veía
él/ella	iba	era	veía
nosotros/as	íbamos	éramos	veíamos
vosotros/as	ibais	erais	veíais
Uds.	iban	eran	veían
ellos/as	iban	eran	veían

- Only the first-person plural forms of **ir** and **ser** have a written accent mark; **ver** uses the regular **-er/-ir** endings, which require a written accent.

¿Comprendes? Select the logical verb to complete each statement: **atendía, estaba, nos probábamos.**

Tú y yo (1) _____ zapatos mientras el dependiente (2) _____ a la otra clienta.
El almacén (3) _____ lleno de gente.

Respuestas: 1. nos probábamos; 2. atendía; 3. estaba

Aplicación

8-5 En la tienda Zara. Cuando estaban en Lima, Elvira, Beto y Andrés visitaron una de las dos tiendas Zara. Selecciona el verbo más lógico para completar lo que dice Andrés sobre la visita.

La tienda no (1) era/tenía muy grande, pero (2) se probaba/había mucha

gente porque todo (3) estaba/pagaba en liquidación. Un dependiente

(4) atendía/regateaba a una señora que (5) había/quería comprar zapatos de tacón

alto, pero (6) calzaba/ponía el número 40 y todos (7) eran/iban más pequeños. Una

joven se probaba una minifalda de rayas que le (8) quedaba/usaba muy bien. Beto y

yo (9) abríamos/buscábamos algunos pantalones cortos cuando Elvira nos dijo que

(10) costaba/estaba cansada y que (11) veía/prefería volver otro día.

8-6 En el mercado de Otavalo. Los mercados turísticos abundan en Perú y Ecuador. El del pueblo de Otavalo, Ecuador, es famoso por sus artesanías, su comida típica y los turistas que lo visitan.

Paso 1   Lee la entrada de diario que Tomás escribió cuando él y su hermana visitaron Otavalo. Completa su historia con la forma apropiada del imperfecto de cada verbo.

El pueblo de Otavalo está situado a tres horas de Quito. Ese día, (1) _____ (hacer) mucho calor y no (2) _____ (llover). Nuestro taxista, Ramón, (3) _____ (ser) muy simpático. Otavalo (4) _____ (parecer) una ciudad impresionante. (5) _____ (Haber) gente por todas partes vendiendo todo tipo de comida, ropa, accesorios y animales. No (6) _____ (poder) creer el espectáculo tan agradable de colores y olores (*smells*). En uno de los puestos (*stands*), algunas mujeres (7) _____ (comprar) camisas; en otro, un hombre (8) _____ (vender) suéteres de lana. En un lugar, algunas personas (9) _____ (preparar) un pavo a la parrilla. Por todas partes los clientes y los vendedores (10) _____ (regatear) el precio de sus cosas.

Cultura en vivo

It is a common practice to bargain with vendors in open markets throughout the Spanish-speaking world; however, bargaining is less common in shops and almost unheard of in department stores. As a buyer, you may offer up to a third less than the asking price, and the seller will respond with a higher price. The haggling continues until both parties are satisfied with the price. Bargaining etiquette requires that you be serious about the purchase, not just curious about the price. Have you ever had success bargaining a lower price for anything?

Quería comprar todas las artesanías que se vendían en Otavalo.

Paso 2   Contesta las preguntas, según el paso anterior.

1. ¿En qué país está Otavalo?
2. ¿Qué tiempo hacía ese día?
3. ¿Qué artículos vendían las personas en el mercado?
4. ¿Qué comida preparaban algunos?
5. ¿Quiénes regateaban?
6. ¿Qué crees que compraban los clientes cuando Tomás y su hermana llegaron?

8-7A ¡Necesito información! Cada uno/a de ustedes tiene una versión diferente del dibujo que muestra lo que pasaba ayer en el almacén. Usen el imperfecto para describir lo que ven y así encontrar seis diferencias en cada versión. **Estudiante B**: por favor, ve al **Apéndice 1**, página A-9.

MODELO: ESTUDIANTE A: *Una mujer se probaba zapatos.*
ESTUDIANTE B: *Es cierto. Una mujer se probaba zapatos.*

Estudiante A:

8-8 En los años 80 y ahora. Los estilos cambian y se reciclan de generación en generación. En parejas, comparen estos ejemplos de estilos populares de la década de los 80 con los del presente. ¿Qué diferencia hay entre esa época y los de hoy? ¿Qué tienen en común?

MODELO: *En los años ochenta, los jóvenes llevaban…, pero yo prefiero llevar… ¿Y tú?*

- ropa casual: chaqueta de vaquero, vaqueros prelavados, ropa demasiado (*too*) grande
- zapatos, sandalias, pulseras y otros accesorios de goma (*jelly*)
- ropa deportiva: sostén deportivo (*sports bra*), camiseta, sudadera, zapatillas de deporte
- ropa de colores neón
- mallas (*leggings*)
- hombreras (*shoulder pads*)

8-9 Sergio Dávila, diseñador. En 2009, el peruano Sergio Dávila fue nombrado "el mejor diseñador de ropa masculina". Busca una foto de él y describe la escena. Usa tu imaginación para inventar detalles y después, preséntale tu descripción a la clase.

MODELO: *Era el dos de julio de 2017. Ese día Sergio Dávila…*

- ¿Dónde estaba?
- ¿Qué tiempo hacía ese día?
- ¿Cómo se sentía en esa ocasión?
- ¿Qué ropa llevaba él?

- ¿Había otras personas allí? ¿Quiénes eran y qué llevaban?
- ¿Adónde iban todos?

Busca: Sergio Dávila diseñador

Ordinal numbers

Puede usar el primer probador.

You've used cardinal numbers (**uno, dos, tres**…) since **Capítulo 1**. Ordinal numbers give the order in which things appear or events occur.

primero/a	*first*	**sexto/a**	*sixth*
segundo/a	*second*	**séptimo/a**	*seventh*
tercero/a	*third*	**octavo/a**	*eighth*
cuarto/a	*fourth*	**noveno/a**	*ninth*
quinto/a	*fifth*	**décimo/a**	*tenth*

- Like other adjectives, ordinal numbers agree in gender and number with the noun they modify.

  Estas son las **primeras** rebajas del año. — *These are the first sales of the year.*

  Clarita compró un **segundo** vestido. — *Clarita bought a second dress.*

- **Primero** and **tercero** are shortened to **primer** and **tercer** before masculine singular nouns.

  La tienda está en el **tercer** piso. — *The store is on the third floor.*

  Juan es el **primer** dependiente en vender un abrigo de cuero. — *Juan is the first sales clerk to sell a leather coat.*

- To express order after **décimo**, use cardinal numbers, following the noun.

  La liquidación es en el piso **doce**. — *The clearance sale is on the twelfth floor.*

- The opposite of **primero** is **último**.

  Olga fue la **primera** en llegar. Antonio fue el **último**. — *Olga was the first to arrive. Antonio was the last.*

¿Comprendes? Select the appropriate word to complete the statements: **primeros, último, tercera**.

En el tren a Lima, nosotros dos fuimos los (1) _____ en subir. La (2) _____ persona fue mi hermana. Después de ella, vino su novio, el (3) _____ en subir.

Respuestas: 1. primeros; 2. tercera; 3. último

Aplicación

8-10 Un viaje a las Islas Galápagos. Individualmente, ordenen los artículos que llevarían (*you would take*) a las Islas Galápagos, según su importancia, de primero a último. Luego, en parejas, comparen sus resultados y explíquense sus razones.

MODELO: *Primero, necesito llevar una camisa de manga larga, porque en las islas hace mucho sol. ¿Y tú?*

Ropa y accesorios	Mi lista	La lista de mi compañero/a
1. unos zapatos de tacón alto	_____	_____
2. una camiseta de algodón	_____	_____
3. unas chanclas	_____	_____
4. un par de zapatillas	_____	_____
5. un traje de rayas	_____	_____
6. una gorra	_____	_____
7. unos vaqueros	_____	_____
8. unos lentes de sol	_____	_____
9. unas botas	_____	_____
10. ¿…?	_____	_____

8-11A ¡Necesito información! Cada uno/a de ustedes tiene una parte del directorio del almacén. Túrnense para pedir información sobre dónde comprar productos o realizar (*carry out*) alguna tarea (*task*). Añadan más información cuando sea posible. **Estudiante B**: por favor, ve al **Apéndice 1**, página A-10.

MODELO: una blusa para tu mamá

ESTUDIANTE A: *Quiero comprar una blusa para mi mamá porque es su cumpleaños.*

ESTUDIANTE B: *La puede buscar en el segundo piso, en Ropa de mujer.*

ESTUDIANTE A: *Muchas gracias.*

Estudiante A:

1. un sándwich y un refresco
2. un traje para un evento formal
3. una corbata para tu tío
4. sandalias de cuero
5. en qué piso solicitar trabajo
6. una raqueta de tenis

saga falabella.

1.er piso	**6.° piso** Muebles para la oficina; Equipo electrónico; Televisores
2.° piso Ropa de mujer (trajes, vestidos, ropa informal)	**7.° piso**
3.er piso Ropa infantil (ambos sexos; tallas neonatal a 4)	**8.° piso** Supermercado
4.° piso	**9.° piso** Artículos en liquidación
5.° piso Todo para la casa (dormitorio, cocina, sala, comedor)	**10.° piso** Cambio de moneda; Caja

¡Conversemos!

Primero, pregúntate si puedes llevar a cabo las siguientes funciones comunicativas en español. Después, júntate con dos o tres compañeros/as de clase para presentar las situaciones. Hagan y respondan a por lo menos cuatro preguntas en cada situación.

✓ CAN YOU ...

☐ talk about clothes and shopping at a department store?

☐ talk about what used to happen and what you used to do in the past?

☐ describe a scene in the past?

WITH YOUR CLASSMATE(S) ...

Situación: En un almacén.

Están en un almacén para hacer algunas compras para una función importante. Expliquen qué quieren comprar; los colores, el estilo, la tela, la talla o el número, etc. Uno/a de ustedes es el/la dependiente/a que también explica en qué piso pueden buscar otros artículos.

Para empezar: *¿En qué puedo servirles?*

Situación: Cuando era pequeño/a.

Usen el imperfecto para hablar de las cosas que les gustaba hacer cuando eran pequeños/as. Incluyan actividades que siempre hacían y actividades que nunca hacían, y por qué.

Para empezar: *Cuando era pequeño/a, iba a las tiendas siempre con mi mamá.*

Situación: Las superestrellas.

Busquen tres fotos en una revista de moda. Usen el imperfecto para describir las escenas, la gente y su ropa.

Para empezar: *En esta foto...*

Perfiles

8.3 Learn about shopping in Peru and traditional Andean music

Mi experiencia

DE COMPRAS EN PERÚ

8-12 Para ti. En EE. UU. y Canadá, ¿compras la comida o la ropa en mercados al aire libre? ¿Se cierran normalmente las tiendas de tu ciudad a la hora de almorzar? ¿Por qué sí o no? Lee el blog de María Antonia, una chica canadiense, en su primer viaje a Perú. Mientras lees, piensa en las diferencias que existen según tu experiencia.

¡Saludos desde Perú y gracias por leer mi blog! Como esta es mi primera visita a Sudamérica, me impresiona todo lo que veo, especialmente cómo se hacen las compras aquí en comparación con Toronto. Primero, todas las ciudades grandes tienen sus almacenes, pero las horas parecen más cortas, desde las once hasta las ocho. No son muchas horas, ¿verdad? También muchas de las tiendas pequeñas cierran para el almuerzo entre las dos y las cuatro. Sin embargo, hay mercados al aire libre, donde puedes comprar de todo, ropa, comida, artesanías y hasta animales. Pero, entre estos dos casos, hay también centros comerciales modernos como Plaza Norte en Lima, con más de 300 tiendas especializadas, un hipermercado, un casino, un hotel de cinco estrellas, un gimnasio, discotecas, un cine con 14 salones y mucho más. Es un lugar de encuentro social donde puedes comprar, pasear o sentarte a ver pasar a la gente. Es muy agradable: no solo se toca música popular, sino que hay también un escenario donde invitan a músicos a dar conciertos. Así es como conocí la música de Yawar, que aquí es un conjunto muy popular. Seguramente voy a buscar algunas de sus canciones en Internet.

8-13 En su opinión. En grupos, comparen su experiencia con la de María Antonia.

1. ¿Dónde compra María Antonia en Perú? ¿Compran ustedes de una manera diferente?
2. ¿Cómo es Plaza Norte en Lima? ¿Conocen ustedes un lugar como ese?
3. ¿Cómo son los mercados al aire libre en Perú? ¿Compran ustedes en uno similar?
4. ¿En cuáles de los lugares que menciona María Antonia creen ustedes que es aceptable regatear? Y en su experiencia, ¿en qué circunstancias regatean el precio?
5. En general, ¿prefieren tener la opción de regatear o prefieren pagar el precio original?

Mi música

"COMPAÑERA" (YAWAR, PERÚ)

Este grupo musical, conocido por todo Perú y Bolivia, toma su nombre *Yawar* de una antigua tradición de los incas. El grupo Yawar se conoce por su original mezcla de ritmos andinos y contemporáneos, en los cuales (*in which*) predominan instrumentos como la zampoña (*panpipe*) y la quena (un tipo de flauta). El grupo también llamó la atención del mundo al interpretar temas de los legendarios Beatles, pero ejecutados con instrumentos andinos.

La zampoña y otros instrumentos musicales andinos producen un sonido muy especial.

ANTES DE VER Y ESCUCHAR

8-14 **"Compañera".** Vas a escuchar estas palabras y expresiones en la canción. Selecciona la opción que mejor corresponde a su equivalente en inglés. Después, adivina (*guess*) el tema de la canción.

1. _____ despedirme
2. _____ vida eterna
3. _____ una luz que ilumina
4. _____ alma
5. _____ emociones
6. _____ esperanza
7. _____ mi pena
8. _____ sin tus besos

a. *soul*
b. *without your kisses*
c. *hope*
d. *emotions*
e. *my pain*
f. *a light that shines*
g. *say good-bye*
h. *eternal life*

PARA VER Y ESCUCHAR

8-15 **La canción.** Busca en Internet un video de "Compañera". Indica con una **X** los instrumentos que escuchas o ves. Pon un **0** si no lo oyes o ves.

_____ el piano   _____ la zampoña

_____ la guitarra   _____ la batería (*drums*)

_____ la quena   _____ la pandereta (*tambourine*)

_____ el acordeón

📍 **Busca:** video Yawar Compañera; letra Yawar Compañera

DESPUÉS DE VER Y ESCUCHAR

8-16 **El video.** Escribe una breve descripción de los músicos y lo que hacían en el video. Usa por lo menos cinco de estos verbos en el imperfecto.

| cantar | estar | haber | llevar | sentirse | ser | tocar |

MODELO: *En el video, había…*

8.2 Segunda parte

Vocabulario

8.4 **Shop for personal care products and jewelry**

Tiendas y productos personales

¿Qué hiciste hoy? Victoria no estaba en casa cuando Lucía la llamó por la mañana.

LUCÍA: Oye, Victoria, esta mañana te llamé tres veces al celular, pero no me contestaste. ¿Dónde estabas? ¿Qué hiciste hoy?

VICTORIA: Disculpa. Estaba en el centro comercial y mi celular no tenía buena recepción.

LUCÍA: Ah, ¿fuiste a **la joyería** a comprarle un regalo a tu mamá? ¿Le compraste **la cadena de plata**?

VICTORIA: Sí, y fui también a **la farmacia** por **un cepillo de dientes** y a **la perfumería** por **jabón** y **loción**. ¿Dónde estás tú ahora?

LUCÍA: Estoy enfrente de **la heladería** Veintiún Sabores. ¿Por qué no vienes y tomamos un helado?

¿Comprendes? Select the correct word to complete each statement: **jabón**, **la joyería**, **un cepillo de dientes**.

1. Victoria compró una cadena de plata en _____.

2. Fue a la farmacia por _____.

3. En la perfumería compró _____.

Respuestas: 1. la joyería; 2. un cepillo de dientes; 3. jabón

))) Vocabulario

En la farmacia y perfumería	In the pharmacy and beauty supply shop
el acondicionador	*conditioner*
el cepillo de dientes	*toothbrush*
la colonia	*cologne*
la crema hidratante / de afeitar	*facial cream / shaving cream*
el desodorante	*deodorant*
la pasta de dientes	*toothpaste*
el perfume	*perfume*
el talco	*talcum powder*

En la joyería	In the jewelry store
el anillo	*ring*
los aretes	*earrings (post)*
la cadena	*chain*
el collar	*necklace*
los pendientes	*earrings (pendant)*
la pulsera	*bracelet*
el reloj inteligente / de pulsera	*smart watch / wristwatch*

Descripciones	Descriptions
de diamantes	*diamond*
de oro	*gold*
de perlas	*pearl*
de plata	*silver*

Más tiendas	More shops
la carnicería	*butcher shop*
la florería	*flower shop*
la heladería	*ice cream shop*
la panadería	*bakery*
la papelería	*stationery shop*
la pastelería	*pastry shop*
la quesería	*cheese shop*
la zapatería	*shoe store*

Verbos	Verbs
devolver (ue)	*to return (something)*
gastar	*to spend*
hacer juego (con)	*to match, to go well with*

Variaciones

- In Mexico, there are variations for **heladería**. For example, **una nevería** sells **nieve** (a water-based product like sherbet), and **una paletería** sells **paletas** (water- or cream-based frozen bars on a stick).
- In Spain, you will hear **floristería** in place of **florería**.

))) Letras y sonidos

The sequences *j*, *ge*, *gi*, and *x*

In Spanish, the letter **j**, as well as **g** before the vowels **e** and **i**, all correspond to the same sound, the *h* sound in English *hip:*

jo-ya   tra-**je**   re-lo**j**   **ge**-ne-ro-so   **gi**m-na-sio

In some Spanish words, the letter **x** also has the *h* sound:

Mé-**x**i-co   **X**a-vier

In most cases, however, the letter **x** creates two sounds, *k* and *s*, as in English *extra:*

e**x**igente → (*e[k-s]i-gen-te*)   e**x**tra → (*e[ks]-tra*)

Aplicación

8-17 Las tiendas especializadas. Selecciona el producto que se vende en cada una de las tiendas especializadas.

1. _____ la joyería   a. carne
2. _____ la perfumería   b. collares de perlas
3. _____ la florería   c. invitaciones
4. _____ la zapatería   d. jabón
5. _____ la quesería   e. pan
6. _____ la papelería   f. quesos
7. _____ la panadería   g. rosas
8. _____ la carnicería   h. sandalias

El heladero en Otavalo vende vainilla y zarzamora (*blackberry*). ¿Cuál prefieres?

8-18 ¡Yo también fui de compras! Lucía también fue de compras ayer. Escucha su conversación con Victoria y selecciona las tiendas que visitó, los artículos que compró y los que devolvió.

Tiendas			
el almacén	la farmacia	la florería	la heladería
la joyería	la librería	la panadería	la papelería
la perfumería	el supermercado	la tienda pequeña	la zapatería

Artículos			
una agenda	una blusa	una camisa	un cepillo de dientes
un desodorante	una falda	un libro de arte	un reloj
unas sandalias	el talco	un té especial	una torta de queso

Tiendas	Compró	Lo/La devolvió

Cultura en vivo

In many countries in South America, it is common to add a little extra to a customer's order as a bonus. The **yapa** is from Quechua, meaning *add-on*. The phrase, **de yapa**, means *for free*. This custom is still practiced in small shops and markets, where a person weighs the goods and tells you the price, and then adds a bit more to the order. Supermarkets with electronic scales would charge you the exact amount, with no **yapa**. Is this practice common in the U.S. or Canada?

8-19 ¿Hacen juego? A Roberto no le interesan las modas y por eso, él siempre se viste con estilos clásicos. En parejas, decidan si para Roberto estos artículos hacen juego. Si no, cámbienlos.

> **MODELO:** un traje de baño y zapatos de cuero
> *Para Roberto, no hacen juego. Es mejor llevar chanclas con un traje de baño.*

1. una camisa de cuadros y pantalones de rayas
2. un vestido de seda y botas de cuero
3. unas sandalias con calcetines
4. una gorra y un traje de lana
5. unos vaqueros y aretes de diamantes
6. un traje con sudadera

8-20 ¿En qué tiendas compran? En parejas, conversen sobre dónde compran cada una de estas cosas y por qué.

> **MODELO:** *Me gusta comprar helado en la heladería La Crema, que está en mi ciudad, porque tiene veintiún sabores deliciosos.*

la ropa informal de todos los días

la ropa elegante

las bebidas para una fiesta

un regalo para una persona especial

los productos de higiene personal

quesos importados

un postre para una cena especial

zapatillas deportivas

Tienda de ropa en Buenos Aires. ¿Dónde compras ropa para el verano?

Presencia hispana

Latina women generally like to **lucir bien**, that is, look good. According to a poll conducted by Univisión, Latinas—especially millennials—are more than twice as likely to buy cosmetics and other personal care items as any other group. They also tend to buy beauty products endorsed by celebrities, or those celebrities who have their own line, such as Salma Hayek and Eva Mendes. In the Univisión poll, 92% of the respondents said they would not leave the house without makeup. Do you think that society puts too much emphasis on how women look?

8-21 Un viaje a Quito. Vas a hacer planes para un viaje a Quito, Ecuador.

Paso 1   Busca un hotel en Internet con estas características:

- Cobra menos de $100 por noche.
- Está cerca del transporte público.
- Incluye el desayuno.
- Tiene Internet o wifi.

> **Busca:** hotel Quito EC

Paso 2   Busca estos lugares cerca del hotel. ¿Es posible ir a pie (*on foot*) o en transporte público, o tienes que tomar un taxi? Escribe un resumen de tu investigación y preséntaselo a la clase.

- una farmacia
- una panadería
- una zapatería
- una joyería

> **Busca:** farmacia, etc. cerca del hotel…

Encontré un hotel en el centro histórico de Quito.

Estructuras

8.5 Narrate in the past, and talk about what people say and believe

Preterit versus imperfect

¿Recuerdas? Indicate if the action of each verb is in the preterit (P) or the imperfect (I).

Cuando (1) <u>éramos</u> estudiantes y (2) <u>estudiábamos</u> química, siempre (3) <u>íbamos</u> al laboratorio los miércoles. Una vez, no (4) <u>fuimos</u> porque el profesor (5) <u>estaba</u> enfermo.

¿Viste las cadenas tan preciosas que llevaba esa chica?

Sí, ¿y viste los pendientes? Eran muy bonitos.

Respuestas: 1, 2, 3. I (imperfect – repetition in the past with no particular beginning or end); 4. P (preterit – completed event in the past); 5. I (imperfect – past condition with no explicit beginning or end)

The preterit and the imperfect reflect the way a speaker views past actions, events, and conditions.

The preterit...	The imperfect...
• reports actions or events that the speaker views as completed or finished. These can be individual events or a series. Las amigas **hablaron** por dos horas. *The friends talked for two hours.* Carlos **entró** en la farmacia, **vio** a su exnovia y **salió** inmediatamente. *Carlos entered the pharmacy, saw his ex-girlfriend, and left immediately.*	• describes an ongoing action, often in relation to another event or time, with no reference to the beginning or end. Rosa **hablaba** por su celular mientras **miraba** las compras. *Rosa was talking on her cell while she was looking at her purchases.*
• expresses the beginning or end of an action. **Llegaste** a la zapatería a las cinco. *You arrived at the shoe shop at five.*	• expresses habitual actions or events. Pedro **compraba** en esa panadería todos los sábados. *Pedro used to shop in that bakery every Saturday*
• expresses changes in mental, physical, and emotional conditions or states. Alejandra **se puso** feliz cuando **vio** el anillo. *Alejandra became happy when she saw the ring.*	• expresses mental, physical, and emotional conditions or states (with no particular beginning or end). Nos **sentíamos** mal cuando estábamos en el centro comercial. *We were feeling sick when we were at the mall.*
• reports weather and scenes as events or within specific time parameters. Ayer **fue** un día horrible. **Llovió** e **hizo** mucho viento. *Yesterday was a horrible day. It rained and was very windy.*	• sets the scene (weather, activities in progress, etc.) for other actions and events that take place. **Hacía** muy mal tiempo y **llovía**. Yo **leía** en mi cuarto y **esperaba** la llamada. *The weather was bad and it was raining. I was reading in my room and waiting for the call.*
	• expresses time or age. **Eran** las once de la noche. *It was eleven o'clock at night.* **Teníamos** seis años en 2006. *We were six years old in 2006.*

- The preterit and the imperfect are often used together. Note how the imperfect describes what was happening or in progress when another action (in the preterit) interrupted and took place.

  Conversábamos con el dependiente cuando Lourdes **entró** en la joyería.

  We were talking with the sales clerk when Lourdes entered the jewelry store.

- Here are some temporal expressions that are frequently (but not always) associated with the imperfect and preterit.

Preterit	Imperfect
anoche	a menudo
anteayer	con frecuencia
ayer	de vez en cuando
de repente (*suddenly*)	mientras
esta mañana	frecuentemente
el fin de semana pasado	todos los lunes/martes/…
el mes pasado	todas las semanas
el lunes/martes/… pasado	todos los días/meses/años
una vez	muchas veces
siempre (*an end point is obvious*)	siempre (*an event is repeated with no particular end point*)

STUDY TIPS — DISTINGUISHING BETWEEN THE PRETERIT AND THE IMPERFECT

1. Analyze the context and decide whether the verb describes the way things were (imperfect), or it tells what happened (preterit).

   Era de noche cuando **volvieron** a casa.

   Era: describes → *It was nighttime. (Imperfect)*

   volvieron: tells what happened → *They returned. (Preterit)*

2. In many instances, both aspects produce a grammatical sentence. Your choice will depend on the message you are communicating.

Preterit		Imperfect	
Así **fue**.	*That's how it happened.*	Así **era**.	*That's how it used to be.*
Ayer **fue** un día horrible.	*Yesterday was a horrible day. (It's completed; not background information.)*	**Era** un día horrible.	*It was a horrible day. (Background information for the actions to be narrated.)*

¿Comprendes? Select the correct verb to complete each statement: **compré**, **gastaba**, **asistía**, **recibí**.

Cuando (1) _____ a la universidad, (2) _____ poco en la ropa. Pero este año, cuando (3) _____ un cheque de mis padres, me (4) _____ un traje nuevo.

Respuestas: 1. asistía; 2. gastaba; 3. recibí; 4. compré

Aplicación

8-22 Guayasamín. El ecuatoriano Oswaldo Guayasamín fue uno de los pintores latinoamericanos más importantes del siglo XX. Muchas de sus obras tienen un tema social.

Paso 1 Lee la selección sobre este famoso artista ecuatoriano y luego, haz una lista con los verbos en el pretérito y otra lista con los verbos en el imperfecto.

La Ternura, Oswaldo Guayasamín

Oswaldo Guayasamín nació en Quito el 6 de julio de 1919. De niño, su familia era muy pobre. Se graduó de pintor y escultor en la Escuela de Bellas Artes de Quito. Tuvo su primera exposición cuando tenía veintitrés años. Durante su vida, recibió muchos premios nacionales y varios internacionales. Tuvo una vida artística muy productiva: hizo cuadros, murales, esculturas y monumentos.

Toda su vida, Guayasamín simpatizó con ideales comunistas y apoyó[1] causas socialistas. Sin embargo, siempre estuvo en contra de todo tipo de violencia. A través de su obra humanista, quiso reflejar la miseria que sufría la mayor parte de la humanidad. Murió[2] el 10 de marzo de 1999, a los setenta y nueve años, antes de poder terminar la obra que él consideraba su más importante: *La capilla[3] del hombre*.

[1]*supported*

[2]*He died*

[3]*chapel*

Paso 2 Contesta las preguntas basadas en el texto sobre Guayasamín.

1. ¿Dónde y en qué año nació?
2. ¿Cuántos años tenía cuando murió?
3. ¿Con qué causas se identificó durante su vida?
4. ¿Qué honores recibió durante su vida?
5. ¿Qué quiso mostrar (*show*) Guayasamín en su obra humanista?
6. ¿En qué trabajaba cuando murió?

Paso 3 Explica el uso del pretérito versus el imperfecto en la biografía de Guayasamín.

MODELO: *nació: completed event*

Cultura en vivo

Many Latin American writers and artists have devoted their work to human rights. Peruvian Mario Vargas Llosa gained international attention with his novel *La ciudad y los perros* (1963), in which he criticized the way of life and military culture (aggressiveness, courage, manhood, sexuality) that he experienced as a boy in a Peruvian military academy. Many of his novels and essays since then have revolved around the quest for justice and human rights. In 2010, Mario Vargas Llosa won the Nobel Prize for Literature. Can you name other Nobel Prize winners dedicated to human justice?

8-23 Mi primer trabajo. Sigue los pasos para completar la actividad.

Paso 1   Lee la historia y selecciona la forma correcta del verbo, según el contexto.

Cuando (1) tuve/tenía 16 años, quería trabajar después de la escuela para ganar un poco de dinero. Mi abuelo, quien (2) vivió/vivía con nosotros, me dio mi primer trabajo en su panadería. Me sentía muy orgulloso de ir todos los días para ayudarlo. Limpiaba las cazuelas, (3) lavé/lavaba el piso, (4) atendí/atendía a los clientes y (5) gané/ganaba lo suficiente para salir con mis amigos los fines de semana y también poner parte del dinero en el banco.

Un sábado, mi abuelo me dijo que él tenía que ir al banco para depositar dinero y que yo (6) estuve/iba a estar a cargo de la panadería. Abrí la tienda como siempre, (7) puse/ponía los panes en la vitrina (*display case*) y esperé a los clientes. De repente, entró un joven con una pistola y me (8) pidió/pedía todo el dinero que había en la caja…

Paso 2   Explica por qué seleccionaste cada verbo, y luego escribe un mínimo de tres oraciones adicionales en el pasado para terminar la historia.

La panadería de mi abuelo

8-24 Queríamos… En parejas, túrnense para completar las oraciones, indicando lo que querían hacer y lo que hicieron, según el contexto. Algunas oraciones deben ser ciertas y otras falsas; a ver si pueden identificar la verdad. Sigan los modelos.

MODELO: Iba a… esta noche, pero…
Iba a ver a mi novio esta noche, pero me llamó y me dijo que estaba cansado.
Yo quería… mientras…
Yo quería estudiar mientras escuchaba música.

1. Ayer venía a clase cuando…
2. Una vez el año pasado…
3. Cuando era más joven, frecuentemente…
4. Esta mañana iba a…
5. Muchas veces en el pasado…
6. Ayer tenía ganas de… mientras…

8-25 ¡Perdí…! Uno/a de ustedes trabaja en la oficina de Servicio al Cliente de un almacén. El/La otro/a es un/a cliente/a que está de compras y se da cuenta de que perdió algunos artículos. Túrnense para hacerse preguntas y describir los artículos para luego identificarlos.

MODELO: ASISTENTE DE SERVICIO AL CLIENTE: *¿En qué puedo servirle?*
CLIENTE: *Perdí…*

Cliente/a: Posibles artículos perdidos

- un guante de (lana, cuero, algodón), de talla (pequeña, mediana, grande), de color…

- unas sandalias de número…, de color…, que costaron….

- una sudadera de talla…, de color… (con/sin capucha), para (niño, mujer, hombre)

- un collar de (oro, plata, perlas, cuero), para (hombre, mujer), que costó…

- un reloj (inteligente, de oro, de plástico), que le dio (sus padres, su novio/a…), que costó…

Asistente: Posibles preguntas

- ¿Cómo era(n)?

- ¿Dónde estaba?

- ¿Con quiénes estaba?

- ¿Qué departamentos visitó?

- ¿Lo/La compró en este almacén?

- ¿Tiene recibo?

- ¿Vio a alguien sospechoso?

- ¿Algún empleado lo/la ayudó? ¿Cómo se llamaba?

Impersonal and passive *se*

In order to attribute actions to no one in particular, you will often see the impersonal **se** on signs, and in instructions and rules.

¿Qué se prohíbe en el Canal?

- Use **se** and the third-person singular of the verb in statements attributed to no one in particular. These are generally followed by an infinitive, an adverb, or a clause introduced by **que**.

Se prohíbe fumar en las heladerías.

Smoking is prohibited in ice cream shops.

Se compra bien en este almacén.

You (One, They) shop well (get good deals) in this department store.

Se dice que hay una liquidación hoy en la zapatería León.

They say there is a clearance sale today in the Leon shoe store.

Se abre el almacén a las nueve.

CERRADO

- Use the pronoun **se** and the third-person singular or plural form of the verb as a substitute for the passive voice to say what is done. Note that the verb agrees with whatever is offered, sold, seen, bought, etc.

Se ofrecen descuentos en Internet.	*Discounts are offered on the Internet.*
Se encontró el anillo en el probador.	*The ring was found in the dressing room.*
Se vendían artículos de segunda mano en esta tienda.	*Secondhand articles used to be sold in this store.*

¿Comprendes? Select the correct verb to complete each statement: **se abren**, **se dice**, **se ofrecen**.

(1) _____ que hay grandes liquidaciones hoy en el centro comercial. (2) _____ artículos por precios muy bajos. ¿Es verdad que las tiendas (3) _____ antes de las nueve?

Respuestas: 1. Se dice; 2. Se ofrecen; 3. se abren

Aplicación

8-26 En Otavalo. ¿Qué pasaba ayer en el mercado de Otavalo? Selecciona el verbo más lógico para completar el párrafo.

En la frutería, (1) se vendía/se vendían plátanos y piñas, pero (2) se prohibía/se prohibían tocarlos. En la sombrerería, (3) se hacía/se hacían sombreros de Panamá. ¡(4) Se dice/Se dicen que son los mismos sombreros que (5) se hace/se hacen en Ecuador! (6) Se ofrecía/Se ofrecían jugo de caña de azúcar por veinte centavos. En muchos puestos, (7) se compraba/se compraban hermosos suéteres de alpaca. (8) Se explicaba/Se explicaban que la lana de alpaca es más suave que la de oveja (*sheep*). (9) Se ofrecía/Se ofrecían descuentos a las personas que llegaban temprano. (10) Se servía/Se servían el almuerzo al mediodía.

En Otavalo, se vendían sombreros para hombres y mujeres.

8-27   Un concierto. En el Anfiteatro del Parque de la Exposición, en Lima, se dan eventos culturales. Aquí tienes información sobre un concierto de música andina.

Paso 1   Selecciona el verbo apropiado para completar el párrafo sobre el concierto.

| se abre   se cierra   se conoce   se ofrece   se presenta   se puede   se recibe   se venden |

Si a usted le apasiona la música andina, lo invitamos este fin de semana a este gran concierto que (1) _____ como uno de los mejores del mundo y donde (2) _____ la música más típica de Perú y de Ecuador. La taquilla donde (3) _____ las entradas (4) _____ a las nueve de la mañana y (5) _____ a las ocho de la noche. Además, (6) _____ una gran variedad de precios para las entradas. (7) _____ un descuento si compran más de cinco entradas. Después del concierto, (8) _____ pasear por los jardines, tomar un pisco sour y conocer a algunos de los músicos.

Gran concierto de
Música andina

Anfiteatro del
Parque de la Exposición

sábado, 15 de octubre
20:00 h

Entradas desde
25 S/

Paso 2   Contesta las preguntas sobre la lectura.

1. ¿Qué se anuncia?
2. ¿Cómo son los precios que se ofrecen?
3. ¿Qué tipo de música se escucha?
4. ¿Qué se puede hacer después del concierto?

8-28   ¿Dónde se encuentra? Ustedes planean un viaje a Machu Picchu y necesitan información para comprar varios artículos para el viaje. En parejas, conversen sobre dónde van a encontrar lo que necesitan. Incluyan estas expresiones: **se dice que; se vende(n); se compra(n); se encuentra(n); se puede; se cree que.**

MODELO: botas de cuero
ESTUDIANTE 1:   *¿Dónde se venden botas de cuero?*
ESTUDIANTE 2:   *Se dice que se venden en…*

1. información sobre el tren a Machu Picchu
2. una lista de hoteles en Cuzco
3. botas impermeables
4. guantes de lana
5. pantalones de algodón
6. un suéter de alpaca
7. crema solar
8. un sombrero de Panamá

8-29   Un negocio nuevo. Ustedes quieren abrir un negocio nuevo (un café, un almacén, una farmacia, etc.), y tienen que decidir todos los detalles del negocio. Conversen sobre estos detalles y sigan el modelo.

MODELO: las horas
ESTUDIANTE 1:   *La joyería se abre a las… y se cierra a las…*
ESTUDIANTE 2:   *No estoy de acuerdo. Se dice que es mejor abrirse a las…*

1. dónde se encuentra
2. las tarjetas de crédito
3. lo que se vende o el servicio que se ofrece
4. lo que se dice sobre el negocio
5. lo que se opina sobre el negocio en las reseñas (*reviews*)

8-30 Planes para este fin de semana. En parejas, hagan planes para hacer algo interesante este fin de semana. Usen una construcción impersonal o una pasiva con **se** para hablar de las posibilidades y hacer sus planes. A continuación tienen algunas expresiones que pueden usar.

> se dice que... se vende(n)... se necesita(n)... se cree que... se abre(n)...
> (no) se permite... se anuncia(n)... se puede... ¿...?

MODELO: ESTUDIANTE 1: *Se dice que el sábado hay un concierto de Adele en el estadio de la universidad. ¿Sabes dónde se venden las entradas?*

ESTUDIANTE 2: *Creo que se venden entradas en Internet o en la taquilla... Se cree que ella...*

¡Conversemos!

Primero, pregúntate si puedes llevar a cabo las siguientes funciones comunicativas en español. Después, júntate con dos o tres compañeros/as de clase para presentar las situaciones. Hagan y respondan a por lo menos cuatro preguntas en cada situación.

✓ CAN YOU ...

☐ shop for personal care products or jewelry?

☐ contrast what happened with something else that was going on?

☐ talk about what people say and believe?

☐ talk about what is done?

WITH YOUR CLASSMATE(S) ...

Situación: De compras.

Uno/a de ustedes necesita comprar varios artículos personales. Explica qué quieres comprar y para quién(es), y decide entre varias opciones. El/La dependiente/a siempre quiere venderles los artículos más caros. Usen las palabras y expresiones de **Vocabulario**.

Para empezar: *Necesito comprar acondicionador y pasta de dientes para mi compañera de cuarto. ¿Tiene alguna rebaja?*

Situación: Un evento importante.

Hablen sobre lo que hacían cuando algo importante ocurrió en el pasado, por ejemplo, recibieron alguna noticia importante, anunciaron la muerte de una persona importante o los resultados de una elección política, tuvieron un accidente, etc. Usen expresiones como **anoche**, **el año pasado**, **ayer**, **mientras**, **de repente**, etc., para describir la acción.

Para empezar: *Ayer veía la televisión, cuando de repente anunciaron...*

Situación: Mi tienda favorita.

Hablen sobre las mejores tiendas de su ciudad donde pueden comprar los mejores productos por un precio bueno, etc. Usen expresiones como **se dice**, **se cree**, etc.

Para empezar: *Se dice que este almacén es el más barato de esta ciudad. ¿Estás de acuerdo?*

Situación: Mis productos favoritos.

Hablen sobre los mejores productos personales, dónde y por cuánto se venden. Usen expresiones como **se vende**, **se ofrece**, **se abre**, etc.

Para empezar: *En mi opinión, la mejor crema hidratante se vende en el salón Bello...*

Club cultura

8.6 Use images to support narration

Machu Picchu, la ciudad perdida de los incas

Estrategia para ver

Use images to support narration. Pay close attention to the images while the narrator is speaking. These will help you connect what you hear with what you see.

ANTES DE VER EL VIDEO

8-31 Una ciudad "perdida" (*lost*). Observa la imagen del video sobre Machu Picchu e indica **sí** o **no** al lado de cada descripción, según la imagen.

1. _____ Está en una ciudad.
2. _____ Está en una montaña.
3. _____ Es difícil llegar aquí.
4. _____ Tiene terrazas.
5. _____ Tiene edificios altos.
6. _____ Está cerca de la costa.

AL VER EL VIDEO

8-32 Imágenes. ¿Cómo ilustra Laura estas ideas en el video? Selecciona la mejor opción para cada idea.

1. _____ La cultura hispana ha tenido (*has had*) infuencia en Perú.
2. _____ Las construcciones incas son perfectas.
3. _____ Los incas tenían una zona agrícola.
4. _____ Los incas tenían una zona urbana.

a. Laura muestra (*shows*) edificios de la ciudad.
b. Laura muestra las terrazas.
c. Laura muestra la Plaza de Armas.
d. Laura no puede insertar una tarjeta de crédito.

DESPUÉS DE VER EL VIDEO

8-33 ¿Comprendiste? Selecciona la opción que mejor completa cada oración.

1. Para llegar a este lugar, tienes que ir en (avión / un todoterreno [*off-road vehicle*] / tren).
2. El símbolo más importante de la civilización inca es (Qorikancha / Machu Picchu / Pachacútec).
3. El nombre significa ("ciudad perdida" / "montaña vieja" / "palacio real [*royal*]").
4. Las construcciones resisten (los huracanes / los tsunamis / los terremotos).
5. El sitio fue abandonado (en el siglo VI / por los españoles / por razones desconocidas [*unknown*]).

8-34 La ciudad perdida. Escribe un párrafo en el pasado describiendo la visita de Laura a Machu Picchu. Usa las imágenes del video como referencia. Incluye una descripción del lugar, el clima y las actividades que hizo.

> MODELO: *Era la primavera cuando Laura visitó Machu Picchu. Ese día hacía buen tiempo, pero estaba nublado…*

8.3 Nuestro mundo

Panoramas

8.7 Identify and research some important cultural aspects of Peru and Ecuador

El imperio inca: Perú y Ecuador

Perú y Ecuador ponen a la vista un tesoro de diversidad cultural, ecológica, gastronómica y topográfica. Ecuador es uno de los países más biodiversos del mundo: tiene más de 20.000 especies de plantas y alrededor de 1.500 de tipos de aves. Además, en los últimos años, Perú experimenta un gran desarrollo económico.

Hay muchos caminos que conducen a Cuzco, pero ninguno como el Camino Inca, el más famoso de las Américas.

El archipiélago de las Islas Galápagos es famoso por su impresionante variedad de vida marítima y terrestre, como los pájaros bobos de patas azules (*blue-footed boobies*). Es aquí también donde el investigador Charles Darwin descubrió que las especies habían evolucionado para adaptarse a las condiciones de cada isla.

La cocina de Perú y la de Ecuador son una fusión de tradiciones andinas y marinas, y hoy cuenta con algunos de los chefs más destacados del mundo. Desde la gran variedad de papas y maíz, hasta los mariscos del famoso ceviche en salsa de limón, chile y sal, hay algo sabroso para todos los gustos.

Puedes descender por un sendero (*path*) entre abundante vegetación, y cruzar el puente colgante (*hanging bridge*) para observar la espectacular vista de la cascada El Pailón del Diablo cerca de Baños, en los altos Andes de Ecuador. Por ser volcánica, la temperatura del agua es de 23° C (o 73° F), todo el año.

El Jirón de la Unión es una calle peatonal en el centro histórico de Lima. Durante muchos años, fue la vía más importante de la ciudad, y donde vivía la gente más acomodada. Hoy es donde la gente pasea para comprar ropa, comer o reunirse con los amigos.

	Perú	Ecuador
Población:	31 millones	16 millones
Lenguas[1]:	español, quechua, aimara y otras amerindias	español, quechua, shuar y otras amerindias
Tarjetas de crédito:	En todas partes, menos en mercados. Es común dar mejor precio cuando se paga en efectivo.	No en tiendas pequeñas, ni en mercados.
Textiles que se exportan:	el algodón Pima, Supima, rayón, telas de punto[2], poliéster	telas planas[3] y telas de punto de lana, algodón y fibras sintéticas

[1]*Both Perú and Ecuador have many indigenous languages which are considered official at the local level.*
[2]*knit*   [3]*woven*

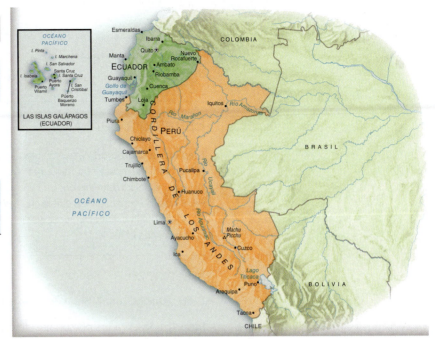

8-35 Identifica. Selecciona la opción correcta según la información de **Panoramas**.

el Camino Inca	el ceviche	Charles Darwin	el Jirón de la Unión	el Pailón del Diablo

1. el científico inglés que hizo investigaciones en las Islas Galápagos
   _____

2. un camino que se puede seguir a pie (*on foot*) hasta llegar a Machu Picchu
   _____

3. donde comprar en Lima _____

4. una cascada impresionante en Ecuador _____

5. un plato de mariscos, limón, chile y sal _____

8-36 Desafío. Identifica la información según el mapa y los datos estadísticos.

1. la capital de Ecuador y la de Perú

2. los países en las fronteras de Perú y de Ecuador

3. el país más grande de los dos

4. dónde se permite usar tarjetas de crédito

5. algunos textiles que se exportan

8-37 Investigación: Perú y Ecuador. Selecciona uno de estos lugares: **Nazca**, **Cuzco**, **Cuenca**, **Islas Galápagos**, **Baños** u otro que te interese de Perú o Ecuador. Usa el modelo para escribir un resumen de tu investigación y luego preséntaselo a la clase. Incluye:

- su nombre y dónde se encuentra
- por qué es importante o interesante
- cómo era en el pasado; cómo es ahora
- si quieres visitarlo o verlo algún día y por qué
- una foto representativa

📍 **Busca:** Nazca; Cuzco; Cuenca EC; Islas Galápagos; Baños

MODELO: *Quito es la capital de Ecuador. Se encuentra a una altura de 2.850 metros y está rodeada de las altas montañas de los Andes...*

Páginas

8.8 **Step into a character**

"Los rivales y el juez" (Ciro Alegría, Perú)

Estrategia para leer

Step into a character. When you read a story, try to identify with one of the characters, such as the hero, the trickster, or the target. Analyze the choices the character makes by asking: Why did the character make this choice? Would you have done the same? Was there an alternative? What was the consequence of this choice? What advice would you give to the character? When you identify with a character, your reading can elicit an emotional response and help deepen your understanding of the text.

ANTES DE LEER

8-38 ¿Quiénes son? Sigue los pasos para completar la actividad.

Paso 1   Observa los personajes de esta fábula y luego, selecciona la descripción que corresponde a cada personaje.

El sapo

La cigarra

La garza

1. _____ el sapo
2. _____ la cigarra
3. _____ la garza

a. pequeño/a, color verde y marrón, seis patas
b. alto/a, gris, elegante, pico largo
c. bajo/a y gordo/a, cuatro patas, feo/a

Paso 2   ¿Cuál de estos personajes te parece el más talentoso? ¿el más bonito? ¿el más inteligente? ¿el más ufano (*conceited*)? Explica tus razones.

AL LEER

8-39 Una historia folclórica. Los cuentos del escritor peruano Ciro Alegría dan vida y validez a las tradiciones y al folclore de los indígenas de Perú. Lee esta fábula para saber qué les pasó a los personajes: el sapo, la cigarra y la garza.

"Los rivales y el juez[1]"

Un sapo estaba muy ufano de su voz y toda la noche se la pasaba cantando: toc, toc, toc.

Y una cigarra estaba más ufana de su voz, y se pasaba toda la noche y también todo el día cantando: chirr, chirr, chirr.

Una vez se encontraron y el sapo le dijo: "Mi voz es mejor".

Y la cigarra contestó: "La mía es mejor".

Se armó una discusión que no tenía cuándo acabar[2].

El sapo decía que él cantaba toda la noche.

La cigarra decía que ella cantaba día y noche.

El sapo decía que su voz se oía a más distancia y la cigarra que su voz se oía siempre.

Se pusieron a cantar alternándose: toc, toc, toc; chirr, chirr, chirr y ninguno se convencía.

Y el sapo dijo: "Por aquí a la orilla[3] de la laguna, se para[4] una garza. Vamos a que haga de juez".

Y la cigarra dijo: "Vamos". Saltaron y saltaron hasta que vieron a la garza.

Y la cigarra gritó: "Garza, queremos únicamente que nos digas cuál de nosotros dos canta mejor".

La garza respondió: "Entonces acérquense[5] para oírlos bien".

El sapo se puso a cantar, indiferente a todo y mientras tanto la garza se comió a la cigarra. Cuando el sapo terminó, dijo la garza: "Ahora seguirá la discusión en mi buche[6]", y también se lo comió. Y la garza, satisfecha de su acción, encogió una pata[7] y siguió mirando tranquilamente el agua.

[1]*judge*

[2]*had no end*

[3]*shore*   [4]*se encuentra*

[5]vengan cerca

[6]*belly*   [7]*drew up a leg*

DESPUÉS DE LEER

8-40 ¿Comprendiste? Contesta las preguntas sobre los personajes y la moraleja (la lección) de la fábula.

1. ¿Quiénes son los personajes?
2. ¿Tiene lugar en una ciudad o en el campo?
3. ¿Es de día o de noche?
4. ¿Quién canta mejor? ¿Quién es el más inteligente?
5. En tu opinión, ¿cuál es la moraleja de esta fábula?

8-41 En su experiencia. En parejas, conversen sobre su experiencia con esta fábula y otros cuentos.

1. ¿Con qué personaje se identifican más y por qué?
2. ¿Conocen otra fábula con una moraleja semejante (*similar*)?
3. Piensen en un personaje de la televisión, del cine o de verdad que, en su opinión, sea como uno de los personajes de esta fábula. ¿Pueden Uds. identificarse con él o ella? ¿Por qué?

Taller

8.9 **Use conventions of storytelling**

Una fábula

Estrategia para escribir

Use conventions of storytelling. Stories follow certain conventions that are predictable to the reader. Fables and fairytales often begin with **Érase una vez...** (*Once upon a time...*) and may end with **Y así fue** (*And that's what happened*). There may also be an explicit **moraleja** (*moral*). Stories often include transitions and contrasts, with expressions like **entonces**, **de repente**, and **por fin** or **finalmente**.

8-42 **Un cuento tuyo.** Escribe una fábula siguiendo el modelo de **Páginas** de este capítulo. Recuerda que los personajes son animales y que debe contener una moraleja explícita o implícita.

ANTES DE ESCRIBIR

- Identifica la moraleja de la historia. Muchas veces es un refrán popular, como "Más vale pájaro en mano que cien volando" o "Antes de pedir dinero a un amigo, piensa bien cuál de las dos cosas necesitas más".

- Identifica los animales que personifiquen la moraleja. Escribe una lista de sus características físicas y psicológicas. Estos son algunos ejemplos:

la araña (*spider*)	la ardilla (*squirrel*)	la culebra (*snake*)
el galápago (*giant tortoise*)	el gato (*cat*)	la iguana
el lobo (*wolf*)	el loro (*parrot*)	el pájaro bobo de patas azules
el pato (*duck*)	el perro	el zorro (*fox*)

- Piensa en el lugar donde la acción ocurre; escribe una lista de sus características.

- Elige expresiones de **Estrategia para escribir** para presentar, añadir coherencia a y concluir tu fábula.

AL ESCRIBIR

- Escribe tu primera versión de la moraleja.

- Empieza tu narración con **Érase una vez....** Escribe dos o tres oraciones en el imperfecto para describir el lugar (*setting*) y los personajes.

- Escribe dos o tres oraciones en el imperfecto para explicar el problema o el conflicto entre los personajes.

- Escribe dos o tres oraciones en el pretérito para contar lo que pasó y cómo se resolvió.

- Si hay una moraleja explícita, escríbela al final para resumir la fábula.

   MODELO: *Érase una vez, en la alta sierra de Ecuador, vivían una alpaca y un cóndor...*

DESPUÉS DE ESCRIBIR

- **Revisar.** Revisa tu fábula para verificar estos puntos:
  - ☐ el uso de las técnicas de **Estrategia para escribir**.
  - ☐ el uso del imperfecto (la escena; las características de los personajes).
  - ☐ el uso del pretérito (lo que pasó; cómo se resolvió).
  - ☐ la ortografía y la concordancia.

- **Intercambiar.** Intercambia tu fábula con la de otro/a compañero/a para hacer correcciones y sugerencias y para comentar sobre la moraleja de la fábula.

- **Entregar.** Crea tu versión final, incorporando las sugerencias de tu compañero/a. Después, entrégasela a tu profesor/a.

En este capítulo...

))) Vocabulario

Primera parte

La ropa y los accesorios	Clothing and accessories
el abrigo	coat
la billetera	wallet
la blusa	blouse
las botas	boots
los calcetines	socks
la camisa	shirt
la camiseta (sin mangas)	t-shirt (tank top)
las chanclas	flip-flops
la chaqueta	jacket, windbreaker
la corbata	tie
la (mini)falda	(mini) skirt
la gorra	baseball cap
los pantalones (cortos)	pants (shorts)
las sandalias	sandals
la sudadera (con capucha)	(hooded) sweatshirt
el suéter	sweater
el traje	suit
los vaqueros	jeans
el vestido	dress
las zapatillas de deporte	running shoes, sneakers
los zapatos (de tacón alto)	(high-heeled) shoes

Los materiales	Materials
el algodón	cotton
el cuero	leather
la lana	wool
la seda	silk

Descripciones	Descriptions
de cuadros	plaid
de manga corta/larga	short-/long-sleeved
de moda	in style
de rayas	striped

Dónde comprar	Where to shop
el almacén	department store
el centro comercial	shopping center, mall
el mercado (al aire libre)	(open-air) market

En la tienda	In the store/shop
la caja	register
el/la cliente/a	customer
el/la dependiente/a	sales clerk
el descuento	discount
la ganga	bargain, good deal
el precio	price
el probador	fitting room
el recibo	receipt

Verbos	Verbs
calzar	to wear (shoes)
estar en rebaja/liquidación	to be on sale/clearance
llevar	to wear
pagar (en efectivo / con tarjeta de crédito / con celular)	to pay (with cash / credit card / cell phone)
probarse (ue)	to try on
regatear	to bargain, to haggle over

Segunda parte

En la farmacia y perfumería	In the pharmacy and beauty supply shop
el acondicionador	conditioner
el cepillo de dientes	toothbrush
la colonia	cologne
la crema hidratante / de afeitar	facial cream / shaving cream
el desodorante	deodorant
la pasta de dientes	toothpaste
el perfume	perfume
el talco	talcum powder

En la joyería	In the jewelry store
el anillo	ring
los aretes	earrings (post)
la cadena	chain
el collar	necklace
los pendientes	earrings (pendant)
la pulsera	bracelet
el reloj inteligente / de pulsera	smart watch / wristwatch

Descripciones	Descriptions
de diamantes	diamond
de oro	gold
de perlas	pearl
de plata	silver

Más tiendas	More shops
la carnicería	butcher shop
la florería	flower shop
la heladería	ice cream shop
la panadería	bakery
la papelería	stationery shop
la pastelería	pastry shop
la quesería	cheese shop
la zapatería	shoe store

Verbos	Verbs
devolver (ue)	to return (something)
gastar	to spend
hacer juego (con)	to match, to go well with

Shopping expressions   See page 251.
Ordinal numbers   See page 258.

Capítulo 9
Vamos de viaje

«Allá donde fueres, haz como vieres».

Fuente: Rafael Campillo / agefotostock

Los ricos, **Fernando Botero. El boterismo** is a style attributed to this Colombian artist in which he depicts people and figures in an exaggerated manner meant to satirize and make fun of political groups and the super wealthy. His work is the most recognizable of any Latin American artist.

Learning Objectives

9.1 Make travel arrangements

9.2 Give reasons and purpose, and describe actions and conditions

9.3 Learn about adventure travel in Venezuela, and hear a renowned Colombian musician

9.4 Describe travel and vacation experiences

9.5 Try to influence others, and give advice

9.6 Summarize what you have seen

9.7 Identify and research some important cultural aspects of Colombia and Venezuela

9.8 Read for purpose

9.9 Give advice

In this Chapter

ENFOQUE CULTURAL: COLOMBIA Y VENEZUELA
Club cultura: Introducción a Colombia

Indica con **C (Cierto)** o **F (Falso)** si escuchas/ves o no esta información en el video.

1. _____ el nombre oficial del país y de la capital

2. _____ la población

3. _____ el Museo de Antropología

4. _____ la ciudad histórica de Cartagena de Indias

5. _____ algunos ejemplos de la biodiversidad

9.1 Primera parte

Vocabulario

9.1 Make travel arrangements

En el aeropuerto

Daniel Mauricio Marisela

De vacaciones. Marisela, Mauricio y Daniel están por **abordar el avión** de Caracas a Bogotá.

MARISELA: ¡Ay! ¡Toda una semana sin clases! ¡Qué chévere!

MAURICIO: Sí, pero primero tenemos que **hacer cola** para pasar por **el control de seguridad**...

DANIEL: ...y quitarnos los zapatos, sacar la portátil de la mochila, ...

MARISELA: Oye, Daniel, ¿tienes tu **tarjeta de embarque** a mano?

DANIEL: ¡Claro, y **el pasaporte**! Por cierto, chicos, ¡el precio del **sitio web de viajes** fue una ganga!

MAURICIO: Es verdad, **paquete de vuelo y hotel** en Cartagena, excursión al Parque Tayrona...

MARISELA: ¡Y todo por solo ochocientos noventa y nueve dólares por persona!

¿Comprendes? Complete the sentences with the correct option: **aborda, hacer cola, el control de seguridad, tarjeta de embarque**.

Antes de pasar por (1) _____, Marisela tiene que (2) _____ y mostrar su (3) _____. Después, (4) _____ el avión.

Respuestas: 1. el control de seguridad; 2. hacer cola; 3. tarjeta de embarque; 4. aborda

))) Vocabulario

En el sitio web de viajes	On the travel web site
el boleto (electrónico)	(e-)ticket
el destino	destination
el equipaje (permitido)	luggage (policy)
el pasaje (de ida y vuelta)	(round-trip) fare, ticket
el paquete de viaje (vuelo/hotel/carro)	(flight/hotel/car) travel package
la reservación / la reserva	reservation

En el aeropuerto	In the airport
la aduana	customs
el/la agente	agent
el avión	plane
el control de seguridad	security checkpoint
el/la inspector/a de aduanas	customs inspector
el mostrador (de la aerolínea)	(airline) counter
el pasaporte	passport
la puerta de embarque	boarding gate
la sala de espera	waiting room
el reclamo de equipaje	baggage claim
la tarjeta de embarque	boarding pass
el/la viajero/a	traveler
el vuelo	flight

En el avión	On the plane
el asiento (de pasillo/ventanilla)	(aisle/window) seat
el/la asistente de vuelo	flight attendant
la clase turista/ejecutiva	coach/business class
el compartimento superior	overhead bin
la demora	delay
la llegada	arrival
el/la pasajero/a	passenger
el/la piloto	pilot
la salida	departure

Verbos	Verbs
abordar (el avión/autobús/barco/tren)	to board (the plane/bus/boat/train)
aterrizar	to land
bajarse (del autobús/avión, etc.)	to get off (of), to get down (from) (the bus/plane, etc.)
despegar	to take off
esperar	to wait for; to hope for
facturar el equipaje	to check baggage
hacer cola	to stand in line
hacer escala	to make a stopover
hacer un crucero	to take a cruise
hacer la maleta	to pack one's suitcase
pasar por seguridad (inmigración/la aduana)	to go through security (immigration/customs)
revisar (el equipaje)	to inspect (the luggage)
viajar por (barco, etc.)	to travel by (ship, etc.)

Variaciones

- In Latin America, you purchase **un boleto**; in Spain, **un billete**.
- Although **el carro** is common throughout the Americas for *car*, you will hear **el auto** (from **el automóvil**) in Argentina and Chile, **el coche** in Spain (where **el carro** means *cart, wagon*), and colloquially, **la nave** (*ship*) in some places.
- You can usually use **el autobús** to mean *intercity bus*, although **el camión** is a *local bus* in Mexico.

Aplicación

9-1 En el aeropuerto. Siempre hay mucha actividad en el Aeropuerto Internacional de Maiquetía (Simón Bolívar), Caracas. Selecciona la frase que mejor completa cada oración.

1. _____ Los pasajeros están esperando en...

2. _____ Antes de abordar el avión, los inspectores de seguridad les revisan...

3. _____ Algunos pasajeros van a pasar sus vacaciones en...

4. _____ El sitio web de viajes les dio un paquete muy económico; fue...

5. _____ El asistente de vuelo les ayudó a subir una mochila...

6. _____ Según el piloto, el avión despega en cinco minutos, y...

a. si no hay demora, aterriza en dos horas.

b. una verdadera ganga.

c. la cola para pasar por el control de seguridad.

d. la ciudad colonial de Cartagena.

e. las maletas y las bolsas.

f. al compartimento superior.

9-2 Planes para un viaje. En parejas, preparen un viaje como el de Marisela y sus amigos. Usen números ordinales para ordenar las actividades lógicamente y poder hacer el viaje. Escriban una última actividad original al final.

Vamos a...

primero pedir dos semanas de vacaciones

_____ bajarnos del avión

_____ abrirle la maleta al aduanero (*customs officer*)

_____ hacer cola para abordar el avión

_____ hacer la maleta

_____ consultar un sitio web de viajes

_____ pedir un taxi para el aeropuerto

_____ darle la tarjeta de embarque al asistente de vuelo

_____ hacer las reservaciones del avión

décimo _____

9-3 Destino: Caracas. Estás en ruta a Caracas a pasar las vacaciones con amigos venezolanos. Completa las oraciones con una palabra o frase del **Vocabulario**.

MODELO: Los pasajeros le piden un refresco al _asistente de vuelo_ .

1. Para las vacaciones, tenemos _____ de ida y vuelta de Cleveland a Caracas.

2. Tenemos asientos en _____ porque es más económica que la ejecutiva.

3. El avión no puede salir a tiempo por la tempestad y los vientos. Hay una _____ de media hora.

4. Si el avión no _____ pronto, vamos a perder nuestra conexión en Miami.

5. Durante el vuelo, el piloto nos informa que tenemos que hacer _____ en Atlanta.

6. A las once de la noche, llegamos a Caracas, donde pasamos por el control de inmigración y recogemos nuestras maletas en el _____ .

7. Después, tenemos que pasar por la _____ , donde el agente nos revisa las maletas para ver si llevamos fruta o plantas prohibidas.

8. Enseguida, tomamos un taxi al hotel donde tenemos una _____ por tres noches.

Cultura en vivo

Before traveling abroad, be sure to check the visa requirements of your destination country or countries. Many have reciprocity agreements with the U.S., which means they require a visa and fee that is equal to what the U.S. charges, and they may require you to apply for the visa months ahead of time. Most tourist visas last for three months, and do not allow you to work. If you plan to stay longer to study, work, or travel, you will have to apply for the appropriate visa (or plan to return to the U.S. during your stay). The U.S. Department of State has a single web site with links to country-specific information. Do you have a passport? Which Spanish-speaking country would you visit first? Do you need a visa for that country?

9-4 Un vuelo en avión. Parece que Marisela, Mauricio y Daniel se equivocaron (*made a mistake*) de vuelo. Escucha el anuncio que ellos oyen en el avión e indica la información correcta del vuelo.

1. aerolínea:
   a. Iberia   b. Conviasa   c. LACSA

2. número:
   a. 895   b. 985   c. 995

3. destino:
   a. San Juan   b. San José   c. San Antonio

4. maletas:
   a. en la cabina de clase   b. en el pasillo   c. en el compartimiento
      ejecutiva   superior

5. película:
   a. cubana   b. venezolana   c. colombiana

6. documentos:
   a. para transporte   b. para el hotel   c. para la aduana
      terrestre (*ground*)

9-5A ¡Necesito información! En parejas, hagan el papel de agente (estudiante A) y viajero/a (estudiante B) en el mostrador del aeropuerto de la aerolínea colombiana Avianca. Tengan una conversación siguiendo la guía. **Estudiante B:** por favor, ve al **Apéndice 1**, página A-10.

MODELO: AGENTE: Saluda al / a la viajero/a.
                        Buenas tardes. ¿En qué puedo servirle?
              VIAJERO/A: Saluda al / a la agente; Dile (*Tell him/her*) adónde viajas hoy.
                        Buenas tardes. Viajo a (Bogotá/Cartagena/Medellín, etc.).

Estudiante A: El/La agente

1. Saluda al / a la viajero/a.

3. Dile la hora de salida, el número del vuelo y el número de la puerta de embarque.

5. No se permiten más de _____ maletas.

7. No se permite llevar más de _____ onzas de líquido en la maleta de mano.

9. Hay asientos en clase ejecutiva, pero hay que pagar _____ dólares.

11. No se sirve comida en el avión, pero puede comprarla en _____.

13. Si es el fin de la conversación, dile "Buen viaje".

9-6 ¿Qué tipo de viajero eres? Contesta las preguntas de la encuesta (*survey*) para saber qué puntuación recibes. Luego, con un/a compañero/a, comparen sus resultados para ver qué tipo de viajero es cada uno, económico o gastador.

1. Si puedo, me gusta viajar...
   a. en clase turista.
   b. en avión privado.
   c. en clase ejecutiva.
   d. en un vuelo con descuento.

2. Para hacer la reservación de un vuelo de vacaciones por el Día de Acción de Gracias (*Thanksgiving*), ...
   a. consulto a un agente de viajes y le pago su comisión.
   b. la hago en el sitio web de mi aerolínea favorita para ganar millas.
   c. busco en varios sitios web para conseguir el mejor precio.
   d. la hago algunos días antes, aunque tenga que pagar más.

3. En el vuelo, las demoras...
   a. son parte de la experiencia.
   b. no me importan porque tengo acceso a la sala de espera VIP de la aerolínea.
   c. no me molestan porque tengo algo que leer.
   d. me preocupan porque temo perder mi conexión.

4. Cuando viajo, ...
   a. llevo todo en una mochila.
   b. facturo una sola maleta para no tener que pagar extra.
   c. pago extra para abordar antes que los otros pasajeros.
   d. muchas veces pago extra por exceso de peso (*weight*) en el equipaje.

5. Para llegar al aeropuerto, ...
   a. llamo un taxi.
   b. un/a amigo/a me lleva.
   c. voy en transporte público.
   d. voy en carro y lo dejo en un estacionamiento con valet.

6. Al llegar a mi destino, ...
   a. busco la salida al metro o al autobús.
   b. el maletero recoge mi equipaje y subo a la limusina que me está esperando.
   c. busco otras personas para compartir un taxi al centro.
   d. hago cola para tomar un taxi solo/a.

Puntos de cada respuesta: 1. a=2, b=4, c=3, d=1; 2. a=3, b=2, c=1, d=4; 3. a=1, b=2, c=4, d=3; 4. a=1, b=2, c=3, d=4; 5. a=3, b=1, c=2, d=4; 6. a=1, b=4, c=2, d=3

Puntuación de la encuesta

6 puntos: Planeas tus viajes con mucho cuidado. Prefieres viajar sencillamente y económicamente.

7–12 puntos: Te gustan los descuentos, y también acumular millas para viajar gratis.

13–18 puntos: Te importa viajar cómodamente. No te importa pagar extra por buen servicio.

19–24 puntos: Tienes un fondo fiduciario (*trust fund*) de un tío rico. El costo del viaje te importa poco.

Estructuras

9.2 Give reasons and purpose, and describe actions and conditions

Por or *para*

¿Recuerdas? You've used the prepositions **por** and **para** in common phrases. Complete the sentences with the correct preposition.

Tengo que trabajar (1) _____ la tarde. Y después salgo (2) _____ la casa. ¿Es posible llamarme más tarde, (3) _____ favor?

Respuestas: 1. por; 2. para; 3. por.

¿Para qué y por cuánto tiempo vienes a Venezuela?

Vengo para estudiar por un mes.

ADUANA

USE *POR* TO EXPRESS . . .

- the time during which an action takes place or its duration (*during, for*).

Vamos al aeropuerto **por la tarde**.	*We are going to the airport during the afternoon.*
Pienso estudiar en Caracas **por un semestre**.	*I am planning to study in Caracas for a semester.*

- motion (*through, by, along, around*).

Pasé **por el control de seguridad**.	*I passed through the security checkpoint.*
Hay muchas maletas **por el reclamo de equipaje**.	*There are a lot of suitcases around the baggage claim.*

- the object/goal of an action or a person being sought after (*for*).

Vamos **por usted** a las dos.	*We'll come by for you at two o'clock.*
Los estudiantes fueron **por el equipaje**.	*The students went for their luggage.*

- *because of, in exchange for,* or *on behalf of.*

Tuve que cancelar el vuelo **por una emergencia**.	*I had to cancel the flight because of an emergency.*
Pagué $250 **por el boleto**.	*I paid $250 for the ticket.*
¿Lo hiciste **por mí**?	*Did you do it for me?*

- the means by or manner in which an action is accomplished (*by*).

¿Recibiste los pasajes **por correo electrónico**?	*Did you receive the tickets by e-mail?*
Hicimos las reservaciones **por Internet**.	*We made the reservations by Internet.*

- You also use **por** in many common idiomatic expressions.

estar por	*to be about to*
por ahora	*for now*
por aquí	*around here*
por cierto	*by the way, indeed*
por Dios	*for heaven's (lit. God's) sake*
por eso	*that's why*
por ejemplo	*for example*
por favor	*please*
por fin	*finally, at last*
por lo general	*in general*
por supuesto	*of course*
por último	*finally (last item in a statement)*

¿Para quién son todas estas frutas?

Son para mí.

ADUANA

USE *PARA* TO EXPRESS . . .

- time limits or specific deadlines (*by, for*).

Necesito el pasaporte **para esta tarde**.	*I need the passport for this afternoon.*
Pienso estar en Cartagena **para las tres de la tarde**.	*I plan to be in Cartagena by three in the afternoon.*

- destination (a place or a recipient).

Mañana salimos **para Maracaibo**.	*Tomorrow we're leaving for Maracaibo.*
Este pasaje es **para ti**.	*This ticket is for you.*

- the purpose of an action (*in order to* + infinitive) or of an object (*for* + *-ing* form of verb).

Vamos a Colombia **para conocer** el país.	*We're going to Colombia in order to get to know the country.*
La cámara es **para sacar** fotos.	*The camera is for taking pictures.*

- a work objective.

Ana estudia **para piloto**.	*Ana is studying to be a pilot.*

- in whose opinion (*for*).

Para mí, siempre es divertido viajar.	*For me, it's always fun to travel.*

STUDY TIPS — DISTINGUISHING BETWEEN *POR* AND *PARA*

1. The uses of **por** and **para** have apparent similarities, which may cause confusion. In some cases it may be helpful to link their uses to the questions **¿por qué?** (*for what reason? what is behind it?*) and **¿para qué?** (*for what purpose? what is ahead of it?*).

   —¿**Por qué** viniste?
   Why (For what reason) did you come?

   —Vine **porque** necesitaba los boletos.
   I came because I needed the tickets.

   —¿**Para qué** viniste?
   For what purpose did you come?

   —Vine **para** pedirte un favor.
   I came (in order) to ask you a favor.

2. In many instances, the use of either **por** or **para** will be grammatically correct, but the meanings will be different. Compare the following sentences:

   Mario viaja **por** Cartagena.
   Mario is traveling through (in) Cartagena. (motion)

   Mario viaja **para** Cartagena.
   Mario is traveling to (toward) Cartagena. (destination)

3. Remember to use the prepositional object pronouns **mí** and **ti** after **por** and **para**.

   Nuestros padres lo hicieron **por mí** y **por ti**.
   Our parents did it for me and for you.

   Para mí, es importante viajar. ¿Y **para ti**?
   For me, it's important to travel. And for you?

¿Comprendes? Complete the sentences with **por** or **para**.

Teníamos pasajes (1) _____ Nueva York. (2) _____ eso, caminamos (3) _____ la terminal y buscamos el mostrador de Avianca. Compramos un sándwich (4) _____ comer en el avión.

Respuestas: 1. para; 2. Por; 3. por; 4. para

Aplicación

9-7 Un viaje a Colombia, Bogotá. Selecciona la respuesta más lógica para cada pregunta.

1. _____ ¿Tienen que hacer escala en Miami?

2. _____ ¿Tienen que hacer cola en el mostrador?

3. _____ ¿De qué puerta sale el avión?

4. _____ ¿Y estos regalos en la maleta?

5. _____ ¡Mira, ya son las 8:30!

a. ¡Por Dios! ¡Tenemos que ir corriendo para no perder el avión!

b. No sabemos el número todavía. El agente dice que debemos esperar por la terminal hasta que se anuncie el vuelo.

c. No. Vamos por Atlanta.

d. Sí, parece que hay una demora para facturar el equipaje.

e. Son algunas cositas para nuestros amigos en Bogotá.

9-8 Una entrevista con el ayudante de Fernando Botero. Este artista colombiano es uno de los pintores más ilustres de nuestro tiempo. Sus pinturas y esculturas aparecen en museos y en lugares públicos por todo el mundo. Lee la entrevista que Carmen le hace a su ayudante y complétala con **por** o **para**, según el contexto.

CARMEN: Buenas tardes. Soy Carmen Domínguez y trabajo (1) _____ el periódico digital *El Universal*. Estoy aquí (2) _____ aprender más sobre la carrera de este importante artista.

SANTIAGO: Claro que sí. Vamos a sentarnos aquí (3) _____ unos minutos para conversar.

CARMEN: Gracias. Bueno, (4) _____ empezar, el Sr. Botero nació en Medellín, pero después se fue a vivir a Bogotá. ¿(5) _____ qué no se quedó en Medellín?

SANTIAGO: Él dice que se fue por todas las oportunidades que se ofrecían en la capital. Ganó varios premios y decidió ir a Europa. (6) _____ supuesto, allí había muchas oportunidades (7) _____ colaborar con artistas de todo el mundo. Ahora financia museos y exhibiciones (8) _____ el público. Es muy generoso.

Este gato monumental por Fernando Botero saluda a las personas que pasan por la calle en Barcelona.

9-9 Un viaje a un lugar interesante. Con un/a compañero/a, hagan planes para visitar algún lugar interesante este verano. Usen estas preguntas para planear el viaje y después hagan un resumen de sus planes.

1. ¿Por qué hacemos el viaje? ¿Para cuándo va a ser? ¿Para dónde vamos?

2. ¿Por cuánto tiempo vamos?

3. ¿Salimos por la mañana o por la tarde?

4. ¿Cuánto vamos a pagar por los pasajes?

5. ¿Cuánto dinero vamos a necesitar para el hotel? ¿Y para la comida?

6. ¿Es necesario cambiar dólares por la moneda nacional para pagar en ese lugar?

9-10A ¡Necesito información! En parejas, conversen sobre los viajes que van a hacer en la primavera. Cada uno/a debe usar la información de su itinerario y las preguntas guía. Luego, deben intentar convencer (*try to convince*) a la otra persona de viajar juntos/as al destino que cada uno/a eligió. **Estudiante B**: por favor, ve al **Apéndice 1**, página A-11.

MODELO: ESTUDIANTE A: *¿Adónde vas para las vacaciones de primavera?*
ESTUDIANTE B: *Voy a... Y tú, ¿adónde vas para las vacaciones?*

Estudiante A:

	Mi viaje	El viaje de mi compañero/a
Destino:	Medellín, Colombia	
Propósito:	hacer servicio en una comunidad rural	
Transporte:	avión, autobús	
Ruta:	Miami, Medellín	
Duración del viaje:	una semana	
Fecha de llegada:	el primero de marzo	

Preguntas:

1. ¿Adónde vas?

2. ¿Por qué ruta vas a ese lugar?

3. ¿Cómo vas a viajar; por tren, por carro, por...?

4. ¿Cuándo es el viaje?

5. ¿Por cuánto tiempo vas?

6. ¿Para qué vas?

Al final, para convencer a tu compañero/a:

7. ¿Por qué no vienes conmigo? Creo que mi viaje va a ser...

Presencia hispana

South Florida has long been a destination for wealthy Venezuelans, first during the oil boom years when many went to shop or to buy property, and then later during the presidency of Hugo Chávez, when immigration included many from the upper and middle classes. For years, South Florida remained a vacation destination for Venezuelans with some 380,000 visitors each year, generating millions of dollars in tourism and merchandise revenue for the Miami area alone. However, with a strong U.S. dollar and hyperinflation in Venezuela, tourism has dropped considerably in recent years. What other economic sectors suffer from a reduction of tourism from any particular country?

Adverbs ending in *-mente*

¿Recuerdas? Provide the meaning of these adverbs in English.

1. frecuentemente: _____   2. igualmente: _____   3. generalmente: _____

Respuestas: 1. frequently; 2. equally (likewise); 3. generally

¡Nos queremos enormemente!

- An adverb modifies a verb, an adjective, or another adverb. In English, many adverbs add *-ly* to an adjective to form an adverb:

  slow → *slowly*   normal → *normally*

- In Spanish, add **-mente** to the feminine form of the adjective. Be sure to keep the accent if the adjective has one.

  lento → lent**a**mente   rápido → rápid**a**mente
  alegre → alegremente   fácil → f**á**cilmente

Teresa canceló el viaje **inmediatamente**.	*Teresa canceled the trip immediately.*
Cartagena de Indias es **particularmente** bella.	*Cartagena de Indias is particularly beautiful.*

¿Comprendes? Complete each sentence with the adverb of the appropriate adjective: **especial, fácil**.

Tenemos una guía de la ciudad; por eso, encontramos el museo (1) _____. Tiene una colección (2) _____ extensa de artefactos precolombinos.

Respuestas: 1. fácilmente; 2. especialmente

Aplicación

9-11 Un viaje a Cartagena de Indias. Hoy Esperanza y Ramón hacen un viaje a Cartagena de Indias. Selecciona el adverbio más lógico para completar la historia, según el contexto.

Antes del viaje, Esperanza y Ramón hacen sus maletas (1) rápidamente/ cuidadosamente para estar seguros que tienen la ropa que van a necesitar. Llegan al aeropuerto (2) puntualmente/especialmente dos horas antes de su vuelo. La agente de la aerolínea los saluda (3) cordialmente/tristemente con una sonrisa. Ella factura (4) correctamente/raramente la maleta de Esperanza. Ramón decide (5) lentamente/prudentemente llevar su maleta a bordo. (6) Elegantemente/ Generalmente, ellos preparan una merienda para llevar en el vuelo, pero esta vez deciden comprar algo en el aeropuerto. Aunque hay una demora de dos horas, ellos esperan (7) posiblemente/pacientemente en la sala de espera sin molestarse.

9-12 En el Museo del Oro de Bogotá. El Museo del Oro exhibe la colección de piezas de oro y otros artefactos prehispánicos más grande del mundo. Para las culturas indígenas de esta región, el oro era sagrado (*sacred*).

Paso 1 Lee el párrafo sobre una visita al Museo del Oro de Bogotá e indica los adverbios que terminan en -**mente**.

Cuando Alina y José vivían en Bogotá, iban frecuentemente al Museo del Oro para ver las diferentes exposiciones que tenían. Para llegar al museo, normalmente pasaban por el parque, especialmente cuando hacía buen tiempo. A José siempre le gustaba caminar lentamente, pero Alina siempre tenía más prisa y caminaba rápidamente. En el museo, José se sentaba en los bancos y tranquilamente leía todos los letreros (*signs*) sobre las piezas, pero Alina solamente sacaba fotos de ellas. Salían puntualmente a la hora que cerraba el museo y generalmente iban a un café donde se sentaban a tomar un refresco y a conversar animadamente sobre la visita. Siempre lo pasaban maravillosamente bien. Ahora que viven en Medellín, usualmente visitan el Museo de Antioquia los domingos porque tiene una gran colección de piezas de Fernando Botero.

Paso 2 Contesta las preguntas sobre el texto que acabas de leer.

1. ¿Cuántas veces iban Alina y José al Museo del Oro?
2. ¿Cómo iban normalmente?
3. ¿Cómo caminaba cada uno?
4. ¿Qué hacía José en el museo? ¿Y Alina?
5. ¿Qué hacían después de visitar el museo?
6. ¿Qué hacen ahora los domingos? ¿Por qué?

Paso 3 Escribe oraciones originales usando cinco de los adverbios que identificaste en el **Paso 1**.

> **MODELO:** *Cuando voy en avión, frecuentemente llevo todo en una mochila.*

9-13A ¡Necesito información! En el aeropuerto, antes de su vuelo a la Isla de Margarita, ustedes están observando lo que está pasando. Túrnense para hacerse preguntas y describir la escena. Contesten cada pregunta con un adverbio que termina en -**mente**. **Estudiante B:** por favor, ve al **Apéndice 1**, página A-11.

> **MODELO:** El inspector de seguridad está revisando una maleta (**especial**) misteriosa.
> ESTUDIANTE A: *¿Qué hace el inspector de seguridad?*
> ESTUDIANTE B: *Él está revisando una maleta especialmente misteriosa.*

Estudiante A:

Preguntas para mi compañero/a	Respuestas para mi compañero/a
1. ¿Qué hace la piloto?	• Él está caminando (**rápido**) hacia la puerta de embarque.
2. ¿Dónde están los pasajeros?	• Los que acaban de llegar están esperando (**paciente**) la llegada de sus maletas.
3. ¿Qué hace el inspector de aduanas?	• No. (**Increíble**) me ofrecieron un asiento en clase ejecutiva sin tener que pagar más.
4. ¿Hay una demora de tu vuelo?	• Sí, hay familias y amigos saludando (**animado**) a las personas que llegan.

9-14 ¿Probable o improbable? Sigue los pasos para completar esta actividad.

Paso 1 Escribe tres oraciones probables y tres improbables usando adverbios formados de diferentes adjetivos. Cada oración debe tener un mínimo de seis palabras y un verbo diferente.

alegre	cómodo	feliz	particular
amable	cuidadoso	frecuente	rápido
animado	difícil	lento	raro
ansioso	fácil	loco	tranquilo

Paso 2 En grupos de tres o cuatro personas, túrnese para leer sus oraciones y determinar si son probables o improbables.

MODELO: ESTUDIANTE 1:   (frecuente) *Viajo frecuentemente a Isla de Margarita.*
ESTUDIANTE 2:   *¡Improbable!*

¡Conversemos!

Primero, pregúntate si puedes llevar a cabo las siguientes funciones comunicativas en español. Después, júntate con dos o tres compañeros/as de clase para presentar las situaciones. Hagan y respondan a por lo menos cuatro preguntas en cada situación.

✓ CAN YOU . . .

☐ make travel arrangements?

☐ request and give travel-related information?

☐ talk about going to and through places?

☐ describe actions and conditions?

WITH YOUR CLASSMATE(S) . . .

Situación: Una conversación con un/a agente.

Hagan el papel de agente y viajero/a y pidan/den información sobre viajes. Usen palabras y expresiones del **Vocabulario** y hagan/contesten por lo menos cinco preguntas.

Para empezar: *Quiero visitar un lugar especialmente interesante y económico...*

Situación: En el aeropuerto.

Hagan el papel de viajero/a y agente en el mostrador de la aerolínea. Pidan/Den información sobre el vuelo (el control de seguridad, la sala de espera, el reclamo de equipaje, etc.).

Para empezar: *Perdone, ¿me puede decir dónde está... / el número de... / cómo puedo...?*

Situación: Por teléfono con un/a amigo/a.

Explíquense qué pasó en el último viaje que hicieron, cómo se prepararon para el viaje, cómo viajaron, por cuánto tiempo fueron, etc. Usen **por** y **para** en sus descripciones.

Para empezar: *Antes de salir, tuve que pasar por... el sitio web de viajes para...*

Situación: Un viaje inolvidable.

Hablen de sus impresiones de un lugar que conocieron. Usen adverbios que terminan en **-mente** para describir qué vieron en ese lugar y qué hicieron allí.

Para empezar: *Vancouver es una ciudad increíblemente bella. Caminamos lentamente por las calles...*

Perfiles

9.3 Learn about adventure travel in Venezuela, and hear a renowned Colombian musician

Mi experiencia

AUYANTEPUY: UN VIAJE DE AVENTURA

9-15 Para ti. ¿Cuáles son algunos de los parques nacionales más importantes de EE. UU. y Canadá? ¿Conoces alguno? ¿Fuiste de camping o hiciste algún viaje de aventura? A continuación Felipe te cuenta de una excursión que hizo a Venezuela. ¿Te gustaría hacer esta excursión también?

¿Qué húbole[1], muchachos (como dicen aquí en Venezuela)? Soy Felipe, de Uruguay. Este verano estoy viajando por Latinoamérica, en mi furgoneta[2], para conocer mejor este tremendo continente. Pienso contarles a todos mis amigos que me siguen por Internet todas mis aventuras. Primero paré unos días en Venezuela e hice un trekking a Auyantepuy, una montaña en el Parque Nacional Canaima.

¡Qué lugar tan misterioso! Tiene paisajes irregulares, cuevas[3] y ríos[4] que aparecen y desaparecen, rocas y murallas de arenisca[5]. Entiendo bien por qué la llaman la "Montaña del Diablo". El viaje duró diez días y cada noche me quedé en un campamento diferente dentro del parque. Además de trekking, hice kayaking por el río Orinoco. El mejor momento del viaje fue cuando llegué al Salto Ángel y vi las cascadas desde un helicóptero. ¡Qué tremendo! Bueno, ahora voy hasta Colombia, la tierra de mi "amigo", Juanes, para conocer Villa de Leyva y las cuevas de la región. ¡Este ha sido[6] el viaje de mi vida!

[1]*What's up?*
[2]*van*
[3]*caves*　[4]*rivers*
[5]*walls of sandstone*
[6]*has been*

9-16 En su opinión. Sigan los pasos para completar esta actividad.

Paso 1　En parejas, indiquen cuáles de estas actividades hace Felipe y después, cuáles les gusta hacer a ustedes, y por qué.

　　MODELO:　*Como a Felipe, me gusta...*

　　_____ bajar un río en kayak

　　_____ hacer un viaje en helicóptero para ver la selva (*jungle*) amazónica

　　_____ hacer trekking por las montañas

　　_____ hacer rafting por un río con fuertes corrientes

　　_____ hacer windsurf

　　_____ explorar cuevas

　　_____ hacer parapente (*hang glide*)

　　_____ hacer camping

　　_____ ¿...?

Paso 2　Después, pongan en orden de preferencia las actividades, añadan otras y comparen sus gustos.

Mi música

"JUNTOS" (JUANES, COLOMBIA)

Según el periódico *Los Angeles Times*, Juanes es hoy en día "la figura más importante de la música latina contemporánea". Es ganador de muchos premios Grammy y Grammy Latinos y, según la revista *Time*, es una de las "cien personas más influyentes del mundo". No solo es el cantante de rock latino con el mayor número de ventas (*sales*), sino un activista social prominente también. En una entrevista para la revista *Woman*, Juanes dijo: "Creo que la música puede ser una poderosa arma de paz y cada uno, como ciudadano, debemos ser parte del cambio". Su nombre es la abreviatura de *Juan Esteban*.

ANTES DE VER Y ESCUCHAR

9-17 McFarland, USA. Esta canción alude a una historia verdadera de un entrenador de un equipo de carrera de campo abierto (*cross-country*) en una escuela en California. El entrenador insiste en que los jóvenes pueden ganar el campeonato del estado si trabajan juntos. Completa el párrafo con **por** o **para** para darte una idea de lo que vas a ver en el video.

El cantante hace un viaje a McFarland (1)_____ conocer a la gente que vive allí. Viaja (2) _____ carro. Da un concierto (3) _____ honrar a los atletas y (4) _____ animar a los residentes. Los que asisten al concierto cantan y bailan (5) _____ horas. (6) _____ fin, todos están de acuerdo que nada importa, lo pueden lograr (*achieve*) si todos trabajan juntos.

PARA VER Y ESCUCHAR

9-18 La canción. Busca en Internet el video y la letra de "Juntos". Indica cuáles de estas expresiones relacionadas con los viajes escuchas en la canción.

1. avión	**Sí No**	5. mar	**Sí No**	
2. camino	**Sí No**	6. horizonte	**Sí No**	
3. carretera (*highway*)	**Sí No**	7. mundo	**Sí No**	
4. guía	**Sí No**	8. navegando (*sailing*)	**Sí No**	

> 📍 **Busca:** Juanes Juntos video; Juanes Juntos letra

DESPUÉS DE VER Y ESCUCHAR

9-19 La vida es como un viaje. En parejas, den su opinión sobre el mensaje de esta canción. ¿Están de acuerdo? Den ejemplos basados en su propia experiencia.

MODELO: La vida es como un viaje.
Estoy de acuerdo. Y es diferente si vas en carro, en autobús o en avión...

1. La vida es como un viaje.

2. La vida es como un libro abierto.

3. No sabemos cuál es nuestro destino.

4. Para tener éxito (*success*) en la vida, todos tenemos que ayudarnos mutuamente.

5. Para tener éxito en la vida, hay que hacer el máximo esfuerzo.

9.2 Segunda parte

Vocabulario

9.4 **Describe travel and vacation experiences**

Los viajes

Gladys

Jairo

Héctor

Planes para mañana. Los viajeros **lo están pasando de maravilla** en sus vacaciones. Ahora están pensando en lo que van a hacer el próximo día.

GLADYS: ¡Qué hermosos **el bosque** y **la catarata**! Pero, mañana voy a **hacer una gira** por **el centro histórico**.

JAIRO: ¡Hoy **recorrimos** toda **la isla**! Mañana voy a **bucear en el lago**.

HÉCTOR: Hoy lo pasé de maravilla. Mañana voy a **subir al volcán a caballo**.

¿Comprendes? Indicate who is going to do each activity: **Gladys, Jairo,** or **Héctor**.

1. Va a hacer un deporte acuático.

2. Va a ver monumentos.

3. Va a hacer una excursión a caballo.

Respuestas: 1. Jairo; 2. Gladys; 3. Héctor

Vocabulario

Para el viaje	For the trip
el cajero automático	ATM
la casa de cambio	currency exchange
el/la guía	tour guide
la guía turística	guidebook
la oficina de turismo	tourist office
el plano de la ciudad	city map
la tarjeta postal	postcard
Atracciones turísticas	**Tourist attractions**
la catedral	cathedral
el centro histórico	historical center
la estatua (del héroe)	statue (of the hero)
el monumento (a la revolución)	monument (to the revolution)
el parque de atracciones	amusement park
la plaza central	town square
Atracciones naturales	**Natural attractions**
el bosque	forest
el glaciar	glacier
la isla	island
el lago	lake
la montaña	mountain
el salto de agua / la catarata	waterfall
el valle	valley
la vista	view
el volcán	volcano
En el hotel/hostal	**At the hotel/hostel**
el/la camarero/a	cleaning staff
el cuarto individual/doble	single/double room
la estadía	stay
el/la gerente	manager
el hotel (económico / de lujo)	(economical/luxury) hotel
la recepción	reception desk

Actividades típicas de los viajeros	Typical activities for travelers
bucear (en el lago/mar)	to scuba dive, to snorkel (in the lake/sea)
comprar recuerdos	to buy souvenirs
hacer una gira	to take a tour
ir de excursión (en todoterreno)	to go on an excursion (in an ATV)
ir en barco	to go by boat
montar a caballo / en bicicleta	to go horseback riding / bicycle riding
pasarlo de maravilla	to have a wonderful time
pescar	to fish
quedarse (en un hostal/hotel)	to stay (in a hostel/hotel)
recorrer (la ciudad / el campo)	to travel around, to tour (the city/ countryside)
sacar fotos	to take pictures
subir al (cerro/glaciar/volcán)	to climb (the hill / the glacier / the volcano)
viajar al extranjero	to travel abroad

Variaciones

- In Spain, you ask for **una habitación doble/sencilla**, and say **la estancia** in place of **la estadía.**
- In Mexico and other parts of Latin America, you will also hear **pasarla de maravilla: ¡La pasé de maravilla en la fiesta!**
- **El centro histórico** can also be **el casco viejo** or **el casco antiguo**, especially in Spain.

Letras y sonidos

The letter *g* in sequences other than *ge* and *gi* in Spanish

Remember that in Spanish, the letter **g** before the vowels **e** and **i** sounds like the *h* in English *hip*. In all other sequences, such as **ga**, **go**, and **gu**, the letter **g** creates one of two sounds, depending on the context. After a pause or the letter **n**, the letter **g** sounds like the *g* in English *good*. In all other contexts, the **g** is softer, like the *g* in English *sugar*.

Hard **g**:	**g**a-lle-ta	**g**us-to	ten-**g**o	**g**uí-a
Soft **g**:	la-**g**a-lle-ta	mu-cho-**g**us-to	ha-**g**o	ham-bur-**g**ue-sa

Note that the letter **u** in the sequences **gue** and **gui** is silent. When two dots (or **diéresis**) are written above the letter **u**, or when **u** is inserted between **g** and **a**, or **g** and **o**, a glide is created: **bi-lin-güe, pin-güi-no, a-gua, an-ti-guo**.

Aplicación

9-20 De viaje. Indica la expresión que no pertenece al grupo y explica por qué.

> MODELO: la catarata – la plaza – el valle – el lago
> *La plaza no es una atracción natural.*

1. hacer una gira – quedarse en un hotel – recorrer la ciudad – ir de excursión
2. el cuarto doble – el camarero – la gira – la recepción
3. el caballo – la bicicleta – el todoterreno – la estadía
4. el cajero automático – el monumento – la estatua – la catedral
5. la tarjeta postal – la guía turística – el plano de la ciudad – el gerente

9-21 De vacaciones en Colombia. Alberto y Delia son dos estudiantes de intercambio que se conocieron en el vuelo a Bogotá. Completa su conversación con la expresión lógica de la lista.

barco	cajero automático	comprar recuerdos	plano	vista
bucear	centro histórico	económico	te quedas	volcán

ALBERTO: ¿Dónde (1) _____ en la ciudad?

DELIA: Tengo un hostal muy (2) _____: solo veinte dólares por noche. ¡Ay de mí! Necesito sacar dinero para poder comer esta noche.

ALBERTO: Vamos a buscar un (3) _____ o una casa de cambio. Oye, el (4) _____ es muy hermoso, ¿no?

DELIA: Sí, los edificios son coloniales. ¿Sabes dónde está la catedral?

ALBERTO: Según el (5) _____, está en la plaza central. Después de visitarla, ¿prefieres ir al parque de atracciones o subir al (6) _____?

DELIA: Vamos para arriba. Tengo mi celular para sacar fotos de la (7) _____ desde arriba. ¿Mañana quieres ir en (8) _____ por el lago?

ALBERTO: Buena idea. Podemos pescar y (9) _____ en el agua.

DELIA: ¡Muy bien! Y después vamos al mercado de artesanías para (10) _____.

))) **9-22 El viaje de Gladys.** Escucha lo que Gladys le cuenta a su novio César de su viaje. Después indica la opción correcta para completar cada oración.

1. Fueron a...
   a. Ecuador.   b. Colombia.   c. Venezuela.

2. Estuvieron allí por...
   a. ocho días.   b. once días.   c. un mes.

3. Fueron de excursión en un...
   a. barco.   b. autobús.   c. todoterreno.

4. Una actividad que no hicieron allí fue...
   a. nadar.   b. montar a caballo.   c. sacar fotos.

5. Les impresionó especialmente...
   a. el volcán.   b. el bosque.   c. el salto de agua.

6. Llegaron al lugar...
   a. en helicóptero.   b. a caballo.   c. por las montañas.

7. Gladys le dice a César que algún día ellos van a...
   a. conocer Venezuela.   c. visitar un lugar más
   b. quedarse en el   económico.
      mismo hotel.

9-23 Sus gustos. En parejas, comparen y luego conversen sobre cómo prefieren pasar sus vacaciones. ¿Qué tienen en común y cómo se diferencian?

Actividad	A mí me gusta...		A mi compañero/a le gusta...	
	Sí	No	Sí	No
hacer una gira organizada				
visitar un lugar por mi cuenta (*on my own*)				
bucear con amigos				
comprar recuerdos para mi familia				
montar a caballo / en bicicleta				
pescar en un lago o en el mar				
ir de excursión en un todoterreno				
hacer un crucero				
viajar al extranjero				
¿...?				

 9-24 Son agentes de viajes. En parejas, tienen que organizar viajes para algunos de estos clientes a diferentes destinos de Latinamérica. Para cada uno, deben planear el lugar, el hotel, el transporte, las actividades y excursiones de viaje y un estimado del costo.

> **MODELO:** ESTUDIANTE 1: *Ana y Carlos quieren visitar un lugar muy exótico...*
> ESTUDIANTE 2: *Muy bien. Deben visitar...*

1. Ana y Carlos son novios y están planeando su luna de miel. Han ahorrado (*They've saved*) mucho dinero para hacer un viaje muy especial. Les gusta la aventura, la buena comida y el lujo.

2. Sandra y Pati son estudiantes de antropología con una semana de vacaciones. Desean visitar un lugar donde puedan conocer a otros jóvenes, la vida nocturna y las atracciones naturales. No quieren gastar mucho en el viaje.

3. Los señores Aguirre son una pareja de 80 años de Maracaibo, Venezuela, donde son hacendados (*ranchers*) ricos. Cuando viajan, prefieren visitar lugares de lujo y con muchas oportunidades culturales. Siempre los acompaña don Luis, su caniche (*poodle*) miniatura.

4. Marisol Rivas es una mujer de negocios de unos 30 años. Es muy trabajadora y raras veces toma vacaciones. Cuando viaja, quiere conocer a otras personas solteras que se interesen en hacer deportes extremos.

9-25 ¿Qué hacen? En parejas, túrnense para contar qué hacen o cómo reaccionan frente a estas situaciones de viaje.

> **MODELO:** Tu cuarto en el hotel no está listo.
> ESTUDIANTE 1: *Cuando mi cuarto en el hotel no está listo, me pongo impaciente y hablo con el gerente.*
> ESTUDIANTE 2: *Pues, salgo a recorrer la ciudad.*

1. Los cuartos de los hoteles están sobrevendidos. No tienen cuartos disponibles.
2. Pediste un cuarto doble, pero te dan uno individual.
3. Cuando abres la ventana del cuarto, tienes una vista preciosa de la plaza central.
4. Quieres ir de excursión al volcán, pero el autobús acaba de salir.
5. Después de comer en un bar, no te permiten pagar con tarjeta de crédito.
6. Quieres ir a un parque de atracciones, pero está cerrado por un mes.

Estructuras

9.5 Try to influence others, and give advice

Introduction to the Spanish subjunctive

¿Recuerdas? Look at these statements. They are both grammatically correct in English, but they have different meanings. Can you explain how they differ?

1. I insist that you **are** on time to class.   2. I insist that you **be** on time to class.

Respuestas: 1. The first is a simple report, a fact.   2. The second is an effort to influence you to get to class on time.

Spanish has more than one mood. Until now, you have used the **indicative** mood in the present, preterit, and imperfect, which expresses *real*, *definite*, or *factual* actions or states of being. Now you will learn about the **subjunctive** mood, which is used to express the *hypothetical* or *subjective*, such as a speaker's wishes, feelings, emotions, or doubts.

USOS GENERALES DEL SUBJUNTIVO

You use the subjunctive when these conditions are true:

1. You have a compound sentence (independent clause + **que** + dependent clause):

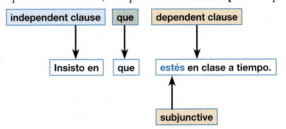

2. The independent (main) clause expresses **influence**, **emotion**, **doubt**, or **denial** about an action in the dependent clause. These expressions imply uncertainty because the action has yet to occur, or is outside of the speaker's experience.

3. The subjects of the two clauses are different in most cases.

    Dudamos que viajes al extranjero este año.   *We doubt you will travel abroad this year.*

    Sientes que nuestra madre no **pueda** ir.   *You're sorry our mother can't go.*

4. If there is no change of subject, and no **que**, you will usually use the infinitive.

    Queremos viajar al extranjero.   *We want to travel abroad.*

LOS VERBOS REGULARES DEL PRESENTE DE SUBJUNTIVO

- For most verbs, begin with the **yo** form of the verb in the present tense, drop the **-o** and add the subjunctive endings, as the table shows. Note that the endings for **-er** and **-ir** verbs are identical.

	hablar	comer	vivir	tener
	habl**ø**	com**ø**	viv**ø**	teng**ø**
yo	habl**e**	com**a**	viv**a**	teng**a**
tú	habl**es**	com**as**	viv**as**	teng**as**
Ud.	habl**e**	com**a**	viv**a**	teng**a**
él/ella	habl**e**	com**a**	viv**a**	teng**a**
nosotros/as	habl**emos**	com**amos**	viv**amos**	teng**amos**
vosotros/as	habl**éis**	com**áis**	viv**áis**	teng**áis**
Uds.	habl**en**	com**an**	viv**an**	teng**an**
ellos/as	habl**en**	com**an**	viv**an**	teng**an**

- Other verbs like **tener** with an irregular **yo** form:

Infinitive	Present indicative first-person singular	Present subjunctive
decir	dig**ø**	diga, digas, diga,...
hacer	hag**ø**	haga, hagas, haga,...
oír	oig**ø**	oiga, oigas, oiga,...
poner	pong**ø**	ponga, pongas, ponga,...
salir	salg**ø**	salga, salgas, salga,...
traer	traig**ø**	traiga, traigas, traiga,...
venir	veng**ø**	venga, vengas, venga,...
ver	ve**ø**	vea, veas, vea,...

- When a verb ends in **-car**, **-gar**, or **-zar**, change the spelling to maintain the original sound, just like in the preterit.

-car:	c → qu	buscar	busque, busques, busque...
-gar:	g → gu	llegar	llegue, llegues, llegue...
-zar:	z → c	abrazar	abrace, abraces, abrace...

- When you have an **-ar** or **-er** stem-changing verb in the subjunctive, you follow the same pattern as the present indicative, that is, the stem-change appears in all forms *except* **nosotros** and **vosotros**.

Espero que llegues pronto.

	pensar (ie)	volver (ue)
yo	p**ie**nse	v**ue**lva
tú	p**ie**nses	v**ue**lvas
Ud.	p**ie**nse	v**ue**lva
él/ella	p**ie**nse	v**ue**lva
nosotros/as	p**e**nsemos	v**o**lvamos
vosotros/as	p**e**nséis	v**o**lváis
Uds.	p**ie**nsen	v**ue**lva
ellos/as	p**ie**nsen	v**ue**lva

- For **-ir** stem-changing verbs, follow the stem changes of both the present indicative and the preterit. Note how you use the preterit stem changes in the **nosotros/as** and **vosotros/as** forms, where the unstressed **-e-** changes to **-i-**, and the unstressed **-o-** changes to **-u-**. The other persons follow the present-tense pattern.

	sentir (ie, i)	pedir (i, i)	dormir (ue, u)
yo	s**ie**nta	p**i**da	d**ue**rma
tú	s**ie**ntas	p**i**das	d**ue**rmas
Ud.	s**ie**nta	p**i**da	d**ue**rma
él/ella	s**ie**nta	p**i**da	d**ue**rma
nosotros/as	s**i**ntamos	p**i**damos	d**u**rmamos
vosotros/as	s**i**ntáis	p**i**dáis	d**u**rmáis
Uds.	s**ie**ntan	p**i**dan	d**ue**rman
ellos/as	s**ie**ntan	p**i**dan	d**ue**rman

LOS VERBOS IRREGULARES DEL PRESENTE DE SUBJUNTIVO

- There are only a few irregular verbs in the present subjunctive.

	dar	estar	ir	saber	ser
yo	dé	esté	vaya	sepa	sea
tú	des	estés	vayas	sepas	seas
Ud.	dé	esté	vaya	sepa	sea
él/ella	dé	esté	vaya	sepa	sea
nosotros/as	demos	estemos	vayamos	sepamos	seamos
vosotros/as	deis	estéis	vayáis	sepáis	seáis
Uds.	den	estén	vayan	sepan	sean
ellos/as	den	estén	vayan	sepan	sean

¡OJO!

The subjunctive form for **hay** is **haya**.

Espero que **haya** música en la fiesta.
I hope there is music at the party.

¿Comprendes? Identify the infinitive form of the verb used in the dependent clause. Then indicate if it is in the indicative (**I**) or subjunctive (**S**) mood.

1. Espero que vayas conmigo a Cartagena.
2. Creo que el hotel es muy lindo.
3. No es cierto que durmamos al aire libre.

Respuestas: 1. ir, S; 2. ser, I; 3. dormir, S

Aplicación

9-26 El arte público en Bogotá. Los artistas de Bogotá reciben apoyo del gobierno para realizar sus trabajos, transformando esta ciudad en un gran museo al aire libre.

Paso 1 Lee la conversación entre dos artistas urbanos de Bogotá que hablan sobre su trabajo en un mural y selecciona el verbo más apropiado en el subjuntivo para completar la conversación.

ERNESTO: ¡Oye, Pilar! Veo que no hay muchas personas aquí para ayudarnos a pintar. Es importante que los oficiales (1) conozcan/llamen a otros artistas.

PILAR: Tienes razón, Ernesto. Voy a hablar con el gerente y decirle que (2) haga/visite una lista de personas interesadas en el proyecto.

ERNESTO: Perfecto. ¿Dónde está la pintura? Hay que pedirles a los ayudantes que nos la (3) traigan/vean ahora mismo, y que también ellos nos (4) pongan/sepan las escaleras (*ladders*). ¿Quieres que nos (5) piensen/busquen sillas también?

ERNESTO: No, sillas no. Es mejor que los artistas no (6) se levanten/se sienten.

PILAR: Y es importante que la prensa (*press*) (7) esté/oiga presente y que los fotógrafos (8) saquen/den muchas fotos para el periódico.

Paso 2 Haz una lista de lo que piden los artistas en el **Paso 1**.

MODELO: *Piden que...*

9-27 ¡A conjugar! Sigan los pasos para completar la actividad.

Paso 1 En parejas, túrnense para decirse el indicativo y el subjuntivo de los verbos de la lista.

> MODELO: ESTUDIANTE 1: *nosotros, tomar*
> ESTUDIANTE 2: *Indicativo: tomamos; Subjuntivo: tomemos.*
> ESTUDIANTE 1: *Correcto.*

1. el avión/despegar
2. tú/hacer
3. yo/salir
4. los niños/pescar
5. nuestros amigos/estar
6. tú/ir
7. nosotros/tener
8. yo/pedir
9. nosotros/dormir

Paso 2 Imagínense que van de vacaciones con algunos amigos. Túrnense para comentar sus deseos y dudas para el viaje, usando el subjuntivo de estos verbos. Pueden empezar con una de estas frases: **Es necesario que... Es bueno que... Es dudoso que...**

> MODELO: *Es bueno que tomemos café antes de ir de excursión.*

 9-28 Unos pedidos (*requests*). En parejas, imagínense que van de vacaciones al Parque Tayrona en Colombia. Túrnense para expresar lo que quieren o no quieren que haga su compañero/a durante sus vacaciones. Usen **quiero** o **no quiero** y el subjuntivo.

> MODELO: sacar muchas fotos
> ESTUDIANTE 1: *Quiero que saques muchas fotos.*
> ESTUDIANTE 2: *¡Claro que sí! (No puedo. No tengo cámara.)*

1. ver muchos animales salvajes (*wild*)
2. conocer gente interesante
3. tener un buen guía
4. bucear solo/a
5. ir de excursión en todoterreno
6. no tomar demasiado (*too much*) sol

Espero que conozcas la playa del Parque Tayrona.

¿Necesitan que los lleve a casa?

The subjunctive to express influence

When you hope to influence someone to do something, you use verbs expressing *wants, wishes, preferences, suggestions, requests,* and *implied commands*. Here are some verbs that suggest influence:

aconsejar	to advise	pedir (i, i)	to ask
decir (i, i)	to tell	permitir	to permit
desear	to wish, to desire	prohibir	to prohibit
insistir (en)	to insist	querer (ie)	to want
mandar	to order	recomendar (ie)	to recommend
necesitar	to need	sugerir (ie, i)	to suggest

- The subject of the verb in the independent clause tries to influence the subject of the dependent clause.

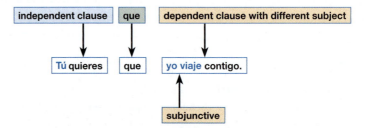

independent clause	que	dependent clause with different subject
Tú quieres	que	yo viaje contigo.

subjunctive

- **Ojalá**[1] is a useful expression to express hope or desire. It originates from an Arabic phrase meaning *God (Allah) willing*, and may be followed with or without **que**. You always use the subjunctive with **ojalá**.

> **Ojalá (que)** visitemos Cartagena.   *I hope (that) we visit Cartagena.*
> **Ojalá (que)** vayas a bucear en el mar.   *I hope (that) you go snorkeling in the sea.*

- You will also find that many impersonal expressions show influence and call for the subjunctive when there is a change of subject introduced by **que**.

es bueno	it's good	es mejor	it's better
es importante	it's important	es necesario	it's necessary
es imposible	it's impossible	es preciso	it's essential
es indispensable	it's crucial	es urgente	it's urgent

> **Es imposible que pasemos** la frontera sin pasaporte.   *It's impossible for us to cross the border without a passport.*
> **Es indispensable que compres** un plano de la ciudad.   *It's crucial that you buy a city map.*

- Use the infinitive when there is no change of subject between the two clauses.
  Sofía (desear) + Sofía (ir)

> **Sofía desea ir** a pescar.   *Sofía wants to go fishing.*

  Es mejor + (conocer)

> **Es mejor conocer** la ciudad a pie.   *It's better to get to know the city on foot.*

- When you use verbs such as **aconsejar, decir, pedir, recomendar,** and **sugerir**, you must also include an indirect object pronoun to refer to the subject of the dependent clause.

> **Le aconsejo** (a Ud.) que recorra la ciudad.   *I advise you to tour the city. (lit., I advise that you tour the city.)*
> **Nos piden que** nos quedemos en este hotel.   *They ask us to stay in this hotel. (lit., They ask that we stay in this hotel.)*

---

[1]From Arabic, *law šá lláh,* "si Dios quiere."

- To simply report information with verbs such as **decir, informar**, and **escribir**, use the indicative in the dependent clause. However, if your intent is to order someone to do something, use the subjunctive.

    Information:

El agente te **informa** que **vuelves** el sábado.	*The agent informs you that you're returning on Saturday.*

    Command:

El agente te **informa** que **vuelvas** el sábado.	*The agent informs you to return on Saturday.*

¿Comprendes? Complete each sentence with the most logical verb: **compremos, haga, subamos**.

1. ¿Quieres que _____ al Cerro de Monserrate en Bogotá?

2. Es necesario que _____ billetes para el teleférico para subir.

3. Ojalá que no _____ frío en las montañas.

Respuestas: 1. subamos; 2. compremos; 3. haga

Aplicación

9-29 La noche de Shakira. Esta noche Shakira, la exitosa cantante colombiana, va a hacer una presentación en los Grammy Latinos. Una reportera para el sitio web Colombia-Hoy entrevista a otros artistas en la alfombra (*carpet*) roja y les pregunta sobre sus expectativas (*expectations*) sobre la noche.

Paso 1 Lee los comentarios que algunos de los invitados le hicieron a la reportera y selecciona el verbo apropiado para completar cada comentario.

JUANES:	Deseo que Shakira (1) baile/duerma y (2) cante/recorra algunas canciones nuevas.
ENRIQUE IGLESIAS:	Insisto en que le (3) den/saquen muchas fotos a ella en la alfombra roja.
RIHANNA:	Es importante que (4) sea/lleve su vestido con lentejuelas (*sequins*) doradas.
SU AGENTE:	Le recomiendo que (5) pierda/tome mucha agua antes de su actuación.
SUS PADRES:	Le sugerimos que (6) haga/corra ejercicio todos los días para mantenerse en forma.
GERARD PIQUÉ:	Quiero que (7) descanse/sienta después y que pronto (8) traiga/vuelva conmigo a España.

Paso 2 Identifica los dos deseos más lógicos, en tu opinión, y los dos menos lógicos y explica por qué.

> **MODELO:** *Creo que Rihanna tiene razón porque...*

Paso 3 Shakira y Carlos Vives ganaron los premios Mejor grabación del año y Mejor canción del año por "Bicicleta" en los Grammy Latinos de 2016. Busca su video en Internet y escribe una descripción de la escena, su estilo y la personalidad de los cantantes.

📍 **Busca:** Shakira; Carlos Vives; Bicicleta video oficial

Presencia hispana

Another well-known Colombian currently residing in the U.S. is racecar driver Juan Pablo Montoya. Mostly known for his open-wheel racing, he achieved the rare feat of becoming a crossover race winner on Formula One, ChampCar, IndiCar, GrandAm, and Nascar. Montoya established the Formula Smiles Foundation to help improve sports facilities and infrastructures in Colombia's poor neighborhoods. What cause would you support if you were a famous athlete or performer?

9-30 Agente de viajes. Una agente de viajes chatea con clientes que tienen preguntas sobre sus viajes. Completa sus consejos con el verbo lógico en el subjuntivo.

> MODELO: Sra. Domínguez, ¿prefiere que yo le _mande_ (buscar – mandar – traer) su itinerario por correo electrónico?

- Sr. López, es necesario que usted (1) _____ (comprar – dar – perder) su pasaje con dos semanas de anticipación. Necesito que usted me (2) _____ (abrir – dar – trabajar) su número de tarjeta de crédito.

- Doña María, sugiero que usted (3) _____ (llegar – perder – poner) las recetas médicas (*prescriptions*) en su bolsa y que (4) _____ (desear – hacer – pensar) copias para poner en la maleta.

- Lupe, es importante que (tú) (5) _____ (comprar – dormir – llegar) al aeropuerto con dos horas de anticipación antes de tu vuelo. Los agentes de seguridad insisten en que los pasajeros no (6) _____ (buscar – conocer – pasar) por seguridad con objetos puntiagudos (*sharp*).

- Señores Echevarría, les recomiendo que ustedes (7) _____ (dormir – salir – vivir) en el avión, porque si no, van a estar muy cansados después de más de siete horas de viaje. Por eso, les sugiero que le (8) _____ (aconsejar – esperar – pedir) café descafeinado al asistente de vuelo.

- Carolina, en países hispanos, vas a escuchar muchos piropos (*compliments*) en la calle. Es importante que no (9) _____ (enojarse – pedir – recorrer) ni que les (10) _____ (responder – salir – viajar), porque es parte de la cultura.

Cultura en vivo

A common custom throughout the Spanish-speaking world is **el piropo**, an expression of admiration, flirtation, or praise that one person calls to another, often on the street. To create **piropos** is almost an art form; usually men, but also sometimes women, can **echar un piropo**, a poetic or imaginative expression of praise. Here are a few you may hear: **"¿Crees en el amor a primera vista o tengo que volver a pasar?" "El amor sin un beso es como los espaguetis sin queso" "¡Vaya, vaya... lo que hace Dios cuando está contento!"** Do similar expressions exist in English? How would you feel or react upon receiving a **piropo**?

9-31 ¿Qué esperan tus amigos y tu familia? Tus amigos y tu familia quieren que lo pases bien en tus vacaciones. Combina frases de las dos columnas con **que** para decir lo que desean ellos.

> MODELO: Mi padre quiere... que yo (no)... poner muchas fotos en mi muro (*wall*).
> *Mi padre quiere que yo ponga muchas fotos en mi muro.*

Mi madre espera...		pasarlo bien
Mi novio/a (esposo/a) desea...		hacer una gira del centro histórico
Mi amigo/a me sugiere...		bucear en el mar
Mi profesor/a de... insiste en...	**que yo (no)**	comprar muchos recuerdos
Mi abuelo/a prefiere...		quedarme en un hotel económico
Mis tíos recomiendan...		no hacer deportes extremos

9-32 ConCalma Viajes. Los seguidores (*followers*) de este sitio web español ofrecen opiniones y consejos sobre viajes a diferentes partes del mundo. Completa cada consejo con la forma correcta del verbo apropiado de la lista. Usa cada verbo solo una vez.

ayudar	entrar	pagar	tener
buscar	ir	pedir	usar

¿Cómo debo prepararme para mi primer viaje a Colombia en octubre?

VIAJERA: Te aconsejo que (1) _____ el pasaporte con varios meses de anticipación para poder visitar Colombia. No es necesario (2) _____ visa para este país.

GUÍAJAIRO: Te sugiero que (3) _____ una buena guía turística en Internet. O también puedes bajar una aplicación en tu teléfono con información y consejos. Recuerda, no se permite que los viajeros (4) _____ al país con frutas u otros comestibles. Es mejor (5) _____ el cajero automático en el aeropuerto.

JUANITOBOGOTÁ: Una vez en Colombia, te recomiendo que (6) _____ al Parque Tayrona en carro privado y con guía. Es un viaje inolvidable. También, te sugiero que (7) _____ en Internet directamente el hotel, porque muchas veces te cuesta menos.

ALIDA: Soy guía turística con una agencia pequeña. Si quieres que nosotros te (8) _____ con el viaje, llámanos al...

9-33 El viaje de sus sueños. En parejas, hagan planes para hacer un viaje a Latinoamérica, teniendo en cuenta los gustos de los/las dos. Usen las expresiones de la lista con el subjuntivo o el infinitivo y las sugerencias de actividades para hacer.

MODELO: hacer surf en el Caribe

ESTUDIANTE 1: *Quiero hacer surf en el Caribe. Ojalá que vayas conmigo.*

ESTUDIANTE 2: *Prefiero... Es mejor que...*

ESTUDIANTE 1: *¿Qué tal si...?*

Es bueno (que)	Ojalá (que)	Te aconsejo que
Es urgente (que)	Prefiero (que)	Te recomiendo que
Insisto en (que)	Quiero (que)	Te sugiero que

- visitar los glaciares en Argentina
- bañarme en las aguas termales de Costa Rica
- pasar en helicóptero sobre el Salto Ángel
- buscar un paquete con todo incluido
- hacer un crucero en el Caribe
- subir a un volcán en Ecuador
- hacer una gira del Parque Nacional Cainama en Venezuela
- quedarme en un hotel (de lujo / económico)
- bucear en el Caribe
- pescar en el río Orinoco

9-34 ¿Cuáles son tus deseos? Escribe cinco deseos que tienes para el futuro. Expresa los deseos con verbos como **querer, desear, ojalá, preferir, es importante**, etc., usando el subjuntivo cuando sea necesario.

MODELO: *Deseo que mis padres vivan muchos años y que siempre tengamos una buena relación. Espero que mis amigos encuentren un buen trabajo y que ganen mucho dinero. Prefiero viajar después de terminar mis estudios.*

¡Conversemos!

Primero, pregúntate si puedes llevar a cabo las siguientes funciones comunicativas en español. Después, júntate con dos o tres compañeros/as de clase para presentar las situaciones. Hagan y respondan a por lo menos cuatro preguntas en cada situación.

✓ CAN YOU . . .

☐ describe travel and vacation experiences?

☐ try to influence others?

☐ give advice to someone?

WITH YOUR CLASSMATE(S) . . .

Situación: Entre amigos.

Cuéntense lo que hicieron en sus últimas vacaciones. Hablen de su hotel, de los lugares que visitaron, de las excursiones que hicieron, de cómo lo pasaron, si compraron algo, etc.

Para empezar: *El año pasado hice un viaje a...*

Situación: Nuestro próximo viaje.

Ustedes no pueden decidir adónde ir en su próximo viaje. Todos tienen opiniones muy fuertes. Usen el subjuntivo para convencerse y finalmente, llegar a un acuerdo.

Para empezar: *Quiero ir a... Insisto en que... Es necesario que... Ojalá...*

Situación: Problemas personales.

Traten de ayudarse con un problema serio, como la falta de dinero, problemas en casa, una clase difícil, un horario imposible, etc. Usen el subjuntivo para darse consejos.

Para empezar: *Te aconsejo que... Es importante que... Insisto en que...*

Club cultura

9.6 Summarize what you have seen

El paraíso venezolano

Estrategia para ver

Summarize what you have seen. Can you state what you have seen and heard in your own words? Doing so will help internalize the content and reveal if you have missed any key information.

ANTES DE VER EL VIDEO

9-35 Lo que sabes de Venezuela. Imagínate que cada palabra vale (*is worth*) un bolívar venezolano. Escribe un resumen de 30 bolívares de lo que ya sabes sobre el país. Incluye esta información:

MODELO: *Venezuela está situada en...*

dónde está	su capital
una riqueza natural	un lugar turístico
los países que lo limitan	una actividad que puedes hacer en Venezuela

AL VER EL VIDEO

9-36 El paraíso venezolano. Indica con **sí** o **no** si escuchas/ves o no estos lugares en el video.

1. el río Orinoco — **Sí   No**
2. el Lago de Maracaibo — **Sí   No**
3. el Relámpago (*lightning flash*) del Catatumbo — **Sí   No**
4. la Isla de Margarita — **Sí   No**
5. la Playa Cuyagua — **Sí   No**
6. el Parque Nacional Canaima — **Sí   No**
7. el Tepuy Roraima — **Sí   No**
8. el Salto Ángel — **Sí   No**

DESPUÉS DE VER EL VIDEO

9-37 Los detalles. Selecciona la opción que mejor describe cada término, según el video.

1. _____ Auyán-tepui
2. _____ el Tepuy Roraima
3. _____ el Relámpago del Catatumbo
4. _____ Jimmy Angel
5. _____ la Playa Cuyagua
6. _____ un tepuy
7. _____ *Up*

a. un fenómeno natural de sonido y luz
b. donde puedes hacer surf
c. película inspirada en la selva venezolana
d. donde se encuentra el Salto Ángel
e. el piloto estadounidense que tuvo un accidente
f. un lugar donde llueve casi todo el año
g. montaña con cima plana (*flat top*) y paredes verticales

9-38 Tu resumen. Usa la información de la actividad anterior para escribir un resumen del video en tus propias palabras. Incluye algunas de estas frases: **Para empezar, Además, También, Lo que más me interesa (fascina/gusta), Para concluir.**

9.3 Nuestro mundo

Panoramas

9.7 Identify and research some important cultural aspects of Colombia and Venezuela

Riquezas naturales e históricas: Colombia y Venezuela

Al mirar el mapa de Colombia y Venezuela, vas a ver que tienen una geografía y topografía muy variadas: montañas, ríos, lagos, mar y océano. Esta variedad es una de las razones por las cuales todos los años estos países atraen a muchos turistas. Además, las riquezas minerales y de energía fósil contribuyen a la economía de la región.

La cuenca (*basin*) del Lago de Maracaibo en Venezuela es donde se han encontrado vastos yacimientos (*deposits*) de petróleo. Aunque por muchos años contribuyó a la economía y el bienestar de sus habitantes, hoy sus refinerías no tienen la capacidad para producir suficiente combustible para su propio uso. Además, el lago sufre de tremenda contaminación por el abuso del medio ambiente (*environment*).

Para llegar al Parque Nacional Canaima en Venezuela, puedes hacer una excursión por canoa motorizada por los ríos Carrao y Churún. Pero debes ir durante la temporada de lluvias, de junio a noviembre.

El oro y las piedras preciosas que abundan en Colombia aparecen en las prendas que llevaban los caciques (*chiefs*) de los indígenas en tiempos pasados. La colección del Museo del Oro en Bogotá exhibe una muestra (*sample*) de las muchas piezas que elaboraron los habitantes originales.

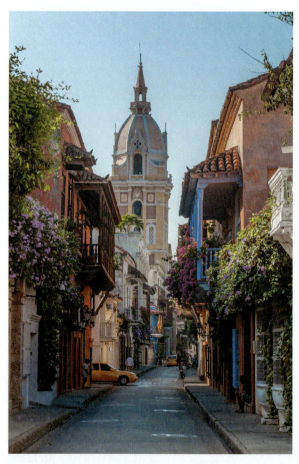

Puedes recorrer la hermosa ciudad de Cartagena de Indias en el mar Caribe a pie, en autobús, en taxi o en coche de caballos. Fundada en 1533, la ciudad colonial hoy es sitio del Patrimonio Mundial de UNESCO.

Bogotá tiene muchos espacios verdes y calles peatonales que benefician la calidad de vida de sus habitantes y de los turistas. Puedes recorrer el centro colonial con facilidad y después subir al Cerro Monserrate por funicular o teleférico para tener una vista preciosa de toda la ciudad.

	La República Bolivariana de Venezuela	La República de Colombia
Población	31 millones	47,2 millones
Sitios de la UNESCO[1]	3	7
Número de turistas/año	857.000	2,5 millones
Número de empleados en turismo	967.000	1,3 millones

[1]Patrimonio de la Humanidad (*UNESCO World Heritage site*)

9-39 Identifica. Identifica la información según **Panoramas**.

1. por qué Bogotá es una "ciudad verde"
2. cómo llegar al Salto Ángel en el Parque Canaima
3. un metal precioso de Colombia
4. medios de transporte para conocer Cartagena de Indias
5. la importancia del Lago de Maracaibo
6. una buena manera de ver toda la ciudad de Bogotá

9-40 Desafío. Identifica el lugar correcto según el mapa y los datos estadísticos.

1. el país que tiene costas en el Caribe y en el Pacífico
2. la capital de Colombia y la de Venezuela
3. el país que emplea más personas en la industria del turismo
4. el número de sitios en los dos países que forman parte del Patrimonio de la Humanidad de la UNESCO

9-41 Investigación: Un viaje a Colombia o Venezuela. Vas a investigar sobre un lugar en Colombia o Venezuela que te interese visitar. Escoge uno de la lista, u otro que te interese, y escribe un resumen en el que incluyas los elementos de la lista. Luego, preséntaselo a la clase. Sigue el modelo.

- dónde está
- por qué es importante o interesante
- cómo era en el pasado; cómo es ahora
- los medios de transporte que usas para llegar
- las actividades que puedes hacer allí
- una foto representativa

📍 **Busca: Colombia:** Laguna de Guatavita, Medellín, el Parque Tayrona
Venezuela: Isla de Margarita, San Andrés, Parque Nacional Henri Pittier

MODELO: *La ciudad de Medellín es "la ciudad más innovadora del mundo", según BBC América...*

Páginas

9.8 Read for purpose

Viajes aventura, un sitio turístico

Estrategia para leer

Read for purpose. When you read for purpose, you go beyond comprehension to analyze text and assess its importance and value to you or others. Does the text make sense? Is it truthful? Is it valuable? Is it feasible? Will I incorporate the information into my knowledge base? Will I act on the knowledge? As you read, analyze the information and apply it to your purpose.

ANTES DE LEER

9-42 Motivos para visitar un lugar. Cada persona tiene diferentes motivos para viajar. Escribe lo que te imaginas que es importante para cada persona o grupo de la lista.

aprender algo nuevo	hacer turismo (en grupo / individualmente)
conocer a gente nueva	motivos profesionales
un desafío / una aventura	tener todo incluido
entender mejor la cultura local	viajar económicamente/cómodamente

1. un club de estudiantes que se especializan en ecología y antropología
2. dos personas que quieren conocerse mejor
3. una mujer de negocios de 30 años que viaja sola
4. una pareja de 80 años
5. una familia con tres niños pequeños
6. un grupo de estudiantes con poca experiencia en viajes
7. amigos que quieren divertirse
8. tú

AL LEER

9-43 Un destino interesante. Antes de hacer planes para un viaje al extranjero, consultas Viajes aventura, un sitio web que tiene información y consejos sobre destinos interesantes. Mientras lees el texto, indica con una **X** los motivos que algunos turistas pueden tener para viajar a la Reserva Natural Calanoa.

_____ 1. para descansar

_____ 2. para conocer culturas y formas de vida diferentes

_____ 3. para salir por la noche a divertirse

_____ 4. para conectarse con la naturaleza

_____ 5. para realizar un estudio de antropología

_____ 6. para quedarse en alojamientos lujosos

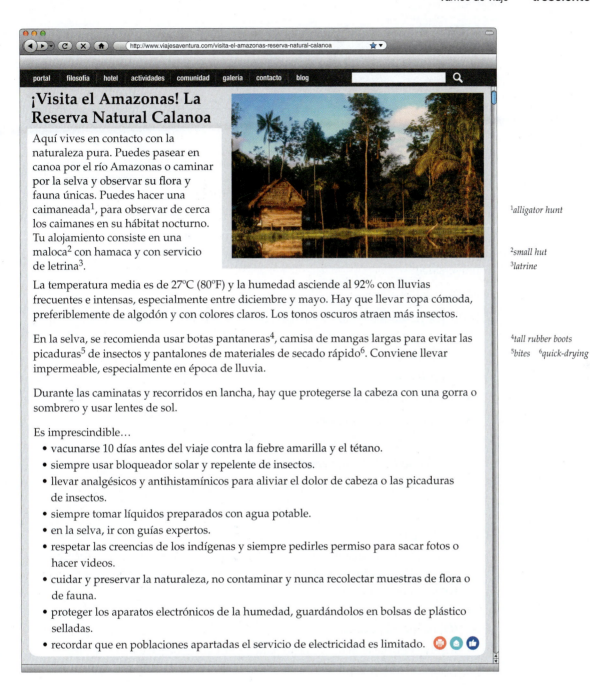

http://www.viajesaventura.com/visita-el-amazonas-reserva-natural-calanoa

portal filosofía hotel actividades comunidad galería contacto blog

¡Visita el Amazonas! La Reserva Natural Calanoa

Aquí vives en contacto con la naturaleza pura. Puedes pasear en canoa por el río Amazonas o caminar por la selva y observar su flora y fauna únicas. Puedes hacer una caimaneada[1], para observar de cerca los caimanes en su hábitat nocturno. Tu alojamiento consiste en una maloca[2] con hamaca y con servicio de letrina[3].

[1]*alligator hunt*

[2]*small hut*
[3]*latrine*

La temperatura media es de 27°C (80°F) y la humedad asciende al 92% con lluvias frecuentes e intensas, especialmente entre diciembre y mayo. Hay que llevar ropa cómoda, preferiblemente de algodón y con colores claros. Los tonos oscuros atraen más insectos.

En la selva, se recomienda usar botas pantaneras[4], camisa de mangas largas para evitar las picaduras[5] de insectos y pantalones de materiales de secado rápido[6]. Conviene llevar impermeable, especialmente en época de lluvia.

[4]*tall rubber boots*
[5]*bites*   [6]*quick-drying*

Durante las caminatas y recorridos en lancha, hay que protegerse la cabeza con una gorra o sombrero y usar lentes de sol.

Es imprescindible…
- vacunarse 10 días antes del viaje contra la fiebre amarilla y el tétano.
- siempre usar bloqueador solar y repelente de insectos.
- llevar analgésicos y antihistamínicos para aliviar el dolor de cabeza o las picaduras de insectos.
- siempre tomar líquidos preparados con agua potable.
- en la selva, ir con guías expertos.
- respetar las creencias de los indígenas y siempre pedirles permiso para sacar fotos o hacer videos.
- cuidar y preservar la naturaleza, no contaminar y nunca recolectar muestras de flora o de fauna.
- proteger los aparatos electrónicos de la humedad, guardándolos en bolsas de plástico selladas.
- recordar que en poblaciones apartadas el servicio de electricidad es limitado.

DESPUÉS DE LEER

9-44 Las condiciones del lugar. Selecciona la opción más lógica para identificar lo que necesitas para el viaje, teniendo en cuenta las condiciones del lugar.

1. _____ para quedarse	a. agua potable
2. _____ para dormir	b. bloqueador solar y repelente de insectos
3. _____ para beber	c. una bolsa de plástico
4. _____ para llevar de ropa	d. una caimaneada
5. _____ para aplicarse sobre la piel (*skin*)	e. una hamaca
6. _____ para guardar el celular	f. una maloca
7. _____ para moverse en la zona	g. pantalones de secado rápido
8. _____ para observar criaturas de noche	h. una persona experta de la zona

9-45 Analizar el viaje. Analiza la información presentada y aplícala a las personas en la actividad **9-42**. ¿Quiénes son los que más van a disfrutar de este viaje, y por qué?

Taller

Conoce mi universidad

Estrategia para escribir

Give advice. Just as when you read for purpose, when you write for purpose, you include information you hope the reader will find interesting, valuable, and useful. Ask yourself the question: will this advice and information fulfill their purpose for reading?

9-46 **Consejos para estudiantes extranjeros.** Vas a preparar una entrada de un blog para estudiantes de Venezuela o Colombia que estén pensando estudiar en tu universidad.

ANTES DE ESCRIBIR

De lo que ya sabes de estos dos países, prepara una lista de consejos y detalles que atraigan y que informen a estudiantes potenciales. Incluye:

- dónde está
- cómo llegar
- por qué es especial
- qué programas excepcionales se ofrecen
- qué actividades se ofrecen
- algunas fotos de la universidad o del lugar
- cómo prepararse para venir (ropa, vacunas, equipo, etc.)

AL ESCRIBIR

Sigue estos pasos:

- Ordena la información y los consejos de una manera lógica. Puedes incluir puntos interesantes sobre la cultura, la historia, el clima, la comida, actividades y fechas importantes, etc.
- Incluye razones importantes para conocer la universidad (**Ojalá que conozcas...**).
- Incluye información de contacto para pedir más información.

DESPUÉS DE ESCRIBIR

- **Revisar.** Revisa tu entrada del blog para verificar los siguientes puntos:
  - ☐ la concordancia de nombres y adjetivos
  - ☐ el uso de **por** y **para**
  - ☐ el uso de adverbios que terminan en **-mente** (**Originalmente la universidad era...**)
  - ☐ el uso del subjuntivo (**Es importante que...**; **Sugerimos que...**; **Es necesario que...**; **Ojalá...**)
- **Intercambiar.** Intercambia tu entrada con la de un/a compañero/a para hacer correcciones y sugerencias y para decidir si quieren visitar el lugar.
- **Entregar.** Prepara la versión final de tu entrada, incorporando las sugerencias de tu compañero/a. Después, entrégasela a tu profesor/a.

En este capítulo...

))) Vocabulario

Primera parte

En el sitio web de viajes	On the travel web site
el boleto (electrónico)	(e-)ticket
el destino	destination
el equipaje (permitido)	luggage (policy)
el pasaje (de ida y vuelta)	(round-trip) fare, ticket
el paquete de viaje (vuelo/hotel/ carro)	(flight/hotel/car) travel package
la reservación/la reserva	reservation

En el aeropuerto	In the airport
la aduana	customs
el/la agente	agent
el avión	plane
el control de seguridad	security checkpoint
el/la inspector/a de aduanas	customs inspector
el mostrador (de la aerolínea)	(airline) counter
el pasaporte	passport
la puerta de embarque	boarding gate
la sala de espera	waiting room
el reclamo de equipaje	baggage claim
la tarjeta de embarque	boarding pass
el/la viajero/a	traveler
el vuelo	flight

En el avión	On the plane
el asiento (de pasillo/ventanilla)	(aisle/window) seat
el/la asistente de vuelo	flight attendant
la clase turista/ejecutiva	coach/business class
el compartimento superior	overhead bin
la demora	delay
la llegada	arrival
el/la pasajero/a	passenger
el/la piloto	pilot
la salida	departure

Verbos	Verbs
abordar (el avión/autobús/barco/ tren)	to board (the plane/bus/boat/train)
aterrizar	to land
bajarse (del autobús/avión, etc.)	to get off (of), to get down (from) (the bus/plane, etc.)
despegar	to take off
esperar	to wait for; to hope for
facturar el equipaje	to check baggage
hacer cola	to stand in line
hacer escala	to make a stopover
hacer un crucero	to take a cruise
hacer la maleta	to pack one's suitcase
pasar por seguridad (inmigración/la aduana)	to go through security (immigration/customs)
revisar (el equipaje)	to inspect (the luggage)
viajar por (barco, etc.)	to travel by (ship, etc.)

Segunda parte

Para el viaje	For the trip
el cajero automático	ATM
la casa de cambio	currency exchange
el/la guía	tour guide
la guía turística	guidebook
la oficina de turismo	tourist office
el plano de la ciudad	city map
la tarjeta postal	postcard

Atracciones turísticas	Tourist attractions
la catedral	cathedral
el centro histórico	historical center
la estatua (del héroe)	statue (of the hero)
el monumento (a la revolución)	monument (to the revolution)
el parque de atracciones	amusement park
la plaza central	town square

Atracciones naturales	Natural attractions
el bosque	forest
el glaciar	glacier
la isla	island
el lago	lake
la montaña	mountain
el salto de agua / la catarata	waterfall
el valle	valley
la vista	view
el volcán	volcano

En el hotel/hostal	At the hotel/hostel
el/la camarero/a	cleaning staff
el cuarto individual / doble	single / double room
la estadía	stay
el/la gerente	manager
el hotel (económico / de lujo)	(economical/luxury) hotel
la recepción	reception desk

Actividades típicas de los viajeros	Typical activities for travelers
bucear (en el lago / mar)	to scuba dive, to snorkel (in the lake / sea)
comprar recuerdos	to buy souvenirs
hacer una gira	to take a tour
ir de excursión (en todoterreno)	to go on an excursion (in an ATV)
ir en barco	to go by boat
montar a caballo / en bicicleta	to go horseback riding / bicycle riding
pasarlo de maravilla	to have a wonderful time
pescar	to fish
quedarse (en un hostal/hotel)	to stay (in a hostel/hotel)
recorrer (la ciudad / el campo)	to travel around, to tour (the city/ countryside)
sacar fotos	to take pictures
subir al (cerro/glaciar/volcán)	to climb (the hill / the glacier / the volcano)
viajar al extranjero	to travel abroad

Expressions with *por* See page 289.
Expressions that may be followed by the subjunctive See page 306.

Capítulo 10
¡Tu salud es lo primero!

«Comamos manzanas todo el año y la enfermedad sufrirá un desengaño».

Fuente: Peter Langer / Design Pics

El juicio final, **Anónimo, Bolivia.** This fresco from the 17th-century Iglesia de Curahuara de Carangas was painted by an indigenous artist who portrayed the story of the Last Judgment as it was told to him. It seems curious that all of the people in the fresco are fair-skinned. Could this be the painter subtly suggesting that the Final Judgment is reserved for Europeans? Or perhaps it was at the direction of the priest who told the story to the artist?

Learning Objectives

10.1 Discuss health-related issues

10.2 Give and follow instructions from an acquaintance, and express feelings about future situations

10.3 Learn about traditional medicine and an influential Bolivian pop rock band

10.4 Talk about how to stay healthy and fit

10.5 Express beliefs and doubts about future situations

10.6 Plan for the viewing/listening task

10.7 Identify and research some important cultural aspects of Bolivia and Paraguay

10.8 Identify the main characteristics in a story

10.9 Create an idea web

In this Chapter

ENFOQUE CULTURAL: PARAGUAY Y BOLIVIA
Club cultura: Introducción a Paraguay

Video

Indica con **C (Cierto)** o **F (Falso)** si escuchas/ves o no esta información en el video.

1. _____ No tiene salida al mar.

2. _____ La base de su economía es la agricultura.

3. _____ Exporta energía.

4. _____ Tiene una población homogénea.

5. _____ Tiene dos lenguas oficiales: el quechua y el castellano (español).

10.1 Primera parte

Vocabulario

10.1 Discuss health-related issues

Las partes del cuerpo humano

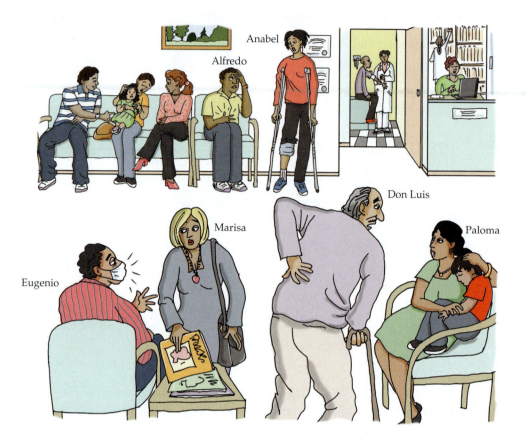

En el consultorio del médico. Muchas personas tienen **cita** con la doctora Méndez. Mientras esperan, hablan de sus **síntomas**.

ANABEL: **Me torcí la rodilla** mientras hacía jogging.

ALFREDO: Y yo, tengo **náuseas**. ¡Qué mal me siento!

DON LUIS: ¡Ay, cuánto **me duele la espalda**! No puedo sentarme.

PALOMA: Mi hijo tiene **fiebre** y no quiere comer nada. No sé si es un simple **resfriado** o algo más serio.

EUGENIO: Tengo mucha **tos** y me duele todo **el cuerpo**. Creo que tengo **gripe**.

MARISA: Es mejor que se lo diga a la doctora y que **siga sus consejos**.

¿Comprendes?   Identify who is described: **Eugenio**, **Marisa**, **don Luis**, **Paloma**, **Alfredo**, or **Anabel**.

1. _____ Debe seguir los consejos de la doctora.

2. _____ Su hijo no tiene una temperatura normal.

3. _____ Se lastimó la rodilla.

Respuestas: 1. Eugenio; 2. Paloma; 3. Anabel

))) Vocabulario

Las partes del cuerpo humano	Parts of the human body
la boca	*mouth*
el brazo	*arm*
la cabeza	*head*
el corazón	*heart*
el dedo (del pie)	*finger (toe)*
la espalda	*back*
el estómago	*stomach*
la garganta	*throat*
la lengua	*tongue*
la muela	*molar*
el oído	*ear (inner)*
la oreja	*ear (outer)*
el pecho	*chest*
el pie	*foot*
la pierna	*leg*
el pulmón	*lung*
la rodilla	*knee*

Problemas de salud	Health problems
doler (ue)	*to hurt*
lastimarse	*to hurt oneself*
romperse (un hueso)	*to break (a bone)*
ser alérgico/a a	*to be allergic to*
tener dolor de cabeza / fiebre (f.) / gripe (f.) / una infección / náuseas / un resfriado / tos (f.)	*to have a headache / a fever / the flu / an infection / nausea / a cold / a cough*
torcerse (ue)	*to twist*
toser	*to cough*

En el consultorio del médico	At the doctor's office
el beneficio y el riesgo	*benefit and risk*
el diagnóstico	*diagnosis*
la enfermedad	*illness*
el examen físico	*checkup*
la inyección	*shot*
el/la paciente	*patient*
la radiografía	*X-ray*
la receta	*prescription*
el síntoma	*symptom*
la sala de urgencias	*emergency room*

Sugerencias y remedios médicos	Medical advice and remedies
dejar de (fumar / tomar bebidas alcohólicas)	*to quit (smoking / drinking alcoholic beverages)*
guardar cama	*to stay in bed due to sickness*
hacer una cita	*to make an appointment*
mejorarse	*to get better, to get well*
respirar (profundamente)	*to breathe (deeply)*
seguir (i, i) los consejos del médico	*to follow the doctor's advice*
tomar la presión / la temperatura	*to take blood pressure / temperature*

Tratamientos	Treatments
la acupuntura	*acupuncture*
el antiácido	*antacid*
el antibiótico	*antibiotic*
la aspirina	*aspirin*
el calmante	*tranquilizer, painkiller*
el jarabe	*cough syrup*
el medicamento herbal	*herbal medicine*
la pastilla	*pill, lozenge*

Variaciones

- Although you will hear **la gripe** almost everywhere, in Mexico the term is **la gripa**.
- You will generally hear **lastimarse** in the Americas, but in Spain, **hacerse daño**.
- In Latin America, use **tomar la presión**, but in Spain, **tomar la tensión**.

Aplicación

10-1 ¿Qué parte del cuerpo? Selecciona la parte del cuerpo que mejor corresponde a cada descripción.

1. __B__ Es indispensable en la circulación de la sangre.
2. __e__ Esta permite apreciar el perfume de las flores.
3. __g__ Tienes dos para ver y leer.
4. __j__ Tienes dos para respirar el aire fresco.
5. __f__ Tienes dos para oír la música.
6. __i__ Con dos de estas, caminas y corres.
7. __h__ En cada uno de estos, tienes cinco dedos.
8. __C__ Es en este donde llega la comida después de comer.
9. __a__ Con esta, comes y hablas.
10. __D__ Si te duele esta, debes consultar al dentista.

a. la boca
b. el corazón
c. el estómago
d. la muela
e. la nariz
f. el oído
g. el ojo
h. el pie
i. la pierna
j. el pulmón

10-2 ¿Qué le pasa? Describe lo que les pasa a estas personas y da una posible causa de su(s) problema(s).

MODELO:

Alicia

A Alicia le duele el estómago porque comió dos pasteles.

1.

Alberto

2.

Ana María

3.

Samuel y Ricardo

4.

Carlos

5.

Ramiro y Marta

10-3 ¡Qué mal me siento! Escucha a doña Carmen mientras habla por teléfono con su médico; indica con una **X** sus síntomas, los diagnósticos y los consejos del médico.

Síntomas	Diagnósticos	Consejos
_____ tos	_____ alergias	_____ tomar aspirina
_____ fiebre	_____ presiones del trabajo	__/__ descansar
__/__ dolor de cabeza	_____ resfriado	_____ comer sopa
_____ dolor de estómago	_____ gripe	__/__ comer mejor
_____ dolor de garganta	_____ úlceras	_____ hacer ejercicio
_____ dolor en una muela	__/__ mala dieta	_____ tomar antibióticos

10-4 ¿Cuándo consultas al médico? Pregúntense si consultan al médico en las siguientes situaciones, y dense más detalles.

MODELO: Te duele la cabeza.

ESTUDIANTE 1: *¿Consultas al médico si te duele la cabeza?*

ESTUDIANTE 2: *No. Por lo general, tomo dos aspirinas y me siento mejor. ¿Y tú?*

1. Tienes tos.
2. Tienes una fiebre alta.
3. Te duele la espalda.
4. Te rompes un hueso.
5. Necesitas un examen físico para el trabajo.
6. Tienes náuseas.
7. Te duele la garganta.
8. Tienes resfriado.

10-5A ¡Necesito información! Hagan el papel de doctor/a (estudiante A) y paciente (estudiante B). Sigan la guía y tengan una conversación de sus síntomas, un diagnóstico lógico y recomendaciones para mejorarse. **Paciente:** por favor, ve al **Apéndice 1**, página A-12.

MODELO: DOCTOR/A: *Buenos días. ¿Cómo se siente? ¿Cuáles son sus síntomas?*

PACIENTE: *Buenos días, doctor/a. Me siento muy mal...*

Estudiante A: Doctor/a

1. Saluda al/a la paciente y pregúntale cuáles son sus síntomas.
3. Pregúntale qué medicinas toma.
5. Pregúntale cuánto ejercicio hace cada día.
7. Pregúntale si fuma, y cuánto.
9. Dale tu diagnóstico. Recomienda que (haga una cita con un especialista, guarde cama, deje de fumar...).

Cultura en vivo

According to the World Health Organization (WHO), traditional medicine is widely practiced in much of Latin America and is often relied on for primary health care. Herbal medicines are the most lucrative form of traditional medicine, generating billions of dollars in revenue. There are over 2,000 documented indigenous medicinal plants in Bolivia alone. Have you ever taken an herbal remedy?

Estructuras

10.2 **Give and follow instructions from an acquaintance, and express feelings about future situations**

Formal commands

¿Recuerdas? You've tried to influence another person by using the subjunctive in a dependent clause. Complete the sentence with the correct forms of **guardar** and **tomar**, according to the context.

Insisto en que usted (1) _____ su medicina y que (2) _____ cama.

Respuestas: 1. tome; 2. guarde

Vaya a su casa y guarde cama. Tome estas pastillas por diez días y llámeme si no se siente mejor.

A more direct way to tell someone to do something is with a command: *Take your medicine! Stay in bed!*

- In Spanish, you use different forms of the command for informal (**tú/vosotros**) and formal (**usted/ustedes**) address. With formal commands, use the same forms as the present subjunctive.

  (Quiero que usted) consulte al médico. → **¡Consulte** al médico!
  (Es necesario que ustedes) hagan ejercicio. → **¡Hagan** ejercicio!

Infinitive	Subjunctive	Formal commands	
		Ud.	**Uds.**
hablar	hable	habl**e**	habl**en**
comer	coma	com**a**	com**an**
escribir	escriba	escrib**a**	escrib**an**
pensar	piense	piens**e**	piens**en**
pedir	pida	pid**a**	pid**an**
saber	sepa	sep**a**	sep**an**
ir	vaya	vay**a**	vay**an**

- Place **no** before a negative command form.

  No guarde cama más de dos días.   *Don't stay in bed for more than two days.*
  No tosan durante un concierto.   *Don't cough during a concert.*

- You may use **usted** or **ustedes** for emphasis. As a rule, place them after the verb.

  Tenga usted cuidado.   *You be careful.*
  No fumen ustedes en el trabajo.   *Don't you smoke at work.*

- Attach object pronouns (direct, indirect) and reflexive pronouns to affirmative commands, and add an accent mark to the stressed vowel.

  ¡Váyase de aquí!   *Leave here!*
  Tómele la presión, por favor.   *Take her blood pressure, please.*

- Place object pronouns and reflexive pronouns before the verb in negative commands.

  No **se tuerza** la rodilla esquiando.   *Don't twist your knee skiing.*
  No **le hagan** una radiografía a la paciente.   *Don't take the patient's X-ray.*

¿Comprendes? Complete each sentence with the correct form of the appropriate verb: **mejorarse**, **respirar**, or **seguir**.

Señor Martínez, (1) _____ profundamente, por favor. Señorita López, (2) _____ mis consejos y va a sentirse mejor. Carlos y Roberto, ¡(3) _____ pronto!

Respuestas: 1. respire; 2. siga; 3. mejórense

Rockford

class work

Aplicación

10-6 En el consultorio médico. La doctora Villalba se confunde un poco cuando les da consejos a sus pacientes, o le pide algo a su asistente.

Paso 1   Lee lo que dice la doctora e indica todos los mandatos.

circle the comands

los mandatos

   MODELO: Señor Álvarez, <u>no me explique</u> sus síntomas, por favor.

DOCTORA: Señora Martínez, usted tiene la gripe porcina (*swine*). Vaya a su casa y guarde cama. Tome mucha agua y no se bañe por un mes.

DOCTORA: Luisa, por favor, llame a la farmacia y dígales que necesitamos una botella grande de aspirinas. Pídales las pastillas grandes, las que no les gustan a los pacientes.

DOCTORA: Sr. Duarte, usted necesita un examen físico completo. Tome esta receta y vaya a un restaurante. Pídale al camarero que le haga el examen.

DOCTORA: Srta. Vera, usted se rompió un dedo. No use la mano durante dos semanas. No cocine ni escriba en la computadora. Tenga cuidado de no lastimarse más.

DOCTORA: Luisa, por favor, vaya al departamento de radiografías y busque la de la Srta. Vera. Explíqueles que la necesito ahora mismo. Si dicen que no la tienen, deles una inyección de penicilina.

DOCTORA: Sr. Fernández, usted tiene los pulmones congestionados. Deje de fumar, haga por lo menos una hora de ejercicio diario, y no respire mucho durante dos semanas. Venga a verme en un mes, y por favor, no se mejore.

Paso 2   En parejas, identifiquen los consejos ilógicos y explíquense por qué.

   MODELO: ESTUDIANTE 1: *En mi opinión, "no se bañe por un mes" es ilógico. Creo que ella debe bañarse para sentirse mejor.*
   ESTUDIANTE 2: *Estoy de acuerdo. Un mes es mucho tiempo.*

10-7 El doctor Chiringa. El doctor Chiringa siempre les da muchas órdenes a sus pacientes. Completa la conversación que tiene con sus pacientes Roberto y Tomás Cruz, usando mandatos formales del verbo lógico.

DR. CHIRINGA: Señores Cruz, ustedes tienen que hacer algo por su salud. No (1) _____ (cenar/guardar) tan tarde y no (2) _se acuesten_ (acostarse/respirar) todos los días después de la medianoche.

ROBERTO: Sí, doctor, pero es que llegamos del trabajo muy tarde.

DR. CHIRINGA: Entiendo, pero (3) _tengan_ (empezar/tener) más cuidado, no (4) _trabajen_ (trabajar/descansar) tanto. (5) _lleguen_ (Seguir/ Llegar) a casa más temprano; (6) _descansen_ (bailar/descansar) más y (7) _pongan_ (comer/poner) más atención a su salud.

TOMÁS: Doctor, es que tenemos muchas presiones. (8) _miren_ (Mirar/ Salir) usted, tenemos que trabajar doce horas para ganarnos la vida.

DR. CHIRINGA: Bueno, no (9) _se enojen_ (divertirse/enojarse). Su salud es lo primero.

Presencia hispana

According to the American Medical Association (AMA), about 5% of U.S. physicians are Hispanic, even though that group represents 17% of the nation's population. In response, the AMA launched the Hispanic Physician Outreach Initiative to discuss strategies for increasing the voice of Hispanic physicians. Why is this outreach important?

will go over tuesday

★ HW

10-8 Servicios médicos de urgencias. Ustedes están entrenándose para ser paramédicos/as. Decidan el orden de importancia de las acciones en cada emergencia y túrnense para darle mandatos a su compañero/a.

MODELO: Un señor no puede respirar: darle oxígeno, darle respiración artificial, llamar a un cardiólogo.

ESTUDIANTE 1: *Primero, dele respiración artificial, después llame a un cardiólogo y, finalmente, dele oxígeno.*

ESTUDIANTE 2: *No, primero llame a un cardiólogo.*

1. Hay un accidente en el centro: avisar al hospital, investigar cuál es el hospital que está más cerca, poner todo el equipo de emergencia en la ambulancia.

2. Un niño tuvo un accidente en su bicicleta: contactar a los padres, llevarlo al hospital, examinarlo para ver si se rompió algún hueso.

3. Hay un escape de gas en una casa de apartamentos: llamar a los bomberos, darles oxígeno a las víctimas, sacar a los residentes del edificio.

4. Un paciente está desorientado: hacerle preguntas, llamar a un familiar, tomarle la presión.

5. Una mujer tiene un tremendo dolor de cabeza: darle un calmante, tomarle la temperatura, preguntarle su nombre.

6. Es necesario preparar el equipo de la ambulancia para empezar un nuevo día: llenar el tanque de gasolina, revisar (*check*) los tanques de oxígeno, reponer (*restock*) las medicinas.

Prepare la ambulancia para una emergencia.

10-9A ¡Necesito información! Ustedes trabajan en la sala de urgencias y tienen que decidir qué hacer en situaciones de emergencia. Túrnense presentando las situaciones y respondiendo con mandatos formales lógicos de su lista. Incluyan una situación original. **Estudiante B**: por favor, ve al **Apéndice 1**, página A-12.

MODELO: ESTUDIANTE A: *El niño tiene gripe.*

ESTUDIANTE B: *Dele muchos líquidos como jugo o agua.*

Estudiante A:

Situaciones urgentes	Acciones
1. El paciente necesita oxígeno.	buscarle un calmante
2. A la niña le duele el estómago.	darle dos aspirinas
3. El bebé está tosiendo mucho.	darle té con limón
4. La señora tiene una infección en el brazo.	hacerle una radiografía
5. El Sr. Pérez tiene una fiebre muy alta.	mandarlo al dentista
6. ¿...?	¿...?

10-10 Consejos sobre la salud. En parejas, piensen en una pregunta o un problema sobre la salud y escríbanlo en un papel. Intercambien papeles con otra pareja y escríbanles seis consejos para remediar su problema o contestar su pregunta. Después, devuélvanse los papeles y escojan el mejor y el peor consejo que recibieron para presentárselos a la clase.

MODELO: *¿Qué hago para dormir mejor?*

The subjunctive to express feelings and emotions

Temo que tu hija tenga una infección de oído.

¿Recuerdas? You used the subjunctive with verbs of influence in this chapter. Complete the sentence with the correct form of **descansar** or **hacer**.

Tienen gripe. Insistimos en que (1) _____ y que no (2) _____ ejercicio.

Respuestas: 1. descansen; 2. hagan

When you express a feeling or an emotion about an action or state, it is the same as expressing uncertainty, or lack of knowledge. These expressions of hope, fear, surprise, regret, pity, anger, joy, and sorrow take the subjunctive in the dependent clause.

Me alegro de que **te sientas** mejor.	*I'm glad (that) you feel better.*
Es una lástima que no **podamos** acompañarte al médico.	*It's a pity (that) we can't go with you to the the doctor.*

- Remember the conditions for using the subjunctive: *two* clauses with *two* different subjects joined by **que**.

Temes que el médico te **dé** una mala noticia.	*You fear (that) the doctor will give you bad news.*
Es ridículo que las pastillas sean tan grandes.	*It's ridiculous (that) the pills are so big.*

- Here are some common verbs and impersonal expressions that may be followed by the subjunctive when there is a change of subject:

Algunos verbos		Algunas expresiones impersonales	
alegrarse (de)	*to be glad*	es bueno/malo/mejor	*it's good/bad/better*
enojar	*to anger*	es extraño	*it's strange*
esperar	*to hope*	es fácil/difícil	*it's easy/difficult*
estar contento/a (de)	*to be happy*	es fantástico	*it's fantastic*
lamentar	*to regret*	es lamentable	*it's regrettable*
molestar	*to bother*	es una lástima	*it's a shame*
sentir (ie, i)	*to regret*	es (i)lógico	*it's (il)logical*
sorprender	*to surprise*	es (im)posible	*it's (im)possible*
temer	*to fear*	es ridículo	*it's ridiculous*
tener (ie) miedo (de)	*to be afraid*	es sorprendente	*it's surprising*

- As a general rule, use the infinitive when there is only one subject.

Carlos lamenta **estar** enfermo.	*Carlos regrets being sick.*
Es fácil **dar** consejos sobre la salud.	*It's easy to give health advice.*

¿Comprendes? Complete each sentence with the correct form of the appropriate verb: **comer, dar, engordar**.

Doctor, temo (1) _____ mucho si como mucha grasa (*fat*). Me sorprende que usted no me (2) _____ una dieta de menos calorías. Es ilógico que yo (3) _____ solo queso y carne.

Respuestas: 1. engordar; 2. dé; 3. coma

[Handwritten margin notes:]

leer,
identificar,
traducier,

Siga/Follow
comience/start
gradualmente/
gradually

conozca/know

Aprenda/Learn
Siga/Follow

use/use
Mantenga/maintain
no tome/Dont take

Descanse/rest
no se/Dont
Tome/take

Siempre haga/always
do

Nunca jueges/Dont
play

no ignore/Dont ignore

Aplicación

10-11 Seis consejos para practicar un deporte. Antes de empezar a practicar un deporte, es importante seguir algunos consejos.

Paso 1 Lee los consejos e indica todos los mandatos.

1. Siga un programa de entrenamiento para estar en forma para su deporte. Comience por caminar o montar en bicicleta durante quince minutos. Gradualmente aumente su entrenamiento con otros ejercicios.

2. Conozca bien y siga las reglas del deporte, especialmente los deportes de contacto. Aprenda de las tácticas de los demás.

3. Use protección apropiada para las rodillas, las manos, los dientes, los ojos y la cabeza. Mantenga la guardia atenta y no tome riesgos innecesarios.

4. Descanse. No se entrene todos los días. Tome días de descanso para evitar lesiones[1].

5. Siempre haga ejercicios de calentamiento para estirar[2] los músculos antes de jugar. Los músculos calientes son menos susceptibles a lastimarse.

6. Nunca juegue si está muy cansado. No ignore el dolor o la fatiga.

[1]*injuries* [2]*stretch*

Paso 2 Escribe cuatro expresiones de emoción para comentar sobre los consejos para practicar un deporte.

MODELO: *Es sorprendente que algunas personas no sigan un programa de entrenamiento.*

10-12 Un examen médico. Completa la conversación entre el médico y el paciente con la forma correcta del verbo entre paréntesis. Usa el subjuntivo o el infinitivo según el contexto.

PACIENTE: Buenos días, doctor. Me siento muy mal.

MÉDICO: Lamento que usted (1) se sienta (sentirse) mal. ¿Qué tiene?

PACIENTE: Me molesta que a mi esposa no le (2) guste (gustar) lo que como.

MÉDICO: Mmmm... Es lógico que ella (3) se preocupe (preocuparse) por usted. Quítese la camisa; voy a ver cómo está del corazón.

PACIENTE: Espero que no (4) sea (ser) nada serio.

MÉDICO: No, pero temo que su comida (5) contenga (contener) demasiado colesterol y grasas trans.

PACIENTE: Me sorprende que (6) digas (decir) eso. Soy vegetariano.

MÉDICO: Mmmm... Me alegro de (7) saber (saber) eso. ¿Qué come para el desayuno?

PACIENTE: Donuts, galletas y panqueques.

MÉDICO: Ah... ¡Ahora entiendo! Es mejor (8) _____ (dejar) de comer comida chatarra (*junk*) y (9) empezar (empezar) a comer más verduras y frutas frescas.

10-13 ¡Mejoremos nuestra salud! ¿Cómo propones cambiar tu vida para mejorar tu salud?

Paso 1 Escribe cinco resoluciones para mejorar la salud que piensas hacer el año que viene.

MODELO: *Espero ir al gimnasio todos los días.*

Paso 2   En parejas, túrnense para expresar sus resoluciones y reaccionar usando una expresión apropiada para cada resolución.

MODELO: ESTUDIANTE 1: *Espero ir al gimnasio todos los días.*
　　　　　　 ESTUDIANTE 2: *Espero que tengas buenos resultados, pero antes,*
　　　　　　　　　　　　　　 es bueno que consultes al médico.

Es bueno/malo/mejor	Es ridículo	Me sorprende
Es fácil/difícil	Es sorprendente	Siento
Es fantástico	Espero	Temo
Es (i)lógico	Me alegro de	¿...?

10-14A   ¡Necesito información!   Hagan el papel de paciente (estudiante A) y doctor/a (estudiante B) en el consultorio médico. El/La paciente explica sus síntomas y el/la doctor/a reacciona y da consejos. Sigan la guía para la conversación y usen expresiones de emoción con el subjuntivo o el infinitivo según el contexto. **Doctor/a**: por favor, ve al **Apéndice 1**, página A-13.

MODELO: PACIENTE: *Doctor/a, temo tener una enfermedad muy rara.*
　　　　　　 DOCTOR/A: *Es mejor que me diga todos sus síntomas.*

Estudiante A: Paciente

1. Temo tener (una enfermedad rara, una infección del / de la..., una condición contagiosa).

3. Es ridículo que (decirme eso, no decirme la verdad, querer saber eso).

5. Es difícil (seguir sus consejos, comer menos, trabajar menos, no usar mi teléfono celular).

¡Conversemos!

Primero, pregúntate si puedes llevar a cabo las siguientes funciones comunicativas en español. Después, júntate con dos o tres compañeros/as de clase para presentar las situaciones. Hagan y respondan a por lo menos cuatro preguntas en cada situación.

✓ CAN YOU . . .

☐ discuss health-related issues?

☐ give and follow instructions from an acquaintance?

☐ express feelings about future actions?

WITH YOUR CLASSMATE(S) . . .

Situación: En un consultorio médico.

Túrnense para hacer los papeles de médico/a y paciente. Pregúntense y explíquense cuáles son los síntomas y los remedios para curarlos. Usen mandatos formales para explicar qué debe hacer el/la paciente o para darle consejos.

Para empezar: *Doctor/a, no sé qué me pasa. Me duele...*

Situación: En la sala de urgencias.

Hagan los papeles de médicos/as en la sala de urgencias que atienden a un paciente que no puede explicar sus problemas. Usen mandatos formales.

Para empezar: *Doctor, deme la radiografía del paciente...*

Situación: Avances médicos.

Hablen sobre avances y problemas médicos que conozcan. Usen expresiones de emoción para expresar su opinión.

Para empezar: *Veo en Internet que hay un nuevo tratamiento para el cáncer. Me alegro de que investiguen... Me sorprende que...*

Perfiles

10.3 Learn about traditional medicine and an influential Bolivian pop rock band

Mi experiencia

LA MEDICINA TRADICIONAL EN BOLIVIA

10-15 **Para ti.** ¿Tienes experiencia con la medicina tradicional (la homeopatía, la acupuntura, la medicina naturista)? ¿Qué piensas de estas prácticas? Lee lo que dice Rosario, una estudiante de antropología biológica en la Universidad de Toronto en su blog desde Bolivia.

[1]*internship*

[2]*healer*

[3]*leaves* [4]*Even though*

[5]*raise funds*

¡Hola! Aquí estoy yo, Rosario, otra vez para contarles sobre mi pasantía[1] aquí en Bolivia con la Organización Panamericana de la Salud (OPS). Esta es la segunda entrada en mi blog desde mi llegada hace dos semanas, y como les dije la última vez, estoy aquí por un año para trabajar en una comunidad remota donde esperamos mejorar la salud de los habitantes y también aprender sobre la medicina tradicional.

La semana pasada terminamos la orientación en Cochabamba y ahora estoy en uno de los pueblos donde voy a trabajar. En la orientación aprendí que en las zonas más remotas es muy común que los habitantes tengan más confianza en los médicos tradicionales que en la medicina moderna. Yo creo que es lógico, pues Bolivia tiene una larga tradición con estas prácticas, tanto que el viceministro de Medicina Tradicional e Interculturalidad, Germán Mamani Huallpa, es un conocido curandero[2]. Cuando llegué a Bolivia hace dos semanas, tenía unos dolores de cabeza terribles a causa de la altura (esto lo llaman **soroche** aquí), y fui a ver a un médico *kallawaya* quien me preparó mate de coca, una infusión hecha de las hojas[3] de coca. Aunque[4] al principio tenía mis dudas, poco a poco empecé a sentirme mejor. Nunca se sabe, ¿verdad?

Durante mi pasantía, vamos a tener un concierto benéfico para recaudar fondos[5] para estas comunidades a la vez que promocionamos el trabajo de la OPS. Entre los artistas, va a tocar Octavia, la banda boliviana más popular de este momento. Vuelvan la semana que viene y les cuento sobre el concierto y más de mis experiencias en este fascinante lugar.

10-16 **En su opinión.** ¿Les gustaría investigar sobre la medicina tradicional?

Paso 1 Individualmente, escriban una lista de los beneficios y los riesgos para cada una de estas sugerencias o tratamientos.

1. el mate de coca para aliviar los síntomas de mal de altura
2. la quiropráctica para aliviar el dolor de espalda
3. el té verde para protegerse del cáncer
4. la acupuntura para aliviar el dolor de la rodilla
5. las bebidas enérgicas para mantenerse fuerte
6. las superfrutas para mantener la buena salud

Paso 2 En parejas, comparen sus opiniones.

MODELO: una copa de vino diaria para proteger el corazón

ESTUDIANTE 1: *En mi opinión, es bueno tomar una copa de vino todos los días para proteger el corazón.*

ESTUDIANTE 2: *No estoy de acuerdo. Las bebidas alcohólicas tienen muchos riesgos y creo que...*

Mi música

"LA CIUDAD QUE HABITA EN MÍ" (OCTAVIA, BOLIVIA)

Al debutar en el MTV Latino, la banda Octavia fue conocida a nivel mundial. Su música—una fusión de pop rock, música andina, electrónica y acústica— recoge la experiencia del boliviano orgulloso (*proud*) de la riqueza de sus raíces étnicas. Los miembros son Omar González (voz), Simón Luján (guitarra), Vladimir Pérez (bajo) y Martín Fox (batería).

ANTES DE VER Y ESCUCHAR

10-17 Las Ciudades Maravillas. En 2014, La Paz fue elegida una de las nuevas Siete Ciudades Maravillas del Mundo. Esta canción es la entrada oficial de la campaña "La Paz: Ciudad Maravilla". En tu opinión, ¿cuáles son algunas características de una ciudad que la hacen una "Ciudad Maravilla"?

> **MODELO:** *Primero, es necesario que la ciudad...*

PARA VER Y ESCUCHAR

10-18 La canción. Busca en Internet el video y la letra de "La ciudad que habita en mí" por Octavia. Haz una lista de las escenas más impresionantes del video que la hagan una Ciudad Maravilla. ¿Cuál es la más extraordinaria para ti personalmente?

> **♀ Busca:** Octavia La ciudad que habita en mí video oficial; Octavia La ciudad que habita en mí letra

DESPUÉS DE VER Y ESCUCHAR

10-19 La ciudad que habita en mí. Esta canción es una fuerte expresión del orgullo que sienten los músicos por ser ciudadanos de La Paz, Bolivia. Busca dos ejemplos de este orgullo en las escenas del video y en la letra de la canción.

> **MODELO:** *La letra dice que la ciudad "habla a través de mí", es decir que el cantante es la voz de la ciudad.*

 **10-20 Un concierto para ayudar a la OPS.** Imagínense que organizan un concierto para la Organización Panamericana de la Salud (OPS). Trabajen juntos/as y hagan una lista de las cosas que deben hacer o de las preocupaciones que tengan antes del concierto de Octavia.

> **MODELO:** *Es necesario que... le escribamos una invitación al agente de Octavia.*

1. Espero que...
2. Es importante que...
3. Me sorprende que...
4. Me alegro de que...
5. Temo que...
6. Es lógico que...

10.2 Segunda parte

Vocabulario

10.4 Talk about how to stay healthy and fit

Los alimentos

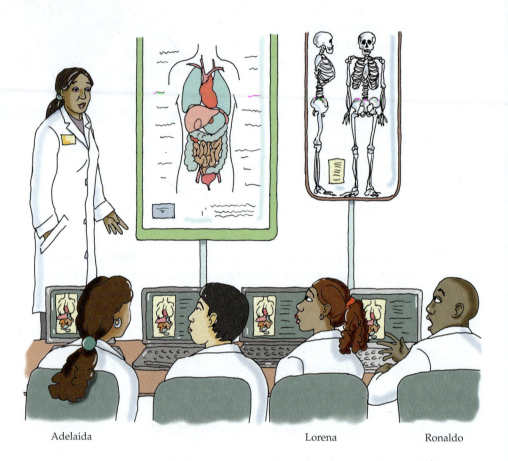

Adelaida   Lorena   Ronaldo

))) **¡Mejora tu salud!** La doctora Duarte da una clase de nutrición.

DRA. DUARTE: ¿Cierto o falso? Se puede **adelgazar** comiendo una dieta de puros **carbohidratos**.

ADELAIDA: Cierto, pero **se engorda** después.

LORENA: Cierto, pero el cuerpo necesita **proteínas** también.

RONALDO: Depende de si son carbohidratos buenos o malos...

DRA. DUARTE: Me gustan todas sus repuestas, pero recuerden que es necesario **seguir una dieta equilibrada**, rica en **fibras**, **grasas monoinsaturadas**, **antioxidantes**, **vitaminas y minerales**. Ahora, ¿quién me puede dar un ejemplo de cada categoría?

¿Comprendes? Indicate whether each statement is **cierto** (**C**) or **falso** (**F**), according to the dialogue.

1. _____ La Dra. Duarte es profesora de anatomía.

2. _____ Según la Dra. Duarte, es importante comer una dieta equilibrada.

3. _____ Es probable que los antioxidantes sean malos.

Respuestas: 1. F; 2. C; 3. F

Vocabulario

Sigan una dieta rica en...	Follow a diet rich in . . .
los antioxidantes	*antioxidants*
los carbohidratos complejos	*complex carbohydrates*
la fibra	*fiber*
las grasas (monoinsaturadas)	*(monounsaturated) fats*
los minerales y las vitaminas	*minerals and vitamins*
las proteínas	*proteins*
En moderación, coman/beban...	**In moderation, eat/drink . . .**
los carbohidratos sencillos	*simple carbohydrates*
el colesterol	*cholesterol*
Eviten...	**Avoid . . .**
el azúcar (los dulces)	*sugar (sweets)*
la comida chatarra	*junk food*
las grasas saturadas (trans)	*saturated (trans) fats*
Algunas condiciones	**Some conditions**
la depresión	*depression*
el estrés	*stress*
el (sobre)peso	*(excess) weight*

Tu peso y tu salud	Your weight and your health
adelgazar	*to lose weight*
bajar/subir de peso	*to lose/gain weight*
cuidar(se)	*to take care (of oneself)*
engordar	*to gain weight*
estar a (seguir una) dieta (equilibrada)	*to be on (to follow) a (balanced) diet*
guardar la línea	*to stay trim, to watch one's figure*
hacer ejercicios aeróbicos	*to do aerobics*
mantenerse[1] en forma	*to stay in shape*
padecer (zc) de (diabetes/cáncer)	*to suffer (from) (diabetes/cancer)*
ponerse en forma	*to get in shape*

Variaciones

- You will hear **la comida chatarra** mainly in Mexico and Uruguay. **La comida basura** and **las porquerías** are common alternatives in other Spanish-speaking countries. Examples of these foods include **las papas fritas** (in the Americas), and **las patatas fritas** (in Spain), for both potato chips and French fries.

 Letras y sonidos

The consonants *r* and *rr*

In Spanish, there are two **r** sounds: a flap (or tap) and a trill. A flap involves one quick touch of the tongue behind the upper front teeth. This sound is similar to the English flap made for the letters *tt* in *butter*. A Spanish trill is a rapid series of two or more flaps. English has no trill, but this sound is approximated when imitating a race car revving up its engine.

The trill sound occurs in Spanish in the contexts:

rr:	pe-**rr**o	pi-za-**rr**a	a-bu-**rr**i-do
Word initial:	**R**o-sa	**R**a-món	**r**á-pi-do
After **l, n,** or **s:**	al-**r**e-de-dor	En-**r**i-que	Is-**r**a-el

In other contexts, the **r** is a single flap:

pe-**r**o	o-pe-**r**ar	es-t**r**és	g**r**a-sa

---

[1]like **tener: (pres.)** *mantengo, mantienes, mantiene, mantenemos...* **(pret.)** *mantuve, mantuviste, mantuvo...*

Aplicación

10-21 ¿Qué comes? Sigue los pasos para completar esta actividad.

Paso 1 Selecciona la descripción que mejor corresponde a cada comida.

1. _g_ la leche
2. _c_ la mantequilla
3. _e_ el aceite de oliva
4. _d_ el vino
5. _h_ la manzana
6. _a_ el pescado
7. _b_ la pizza
8. _f_ el helado

a. Es un plato saludable del mar que contiene mucha proteína y que no engorda. Además, contiene vitamina E.

b. Para muchos, es comida chatarra porque contiene poca proteína y mucha grasa.

c. Es un producto sólido, derivado de la crema y que contiene grasas saturadas.

d. Es una bebida alcohólica que se debe tomar con moderación.

e. Es un aceite que contiene grasas monoinsaturadas, que son buenas para el corazón.

f. Es un postre que contiene grasas saturadas y azúcar.

g. Es una bebida rica en proteína, calcio y vitaminas.

h. Es una fruta que contiene vitamina C y fibra.

Paso 2 En parejas, conversen sobre las comidas en el **Paso 1**. ¿Cuáles comen con frecuencia y cuáles comen raramente? ¿Por qué?

MODELO: *Como pizza con frecuencia, no porque es buena para la salud, sino porque...*

10-22 En la oficina de la Dra. Menéndez. Completa los consejos de la Dra. Menéndez con una palabra o expresión del **Vocabulario**. Conjuga los verbos si es necesario.

MODELO: Sra. García, es bueno __guardar la línea__, es decir, no subir ni bajar mucho de peso.

1. Sra. García, usted tiene mucho _estrés_ en su vida. Quiero que tome calmantes y que se vaya de vacaciones por una semana.

2. Sra. López, su hijo _padece_ de alergias a los productos lácteos. No debe beber leche ni comer helado.

3. Sr. González, para mantenerse en forma, usted debe hacer _ejercicio_ como el jogging o el tenis. Pronto va a _rajar de peso_

4. Srta. Casals, usted está demasiado delgada. No debe seguir _a delegazar_ tan rígida de solo verduras.

5. Sr. Rojas, usted perdió dos kilos este mes. ¿Cómo _bajo de peso_?

Presencia hispana

High blood pressure is strongly linked to cardiovascular diseases such as stroke and heart attack, but it is also very treatable. According to a recent U.S. government survey, black and Hispanic Americans are considerably less likely to receive adequate treatment for high blood pressure than white Americans, whether they have health insurance or not. What strategies could the health care community use to serve at-risk groups better?

10-23 Una encuesta médica. La señora Ramírez participa en una encuesta (*survey*) por teléfono. Selecciona la frase que mejor completa cada oración.

1. El agente representa...
   a. a un candidato para la presidencia.
   b. una empresa de farmacéuticos.
   c. el Servicio de Seguros Sociales.

2. La encuesta colecciona datos sobre...
   a. el nivel (*level*) de educación de los habitantes.
   b. el estado de salud de la ciudad.
   c. el número de inmigrantes en la comunidad.

3. La señora dice que su esposo...
   a. fuma mucho y tiene tos.
   b. va al gimnasio con regularidad.
   c. consulta al médico cuando no es necesario.

4. Ella no come...
   a. carne.
   b. pescado.
   c. verduras.

5. Ella hace ejercicio...
   a. raramente.
   b. los fines de semana.
   c. con sus amigas.

6. Tiene una buena colección de...
   a. libros de autoayuda.
   b. recetas saludables.
   c. medicamentos.

7. Es probable que ella...
   a. sepa más que su médico.
   b. padezca de alguna enfermedad.
   c. busque un especialista en acupuntura.

10-24 ¿Cuánto estrés tienes en tu vida? Sigue los pasos para completar la actividad.

Paso 1 Indica los factores que hayas experimentado (*may have experienced*) en los últimos 12 meses. Después, suma el total según la clave (*key*).

	Sí	No
En lo personal		
1. Duermes menos de siete horas por noche.		
2. Trabajas más de 40 horas por semana.		
3. Es el comienzo o el fin del semestre.		
En las relaciones	Sí	No
4. Te casaste.		
5. Te separaste o divorciaste.		
6. Tienes problemas familiares.		
En el trabajo	Sí	No
7. Empiezas un trabajo nuevo.		
8. Tuviste un cambio de horario o de responsabilidades.		
9. Tienes problemas con el jefe (*boss*).		
Cambios extremos	Sí	No
10. Cambiaste de universidad o de casa.		
11. Cambiaste de religión o amistades.		

Clave: Cada respuesta **Sí** = 1 punto.

0–4 puntos: Tienes mucha suerte porque tienes poco estrés en tu vida. Debes ser un/a buen/a amigo/a para los que padezcan de estrés y te necesiten.

5–8 puntos: Tienes un nivel de estrés normal. Debes seguir trabajando para mantener un buen estado de ánimo.

9–11 puntos: Tu nivel de estrés está a un grado crítico. Debes consultar a un profesional que te pueda ayudar a manejar los factores estresantes en tu vida. Los amigos y los familiares son importantes también.

Paso 2   En parejas, conversen sobre las estrategias que ustedes emplean cuando padecen de estrés. ¿Cuáles son más efectivas y cuáles son menos efectivas en diferentes contextos? ¿Cuáles tienen en común?

MODELO: *En época de exámenes, me ayuda... para combatir el estrés. ¿Qué haces tú?*

10-25 Consejos para un/a amigo/a.   Creen que su amigo/a tiene un problema y quieren intervenir para ayudarlo/la. Elijan una de estas situaciones y trabajen juntos/as para llegar a un plan de acción. Usen el subjuntivo cuando sea necesario. Preséntenle su plan a la clase.

MODELO: ESTUDIANTE 1: *Nuestra amiga es demasiado flaca. No come más que...*
ESTUDIANTE 2: *Es evidente que... Debemos recomendarle que...*
Es crucial que... Debes decirle que...

Posibles problemas:

1. Su amigo/a tiene un nivel de azúcar muy alto y temen que padezca de _____. No hace ejercicio y siempre está cansado/a. Además, no tiene seguro médico.

2. Su amigo/a tiene una tos tremenda. Fuma más de _____ paquetes de cigarillos al día. No duerme más de _____ horas cada noche. Además, come mucha comida chatarra.

3. Su amigo/a es un/a fanático/a del ejercicio. Siempre está entrenándose para la próxima prueba de Ironman. Sigue una dieta que bajó de Internet y come solo _____. Cuando sus amigos lo/la invitan a tomar _____ o a salir, siempre tiene una excusa.

4. Creen que su amigo/a es hipocondríaco/a. Siempre dice que padece de una lista de enfermedades. Si alguien tiene _____ (gripe, resfriado, etc.), él/ella también lo tiene. Toma todo tipo de remedios: medicamentos herbales, antiácidos, calmantes...

Cultura en vivo

Una farmacia is a place to buy health-related products, not the wide range of sundries typical in U.S. or Canadian stores. In many countries, you can purchase prescription medicines over the counter in a pharmacy. The pharmacist is usually helpful in identifying the appropriate medication and dosage. When you travel, be sure to carry a list of the generic name and exact dosage of any medications.

Estructuras

10.5 Express beliefs and doubts about future situations

The subjunctive to express doubt and denial

¿Recuerdas? You've used the subjunctive in dependent clauses when (1) you express influence or emotion in the main clause, and (2) there is a change of subject, usually introduced by **que**.

Complete each sentence with the correct form of the verb in parentheses.

Es una lástima que tú (1) _____ (sentirse) mal. Ojalá que (2) _____ (mejorarse) pronto.

Respuestas: 1. te sientas; 2. te mejores

Dudo que el azúcar y la grasa saturada sean buenos para la salud.

You also use the subjunctive in dependent clauses after expressions of *doubt*, *uncertainty*, or *denial*. These expressions suggest that the action in the dependent clause is outside of the speaker's experience.

Algunos verbos		**Algunas expresiones impersonales**	
dudar	to doubt	**es dudoso**	it's doubtful
negar (ie)	to deny	**no es cierto**	it's not certain
no pensar (ie)	to not think	**es increíble**	it's incredible
no creer	to not believe	**no es verdad**	it's not true
no estar seguro/a (de)	to not be sure (of)		

No es cierto que Camilo **padezca** de artritis.
It's not certain that Camilo suffers from arthritis.

No creo que el médico **sepa** el diagnóstico.
I don't believe that the doctor knows the diagnosis.

El médico niega que una megadosis de vitaminas **beneficie** la salud.
The doctor denies that a megadose of vitamins is beneficial for health.

- When there is *no* doubt, uncertainty, or disbelief about an action or event, use the indicative in the dependent clause.

Es cierto que Camilo **padece** de artritis.
It's certain that Camilo suffers from arthritis.

Creo que el médico **sabe** el diagnóstico.
I believe that the doctor knows the diagnosis.

El médico no niega que una megadosis de vitaminas **beneficia** la salud.
The doctor doesn't deny that a megadose of vitamins is beneficial for health.

- When you ask a question with **creer** and you expect a negative response, use the subjunctive in the dependent clause. If you have no opinion, or don't expect a negative response, use the indicative.

¿Crees que el alcohol **afecte** el corazón?
Do you believe (think) that alcohol affects the heart? (you imply doubt)

¿Crees que el alcohol **afecta** el corazón?
Do you believe (think) that alcohol affects the heart? (you have no opinion)

- Use the infinitive if there is no change of subject.

Carlos niega tomar bebidas alcohólicas.
Carlos denies drinking alcoholic beverages.

Es increíble ver cuántas calorías tiene una hamburguesa.
It's unbelieveable seeing how many calories a hamburger has.

EL SUBJUNTIVO CON *TAL VEZ* Y *QUIZÁ(S)*

- Use the subjunctive to convey uncertainty or doubt with the expressions **tal vez** and **quizá(s)**, meaning *perhaps* or *maybe*. These expressions omit **que**.

Tal vez funcione no comer tanto azúcar. — *Perhaps not eating so much sugar will work.*

Quizás el ejercicio me **haga** sentir mejor. — *Maybe exercise will make me feel better.*

RESUMEN DE LOS USOS DEL SUBJUNTIVO

You have now practiced using the subjunctive in dependent clauses when the main clause expresses *influence*, *emotion*, *doubt*, or *denial* and (with the exception of **tal vez** and **quizás**), there is a change in subject between the two clauses. All of these uses suggest that the action in the dependent clause is outside of the speaker's experience.

Queremos que **te cuides** mejor. — *We want you to take better care of yourself.*
Dudas que yo **haga** ejercicio todos los días. — *You doubt that I exercise every day.*
Es una lástima que la madre de Jorge **esté** enferma. — *It's a shame Jorge's mother is sick.*
Ojalá (que) **se mejore**. — *I hope that she gets better.*
Tal vez el médico me **dé** antibióticos. — *Perhaps the doctor will give me antibiotics.*

Es importante que estudies para ser médico.

¿Comprendes? Complete the sentences with the correct form of the appropriate verb: **necesitar**, **ser**, **tener**.

Doctora: Creo que usted (1) _____ una infección del oído, pero dudo que (2) _____ grave. Tal vez (3) _____ una inyección.

Respuestas: 1. tiene; 2. sea; 3. necesite

Aplicación

10-26 Leryn Franco, supermujer. La paraguaya, Leryn Franco, tiene fama no solo por ser supermodelo y presentadora de televisión, sino también por representar a Paraguay como lanzadora de jabalina en los Juegos Olímpicos.

Paso 1 Lee la entrevista entre un periodista y el entrenador de Leryn Franco y selecciona el verbo más lógico para cada opción.

PERIODISTA: Buenas tardes, Sr. Villalba. Lamento que Leryn no (1) pueda/niegue participar en esta entrevista. Ojalá que (2) se vista/se encuentre bien.

ENTRENADOR: ¡Claro que sí! En este momento está en el estudio de televisión. No creo que (3) se tuerza/termine a tiempo para estar con nosotros. Pero tal vez usted (4) sienta/quiera hacerme a mí algunas preguntas sobre su carrera.

PERIODISTA: ¡Ah, sí! ¡Es cierto que ella (5) es/debe presentadora de televisión también! Quizás usted (6) pueda/trabaja hablarme un poco sobre cómo se mantiene en forma como atleta, supermodelo y también presentadora.

ENTRENADOR: Pues, es verdad que ella (7) pierde/tiene un régimen muy estricto para mantenerse en forma. Es importante que (8) encuentre/vaya todos los días al gimnasio y también que corra tres veces a la semana. Ella es muy dedicada, y dudo que (9) busque/pierda una sola sesión de entrenamiento.

PERIODISTA: ¿También sigue una dieta especial?

ENTRENADOR: Sí, es crucial que (10) espere/coma mucha proteína, verduras y frutas. Casi no come carbohidratos sencillos.

PERIODISTA: Ahora entiendo. Gracias por su atención, y espero que la señorita Franco (11) continúe/se enferme teniendo mucho éxito (*success*) como modelo, presentadora y atleta.

Paso 2 Vuelve a leer la entrevista sobre Leryn Franco y contesta las preguntas.

1. ¿Quién es Leryn Franco? ¿Cuál es su nacionalidad?

2. ¿Por qué no va a llegar para la entrevista?

3. ¿Qué hace para mantenerse en forma?

4. ¿Cómo es la dieta que sigue?

5. ¿Cuál es tu opinión de su régimen de ejercicio y dieta? Usa algunas de estas frases: (No) Creo que... Niego que... Dudo que... Espero que...

10-27 En el Spa-Hotel Hacienda La Fortuna. Aquí tienes un anuncio para un spa en Bolivia. Contesta las siguientes preguntas, usando una expresión diferente de duda, negación o emoción para cada una.

Bienvenidos a la Hacienda La Fortuna
Spa-Hotel, Lago Titicaca, Bolivia

La Hacienda La Fortuna le ofrece un servicio único y personal. Nuestro spa-hotel tiene todo lo que pueda desear en un solo lugar con un ambiente de total relajamiento. Contamos con[1] 23 habitaciones de lujo con vistas espectaculares, así como jacuzzi y piscina con agua de manantiales[2] termales.

PLANES
Adelgazamiento
• sauna, masajes, baños termales, yoga, caminatas • consulta médica • lodo[3] medicinal
• dieta de baja grasa • entrenador personal

Antiestrés
• masajes • baño con esencias botánicas • manicura, pedicura

Tratamiento para enfermedades crónicas
• acupuntura • reflexología • baño con barro[4] • dieta de alta proteína y bajos carbohidratos
• control de peso

Contamos con el ambiente perfecto para que sus vacaciones sean inolvidables y muy saludables. Nuestros paquetes le ofrecen planes de adelgazamiento, antiestrés, tratamiento para las enfermedades crónicas, clases de cocina y todo tipo de actividades para que usted pueda olvidarse del estrés.
La variedad de servicios le deja crear su propia experiencia...

Consulte nuestra página web para ver tarifas y fechas.

[1]*We have*

[2]*springs*

[3]*mud*

[4]*earth*

MODELO: ¿Vas a bañarte en las aguas termales?
Tal vez me bañe. (No creo que... Estoy seguro/a de que...)

1. ¿Vas por más de una semana?

2. ¿Vas a seguir los consejos del entrenador?

3. ¿Vas a hacer alguna excursión?

4. ¿Tienes una cita para hacerte la pedicura?

5. ¿Vas a caminar o hacer otro ejercicio?

6. ¿Vas a divertirte mucho?

10-28A **¡Necesito información!** El Spa-Hotel tiene un centro naturista donde los clientes pueden recibir consejos de un/a naturista y comprar todo tipo de productos naturales. Hagan los papeles de naturista (estudiante A) y cliente/a (estudiante B) en la tienda. Sigan la guía para la conversación. **Cliente/a:** por favor, ve al **Apéndice 1**, página A-13.

> MODELO: NATURISTA: *Buenos días, (señor/señora/señorita). ¿En que puedo servirle?*
> CLIENTE/A: *Buenos días. Necesito algo para...*

Estudiante A: Naturista

1. Saluda al/a la cliente/a y pregúntale cómo lo/la puedes ayudar.

3. Pregúntale cuáles son sus síntomas.

5. Dile que tienes el remedio perfecto para él/ella. Es (una botella de_____, un té de _____, una dieta especial, hacerle acupuntura, un régimen de ejercicios...).

7. Explícale que depende del/de la (peso, edad, estado físico, estado de ánimo...) de la persona.

9. Contéstale que (es posible que..., es dudoso que..., es importante que...).

10-29 **Un infocomercial.** Ustedes escriben anuncios publicitarios para la industria farmacéutica o la naturista. Trabajen en parejas para escribir y presentar un infocomercial para vender un medicamento o un tratamiento nuevo para combatir alguna enfermedad o condición física. Usen expresiones del **Vocabulario** y también las que usan el subjuntivo, el indicativo o el infinitivo, según el contexto.

> MODELO: *¿Padece usted de...? ¿Busca un remedio natural, económico y sin riesgo?*
> *Le recomendamos que hable con su médico sobre los beneficios de...*
> *Mire Ud. los testimonios de personas que toman este medicamento...*
> *Tenga en cuenta (Keep in mind) que hay algunos riesgos, por ejemplo...*

¡Conversemos!

Primero, pregúntate si puedes llevar a cabo las siguientes funciones comunicativas en español. Después, júntate con dos o tres compañeros/as de clase para presentar las situaciones. Hagan y respondan a por lo menos cuatro preguntas en cada situación.

✓ CAN YOU ...	WITH YOUR CLASSMATE(S) ...
☐ talk about how to stay healthy and fit?	**Situación: En un gimnasio.** Hagan los papeles de entrenador/a personal y cliente/a. Háganse preguntas y dense consejos para mantenerse en forma. **Para empezar:** CLIENTE/A: *¿Qué hago para sentirme mejor?* ENTRENADOR/A: *Es muy importante que usted siga una dieta equilibrada. Por ejemplo...*
☐ express beliefs and doubts about future situations?	**Situación: En un restaurante.** Ustedes están leyendo el menú en un restaurante de comida rápida y opinan sobre la comida y sus ingredientes. Usen expresiones como **Dudo que...**, **No pienso que...**, **Creo que...**, **Es increíble que...** y otras para expresar sus opiniones y creencias. **Para empezar:** *Aquí todo es comida chatarra... Es increíble que... Dudo que...*

Club cultura

10.6 **Plan for the viewing/listening task**

La medicina tradicional y la medicina moderna en Bolivia

Estrategia para ver

Plan for the viewing/listening task. Before viewing/listening, plan by thinking about the strategies you will use. What do you already know about the topic? Will you listen for the main idea or for specific details? Will you try to summarize the content to check your comprehension?

ANTES DE VER EL VIDEO

10-30 **Anticipar el contenido.** En este video vas a ver y oír sobre algunas prácticas de medicina tradicional, por ejemplo, el uso de hierbas medicinales y talismanes.

Paso 1   Revisa rápidamente las actividades 10-31 y 10-32 para decidir qué estrategias vas a usar para la comprensión del video: ¿enfocarte en la idea principal o en los detalles secundarios?, ¿identificar el propósito?, etc.

Paso 2   Anota los usos de la medicina tradicional que ya conozcas, y al ver el video, trata de identificar los que usan en Bolivia.

AL VER EL VIDEO

10-31 **En el video...** Indica con **Sí** o **No** si escuchas/ves o no esta información en el video. Después, describe las estrategias que usaste para entenderlo. ¿Usaste más de una? ¿Usaste una más que las otras?

1. _____ En Bolivia, se practica la medicina tradicional en los hospitales modernos.
2. _____ Hay hospitales públicos y privados en Bolivia.
3. _____ Para una gran parte de la población, las prácticas tradicionales son más importantes que las modernas.
4. _____ El feto (*fetus*) de la llama es un talismán que trae buena suerte.
5. _____ Es común masticar (*chew*) hoja de coca para aliviar el hambre, el cansancio y el mal de altura.

DESPUÉS DE VER EL VIDEO

10-32 **¿Qué dudas tienes?** Escribe tres preguntas que tengas sobre la información presentada en el video e investiga una de ellas en Internet. Escribe un párrafo sobre lo que encuentres y preséntale la información a la clase.

   MODELO: *¿Se permite exportar el mate de coca a otros países?*

10.3 Nuestro mundo

Panoramas

10.7 Identify and research some important cultural aspects of Bolivia and Paraguay

Bolivia y Paraguay: Riquezas por descubrir

No podemos ignorar las riquezas naturales, históricas, culturales y lingüísticas de Bolivia y Paraguay. Su herencia indígena y española, sus recursos minerales, la energía natural, la agricultura y sus idiomas contribuyen a las riquezas por descubrir de estos dos países.

La represa (*dam*) de Itaipú en el río Paraná entre Paraguay y Brasil es la más larga del mundo. Proporciona toda la electricidad que necesita Paraguay y el 25% de la electricidad que usa Brasil. La American Society of Civil Engineers la nombró una de las "siete maravillas del mundo moderno".

El salar de Uyuni en Bolivia es el desierto de sal más grande y más alto del mundo, y cuenta con la reserva de litio (*lithium*) más grande, con el 50–70% de la reserva mundial. El litio tiene muchos usos, pero es indispensable en las baterías recargables para los aparatos electrónicos y los automóviles eléctricos.

La quinua que se cultiva en Bolivia desde hace unos 5.000 años juega un papel importante en la dieta andina. Posee un excepcional equilibrio de proteínas, grasas y carbohidratos. Además, es rica en aminoácidos importantes para el desarrollo humano durante la infancia. Es rica en minerales como hierro, calcio, fósforo y vitaminas, mientras que es pobre en grasas.

Paraguay no solo produce carne y azúcar, sino también plantas medicinales, como la moringa. Esta planta está llena de nutrientes: proteína, calcio, beta caroteno, vitamina C, potasio y más. Según muchos especialistas de la salud, puede usarse para bajar el colesterol, la presión y el nivel de azúcar sanguíneo de los diabéticos. Por eso, algunos la llaman "el árbol de la eterna juventud".

La riqueza de la herencia indígena es evidente no solo en sus prácticas culturales, sino también en el orgullo por los idiomas indígenas. En Paraguay, el español y el guaraní son idiomas oficiales y enseñados en las escuelas. En Bolivia, el gobierno protege 36 lenguas indígenas, de las cuales predominan el aimara, el quechua y el guaraní.

	Bolivia	Paraguay
Población:	11 millones	7 millones
Enfermedades:	dengue, malaria, fiebre amarilla	dengue
Expectativa de vida:	69 años	77 años
Obesidad:	15,8%	15%
PIB[1] gastado en la salud:	6,3%	9,8%

[1]Producto Interno Bruto = *GDP (Gross Domestic Product)*

10-33 Identifica. Identifica la información sobre Bolivia y Paraguay, según **Panoramas**.

1. las lenguas indígenas que predominan
2. la importancia del litio
3. el país con terreno montañoso, y la dificultad que esto causa
4. la importancia de la represa de Itaipú
5. algunos productos agrícolas importantes en Bolivia
6. un producto de Paraguay que se cree muy saludable

10-34 Desafío. Identifica el lugar o los lugares según el mapa y los datos estadísticos.

1. el país que gasta más de su PIB por persona para mantener la salud
2. el país que tiene la más alta expectativa de vida
3. el país más poblado
4. el país más grande
5. sus capitales

10-35 Investigación: Bolivia y Paraguay. Selecciona un lugar, una persona o un tema (*theme*) que te interesa, como, por ejemplo, **la medicina tradicional o moderna, el cultivo de coca o de quinua, la minería, el salar de Uyuni, la represa de Itaipú, los guaraníes**, etc. Busca imágenes en Internet y escribe un resumen de tu investigación. Luego preséntaselo a la clase. Debes incluir:

- el lugar o el tema
- cómo es; por qué es importante/interesante
- los recursos naturales y los productos si hay
- una foto representativa

📍 Busca: medicina tradicional Bolivia; guaraníes Paraguay, etc.

MODELO:　*Los guaraníes son indígenas de Paraguay, de partes de Brasil y de Argentina. Tienen su propio idioma, pero muchos son bilingües en español o portugués y guaraní y tienen sus propias tradiciones culturales...*

Páginas

10.8 Identify the main characteristics in a story

"La azucena del bosque" (Mito guaraní)

Estrategia para leer

Identify the main characteristics in a story. Stories typically have a certain structure: an introduction giving the context, a complication, and a resolution, as well as characters that contribute to the development of the plot line. When you identify the basic elements of structure, plot, and characters, you can anticipate the progression and meaning of the story.

ANTES DE LEER

10-36 Características del cuento. Sigue los pasos para completar esta actividad.

Paso 1 Lee el primer párrafo del cuento e indica la opción que mejor completa cada oración.

1. La historia tiene lugar en (un bosque / una ciudad / un lago).
2. Allí hay (una civilización primitiva / plantas medicinales / solo animales).
3. Tupá es (un animal / el dios creador / un hombre).
4. I-Yara es (el dios sol / el dueño de las aguas / la primera esposa).
5. Tupá decide darles a los hombres más (inteligencia / potencia / valor) que a los animales.

Paso 2 Identifica **el contexto** y **los personajes** de la historia según lo que leíste en el primer párrafo, y adivina (*guess*) una posible **complicación**.

AL LEER

 10-37 El mito. Lee este mito guaraní para ver si puedes confirmar **el contexto, los personajes**, e identificar **la complicación** y **la resolución**.

---

[1]*There once was*

[2]*ferocious*

[3]*kneaded*

[4]*skin*

[5]*rubbed* [6]*stones* [7]*sparks*
[8]*by chance* [9]*wild pig*
[10]*had lit* [11]*threw*
[12]*flames* [13]*emitted*

[14]*hunt*

"La azucena del bosque" (Mito guaraní)

Había una vez[1] una hermosa región de la tierra donde solo existían animales. Pasó por allí Tupá, el dios sol, que había creado los animales y los bosques, y decidió crear a los hombres, con suficiente inteligencia para poder gobernar hasta los animales más feroces[2]. Entonces le pidió a I-Yara, el dueño de las aguas, que trajera un poco de tierra de ese lugar. Tupá amasó[3] la tierra y le dio forma humana, creando dos hombres, uno con la piel[4] roja llamado Pitá y otro con la piel blanca llamado Morotí.

Estos hombres necesitaban compañeras y Tupá ordenó a I-Yara que, con un poco más de tierra, hiciera a dos mujeres. Y Pitá y Morotí tuvieron muchos hijos con sus mujeres y vivían felices en la selva comiendo de sus frutos.

Pero un día, Pitá frotó[5] dos piedras[6] y salieron unas chispas[7] y descubrió el fuego. Ese mismo día, por casualidad[8], Morotí tuvo que matar un jabalí[9] que lo atacaba. Al ver que Pitá había encendido[10] un hermoso fuego, arrojó[11] el animal muerto a las llamas[12]. Al poco rato, se desprendió[13] de la carne un olor delicioso y cuando probaron la carne, les pareció exquisita. Desde ese momento, abandonaron la recolección de las frutas y comenzaron a cazar[14] para comer.

Con los años fueron perfeccionando sus armas, y de esa forma inventaron el arco, la flecha[15] y la lanza. Debido a que la caza[16] era cada vez más escasa[17], empezaron a competir entre ellos y tan grande fue el rencor y el odio[18] que sintieron entre las dos familias que decidieron separarse.

Tupá decidió castigarlos[19] por necios[20]. El castigo serviría para que no olvidaran que Tupá los había puesto en el mundo para vivir en paz y para amarse los unos a los otros. Provocó entonces una terrible tormenta que duró tres días y tres noches, al cabo de los cuales[21] salió el sol, y por uno de sus rayos bajó a la Tierra I-Yara.

I-Yara llamó a todas las tribus y las reunió en un claro[22] del bosque. Allí les habló de esta forma:

—Tupá, nuestro creador me mandó— les dijo a los dos hermanos. —La furia se ha apoderado[23] de él al conocer la ingratitud de ustedes. Él los creó para que el amor y la paz guiaran sus vidas, pero la codicia[24] pudo más y se dejaron llevar por la intriga y la envidia. Ustedes son hermanos, hijos de hermanos. Tupá me envía para que hagan la paz entre ustedes.

—¡Pitá!, ¡Morotí!, ¡Abrácense, Tupá lo manda!

Arrepentidos y avergonzados[25], los hermanos se abrazaron y, allí, en presencia de todos, fueron perdiendo sus formas humanas y se fueron fundiendo[26] hasta convertirse en un solo cuerpo, que se hizo una planta de donde salían ramas[27], y de las ramas, hojas[28] y flores.

Y las flores fueron rojas al principio como la piel de Pitá, y con el tiempo, perdían su color hasta llegar a ser blancas, como la piel de Morotí. Eran Pitá y Morotí que, convertidos en flores, simbolizaban la unión y la paz entre hermanos.

Así nació la Azucena del Bosque, que Tupá dejó en la Tierra para recordarles a los hombres que deben vivir en paz.

Así nació la Azucena del Bosque...

[15]*bow, arrow* [16]*Debido... caza: Due to the fact that the game*
[17]*scarce*
[18]*hatred*

[19]*punish them* [20]*fools*

[21]*al... cuales: at the end of which*
[22]*clearing*

[23]*has taken hold*
[24]*greed*

[25]*ashamed*
[26]*melting*
[27]*branches*
[28]*leaves*

DESPUÉS DE LEER

10-38 ¿En qué orden? Pon las oraciones en el orden cronológico de la historia. Luego, termina la historia con la complicación y la resolución.

_____ También creó a dos mujeres y entre ellos tuvieron muchos hijos.

_____ Así descubrieron la delicia de la carne asada.

_____ Uno de ellos era de piel roja; el otro de piel blanca.

_____ Había un hermoso lugar lleno de animales y flores.

_____ Un día, uno de los hombres descubrió el fuego y el otro mató un jabalí.

_____ El dios sol decidió crear un par de hombres para dominar la naturaleza.

A ver si ahora puedes terminar la historia...

La complicación: _____

_____

La resolución: _____

10-39 Entrevista. En grupos de cuatro personas, divídanse en dos grupos. Un grupo representa a Tupá y el otro representa a los dos hermanos. Preparen preguntas para hacerle al otro grupo, y luego háganselas y contéstenselas.

MODELO: GRUPO 1: *Tupá, ¿por qué decidió crear dos hombres en vez de uno?*
GRUPO 2: *Porque...*

10-40 Los valores. Las leyendas y los mitos transmiten los valores de una sociedad. Da ejemplos de estos valores en la historia: **la paz, el amor fraternal, la rivalidad**. Da también un ejemplo de una leyenda que conozcas que transmita uno o más de estos valores.

Taller

10.9 Create an idea web

Un artículo sobre la salud

Estrategia para escribir

Create an idea web. There are several kinds of diagrams that can help guide you in writing. An idea web is a visual tool to help you make your main and supporting ideas concrete.

10-41 Consejos. En sitios populares para la salud es común encontrar artículos que dan consejos. En este taller vas a escribir un artículo al estilo de uno de estos sitios.

ANTES DE ESCRIBIR

Completa un esquema web como este para orientarte antes de escribir.

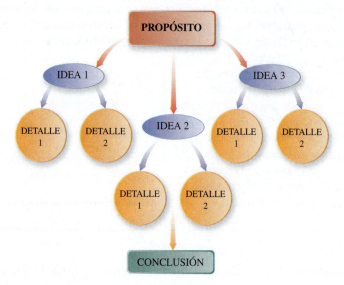

AL ESCRIBIR

Usa tu esquema web para escribir el artículo:

- Presenta el propósito o el problema.
- Apoya tu propósito en dos o tres párrafos. Incluye tus ideas, los detalles y tus consejos.
- Concluye el artículo de una manera positiva, explicándoles a los lectores cómo van a sentirse mejor si siguen tus consejos.
- Incluye alguna foto o algún dibujo que ilustre el propósito o el problema.

    MODELO: *Los tratamientos naturales: La manzanilla. La flor de manzanilla tiene muchos usos...*

DESPUÉS DE ESCRIBIR

- **Revisar.** Revisa tu artículo para verificar los siguientes puntos:
    - ☐ el vocabulario relacionado a la salud
    - ☐ los diferentes usos del subjuntivo
    - ☐ la ortografía y la concordancia
- **Intercambiar.** Intercambia tu artículo con el de un/a compañero/a para hacer correcciones y sugerencias, y para comentar sobre el contenido.
- **Entregar.** Pon tu artículo en limpio, incorporando las sugerencias de tu compañero/a. Después, entrégaselo a tu profesor/a.

En este capítulo...

))) Vocabulario

Primera parte

Las partes del cuerpo humano	Parts of the human body
la boca	mouth
el brazo	arm
la cabeza	head
el corazón	heart
el dedo (del pie)	finger (toe)
la espalda	back
el estómago	stomach
la garganta	throat
la lengua	tongue
la muela	molar
el oído	ear (inner)
la oreja	ear (outer)
el pecho	chest
el pie	foot
la pierna	leg
el pulmón	lung
la rodilla	knee
Problemas de salud	**Health problems**
doler (ue)	to hurt
lastimarse	to hurt oneself
romperse (un hueso)	to break (a bone)
ser alérgico/a a	to be allergic to
tener dolor de cabeza / fiebre (f.) / gripe (f.) / una infección / náuseas / un resfriado / tos (f.)	to have a headache / a fever / the flu / an infection / nausea / a cold / a cough
torcerse (ue)	to twist
toser	to cough
En el consultorio del médico	**At the doctor's office**
el beneficio y el riesgo	benefit and risk
el diagnóstico	diagnosis
la enfermedad	illness
el examen físico	checkup
la inyección	shot
el/la paciente	patient
la radiografía	X-ray
la receta	prescription
el síntoma	symptom
la sala de urgencias	emergency room
Sugerencias y remedios médicos	**Medical advice and remedies**
dejar de (fumar / tomar bebidas alcohólicas)	to quit (smoking / drinking alcoholic beverages)
guardar cama	to stay in bed due to sickness
hacer una cita	to make an appointment
mejorarse	to get better, to get well
respirar (profundamente)	to breathe (deeply)

Sugerencias y remedios médicos	Medical advice and remedies
seguir (i, i) los consejos del médico	to follow the doctor's advice
tomar la presión / la temperatura	to take blood pressure / temperature
Tratamientos	**Treatments**
la acupuntura	acupuncture
el antiácido	antacid
el antibiótico	antibiotic
la aspirina	aspirin
el calmante	tranquilizer, painkiller
el jarabe	cough syrup
el medicamento herbal	herbal medicine
la pastilla	pill, lozenge

Segunda parte

Sigan una dieta rica en...	Follow a diet rich in . . .
los antioxidantes	antioxidants
los carbohidratos complejos	complex carbohydrates
la fibra	fiber
las grasas (monoinsaturadas)	(monounsaturated) fats
los minerales y las vitaminas	minerals and vitamins
las proteínas	proteins
En moderación, coman/beban...	**In moderation, eat/drink . . .**
los carbohidratos sencillos	simple carbohydrates
el colesterol	cholesterol
Eviten...	**Avoid . . .**
el azúcar (los dulces)	sugar (sweets)
la comida chatarra	junk food
las grasas saturadas (trans)	saturated (trans) fats
Algunas condiciones	**Some conditions**
la depresión	depression
el estrés	stress
el (sobre)peso	(excess) weight
Tu peso y tu salud	**Your weight and your health**
adelgazar	to lose weight
bajar/subir de peso	to lose/gain weight
cuidar(se)	to take care (of oneself)
engordar	to gain weight
estar a (seguir una) dieta (equilibrada)	to be on (to follow) a (balanced) diet
guardar la línea	to stay trim, to watch one's figure
hacer ejercicios aeróbicos	to do aerobics
mantenerse en forma	to stay in shape
padecer (zc) de (diabetes/cáncer)	to suffer (from) (diabetes/cancer)
ponerse en forma	to get in shape

Verbs and expressions of emotion   *See page 327.*
Verbs and expressions of doubt and denial   *See page 337.*

Capítulo 11
¿Para qué profesión te preparas?

«El trabajo no deshonra; dignifica».

Sin título, **Florencio Molina Campos.** The drawing depicts the lonely life of a **gaucho** herding sheep, perhaps going months without seeing another human being on the Argentine Pampas.

Fuente: Christie's Images Ltd.

Learning Objectives

11.1 Discuss professions and job qualifications

11.2 Give and follow instructions from a friend, and communicate future plans

11.3 Learn about job hunting in a hard economy and an award-winning Uruguayan musician

11.4 Discuss job hunting, and interview for a position

In this Chapter

ENFOQUE CULTURAL: ARGENTINA Y URUGUAY
Club cultura: Introducción a Argentina

Indica con **C (Cierto)** o **F (Falso)** si escuchas/ves o no esta información en el video.

1. _____ la población
2. _____ el nombre de la capital
3. _____ la producción de carne
4. _____ los glaciares y la Pampa
5. _____ el Cerro Aconcagua, la montaña más alta del continente
6. _____ las cataratas del Iguazú

11.1 Primera parte

Vocabulario

11.1 **Discuss professions and job qualifications**

El mundo del trabajo

Dra. Messi

Sr. Fernández

Oficina de Empleo

Angélica   Sergio

En la Oficina de Empleo. Muchas personas esperan su turno.

SR. FERNÁNDEZ: Dale tu **currículum vitae** al **ayudante administrativo**. Creo que hay muchas oportunidades con buenos **beneficios** para personas con tu **formación**.

DRA. MESSI: Ya se lo di. Ojalá que **consiga** un buen **puesto** como **supervisora** clínica.

SERGIO: Hace un mes que **estoy sin trabajo**. Tengo muy buenas **cualificaciones** y espero **conseguir** trabajo **a tiempo completo** en **una empresa** que me pague bien y no **el sueldo mínimo**.

ANGÉLICA: Nunca aceptes el sueldo mínimo sin antes negociar el contrato.

¿Comprendes? Select the correct person for each description: **el Sr. Fernández**, **la Dra. Messi**, **Angélica**, or **Sergio**.

1. _____ En este momento está sin trabajo.

2. _____ Le dio su currículum vitae al recepcionista.

3. _____ Aconseja que no acepte el sueldo mínimo.

Respuestas: 1. Sergio; 2. la Dra. Messi; 3. Angélica

))) Vocabulario

Los oficios y las profesiones	Occupations and professions
el/la abogado/a	*lawyer*
el/la analista (financiero/a, de sistemas)	*(financial/systems) analyst*
el/la arquitecto/a	*architect*
el/la ayudante (administrativo/a, clínico/a)	*(administrative/clinical) assistant*
el/la carpintero/a	*carpenter*
el/la científico/a	*scientist*
el/la cocinero/a	*cook, chef*
el/la contador/a	*accountant*
el/la dentista	*dentist*
el/la emprendedor/a	*entrepreneur*
el/la enfermero/a	*nurse*
el hombre / la mujer de negocios	*businessman/woman*
el/la ingeniero/a (eléctrico/a, civil, mecánico/a)	*(electrical/civil/mechanical) engineer*
el/la intérprete	*interpreter*
el/la mecánico/a	*mechanic*
el/la obrero/a de construcción	*construction worker*
el/la organizador/a de eventos	*events organizer*
el/la peluquero/a	*hairdresser*
el/la periodista	*journalist*
el/la plomero/a	*plumber*
el/la profesional de la salud	*healthcare worker*
el/la psicólogo/a	*psychologist*
el/la veterinario/a	*veterinarian*

Cargos	Positions
el/la director/a	*director*
el/la empleado/a	*employee*
el/la jefe/a (ejecutivo/a)	*boss (CEO)*
el/la supervisor/a	*supervisor*

Términos y expresiones de trabajo	Work-related terms and expressions
los beneficios	*benefits*
las cualificaciones	*qualifications*
el currículum vitae	*curriculum vitae (vita)*
el (des)empleo	*(un)employment*
la empresa	*company, firm*
el entrenamiento	*training*
la formación	*education*
la meta	*goal*
el puesto	*position (job)*
el sueldo (mínimo)	*(minimum) wage*
la (des)ventaja	*(dis)advantage*

¡Manos a la obra!	Let's get to work!
conseguir[1] (i, i)	*to get, to obtain*
diseñar	*to design*
estar sin trabajo	*to be out of work*
reparar	*to repair*
repartir	*to deliver, to distribute*
trabajar a tiempo completo/ parcial	*to work full-time / part-time*

Variaciones

- You will hear **el/la contador/a** in Latin America, but usually **el/la contable** in Spain. Likewise, **el/la plomero/a** is used in the Americas and **el/la fontanero/a** in Spain.
- **El/La jefe/a** may also be **director/a**, **presidente/a**, or **el/la principal oficial**; common in Puerto Rico.
- You will also hear **estar en paro** in Spain or **estar desempleado/a**.

---

[1]conjugated like **seguir**: *consigo, consigues, consigue, conseguimos, conseguís, consiguen...*

Presencia hispana

According to the Stanford Latino Entrepreneurship Initiative, there are 1,432,746 Latino-owned businesses in the U.S., and this number is growing at three times the rate of the national average. Although the trend is for these to be small businesses, they serve a diverse clientele, not just Latino customers. In addition, they are predominantly family-owned, with a clear preference to keep the business within the family. How many Latino-owned businesses are in your community?

Aplicación

11-1 ¿A quién llamas? ¿A qué profesionales llamas en estas situaciones? Selecciona la opción que mejor corresponde a cada descripción. Después, explica tu selección.

MODELO: Tienes el pelo muy largo y necesitas un corte nuevo.
Llamo a mi peluquera. Siempre voy a PeloBello donde me atienden puntualmente.

1. __F__ No hay agua en el baño.
2. __g__ Necesitas resolver algunos problemas personales.
3. __h__ Tu perro está enfermo.
4. __C__ Quieres reparar unas sillas de tu comedor.
5. __D__ Necesitas ayuda para hacer los impuestos (*taxes*).
6. __B__ Quieres un diseño original para tu casa nueva.
7. __a__ Necesitas una persona experta en cuestiones legales.
8. __e__ Necesitas reparar tu carro.

a. abogado/a
b. arquitecto/a
c. carpintero/a
d. contador/a
e. mecánico/a
f. plomero/a
g. psicólogo/a
h. veterinario/a

11-2 Busco trabajo. Manuel está en la oficina de empleo donde tiene una cita con una consejera. Selecciona la expresión que mejor completa el diálogo.

a tiempo completo	conseguir	una empresa	formación	sin trabajo
analista	cualificaciones	entrenamiento	un puesto	supervisora

SRA. SOSA: Buenas tardes, siéntese, por favor.

MANUEL: Gracias. Soy Manuel Vázquez y busco (1) __un puesto__ en (2) __una empresa__ internacional. Prefiero trabajar de 40 a 50 horas por semana, es decir, (3) __a tiempo completo__. Hace seis meses que estoy (4) __sin trabajo__ y necesito (5) __conseguir__ un buen trabajo para mantener a mi familia.

SRA. SOSA: Entiendo su situación. Hábleme de su (6) __entrenamiento__ académica y su (7) __formación__ práctico.

MANUEL: Soy (8) __analista__ de sistemas. Tengo muy buenas (9) __cualificaciones__: un título universitario en ingeniería y tres años trabajando en una empresa de ciberseguridad. Aquí tiene el número de teléfono de la (10) __supervisora__, la Dra. González. Ella me dio una carta de recomendación.

11-3 Las profesiones y los oficios. Escucha a las siguientes personas y selecciona la profesión u oficio que le interesa a cada una.

MODELO: Soy bilingüe. Tengo experiencia ayudando al jefe administrativo de una empresa grande. Manejo su calendario y le hago las citas.
ayudante administrativo/a

a. profesional de la salud	c. cocinero/a	e. dentista	g. peluquero/a
b. arquitecto/a	d. científico/a	f. mecánico/a	h. periodista

1. __F__ 3. __h__ 5. __g__ 7. __e__
2. __B__ 4. __c__ 6. __a__ 8. __d__

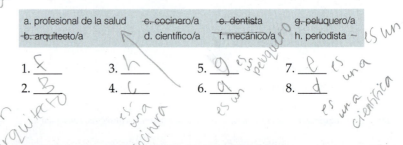

11-4 ¿En qué orden? Sigue los pasos para completar esta actividad.

Paso 1 Pon los siguientes aspectos de un trabajo en orden de importancia para ti personalmente. (**1:** más importante – **7:** menos importante)

_____ la oportunidad de aprender más _____ un buen horario de trabajo

_____ un sueldo o un salario adecuado _____ buenos beneficios

_____ un/a jefe/a paciente _____ un trabajo a comisión

  _____ ¿otro?

Paso 2 En parejas, comparen sus listas. Cuando no estén de acuerdo, explíquense sus puntos de vista.

MODELO: ESTUDIANTE 1: *Quiero un trabajo interesante porque no quiero estar aburrido/a.*

ESTUDIANTE 2: *Bueno, para mí el horario de trabajo es lo más importante. Prefiero no tener que levantarme demasiado temprano. Después, para mí es...*

11-5 Avisos clasificados en Internet. En BolsaTrabajo, un sitio web uruguayo, la gente pone y responde a avisos (*ads*) clasificados.

Paso 1 Lee los avisos y contesta las preguntas a continuación.

LA TIENDA DE COCINAS Y BAÑOS

necesita

VENDEDORES

–ambos sexos–

SE REQUIERE:
- Experiencia en venta de servicios.
- Capacidad de trabajo y ganas de superación.

SE OFRECE:
- Integración en la primera empresa del sector.
- Incorporación inmediata.
- Ingresos superiores a 13.000 pesos argentinos, entre sueldo fijo y comisiones.

Para entrevista personal, llamar al teléfono **4978 0875.**

CASALINDA

EMPRESA DE ÁMBITO NACIONAL QUE FABRICA CASAS MODULARES PRECISA PARA SU DELEGACIÓN EN MONTEVIDEO

ARQUITECTO TÉCNICO

- Con experiencia mínima de un año para incorporarse a empresa líder en el sector.

- Responsabilidades: realizar proyectos de producto, nuevos diseños de casas y promoción de productos.

- Cualidades necesarias: iniciativa, facilidad de trabajo con la gente, facilidad para convencer, capacidad de trabajo y espíritu competitivo.

- Salario mínimo inicial 52.000 pesos uruguayos al mes.

- Gastos de kilometraje y comida.

Interesados enviar C.V., con carta de presentación escrita a mano y fotografía reciente, al apartado de Correos 20-037, Montevideo.

Pilotos de ambos sexos para nueva aerolínea uruguaya con sede en Montevideo. Se requiere un mínimo de seis años de experiencia con aviones en rutas regionales. Salario y beneficios. Llamar Oficina de Personal de AeroUR al 8989 3411.

---

1. ¿Cuál(es) de estos avisos tiene(n) puestos para hombres y mujeres?
2. ¿Qué empresa busca gente entrenada en aviación?
3. ¿Cuál(es) paga(n) salario y comisión?
4. ¿Cuál(es) paga(n) los gastos de viaje?
5. ¿Cuál de los puestos te atrae más y por qué?

Paso 2 Eres jefe/a de personal. Escribe un aviso clasificado para este sitio web para anunciar un puesto en tu empresa.

Paso 3 En parejas, túrnense para llamar a sus empresas con vacantes y hacerse más preguntas sobre la posición.

MODELO: ESTUDIANTE 1: *Buenas tardes. AeroEur. ¿A quién le dirijo su llamada?*

ESTUDIANTE 2: *Al jefe de personal, por favor...*

Estructuras

11.2 Give and follow instructions from a friend, and discuss future plans

Tú commands

¿Recuerdas? In **Capítulo 10** you used *formal* commands, which use the forms of the subjunctive. Complete this sentence with the logical commands of **ir**, **pedir**.

(1) _____ usted a la oficina de empleo y (2) _____ una cita con la señora Ramírez.

Respuestas: 1. Vaya; 2. pida

Here are the *informal* (**tú**) commands. Note how the affirmative and negative differ.

Infinitive	Affirmative	Negative	(Subjunctive)
comprar	compr**a**	**no** compr**es**	(compres)
comer	com**e**	**no** com**as**	(comas)
escribir	escrib**e**	**no** escrib**as**	(escribas)
pensar	piens**a**	**no** piens**es**	(pienses)
dormir	duerm**e**	**no** duerm**as**	(duermas)
pedir	pid**e**	**no** pid**as**	(pidas)
traer	tra**e**	**no** traig**as**	(traigas)

Toma estos formularios y rellénalos con tus datos personales. No te olvides de incluir una foto.

- Use the third-person singular of the present indicative for regular affirmative **tú** commands.

  Estudia para ser abogada.   *Study to be a lawyer.*
  Lee los avisos clasificados.   *Read the classified ads.*

- Use the subjunctive for negative **tú** commands.

  No trabajes a comisión.   *Don't work on commission.*
  No estés sin trabajo.   *Don't be out of work.*

- Irregularities in the subjunctive will also appear in the negative **tú** command.

  No empieces a trabajar.   *Don't start working.*
  No vayas a la oficina hoy.   *Don't go to the office today.*

MANDATOS AFIRMATIVOS IRREGULARES DE LA FORMA *TÚ*

- A few common verbs have irregular **affirmative** command forms:

decir	**di**	**Di** por qué.	*Tell (Say) why.*
hacer	**haz**	**Haz** el informe.	*Do the report.*
ir	**ve**	**Ve** a la oficina de empleo.	*Go to the employment office.*
poner	**pon**	**Pon** tu solicitud aquí.	*Put your application here.*
salir	**sal**	**Sal** a tiempo.	*Leave on time.*
ser	**sé**	**Sé** amable con la jefa.	*Be nice to the boss.*
tener	**ten**	**Ten** paciencia.	*Be patient.*
venir	**ven**	**Ven** a mi oficina ahora.	*Come to my office now.*

Ten paciencia y vas a ver muchos pájaros exóticos.

- Attach pronouns to the affirmative command. If the command has more than one syllable, remember to place an accent on the next-to-last syllable of the verb, in order to maintain its original stress. For negative commands, place pronouns between **no** and the conjugated verb.

  Tenlo para esta tarde.   *Have it by this afternoon.*
  Háblale mañana.   *Talk to her tomorrow.*
  Por favor, ¡**no te vayas**!   *Please, don't leave!*

¿Comprendes? Complete the sentence with the commands of **poner**, **ser**.

(1) _____ respetuoso; no (2) _____ los pies en el escritorio.

Respuestas: 1. Sé; 2. pongas

Aplicación

11-6 El Café Tortoni. Selecciona el mandato más lógico para completar la conversación entre dos turistas que visitan este famoso café de Buenos Aires.

GLORIA: (1) Mira/Trae, Enrique, en la pared hay muchas fotos de personas famosas que frecuentaban el café. (2) Pon/Ve a ver quiénes son.

ENRIQUE: (3) Búscalas/Acompáñame, Gloria. Hay muchísimas fotos interesantes. (4) Léeme/Hazme los nombres bajo esta.

GLORIA: (5) Oye/Sé, Enrique. Aquí hay una del famoso tanguista, Carlos Gardel. ¡Qué guapo!

ENRIQUE: Está bien, Gloria. Pero (6) acuéstate/siéntate ahora. Aquí viene el mesero. Mozo, (7) tráenos/escríbenos el menú, por favor.

MESERO: Enseguida, señor.

GLORIA: (8) Dime/Pídeme un cafecito y una medialuna, Enrique. Voy a volver a ver las fotos en la pared.

ENRIQUE: Está bien, pero no (9) tardes/comas mucho. ¡Tengo hambre!

Fundado en 1858, este café es famoso por ser un sitio de reunión de escritores, músicos y otros artistas argentinos durante más de 150 años. Lo puedes visitar hoy para tomar un café y apreciar su entorno histórico.

11-7 En una empresa multinacional. Una jefa ejecutiva le da muchas órdenes a su personal. Decide y luego explica cuáles son lógicas y cuáles ilógicas.

MODELO: María, tráeme los periódicos de hoy.
Lógica.
María, prepárame una empanada.
Ilógica, porque no se cocina en una oficina.

1. Tomás, no trabajes más de cinco horas diarias.

2. Clarisa, escribe este informe en latín.

3. Ramón, ve a la piscina y nada por tres horas.

4. Josefina, búscame el informe del departamento de finanzas.

5. Julia, descansa. No hagas tu trabajo.

6. Conchita, sé amable con los visitantes.

7. Eduardo, pon las sillas alrededor de la mesa para la reunión.

11-8A ¡Necesito información! Ustedes son el/la ayudante administrativo/a (estudiante A) y el/la organizador/a de eventos (estudiante B) en una empresa donde hoy va a haber una reunión importante, y tienen que resolver situaciones urgentes. Respondan de una manera apropiada a las urgencias que se presentan. **Organizador/a de eventos**: por favor, ve al **Apéndice 1**, página A-14.

> MODELO: AYUDANTE ADMINISTRATIVO/A: *La reunión es ahora, pero no hay café.*
> ORGANIZADOR/A DE EVENTOS: ¡(Llamar) al restaurante ahora mismo!
> *¡Llama al restaurante ahora mismo!*

Estudiante A: Ayudante administrativo/a

Situaciones urgentes	Posibles soluciones para el/la organizador/a de eventos
1. Hay un carpintero que necesita arreglar la mesa en el salón de reuniones.	• ¡(Dársela) enseguida!
2. La fotocopiadora no tiene papel.	• ¡(Llamar) a la agencia de intérpretes!
3. La supervisora insiste en que yo repare su computadora portátil.	• ¡(Pedir) la opinión de otro contador!
4. Uno de lo invitados se siente mal.	• ¡(No tocar) nada eléctrico! ¡(Llamar) al plomero ahora mismo!
5. Un periodista pide información confidencial.	• ¡(Explicarle) que es imposible irse de vacaciones ahora!

11-9 Consejos en el trabajo. En parejas, túrnense para leer los problemas y darse consejos sobre el trabajo.

> MODELO: ESTUDIANTE 1: *El jefe quiere que yo lo haga todo inmediatamente.*
> ESTUDIANTE 2: *¡Hazlo! No quieres perder tu puesto.*
> ESTUDIANTE 1: *Tienes razón. ¡Buen consejo! / Me parece razonable porque...*

Problemas:

1. Gano muy poco por todo lo que tengo que hacer.
2. Necesito encontrar otro trabajo para pagar mis estudios.
3. Quiero estudiar para ser veterinario/a, pero soy alérgico/a a ciertos animales.
4. La computadora de mi oficina es muy vieja y necesito una nueva.
5. Temo que la empresa vaya a eliminar mi puesto.
6. Tengo buenas cualificaciones, pero no hay muchas oportunidades de trabajo ahora.

Verbos para expresar consejos:

buscar	decir	ir	poner
comprar	estudiar	pedir	salir
consultar	hacer	pensar	trabajar

The subjunctive and the indicative with adverbial conjunctions

¿Recuerdas? You've used prepositional phrases, such as **antes de** and **después de**, to indicate when something takes place. Complete this sentence with the logical preposition (**antes de**, **después de**).

Me levanto (1) _____ ducharme, y me acuesto (2) _____ cepillarme los dientes.

Respuestas: 1. antes de; 2. después de

A conjunction introduces a dependent clause with a conjugated verb, rather than an infinitive. antes de → antes de **que**

> Me levanto **antes de que suene**   *I'll get up before the alarm clock rings.*
> el despertador.

CONJUNCIONES QUE SIEMPRE REQUIEREN EL SUBJUNTIVO

Some conjunctions always take the subjunctive because they express purpose, intent, condition, anticipation, or uncertainty.

independent clause	conjunction always takes subjunctive	dependent clause in subjunctive
Voy a la oficina de empleo *I'm going to the employment office*	**antes de que** *before*	**se cierre.** *it closes.*

a fin de que	*in order that*	**en caso de que**	*in case*
a menos que	*unless*	**para que**	*in order that, so that*
antes de que	*before*	**sin que**	*without*
con tal de que	*provided (that)*		

> Reparte los informes   *Distribute the reports so that everyone*
> **para que** todos los **lean**.   *reads them.*

CONJUNCIONES QUE USAN EL SUBJUNTIVO O EL INDICATIVO

Some other conjunctions take the subjunctive when the action in the dependent clause has not yet taken place. In these cases, the verb in the main clause is in any tense that suggests the future (for example, **ir a...**, **pensar/poder/querer** + *inf.*, command form, present tense with future meaning, future tense, etc.).

future action	conjunction	dependent clause in subjunctive
Voy a solicitar el puesto *I'm going to apply for the job*	**en cuanto** *as soon as*	**reciba la solicitud.** *I receive the application.*

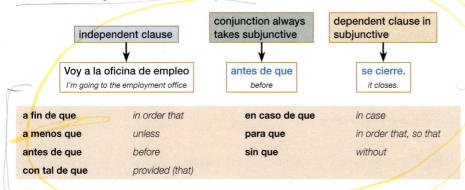

cuando	*when*	**hasta que**	*until*
después de que	*after*	**luego que**	*as soon as*
donde	*where*	**mientras que**	*as long as, while*
en cuanto	*as soon as*	**tan pronto como**	*as soon as*

> José, pon los informes **donde**   *José, put the reports where the manager*
> el gerente te **indique**.   *indicates.*

Vamos a entrevistarlos hasta que encontremos al mejor candidato.

- But, if the action in the dependent clause is *habitual* or *has already taken place*, use the *indicative* with these conjunctions.

independent clause	conjunction	dependent clause in indicative
Siempre solicito un puesto *I always apply for a job*	**en cuanto** *as soon as*	**recibo la solicitud.** *I receive the application.* (habitual)

Ana preguntó por el sueldo **cuando tuvo** una entrevista.	*Ana asked about the salary when she had the interview.* (has already taken place)

- Always use the infinitive after these prepositions when there is no change of subject: **a fin de, con tal de, antes de, después de, en caso de, para,** and **sin.**

Van a comprar un teléfono celular **después de hablar** con el dependiente.	*They are going to buy a cell phone after talking with the clerk.*
No puedes preparar un contrato **sin usar** una computadora.	*You can't prepare a contract without using a computer.*

¿Comprendes? Complete each sentence with the correct form (indicative, subjunctive, infinitive) of **hacer** or **terminar.**

Tu jefa va a estar contenta con tal de que (1) _____ bien tu trabajo. No salgas para tu casa antes de (2) _____ lo necesario.

Respuestas: 1. hagas; 2. terminar

Aplicación

11-10 Soy gaucha. El gaucho es una figura popular que se asocia con las pampas argentinas y uruguayas.

Paso 1 Lee la descripción de la vida diaria de Juana María e indica todas las conjunciones adverbiales y su verbo.

> **MODELO:** Hoy voy a trabajar <u>hasta que se ponga</u> el sol.

[1]*gourd*

[2]*I mash* [3]*leaves*

[4]*hay*

[5]*sheep*

Hoy en día no todos los gauchos son hombres.

Soy Juana María Soldado y soy "gaucha" de profesión. Todos los días, antes de que salga el sol, me levanto, me visto y preparo mi yerba mate. Siempre pongo a calentar agua, y tan pronto como está caliente, la echo a una calabaza[1] que ya tiene yerba mate. Machaco[2] las hojas[3] para que se mezclen bien con el agua caliente. Es una bebida sabrosa y saludable. (Y además, ¡tiene la cafeína que necesito cuando me levanto tan temprano!) Después de tomar el mate, le doy agua y heno[4] a Diablo, mi caballo. En la estancia (el rancho) donde trabajo, tenemos cinco mil ovejas[5] y hoy es el día para llevarlas al mercado. Le pongo la silla a mi caballo y la ajusto para que esté segura. Lo monto y me dirijo hacia las pampas donde encuentro las ovejas. A menos que sea un día extraordinario, es imposible atraparlas a todas, pero Diablo y yo lo intentamos. Al final del día, mis compañeros y yo preparamos una parrillada (una barbacoa) y nos acostamos temprano a fin de poder levantarnos bien temprano al día siguiente y continuar con nuestro trabajo.

Paso 2   Contesta las preguntas basándote en la lectura sobre Juana María.

1. ¿Cuándo se levanta Juana María?
2. ¿Cuándo va a preparar su mate mañana?
3. ¿Por qué le gusta tomar yerba mate?
4. ¿Qué hace después de tomarla?
5. ¿Por qué es imposible atrapar todas las ovejas?
6. ¿Por qué se acuestan temprano los gauchos?

11-11   Dos empresas rivales.   El director de una empresa que fabrica artículos de plástico espera piratear a algunos ingenieros de una empresa rival, Mundiplásticos. Selecciona la conjunción más lógica para completar lo que dice el director.

Hoy es 17 de mayo, y mi plan es piratear a cinco ingenieros de la empresa Mundiplásticos, (1) para que / tan pronto como pueda. Estudié todos los documentos (2) para / sin entender bien su organización. Quiero hablar con todos los empleados (3) en cuanto / a menos que me lo impidan. Quiero invitarlos a mi fábrica (4) a fin de que / cuando vean las máquinas modernas que tenemos aquí. ¡Estoy decidido! Voy a aumentar el número de empleados de mi empresa (5) antes de que / mientras que sea demasiado tarde. El jefe de Mundiplásticos va a estar muy sorprendido (6) cuando / sin que sus ingenieros renuncien a su posición.

11-12   En la oficina de empleo.   Aquí tienes algunos consejos de la directora de empleos. Escribe la forma correcta del verbo entre paréntesis. Ten cuidado de usar el indicativo (presente o pasado), el subjuntivo o el infinitivo, según el contexto.

1. Le voy a enseñar los avisos clasificados para que (Ud.: ver) _____ los nuevos empleos que publicamos hoy.
2. Ayer recibimos avisos nuevos después de que (Ud.: salir) _____ de la oficina.
3. Voy a obtenerle una entrevista tan pronto como (yo: hablar) _____ con el jefe de personal.
4. Usted debe hacer copias de su currículum vitae antes de (Ud.: ir) _____ a la entrevista.
5. Vamos a ensayar (*rehearse*) su entrevista para que (Ud.: sentirse) _____ cómodo/a.
6. A menos que el taxi le (costar) _____ demasiado, usted debe usarlo para ir a la entrevista en vez del autobús.
7. Va a conocer a la supervisora cuando los empleados le (enseñar) _____ la línea de producción.
8. Ellos van a estar impresionados tan pronto como usted les (decir) _____ que tiene experiencia en este tipo de industria.

11-13   Estoy decidido/a.   Escriban individualmente cinco resoluciones que tengan para el resto de este año. Luego, en parejas, comparen sus resoluciones para ver qué tienen en común. Empiecen las cláusulas dependientes con algunas de estas conjunciones: **después de que, antes de que, cuando, a menos que, a fin de que, con tal de que, hasta que**.

MODELO: Este año voy a... después de que...
Este año voy a buscar trabajo después de que terminen mis clases.

11-14 En el trabajo. A veces es necesario dar explicaciones en el trabajo.

Paso 1 Primero, escribe un mensaje por correo electrónico para explicarle a tu jefe/a cuándo vas a terminar el trabajo para hoy. Puedes completar las oraciones a continuación en tu mensaje.

> **MODELO:** *Estimada Directora:*
>
> *Espero terminar el informe en cuanto reciba la información necesaria.*

- Le prometo que voy a terminar el informe mientras que...
- Mi colega promete ayudarme a menos que...
- Quiero reunirme con el resto del equipo para que...
- Pienso trabajar hasta que...
- Voy a estar en la oficina mañana antes de que...
- Siempre puedo terminar mi trabajo cuando...

Paso 2 Intercambia correos con un/a compañero/a de clase y contéstalo de una manera lógica, como si fueras (*as if you were*) el/la jefe/a.

> **MODELO:** *Estimado/a...*
>
> *Me alegro de que usted quiera trabajar en el proyecto hasta que...*

Me gusta caminar a la oficina en Buenos Aires cuando hace buen tiempo.

11-15 ¿Cuándo vas a...? En parejas, túrnense para entrevistarse sobre sus planes para el futuro.

> **MODELO:** ESTUDIANTE 1: *¿Cuándo vas a comprar un carro?*
>
> ESTUDIANTE 2: *Voy a comprar un carro cuando consiga un buen puesto.*

1. ¿Cuándo vas a terminar tus estudios? (tan pronto como)
2. ¿Cuándo vas a buscar trabajo? (después de que)
3. ¿Hasta cuándo vas a estudiar español? (hasta que)
4. ¿Cuándo vas a escribir tu currículum vitae? (en cuanto)
5. ¿Cuándo vas a tener tu entrevista con el jefe de la empresa? (con tal de que)
6. ¿Cuándo vas a trabajar en Argentina o Uruguay? (luego que)

Cultura en vivo

In contrast to the U.S. or Canada, applicants in some Spanish-speaking regions may be expected to include a photo with their application. What concerns might you have either as an applicant or as an employer about including a photograph in an application?

¡Conversemos!

Primero, pregúntate si puedes llevar a cabo las siguientes funciones comunicativas en español. Después, júntate con dos o tres compañeros/as de clase para presentar las situaciones. Hagan y respondan a por lo menos cuatro preguntas en cada situación.

✓ CAN YOU ...

☐ discuss professions and job qualifications?

☐ talk about the advantages of different professions?

☐ give and follow instructions from a friend?

☐ communicate future plans?

WITH YOUR CLASSMATE(S) ...

Situación: En la oficina de empleo.

En tu empresa, hay varias oportunidades de empleo. Explica los requisitos y las responsabilidades de cinco de los puestos vacantes.

Para empezar: *Tenemos cinco vacantes: ingeniero, plomero, arquitecto, mecánico y...*

Situación: Consejos.

Explícale a un nuevo estudiante cuáles son las ventajas y desventajas de estudiar para ciertas profesiones u oficios. Usa las palabras y expresiones del **Vocabulario**.

Para empezar: *Si te interesan los animales, debes estudiar para ser veterinario/a porque...*

Situación: En la universidad.

Usa mandatos de **tú** para decirle a un/a compañero/a lo que tiene que hacer para conseguir un buen trabajo.

Para empezar: *Primero, entra en Internet y busca un sitio con avisos clasificados para trabajo...*

Situación: En casa.

Explícales a tus padres (o a tu pareja) cuándo vas a terminar los estudios. Usa una variedad de conjunciones (**antes de que, para que, cuando, tan pronto como**, etc.) con el infinitivo, el subjuntivo o el indicativo según el caso.

Para empezar: *Voy a terminar mis estudios cuando... a menos que...*

Perfiles

11.3 Learn about job hunting in a hard economy and an award-winning Uruguayan musician

Mi experiencia

LOS EMPLEOS Y LAS RECOMENDACIONES

11-16 Para ti. ¿Tienes un trabajo en este momento? ¿Qué hiciste para conseguirlo? ¿Tuviste que conocer a alguien importante en la empresa para conseguir tu puesto? A la hora de conseguir trabajo, ¿qué crees que es más importante, tener buenos contactos o tener experiencia? Lee lo que dice Cristina, una joven que estudia y trabaja en Buenos Aires.

Hola, soy Cristina y estudio ciencias de comunicación social en la Universidad de Buenos Aires. Ahora estoy en mi último año y espero recibir mi título dentro de unos pocos meses. Este año tuve la oportunidad de hacer una pasantía[1] con el periódico *Clarín*, el más importante de Argentina. ¡Fue bárbaro y aprendí un montón! Espero que esta experiencia me ayude a conseguir un buen trabajo. ¡Pero es difícil en esta economía! Se dice que la tasa[2] de desempleo entre los jóvenes argentinos es de más del 20%. Por eso, a la hora de buscar empleo es crucial conocer personalmente a una persona dentro de la organización que pueda ayudarle a uno. En Argentina, como en muchas partes del mundo hispano, "a quién se conoce" muchas veces es la clave[3] para obtener un puesto. Así pues, lo que voy a hacer primero es hablar con la esposa de mi primo, que es editora de un periódico regional. Ella sabe que soy seria y que merezco[4] una posición dentro de mi campo de estudios. Y si tan solo hay un trabajo a tiempo parcial, lo voy a aceptar porque es importante "tener el pie dentro" de la organización. Luego, en el futuro, cuando consiga una posición de tiempo completo, seguramente voy a hacer algo similar por un amigo o una amiga que también necesite ayuda.

Y así están las cosas por ahora. Por eso, cuando me llegan esos momentos de poca inspiración, me gusta escuchar la música de Jorge Drexler, el cantautor uruguayo que es popularísimo desde que ganó un Óscar. Si no conocen su música, les recomiendo que escuchen "Todo se transforma". ¡Verán[5] cómo se animan!

[1]*internship*

[2]*rate*

[3]*key*

[4]*I deserve*

[5]*You'll see*

11-17 En su opinión. Conversen en grupos de tres o más sobre las ventajas y desventajas de conseguir un puesto de trabajo a través de una recomendación familiar o de un/a amigo/a y preparen una lista.

Ventajas de entrar con recomendación	Desventajas de entrar con recomendación
Puede ayudarte cuando hay mucho desempleo.	*Los otros empleados te pueden tener envidia a ti.*

Mi música

"TODO SE TRANSFORMA" (JORGE DREXLER, URUGUAY)

Jorge Drexler se apasionó por la música y la literatura de muy joven cuando estudiaba piano, guitarra clásica, composición y técnica vocal. En la universidad, ganó premios en poesía y cuento corto, y después, en música original. Su canción "Al otro lado del río", que figuró en la película *Diarios de motocicleta*, ganó el premio Óscar a la Mejor canción original.

ANTES DE VER Y ESCUCHAR

11-18 Cada acción crea una reacción. En esta canción, el cantautor propone que cada acción resulta en un efecto, que luego es una acción que tiene otro efecto, etc., y que, eventualmente, la primera acción vuelve a su principio. Es decir, todo se transforma, pero al final es lo mismo. Por ejemplo: el agua → el vapor → la lluvia → el agua. Escribe otro ejemplo basado en tu experiencia.

PARA VER Y ESCUCHAR

11-19 Todo se transforma. Busca en Internet el video y la letra de "Todo se transforma" por Jorge Drexler. Pon en orden la sequencia de la transformación, según la canción.

1. beber el vino
2. el aspa del molino (*windmill blade*)
3. el beso
4. el calor
5. el sudor (*sweat*)
6. el vapor
7. el viento
8. movimiento
9. pisar (*crush*) el vino

____ → ____ → ____ → ____ → ____ → ____ → ____ → ____ → __

📍 **Busca:** video Todo se transforma Jorge Drexler; letra Todo se transforma Jorge Drexler

DESPUÉS DE VER Y ESCUCHAR

11-20 La filosofía de Jorge Drexler. Es posible que la línea "Cada uno da lo que recibe y recibe lo que da" resuma la filosofía de Jorge Drexler. Explica cómo te imaginas que se manifiesta en su vida y en la tuya. ¿Tienen la misma filosofía?

> **MODELO:** *Creo que para Jorge Drexler cada acción tiene una reacción. Si respeta a los demás, él recibe el respeto de ellos. Para mí,...*

11-21 Jorge Drexler. Busca información sobre Jorge Drexler para saber más sobre él. Escribe un párrafo con estos detalles:

- su nombre completo
- su lugar de nacimiento
- la edad cuando empezó su carrera musical
- la razón por qué su familia vivió por algún tiempo en Bolivia
- su otra carrera

📍 **Busca:** Jorge Drexler biografía

11.2 Segunda parte

Vocabulario

11.4 Discuss job hunting, and interview for a position

La búsqueda de empleo

En la entrevista. Es importante que **el aspirante** a **una vacante** dé una buena impresión.

DRA. MENÉNDEZ: Buenas tardes, Sr. Torres. Siéntese, por favor.

SR. TORRES: Mucho gusto, Dra. Menéndez. Gracias por su interés en mi **solicitud**.

DRA. MENÉNDEZ: De nada. Pues, veo que usted tiene mucha experiencia y buenas **cartas de recomendación**. ¿Cómo **se enteró de** la vacante?

SR. TORRES: Vi la información en **los avisos clasificados** y me interesó mucho. Por eso pedí la solicitud y la **rellené** enseguida.

DRA. MENÉNDEZ: El Sr. Torres me dio una muy buena impresión. Según sus cartas, es **capaz**, **entusiasta** y **honrado**. Vamos a **contratarlo** para el puesto de analista financiero.

ALICIA: Perfecto. Voy a rellenar **los formularios** necesarios. ¿Quiere usted que le explique el plan de **beneficios**?

¿Comprendes? Select the logical word or phrase to complete the sentence: **aspirante**, **cartas de recomendación**, **solicitud**.

El (1) _____ para el puesto en la sección de finanzas presentó su (2) _____ y sus (3) _____.

Respuestas: 1. aspirante; 2. solicitud; 3. cartas de recomendación

))) Vocabulario

La búsqueda de empleo	The job search
el/la aspirante	*applicant*
los avisos clasificados	*classified ads*
la carta de presentación/ recomendación	*letter of introduction/ recommendation*
el contrato	*contract*
la entrevista	*interview*
el formulario	*form*
la solicitud de empleo	*employment application*
la vacante	*vacancy*
Los beneficios	**Benefits**
el aumento	*raise*
la bonificación anual	*yearly bonus*
la guardería	*daycare center*
la licencia por enfermedad/ maternidad	*sick/maternity leave*
el plan de retiro	*retirement plan*
el seguro médico	*health insurance*

Verbos	Verbs
ascender (ie) (a un/a empleado/a)	*to promote (an employee)*
contratar	*to hire*
dejar de	*to stop doing something*
despedir (i, i) (a un/a empleado/a)	*to fire (an employee)*
enterarse de	*to find out*
retirarse (de una empresa)	*to retire (from a company)*
rellenar[1]	*to fill completely, to fill out*
Adjetivos	**Adjectives**
capaz	*capable*
entusiasta	*enthusiastic*
honrado/a, honesto/a	*honest*
justo/a	*fair*

Variaciones

- You will hear **retirarse** in much of Latin America, **jubilarse** in Spain, and **pensionarse** in Mexico.
- In Mexico, a colloquial alternative to **despedir** is the verb **correr** as in, **Lo corrieron del trabajo** (lit. *They ran him off*).

))) Letras y sonidos

The consonants *b* and *v*

In Spanish, the letters **b** and **v** sound identical, with no distinction between them, as there is in English. While **b** and **v** are identical, two different sounds correspond to them, depending on the context. After a pause or the letters **m** or **n**, the sound for **b** and **v** is like the *b* in English *base*.

Hard bilabial:

bús-que-da   **v**e-te-ri-na-rio   **b**om-**b**e-ro   con-**v**en-to

In all other positions, especially between vowels, the sound for **b** and **v** is softer. English has no sound similar, but this sound is approximated when one imitates the steady murmur of a motor boat in the distance.

Soft bilabial:

la-**b**ús-que-da   el-**v**e-te-ri-na-rio   con-ta-**b**le   a-**v**ión

---

[1] Also: **completar, llenar** (*to fill*)

Aplicación

11-22 En busca de empleo. Selecciona la opción que mejor completa cada descripción.

1. Cuando hay una recesión económica, _h_ necesita excelentes cualificaciones.

2. Tu último jefe escribió excelentes comentarios en _g_.

3. Acepta el puesto si la empresa tiene _d_ para cuidar a tus hijos durante las horas de trabajo.

4. Pienso que _b_ médico es un beneficio esencial para cuidar la salud de los empleados.

5. Debes firmar _f_ con los términos de tu puesto.

6. Si trabajas bien, es posible que te suban el sueldo, es decir que te den _a_ en el segundo año.

7. Si necesitas dejar tu trabajo temporalmente por un problema grave de salud, pides _e_.

8. Si tu título en el trabajo cambia de ayudante administrativo a jefe ejecutivo, es _c_ importante.

a. un aumento
b. el seguro
c. un ascenso
d. una guardería _daycare_
e. la licencia por enfermedad
f. un contrato _contract_
g. su carta de recomendación
h. el/la aspirante

11-23 La solicitud de empleo. Trabajas en una agencia de empleo y Alejandra es una clienta. Escucha a Alejandra mientras explica su formación y su experiencia. Luego completa su solicitud de empleo.

SOLICITUD DE EMPLEO: AGENCIA LÓPEZ

NOMBRE: _____ APELLIDOS: _____ _____

EDAD: _____ TEL: _____ DIRECCIÓN: _____ NO. _____

EMPLEO DESEADO: _____ SUELDO MÍNIMO: _____

DONDE ESTUDIÓ: _____ NO. DE AÑOS: _____ ¿TÍTULO? **SÍ NO**

AÑOS DE EXPERIENCIA: _____ EMPRESA: _____

IDIOMAS: _____ ; _____ ; _____

REFERENCIA(S): **SÍ NO** NOMBRE(S): _____

Cultura en vivo

Although it used to be common to advertise positions as typically male or typically female, that is becoming less true as attitudes and laws are changing to not discriminate between men and women. In the case of Spain, for example, the European Union has established a set of guidelines that guarantees equal pay for equal work, regardless of gender. Have you noticed attitudes change regarding academic majors for men or for women?

11-24 ¿En qué orden? Trabajen en parejas para ordenar estos pasos para conseguir un puesto. Si no están de acuerdo, explíquense sus razones.

_____ llamar para hacer una cita con el/la jefe/a de personal

_____ volver a casa y esperar una llamada

__1__ leer los avisos clasificados en un sitio web de empleo

_____ rellenar la solicitud de empleo en Internet

_____ hacer preguntas sobre los beneficios del puesto

_____ ir a la entrevista

_____ contestar las preguntas sobre mi formación académica y experiencia

_____ preguntar sobre el sueldo

11-25 Una bolsa de empleo. Puedes encontrar ofertas de empleo en Internet.

Paso 1 Busca un sitio en Internet para ver los avisos clasificados en Argentina o Uruguay. Escoge uno que te interese y contesta estas preguntas.

1. ¿Cómo se llama el sitio?

2. ¿Cómo se llama la empresa?

3. ¿Qué vacante se anuncia? ¿Dónde está?

4. ¿Por qué te parece interesante?

5. ¿Qué tienes que hacer para solicitar el puesto?

> **Busca:** bolsa empleo Argentina/Uruguay

Paso 2 Escribe una lista de las cualificaciones que crees necesarias para el empleo que encontraste. Incluye el tipo de formación, de experiencia y de personalidad o de características físicas que requiere el puesto.

MODELO: analista de sistemas
> FORMACIÓN: *título universitario...*
> EXPERIENCIA: *2 años...,* etc.
> PERSONALIDAD: *paciente, trabajador...*

11-26A ¡Necesito información! Hagan los papeles de jefe/a de personal (estudiante A) y de aspirante (estudiante B) para dramatizar una entrevista de trabajo. **Aspirante**: por favor, ve al **Apéndice 1**, página A-14.

MODELO: JEFE/A DE PERSONAL: *Bienvenido/a. Soy... Siéntese, por favor.*
> ASPIRANTE: *Gracias. Soy... y quiero....*

Estudiante A: Jefe/a de personal

1. Saluda al / a la aspirante. Dile tu nombre. Dile que se siente.

3. Responde con interés. Pregúntale qué experiencia tiene.

5. Pregúntale si tiene nombres de referencias.

7. Responde que esta es una referencia muy (sorprendente/impresionante/dudosa). Pregúntale qué sueldo espera recibir.

9. Respóndele que esta cantidad es (razonable/mucha/imposible), y que puede empezar (mañana / la semana que viene / cuando tenga más experiencia).

Estructuras

11.5 Describe people and things that do or do not exist

The subjunctive with indefinite people and things

> Buscamos una persona que tenga experiencia con análisis de sistemas.

¿Recuerdas? An adjective describes, limits, or modifies a noun. Provide the correct form of the logical adjective: **bueno**, **uruguayo**.

Busco a la mujer (1) _____ que tiene (2) _____ cualificaciones.

Respuestas: 1. uruguaya; 2. buenas

- An adjective *clause* includes a verb.

Adjective	Adjective clause
Estos son aspirantes **cualificados**.	Estos son aspirantes **que tienen** buenas cualificaciones.
These are qualified applicants.	*These are applicants who have good qualifications.*

- Use the indicative when the adjective clause refers to a person, thing, or event that exists, or is within your experience.

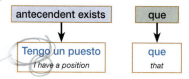

antecendent exists	que	dependent clause in indicative
Tengo un puesto *I have a position*	que *that*	me paga bien. *pays me well.*

- Use the subjunctive when the adjective clause refers to a person, thing, or event that is *unknown* or *does not* exist.

antecendent unknown	que	dependent clause in subjunctive
Necesito un puesto *I need a position*	que *that*	me pague bien. *pays me well.*

No hay nadie **que sepa** reparar mi computadora vieja.	*There is no one who knows how to repair my old computer.*

- Use the subjunctive in a question when asking whether something or someone exists.

¿Conoce usted una empresa **que tenga** vacantes?	*Do you know any company that has vacancies?*

¿Comprendes? Complete the sentences with the logical form (indicative or subjunctive) of these verbs: **necesitar**, **tener**.

¿Sabes si hay alguna empresa que (1) _____ técnicos en computadoras? Tengo una amiga que (2) _____ muy buenas cualificaciones.

Respuestas: 1. necesite; 2. tiene

Aplicación

11-27 Las cataratas del Iguazú. Estas cataratas monumentales atraen a miles de personas cada año.

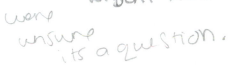

[handwritten: Si ind. No sub]

Paso 1   Selecciona el verbo que mejor completa cada oración.

1. Quiero visitar las cataratas que (están)/estén en el río Iguazú en la frontera entre Brasil y Argentina. *[handwritten: indicative B/c exists]*

2. Las cataratas tienen un nombre que (viene)/venga del guaraní. *[handwritten: indicativ it exists]*

3. Es un nombre que (significa)/signifique "grandes aguas". *[handwritten: indicative name that exists]*

4. Hay una leyenda guaraní que (explica)/explique que un dios creó las cataratas. *[handwritten: indicative exists]*

5. Hay mucha gente que las (visita)/visite todos los años. *[handwritten: indicative]*

6. Voy a buscar un guía que me da/(dé) una orientación a la región. *[handwritten: subjuntiv uncurrently]*

7. No hay nadie que no se impresiona/(se impresione) de su grandeza y de su hermosura. *[handwritten: Doesnt exits subjuntile we Dont know]*

8. ¿Hay otra catarata que (es)/sea más grande que esta? *[handwritten: subjunctive were unsure its a question.]*

Las cataratas del Iguazú, cuatro veces más grandes que las del Niágara, son parte del Patrimonio de la Humanidad de la UNESCO.

Paso 2   Contesta las siguientes preguntas sobre las cataratas del Iguazú.

1. ¿Dónde están situadas?

2. ¿Cuál es el origen del nombre?

3. ¿Por qué crees que los indígenas las consideraron sagradas (*sacred*)?

4. ¿Hay alguna otra cascada en el mundo que sea más grande?

5. ¿Conoces a alguien que las conozca?

6. ¿Quieres visitarlas algún día? Explica.

11-28 Isabelle Chaquiriand, una emprendedora con corazón. Isabelle Chaquiriand es la directora de Xcala, una empresa uruguaya que ayuda a mujeres emprendedoras e inversoras. Su meta es ayudar a crear puestos y contribuir al desarrollo económico y el bienestar de la región. Haz el papel de su ayudante y explica qué tipo de empleados se necesitan en la empresa. Incluye información de la lista en tus descripciones y crea una descripción original.

> MODELO: *Busco una ayudante administativa que... Necesito un contador que...*

intérprete	entender mi misión
abogado/a	poder organizar la oficina
supervisor/a	ser honrado/a y capaz
contador/a	hablar tres idiomas
ingeniero/a	entender nuestra red de computadoras
analista de sistemas	querer trabajar los fines de semana
¿...?	tener experiencia diplomática
	conocer bien el código civil
	¿...?

 11-29A ¡Necesito información! Hagan los papeles de emprendedor/a (estudiante A) y ayudante administrativo/a (estudiante B) en una empresa incipiente (*startup*) multinacional. Háganse y contesten preguntas sobre lo que necesitan para su empresa. **Ayudante administrativo/a**: por favor, ve al **Apéndice 1**, página A-14.

> MODELO: Dile que necesitan empleados que (**tener**) experiencia.
>> EMPRENDEDOR/A: *Necesitamos empleados que tengan experiencia.*
>> AYUDANTE ADMINISTRATIVO/A: *Tengo muchas solicitudes de personas que tienen experiencia.*

Estudiante A: Emprendedor/a

1. Pregúntale si hay muchas vacantes que (**necesitar**) ingenieros.

3. Dile que sí, pero que no hay nadie que lo (**poder**) hacer todo. Pregúntale si hay alguien que (**saber**) inglés, español y portugués.

5. Dile que no, que en este momento no hay nadie que (**ser**) el candidato perfecto. Pregúntale si hay alguien que ustedes (**poder**) ascender.

7. Dile que está bien y que van a ascender a una persona que ya (**trabajar**) en la empresa.

11-30 Las profesiones y los oficios. Entrevístense en grupos de tres o cuatro para saber sus planes después de graduarse. Luego, hagan un resumen de sus planes. Usen las frases siguientes para hacer las preguntas.

> MODELO: querer ser ingeniero/a
>
> ESTUDIANTE 1: *¿Hay alguien que quiera ser ingeniero o ingeniera?*
>
> ESTUDIANTE 2: *Sí, quiero ser ingeniero/a porque…*

1. **querer** ser periodista
2. **pensar** ser emprendedor/a
3. **desear** ser contador/a
4. **soñar** con recibir un aumento su primer año
5. **preferir** ser dentista
6. **creer** que ciertos oficios son mejores que ciertas profesiones
7. **pensar** estudiar para veterinario/a
8. no **querer** un puesto que no **ofrecer** beneficios
9. ¿…?

11-31 En mi opinión. ¿Cúales son tus opiniones y deseos sobre el lugar donde vives?

Paso 1 Completa las oraciones para expresar tu opinión, tus deseos y tus experiencias de vivir en esta ciudad o en este pueblo. Usa el subjuntivo o el indicativo, según el caso. Tus respuestas pueden ser serias o cómicas.

> MODELO: *En esta ciudad / este pueblo no hay nadie que quiera vivir en otro lugar.*

- tengo amigos que…
- me alegro de que mis amigos…
- no conozco a nadie que…
- mis padres dudan que yo…
- no quiero que mis amigos…
- busco un lugar que…
- ojalá que…
- conozco un café donde…

Paso 2 En parejas, túrnense para expresar sus opiniones y comentarlas. Usen expresiones como: **Me alegro que…**, **Dudo que…**, **Es posible que…**, **Es increíble que…**, etc.

> MODELO: ESTUDIANTE 1: *En esta ciudad / este pueblo no hay nadie que quiera vivir en otro lugar.*
>
> ESTUDIANTE 2: *Dudo que tengas razón. Conozco a muchas personas que prefieren vivir en…*

¡Conversemos!

Primero, pregúntate si puedes llevar a cabo las siguientes funciones comunicativas en español. Después, júntate con dos o tres compañeros/as de clase para presentar las situaciones. Hagan y respondan a por lo menos cuatro preguntas en cada situación.

✓ CAN YOU . . .

☐ discuss job hunting?

☐ interview for a job?

☐ describe people and things that do or do not exist?

WITH YOUR CLASSMATE(S) . . .

Situación: En casa con amigos/as.

Hagan los papeles de amigos/as que están buscando empleo en los avisos clasificados de Internet. Hablen sobre por qué les interesan o no las ofertas. Posibles puestos: **científico/a nuclear**, **dentista**, **periodista**, **profesional de la salud**, **psicólogo/a**, **veterinario/a**, **entrenador/a personal**.

Para empezar: *Aquí hay un aviso para... ¿Crees que es una buena opción para ti? ¿Por qué?*

Situación: En una entrevista.

Hagan los papeles de aspirante y director/a de una empresa. El/La directora/a le hace preguntas sobre sus cualificaciones. El/La aspirante le explica que es el/la mejor candidato/a porque...

Para empezar: *Buenas tardes. En su carta, usted dice que tiene experiencia en...*

Situación: En el trabajo.

Conversen sobre los beneficios que tienen en su trabajo y el trabajo que esperan tener algún día.

Para empezar: *Tengo un puesto de cocinero que no me paga muy bien. Cuando termine mis estudios, voy a buscar un puesto que...*

Club cultura

11.6 Put yourself into the scene

Introducción a Uruguay

Estrategia para ver

Put yourself into the scene. When you imagine that you are a participant in the video, you become its representative and can adopt the experiences as if they were yours. As you watch and listen, try to make a list of the important points that you can tell another person about your experience. Then, later, you become its advocate.

ANTES DE VER EL VIDEO

11-32 Eres uruguayo/a. Imagínate que eres uruguayo/a y quieres hacer un video de tu país para que turistas internacionales lo visiten. ¿Cuáles de estos aspectos de Uruguay te gustaría incluir en el video?

su comida	sus deportes	su economía
sus festivales	su gente	su música
sus playas	sus zonas históricas	sus zonas naturales

AL VER EL VIDEO

11-33 ¿Se incluyen? Indica con **Sí** o **No** si escuchas/ves o no estos aspectos en el video. ¿Hay otro que no aparezca o que quieras enfatizar más?

1. _____ su gente
2. _____ sus playas
3. _____ su comida
4. _____ sus deportes
5. _____ sus festivales
6. _____ su economía
7. _____ sus zonas naturales
8. _____ su música
9. _____ sus zonas históricas

DESPUÉS DE VER EL VIDEO

11-34 Comprensión. Indica la opción que mejor completa cada oración, según el video.

1. Uruguay es (más grande que / más pequeño que / tan pequeño como) Inglaterra.
2. Tiene frontera con Brasil al (norte / sur / oeste).
3. El 50% de la población vive en (Punta del Este / Montevideo / Buenos Aires).
4. La economía depende mucho de (la fabricación de automóviles / la agricultura / la ciberseguridad).
5. Muchos turistas asisten a sus festivales de cine y de (ópera / tango / jazz).

11-35 ¡Visita Uruguay! Trabajas en el Departamento de Turismo de Uruguay. Escribe un anuncio publicitario con los puntos más importantes sobre el país, en tu opinión.

  MODELO: *¡Visita Uruguay y conoce el paraíso! No hay ningún lugar del mundo que...*

11.3 Nuestro mundo

Panoramas

11.7 **Identify and research some important cultural aspects of Argentina and Uruguay**

El virreinato del Río de la Plata: Argentina y Uruguay

Las sociedades argentina y uruguaya fusionan vastas áreas salvajes y agrícolas con ciudades de gran actividad cultural y comercial.

La economía de Argentina y Uruguay depende mayormente de sus productos agrícolas como la soya, los granos y el vino, así como de la producción de carne de res (*beef*) y de cordero (*lamb*).

La infusión hecha de yerba mate es ubicua en Argentina y Uruguay, donde no solo se toma individualmente, sino que también simboliza la amistad cuando se comparte entre conocidos. El mate forma parte de la actividad diaria en casa, y también en muchas empresas donde es muy común ver a profesionales trabajando frente a sus computadoras con el termo de agua caliente y el mate acompañando su trabajo.

El turismo es importante para la economía de Uruguay y Argentina. Desde los glaciares de la Patagonia hasta las cataratas del Iguazú en Argentina, y las hermosas playas de Punta del Este, los dos países atraen a visitantes de todo el mundo.

La transformación del Puerto Madero es el proyecto de renovación urbana más importante de la ciudad de Buenos Aires. De ser un puerto obsoleto hasta fines del siglo XX, es hoy un centro de gran expansión comercial, con oficinas, hoteles, restaurantes, viviendas familiares, centros culturales y un nuevo recorrido turístico con su propia identidad.

El desfile (*parade*) de las Llamadas es una fiesta popular que tiene lugar en Montevideo durante la época de carnaval. Durante dos noches, desfilan unas 40 sociedades de afrodescendientes por las calles de la capital. Es una de las más puras manifestaciones de la cultura afrouruguaya.

	Argentina	Uruguay
Población:	44 millones	3,4 millones
Desempleo:	8%	7,6%
Fuerza laboral femenina:	55%	67%
Sueldos F/M:	51/100	56/100
Vacaciones anuales:	21 días	25 días
Licencia por paternidad:	3 meses	3 meses

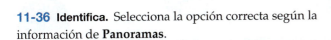

11-36 Identifica. Selecciona la opción correcta según la información de **Panoramas**.

> hoteles, restaurantes y recorrido turístico
> Punta del Este
> la carne de res y de cordero, los granos, el vino
> las Llamadas
> la Patagonia

1. productos agrícolas que se exportan _____

2. un lugar donde hay glaciares _____

3. una tradición afrouruguaya _____

4. una playa popular uruguaya _____

5. los atractivos de Puerto Madero _____

11-37 Desafío. Identifica el lugar o los lugares según el mapa y los datos estadísticos.

1. la capital de Argentina y la de Uruguay

2. el país donde las mujeres ganan más

3. el país donde los trabajadores tienen derecho a tres semanas de vacaciones

4. el país con menor población y desempleo

5. el río que forma la frontera entre Argentina y Uruguay

11-38 Investigación: Argentina/Uruguay. Selecciona un lugar, una persona o un tema (*theme*) que te interesa, como, por ejemplo, **las Llamadas**, **el vino argentino/uruguayo**, **la economía argentina/uruguaya**, **Jorge Drexler**, **un/a artista famoso/a**, etc. Usa el modelo para escribir un resumen de tu investigación y luego preséntaselo a la clase.

📍 **Busca:** las Llamadas Uruguay, etc.

MODELO: *Uno de los productos agrícolas más importantes de Argentina es la carne.*
Según las estadísticas hay entre 50 y 55 millones de cabezas de ganado
(cattle) principalmente en las pampas argentinas...

Páginas

11.8 **Use illustrations to aid comprehension**

¿Qué tipo de jefe tienes tú?

Estrategia para leer

Use illustrations to aid comprehension. Writers may communicate their message by adding illustrations that clarify or exaggerate, such as caricatures. A good illustration will help guide you in comprehending a passage; a poor illustration may cause confusion. When you read, be an active critic of the value of any illustrations.

ANTES DE LEER

11-39 **Las caricaturas.** Selecciona la mejor descripción para cada caricatura.

1. _____    2. _____   3. _____   4. _____

a. Esta persona va a subir sin importarle quién o qué esté en su camino.

b. Esta persona quiere ser amigo/a de todo el mundo.

c. Esta persona sigue un solo camino, nunca va a aceptar ideas nuevas o innovadoras.

d. Esta persona hace mil cosas a la vez y no siempre las hace todas bien.

AL LEER

11-40 **¿Te ayudan las caricaturas?** Lee las descripciones a continuación y decide si te ayudan o no las caricaturas. ¿Con cuáles de los jefes tienes experiencia?

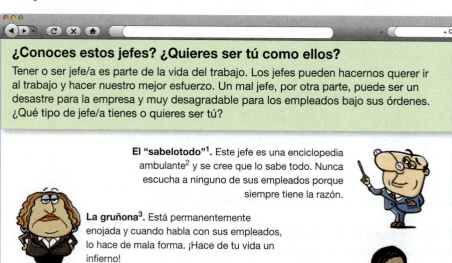

¿Conoces estos jefes? ¿Quieres ser tú como ellos?

Tener o ser jefe/a es parte de la vida del trabajo. Los jefes pueden hacernos querer ir al trabajo y hacer nuestro mejor esfuerzo. Un mal jefe, por otra parte, puede ser un desastre para la empresa y muy desagradable para los empleados bajo sus órdenes. ¿Qué tipo de jefe/a tienes o quieres ser tú?

[1]*know-it-all*
[2]*walking*

El "sabelotodo"[1]. Este jefe es una enciclopedia ambulante[2] y se cree que lo sabe todo. Nunca escucha a ninguno de sus empleados porque siempre tiene la razón.

[3]*el gruñón / la gruñona:*
grumpy

La gruñona[3]. Está permanentemente enojada y cuando habla con sus empleados, lo hace de mala forma. ¡Hace de tu vida un infierno!

La ambiciosa. Lo que desea es mejorar su posición dentro de la empresa y quedar bien con sus jefes para que la asciendan.

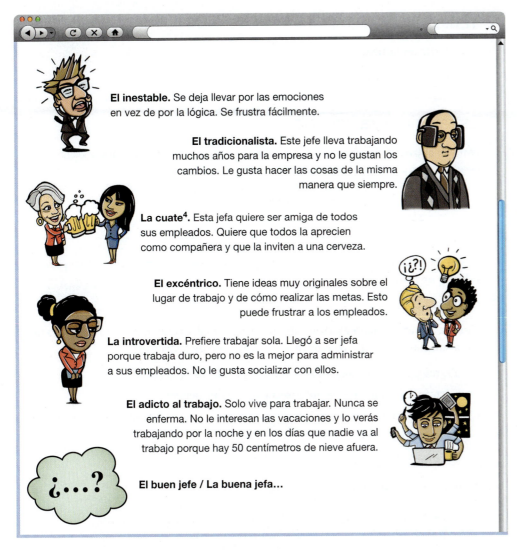

El inestable. Se deja llevar por las emociones en vez de por la lógica. Se frustra fácilmente.

El tradicionalista. Este jefe lleva trabajando muchos años para la empresa y no le gustan los cambios. Le gusta hacer las cosas de la misma manera que siempre.

La cuate[4]. Esta jefa quiere ser amiga de todos sus empleados. Quiere que todos la aprecien como compañera y que la inviten a una cerveza.

[4]el/la cuate: *buddy* (Mex.)

El excéntrico. Tiene ideas muy originales sobre el lugar de trabajo y de cómo realizar las metas. Esto puede frustrar a los empleados.

La introvertida. Prefiere trabajar sola. Llegó a ser jefa porque trabaja duro, pero no es la mejor para administrar a sus empleados. No le gusta socializar con ellos.

El adicto al trabajo. Solo vive para trabajar. Nunca se enferma. No le interesan las vacaciones y lo verás trabajando por la noche y en los días que nadie va al trabajo porque hay 50 centímetros de nieve afuera.

¿…?

El buen jefe / La buena jefa…

DESPUÉS DE LEER

11-41 ¿Quién es? Selecciona la opción que mejor describe a cada jefe, según el artículo.

1. _____ el ambicioso
2. _____ el cuate
3. _____ el excéntrico
4. _____ el gruñón
5. _____ el sabelotodo
6. _____ el tradicionalista

a. Se enoja fácilmente.
b. Cree que es más inteligente y mejor informado que los demás.
c. No le gusta la innovación.
d. Siempre está pensando en ideas raras.
e. No mantiene distancia profesional con sus empleados.
f. Lo importante es seguir subiendo sin preocuparse de los demás.

11-42 En tus palabras. En parejas, túrnense para describir a estos jefes en sus propias palabras y dar un ejemplo de cada uno.

1. el/la inestable
2. el/la adicto/a al trabajo
3. el/la introvertido/a

11-43 El/La jefe/a ideal. En un párrafo, describe y da un ejemplo de una persona que tenga todas la cualifaciones de buen/a jefe/a. Dibuja o busca un dibujo de una caricatura de esta persona.

MODELO: *El buen jefe respeta a sus empleados…*

Taller

11.9 **Write an outline**

Una carta formal

Estrategia para escribir

Write an outline. With formal writing, it is helpful to write an outline to help guide you from main ideas to supporting details. Here is an example:
- Short introductory paragraph with thesis statement
- Topic 1 (etc.): Topic sentence; supporting details; summary sentence
- Closing summary

11-44 **Solicitar un trabajo.** En esta actividad, vas a escribir una carta formal para solicitar un puesto de trabajo.

ANTES DE ESCRIBIR

Sigue la **Estrategia para escribir** para tu carta formal. Primero, inventa el puesto que vas a solicitar. ¿Qué tipo de empresa es? ¿Qué tipo de trabajo es?

- Párrafo 1: Te presentas (tu nombre y el propósito de la carta).
- Párrafo 2: Detalles de tus intereses y tus cualificaciones.
- Párrafo 3: Un resumen y tu interés en el puesto. Tu agradecimiento por su atención.
- Despedida y firma.

AL ESCRIBIR

Algunas expresiones útiles para tu carta:

Saludos: Estimado/a señor/a:

Despedidas: Atentamente, Cordialmente, Lo(s)/La(s) saluda atentamente,

Sigue el modelo para escribir tu carta de solicitud.

MODELO:

(Tu nombre e información de contacto)

(Nombre de la persona a quién se dirige)

(Nombre y dirección de la empresa)

(Dirección de la empresa)

(Fecha de hoy)

(Saludo):

(Presentación) Soy... Escribo esta carta para solicitar el puesto que apareció en el sitio web de... con fecha..., en el que se solicitan personas con el título de....

(Párrafo 2) El año pasado terminé mis estudios en... y además hice...

(Párrafo 3) Para concluir, ... Le aseguro que soy una persona....

(Despedida),

(Firma)

DESPUÉS DE ESCRIBIR

- **Revisar.** Revisa tu carta para verificar los siguientes puntos:
  - ☐ las expresiones para una carta formal
  - ☐ el uso de los tiempos verbales (presente y pretérito) y del subjuntivo
  - ☐ la ortografía y la concordancia
- **Intercambiar.** Intercambia tu carta con la de un/a compañero/a para hacer correcciones y sugerencias, y para comentar sobre el contenido.
- **Entregar.** Pon tu carta en limpio, incorporando los comentarios de tu compañero/a. Después, entrégasela a tu profesor/a.

En este capítulo...

))) Vocabulario

Primera parte

Los oficios y las profesiones	Occupations and professions
el/la abogado/a	*lawyer*
el/la analista (financiero/a, de sistemas)	*(financial/systems) analyst*
el/la arquitecto/a	*architect*
el/la ayudante (administrativo/a, clínico/a)	*(administrative/clinical) assistant*
el/la carpintero/a	*carpenter*
el/la científico/a	*scientist*
el/la cocinero/a	*cook, chef*
el/la contador/a	*accountant*
el/la dentista	*dentist*
el/la emprendedor/a	*entrepreneur*
el/la enfermero/a	*nurse*
el hombre / la mujer de negocios	*businessman/woman*
el/la ingeniero/a (eléctrico/a, civil, mecánico/a)	*(electrical/civil/mechanical) engineer*
el/la intérprete	*interpreter*
el/la mecánico/a	*mechanic*
el/la obrero/a de construcción	*construction worker*
el/la organizador/a de eventos	*events organizer*
el/la peluquero/a	*hairdresser*
el/la periodista	*journalist*
el/la plomero/a	*plumber*
el/la profesional de la salud	*healthcare worker*
el/la psicólogo/a	*psychologist*
el/la veterinario/a	*veterinarian*

Cargos	Positions
el/la director/a	*director*
el/la empleado/a	*employee*
el/la jefe/a (ejecutivo/a)	*boss (CEO)*
el/la supervisor/a	*supervisor*

Términos y expresiones de trabajo	Work-related terms and expressions
los beneficios	*benefits*
las cualificaciones	*qualifications*
el currículum vitae	*curriculum vitae (vita)*
el (des)empleo	*(un)employment*
la empresa	*company, firm*
el entrenamiento	*training*
la formación	*education*
la meta	*goal*
el puesto	*position (job)*
el sueldo (mínimo)	*(minimum) wage*
la (des)ventaja	*(dis)advantage*

¡Manos a la obra!	Let's get to work!
conseguir (i, i)	*to get, to obtain*
diseñar	*to design*
estar sin trabajo	*to be out of work*
reparar	*to repair*
repartir	*to deliver, to distribute*
trabajar a tiempo completo/ parcial	*to work full-time / part-time*

Segunda parte

La búsqueda de empleo	The job search
el/la aspirante	*applicant*
los avisos clasificados	*classified ads*
la carta de presentación/ recomendación	*letter of introduction/ recommendation*
el contrato	*contract*
la entrevista	*interview*
el formulario	*form*
la solicitud de empleo	*employment application*
la vacante	*vacancy*

Los beneficios	Benefits
el aumento	*raise*
la bonificación anual	*yearly bonus*
la guardería	*daycare center*
la licencia por enfermedad/ maternidad	*sick/maternity leave*
el plan de retiro	*retirement plan*
el seguro médico	*health insurance*

Verbos	Verbs
ascender (ie) (a un/a empleado/a)	*to promote (an employee)*
contratar	*to hire*
dejar de	*to stop doing something*
despedir (i, i) (a un/a empleado/a)	*to fire (an employee)*
enterarse de	*to find out*
retirarse (de una empresa)	*to retire (from a company)*
rellenar	*to fill completely, to fill out*

Adjetivos	Adjectives
capaz	*capable*
entusiasta	*enthusiastic*
honrado/a, honesto/a	*honest*
justo/a	*fair*

Adverbial conjunctions   *See page 357.*

Capítulo 12
¡El futuro es tuyo!

«Hay tres cosas que el ser humano necesita en su vida: alguien a quien amar, algo que hacer y una esperanza para el futuro».

Fuente: "Humanscape 65", Mel Casas, Acrylic, 72" x 96", Collection of Jim & Ann Harithas, New York, New York

***Humanscape 65* de Melesio Casas.** The artist was also an activist, writer, and teacher. His visual statements, such as this one, are meant to address cultural stereotypes. He is best known for his series of 150 large-scale paintings called *Humanscapes*.

Learning Objectives

12.1 Discuss technology and ways to communicate

12.2 Describe people and things, and discuss what has happened

12.3 Learn about gaming and a popular Mexican American pop rock artist

12.4 Discuss environmental challenges

12.5 Discuss future and contingent actions, and speculate on events

12.6 Gather information

12.7 Identify and research some important Hispanic Americans

12.8 Look for the main idea and supporting evidence

12.9 State the main idea and add supporting evidence

In this Chapter

ENFOQUE CULTURAL: LOS HISPANOS EN ESTADOS UNIDOS
Club cultura: Introducción a Estados Unidos

Indica con **C (Cierto)** o **F (Falso)** si escuchas/ves o no esta información en el video.

1. _____ dónde está Sharinna en este momento

2. _____ su herencia hispana y dónde estudió

3. _____ la población hispana en EE. UU.

4. _____ el porcentaje de cubanos en la Florida

5. _____ el tratado con México que cedió parte de su territorio a EE. UU.

6. _____ algunos personajes importantes hispanos

12.1 Primera parte

Vocabulario

12.1 **Discuss technology and ways to communicate**

La tecnología

el Dr. Jorge Díaz

Carmen

Raúl

Un proyecto digital. El Dr. Jorge Díaz enseña clases **a distancia** por **videoconferencia** desde un salón en la UNAM a estudiantes en otras universidades. Tienen **una comunidad virtual** en la que todos **colaboran** en proyectos.

DR. DÍAZ: Para la próxima clase, necesitan **acceder al sitio web** de la clase para **bajar** las instrucciones para su tarea. Van a colaborar en grupos de tres para investigar y escribir un proyecto sobre **los medios digitales**. Insisto en que sus colaboradores sean de otras universidades y que **compartan** sus proyectos en el sitio web de la clase.

CARMEN: ¿Viste **el tuit** de Julieta Venegas? Hay **un hipervínculo** a su video musical nuevo.

RAÚL: Espera, no te oigo bien. Tengo que quitarme **los auriculares**.

¿Comprendes? Identify the character in each description: **el Dr. Díaz**, **Carmen**, or **Raúl**.

1. _____ Le explica la tarea a la clase.

2. _____ Lleva auriculares.

3. _____ Quiere abrir un hipervínculo.

Respuestas: 1. el Dr. Díaz; 2. Raúl; 3. Carmen

))) Vocabulario

Los aparatos electrónicos	Electronic devices
la antena parabólica	*satellite dish*
los auriculares	*earbuds, headphones*
el escáner	*scanner*
el lector de libros electrónicos	*eBook reader*
la marca	*brand*
la pantalla	*screen*
el ratón (inalámbrico)	*(wireless) mouse*
la tableta	*tablet*
el teclado	*keyboard*

En Internet	On the Internet
la alerta	*alert*
la aplicación	*app*
el aprendizaje a distancia	*distance learning*
la comunidad virtual	*online community*
el fraude electrónico	*phishing*
el hipervínculo	*hyperlink*
la impresora	*printer*
el juego electrónico	*computer (electronic) game*
los medios digitales	*digital media*
la página (el sitio) web	*web page (website)*
el servidor	*server*
el/la trol	*Internet troll*
el tuit	*tweet*
la videoconferencia	*videoconference*

Verbos	Verbs
acceder	*to access*
actualizar (un programa)	*to update (a program)*
almacenar (en la nube)	*to store (in the cloud)*
apagar	*to turn off*
bajar	*to download*
borrar	*to erase*
colaborar	*to collaborate*
compartir	*to post (share) online*
encender	*to turn on*
enviar	*to send*
fallar	*to break down (e.g., computer)*
funcionar	*to function, to work*
grabar	*to record*
guardar (un documento)	*to save (a document)*
hacer clic	*to click on*
imprimir[1]	*to print*
(des)instalar	*to (un)install*
programar	*to program*
subir	*to upload*
tuitear	*to tweet*
unirse (a un sitio social)	*to join (a social media site)*

Variaciones

- *Headphones* are also **los cascos** in Spain, and **los audífonos** in Mexico and Central America.
- The *Internet* can be **la red (informática), la red mundial**, and **el/la Internet**.
- **Hacer clic** can also be **pulsar**.

---

[1]There are two past participle forms: the regular form **imprimido** and the irregular **impreso**. They can be used interchangeably: **Hemos imprimido/impreso los documentos. Los documentos están imprimidos/impresos.**

Aplicación

12-1 ¿Qué es? Selecciona la opción que mejor corresponde a cada descripción.

1. _____ el hipervínculo
2. _____ el fraude electrónico
3. _____ la antena parabólica
4. _____ la alerta
5. _____ el/la trol
6. _____ la aplicación
7. _____ el tuit
8. _____ almacenar en la nube

a. recibe transmisiones internacionales
b. un programa para un uso específico, como acceso a un servicio de música
c. un mensaje corto enviado por una red social
d. tiene el objetivo de conseguir datos financieros de los usuarios sin su consentimiento
e. guardar datos de forma remota en servidores en otro sitio
f. para dirigirte a una página en la web
g. una persona que escribe mensajes provocadores, irrelevantes o fuera de tema en una comunidad en línea
h. un sonido o mensaje para recordarte de algo

12-2 No pude hacer la tarea. Carmen quiere explicar por qué no pudo hacer la tarea. Selecciona el verbo que mejor completa cada oración.

| acceder | bajar | encendí | falló | hice clic |
| apagué | borrar | envié | funcionó | instalar |

Esta mañana quise (1) _____ al sitio web que tenía la tarea para mi clase. (2) _____ mi portátil e (3) _____ en el hipervínculo que tenía. Pero, por alguna razón, no (4) _____. ¡De repente, (5) _____ el sistema totalmente! Pensé, esto es imposible. (6) _____ mi computadora y esperé un minuto. Volví a encender la computadora y entré en mi cuenta de correo electrónico. Le (7) _____ un mensaje a la profesora diciéndole que no podía encontrar la tarea. Ella me respondió que debía (8) _____ la tarea de otro sitio porque el hipervínculo que yo tenía era sospechoso, y que lo debía (9) _____. ¿Lo crees? Voy a tener que (10) _____ un programa antivirus.

12-3 Un sitio web. Puedes encontrar cualquier aparato electrónico en este sitio web. Escucha el anuncio y selecciona la opción que mejor completa cada oración.

1. El anuncio es para un sistema de...
   a. audio.
   b. computadora.
   c. servidor.
2. No incluye...
   a. altavoces (*speakers*).
   b. receptor.
   c. televisor.
3. A la persona que compre este sistema, le gusta(n)...
   a. la fotografía.
   b. los juegos electrónicos.
   c. la música.
4. Puedes comprar este sistema en...
   a. seis meses.
   b. un año.
   c. un año y medio.
5. Se compra este sistema...
   a. directamente de la fábrica.
   b. en Internet.
   c. en tiendas especializadas.

12-4 Los mensajes de texto. Los mensajes de texto usan emoticonos y abreviaturas en español tanto como en inglés.

Paso 1 Selecciona la descripción que mejor corresponde a cada emoticono.

1. _____ :(h   a. alegría *happy*
2. _____ :'(e   b. indiferencia o molestia
3. _____ :S c   c. confusión *confusion*
4. _____ :) g   d. guiño (un gesto con el ojo) *a gesture with a eye*
5. _____ :D a   e. mucha tristeza *really sad*
6. _____ ;) d   f. sacar la lengua *stick out tongue*
7. _____ :p f   g. sonrisa *smile*
8. _____ :-/ b   h. tristeza *sadness*

Paso 2 Estos son mensajes que le envió una estudiante a su amigo. ¿Los puedes leer? Selecciona la frase que mejor corresponde a cada mensaje.

1. __C__ grax p t msj :)
2. __D__ porfa llama mi mov bss ;)
3. __A__ q pasa no te vi en kls :(
4. __F__ slmos fin d smn? :D
5. __B__ vas sab fsta Julia? :p
6. __E__ xdon el prf dice xam vrns :-/

a. ¿Qué pasa que no te vi en clase?
b. ¿Vas a la fiesta de Julia el sábado?
c. Gracias por tu mensaje. *— phone*
d. Por favor, llama a mi móvil. Besos.
e. Perdón, el profesor dice que hay examen el viernes. *Friday*
f. ¿Salimos este fin de semana?

Paso 3 Busca otras abreviaturas en Internet y escribe tres mensajes originales. Incluye un emoticono en cada uno.

> 📍 **Busca:** abreviaturas mensajes de texto español

12-5 Problemas tecnológicos. Aquí tienen algunos inconvenientes tecnológicos. En parejas, trabajen para resolver tres o cuatro de ellos. Empleen terminología del **Vocabulario** en su discusión.

MODELO: Necesitan imprimir la tarea, pero la impresora no funciona.

ESTUDIANTE 1: *Le podemos escribir un mensaje a la profesora explicándole el problema.*

ESTUDIANTE 2: *No creo que ella acepte la excusa. Es mejor que la subamos al sitio web de la clase o que se la mandemos por correo electrónico.*

1. No entienden cómo llegar a la página web que tiene información sobre las abreviaturas en español. → *Vam*

2. Hay un trol que hace comentarios feos en la red social de uno/a de ustedes.

3. Tenían que colaborar en un proyecto, pero no encuentran dónde lo guardaron en la computadora.

4. Hay un video que deben ver para su clase mañana, pero no pueden acceder a Internet desde su casa.

5. Recibieron un mensaje de una persona prometiéndoles $499.000 y que solo tienen que hacer clic en el hipervínculo en el mensaje.

6. Uno/a tiene que hacer una transferencia entre las cuentas de su banco, pero el banco está cerrado.

[handwritten margin notes:]
→ No, podemos a preguntar por ayuda a los compañeros de clase.
= les voy a enviar mensaje por el chat

Estructuras

12.2 Describe people and things, and discuss what has happened

The past participle

¿Recuerdas? You've used some adjectives that end in **-do**, such as **cansado** and **casado**. Complete the sentence with the correct form of the logical adjectives.

Miguel y Sara se casaron hace diez años, pero no están (1) _____ de estar (2) _____ .

Respuestas: 1. cansados; 2. casados

- In English, the past participle is usually the *-ed* or *-en* form of the verb. In Spanish, you add **-ado** to the stems of **-ar** verbs, and **-ido** to the stems of **-er** and **-ir** verbs to form regular past participles.

guardar	guard**ado**	*saved*
encender	encend**ido**	*turned on*
subir	sub**ido**	*uploaded*

- You can use the past participle as an adjective in Spanish and in English.

Tengo muchos documentos **guardados** en la nube.

I have many documents saved in the cloud.

- Add an accent mark when a past participle has the combination of vowels **ai**, **ei**, or **oi**.

creer	**creído**	*believed*	oír	**oído**	*heard*
leer	**leído**	*read*	traer	**traído**	*brought*

- Some of the more common verbs have irregular past participles.

abrir	**abierto**	*opened*	ir	**ido**	*gone*
cubrir	**cubierto**	*covered*	morir	**muerto**	*dead*
decir	**dicho**	*said*	poner	**puesto**	*put, placed*
descubrir	**descubierto**	*discovered*	romper	**roto**	*broken*
escribir	**escrito**	*written*	ver	**visto**	*seen*
hacer	**hecho**	*done, made*	volver	**vuelto**	*returned*

El documento está **abierto**.

The document is open.

La pantalla de mi computadora está **rota**.

My computer monitor is broken.

- When you use the past participle as an adjective, remember that it agrees in gender and number with the noun it modifies.

Vimos las conferencias **subidas** por nuestro supervisor.

We saw the lectures uploaded by our supervisor.

¿Tienes programas **abiertos** en este momento?

Do you have programs open now?

- When you use the verb **estar** with the past participle, you describe a state or condition that is the result of a previous action.

La impresora **está encendida**; el ayudante la encendió.

The printer is turned on; the assistant turned it on.

Los documentos confidenciales **están borrados**; los borró el jefe ejecutivo.

The confidential documents are erased; the CEO erased them.

Los programas están instalados y los documentos están subidos a la nube.

¿Comprendes? Provide the correct form of the past participle of a logical verb:
cubrir, encender.

—No veo la luz verde en la impresora. ¿Está (1) _____?

—No funciona. Mira cómo todo está (2) _____ de tinta (*ink*).

Respuestas: 1. encendida; 2. cubierto

Aplicación

12-6 En el centro de computación. Los ayudantes en el centro de computación tienen
una lista de tareas que necesitan cumplir antes de terminar su turno (*shift*). Escribe la
forma correcta del participio pasado del verbo más lógico.

   MODELO: el mensaje a la comunidad virtual (escribir, fallar, funcionar): ___*escrito*___

1. las alertas (atender, decir, colaborar): ___atendidas___

2. las aplicaciones (decir, instalar, hacer): ___instaladas___

3. los documentos (programar, funcionar, subir): ___subidos___ a la nube

4. las pantallas (abrir, escribir, limpiar): ___limpias___

5. la dirección del correo electrónico (acceder, añadir, encender): _____ a la lista
   de contactos

6. el servidor (actualizar, bajar, guardar): _____

7. los mensajes del trol (apagar, borrar, fallar): _____

8. los tuits (colaborar, enviar, instalar): ___enviados___

12-7 La Calle Ocho. La Calle Ocho está en el centro de la Pequeña Habana en Miami.
Completa la conversación entre dos turistas cubanas que están visitando el barrio.
Escribe la forma correcta del participio pasado de los verbos en la lista.

abrir	morir	pintar	preparar
hacer	perder	poner	vestir

FLOR: Vamos, Rosa. Dame las llaves del carro y vamos a pasear por la
       Calle Ocho.

ROSA: ¿Y dónde están las llaves? ¡No me digas que están (1) ___perdidas___
       otra vez!

FLOR: Aquí están. ¡Qué día más bonito! Deja la ventana (2) ___abierta___ en
       el carro. Me gusta el aire fresco.

ROSA: ¿Qué te parece ese mural (3) ___pintado___ en la pared?

FLOR: Es lindo, pero ¡mira a esas mujeres tan elegantes! Están (4) ___vestidas___
       para ir a bailar.

ROSA: Y las guayaberas[1] blancas que llevan los músicos son bonitas.
       ¿Son (5) ___hechas___ aquí o en Panamá?

FLOR: Aquí, creo. Mira, allí está el restaurante cubano recomendado en la
       guía. Es la una y estoy (6) ___muerta___ de hambre.

ROSA: Voy a aparcar aquí mismo. Las mesas ya están (7) _____ y la
       comida está (8) _____.

Gallos vestidos, la Pequeña Habana

---

[1]Men's shirt typical of the Caribbean, usually with four pockets in front.

12-8 ¡Juego! En grupos de tres personas, desafíense (*challenge each other*) a hacer frases usando participios pasados como adjetivos. Luego, díganse si la respuesta es lógica o no.

MODELO: ESTUDIANTE 1: la computadora *2 oraciones*
ESTUDIANTE 2: *La computadora está rota.*
ESTUDIANTE 3: *Es lógico.* *estar*

Posibles sustantivos	
los auriculares	la música
la impresora	los videos
el lector de libros electrónicos	las fotos
el escáner	el tuit
el ratón	los documentos
los programas	el teclado

Posibles verbos	
abrir	guardar
actualizar	hacer
apagar/encender	instalar
bajar/subir	perder
borrar	preparar
grabar	romper

12-9 La avenida Bergenline, Union City, NJ. Esta avenida comercial, la más larga del estado, tiene más de 300 tiendas y restaurantes. Es también el sitio de celebraciones cubanas y dominicanas por el gran número de hispanos que viven en Nueva Jersey. Hagan el papel de dos amigos/as que estuvieron allí, y pregúntense cómo se sentían. Usen participios pasados para expresarse.

MODELO: ESTUDIANTE 1: *¿Cómo te sentías cuando llegaste a Union City?*
ESTUDIANTE 2: *Me sentía emocionado/a. ¿Y tú?*

cansar	enojar	morir	sorprender
desilusionar	frustrar	preocupar	(bien/mal) vestir
encantar	interesar	preparar	¿...?

¿Cómo te sentías...

1. en el club bailando salsa?
2. cuando perdiste tu tarjeta de crédito?
3. después de ver un concierto de Prince Royce?
4. en la fiesta de unos amigos cubanos?
5. cuando perdiste (*missed*) el tren a Manhattan?
6. cuando cenaste en el restaurante dominicano?

The present perfect indicative

The present perfect in English and Spanish is a *compound* tense because it requires two verbs. In English, you use the present tense of the auxiliary verb *to have* + past participle. In Spanish, you use the present tense of **haber** + *past participle*.

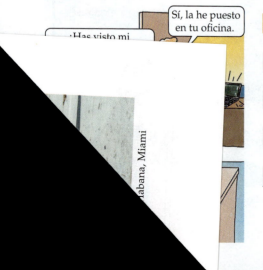

Sí, la he puesto en tu oficina.

¿Has visto mi...

Habana, Miami

	haber	participio pasado	*to have*	past participle
yo	**he**		*I have*	
tú	**has**		*you have*	
Ud.	**ha**	**tomado**	*you (for.) have*	*taken*
él/ella	**ha**	**comido**	*he/she has*	*eaten*
nosotros/as	**hemos**	**vivido**	*we have*	*lived*
vosotros/as	**habéis**		*you (pl.) have*	
Uds.	**han**		*you (for. pl.) have*	
ellos/as	**han**		*they have*	

- In general, use the present perfect to refer to a past action or event that you perceive as having some bearing on the present.

¿Ya **has usado** la impresora?	*Have you already used the printer?*
No. La **he instalado**, pero no la **he usado** todavía.	*No. I've installed it, but I haven't used it yet.*

- Be sure that **haber** agrees with the subject of the sentence. The past participle is invariable in the perfect tense.

Mi jefa me **ha dado** un ratón inalámbrico.	*My boss has given me a wireless mouse.*
Los ayudantes **han preparado** la videoconferencia.	*The assistants have prepared the videoconference.*

- Always place object pronouns and negative words before **haber**; do not insert anything between **haber** and the past participle.

¿Me has grabado el video?	*Have you recorded the video for me?*
No, **no te lo he terminado**.	*No, I haven't finished it for you.*

¡OJO!

- Don't confuse **haber** with **tener**. Use **haber** as an auxiliary verb with the past participle. Use **tener** to mean *to have* or *to own*.

Julia **tiene** muchos aparatos electrónicos, pero nunca **ha almacenado** sus fotos en la nube.	*Julia has many electronic devices, but she has never stored her photos in the cloud.*

Expansión   **More on structure and usage**

Some common expressions used with the present perfect include **alguna vez** (*ever, once*), **ya** (*already*), and **todavía no** (*not yet*).

¿Alguna vez has querido ser astronauta?
Have you ever wanted to be an astronaut?

¿Ya has escuchado toda la música en tu celular?
Have you already listened to all the music on your cell phone?

No, **todavía** no la he escuchado toda.
No, I haven't listened to all of it yet.

ACABAR DE + INFINITIVE

You can use the present tense of **acabar de** + *infinitive* to describe an event that has just happened.

Acabo de compartir mi video.	*I've just shared my video.*

¿Comprendes? Provide the correct form in the present perfect of a logical verb: **almacenar**, **borrar**.

Nosotros (1) _____ los documentos viejos y tú (2) _____ los nuevos en la nube.

Respuestas: 1. hemos borrado; 2. has almacenado

Aplicación

12-10 Cuestiones tecnológicas. Tu amigo siempre te pide ayuda con dudas tecnológicas. Selecciona la respuesta que mejor corresponde a cada duda suya.

1. _____ No encuentro mi lector de libros. ¿Sabes dónde está?

2. _____ Debo mandarle este artículo a mi hermano. ¿Sabes cómo hacerlo?

3. _____ No sé por qué no funciona mi ratón. ¿Crees que está roto?

4. _____ He recibido varias alertas de mi banco. No sé qué está pasando.

5. _____ Mira los comentarios feos que he recibido en esta red social.

6. _____ Me gustaría facilitar el acceso a los medios digitales en zonas rurales. ¿Qué hago?

7. _____ Esta aplicación no funciona.

8. _____ Estoy en el sitio web, pero no encuentro la información que busco. ¿Qué hago ahora?

a. ¿Has entrado al sitio web para ver si hay actividad sospechosa en tu cuenta?

b. ¿Has hecho clic en el hipervínculo que dice: "MÁS INFORMACIÓN"?

c. ¿La has quitado de tu tableta y vuelto a instalar para ver si luego te funciona?

d. ¿Te has puesto en contacto con una comunidad virtual que se interese en el acceso a Internet para gente que vive en el campo?

e. Creo que te está siguiendo un trol. ¿Has notificado al administrador de la aplicación?

f. Es inalámbrico, ¿no? ¿Has cambiado las pilas (*batteries*)?

g. Lo puedes escanear y mandárselo por correo electrónico. ¿Has encendido el escáner?

h. Te he visto leyendo un libro antes de dormirte. Debe estar en tu cama.

12-11 Sandra Cisneros. Esta escritora chicana (*House on Mango Street*, *Caramelo*, *Woman Hollering Creek*) es una de las más importantes de su generación. Aquí tienes un resumen de algunas de sus experiencias.

Paso 1 Lee el resumen y complétalo con la forma del presente perfecto del verbo más lógico.

Sandra Cisneros, de padres mexicanos, nació en Chicago, y durante su vida (1) _____ (subir / vivir) en muchos lugares: en Iowa, en San Antonio, y ahora en San Miguel de Allende, México, donde dice que se siente "en casa". En su vida, (2) _____ (borrar / tener) muchas experiencias que (3) _____ (influir / ver) en sus cuentos, por ejemplo, (4) _____ (imprimido / trabajar) como maestra y consejera para alumnos desertores (*dropouts*), (5) _____ (grabar / servir) como escritora en residencia en universidades donde (6) _____ (dar / dejar) clases de escritura creativa y (7) _____ (contratar / ser) administradora de artes. (8) _____ (diseñar / ganar) muchos premios, por ejemplo, el MacArthur Fellowship Award, el PEN Center USA Literary Award, y en 2016, la National Medal of Arts presentada por el presidente Obama. Finalmente, (9) _____ (despedir / fundar) dos organizaciones que apoyan a escritores jóvenes.

Paso 2 Contesta las preguntas sobre el texto que acabas de leer.

1. ¿Dónde nació y cuál es su nacionalidad?

2. ¿Dónde ha vivido? ¿Dónde vive ahora?

3. ¿Qué trabajos ha tenido?

4. ¿Cómo sabemos que ha tenido éxito (*success*)?

5. ¿Has leído alguna obra suya? ¿Cuál? ¿Te ha gustado?

Paso 3   En parejas, escriban individualmente tres preguntas que les gustaría hacerle a Sandra Cisneros. Túrnense para hacer el papel de Cisneros y contestar las preguntas de su compañero/a. Usen el presente perfecto.

MODELO: ESTUDIANTE 1: *Señorita Cisneros, ¿ha vivido en otras casas en México?*
ESTUDIANTE 2: *Sí. He vivido en la capital…*

12-12   **¿Alguna vez han...?**   En grupos de tres o cuatro, háganse preguntas para saber qué experiencias han tenido con la tecnología. Explíquense qué les ha pasado.

MODELO: perder un documento en la computadora
ESTUDIANTE 1: *¿Alguna vez han perdido un documento en la computadora?*
ESTUDIANTE 2: *No, todavía no he perdido ningún documento.*
ESTUDIANTE 3: *¡Yo sí, he perdido muchos! Por ejemplo, una vez…*

1. borrar un documento sin querer
2. instalar una aplicación maliciosa
3. recibir mensajes provocadores de un trol
4. no poder desinstalar una aplicación
5. subir fotos sin querer a un sitio social

6. quitar tu perfil de un sitio social
7. subir un video a YouTube
8. unirse y después salir de un sitio social
9. hacer clic en un hipervínculo sospechoso
10. ser víctima de fraude electrónico

12-13   **Mis experiencias.**   Túrnense para hablar de experiencias que han tenido y también de experiencias que no han tenido, pero que desean tener.

MODELO: ver
ESTUDIANTE 1: *¿Qué películas has visto este año?*
ESTUDIANTE 2: *Acabo de ver la película que ganó el premio Óscar al Mejor Director, …*
ESTUDIANTE 1: *¿Has visto otras películas dirigidas por él/ella?*
ESTUDIANTE 2: *Sí, ya he visto... / No, todavía no, pero...*

| comer | escribir | hacer | leer | trabajar | visitar |
| conocer | estudiar | ir | salir | ver | volver |

¡Conversemos!

Primero, pregúntate si puedes llevar a cabo las siguientes funciones comunicativas. Después, júntate con dos o tres compañeros/as de clase para presentar las situaciones. Hagan y respondan a por lo menos cuatro preguntas en cada situación.

✓ CAN YOU . . .

WITH YOUR CLASSMATE(S) . . .

☐ discuss technology and ways to communicate?

Situación: En casa.

A ustedes les gusta tener los aparatos más novedosos. Hablen de los que han visto y los que quieren comprar.

Para empezar: *Hoy he visto en un sitio web…*

☐ describe people and things?

Situación: Después de una fiesta en su casa.

Describan a las personas y las cosas que observen en su casa el día después de tener una fiesta. Usen participios pasados como adjetivos.

Para empezar: *Mira, la casa está destruida. Hay platos rotos en el piso…*

☐ talk about what has happened?

Situación: En una cena entre amigos.

A ustedes les gusta contar historias sobre sus experiencias. Hablen de las más interesantes que han tenido. Reaccionen con preguntas y comentarios a lo que les dice su compañero/a.

Para empezar: *He viajado varias veces a...*

[handwritten notes in margin: Answer: Q1: No, no he hecho alguna consulta en ningún foro. Q2: ningún tipo]

Perfiles

12.3 **Learn about gaming and a popular Mexican American pop rock artist**

Mi experiencia

LA TECNOLOGÍA Y EL FUTURO

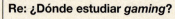

12-14 **Para ti.** ¿Has hecho una consulta alguna vez en algún foro? ¿Qué tipo de consulta has hecho? ¿Te ha servido la respuesta? Lee la consulta que hace un joven argentino en Internet y la respuesta de un estadounidense.

Respuesta.com: Juegos

Jugador Argentina 	**¿Dónde estudiar *gaming*?** Bueno, gente, les digo que tengo 22 años y estoy terminando una carrera corta en sistemas, realmente no quiero continuar con la rama[1], y mi sueño es meterme[2] en el mundo de los videojuegos como *game developer*. Estuve viendo las "carreras" en algunos sitios de cursos virtuales y, además de ser caras, realmente no me parecen nada serias. También estuve viendo la carrera de cine de animación y multimedia, que parece copada[3] y "en teoría" puede ayudar a meterte en el mundo del *gaming*, pero tampoco estoy seguro de cómo son los programas aquí en Argentina para este tipo de cosas. Si me pueden tirar[4] nombres u opiniones, me hacen un gran favor.
Baco EE. UU. 	**Re: ¿Dónde estudiar *gaming*?** ¡Ja! mira, por lo que sé, hay cientos de carreras relacionadas con videojuegos en EE. UU., Japón, Nueva Zelanda y otros. Supongo que buscas una carrera en cine de animación y multimedia, y por ahora me estoy en esa[5]. Recuerda que para dedicarte a la parte artística, no necesitas ser programador. En esa carrera lo más importante es tener título universitario... no es un curso. Estudias mil cosas además de animación que te preparan muy bien, como literatura, guion[6], inglés, música, etc. Por ejemplo, aquí en Los Ángeles (el corazón del cine) hay un programa de diseño de videojuegos que es muy destacado[7], pero solo admiten 50 estudiantes al año. Pero es genial, y un buen camino si tienes éxito[8]. Oye, hablando de caminos, si no conoces la música de Julieta Venegas, vale la pena ver algunos videos suyos. Es una artista que sabe jugar con los efectos especiales.

[1]*branch* [2]*to get involved in* or *to get into*

[3]*cool* (Argentina)

[4]*throw my way*

[5]*that's what I'm involved in*

[6]*script-writing*

[7]*outstanding*

[8]*you are successful*

12-15 **En su opinión.** Trabajen en parejas para contestar las preguntas.

1. ¿Qué información busca Jugador en el foro?

2. ¿Creen que la respuesta de Baco fue buena? ¿Por qué?

3. Según él, ¿es necesario ser programador?

4. ¿Es competitivo el programa de diseño donde vive Baco? ¿Por qué?

5. ¿Se ofrece un programa de diseño de videojuegos en tu universidad? ¿Conocen ustedes a alguien que lo siga?

Mi música

"ESE CAMINO" (JULIETA VENEGAS, MÉXICO/EE. UU.)

Julieta Venegas se siente tan cómoda en Estados Unidos (donde nació), como en México (donde se crió y primero se estableció como artista). La compositora, cantante y activista es una de las artistas hispanas más reconocidas a nivel mundial. Ha apoyado varias causas sociales, por las que ha sido nombrada Embajadora de Buena Voluntad por la UNICEF en México, y también Embajadora Cultural de Buena Voluntad por el Consejo de Ministros de Las Mujeres de Centroamérica. La canción "Ese camino" aparece en *Algo sucede*, el álbum que ganó el Grammy Latino en 2016 por Mejor álbum pop/rock.

ANTES DE VER Y ESCUCHAR

12-16 El camino de la vida. Piensa en cinco cosas que has hecho en tu vida o eventos que han ocurrido desde tu niñez. Describe cuáles son los más importantes para ti personalmente.

> **MODELO:** *Durante mi vida, ha habido muchos inventos tecnológicos, por ejemplo, el teléfono inteligente…*

PARA VER Y ESCUCHAR

12-17 Mirar atrás. Cuando miramos atrás lo que hemos hecho y lo que nos ha pasado, es posible que sintamos nostalgia por una época más inocente. Al ver el video y escuchar la canción, toma nota de los sentimientos de la cantante. ¿Está triste, alegre, sentimental? ¿Crees que quiere ir para atrás o seguir adelante? ¿Por qué?

> ⦿ **Busca:** Julieta Venegas Ese camino video; Julieta Venegas Ese camino letra

DESPUÉS DE VER Y ESCUCHAR

12-18 Traigo una historia en mí. En parejas, conversen sobre cómo esta frase en la canción puede ser la historia que trae ella, y cómo se compara con la de ustedes. ¿Creen que han tenido algunas experiencias en común? ¿Cuáles son?

> **MODELO:** *Ella ha vivido en EE. UU. y México. Nosotros/as…*

12-19 Sueños para el futuro. Ponte en los zapatos de un/a niño/a que tenga sueños para el futuro. ¿Cómo brilla tu camino? ¿Cómo vas a realizar tus sueños?

> **MODELO:** *Mi sueño es ser una estrella de cine. Voy a estudiar teatro y algún día me va a descubrir un director famoso…*

12.2 Segunda parte

Vocabulario

12.4 Discuss environmental challenges

El medio ambiente

¿Cómo proteger nuestro futuro? Los jóvenes hispanos de hoy se preocupan por **el medio ambiente**. A pesar de los amplios **recursos naturales, el desarrollo** industrial y la falta de protección por los gobiernos **perjudican** el mundo para futuras generaciones.

SALVADOR: **Los desechos** de **la energía nuclear** perjudicarán los lagos y los ríos.

GONZALO: ¡Estás loco! **La planta nuclear** nos **asegurará** muchos años de energía económica.

PACO: ¡Están equivocados! **La energía alternativa** es nuestro futuro.

CRISTINA: ¡Ridículo! Hay todavía grandes reservas de **combustible fósil**.

¿Comprendes? Complete each sentence with the correct word: **alternativa, desechos, fósiles, nucleares.**

Cristina prefiere usar los combustibles (1) _____. Paco prefiere la energía (2) _____. A Gonzalo le gustan las plantas (3) _____. Salvador se preocupa por los (4) _____.

Respuestas: 1. fósiles; 2. alternativa; 3. nucleares; 4. desechos

Vocabulario

Nuestro mundo y el medio ambiente	Our world and the environment
el bosque (pluvial)	(rain) forest
el carbón	coal
el combustible fósil	fossil fuel
el desarrollo (sostenible)	(sustainable) development
la energía (alternativa/solar/verde)	(alternative/solar/green) energy
las especies (en peligro de extinción)	(endangered) species
la naturaleza	nature
el reciclaje	recycling
el recurso natural	natural resource
la reforestación	reforestation
la selva	jungle

Amenazas al medio ambiente	Threats to our environment
el cambio climático	climate change
la contaminación	pollution
la deforestación	deforestation
el derrame (de petróleo)	(oil) spill
los desechos (nucleares)	(nuclear) waste
el envase (de aluminio / de plástico / de vidrio)	(aluminum/plastic/glass) container
la escasez	shortage
la fábrica	factory
el humo	smoke
la inundación	flood

Amenazas al medio ambiente	Threats to our environment
el oleoducto	(oil) pipeline
la planta nuclear	nuclear plant
los pesticidas	pesticides
la radioactividad	radioactivity
la sequía	drought

Verbos	Verbs
asegurar	to ensure
conservar	to conserve, to preserve
consumir	to consume
contaminar	to contaminate, to pollute
multar	to fine
perjudicar	to harm
proteger (j)	to protect
reciclar	to recycle
tirar	to throw (away, out)

Variaciones

- You will hear **la deforestación** and **la reforestación** in Latin America, and **la despoblación** and **la repoblación forestal** in Spain.

Letras y sonidos

The consonants *t* and *d*

In Spanish, the letter **t** sounds like the *t* in English *stop*.

Hard **t**:   te-lé-fo-no   tra-í-do   vuel-to   au-to-má-ti-co

The letter **d** in Spanish creates one of two sounds, depending on the context. After a pause, or the letters **n** or **l**, the letter **d** sounds like the *d* in English *den*.

Hard **d**:   dis-co   un-di-se-ño   don-de   el-di-se-ño   suel-do

In all other contexts, especially between vowels, the sound is softer, like the *th* in English *then* or *father*.

Soft **d**:   los-di-se-ños   me-di-da   le-í-do   ver-dad   la red

In sum, Spanish has the same three sounds found at the beginning of the English words *ten* (but with less air expelled), *den* (hard **d**), and *then* (soft **d**). However, in Spanish, all three of these sounds are created with the tongue tip behind the upper front teeth only.

Aplicación

12-20 ¿Qué solución hay? Selecciona la solución que mejor corresponde a cada problema.

1. __F__ la contaminación del aire
2. __E__ la deforestación
3. __a__ basura en el parque
4. __h__ los desechos industriales
5. __C__ la escasez de energía durante el día
6. __B__ una sequía
7. __d__ envases de plástico en la calle
8. __g__ un derrame de petróleo de un oleoducto

a. poner más basureros en el parque
b. conservar agua
c. montar paneles solares *solar panel*
d. establecer programas de reciclaje
e. plantar más árboles
f. usar un programa de inspección de las emisiones de automóviles *program*
g. llamar inmediatamente a la agencia de protección del medio ambiente *protection agency*
h. multar a las fábricas *find factory*

Cultura en vivo

Spain is the world's fifth largest producer of wind power and, with its ample sunshine, one of the most advanced countries in the development of solar energy. The Spanish government has committed to achieve a target of 20% of primary energy from renewable sources by 2020, one of the highest in the European Union. Costa Rica has managed months at a time running only on renewable energy. What are the goals in the U.S. and Canada?

12-21 En las noticias. Completa cada titular (*headline*) con la forma correcta de un verbo lógico.

MODELO: La ciudad de San Francisco __*recicla*__ el 80 por ciento de sus desechos

conservar	consumir	contaminar	multar	proteger

1. Accidente en plataforma petrolífera _____ las aguas del Golfo de México

2. Californianos _____ agua después de meses de sequía

3. La Agencia de Protección del Medio Ambiente _____ a una mina de carbón por desechos tóxicos

4. Manifestantes insisten en que el gobierno _____ el medio ambiente

5. EE. UU. _____ más energía por persona que cualquier otro país del mundo

(handwritten top: — Miedo ambientes)

))) **12-22 Un anuncio público.** Escucha el anuncio de la radio y selecciona la opción que mejor completa cada oración.

1. El anuncio habla de un programa...
   a. del gobierno.
   b. de una organización no gubernamental.
   c. de la ONU.

2. Los participantes son...
   a. niños y jóvenes.
   b. ancianos.
   c. amas de casa (*housewives*).

3. Van a trabajar en la limpieza de las playas y...
   a. el control de los pesticidas.
   b. el reciclaje.
   c. la reforestación.

4. El trabajo va a ser durante....
   a. las vacaciones.
   b. el año escolar.
   c. la Semana Santa.

5. Según el anuncio, el proyecto es...
   a. pagado por una empresa estadounidense.
   b. la obligación de todos.
   c. una manera de ganar dinero.

12-23 Un plan de acción. ¿Qué problemas y soluciones ven para el futuro? *(handwritten: partner:)*

Paso 1 Trabajen en parejas para elegir cinco de los problemas más importantes para el futuro del mundo. Si hay uno que no está en la lista, añádanlo.

(handwritten: Select Bigger problem-to small · select 5 important ones.)

MODELO: ESTUDIANTE 1: *En tu opinión, ¿cuáles son los problemas más importantes para el futuro del mundo?*
(handwritten: Write Solution)
ESTUDIANTE 2: *Creo que el número uno es... porque...*

5 la escasez de agua
___ el sobreconsumo de los recursos naturales
___ el sobreuso de pesticidas
4 la contaminación del aire
___ la contaminación nuclear

2 la sobrepoblación *(handwritten: deberíamos porque apoyar programas de anticoncepivos)*
___ las especies en peligro de extinción
___ la deforestación
1 el cambio climático *(handwritten: debemos solution, apoyar la industria de energia renovable.)*
___ ¿...?

Paso 2 Propongan soluciones a los problemas que identificaron en el **Paso 1**. A continuación hay algunas sugerencias.

(handwritten: can use or use your own)

MODELO: *Para combatir la deforestación, los gobiernos del mundo deben...*

(handwritten: propongo que)

aumentar el precio de la energía
apoyar (*support*) la industria de energía renovable
apoyar programas de anticonceptivos
desarrollar nuevos recursos de energía
implementar un sistema de transporte público
limitar el número de autos por familia
limitar el consumo de energía por persona

mejorar la economía de la región
montar una campaña publicitaria
multar a... *(handwritten: matamos las fábricas → Sugiero que multamos a las fabricas)*
prohibir el uso de carbón para generar la electricidad
proponer leyes más fuertes
¿...?

(handwritten bottom: Tal vez podríamos limitar la cantidad de uso de agua por persona)

Los nuevos teléfonos serán aún más potentes.

Estructuras

12.5 **Discuss future and contingent actions, and speculate on events**

The future tense

We use the future tense in Spanish, as in English, to communicate future actions and events. The English equivalent is *will* + verb.

¿Quién **protegerá** el medio ambiente?	*Who will protect the environment?*
Creo que los pesticidas **contaminarán** el río.	*I think the pesticides will pollute the river.*

- Form the future tense with the same set of endings for all verbs. For regular verbs, attach the endings to the infinitive (do not drop the **-ar**, **-er**, or **-ir**). Note that all endings, except for the **nosotros/as** forms, have written accent marks.

	tomar	**comer**	**vivir**
yo	tomar**é**	comer**é**	vivir**é**
tú	tomar**ás**	comer**ás**	vivir**ás**
Ud.	tomar**á**	comer**á**	vivir**á**
él/ella	tomar**á**	comer**á**	vivir**á**
nosotros/as	tomar**emos**	comer**emos**	vivir**emos**
vosotros/as	tomar**éis**	comer**éis**	vivir**éis**
Uds.	tomar**án**	comer**án**	vivir**án**
ellos/as	tomar**án**	comer**án**	vivir**án**

- Form the future of irregular verbs by adding the future endings to an irregular stem. There are three categories of irregular stems.

  1. Drop *two* letters to form the future stem.

decir	**dir-**	diré, dirás, ...		hacer	**har-**	haré, harás, ...

  2. Drop the **e** of the infinitive ending to form the future stem.

haber	**habr-**	habrá		querer	**querr-**	querré, querrás, ...
poder	**podr-**	podré, podrás, ...		saber	**sabr-**	sabré, sabrás, ...

  3. Replace the **e** or the **i** of the infinitive ending with **d** to form the future stem.

poner	**pondr-**	pondré, pondrás, ...		tener	**tendr-**	tendré, tendrás, ...
salir	**saldr-**	saldré, saldrás, ...		venir	**vendr-**	vendré, vendrás, ...

Haremos un estudio sobre la contaminación del agua.	*We will do a study on water pollution.*
Habrá menos humo con la nueva fábrica.	*There will be less smoke with the new factory.*
Los técnicos **vendrán** a las ocho.	*The technicians will come at eight.*

- You can also express conjecture or speculation in the present by using the future tense. In English, this use is the equivalent of *probably, can, may, must, I wonder*, etc.

¿Dónde **estará** mi celular?	*I wonder where my cell phone might be.*
Estará en tu mochila.	*It's probably in your backpack.*
¿Qué hora **será**?	*What time can it be?*
Serán las seis.	*It must be six o'clock.*

La computadora estará pensando.

A FEW THINGS TO REMEMBER…

- You can also express the future with the present tense of **ir a** + *infinitive*.

  Voy a consumir menos energía.　　*I am going to consume less energy.*

  ¿Vas a tirar los envases en el　　*Are you going to throw the containers in*
  basurero?　　　　　　　　　　　*the trash can?*

- You can use the present tense to express the immediate future in Spanish.

  Mañana **reclicamos** los envases.　　*Tomorrow we will recycle (are recycling)*
  　　　　　　　　　　　　　　　　the cans.

  Termino mi trabajo esta tarde.　　*I will finish my paper/work this afternoon.*

- But, to express the idea of willingness, use verbs like **querer** or the simple present tense.

  ¿Quieres ayudarme con el　　*Will you help me with the recycling?*
  reciclaje?

  ¿Me **traes** el informe sobre la　　*Will you bring me the report on the*
  planta nuclear?　　　　　　　*nuclear plant?*

¿Comprendes? Complete the paragraph with the correct form of a logical verb: **poder, ser**.

Cuando termine mis estudios (1) _____ ingeniera ambiental y (2) _____ trabajar en una empresa que proteja el medio ambiente.

Respuestas: 1. seré; 2. podré

Aplicación

12-24 Óscar Muñoz, jefe ejecutivo. Óscar Muñoz es uno de solo diez jefes ejecutivos hispanos que dirigen una empresa *Fortune 500.* Cuando fue nombrado a su posición en United Airlines, hizo varias promesas y predicciones para cambiar el pronóstico financiero de la aerolínea.

Paso 1 Escribe la forma correcta en el futuro del verbo entre paréntesis.

1. Nosotros _elevaremos_ (elevar) el estatus de la aerolínea entre los consumidores.

2. (Yo) _estableceré_ (establecer) un sitio para recibir quejas y consejos para mejorar la aerolínea.

3. (Yo) _escucharé_ (escuchar) a todos los que me quieran hablar.

4. Los aviones ~~llegan~~ _llegarán_ (llegar) a tiempo.

5. (Nosotros) _tendremos_ (tener) una nueva clase de pasaje económico.

6. Los técnicos _instalaran_ (instalar) wifi en todos los aviones.

7. (Nosotros) _mejoraremos_ (mejorar) la moral del personal.

8. (Nosotros) _negociaremos_ (negociar) un mejor contrato con los empleados de los sindicatos.

Óscar Muñoz con miembros de Team USA en ruta a Río de Janeiro.

Paso 2 En parejas, hablen de cuáles de estas iniciativas les parecen las mejores para (1) los pasajeros, (2) los empleados y (3) ustedes, personalmente. Explíquense sus razones.

MODELO: *En mi opinión, es importante que los aviones lleguen a tiempo porque…*

12-25 Una entrevista con Ecoverde. Isela tiene una entrevista con una empresa que se dedica a proteger el medio ambiente. Completa de una manera lógica la conversación entre ella y el director de personal, usando el futuro de los verbos a continuación.

*Futuro
Verbo*

decir	informar	poder	tener
haber	llamar	saber	trabajar

ISELA: Si no le importa, tengo algunas preguntas sobre el puesto. ¿Me puede decir cuántas horas (1) _trabajaré_ (yo)?

DIRECTOR: Sí, los nuevos investigadores trabajan ocho horas diarias.

ISELA: ¿(2) _Podré_ (yo) trabajar con alguno de los investigadores veteranos?

DIRECTOR: Sí, (3) _habrá_ oportunidades para trabajar con varias personas con experiencia. Naturalmente, los nuevos (4) _tendrá_ que ayudar a los veteranos.

ISELA: ¿Cuándo (5) _sabré_ (yo) su decisión?

DIRECTOR: La (6) _llamaré_ (yo) por teléfono mañana por la mañana.

ISELA: ¿Usted me (7) _dirá_ entonces cuánto me van a pagar?

DIRECTOR: Sí, yo (8) le _informaré_ sobre su sueldo cuando tomemos nuestra decisión.

12-26A ¡Necesito información! Vean las situaciones y túrnense para hacer conjeturas (*guesses*) sobre por qué serán. Respondan de una manera lógica para cada situación. **Estudiante B:** por favor, ve al **Apéndice 1**, página A-15.

MODELO: Recibes una llamada por teléfono a las siete de la mañana.
ESTUDIANTE A: *Será algo urgente de mi jefa.*
ESTUDIANTE B: *Tendrás que salir para la oficina ahora mismo.*

Situaciones	Conjeturas
1. Hay humo en la oficina.	• (estar) fallando un oleoducto
3. Hay algunos electricistas en el techo (*roof*) de tu casa.	• (ser) por la sequía
5. Está lloviendo mucho y hay agua en el piso.	• (tener) un virus
7. Se han plantado muchos árboles en las áreas donde minan carbón.	• ellos (hacer) mantenimiento rutinario de la planta

12-27 ¿Qué harán? Ustedes son administradores/as para una agencia que protege el medio ambiente. Hablen sobre qué deberán hacer si ocurren estas situaciones.

MODELO: ESTUDIANTE 1: *Hay un derrame del oleoducto cerca de una escuela.*
ESTUDIANTE 2: *Tendremos que… Los estudiantes…*

1. Necesitan ingenieros que entiendan la energía nuclear.

2. Los científicos predicen que el cambio climático va a resultar en tormentas más severas.

3. Según los estudios, hay varias especies en peligro de extinción en su estado.

4. Parece que los pesticidas agrícolas han perjudicado los pájaros en su región.

5. Hay una empresa química que pide permiso para construir una fábrica cerca de una población urbana.

The conditional tense

We use the conditional tense, both in Spanish and in English, to communicate an action that is conditional upon another action, or an action that is future to a past action (*would/could/should* + action).

- Use the conditional to say what you would do under certain circumstances.

  ¿Qué **harías** para mejorar el medio ambiente? ¿**Pondrías** paneles solares en tu casa?

  What would you do to improve the environment? Would you put solar panels on your house?

- You can also use the conditional to refer to an event that is future to another past event.

  Nos dijeron que **multarían** a la fábrica que contaminaba el agua.

  They told us (that) they would fine the factory that polluted the water.

- You can use the verb **deber** in the conditional tense to mean *should* + infinitive.

  Deberías conservar recursos.

  You should conserve resources.

- You can also use the conditional to express probability or speculate about a past event.

  ¿A qué hora **sería** la conferencia de prensa?

  I wonder what time the press conference was (at).

  Sería a las cuatro.

  It was probably at four.

- Form the conditional in Spanish in a similar manner as the future. Add the **-er/-ir** imperfect endings (**-ía, ías, ía, íamos, íais, ían**) to the infinitive of regular verbs or the irregular stem.

	tomar	comer	vivir
yo	tomar**ía**	comer**ía**	vivir**ía**
tú	tomar**ías**	comer**ías**	vivir**ías**
Ud.	tomar**ía**	comer**ía**	vivir**ía**
él/ella	tomar**ía**	comer**ía**	vivir**ía**
nosotros/as	tomar**íamos**	comer**íamos**	vivir**íamos**
vosotros/as	tomar**íais**	comer**íais**	vivir**íais**
Uds.	tomar**ían**	comer**ían**	vivir**ían**
ellos/as	tomar**ían**	comer**ían**	vivir**ían**

- The conditional has the same irregular stems as the future.

decir	**dir-**	**diría, dirías, ...**	saber	**sabr-**	**sabría, sabrías, ...**
hacer	**har-**	**haría, harías, ...**	poner	**pondr-**	**pondría, pondrías, ...**
haber	**habr-**	**habría**	salir	**saldr-**	**saldría, saldrías, ...**
poder	**podr-**	**podría, podrías, ...**	tener	**tendr-**	**tendría, tendrías, ...**
querer	**querr-**	**querría, querrías, ...**	venir	**vendr-**	**vendría, vendrías, ...**

¿Comprendes? Provide the correct form of a logical verb in the conditional: **comprar, usar**.

Las empresas automovilísticas prometieron que los modelos nuevos (1) _____ menos combustible. Por eso, decidí que no (2) _____ uno eléctrico este año.

Respuestas: 1. usarían; 2. compraría

Aplicación

12-28 **Profesor, hidrogeólogo y astronauta.** Joseph Acaba fue la primera persona de origen puertorriqueño en llegar a ser astronauta de la NASA. Antes de su primer vuelo al espacio, completaría varias metas suyas y planearía otras.

Paso 1   Completa las oraciones con el verbo que mejor corresponde en el condicional.

asignaría	estudiaría	se quedaría	tendría
se dedicaría	gustaría	serviría	viajaría

1. De joven, dijo que algún día sería astronauta y que _viajaría_ al espacio.
2. Le gustaban mucho las ciencias y decidió que _estudiaría_ para ser geólogo.
3. Antes de tratar de ser astronauta, pensó que le _gustaría_ servir en el Cuerpo de Paz en la República Dominicana.
4. Al regresar a EE. UU., la NASA decidió que lo _asignaría_ al equipo de la estación espacial.
5. Sus entrenadores le dijeron que _serviría_ como ingeniero de vuelo a bordo de la Estación Espacial Internacional.
6. En su misión, _tendría_ que instalar paneles solares en la estación espacial. _space station_
7. En su primer viaje, _se quedaría_ en el espacio por cuatro meses.
8. Al volver a la Tierra, Joseph Acaba decidió que _se dedicaría_ a promover el estudio de las matemáticas y las ciencias entre estudiantes y maestros estadounidenses.

Paso 2   Contesta las preguntas siguientes sobre el texto que acabas de leer.

1. ¿Quién es Joseph Acaba y cuál es su profesión?
2. ¿Qué dijo de joven?
3. ¿Dónde sirvió en el Cuerpo de Paz?
4. ¿Qué haría en su misión al espacio?
5. ¿A qué se dedicaría al volver a la Tierra?
6. ¿Te gustaría ser como Joseph Acaba? Explica.

Presencia hispana

José Hernández is another NASA astronaut. As the son of migrant farm workers, he spent much of his youth picking fruit alongside his parents and siblings, traveling every year from Mexico to Southern California and back. Despite not learning English until he was 12, he excelled in school and earned scholarships to attend college. In space, he was part of a successful mission to perform repairs on the space platform and was the first astronaut to send bilingual Twitter updates from space. His first: **"¡Espero [que] la cosecha de mi sueño sirva como inspiración a todos! Acabo de configurar las computadoras. ¡Buenas noches!"**

12-29A ¡Necesito información! Hagan los papeles de periodista investigador/a (estudiante A) y jefe/a ejecutivo/a de una planta nuclear (estudiante B). Individualmente, preparen sus preguntas y sus respuestas para la entrevista. **Jefe/a ejecutivo/a**: por favor, ve al **Apéndice 1**, página A-15.

> MODELO: **reciclar** los desechos de la planta nuclear
> PERIODISTA INVESTIGADOR/A: *Usted dijo que reciclaría los desechos de la planta nuclear.*
> JEFE/A EJECUTIVO/A: *Tiene razón. Pero también dije que este proyecto tomaría su tiempo.*

Estudiante A: Periodista investigador/a
Usted dijo que...

1. **ser** una planta nuclear ejemplar
2. **proteger** la naturaleza alrededor de la planta
3. **pagar** las multas de la EPA
4. no **contaminar** el agua del mar
5. **trabajar** en la reforestación de las montañas
6. **permitirnos** filmar dentro de su fábrica

12-30 Lo que harían en estas situaciones. Trabajen en parejas para decidir qué harían en estas situaciones. Usen el condicional en sus respuestas.

> MODELO: Su computadora ha fallado y se han perdido algunos documentos importantes.
> ESTUDIANTE 1: *Llamaría a un técnico.*
> ESTUDIANTE 2: *Instalaría un programa antivirus.*

Algunas acciones				
buscar	decir	escribir	multar	protestar
consumir	eliminar	hacer	proteger	tener

1. Hace un año que no llueve en el bosque pluvial del Amazonas.
2. El proveedor de electricidad afirmó que iba a usar carbón para generar energía.
3. Cada año hay más especies en peligro de extinción.
4. Según la agencia NOAA, la temperatura del planeta ha subido un grado centígrado en los últimos diez años.
5. Si llega un huracán de categoría 5, va a haber graves inundaciones en la costa.
6. Una empresa de petróleo va a construir un oleoducto que pasará por tierras indígenas.

El mono aullador está en peligro de extinción.

¡Conversemos!

Primero, pregúntate si puedes llevar a cabo las siguientes funciones comunicativas. Después, júntate con dos o tres compañeros/as de clase para presentar las situaciones. Hagan y respondan a por lo menos cuatro preguntas en cada situación.

✓ CAN YOU . . .

☐ discuss environmental challenges?

☐ discuss what will happen in the future?

☐ speculate on actions?

☐ speculate about future events?

WITH YOUR CLASSMATE(S) . . .

Situación: Una conversación.

Túrnense para hablar de los problemas del medio ambiente que consideran los más importantes hoy en día. Usen palabras y expresiones del **Vocabulario**.

Para empezar: *Creo que el cambio climático es uno de los problemas más grandes que tenemos que solucionar porque...*

Situación: Una discusión sobre el medio ambiente.

Túrnense para contarse lo que pasará si no protegemos el medio ambiente.

Para empezar: *En el futuro, tendremos que proteger los espacios verdes, los ríos y los lagos...*

Situación: Una campaña.

Túrnense para contarse lo que harían para mejorar el medio ambiente. Usen palabras y expresiones del **Vocabulario** y los verbos en el condicional.

Para empezar: *Trabajaría para reducir las emisiones de las plantas de carbón...*

Situación: Predicciones.

Túrnense para contarse qué dijo o prometió la gente que pasaría en el futuro.

Para empezar: *Mis padres dijeron que yo estudiaría medicina. Mis profesores dijeron que estudiaría arte, pero yo les dije que sería ingeniero...*

Club cultura

12.6 Gather information

EE. UU.: Los medios de comunicación en español

Estrategia para ver

Gather information. When you don't know much about a topic, your purpose is to learn as much as you can in order to be able to speak about it afterward. As you watch and listen, try to record at least three pieces of information you didn't know previously.

ANTES DE VER EL VIDEO

12-31 Los medios de comunicación. Escribe una lista de tres medios de comunicación que usas todos los días. De estos, ¿cuál crees que es el más importante para la comunidad hispana en Estados Unidos? ¿Cuál podría ser el más útil para mejorar tu comprensión de la lengua? ¿Con cuál has tenido alguna experiencia?

AL VER EL VIDEO

12-32 ¿Qué medios de comunicación? Al ver el video, anota lo siguiente.

1. De los medios de comunicación que escribiste en la actividad anterior, ¿cuáles se mencionan en el video?

2. Según la presentadora, ¿cuáles pueden ayudarte a aprender español?

3. ¿Cuántas estaciones de radio hay en EE. UU.?

4. ¿Qué es Buenavisión?

5. ¿Por qué es importante?

6. ¿Cuáles de estos puntos no sabías antes de ver el video?

DESPUÉS DE VER EL VIDEO

12-33 En tus propias palabras. Usa tus respuestas a la Actividad **12-32** para escribir un párrafo sobre el contenido del video. Incluye el tema, la información que aprendiste, la importancia y una conclusión personal.

12.3 Nuestro mundo

Panoramas

12.7 Identify and research some important Hispanic Americans

Los hispanos en Estados Unidos

La meta de la Hispanic Heritage Foundation es identificar, inspirar, preparar y posicionar a líderes hispanos en el salón de clase, la comunidad y el trabajo. Cada año premia a algunos miembros de la comunidad por sus logros (*achievements*) en las artes, los deportes, las ciencias, la tecnología y el liderazgo. Aquí hay algunos de ellos que han recibido este honor.

El doctor **Pedro "Joe" Greer, Jr.**, médico y administrador universitario de herencia cubana, ganador de la Presidential Medal of Freedom, el MacArthur Fellowship Award y el premio Great Floridian. Sirve como miembro de la junta directiva de Comic Relief, una organización que recauda fondos para personas sin hogar (*homeless*).

Monika Mantilla, Presidenta y Jefa Ejecutiva de Altura Capital, de herencia colombiana, una de las más prominentes figuras y líder en la comunidad financiera latina.

Óscar Jerome Hijuelos novelista de herencia cubana; el primer escritor hispano en ganar el premio Pulitzer de ficción por *The Mambo Kings*, la que después se adaptó al cine.

Richard Alfred Tapia, matemático y profesor de herencia mexicana, y promotor de las ciencias para las minorías no representadas, ganador de la National Medal of Science.

Ileana Ros Lehtinen, de herencia cubana, la primera mujer hispana electa al Congreso de EE. UU. y hasta su jubilación en 2018, la mujer que llevó más tiempo en el Congreso.

América Ferrera, actriz de herencia hondureña (*Real Women Have Curves*, *Ugly Betty*, *Superstore*), ganadora de premios Emmy, Golden Globe y Screen Actors Guild.

Los hispanos en Estados Unidos

Hispanos en EE. UU.[1]:	57 millones
Oficialmente bilingüe:	Puerto Rico
Hablan español en casa:	73%
Son competentes en inglés:	89%
Les importa proteger el medio ambiente[2]:	93%

[1]Source: Pew Hispanic Center
[2]Source: latinodecisions

12-34 Identifica. Selecciona la opción correcta según la información de **Panoramas**.

artes	congresista	líderes
ciencias	liderazgo	minorías

1. El propósito de la Hispanic Heritage Foundation es identificar, inspirar, preparar y posicionar a _____ hispanos en el salón de clase, la comunidad y el trabajo.

2. La fundación honra los campos de las artes, los deportes, las _____ y el liderazgo.

3. Ileana Ros Lehtinen era una _____ y ha recibido muchos reconocimientos.

4. Óscar Hijuelos recibió el premio de la HHF en las _____.

5. Richard Alfred Tapia promueve las ciencias para las _____ no representadas.

6. Monika Mantilla lo recibió en el campo del _____.

12-35 Desafío. Identifica esta información según el mapa y los datos estadísticos.

1. el número de hispanos en EE. UU.

2. si están a favor o en contra de la protección del medio ambiente

3. las lenguas oficiales de Puerto Rico

4. el porcentaje de hispanos que son competentes en inglés

12-36 Investigación: Hispanos en EE. UU. Selecciona otra persona honrada por la Hispanic Hertitage Foundation, por ejemplo, **Isabel Allende** (novelista), **Pedro Martínez** (beisbolista), **Salma Hayek** (actriz), **Sonia Sotomayor** (jueza), **Luis von Ahn** (científico, profesor, inventor), **Guillermo del Toro** (cineasta), **Julia Álvarez** (novelista, cuentista, poeta), **Gina Rodríguez** (bailadora de salsa, actriz), **Soledad O'Brien** (corresponsal, productora), **Prince Royce** (cantante y compositor), **Óscar de la Hoya** (boxeador), **Eduardo Padrón** (educador). Usa el modelo para escribir un resumen de tu investigación, y prepárate para presentarlo a la clase. Debes incluir:

- su nombre y su herencia hispana
- su profesión y dónde vive
- por qué fue honrado/a
- una foto representativa

Busca: (Prince Royce, etc.) premio Hispanic Heritage

MODELO: *Tony Jiménez, de herencia costarricense, es el fundador y jefe ejecutivo de MicroTech, una empresa que ayuda a veteranos deshabilitados. La empresa, situada en Virginia, tiene oficinas por todo el mundo. En 2016, el señor Jiménez recibió el premio de tecnología, no solo por sus logros en la tecnología, sino también por ser veterano, innovador, líder y emprendedor...*

Páginas

12.8 Look for the main idea and supporting evidence

El cambio climático es en serio para la comunidad latina

Estrategia para leer

Look for the main idea and supporting evidence. When reading an essay or article, you can expect to identify the main idea, followed by evidence to support it. Be sure to examine the evidence to see if it advances the argument of the essay. Finally, is there sufficient information in the supporting details to convince you as a reader?

ANTES DE LEER

12-37 La idea principal. Lee el título y el primer párrafo e identifica la idea principal del artículo.

a. El cambio climático amenaza las costas de la Florida.

b. El cambio climático afecta especialmente a los hispanos.

c. El gobierno debe tomar medidas para proteger el medio ambiente.

AL LEER

12-38 ¿Qué evidencia? Sigue los pasos para completar esta actividad.

Paso 1 Escanea los primeros párrafos para identificar una declaración que apoye la idea principal. ¿Te parece evidencia sólida u opinión del escritor? ¿Por qué?

Paso 2 Sigue leyendo el artículo e identifica otras declaraciones que apoyen la idea principal. ¿Cuál es la más sólida, en tu opinión?

LA OPINIÓN DEL PUEBLO

El cambio climático es en serio para la comunidad latina

REYNALDO SANTOS
ReynaldoSantos@laopiniondelpueblo.com

Residentes de Miami Beach tratan de protegerse de las lluvias torrenciales.

Un estudio reciente publicado por el Consejo para la Defensa de Recursos Naturales (NRDC) y Voces Verdes informa sobre las amenazas que se presentan particularmente a la comunidad hispana, y cómo pueden colaborar para mejorar su futuro. En su investigación, han tomado en cuenta datos sobre el clima, la salud, la demografía y la opinión pública.

El estudio afirma que la comunidad hispana está creciendo[1] no solo en tamaño[2] sino también en influencia. En números, se predice que para el año 2060, será un 29 por ciento de la populació del país, pero que además, estará cada vez más presente en el mundo de la política y los negocios, por lo que su voz contará aún más que hoy.

Del estudio, es evidente que la mayoría de los hispanos en EE. UU. espera que el gobierno no solo se encargue[3] de limitar las emisiones de dióxido de carbono, sino que también tome medidas concretas para frenar[4] el cambio climático.

[1]*growing* [2]*size*

[3]*take responsibility*
[4]*slow down*

Las razones por su preocupación son evidentes: los hispanos son especialmente vulnerables a las amenazas del clima: el calor, la contaminación del aire y del agua, los pesticidas y las inundaciones.

Para empezar, unos 24 millones viven en las 15 ciudades de EE. UU. con la mayor contaminación del aire. Además, en el estado de la Florida, un 40 por ciento vive en lugares más amenazados por las inundaciones por las mareas[5] altas.

[5]*tides*

Los que trabajan al aire libre enfrentan[6] el calor extremo, y los que trabajan en la agricultura, también son afectados por los pesticidas que se usan. Y la combinación de calor y humedad son condiciones ideales para la proliferación del mosquito *Aedes aegypti*, que transmite el zika, el dengue y la chikunguya.

[6]*face*

Para colmo[7], los hispanos, especialmente los indocumentados, tienen menor acceso al seguro y al cuidado médico.

[7]*To top it all*

Pero estos desafíos también le presentan oportunidades a la comunidad hispana. Por ejemplo, la industria de la energía renovable sigue creciendo, lo que creará empleos bien remunerados[8] a la vez que disminuye el uso del combustible fósil. Además, la voz de la comunidad hispana seguirá creciendo y tendrá más y más influencia al nivel local, estatal y nacional. Para concluir, el futuro dependerá no solo de los avances tecnológicos, sino también de la colaboración de la comunidad.

[8]*paid*

DESPUÉS DE LEER

12-39 ¿Apoya la idea principal? Indica con **Sí** o **No** si estas declaraciones presentan o no presentan evidencia para apoyar la idea principal.

1. _____ Hubo un estudio de una organización sin fines de lucro (*nonprofit*) que presenta resultados sobre las opiniones de la comunidad hispana.

2. _____ Según el estudio, los hispanos creen qué el gobierno es responsable de proteger el medio ambiente.

3. _____ Muchos hispanos viven en zonas del país afectadas por el cambio climático.

4. _____ Muchos hispanos padecen de zika, una enfermedad contagiosa.

5. _____ Muchos hispanos trabajan al aire libre donde les afecta más el calor, la contaminación del aire y los pesticidas.

6. _____ Muchos hispanos viven en ciudades donde hay peligro de inundaciones.

7. _____ El gobierno subvenciona (*subsidizes*) el seguro médico de los trabajadores indocumentados.

12-40 En tus propias palabras. Escribe un párrafo para resumir el artículo y dar tu opinión sobre lo que has leído. ¿Ha presentado el escritor un argumento sólido? ¿Te ha convencido del problema que existe? ¿Necesitas más información? Explica.

Taller

12.9 **State the main idea and add supporting evidence**

Un artículo serio

Estrategia para escribir

State the main idea and add supporting evidence. When you write an essay or article, you first state your thesis or main idea, and then add evidence in support of your thesis. Be careful to avoid giving opinions that cannot be supported by the evidence.

12-41 **Un desafío para el medio ambiente.** En tu artículo, vas a presentar una tesis y evidencia que la respalde (*supports it*), semejante al artículo que leíste en **Páginas**. Por ejemplo, el tema puede ser sobre la energía (fósil o renovable), una especie en peligro de extinción, el cambio climático, la contaminación (del aire, del agua), la sobrepoblación, los recursos naturales, etc.

ANTES DE ESCRIBIR

- **El problema.** Piensa en un problema que quieras presentar en tu artículo. Investiga en Internet la evidencia que necesites para apoyar tu tesis.

AL ESCRIBIR

- **Introducción.** Presenta tu tesis.
- **Discusión.** Presenta la evidencia que has encontrado.
- **Conclusión.** Resume el tema.

    MODELO: *El uso de las bolsas de plástico afecta enormemente el medio ambiente. Según un estudio… Primero, … Además, … En conclusión, …*

DESPUÉS DE ESCRIBIR

- **Revisar.** Revisa tu artículo para verificar los siguientes puntos:
    - ☐ el uso del presente perfecto
    - ☐ el uso del futuro y del condicional
    - ☐ la concordancia y la ortografía
- **Intercambiar.** Intercambia tu artículo con el de un/a compañero/a. Hagan comentarios y sugerencias sobre el contenido, la estructura y la gramática.
- **Entregar.** Pon tu artículo en limpio, incorporando las sugerencias de tu compañero/a. Después, entrégaselo a tu profesor/a.

En este capítulo...

)) Vocabulario

Primera parte

Los aparatos electrónicos	Electronic devices
la antena parabólica	*satellite dish*
los auriculares	*earbuds, headphones*
el escáner	*scanner*
el lector de libros electrónicos	*eBook reader*
la marca	*brand*
la pantalla	*screen*
el ratón (inalámbrico)	*(wireless) mouse*
la tableta	*tablet*
el teclado	*keyboard*

En Internet	On the Internet
la alerta	*alert*
la aplicación	*app*
el aprendizaje a distancia	*distance learning*
la comunidad virtual	*online community*
el fraude electrónico	*phishing*
el hipervínculo	*hyperlink*
la impresora	*printer*
el juego electrónico	*computer (electronic) game*
los medios digitales	*digital media*
la página (el sitio) web	*web page (website)*
el servidor	*server*
el/la trol	*Internet troll*
el tuit	*tweet*
la videoconferencia	*videoconference*

Verbos	Verbs
acceder	*to access*
actualizar (un programa)	*to update (a program)*
almacenar (en la nube)	*to store (in the cloud)*
apagar	*to turn off*
bajar	*to download*
borrar	*to erase*
colaborar	*to collaborate*
compartir	*to post (share) online*
encender	*to turn on*
enviar	*to send*
fallar	*to break down (e.g., computer)*
funcionar	*to function, to work*
grabar	*to record*
guardar (un documento)	*to save (a document)*
hacer clic	*to click on*
imprimir	*to print*
(des)instalar	*to (un)install*
programar	*to program*
subir	*to upload*
tuitear	*to tweet*
unirse (a un sitio social)	*to join (a social media site)*

Segunda parte

Nuestro mundo y el medio ambiente	Our world and the environment
el bosque (pluvial)	*(rain) forest*
el carbón	*coal*
el combustible fósil	*fossil fuel*
el desarrollo (sostenible)	*(sustainable) development*
la energía (alternativa/solar/ verde)	*(alternative/solar/green) energy*
las especies (en peligro de extinción)	*(endangered) species*
la naturaleza	*nature*
el reciclaje	*recycling*
el recurso natural	*natural resource*
la reforestación	*reforestation*
la selva	*jungle*

Amenazas al medio ambiente	Threats to our environment
el cambio climático	*climate change*
la contaminación	*pollution*
la deforestación	*deforestation*
el derrame (de petróleo)	*(oil) spill*
los desechos (nucleares)	*(nuclear) waste*
el envase (de aluminio / de plástico / de vidrio)	*(aluminum/plastic/glass) container*
la escasez	*shortage*
la fábrica	*factory*
el humo	*smoke*
la inundación	*flood*
el oleoducto	*(oil) pipeline*
la planta nuclear	*nuclear plant*
los pesticidas	*pesticides*
la radioactividad	*radioactivity*
la sequía	*drought*

Verbos	Verbs
asegurar	*to ensure*
conservar	*to conserve, to preserve*
consumir	*to consume*
contaminar	*to contaminate, to pollute*
multar	*to fine*
perjudicar	*to harm*
proteger (j)	*to protect*
reciclar	*to recycle*
tirar	*to throw (away, out)*

EXPANSIÓN Expressions used with the present perfect indicative   *See page 389.*

Capítulo 13
¿Oíste las noticias?

«Cree lo que vieres (veas) y no lo que oyeres (oigas)».

La Alhambra, Granada, Spain.
A UNESCO World Heritage site, the palace and fortress display Spain's most celebrated Islamic architecture. Over the centuries, it has inspired countless stories, poems, and musical pieces.

Learning Objectives

13.1 Discuss print and electronic media

13.2 Express uncertainty in the past; emphasize possession and avoid repetition

13.3 Learn about a symbol of press freedom in Spain and a popular rumba flamenco band

13.4 Discuss popular media: television, movies, and other entertainment

13.5 Hypothesize about what you and others will or would do

13.6 First identify topics, then summarize main ideas

13.7 Identify and research key elements of Spain's cultural heritage

13.8 Evaluate what you read

13.9 Express and support an opinion

In this Chapter

ENFOQUE CULTURAL: LA HERENCIA CULTURAL DE ESPAÑA
Club cultura: El País Vasco, destino cultural y deportivo

Selecciona la opción más lógica, según el video.

1. El País Vasco está situado en el extremo...
   a. sur.   b. este.   c. noreste de España.

2. Además del español, allí se habla...
   a. eusquera.   b. catalán.   c. valenciano.

3. Entre los atractivos turísticos, puedes visitar...
   a. el estadio Bernabéu del Real Madrid.
   b. el museo Guggenheim.
   c. la Sagrada Familia.

4. La escultura enfrente del sitio está hecha de...
   a. bronce.   b. titanio.   c. flores.

13.1 Primera parte

Vocabulario

13.1 Discuss print and electronic media

Los medios de comunicación

En la sala de redacción. Hay mucho movimiento para actualizar **el periódico digital** *El Mundo*. **La directora**, Soledad, insiste en que **las noticias de última hora** incluyan **los titulares** más importantes.

PATRICIA: ¿De quién es esta **reseña**?

ROGELIO: Es mía. Es de una novela nueva de Carlos Ruiz Zafón. Según **los críticos**, es su mejor hasta la fecha.

PATRICIA: Uy, ¡qué guay[1]! Es **un superventas**, ¿no? Tiene millones de **lectores**.

ROGELIO: Sí. Acabo de ver una entrevista con él en **la televisión** y **el presentador** dijo que habría una versión digital y un audiolibro también.

SOLEDAD: ¡Vamos, colegas! ¿Dónde están las noticias **financieras** y las **deportivas**?

GARCÍA: ¡Las voy a subir ahora mismo!

¿Comprendes? Identify the character in each description: **Soledad**, **Patricia**, **Rogelio**, **García**.

1. _____ Escribió una reseña de una novela.

2. _____ Tiene prisa para terminar la edición.

3. _____ Ha terminado la página financiera y la deportiva.

4. _____ Quiere saber de quién es la reseña.

Respuestas: 1. Rogelio; 2. Soledad; 3. García; 4. Patricia

---
[1]*How cool!* (Spain)

))) Vocabulario

La prensa	The press
el artículo	article
la caricatura política	political cartoon
la cartelera	entertainment section
el consultorio sentimental	advice column
el editorial[1]	editorial section
el horóscopo	horoscope
las noticias (de última hora)	(latest) news
la primera plana	front page
la reseña	review (of books, movies, etc.)
la revista (del corazón)	(celebrity) magazine
la sección deportiva	sports section
la sección financiera	financial section
el superventas	bestseller
el titular	headline

Noticias en línea	Online news
el buscador	search engine
el inicio	home
el periódico digital	online newspaper

Noticias en la televisión y en la radio	News on television and radio
el noticiero	newscast
el reportaje	feature

Gente en los medios	People in the media
el/la comentarista	newscaster, commentator
el/la comentarista deportivo/a	sportscaster
el/la crítico/a[2]	critic
el/la director/a	editor in chief
el/la meteorólogo/a	meteorologist
el/la presentador/a	host (on television, radio), announcer
el/la reportero/a	reporter

El público	The audience
el/la lector/a	reader
el/la radioyente	listener
el/la oyente de podcast	podcast listener

Verbos	Verbs
informar	to report
revisar	to check
tener éxito	to be successful
transmitir	to broadcast

Variaciones

- You will hear **el/la meteorólogo/a** throughout the Spanish-speaking world; however, **el hombre/la mujer del tiempo** is also common.
- The front page of a newspaper is **la primera plana** in Latin America and **la portada** in Spain.

[1]**El editorial** refers to an editorial; **la editorial** to a publishing house.

[2]**El/la crítico/a** is a film or book critic. **La crítica** (when not referring to a person) is criticism in a general sense.

Aplicación

13-1 Los medios de información. Selecciona la opción que mejor corresponde a cada descripción.

1. _____ la caricatura política
2. _____ el editorial
3. _____ la primera plana
4. _____ la cartelera
5. _____ el titular
6. _____ el/la reportero/a
7. _____ el/la comentarista
8. _____ el noticiero

a. la sección donde se da la opinión del periódico

b. la sección con información sobre películas y conciertos

c. una persona que ofrece su opinión por radio o televisión

d. el título de un artículo en un periódico o una revista

e. la página del periódico donde aparecen las noticias más importantes

f. un programa que informa sobre lo más importante del día

g. un dibujo que parodia a una persona o situación política

h. una persona que hace investigaciones y escribe artículos o informes

13-2 Los medios de comunicación. Vas a oír un reportaje sobre la importancia de los hispanos en los medios de comunicación estadounidenses. Después de escucharlo, selecciona la opción que mejor completa cada una de las frases.

1. La presencia de los hispanos en EE. UU...
   a. sigue igual que hace veinte años.
   b. está disminuyendo.
   c. está aumentando.

2. Las grandes compañías de productos de consumo quieren saber cómo...
   a. aumentar el mercado hispano.
   b. vender más productos en Hispanoamérica.
   c. hablar español mejor.

3. En Los Ángeles, Nueva York y Miami...
   a. hay muchos periódicos hispanos.
   b. necesitan más periódicos hispanos.
   c. hay mucho interés en la política.

4. *La Opinión* es un periódico publicado en...
   a. Los Ángeles.
   b. Chicago.
   c. Miami.

5. *Vanidades* es...
   a. una revista popular.
   b. un periódico publicado en Miami.
   c. una telenovela bilingüe.

6. El mercado hispano cada vez va adquiriendo más...
   a. dinero.
   b. importancia.
   c. público de habla inglesa.

13-3 Su punto de vista. Lean las siguientes oraciones y expliquen por qué están de acuerdo o no con cada una de ellas.

MODELO: La prensa en EE. UU. es muy sensacionalista.
ESTUDIANTE 1: *Estoy de acuerdo. Algunos ejemplos son...*
ESTUDIANTE 2: *No estoy de acuerdo. Leo varios periódicos digitales y...*

1. En EE. UU. y Canadá no hay libertad total de prensa.
2. Muchas de las noticias publicadas son falsas.
3. La censura de la prensa es necesaria para proteger la seguridad nacional.
4. En general, la gente pasa demasiado tiempo en sitios sociales.
5. Los periódicos impresos están pasados de moda. Todo se lee en línea.
6. No leo las noticias; solo veo los videos humorísticos de gatos.

13-4 Radio Cádiz. Con más de 80 años en existencia, Radio Cádiz continúa transmitiendo desde la ciudad de Cádiz en España.

Paso 1 Usa el aviso de Radio Cádiz como modelo y prepara un anuncio para un programa de tu estación favorita. Incluye esta información.

- el nombre o las siglas (*call letters*) de la estación de radio
- un lema publicitario (*slogan*)
- una mascota o un símbolo de la estación de radio
- el tipo de programación
- la gente que la escucha
- el nombre de un/a comentarista
- otra información para atraer a los radioyentes

Paso 2 Usa el aviso que preparaste para hacer un anuncio en la radio. Preséntale el anuncio a la clase.

MODELO: *Radio Río, KRMP, es tu estación de radio de música guay. Te invitamos a escuchar las mejores entrevistas...*

EN EL FIN DE SEMANA, SIEMPRE HAY TIEMPO...
para compartir y disfrutar la mejor música.
Música elegida y presentada por Begoña Lomas los sábados de 13 a 19 y los domingos de 12:30 a 15. Y en el momento oportuno, noticias, comentarios, todo lo que usted quiere saber y con la agenda cultural más completa. Calidad inconfundible de Begoña Lomas y Radio Cádiz. Porque para descansar y divertirse, siempre hay tiempo en Cádiz.
SIEMPRE HAY TIEMPO.
Sábados de 13 a 19.
Domingos de 12:30 a 15.
EN EL *640* DEL DIAL **CÁDIZ** SIEMPRE MÁS RADIO

 13-5 ¿Cuánto confías? Responde a la encuesta para saber qué puntuación recibes. Luego, con un/a compañero/a, comparen sus resultados para ver quién confía (*trusts*) más.

MODELO: ESTUDIANTE 1: *¿Cuánto confías en...?*
ESTUDIANTE 2: *...*

Indica cuánto confías en la información presentada en estos medios (**1:** poco – **5:** mucho).
1. _____ los medios convencionales (*mainstream*)
2. _____ la prensa sensacionalista
3. _____ la radio alternativa
4. _____ la radio pública
5. _____ los noticieros en la televisión pública
6. _____ las redes sociales

Puntos de cada respuesta: **Preguntas 1, 4, 5:** 5 = 5, 4 = 4, 3 = 3, 2 = 2, 1 = 1 **Preguntas 2, 3, 6:** 5 = 1, 4 = 2, 3 = 3, 2 = 4, 1 = 5

Puntuación de la encuesta

20–30: Confías en los medios convencionales que ofrecen más de un punto de vista. Resistes la atracción de las noticias sensacionalistas.

10–19: No eres muy aficionado/a a los medios de comunicación. No prefieres ninguno en particular.

6–9: Tiendes a buscar información sensacionalista, o en la prensa alternativa o en las redes sociales. No confías mucho en los medios convencionales para informarte sobre las noticias; no importa su punto de vista. Tal vez pases más tiempo en actividades de entretenimiento en Internet en lugar de leer o escuchar las noticias.

Estructuras

13.2 Express uncertainty in the past; emphasize possession and avoid repetition

The imperfect subjunctive

¿Recuerdas? You've used the present subjunctive to express influence, emotion, doubt, and denial in the present or future.

Complete the sentence with the correct form of the logical verb: **buscar**, **informar**.

La profesora quiere que nosotros (1) _____ una estación que (2) _____ sobre las noticias en España.

Respuestas: 1. busquemos; 2. informe

Use the subjunctive in the past under the same hypothetical or subjective contexts as in the present: uncertainty, attitudes, emotions, or wishes. The verb in the main clause is in the past tense (preterit or imperfect), or in the conditional (would/could).

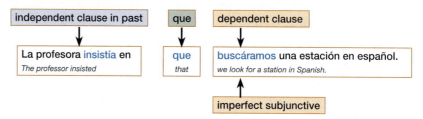

- Form the imperfect subjunctive of both regular and irregular verbs by dropping the **-ron** ending of the third-person plural of the preterit and adding the endings: **-ra, -ras, -ra, -ramos, -rais, -ran**. Note the accent on the **nosotros/as** form.

buscar	→	buscaron	→	buscara...
comer	→	comieron	→	comiera...
vivir	→	vivieron	→	viviera...

salir			
yo	**saliera**	nosotros/as	**saliéramos**
tú	**salieras**	vosotros/as	**salierais**
Ud.	**saliera**	Uds.	**salieran**
él/ella	**saliera**	ellos/as	**salieran**

- Note that any verb that is irregular in the preterit will follow the same pattern in the imperfect subjunctive. For example:

Infinitive	Third-person plural Preterit	First-person singular Imperfect subjunctive
creer	creyeron	**creyera**
decir	dijeron	**dijera**
estar	estuvieron	**estuviera**
ir	fueron	**fuera**
leer	leyeron	**leyera**
poder	pudieron	**pudiera**
poner	pusieron	**pusiera**

Infinitive	Third-person plural Preterit	First-person singular Imperfect subjunctive
querer	quisieron	**quisiera**
saber	supieron	**supiera**
ser	fueron	**fuera**
tener	tuvieron	**tuviera**
traer	trajeron	**trajera**
venir	vinieron	**viniera**

Buscaba a alguien que **siguiera** su horóscopo. *I was looking for someone who followed his/her horoscope.*

- The imperfect subjunctive of **hay** is **hubiera**.

El director insistió en que **hubiera** un editorial sobre el accidente nuclear. *The editor in chief insisted that there be an editorial about the nuclear accident.*

- Use the imperfect subjunctive with **ojalá** when it means *I wish.*

  ¡Ojalá (que) no **cancelaran** mi
  telenovela favorita!

  *I wish they wouldn't cancel my favorite
  soap opera!*

- You can also use the imperfect subjunctive of **querer**, **poder**, or **deber** to make
  polite requests or statements.

  Quisiera leer la primera plana.

  I would like to read the front page.

  ¿Pudieras darme la sección
  deportiva?

  Could you give me the sports section?

  Debiéramos escribir una carta al
  director.

  We should write a letter to the editor.

¿Comprendes? Complete each sentence with the correct form of the logical
verb: **creer**, **decir**.

Era importante que nadie (1) _____ las noticias falsas. Por eso, buscábamos a alguien
que (2) _____ la verdad.

Respuestas: 1. creyera; 2. dijera

Aplicación

13-6 Alejandro Sanz. El cantautor español Alejandro Sanz siempre ha estado
dispuesto (*willing*) a responder a las preguntas de sus aficionados. Aquí hay una
selección de preguntas y respuestas que aparecieron en un foro en Internet.

Paso 1 Selecciona el verbo correcto y explica por qué lo seleccionaste.

ATILA: ¿Cómo te sentías cuando algunas estaciones de radio no quisieron que
(1) tocabas/tocaras tu canción "No es lo mismo"?

SANZ: Me dio mucha lástima que (2) decidieron/decidieran censurar
esa canción. Compuse "No es lo mismo" para que la gente
(3) entendió/entendiera mi opinión sobre la censura.

MAMITA: ¿Cómo te sentías cuando nació tu hija?

SANZ: ¡Pura felicidad! No podía creer que (4) tenía/tuviera una cosita tan
preciosa entre mis brazos y que (5) era/fuera mía (*mine*).

BELLACHICA: Imagínate que eres un político importante y muy influyente. ¿A quién
seleccionarías como presidente y a quién como primera dama?

SANZ: Insistiría en que la primera dama (6) era/fuera Madonna, y el presidente
Danny DeVito. Creo que (7) harían/hicieran una pareja estupenda.

SOLTERO: ¿Con quién harías un dueto?

SANZ: No sé, con Seal, con Aretha Franklin, con Elton John. Me gustaría hacer
un dueto con alguien que (8) sentía/sintiera la misma pasión que yo.

Paso 2 Vuelve a leer las respuestas de Alejandro Sanz para identificar esta
información.

1. el momento más feliz de su vida
2. una canción de él que fue censurada por algunas estaciones de radio
3. a quiénes nombraría presidente y primera dama
4. el tipo de persona con quien le gustaría hacer un dueto
5. ¿Conoces otra canción o artista que fuera censurada por su opinión?

13-7 José Díaz-Balart. Presentador para el *Noticiero Telemundo, NBC Nightly News*, además de un noticiero en MSNBC, el cubano-americano José Díaz-Balart es uno de los más premiados de la televisión. Aquí entrevista a un periodista que publica sus reportajes en Internet de manera anónima. Completa la entrevista con la forma correcta del imperfecto de subjuntivo de un verbo lógico de la lista.

hacer	poder	reconocer	ser
invitar	recibir	saber	tener

JOSÉ: Buenas tardes, señor X. Nos alegró mucho de que usted (1) _____ estar aquí con nosotros en persona, aunque con la cara cubierta. ¡Fue bueno que nadie lo (2) _____ en el viaje!

PERIODISTA: Hola, José. Sí, fue un honor tremendo que ustedes me (3) _____ a hablar.

JOSÉ: Bueno, vamos a hablar de su último libro publicado en inglés y español. ¿Le sorprendió que (4) _____ tanto éxito?

PERIODISTA: Bueno, me sentí verdaderamente feliz que el público lo (5) _____ con tanto entusiasmo. Le pedí a mi agente que (6) _____ una buena campaña publicitaria para el libro sobre la libertad de prensa. Era importante que el público (7) _____ que en muchos países los periodistas temen por su vida solo por informar sobre hechos verdaderos.

JOSÉ: ¡Qué lástima! Ojalá que no (8) _____ así. Todos tenemos que resistir la tiranía y defender la libertad de expresión.

Presencia hispana

The National Association of Hispanic Journalists (NAHJ) is dedicated to the recognition and professional advancement of Hispanics in the news industry. According to their website, its mission is "to organize and provide support for Hispanic journalists, encourage and support the study and practices of journalism and communications by Hispanics, promote accurate and fair treatment of Hispanics by the news media, further employment opportunities and career development for Hispanics in the news media, and foster greater understanding of the unique cultural identity, interests, and concerns of Hispanic journalists." Which of these goals would be most important to students of journalism?

13-8 La mesa redonda. Explica lo que pasó anoche en una reunión del director con los reporteros. Escribe por lo menos ocho oraciones completas en español. Para cada oración, combina un elemento de cada columna y completa la idea.

MODELO: el director / insistir en que / los reporteros / terminar
El director insistió/insistía en que los reporteros terminaran a tiempo.

A	B	C		D
el director	insistir en que	el periódico		publicar
nosotros	dudar que	los lectores		entender
un meteorólogo	temer que	el presidente	(no)	decir
unos periodistas	sentir que	el público		ser
los críticos	esperar que	la comentarista		escribir

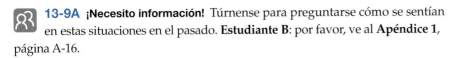

13-9A ¡Necesito información! Túrnense para preguntarse cómo se sentían en estas situaciones en el pasado. **Estudiante B**: por favor, ve al **Apéndice 1**, página A-16.

MODELO: ESTUDIANTE A: *De joven, ¿qué querías que hicieran tus amigos?*
ESTUDIANTE B: invitarme a su casa a jugar videojuegos
Quería que me invitaran a su casa a jugar videojuegos.

Estudiante A:

Mis preguntas	Posibles respuestas a las preguntas de mi compañero/a
1. En clase, ¿qué temías que hiciera tu profesora favorita?	• despedirme si llegaba tarde
3. En casa, ¿qué dudabas que hicieran tus padres?	• olvidarme de todas las respuestas
5. En una fiesta con tu mejor amigo o amiga, ¿qué deseabas que pasara?	• publicarse mi carta al director
7. En el cine, ¿qué esperabas que pasara al final de la película?	• traernos la comida sin demora

13-10 Quisiera pedirte un favor. En parejas, usen el imperfecto de subjuntivo de **querer**, **poder** y **deber** para pedirse tres favores. Respondan de una manera apropiada.

MODELO: ESTUDIANTE 1: *Quisiera pedirte un favor. Mañana tengo examen de cálculo. ¿Pudieras prestarme tu calculadora?*
ESTUDIANTE 2: *Me gustaría, pero tengo el mismo examen y la necesito también.*

13-11 ¡Ojalá que la prensa fuera perfecta! En parejas, conversen sobre estas cuestiones relacionadas con los medios de comunicación.

MODELO: ESTUDIANTE 1: *¿Reportan siempre la pura verdad los periódicos?*
ESTUDIANTE 2: *¡Ojalá la reportaran! La verdad es que hay reporteros que no son honrados.*

1. ¿Respetan siempre los reporteros la privacidad de las celebridades?
2. ¿Siempre encuentran la verdad los reporteros políticos?
3. ¿Son acertadas (*accurate*) las caricaturas políticas?
4. ¿Tiene razón siempre el meteorólogo cuando pronostica el tiempo?
5. ¿Hay sitios en Internet que nunca informan sobre noticias falsas?

13-12 Un periódico digital. Ustedes son miembros de un equipo de reporteros investigadores para un periódico que se publica en línea. Trabajen en parejas para completar las frases y explicar cómo se originó su organización. Escriban sus respuestas para después presentárselas a la clase. OJO: No todas las frases usan el subjuntivo.

MODELO: *Era importante que todos trabajáramos juntos.*

1. Era esencial que…
2. Había un grupo de personas que…
3. Pero no había nadie que…
4. Queríamos crear un sitio que…
5. Esperábamos que…
6. Íbamos a publicar el sitio cuando…

Cultura en vivo

Being a journalist can be dangerous business. According to the Committee to Protect Journalists (CPJ), some 1,840 journalists and media workers have been killed since they began keeping statistics in 1992. These deaths have occurred all over the world, including many in Latin America and Europe, with the most dangerous assignments being politics, war, human rights, and corruption. The CPJ emphasizes that although "murder is the ultimate censorship," 90% of the perpetrators go free. What can we do to protect a free press?

Long-form possessive adjectives and pronouns

¿Recuerdas? In **Capítulo 3**, you learned the short (unstressed) possessive adjectives (**mi/s, tu/s, su/s, nuestro/a/s**).

Complete this sentence with the logical possessive adjectives:

Buscábamos (1) _____ portátil, pero lo tenías en (2) _____ mochila.

Respuestas: 1. nuestro; 2. tu

Use long-form possessives to add emphasis or contrast, or as a pronoun to replace a noun already mentioned.

<table>
<tr><th>Short form</th><th>Long form</th></tr>
<tr><td>Es mi amigo.
He's my friend.</td><td>Es un amigo mío.
He's a friend of mine.</td></tr>
<tr><td>Nuestros reporteros son mejores
que tus reporteros.
Our reporters are better than your reporters.</td><td>Los nuestros son mejores
que los tuyos.
Ours are better than yours.</td></tr>
</table>

Here are the long (stressed) forms:

Possessive adjectives and pronouns (long forms)			
Subject Pronoun	Singular	Plural	
yo	**mío/a**	**míos/as**	*my, (of) mine*
tú	**tuyo/a**	**tuyos/as**	*your (fam.), (of) yours*
Ud.	**suyo/a**	**suyos/as**	*your (form.), (of) yours*
él/ella	**suyo/a**	**suyos/as**	*his/her, (of) his/hers, (of) its*
nosotros/as	**nuestro/a**	**nuestros/as**	*our, (of) ours*
vosotros/as	**vuestro/a**	**vuestros/as**	*your (fam. pl.), (of) yours*
Uds.	**suyo/a**	**suyos/as**	*your (form. pl.), (of) yours*
ellos/ellas	**suyo/a**	**suyos/as**	*their, (of) theirs*

- Note that the long forms of possessive adjectives follow nouns and agree with the nouns in gender and number.

  La revista **tuya** está en la mesa.   *The magazine of yours is on the table.*
  Aquí tienes dos reseñas **mías**.   *Here you have two reviews of mine.*

- When you omit the noun, the long-form possessive adjective becomes a pronoun. Be sure to keep the definite article in this case.

  Los presentadores **nuestros** son   *Our announcers are very good.*
  muy buenos.
  Los **nuestros** son muy buenos.   *Ours are very good.*

- As with the short form of **su(s)**, you can clarify the identity of **suyo/a(s)** with the construction **de** + *pronoun*. Remember that the definite article must agree in gender and number with the *noun* it replaces.

  —**La** crítica **suya** es imposible.   —*His criticism is impossible.*
  —¿**La** crítica **de quién**?   —*Whose criticism?*
  —**La de Juan**.   —*Juan's criticism.*

- Finally, you can omit the article from the possessive pronoun when it follows **ser**.

  ¿De quién es esta caricatura   *Whose political cartoon is this? Is it*
  política? **¿Es tuya?**   *yours?*

STUDY TIPS – POSSESSIVE ADJECTIVES AND PRONOUNS
In order to have the right form of a possessive adjective or pronoun, always focus on the thing possessed, rather than the possessor. Is the thing possessed singular or plural, masculine or feminine?

¿Comprendes? Complete these sentences with the correct form of the logical possessive: **mío**, **suyo**.

Esta es la sección financiera de José y Carmen. Es (1) _____. No encuentro la (2) _____.

Respuestas: 1. suya; 2. mía

Aplicación

13-13 *En la tuya o en la mía.* En este programa de entrevistas en la televisión española, el presentador, Bertín Osborne, les da a los entrevistados la opción de reunirse con él o en la casa suya o en la de ellos. Allí, además de tener una conversación, la celebridad prepara un plato favorito. Lee la entrevista que hace con un famoso cantante de ópera y selecciona el posesivo más lógico.

PRESENTADOR:	¿Hacemos la entrevista en mi casa o en (1) el tuyo/la tuya?
INVITADO:	Tienes una cocina más grande que (2) el mío/la mía. Creo que es mejor en (3) el tuyo/la tuya.
PRESENTADOR:	Está bien. Luego puedes conocer a mi esposa y a los hijos (4) suya/suyos.
INVITADO:	¿Y (5) los nuestros/los tuyos? ¿No viven en casa?
PRESENTADOR:	No, ellos ya están muy grandes y viven en casas (6) tuyas/suyas. Pero los de mi segunda esposa son más jóvenes. (7) Los de ella/Los de ellos viven con nosotros.
INVITADO:	¿Dónde viven tus hijos?
PRESENTADOR:	(8) Los míos/Los nuestros viven en España y Nueva York.
INVITADO:	¡Qué bien! Las hijas (9) mías/míos también viven en Nueva York. ¡Qué mundo más pequeño es (10) los nuestros/el nuestro!

13-14 En Univisión. Univisión es la cadena de televisión estadounidense más grande que transmite en español. Completa la conversación entre el director de noticias y su ayudante con la forma correcta del posesivo pleno (*long-form*), según el contexto.

MODELO: JEFE: Oye, ¿está listo tu informe sobre las noticias políticas?

AYUDANTE: Sí, *el mío* está listo, pero no el del comentarista.

JEFE: ¿Y por qué no está listo *el suyo / el de él*?

JEFE: ¿Dónde está nuestra campaña publicitaria?

AYUDANTE: (1) _____ está en el estudio.

JEFE: Por cierto, ¿sabes dónde está mi taza de café?

AYUDANTE: Seguramente la taza (2) _____ está en tu escritorio.

JEFE: Ah, sí, ahora la veo. ¿Tiene la meteoróloga sus informes sobre el tiempo?

AYUDANTE: Creo que ella tiene los informes (3) _____ pero aún necesita las imágenes del satélite.

JEFE: Aquí están las noticias de la comentarista deportiva para hoy. Míralas para ver si están bien.

AYUDANTE: Sí, (4) _____ están al día, pero tengo que buscar las del comentarista político. ¿Sabes cuándo me va a dar (5) _____?

JEFE: Bueno, ahora se lo pregunto. ¿Está ya en la oficina? Me dijo que tenía problemas con su carro.

AYUDANTE: Es verdad. ¡Ese carro (6) _____ es un desastre!

JEFE: Mira, la crítica de nuestra estación es más positiva esta semana.

AYUDANTE: Es verdad. (7) _____ es mucho mejor que la de nuestros competidores.

13-15 En la oficina del periódico. En parejas, túrnense para identificar de quiénes son las siguientes cosas. Usen la imaginación para dar la respuesta.

MODELO: el consultorio sentimental / tú
ESTUDIANTE 1: *¿De quién es el consultorio sentimental? ¿Es tuyo?*
ESTUDIANTE 2: *No, no es mío. Es de Amy Dickinson…*

1. los editoriales / ustedes

2. la cartelera / nosotros

3. el horóscopo / los estudiantes colombianos

4. las reseñas / tú

5. la sección financiera / los editores

6. la revista del corazón / yo

7. la sección deportiva / la comentarista

8. la entrevista con Jorge Ramos / Michelle Galván

13-16 ¿Quién tiene la responsabilidad? En parejas, conversen para decidir quién tiene la responsabilidad, la culpa o el crédito en las siguientes situaciones. Usen los posesivos cuando sea posible.

MODELO: la violencia en los videojuegos
ESTUDIANTE 1: *La culpa es de los programadores de los videojuegos.*
ESTUDIANTE 2: *No, no es suya. Es de los padres que permiten que sus hijos los jueguen.*
ESTUDIANTE 3: *No estoy de acuerdo. Creo que es de los programadores, porque...*

- la censura de los medios de comunicación en tiempos de crisis
- el tiempo que dedicamos a los sitios sociales en Internet
- el costo de tener acceso a Internet
- las noticias falsas
- el sensacionalismo en la prensa

¡Conversemos!

Primero, pregúntate si puedes llevar a cabo las siguientes funciones comunicativas. Después, júntate con dos o tres compañeros/as de clase para presentar las situaciones. Hagan y respondan a por lo menos cuatro preguntas en cada situación.

✓ CAN YOU...

☐ discuss print and electronic media?

☐ express requests or uncertainty in the past?

☐ emphasize possession and avoid repetition?

WITH YOUR CLASSMATE(S)...

Situación: En la residencia.

Ustedes tienen una suscripción a un periódico digital y pasan todo el día del domingo leyéndolo. Explíquense las secciones que prefieren leer primero y por qué.

Para empezar: *Me gusta leer... primero porque...*

Situación: Testigo (*Witness*).

Uno/a de ustedes es reportero/a y el/la otro/a es testigo de un accidente. Háganse y respondan a preguntas en el pasado.

Para empezar: *¿Dudaba que fuera un accidente? ¿Insistió el policía en que usted lo acompañara? ¿Era necesario que...?*

Situación: Entre amigos/as.

Al final del semestre, ustedes tienen que dividir sus pertenencias (*belongings*), pero no recuerdan de quiénes son. Háganse por lo menos cuatro preguntas para determinar de quiénes son.

Para empezar: *¿De quién son estas revistas? ¿Son tuyas? No, son de...*

Perfiles

13.3 Learn about a symbol of press freedom in Spain and a popular rumba flamenco band

Mi experiencia

EL PAÍS, VOZ DE LA DEMOCRACIA

))) **13-17 Para ti.** ¿Existe un periódico nacional en EE. UU. o Canadá? ¿Cómo se llama? ¿Lo lees en línea o impreso? ¿En qué sentido tienen los periódicos en EE. UU. y en Canadá influencia en la política? Lee la siguiente descripción de Renata sobre un periódico muy conocido en España.

Hola, soy Renata y vivo en Bilbao, donde estudio periodismo. Me fascina estudiar los medios de comunicación y ver las diferentes perspectivas de las noticias que se ofrecen. Aquí en España tenemos muchos periódicos regionales y varios nacionales, pero el que tiene más historia y la mayor circulación es *El País.* Empezó a publicarse en 1976 durante el proceso de transición de la dictadura de Francisco Franco a una democracia bajo una monarquía constitucional. Sin embargo, como muchos periódicos, se ha dedicado más al público digital que al impreso, hasta el punto en que tal vez deje de publicar el impreso.

En mi opinión, es importante ver más de un punto de vista en cuestiones de política. Por eso, frecuentemente leo periódicos de otros países tales como *La Opinión* de Los Ángeles, *El Mercurio* de Santiago de Chile y el *Clarín* de Buenos Aires. Además de las noticias, me gusta que siempre haya una sección de cartelera donde tienen noticias sobre las estrellas del día, como Shakira, Juanes y por supuesto, ¡un grupo europeo muy talentoso, los Gipsy Kings!

13-18 En su opinión. Conversen sobre Renata y cómo su perspectiva se compara con la de ustedes.

1. ¿Por qué estudia Renata periodismo? ¿Tienen ustedes la misma perspectiva que ella? Expliquen.

2. ¿Conocen un periódico en EE. UU. o Canadá que se considere protector de la democracia como *El País*?

3. ¿Por qué lee Renata periódicos internacionales? ¿Cuáles leen ustedes y por qué?

4. ¿Qué sistema político tenía España durante la época de Francisco Franco? ¿Qué sistema tiene hoy? ¿Por qué sería importante una prensa independiente durante la transición?

Mi música

"BAILA ME" (GIPSY KINGS, ESPAÑA)

Los miembros de este grupo nacieron en Francia, pero son hijos de gitanos catalanes que huyeron de España durante la Guerra Civil (1936–39). Hablan francés y caló, la lengua tradicional de los gitanos españoles, y cantan en un argot español que es la misma forma del español que se utiliza en la música tradicional del flamenco. Su música es un tipo de flamenco popular que ha tenido mucho éxito en Europa y en EE. UU.

ANTES DE VER Y ESCUCHAR

13-19 ¡Baila! En esta canción, los Gipsy Kings animan a todos a bailar para disfrutar del momento, del presente. ¿Qué otras cosas le dirías a un/a amigo/a para vivir el momento? Usa mandatos informales (**tú**) afirmativos y negativos para animarlo/la.

> **MODELO:**   escuchar
> *Escucha la música. No pienses en los problemas.*

1. bailar
2. cantar
3. irse
4. ponerse

5. ir
6. levantarse
7. sonreír
8. hablar

PARA VER Y ESCUCHAR

13-20 La canción. El instrumento musical predominante de la música flamenca es la guitarra, pero también los músicos usan las manos para golpear (*thump*) la guitarra o para hacer palmadas, y los pies para acompañar el ritmo. En la rumba, el tambor (*drum*) también predomina. Observa el video de los Gipsy Kings e indica con **sí** o **no** los instrumentos y técnicas musicales que oyes y ves.

1. _____ el acordeón
2. _____ las castañuelas (*castanets*)
3. _____ los golpes (con el dedo en la guitarra)
4. _____ la guitarra
5. _____ las palmas (con las manos)
6. _____ la pandereta (*tambourine*)
7. _____ el violín
8. _____ el zapateo (percusión con el pie)

> **⊙ Busca:** Gipsy Kings Baila me video; Gipsy Kings Baila me letra

DESPUÉS DE VER Y ESCUCHAR

13-21 Música que mezcla estilos. La música de los Gipsy Kings mezcla estilos: el flamenco tradicional, el pop rock, la rumba. Compara su música con la de otro artista o grupo que conozcas que también mezcle estilos.

> **MODELO:**   *Shakira es una artista que mezcla estilos. Por ejemplo, …*

13.2 Segunda parte

Vocabulario

13.4 Discuss popular media: television, movies, and other entertainment

El cine, el teatro y la televisión

Sábado de Estrellas. Este es **un programa** popular que cada semana invita a una celebridad a ser presentador o presentadora. Esta persona también **representa** una serie de pequeñas **parodias** durante el programa. Hace poco, la presentadora fue **una** famosa **actriz** de 82 años, y así empezó la noche...

ENTREVISTADORA:	Buenas tardes, señora. Represento una organización que **sondea** a **los televidentes** para saber sus gustos. ¿Cuál es su **telenovela** favorita?
SEÑORA:	Me gustan especialmente **los documentales** sobre los gatos (*cats*).
ENTREVISTADORA:	Ah... entiendo. ¿Ve usted **la televisión por cable** o **por satélite**?
SEÑORA:	Prefiero **la televisión en vivo**. Me gusta mucho **el galán** de *Noticias Esta Noche*.
ENTREVISTADORA:	Pero, señora, ese es un noticiero y él es presentador, no es galán.
SEÑORA:	Bueno, pero no me gusta nada **la primera actriz** que siempre está con él.
ENTREVISTADORA:	Señora, ¡por favor! ¡Esto es algo serio! ¿Hay algún **drama** que le guste?
SEÑORA:	Sí, sí. Me encanta **el concurso** *Baila con una estrella*. Espero ser **concursante** algún día...

¿Comprendes? Identify the character in each description: **E** (**la entrevistadora**) or **S** (**la señora**).

1. _____ Entrevista a los televidentes.

2. _____ Quiere participar en un programa de baile.

3. _____ Cree que el presentador de un noticiero es un galán.

Respuestas: 1. E; 2. S; 3. S

Vocabulario

El cine, el teatro y la televisión	Film, theater, and television
la cadena	network
el canal	channel
el ensayo	rehearsal
el estudio	studio
el guion	script
la obra	play (theater)
el papel	role (in a play, movie, or television show)
el premio	prize
la televisión por cable	cable television
por satélite	satellite television
en directo / en vivo	live (on television)

Los programas	Programs
la comedia	comedy
el concurso	game show, pageant
el documental	documentary
el drama	drama
la parodia	spoof
la telenovela	soap opera
la tragedia	tragedy

Los personajes	Characters
el/la concursante	contestant
el/la espectador/a	spectator
el galán	leading man
la primera actriz	leading lady
el/la productor/a	producer
el/la protagonista	protagonist, star
el/la televidente	TV viewer

Verbos	Verbs
actuar (actúo, actúas...)	to act (I act, you act . . .)
filmar	to film
ensayar	to rehearse
representar	to perform
sondear	to survey

Otras palabras y expresiones	Other words and expressions
el final	end
el principio	beginning

Variaciones

- The term **galán** expresses different meanings in Latin America versus Spain. In Latin America, where **la telenovela** is a very popular television genre, **el galán** refers to a handsome, savvy leading man. In Spain, however, **un galán** may not be handsome at all; the term is synonymous with *a courteous gentleman* and refers strictly to how a man treats a woman.
- In some countries, such as Spain, the verb **representar** is more commonly **interpretar**.

Letras y sonidos

The consonants *y*, *l*, and the sequence *ll*

As you already know, the letter **y** at the end of a word in Spanish corresponds to a glide sound as in **soy**, and alone, it can sound like a vowel, as in **Juan y María**. In other contexts, however, the letter **y** produces a consonant, which is stronger and usually sounds like the *y* in English *you* or *yellow*.

o-**y**e   pla-**y**a   **y**er-no   in-clu-**y**e   le-**y**e-ron

In most varieties of Spanish, the sequence **ll** sounds the same as **y**. Similarly, words that begin with the letters **hie-** in Spanish are pronounced like **ye-**.

lle-var   ta-**ll**a   a-ma-ri-**ll**o   **hie**-lo   **hie**r-ba

Finally, the letter **l** in Spanish sounds like the *l* in English *low*.

la-go   re-**l**oj   vo**l**-cán   mi**l**   fa-ta**l**   ge-ne-ra**l**

Aplicación

13-22 El cine, el teatro y la televisión. Selecciona la mejor definición o descripción para cada expresión.

1. _____ la comedia
2. _____ el documental
3. _____ el/la protagonista
4. _____ los espectadores
5. _____ el ensayo
6. _____ el guion
7. _____ la telenovela
8. _____ el papel

a. la preparación de una obra antes de presentarla
b. el actor o la actriz principal de la obra
c. una obra que divierte
d. un drama en la televisión en el que siempre hay mucha tensión dramática entre los personajes
e. una película informativa, por ejemplo, en un canal público
f. la parte que le corresponde a un actor en una obra
g. los que van a ver una obra
h. el material que los actores se memorizan, o las noticias que leen los presentadores

13-23 La guía de hoy. Lee el horario de algunos canales de televisión de España y contesta las preguntas a continuación.

08 abr	TV1	TV2	La Sexta	Cuatro	Teledeporte HD
20:30	…Gente	Tu salud	Serie: "La oficina"	Novela: "Amar en tiempos revueltos"	Fútbol: Real Madrid-Barcelona
21:00		Documental: *El mundo en crisis*	Serie: "Investigación criminal"		
21:30	Serie: "Anatomía de Grey"			Concurso: "¡Quiero bailar!"	
22:00			Cine: *La pantera rosa*		
22:30	Noticias	El tiempo			Tenis: Nadal-Federer
23:00		Cocina con Rubén		La 4 Noticias	

1. ¿Cuál es el canal con programas educativos?
2. ¿En qué canales hay noticieros?
3. ¿Qué programas son de EE. UU.?
4. ¿Qué documentales, películas y telenovelas se ofrecen?
5. ¿Qué concurso hay? ¿Es semejante a concursos en la televisión estadounidense?
6. Si te gustan los deportes, ¿qué canal te interesa?

13-24 Una escena de *Sábado de Estrellas*. Usa las palabras a continuación para completar las instrucciones del director de esta telecomedia popular en la televisión.

ensayar	espectadores	galán	papel	protagonistas
en vivo	filmar	guion	premio	

¡Atención! Hoy vamos a (1) _____ la escena del noticiero con la primera actriz y el (2) _____ para la presentación el sábado. Quiero que ustedes estén bien preparados. Por eso, el camarógrafo va a (3) _____ la escena para que después puedan verse y criticarse. Les quiero recordar que este es un programa (4) _____; el teatro estará lleno de (5) _____. Aunque es una comedia, es importante que los (6) _____ no se rían (*don't laugh*) en la escena. Estudien bien el (7) _____, especialmente donde deben hacer pausas. Memoricen su (8) _____ y no les presten atención a los espectadores cuando se rían. Ustedes pueden ayudarnos a ganar otro (9) _____ Emmy por nuestra comedia.

13-25 Jorge Ramos. Jorge Ramos es un presentador de renombre en el canal hispanohablante más visto de EE. UU.

Paso 1 Escucha el informe sobre él e identifica la información.

1. su profesión _____

2. la cadena de televisión que representa _____

3. el número de Emmy que ha ganado _____

4. gente que ha entrevistado _____

5. otras actividades profesionales _____
_____

6. su opinión sobre la diversidad _____
_____

Paso 2 Busca más información sobre Jorge Ramos en Internet para contestar estas preguntas.

1. ¿Quiénes son algunas de las personalidades que ha entrevistado?

2. ¿Cuáles son algunos de los temas sobre los que opina?

3. ¿Cuáles son algunos de los libros que ha escrito? ¿Has leído alguno?

📍 **Busca:** Jorge Ramos Univisión

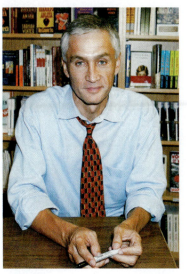
Jorge Ramos

13-26 Una serie en la televisión. Las telenovelas y las series dramáticas siempre exageran las cualidades y los defectos de sus protagonistas y las situaciones en que se encuentran. Trabajen en parejas para describir las características y las acciones de los personajes en una serie o telenovela que conozcan.

- el hombre diabólico
- la mujer perversa
- la mujer inocente
- el hombre de buen corazón

13-27 *Cara a cara*. Uno/a de ustedes es presentador/a de *Cara a cara*, un segmento de entrevistas dentro del *Noticiero 41*. El/La otro/a es una celebridad del cine o de la televisión. Háganse y respondan a las preguntas de una manera apropiada.

MODELO: PRESENTADOR/A: *¿Cuándo empezó su carrera?*
CELEBRIDAD: *La empecé en...*

Algunos temas de conversación

- su vida personal
- un escándalo
- su próxima película o presentación
- sus compañeros de reparto (*co-stars*)
- una experiencia inolvidable (*unforgettable*)

13-28 Una serie suya. Ustedes tienen un guion para una serie que quieren filmar. En grupos de tres o cuatro personas, preparen los siguientes elementos de su guion para vender un episodio piloto a un/a patrocinador/a (*sponsor*).

1. ¿Dónde ocurren el principio y el final del episodio?

2. ¿Quiénes serán el/la director/a, el galán y la primera actriz?

3. Describan las cualidades y los defectos de sus protagonistas.

4. ¿En qué situaciones se encontrarán?

5. ¿Cuántos episodios habrá? ¿A qué público le interesará la serie?

Cultura en vivo

Telenovelas are very popular in Latin America, and may last from six months to a year and a half, depending on their popularity. Among television viewers, **telenovelas** are part of their daily conversation, as they follow the actors and the plot twists and turns. In the U.S., the award-winning program *Jane, the Virgin* is loosely based on a Venezuelan **telenovela**, *Juana la Virgen*. What programs with an ongoing plot line do you watch? How long does it take for the story to come to a conclusion?

Si lo comemos todo, ganamos el concurso.

Estructuras

13.5 Hypothesize about what you and others will or would do

Si clauses

CLÁUSULAS CON *SI* EN EL INDICATIVO

¿Recuerdas? You have used the conjunction **si** in the present to refer to true and verifiable condition: **Vamos a la playa si no llueve.** *We'll go to the beach if it doesn't rain.*

Complete the sentence with the correct form of the logical verb: **ensayar, filmar.**

Si los actores (1) _____ bien la obra, el director (2) _____ la escena mañana.

Respuestas: 1. ensayan; 2. filma/filmará

When you begin a clause with **si**, you state a condition that must be met in order for something else to occur. If you are stating a fact, the verb in the **si** clause is usually in the present indicative, and the verb in the main clause is in the present or future tense, or is a command.

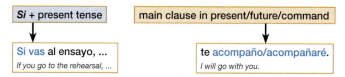

Si + present tense	main clause in present/future/command
Si vas al ensayo, ...	te **acompaño/acompañaré**.
If you go to the rehearsal, ...	*I will go with you.*

CLÁUSULAS CON *SI* PARA EXPRESAR HIPÓTESIS E INFORMACIÓN EN CONTRA DE LOS HECHOS

Si prefirieras escuchar el audiolibro, podríamos pedírselo.

- When the condition is hypothetical or contrary-to-fact, use the imperfect subjunctive after **si** and the conditional tense in the main clause.

Si + imperfect subjunctive	main clause in conditional tense
Si entendieras italiano, ...	el documental sobre Italia **sería** más interesante.
If you understood Italian, ...	*the documentary about Italy would be more interesting.*

- Note that you can reverse the order of the **si** clause and the conditional clause.

| **Si conociera** a Jorge Ramos, lo **invitaría** a cenar. | *If I knew Jorge Ramos, I'd invite him to dinner.* |
| **Invitaría** a cenar a Jorge Ramos **si lo conociera**. | *I'd invite Jorge Ramos to dinner if I knew him.* |

- Always use the imperfect subjunctive with the expression **como si** (*as if*) because it connotes a contrary-to-fact situation.

| El galán actúa **como si fuera** el más atractivo de la telenovela. | *The leading man acts as if he were the most attractive in the soap opera.* (He's not.) |
| ¡No me mires **como si** yo no **supiera** nada! | *Don't look at me as if I didn't know anything!* (I do.) |

¿Comprendes? Complete the sentences with the correct present indicative or imperfect subjunctive form of the logical verb: **estar, ser.**

Los directores hablan como si el programa (1) _____ un gran éxito. Pero si el índice de audiencia (*ratings*) (2) _____ muy bajo, la cadena va a cancelar el programa.

Respuestas: 1. fuera 2. está

Aplicación

13-29 *Primer Impacto.* Michelle Galván y Pamela Silva Conde son dos presentadoras de *Primer Impacto*, un noticiero de Univisión que cuenta con uno de los índices más altos de audiencia en EE. UU. y en 12 países de Latinoamérica.

Paso 1   Lee la conversación entre las dos presentadoras y selecciona el verbo más lógico.

PAMELA: Hola, Michelle. Si (1) tienes/tuvieras las estadísticas demográficas para las elecciones presidenciales, dámelas ahora para que las repase antes de empezar.

MICHELLE: No las tengo, pero si quieres, (2) podemos/podríamos hablar con la persona que está haciendo la investigación.

PAMELA: Ah, mira esto. Parece que el número de votantes hispanos aumenta todos los años. Si los políticos (3) entienden/entendieran el impacto de sus votos, les darían más atención.

MICHELLE: Tienes razón. Y si un candidato hispano (4) tiene/tuviera éxito en las próximas elecciones presidenciales, o mejor, si (5) es/fuera electa una presidenta hispana, no habría duda de que la voz hispana es muy importante en este país.

DIRECTOR: Atención. Si me (6) hacen/hicieran el favor, el programa empieza en cinco, cuatro, tres, dos, uno...

Paso 2   Ahora vuelve a leer la conversación entre Michelle y Pamela y contesta las preguntas.

1. ¿Quién necesita más información para el noticiero de esta noche? ¿Por qué?

2. ¿Qué van a hacer para obtener la información?

3. ¿Por qué deberían los políticos dar más atención a los votantes hispanos?

4. ¿Qué le gustaría a Michelle que pasara en las próximas elecciones presidenciales?

5. ¿Votarías por un candidato hispano en las elecciones presidenciales si se presentara uno/a con buenas calificaciones?

13-30 **Comedia en Internet.** Antes, era necesario ver las comedias en la televisión o en un club. Ahora reina Internet y hay una nueva generación de jóvenes cómicos. Entre ellos, el dominicano Félix Mejía tiene una presencia notable. Aquí explica sus razones por ser cómico. Escribe la forma correcta del presente del indicativo de un verbo lógico para completar su explicación.

deber	encontrar	preferir	representar
decir	ir	reírse	tener

Para mí, lo importante es entretener a mi audiencia. Si el público (1) _____, (2) _____ éxito. Si la gente no (3) _____ chistosas mis pequeñas comedias, (4) _____ inventar algo nuevo. Pero hay que representar la realidad de la cultura hispana, en mi caso, la dominicana. Todos (5) _____ a reconocer a la madre dominicana, a la novia dominicana o al amigo dominicano si yo los (6) _____ fielmente. Es una meta que cumplo de buen corazón. Si mis seguidores (7) _____ otra cosa, me lo (8) _____.

13-31 **¿Qué pasaría si...?** Los cinematógrafos están discutiendo las consecuencias de sus posibles acciones. Completa la conversación con la forma correcta del condicional o del imperfecto de subjuntivo de cada verbo entre paréntesis.

PRODUCTORA: Si (1: nosotros) _____ (contratar) a Penélope Cruz, (2) _____ (tener) que pagarle más de un millón de dólares.

DIRECTOR: Es verdad, pero si ella (3) _____ (trabajar) para nosotros, nuestra película (4) _____ (tener) mucho más éxito.

PRODUCTORA: Mi amigo Javier la conoce bien. Pero, seguramente no le (5) _____ (decir) nada a la prensa si yo lo (6) _____ (llamar). Es muy discreto.

DIRECTOR: Es bueno que tengas esas conexiones. Si yo (7) _____ (poder) usar alguna conexión, ¡(8) _____ (usar) esa ventaja!

PRODUCTORA: Bueno, ¡lo llamo ahora mismo!

Presencia hispana

Until the last decade, most well-known Hispanic directors worked from abroad. That is changing, both with Hispanic directors born and raised in the U.S., such as Aurora Guerrero (*Mosquita y Mari*), and others who have emigrated, such as Rodrigo García. García has earned a place in the arts as a screenwriter, producer, and director for HBO (*The Sopranos, In Treatment*), and for independent films (*Things You Can Tell by Looking at Her, Nine Lives, Mother and Child*). About his art, García says his vision is through the eyes of an immigrant. How might his experience influence his work?

13-32A **¡Necesito información!** Túrnense para reflexionar sobre lo que harían en estas situaciones hipotéticas. **Estudiante B**: por favor, ve al **Apéndice 1**, página A-16.

> MODELO: subir los precios de las entradas del cine
>
> ESTUDIANTE A: *¿Qué harías si subieran los precios de las entradas del cine?*
>
> ESTUDIANTE B: *Pues, iría menos...*

Estudiante A:

Mis preguntas	Posibles respuestas a las preguntas de mi compañero/a
¿Qué harías si...?	
1. (yo) invitarte a un concierto de rock	• pedir dos millones de dólares
3. (tú) tener que comprar un televisor de alta definición	• prestarte el dinero que necesitaras
5. (tú) ganar un concurso en la televisión	• aceptar el papel de extra con mucho gusto
7. (tú) conocer una personalidad famosa	• regalarle una a mi profesor de drama
9. (tú) visitar Hollywood	• invitarla a cenar a mi casa

 13-33 **Los valores sociales, el público y el dinero.** Hay muchos factores que afectan lo que vemos en el cine y la televisión. En parejas, hablen sobre algunos de estos factores.

> MODELO: Si los padres controlaran mejor los programas en la televisión...
>
> *sus hijos no verían programas violentos.*

Posibles temas

1. No habría odio (*hatred*) contra los grupos minoritarios...
2. Si hubiera papeles positivos para personas mayores en el cine...
3. Habría más películas apropiadas para niños...
4. Los documentales serían más populares...
5. Yo siempre vería el noticiero de Univisión...
6. Si no hubiera tantos anuncios comerciales en la televisión...

 13-34 **Si yo fuera...** Túrnense para decir lo que harían si fueran estrellas en el mundo del espectáculo por un día.

cantar	ir
dar	jugar
decir	participar
ganar	recibir
hacer	ver
invitar	visitar

Algunas posibilidades: Lady Gaga, Will Smith, Jorge Ramos, Tina Fey, Eva Mendes, Ashton Kutcher, Maggie Q, Viola Davis, Jon Stewart, Taylor Swift, Queen Latifah

> MODELO: ESTUDIANTE 1: *Si yo fuera Jorge Ramos, pasaría mis vacaciones en Cancún...*
>
> ESTUDIANTE 2: *¿Por qué irías a Cancún y no a Acapulco?*

¡Conversemos!

Primero, pregúntate si puedes llevar a cabo las siguientes funciones comunicativas. Después, júntate con dos o tres compañeros/as de clase para presentar las situaciones. Hagan y respondan a por lo menos cuatro preguntas en cada situación.

✓ CAN YOU. . .

☐ discuss television shows, movies, and entertainment?

☐ talk about what will happen given certain conditions or circumstances?

☐ talk about hypothetical situations and what you and others would do?

WITH YOUR CLASSMATE(S). . .

Situación: En un café.

Hablen de sus programas y estrellas favoritos y describan los aspectos que les gustan de ellos. Incluyan también los programas y estrellas que no toleran y expliquen por qué.

Para empezar: *¿Cuál es tu programa favorito?*

Situación: Planes.

Hagan planes para el sábado, pero propongan las condiciones o circunstancias necesarias para poder llevar a cabo sus planes. Usen cláusulas con **si** en el indicativo.

Para empezar: *Si no llueve, vamos a hacer un pícnic, pero si llueve, vamos a...*

Situación: En otra vida.

Hablen de cómo cambiaría su vida si algunas cosas fueran diferentes. Piensen en los amigos, trabajos, clases, etc., que tienen ahora y cómo cambiarían bajo otras circunstancias.

Para empezar: *Si no estudiara ingeniería, querría estudiar arte porque...*

Club cultura

13.6 First identify topics, then summarize main ideas

San Sebastián y el Festival Internacional del Cine

Estrategia para ver

First identify topics, then summarize main ideas. When you read, you can stop, reread, mark passages, and write notes in the margin. But when you watch, these strategies do not easily apply. Instead, try watching in chunks to first identify the topic, and then again to summarize the content. Watch as many times as necessary to identify enough information to be able to restate it in your own words.

ANTES DE VER EL VIDEO

13-35 ¿Qué sabes de San Sebastián, España? Escribe **C** o **F** para indicar si la información es cierta o falsa para darte una idea sobre los temas de este video.

1. _____ San Sebastián está en la costa sur.
2. _____ Tiene un lugar estratégico por su comercio con Asia.
3. _____ Tiene una playa que se llama la Concha (*Shell*).
4. _____ Eduardo Chillida es un artista famoso de San Sebastián.
5. _____ Todos los años hay un importante festival de cine en San Sebastián.

AL VER EL VIDEO

13-36 Los temas del video. Mira el video y escribe los tres temas más importantes. Luego, velo otra vez y escribe un pequeño resumen sobre cada tema.

DESPUÉS DE VER EL VIDEO

13-37 ¿Comprendiste? Selecciona la opción que mejor completa cada oración.

1. El *Peine del Viento* es…
   a. una escultura.   b. un poema.   c. una roca en la costa.

2. El nombre **San Sebastián** en vasco es…
   a. Llanes.   b. Donostia.   c. Gijón.

3. El premio más importante del festival reconoce…
   a. al primer actor.   b. la carrera   c. la mejor película.
                              cinematográfica.

4. Entre los premiados se incluye…
   a. Rodrigo García.   b. *Titanic*.   c. Meryl Streep.

5. Si asistes al festival, puedes participar en…
   a. las fiestas.   b. el *photocall*.   c. el Premio del Público.

13-38 Si asistieras al Festival. Escribe un párrafo para contar lo que verías y harías si asistieras al Festival de San Sebastián. Incluye por lo menos cinco oraciones con **si** y el condicional.

   MODELO: *Si pudiera asistir al Festival, participaría en el Premio del Público…*

13.3 Nuestro mundo

Panoramas

13.7 **Identify and research key elements of Spain's cultural heritage**

La herencia cultural de España

La rica herencia cultural de España se refleja en su lengua, sus monumentos, su arte, su comida, y su gente, y se debe a la diversidad de pueblos que han habitado la península ibérica. Aunque la lengua española se derive del latín, por su historia, otras muchas culturas también la han influenciado enormemente.

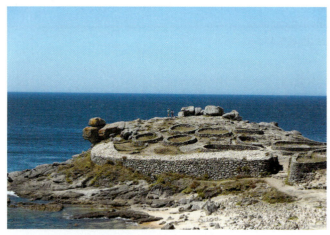

¿A que no sabías que los celtas se establecieron en el norte de España? Algunos vestigios de sus fortalezas quedan, especialmente en Galicia. La fortaleza celta Castro de Barona fue establecida y habitada en Galicia entre 1000 a.C. y 1000 d.C. En el léxico, sabemos que las palabras **la camisa**, **la cerveza** y **el carpintero** tienen origen celta. En la música, nos queda **la gaita** (*bagpipe*).

Desde su llegada en 711 hasta su expulsión en 1492, los moros influyeron en las matemáticas, la ingeniería, las artes y la literatura. Por ejemplo, la Mezquita de Córdoba, construida en 784, es un fenómeno que reúne su vasto conocimiento de la arquitectura. En el léxico, numerosas palabras que empiezan con **al** son de origen árabe: **alcohol**, **álgebra**, **alfombra**, **algodón**. En la cocina, introdujeron **la berenjena** (*eggplant*), **la espinaca**, **la caña de azúcar**, **el arroz** y **las naranjas amargas** (*bitter*).

Los judíos jugaron un papel importante en muchas partes de España, pero especialmente en Toledo, donde puedes apreciar los antiguos barrios con sus callejuelas estrechas y empedradas con adoquines (*paved with cobblestones*). En el léxico encontramos expresiones de origen hebreo, como **aleluya**, **el sábado** y **amén**. En la cocina, introdujeron **el gazpacho** preparado con **pan ácimo** (*unleavened*) y **los estofados** (*stews*) que se preparaban el día antes del *sabbat*. Tradicionalmente, los judíos dominaban los campos de la medicina, la educación y las finanzas.

Con la Reconquista de la Península en 1492 y la expulsión de los judíos y los moros, España se convirtió en un país nominalmente cristiano. Las tradiciones cristianas siguen presentes hoy por toda la Península, pero en ningún lugar más que en Sevilla en Semana Santa, una celebración que data del siglo XVI. La figura de la "Macarena", la Virgen María de mayor devoción, sale en procesión el Viernes Santo.

España

Sitios de la UNESCO:	49
Sitios nominados:	30[1]
Periódicos independientes:	*El País, El Mundo, ABC*
Televisión nacional:	TVE
Radio nacional:	RNE
Libertad de prensa:	1977[2]

[1]UNESCO
[2]PressReference.com

13-39 Identifica. Selecciona la opción correcta según la información de **Panoramas**.

la cerveza	Galicia	palabras que empiezan con **al**
la cultura judía	la mora, la judía y la cristiana	la Virgen de la Macarena

1. tres culturas que existieron simultáneamente _____

2. donde se establecieron los celtas _____

3. una figura importante en Semana Santa en Sevilla _____

4. la influencia mora en la lengua _____

5. el origen del gazpacho preparado con pan ácimo _____

6. una bebida cuyo nombre tiene origen celta _____

13-40 Desafío. Identifica la información según el mapa y los datos estadísticos.

1. tres islas españolas en el Mediterráneo

2. una ciudad española situada en África

3. el río que pasa por Toledo

4. las montañas que forman la frontera con Francia

5. cuándo se hizo ley la libertad de prensa

6. el número de sitios de la UNESCO

13-41 Investigación: Herencia cultural de España. Investiga un sitio español del Patrimonio de la Humanidad y escribe un resumen del lugar. Luego, preséntaselo a la clase. Incluye:

- su nombre y dónde se encuentra
- por qué es importante o interesante
- cómo era en el pasado; cómo es ahora
- qué harías si algún día lo visitaras
- una foto representativa

Busca: España sitios UNESCO

Páginas

13.8 **Evaluate what you read**

La diversidad en el cine, el teatro y la televisión (Erasmo Santiago del Toboso, España)

Estrategia para leer

Evaluate what you read. Beyond summarizing, we need to think about what we read, and to evaluate the reasoning. To begin, look at the key question: Is it stated or implied? Is it clear and unbiased? Does it reflect the complexity of the issue? Then, focus on the information: Is there relevant evidence, first-hand experiences, or information essential to the issue? Is the information accurate?

ANTES DE LEER

13-42 **¿Es parcial (*biased*) o imparcial?** Estas son las primeras frases de tres ensayos diferentes. Identifica si son parciales (**P**) o imparciales (**I**). Explica tu razón.

1. _____ Según la investigación, las carreras del futuro dependerán de la tecnología, y no del trabajo manual.

2. _____ En mi experiencia, es mejor seguir la carrera que uno quiera y no la que quieran los padres.

3. _____ Para 2025, temo que el gobierno controle nuestros pensamientos.

AL LEER

13-43 **El argumento.** Primero, dale una mirada rápida (*skim through*) a la carta para identificar el argumento principal. Luego, evalúa la información: ¿es parcial o imparcial? ¿Incluye experiencias o información verificable para apoyar su argumento? Da ejemplos de tu evaluación.

Nombre* | Erasmo Santiago del Toboso

Correo* | erasmosantiagodeltoboso@manchanet.com

Asunto | La diversidad en el cine, el teatro y la televisión

Mensaje*

Estimado Director de *El Campo*:

En estos días, se lee mucho sobre la necesidad de tener más diversidad en el cine, el teatro y la televisión. Por ejemplo, muchas personas dicen que el gobierno va a implementar una ley que requiere que haya cierto número de papeles para cada grupo étnico y también que haya categorías de premios reservadas para hombres y mujeres (p. ej., "mejor película femenina", "mejor guion femenino", etc.). Además, muchas personas comentan que si hay un papel masculino heroico, que debería haber un papel femenino heroico en la misma película. Y no me pregunte sobre cómicos o cómicas. No hay ninguna mujer que me haga reír como los cómicos masculinos de la televisión de noche. ¿Se ha preguntado por qué la mayoría son hombres y no mujeres? ¿Y qué de los salarios? ¡Hombre! ¿Debe la primera actriz ganar tanto como el galán? Yo digo que no, no solo porque el público prefiere ver un hombre fuerte que una mujer fuerte, sino también porque, en general, los hombres son más talentosos que las mujeres. En fin, es toda una conspiración de un grupo de radicales que espera controlar lo que vemos en la televisión, el teatro y el cine. Tenemos que resistir.

Con todo respeto,

Erasmo Santiago del Toboso, Madrid

*Campo requerido

MANDAR

DESPUÉS DE LEER

13-44 La carta al director. Indica si es probable (**P**) o improbable (**I**), según lo que has leído. Después, explica por qué lo crees.

1. _____ El escritor es un hombre.

2. _____ Su argumento es que hay mucha discriminación en el cine, el teatro y la televisión.

3. _____ Para esta persona, es importante que el gobierno regule la industria cinematográfica.

4. _____ Para esta persona, hay grandes diferencias entre los talentos masculinos y los femeninos.

5. _____ Para esta persona, es lógico que la mujer gane tanto como el hombre.

6. _____ Esta persona da la impresión de que está en control de su situación.

13-45 Resume y evalúa. Primero, escribe un resumen del argumento del escritor. Después, contesta estas preguntas para evaluar su contenido. ¿Es claro o implícito su argumento? ¿Es su posición parcial o imparcial? ¿Representa bien un tema complejo? ¿Es relevante su experiencia o la evidencia que presenta? ¿Es acertada (*accurate*) la información? Explica.

13-46 La diversidad en los medios. El Consejo Estatal del Pueblo Gitano en España ha pedido que se retiren programas de televisión (especialmente los de *reality*) que promueven estereotipos ofensivos de su etnia. El Consejo ha organizado una campaña publicitaria para concienciar a la población española que estas caricaturas fomentan el prejuicio y la discriminación contra el pueblo gitano.

Paso 1 Busca un video de la campaña del Consejo y escribe tu reacción sobre su mensaje. ¿Te parece efectivo? ¿Por qué? ¿Te hace pensar en cómo la televisión representa a otras etnias? Da un ejemplo positivo y otro negativo.

📍 **Busca:** TelebasuraNoEsRealidad

Los programas de televisión *reality* promueven estereotipos del pueblo gitano.

Paso 2 En parejas, hablen de la diversidad en los medios de comunicación y el mundo del entretenimiento. En los noticieros, ¿hay suficiente representación de mujeres, de diversos grupos étnicos y de personas mayores? Den ejemplos concretos para su opinión. ¿Creen que son justos los papeles en la televisión para afroamericanos, musulmanes, hispanos y asiáticos? Den ejemplos para respaldar su opinión. ¿Qué películas o programas en la televisión podrían servir como modelo para la diversidad? ¿Han tenido éxito?

Taller

13.9 Express and support an opinion

Una carta al director

Estrategia para escribir

Express and support an opinion. It's simple to find opinions on almost any topic in the press, on TV and on the Internet, but what is often lacking is concrete, verifiable evidence for the opinion. When you write an opinion piece, first, state the issue clearly. Then, provide relevant evidence, experiences, or essential information to support your view.

13-47 En mi opinión. Vas a escribir una carta al director de un periódico sobre algún tema que te interese. Puede ser sobre la prensa, el cine, la música, algún artista, la política, etc. Primero, quieres que el director decida publicar tu carta y segundo, esperas convencer a los lectores que tienes razón.

ANTES DE ESCRIBIR

- **Ideas.** Busca el sitio web de algún periódico del mundo hispano y dale una mirada rápida a las secciones para ver lo que contienen. Elige un tema que quieras comentar.
- **Tu opinión.** Escribe una oración que introduzca tu posición sobre el tema y por lo menos tres razones concretas que apoyen tu opinión.

AL ESCRIBIR

- **Presentación.** Escribe el saludo y la razón por qué le escribes la carta. Escribe una o dos oraciones para explicar por qué te importa este tema.
- **Apoya tu opinión.** Explica las razones explícitas por las que tienes esta opinión sobre el tema. Incluye experiencias y evidencia concretas y verificables.
- **Resumen.** Resume tu argumento y agradécele su tiempo.
- **Cierre.** Cierra la carta de una manera respetuosa.

DESPUÉS DE ESCRIBIR

- **Revisar.** Revisa tu carta para verificar los siguientes puntos:
  - ☐ el uso del imperfecto del subjuntivo, el condicional y las cláusulas con **si**
  - ☐ el uso de los adjetivos y pronombres posesivos
  - ☐ la concordancia y la ortografía
- **Intercambiar.** Intercambia tu carta con la de un/a compañero/a. Mientras leen las cartas, hagan comentarios y sugerencias sobre el contenido, la estructura y la gramática. Reaccionen también a las cartas.
- **Entregar.** Pon tu carta en limpio, incorporando las sugerencias de tu compañero/a. Después, entrégasela a tu profesor/a.

En este capítulo...

))) Vocabulario

Primera parte

La prensa	The press
el artículo	article
la caricatura política	political cartoon
la cartelera	entertainment section
el consultorio sentimental	advice column
el editorial	editorial section
el horóscopo	horoscope
las noticias (de última hora)	(latest) news
la primera plana	front page
la reseña	review (of books, movies, etc.)
la revista (del corazón)	(celebrity) magazine
la sección deportiva	sports section
la sección financiera	financial section
el superventas	bestseller
el titular	headline

Noticias en línea	Online news
el buscador	search engine
el inicio	home
el periódico digital	online newspaper

Noticias en la televisión y en la radio	News on television and radio
el noticiero	newscast
el reportaje	feature

Gente en los medios	People in the media
el/la comentarista	newscaster, commentator
el/la comentarista deportivo/a	sportscaster
el/la crítico/a	critic
el/la director/a	editor in chief
el/la meteorólogo/a	meteorologist
el/la presentador/a	host (on television, radio), announcer
el/la reportero/a	reporter

El público	The audience
el/la lector/a	reader
el/la radioyente	listener
el/la oyente de podcast	podcast listener

Verbos	Verbs
informar	to report
revisar	to check
tener éxito	to be successful
transmitir	to broadcast

Segunda parte

El cine, el teatro y la televisión	Film, theater, and television
la cadena	network
el canal	channel
el ensayo	rehearsal
el estudio	studio
el guion	script
la obra	play (theater)
el papel	role (in a play, movie, or television show)
el premio	prize
la televisión por cable	cable television
por satélite	satellite television
en directo / en vivo	live (on television)

Los programas	Programs
la comedia	comedy
el concurso	game show, pageant
el documental	documentary
el drama	drama
la parodia	spoof
la telenovela	soap opera
la tragedia	tragedy

Los personajes	Characters
el/la concursante	contestant
el/la espectador/a	spectator
el galán	leading man
la primera actriz	leading lady
el/la productor/a	producer
el/la protagonista	protagonist, star
el/la televidente	TV viewer

Verbos	Verbs
actuar (actúo, actúas...)	to act (I act, you act. . .)
filmar	to film
ensayar	to rehearse
representar	to perform
sondear	to survey

Otras palabras y expresiones	Other words and expressions
el final	end
el principio	beginning

Long-form possessive adjectives and pronouns   *See page 422.*

Capítulo 14
¡Seamos cultos!

«De músico, poeta y loco, todos tenemos un poco».

Fuente: Christie's Images Ltd.

Deux figures de **Wifredo Lam.** The figures in Lam's paintings often depict characters central to **santería**, an Afro-Caribbean religion that fuses Yoruba and Christian beliefs.

Learning Objectives

14.1 Discuss music and dance

14.2 Report how long something has been going on, and convince others to join you to do something

14.3 Discuss types of dance, and learn about an eclectic Colombian band

In this Chapter

ENFOQUE CULTURAL: COLOMBIA
Club cultura: Medellín, símbolo de la Colombia moderna

Indica con **C (Cierto)** o **F (Falso)** si escuchas/ves o no esta información en el video.

1. _____ la población de Medellín

2. _____ los proyectos artísticos y culturales

3. _____ el sistema de transporte

4. _____ el artista Botero

5. _____ la conciencia social de la gente

14.1 Primera parte

Vocabulario

14.1 Discuss music and dance

La música y el baile

Salvador

Maripaz

))) En un concierto. El joven **director** de **orquesta** impresiona al **público**.

SALVADOR: **El compositor** de esta **pieza musical** es muy **talentoso**, ¿no crees?

MARIPAZ: Sí, y **los músicos** son impresionantes. Escucha a **la solista**, ¡tiene **una voz** fenomenal!

SALVADOR: También el director es extraordinario. Ha llevado **la orquesta sinfónica** en giras a las más importantes ciudades del mundo. El público siempre **aplaude** mucho y le da **una ovación de pie**.

MARIPAZ: Eso explica por qué fue tan difícil conseguir boletos. El año que viene, compremos una suscripción para toda la temporada.

¿Comprendes? Indicate who each statement describes: **el director**, **Maripaz**, **el público**, **la solista**.

1. _____ Aplaude entusiasmadamente.

2. _____ Canta excelentemente.

3. _____ Viaja mucho con la orquesta.

4. _____ Va a planear mejor el próximo año.

Respuestas: 1. el público; 2. la solista; 3. el director; 4. Maripaz

Vocabulario

La ópera, la música clásica y el jazz	Opera, classical music, and jazz
la audición	audition
el bailarín / la bailarina	dancer
la comedia musical	musical comedy
el/la compositor/a	composer
el/la coreógrafo/a	choreographer
el/la director/a	conductor, director
el escenario	stage
el/la músico/a	musician
la ópera	opera
la ovación de pie	standing ovation
la pieza (musical / de baile)	(musical/dance) piece
el público	audience
la sinfonía	symphony
el/la solista	soloist
talentoso/a	talented
la voz	voice

Verbos	Verbs
aplaudir	to clap, applaud
cantar	to sing
componer	to compose
improvisar	to improvise

Los grupos musicales	Musical groups
la banda	band
el conjunto	musical group
el cuarteto	quartet
la orquesta sinfónica	symphony orchestra

Los instrumentos musicales	Musical instruments
el arpa	harp
la batería	drums
el chelo	cello
el clarinete	clarinet
el contrabajo	bass
la corneta	cornet, horn
la flauta	flute
la guitarra	guitar
las maracas	maracas
la marimba	marimba
el piano	piano
el saxofón	saxophone
el tambor	drum
el trombón	trombone
la trompeta	trumpet
el violín	violin

Algunos bailes	Some dances
el baile de salón	ballroom dancing
el ballet	ballet
la danza moderna	modern dance
el flamenco	flamenco

Variaciones

- **La guitarra** has different names, depending on its size and where it is popular. In traditional **mariachi** music, you have a small five-stringed **vihuela**, the traditional six-stringed **guitarra acústica**, and the very large **guitarrón**. A **charango** is a small ten-stringed instrument, traditionally made from the shell of an armadillo, and popular throughout the Andes.
- **El chelo** is also called **el violonchelo**.

Aplicación

14-1 La música. Indica si estos instrumentos musicales son de cuerda (*string*), de percusión o de viento.

el arpa	el contrabajo	las maracas	el tambor
la batería	la corneta	la marimba	el trombón
el chelo	la flauta	el piano	la trompeta
el clarinete	la guitarra	el saxofón	el violín

de cuerda	de percusión	de viento
la viola	*el triángulo*	*la tuba*

14-2 **En el escenario.** Selecciona el significado de cada palabra.

1. _____ el/la solista
2. _____ la audición
3. _____ el/la director/a
4. _____ la sinfonía
5. _____ el conjunto
6. _____ el/la coreógrafo/a
7. _____ el/la compositor/a
8. _____ el escenario

a. miembros de un grupo musical que tocan y cantan juntos

b. la persona que canta o toca sola

c. una persona que compone música

d. la persona que dirige la orquesta

e. la persona que crea los pasos de los bailarines

f. el lugar en el teatro donde se presenta un drama

g. una pieza musical con movimientos

h. un tipo de prueba en que el músico toca o canta

 14-3 **Un genio causa sensación en Los Ángeles.** Es muy raro que una persona tan joven adquiera tanto prestigio en tan poco tiempo.

Paso 1 Escucha el informe sobre Gustavo Dudamel y contesta brevemente las siguientes preguntas.

1. ¿Cuál es su nacionalidad y su profesión?
2. ¿A qué se debe su éxito, según él?
3. ¿Qué oportunidad tienen los jóvenes con talento en su país?
4. ¿Qué habilidad especial tiene Dudamel?
5. En tu opinión, ¿por qué lo ha llamado la revista *Time* una de las personas más influyentes del mundo?

Paso 2 Busca en Internet un fragmento de una función en la que aparece Gustavo Dudamel. Escribe un párrafo describiendo lo que ves y escuchas.

 **Busca:** Gustavo Dudamel video

Gustavo Dudamel

Presencia hispana

Because of their multicultural heritage, many Hispanic-American composers explore the theme of identity in their music. Born in Berkeley, California in 1972, Gabriela Lena Frank is an up-and-coming composer who incorporates her Peruvian, Chinese, Lithuanian, and Jewish ancestry into her work. After winning her first Latin Grammy, her works have been commissioned by major U.S. and international orchestras and performers, such as Yo-Yo Ma. What parts of your heritage would you include if you were a composer?

Cultura en vivo

The major cities in Latin America and Spain are known for their opera houses and theaters. The Teatro de Colón in Buenos Aires, Teatro Solís in Montevideo, Teatro Municipal in Santiago de Chile, and Teatro Real in Madrid are just a few of the fabulously ornate and acoustically perfect venues for classical music and opera. Tickets are relatively inexpensive in many places, and events are regularly sold out. How would the cost of tickets affect the popularity of attending live classical music concerts?

 14-4 La vida de los músicos. En parejas, hagan una lista de las cualidades y talentos que deben tener las personas dedicadas a la música o al baile.

MODELO: *Deben tener mucha perseverancia; por eso hay muy pocas estrellas.*

 14-5 Una fundación cultural. Ustedes son miembros de un comité de una fundación cultural y tienen que distribuir sus fondos entre varios programas.

Paso 1 En grupos de tres o cuatro estudiantes, decidan entre ustedes cómo van a distribuir los fondos y preparen sus razones para justificar sus recomendaciones. Tienen un presupuesto (*budget*) de $3.000.000.

MODELO: ESTUDIANTE 1: *Creo que debemos donarle... a...*
ESTUDIANTE 2: *No estoy de acuerdo. Es mucho dinero y...*

PROYECTOS:

1. una exposición de murales de pintores del barrio del este de Los Ángeles (costo: $500.000)
2. un programa educativo para llevar la música clásica a las escuelas de Appalachia (costo: $1.000.000)
3. un concierto abierto al público de música de compositores jóvenes no muy conocidos (costo: $750.000)
4. un programa para reparar y donarles instrumentos musicales a las escuelas (costo: $250.000)
5. una gira de una compañía de ballet por Europa (costo: $2.000.000)
6. una gira de esculturas de artistas jóvenes por EE. UU. (costo: $450.000)

Paso 2 Júntense con el resto de la clase para debatir sus selecciones y llegar a un consenso. Usen las siguientes expresiones para expresar su opinión.

- (No) Estoy de acuerdo.
- (No) Tienes razón.
- Pienso que...
- En mi opinión, ...
- Entiendo lo que dices, pero...
- Por otro lado, ... (*On the other hand, ...*)

Estructuras

14.2 **Report how long something has been going on, and convince others to join you to do something**

Hacer in time expressions

¿Recuerdas? In **Capítulo 6** you learned to express how long ago an event took place with the expression **hace... que...** (event in the preterit): **Hace diez años que estudié violín.** *I studied violin ten years ago.*

Answer in Spanish: ¿Cuánto tiempo hace que empezaste a estudiar español?

Respuestas: 1. *Answers will vary:* Hace (seis meses, un año, dos años, etc.) que empecé a estudiar español.

...iiiiiiiiiiiiiiiiiiiiiiiiiiiiiiiiii

¿Cuánto tiempo hace que canta esa nota?

To express the idea that an action began in the past and is still going on in the present, use these constructions with the verb **hacer**:

- To ask *how long* a certain action has been going on, use the following construction.

¿Cuánto (tiempo) hace que + verb phrase in the present tense**?**

¿Cuánto tiempo hace que Gustavo Dudamel dirige la orquesta filarmónica?	*How long has Gustavo Dudamel been conducting the philharmonic orchestra?*
¿Cuántas horas hace que esperas la audición?	*How many hours have you been waiting for the audition?*

- To answer these questions, use these constructions with **hacer**.

hace + time expression + **que** + verb phrase in the present

Hace dos horas que espero la audición.	*I have been waiting for the audition for two hours.*

- When the question is negative, it expresses how long it has been since something occurred.

¿Cuántos años hace que **no** tocas el violín?	*How many years has it been since you played the violin?*

- Note that in Spanish, the verb **hacer** and the main verbs are in the present tense; the English equivalent, however, uses *has* or *have been*.

¿Comprendes? Complete the sentence with the correct form of the logical verb: **aplaudir, hacer.**

(1) _____ tres minutos que el público (2) _____ a la solista.

Respuestas: 1. Hace; 2. aplaude

Aplicación

14-6 Juan Diego Flórez. El tenor peruano Juan Diego Flórez ha recibido mucha atención crítica por sus representaciones en los principales teatros del mundo.

Paso 1 Selecciona la respuesta que mejor contesta cada pregunta que le hace un reportero.

1. _____ ¿Cuánto tiempo hace que usted es aficionado a la música?

2. _____ ¿Cuánto tiempo hace que usted canta ópera?

3. _____ ¿Cuánto tiempo hace que usted compone música también?

4. _____ ¿Cuánto tiempo hace que usted estudió en el Instituto Curtis?

5. _____ ¿Cuánto tiempo hace que usted hizo su primera audición en Bolonia, Italia?

6. _____ ¿Cuánto tiempo hace que usted sirve como Embajador de Buena Voluntad de la UNESCO?

a. Creo que cualquier músico debe saber componer además de representar. Empecé a componer cuando empecé mis estudios en el conservatorio.

b. En 1989, decidí estudiar y cantar ópera en serio.

c. Fue un gran honor ser invitado a una audición en el Festival de Rossini en 1996.

d. Me nombraron al puesto en 2014. Es un placer representar esa organización mundial.

e. Quería conocer el mundo, por eso, en 1993 fui a estudiar en EE. UU.

f. Siempre me ha gustado la música, y de joven cantaba música pop y rock.

Paso 2 Contesta las preguntas basadas en el **Paso 1**.

1. ¿Cuánto tiempo hace que Juan Diego canta ópera?

2. ¿Cuánto tiempo hace que estudió en el Instituto Curtis?

3. ¿Cuánto tiempo hace que hizo su primera audición en Bolonia, Italia?

4. ¿Cuánto tiempo hace que sirve como Embajador de Buena Voluntad de la UNESCO?

Paso 3 En 2017, Perú sufrió devastadoras lluvias y deslizamientos de tierra (*mudslides*) que destruyeron muchas zonas rurales y causaron unas 120 muertes. En su página de Facebook, Juan Diego hizo un llamamiento para donaciones para ayudar a las víctimas de la tragedia. Busca su versión de la canción "Contigo Perú" y escribe tu reacción a su representación.

⚲ Busca: Juan Diego Flórez Contigo Perú

14-7 Antes de la función. La función va a empezar a las ocho y todos se están preparando. Forma oraciones completas para explicar cuánto tiempo hace que las siguientes personas hacen las acciones indicadas, y luego explica cómo se sienten o de qué se quejan (*they complain*).

> MODELO: la violinista: practicar / cinco horas
> *Hace cinco horas que la violinista practica y ahora está cansada.*

1. la soprano: buscar su vestido / treinta minutos

2. los bailarines: bailar sin música / diez minutos

3. los miembros de la orquesta: esperar al solista / mucho tiempo

4. los chelistas: hablar con el director / quince minutos

5. el director: trabajar con la orquesta / una semana

6. el público: esperar entrar / una hora

14-8A ¡Necesito información! A continuación tienen información sobre dos famosos artistas. Háganse y contesten preguntas sobre cuánto tiempo hace que participan en su arte o sobre actividades o eventos que les ocurrieron en el pasado. **Estudiante B**: por favor, ve al **Apéndice 1**, página A-17.

> MODELO: Miguel Zenón toca jazz desde (*since*) 1995
>
> ESTUDIANTE A: *¿Cuánto tiempo hace que Miguel Zenón toca jazz?*
>
> ESTUDIANTE B: *Hace... años que lo toca. Empezó en 1995.*

Estudiante A:

Preguntas sobre Miguel Zenón	Perfil de Dafnis Prieto

1. ¿Cuántos años hace que nació? ¿Dónde nació?	• lugar y fecha de nacimiento: Cuba, 1974
3. ¿Cuántos años hace que recibió un premio artístico?	• salió de Cuba en 1999
5. ¿Cuántos años hace que fue nombrado el mejor artista de jazz?	• es profesor de música en la Universidad de Miami desde 2014
7. ¿Cuánto tiempo hace que hizo una gira por África?	• fue nominado al Grammy Latino en 2007
9. ¿Cuántos años hace que fue nominado al Grammy?	• recibió el MacArthur Fellowship Award en 2011

14-9 Soy famoso/a. Asume la identidad de una persona famosa en las artes (músico/a, director/a, bailarín/bailarina, cantante, etc.).

Paso 1 Escribe una autodescripción de tu personaje para después presentarla en grupos pequeños. Incluye un mínimo de cinco datos personales o profesionales sobre la experiencia de tu personaje.

 Paso 2 Túrnense para presentarse su autodescripción y preguntarse sobre sus experiencias. Usen las expresiones **¿Cuánto tiempo hace que...? / Hace... que...**

> MODELO: ESTUDIANTE 1: *Me llamo Dafnis Prieto y soy percusionista de jazz...*
>
> ESTUDIANTE 2: *¿Cuánto tiempo hace que toca los tambores?*
>
> ESTUDIANTE 1: *Hace...*

14-10 Tu vida personal. ¿Cuánto tiempo hace que (no) haces o que hiciste las actividades a continuación?

Paso 1 Indica tus actividades y experiencias.

MODELOS: venir a esta universidad: ___2018___
estudiar español: _seis meses_
no limpiar mi apartamento: _dos semanas_

1. asistir a un concierto: _____

2. escuchar música jazz: _____

3. (no) ver ballet: _____

4. invitar a un amigo a una fiesta: _____

5. tocar un instrumento musical: _____

6. (no) tomar clases de baile/música: _____

Paso 2 Ahora, escribe oraciones completas usando **hace que**. Piensa en si la acción ya pasó, o si todavía continúa, para determinar qué tiempo del verbo debes usar, el presente o el pretérito.

MODELOS: venir a esta universidad: _2018_
Hace... año(s) que <u>vine</u> a esta universidad.
estudiar español: _seis meses_
Hace seis meses que <u>estudio</u> español.
no limpiar mi apartamento: _dos semanas_
Hace dos semanas que <u>no limpio</u> mi apartamento.

Paso 3 En parejas, túrnense para hacerse y responder a preguntas usando **hacer que**... + el presente o el pretérito.

MODELO: ESTUDIANTE 1: *¿Cuánto tiempo hace que...?*
ESTUDIANTE 2: *Hace... año(s) que...*

Nosotros commands

¿Recuerdas? In **Capítulo 10** you learned **usted** and **ustedes** commands, for example, **¡Practiquen ustedes la pieza musical!** *Practice the musical piece!*

Provide the correct form for each command: **aplaudir, ir**.

¡(1) _____ usted al concierto y (2) _____ mucho al final!

Respuestas: 1. Vaya; 2. aplauda

- There are two ways to give a direct command to a group of persons that includes yourself: **vamos a** + *infinitive* or the **nosotros/as** form of the present subjunctive.

  ¡**Vamos a asistir** al concierto de Juan Diego Flórez!
  ¡**Asistamos** al concierto de Juan Diego Flórez! } *Let's attend the Juan Diego Flórez concert!*

- As with all command forms, attach object pronouns to the affirmative forms. Add an accent mark on the stressed syllable of an affirmative command to maintain the original stress. With negative commands, place object pronouns between **no** and the verb.

  Busquemos a la solista.   *Let's look for the soloist.*
  Busquémosla.   *Let's look for her.*
  No la busquemos.   *Let's not look for her.*

La próxima vez, ¡compremos los boletos en Internet!

¡Director Dudamel!

- To express *Let's go*, use the indicative **vamos**. For the negative *Let's not go...*, however, you must use the subjunctive form.

Vamos a la audición para la comedia musical.	*Let's go to the audition for the musical comedy.*
No, no vayamos a la audición ahora.	*No, let's not go to the audition now.*

- When you attach the pronouns **nos** or **se** to the **nosotros/as** affirmative command, delete the final **-s** from the verb ending.

¡Vámonos!	*Let's leave! / Let's get out of here!*
Démoselo.	*Let's give it (**el libro**) to him/her/you/them.*

¿Comprendes? Complete the sentences with the **nosotros** command of the logical verb: **bailar, cantar, improvisar.**

Amigos, ¡(1) _____ una escena cómica para la clase! ¡(2) _____ tango y (3) _____ una pieza de ópera!

Respuestas: 1. improvisemos / vamos a improvisar; 2. Bailemos / Vamos a bailar; 3. cantemos / vamos a cantar.

Aplicación

14-11 Una gira de la orquesta sinfónica. El director artístico y el gerente general están planeando los conciertos y las giras para el año que viene.

Paso 1   Lee la conversación y selecciona los mandatos con la forma de **nosotros.**

DIRECTOR: ¡Oye, Luis! (1) Hagamos/Perdamos nuestros planes para el año que viene. ¿Hacemos una gira por Europa o vamos esta vez a Sudamérica?

GERENTE: (2) Representemos/Vamos a planear dos giras. Es muy probable que nos inviten a las grandes ciudades de los dos continentes.
(3) Escribamos/Leamos las últimas reseñas en el periódico. El público está pidiéndonos más conciertos para el año que viene.

DIRECTOR: Pero antes, tenemos que considerar el presupuesto (*budget*).
(4) Informémoslo/Revisémoslo con cuidado antes de hacer una decisión definitiva.

GERENTE: Es verdad, pero (5) ganemos/pensemos en los beneficios de dos giras. A ver, podremos llevar nuestra música a una variedad de públicos; conocerán el gran talento de la sinfónica; podremos experimentar con música nueva. ¡(6) Hagámoslo/Olvidémoslo, es una gran oportunidad!

Paso 2   Contesta las preguntas, basándote en la conversación anterior.

1. ¿Qué quieren hacer el director artístico y el gerente general?

2. ¿Cuántas giras quiere hacer el gerente general? ¿Adónde? ¿Y el director?

3. ¿Cuáles son algunos de los beneficios de hacer dos giras?

4. En tu opinión, ¿cuál es una desventaja de hacer dos giras?

14-12 En un ballet. En parejas, decidan cuáles de estas acciones deben hacer durante una función de ballet y cuáles no deben hacer. Usen mandatos de **nosotros**.

MODELO: fumar en el auditorio   *¡No fumemos en el auditorio!*
          pedir el programa   *Pidamos el programa. / Pidámoslo.*

1. sentarnos cerca del escenario
2. salir durante la función
3. apagar los celulares
4. filmar la función
5. comer caramelos envueltos (*wrapped*) en celofán
6. aplaudir al final
7. pedirles los autógrafos a los bailarines
8. dirigir la orquesta

14-13 Este fin de semana. Hay muchas oportunidades culturales en su universidad. Túrnense para sugerir actividades usando mandatos de **nosotros** afirmativos y negativos. Decidan cuáles de las actividades son las más interesantes, factibles (*doable*), caras, etc. Infórmenle a la clase de sus planes finales.

MODELO: ESTUDIANTE 1: *¡Cantemos en un concierto de jazz!*
          ESTUDIANTE 2: *¡No, no cantemos en un concierto de jazz!*
                              ¡No sé cantar! Escuchemos música clásica.

¡Conversemos!

Primero, pregúntate si puedes llevar a cabo las siguientes funciones comunicativas. Después, júntate con dos o tres compañeros/as de clase para presentar las situaciones. Hagan y respondan a por lo menos cuatro preguntas en cada situación.

✓ CAN YOU . . .

☐ talk about music, art, and dance?

☐ say how long something has been going on?

☐ invite or convince others to do something?

WITH YOUR CLASSMATE(S) . . .

Situación: Hacer planes.

Ustedes quieren asistir a un concierto de música clásica o de jazz o a una función de baile. Hablen sobre lo que quieren ver y por qué. Incluyan información sobre el/la director/a, el/la artista o el/la compositor/a y el estilo de música.

Para empezar: *Hay un concierto de música jazz esta noche... Toca...*

Situación: Una entrevista.

Uno/a de ustedes tiene una entrevista para dar clases de música. Hablen sobre sus experiencias y cuánto tiempo hace que les interesa la música.

Para empezar: *Hace diez años que estudio piano...*

Situación: Planes para el verano.

Hagan planes para el verano. Pueden incluir sus planes para viajar, trabajar y pasarlo bien. Usen mandatos de **nosotros**.

Para empezar: *Vamos a buscar un buen trabajo para el verano. Busquemos oportunidades de empleo en...*

Perfiles

14.3 Discuss types of dance, and learn about an eclectic Colombian band

Mi experiencia

¿BAILE O BALLET? ¡ESA ES LA CUESTIÓN!

 14-14 Para ti. ¿Tocas algún instrumento? ¿Cuál? ¿Has escuchado un concierto de música flamenca? ¿Te gusta bailar? ¿Has tomado clases de baile, por ejemplo, de salsa, de jazz o de ballet? ¿Prefieres el ballet clásico o el moderno? Lee sobre las experiencias de Carlos Perreira Carreras, un estudiante de música.

Hola, soy Carlos Perreira Carreras y soy de Venezuela. Desde pequeño, siempre me ha encantado la guitarra, y la música flamenca en particular. Hace diez años que estudio guitarra en Caracas y este año tuve la oportunidad de venir a España para estudiar en el Conservatorio Joaquín Turina en Madrid. Los fines de semana, mis compañeros y yo vamos mucho a los pequeños bares donde se toca auténtica música flamenca. ¡Está bien pepia'o!¹

La verdad, no soy muy aficionado a la música clásica sinfónica ni al ballet (prefiero salsa ☺), pero en el conservatorio insisten en que asistamos a diferentes funciones para que nos familiaricemos con todo tipo de "cultura". Por eso, he ido bastante al teatro, a la sinfónica y, el fin de semana pasado, ¡fui a un ballet! No pueden imaginarse mi sorpresa cuando vi "Soleá", un ballet coreografiado para los bailarines principales, Ángel y Carmen Corella (te juro que aquí en Europa estos hermanos son una sensación impresionante). Jamás en mi vida había visto una pieza con tanto control físico y mental. ¡Esos chamos² no son solo artistas, sino también gimnastas. Y además, lo que más me gustó fue que ¡la obra tenía un tema flamenco! Ahora tengo un nuevo aprecio por este tipo de arte. Pero esta noche, me relajo escuchando a un grupo fantástico colombiano, Monsieur Periné. (¡Sí, los miembros son colombianos!) ¡Chaito³ pues!

¹¡Es estupendo! *(Venezuela)*

²chicos *(Venezuela)*

³Chao

14-15 En su opinión. En parejas, expliquen su opinión y den ejemplos.

1. ¿Cómo es la música que se toca en los bares en Madrid, según Carlos? ¿Es semejante a la música que ustedes conocen en EE. UU. o Canadá?

2. ¿Es clásico o popular el ballet que vio? ¿Han asistido ustedes a un ballet de ese tipo?

3. ¿Es posible que el arte sea tanto para un público intelectual como para uno popular?

14-16 Soleá. De niño, Ángel Corella no tenía mucha habilidad para los deportes típicos de los jóvenes de su edad, pero sí tenía vocación para el ballet. Busca una representación de "Soleá" en Internet y escribe un párrafo sobre lo que veas: el baile, los participantes, si es un ballet clásico o moderno, etc.

📍 **Busca:** Soleá Corella video

Mi música

"SUIN ROMANTICÓN" (MONSIEUR PERINÉ, COLOMBIA)

La música de este grupo fusiona elementos de cumbia, tango, danzón, bolero, jazz, pop y swing. La voz es Catalina García; Nicolás Junca toca la guitarra; Santiago Prieto toca el charango, el violín y la guitarra; Adinda Meertins, el contrabajo; Jairo Alfonso, los vientos (saxofón, clarinete); Abstin Caviedes, trombón y bugle; Miguel Guerra es el percusionista y Darwin Páez toca la batería. El grupo recibió un Grammy Latino en 2015 por "Best New Artist".

ANTES DE VER Y ESCUCHAR

14-17 ¡Volvamos al pasado! En esta canción, la vocalista anima a su amor que vuelva con ella a un momento cuando eran felices, todo al compás (ritmo) de un "suin" romanticón (*swing* sentimental). Completa los pedidos con mandatos de **nosotros** afirmativos y negativos para ayudar a animarlo.

bailar	ir	ponerse
cantar	perder	ser

MODELO: (pensar) No *pensemos* en los problemas.

1. _____ al lugar donde todo empezó.
2. _____ el control.
3. _____ al compás de mi suin romanticón.
4. _____ una canción sentimental.
5. _____ felices.
6. No _____ serios.

PARA VER Y ESCUCHAR

14-18 La canción. Observa el video de "Suin romanticón" e indica con **C (Cierto)** o **F (Falso)** si oyes/ves o no estos instrumentos.

1. _____ la batería
2. _____ el contrabajo
3. _____ la flauta
4. _____ la guitarra
5. _____ el piano
6. _____ la trompeta

> **Busca:** Suin romanticón video oficial; Suin romanticón letra

DESPUÉS DE VER Y ESCUCHAR

14-19 Un evento cultural. En grupos pequeños, planeen un evento en que invitan a la banda Monsieur Periné a dar un concierto en su universidad. Usen mandatos de **nosotros** en su discusión.

MODELO: ESTUDIANTE 1: *Vamos a invitar a la banda Monsieur Periné a dar un concierto.*
ESTUDIANTE 2: *Buena idea, invitemos también a...*
ESTUDIANTE 3: *Y pidámosle el dinero a...*

14.2 Segunda parte

Vocabulario

14.4 Talk about fashion

La moda

)) **Elegancia total.** Cibeles Madrid Fashion Week es uno de **los desfiles de moda** más importantes del mundo.

PERIODISTA: Nunca había asistido a un desfile de moda de Ágatha Ruiz de la Prada. ¡Qué explosión de colores!

CAMARÓGRAFA: Cibeles Madrid Fashion Week es estupendo. Mira, dicen que los desfiles de este año están llenos de más **novedades** y sorpresas que en años anteriores.

PERIODISTA: Efectivamente. La originalidad de algunos de **los diseñadores** es increíble. ¿Viste a **las modelos** que llevaban trajes de baño de **estilo** 1920, hechos de **seda** y **lentejuelas**?

CAMARÓGRAFA: Sí, pero prefiero **las prendas** de Amaya Arzuaga. Sus **conjuntos** son a la vez prácticos y originales para la mujer moderna, que quiere sentirse tan cómoda en la oficina como en la casa. Debe recibir otro Premio Nacional de Diseño de Moda.

¿Comprendes? Select the correct word to complete each statement: **desfile de moda, estilos, diseñadores**.

Cibeles Madrid Fashion Week es un (1) _____. Los mejores (2) _____ presentan sus (3) _____ más novedosos.

Respuestas: 1. desfile de moda; 2. diseñadores; 3. estilos

))) Vocabulario

La moda	Style
la alta costura	*high fashion*
el conjunto	*outfit*
el desfile de moda	*fashion show*
el/la diseñador/a	*designer*
el disfraz	*costume, disguise*
el esmoquin	*tuxedo*
el estilo	*style*
el/la modelo	*model*
el modo (de vestir)	*way, manner (of dressing)*
la novedad	*latest fashion*
la prenda	*garment*
la sencillez	*simplicity*
el traje de noche	*evening gown*

Telas y materiales	Fabrics and materials
el elástico	*elastic*
las lentejuelas	*sequins*
el nilón	*nylon*
la paja	*straw*
la pana	*corduroy*
la piel	*leather, fur*
el poliéster	*polyester*
el rayón	*rayon*
el terciopelo	*velvet*
el tul	*tulle (silk or nylon net)*

Otras palabras y expresiones[1]	Other words and expressions
encantador/a	*enchanting, delightful*
bien hecho/a	*well made*

Repaso[2]	
el algodón	
el cuero	
la lana	
la seda	
estar de moda	

Variaciones

- **El cuero** is typically used to refer to leather for shoes or furniture. For finer items, you will hear **un bolso de piel** or **una chaqueta de piel**.
- In Venezuela, **una prenda** is also a jewel added as an adornment, and in various parts of Latin America, **mi prenda** is a term of endearment.

))) Letras y sonidos

The consonants *m*, *n*, and *ñ*

Generally, the letter **m** sounds like the *m* in English *mice* and the letter **n** like the *n* in English *nice*. Although the letter **ñ** does not exist in English, its sound in Spanish is approximated by the *ny* sequence in English *canyon*.

  mo-da   la-**na**   ni-**ño**   se-**ñor**   fil-**mar**   es-**mo**-qui**n**

When **n** falls at the end of a syllable, its pronunciation in Spanish is affected by the consonant after it. For example, before the letters **p, b, v,** or **m,** the letter **n** is pronounced like the *m* sound, as in the following examples.

  u**n** po-co   u**n** be-so   u**n** va-so   u**n** mes   i**n**-mi-gra-ción

---

[1]Many cognates can help you describe clothing: **elegante**, **formal**, **informal**, and **simple**.
[2]*Review*; you learned these words in **Capítulo 8**.

Aplicación

14-20 El desfile de moda. Selecciona la palabra o expresión que mejor completa los comentarios del reportero de un desfile de moda.

alta costura	desfile de moda	diseños	lentejuelas	paja
conjunto	diseñadora	estilos	modelos	terciopelo

Buenas tardes, señoras y señores. Estamos aquí esta tarde para presenciar el (1) _____ de la famosa (2) _____ Carolina Herrera. Dentro de unos pocos minutos, van a salir las primeras (3) _____. En el mundo de la (4) _____, no hay nadie que ilustre mejor la feminidad que la Sra. Herrera. Sus (5) _____ siempre complementan las bellas figuras de sus modelos. Bueno, aquí sale la primera: lleva un vestido largo de (6) _____ que sirve tanto para asistir a un concierto, como a una cena elegante. Lleva también un pequeño bolso cubierto de (7) _____. ¡Qué bonito (8) _____! La tercera modelo lleva un vestido corto y un sombrero ancho de (9) _____. Bueno, señoras y señores, hemos visto los nuevos (10) _____ de la Casa Herrera.

Cultura en vivo

Fashion Weeks allow designers, brands, or "houses" to display their latest collections in runway shows, and buyers to take a look at the latest trends. In addition to the four major international venues, there are many other shows that cater to national designers. In Mexico, the major fashion event is Mercedes-Benz Fashion Week, held twice a year since 1998. What are the four major international venues for Fashion Week?

14-21 Cibeles Madrid Fashion Week. Escucha la narración sobre este famoso desfile de moda en España y completa las frases que siguen.

1. La Sra. Cifuentes asistió a Cibeles Madrid Fashion Week para...
   a. presentar a los nuevos diseñadores.
   b. anunciar el premio L'Oreal.
   c. abrir la feria.

2. En el mundo de la moda, se espera que Madrid sea...
   a. un destino a nivel internacional.
   b. atractiva a diseñadores franceses e italianos.
   c. donde se fabrique la ropa de los diseñadores.

3. El primer diseñador presenta una colección de...
   a. vestidos de rayón.
   b. camisetas pintadas.
   c. trajes de terciopelo.

4. La línea de Ruiz de la Prada es ropa...
   a. para la oficina.
   b. para la playa.
   c. de noche.

5. No se permitió que algunas de las modelos participaran porque...
   a. no eran españolas.
   b. estaban demasiado delgadas.
   c. suspendieron la prueba de drogas.

14-22 Las telas. En parejas, túrnense para comentar si consideran las telas para ropa formal o informal, y den un ejemplo de una prenda y cuando la llevarían.

MODELO: el tul

El tul es para ropa formal femenina, o para un disfraz de ballet, por ejemplo, un tutú. Personalmente, nunca llevaría un tutú...

- el algodón
- el cuero
- las lentejuelas
- la paja
- la pana
- la piel
- el poliéster
- el rayón
- el terciopelo

14-23 En orden de importancia. Cuando las personas van de compras, tienen en mente ciertas características de la ropa que quieren comprar.

Paso 1   Pon en orden de importancia para ti estos aspectos de la moda y de prendas específicas que has comprado o que comprarías.

_____ el costo
_____ la marca
_____ el color
_____ si me queda bien o mal
_____ la tela sintética o la natural
_____ el uso de pieles de animales
_____ los gustos de los amigos
_____ la durabilidad
_____ la sencillez
_____ la modestia
_____ la comodidad
_____ la última moda

 Paso 2   En parejas, comparen sus respuestas y digan qué tienen en común y cómo se diferencian. Den ejemplos de sus gustos.

MODELO: la durabilidad

ESTUDIANTE 1: *Para mí, la durabilidad es muy importante, por ejemplo,...*
ESTUDIANTE 2: *De acuerdo. No me importa pagar más por la calidad.*

Presencia hispana

Fashion designer Bryan Hearns was born in East L.A. to a Mexican mother and African American father. Regarding his style, he says he was always drawn to the Latino "gangster" street style, but is also influenced by Spanish architecture from the 1920s. Using texture as his signature design aesthetic, he mixes leather, denim, sweatshirt fabrics, strappy looks, and hardware, making everything very relaxed-looking. He calls his collection "confident, feminine, and dangerous." His celebrity patrons include Selena Gómez, Tyra Banks, and Ariana Grande. How do our daily surroundings affect our preferences for clothing styles?

Antes de esta temporada, este diseñador nunca había creado moda para las masas.

Estructuras

14.5 Talk about what had happened before another past action or event

The pluperfect indicative

¿Recuerdas? In **Capítulo 12**, you learned the present perfect to refer to a past action or event that you perceive as having some bearing on the present, for example:

He asistido a un desfile de moda. *I have attended a fashion show.*

Complete the sentence with the present perfect of the logical verb: **comprar, llevar.**

Yo (1) _____ pantalones de terciopelo, pero no los (2) _____ a clase.

Respuestas: 1. he comprado; 2. he llevado

- Use the pluperfect to refer to an action or event that had occurred before another past action or event. Compare the following sentences with the time line.

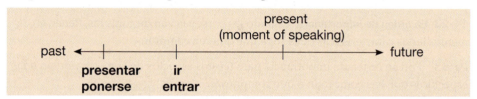

La diseñadora **había presentado** sus diseños en Madrid antes de **ir** a Barcelona.

The designer had presented her designs in Madrid before going to Barcelona.

Cuando **entramos**, la modelo ya **se había puesto** el vestido.

When we entered, the model had already put on her dress.

- Like the present perfect tense, the pluperfect (or past perfect) is a compound tense. Use the imperfect tense of **haber** + *past participle.*

	imperfect tense of *haber*	past participle	past tense of *to have*	past participle
yo	había		I had	
tú	habías		you had	
Ud.	había		you (for.) had	
él/ella	había	tomado	he, she had	taken
		comido		eaten
nosotros/as	habíamos	vivido	we had	lived
vosotros/as	habíais		you (pl. fam.) had	
Uds.	habían		you (pl.) had	
ellos/as	habían		they had	

¡OJO!

Remember that some past participles have irregular forms, such as **abierto**, **escrito**, and **hecho**. See page 386 for a more complete list.

- **Haber** agrees in number with the subject; the past participle is invariable.

Los modelos **habían llegado** tarde.   *The models had arrived late.*

- Finally, any object pronouns precede the auxiliary **haber**.

La modelo **se** había puesto el conjunto antes del desfile.

The model had put on the outfit before the show.

¿Comprendes? Complete the sentences with the present perfect of the logical verb: **hablar, sacar.**

Los diseñadores (1) _____ con las modelos y el fotógrafo (2) _____ muchas fotos antes de la presentación.

Respuestas: 1. habían hablado; 2. había sacado

Aplicación

14-24 Lineisy Montero abre camino. Esta modelo dominicana causó una sensación en Milán.

Paso 1 Lee el artículo sobre Lineisy Montero y selecciona el verbo apropiado para completarlo.

había abierto	había pensado
había aparecido	había seleccionado
se había concentrado	había viajado
había decidido	

Con apenas (*barely*) 19 años, Lineisy Montero creó una tremenda sensación cuando apareció en el desfile de moda de Prada en Milán, Italia, y las revistas especializadas en moda la declararon el descubrimiento (*discovery*) del año. Fue su primer show como modelo profesional, y antes de ella, no (1) _____ ninguna modelo negra en Prada, ni menos una modelo con su estilo de pelo natural. Antes, Prada siempre (2) _____ a modelos blancas.

Lineisy fue descubierta en un parque de diversiones en la República Dominicana, su país natal. Nunca (3) _____ al extranjero, ni tampoco (4) _____ en ser modelo. Su vida (5) _____ en sus estudios y su familia.

A la temporada siguiente, durante el mes de septiembre, Montero caminó en más desfiles que cualquier otra modelo. Por fin, el mundo de la moda (6) _____ mostrar una verdadera diversidad de la belleza. En una industria donde la gran mayoría de los modelos son blancos, Lineisy (7) _____ un camino importante.

 Paso 2 En parejas, conversen sobre Lineisy Montero y por qué el artículo dice que ha abierto un camino.

1. En su opinión, ¿por qué por fin ha tomado esta decisión el mundo de la moda?

2. ¿En qué otras profesiones hay menos oportunidades para personas de color o para mujeres?

3. En su opinión, ¿quiénes tienen la responsabilidad para asegurar su participación en esas profesiones?

 14-25 Antes de asistir a la universidad. Conversen entre ustedes para comparar las experiencias culturales que no habían tenido antes de asistir a la universidad.

MODELO: *Antes de cumplir dieciséis años, nunca había asistido a una ópera, pero vi una el año pasado.*

14-26 **Antes de...** Expliquen lo que no había ocurrido antes de ciertas fechas. A continuación hay una lista de verbos que pueden usar.

cantar	ganar	necesitar	perder	tener	ver
elegir	ir	pagar	presentar	trabajar	votar

MODELO: *Antes de 2004 no habíamos aterrizado en el planeta Marte* (Mars).

1. 1920
2. 2001
3. 2008
4. nacer mis padres
5. venir a la universidad
6. este año

14-27 **Una entrevista con...** ¿Qué le preguntarías a una persona famosa en las artes?

Paso 1   Prepara algunas preguntas que le harías a un/a diseñador/a o artista como Ágatha Ruiz de la Prada, Lineisy Montero, Juan Diego Flórez, Ángel Corella, Gustavo Dudamel, Wifredo Lam, etc. Usa el pluscuamperfecto (*pluperfect*) en tus preguntas.

MODELO: *Sra. Ruiz de la Prada, ¿había visitado usted París antes de presentar su primera colección?*

Paso 2   En parejas, túrnense para hacer los papeles de artista y de entrevistador/a.

MODELO: ESTUDIANTE 1: *Sra. Ruiz de la Prada, ¿había visitado usted París antes de presentar su primera colección?*

ESTUDIANTE 2: *Sí, había visitado París varias veces con mi familia.*

¡Conversemos!

Primero, pregúntate si puedes llevar a cabo las siguientes funciones comunicativas. Después, júntate con dos o tres compañeros/as de clase para presentar las situaciones. Hagan y respondan a por lo menos cuatro preguntas en cada situación.

✓ CAN YOU . . .

☐ talk about fashion?

☐ say what had happened before another action or event in the past?

WITH YOUR CLASSMATE(S) . . .

Situación: En una tienda de moda.

Uno/a de ustedes busca una prenda para un evento formal. Hablen de lo que buscan, las telas, los estilos, y algún diseñador/a en particular.

Para empezar: *Busco un traje de noche de seda...*

Situación: Sus intereses.

Hablen de sus intereses y lo que habían hecho y no habían hecho antes de este año.

Para empezar: *El año pasado ya había visitado... pero todavía no había conocido...*

Club cultura

14.6 Create an idea chart

Arte moderno en Quito

Estrategia para ver

Create an idea chart. While viewing the video, jot down some of the sights and ideas that you believe important. Arrange these with the most important in the middle and the others around it. Watch the video again to review your chart and make changes or add details.

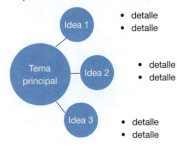

ANTES DE VER EL VIDEO

14-28 Empieza tu representación gráfica de ideas. Usa el título del video, *Arte moderno en Quito*, para inferir el tema principal del video. Luego, haz una lista de dos o tres escenas o ideas que posiblemente verás u oirás.

AL VER EL VIDEO

14-29 Completa tu representación gráfica de ideas. Ve el video para completar tu representación gráfica de ideas. Añade detalles bajo cada idea. Vuelve a ver el video para asegurarte de que la información esté completa.

DESPUÉS DE VER EL VIDEO

14-30 ¿Comprendiste? Selecciona la opción que mejor completa cada oración.

1. El tema principal es (el arte antiguo en Quito / el arte moderno en Quito / el arte de Guayasamín).

2. Laura visita (un barrio / un museo / un parque).

3. Los artistas son (ecuatorianos / profesores de arte / profesionales e interesados).

4. El artista Apitatán dice que, después de pintar un muro, pertenece a (*it belongs to*) (la calle / la ciudad / la universidad).

5. Con el tiempo, los murales (pierden sus colores / se hacen más populares / son vandalizados).

6. El artista cree que aprende (en su estudio / de otros artistas / en la calle).

14-31 Un resumen. Usa tu representación gráfica de ideas para escribir un resumen del video. Incluye por lo menos tres ideas y algunos detalles para cada una.

14.3 Nuestro mundo

Panoramas

14.7 Identify and research some modern art in the Spanish-speaking world

El arte moderno hispano

El arte moderno hispano incluye una diversidad de medios, estilos y temas. Los artistas han recibido renombre en sus propios países y también en el foro internacional. ¿Te acuerdas de algunas de las piezas de arte modeno que has conocido en otros capítulos, por ejemplo, la de Pablo Picasso (Capítulo 2), la de Ramón Oviedo (Capítulo 7) o la de Fernando Botero (Capítulo 9)? Vuelve a ver las obras al comienzo de cada capítulo y compara el estilo con el de los artistas en esta página.

Otto Por Tre. El artista chileno Roberto Matta añadió una dimensión social y política a sus obras. En estas figuras fantásticas, explora la mente inconsciente y el temor que uno siente al odio.

Niñas con sandía. María Izquierdo nunca recibió el reconocimiento que merecía durante su vida. Sin embargo, en 2002 el gobierno mexicano la nombró "Monumento Artístico de la Nación". Según Izquierdo, una pintura es como una ventana al mundo de la imaginación.

Gare do Oriente (Estación de Oriente), Lisboa, Portugal. El arquitecto español Santiago Calatrava es uno de los más innovadores de este siglo. Sus creaciones aparecen en las grandes ciudades por todo el mundo.

© Successio˙ Miro´ / Artists Rights Society (ARS), New York / ADAGP, Paris 2017

Estudio para Detrás del espejo. Las pinturas del surrealista catalán Joan Miró incluyen formas tales como pájaros, peces y perros.

New York Street Scene. El uruguayo Joaquín Torres-García vivió un tiempo en Nueva York, lo que figura en algunas de sus obras. Además de ser pintor, era un gran intelectual y publicó más de 150 libros y artículos teóricos sobre el arte en catalán, francés, español e inglés.

Algunas obras excepcionales

Artista	Obra	Se vendió por...
Pablo Picasso (España)	*Les femmes d'Alger (Version O)*	$179 millones (2015)
Santiago Calatrava (España)	*World Trade Center Transportation Hub*	$80 millones (2016)*
Joan Miró (España)	*Estrella azul*	$39 millones (2012)
Frida Kahlo (México)	*Dos desnudos en el bosque (La tierra misma)*	$8 millones (2015)
Rufino Tamayo (México)	*Trovador*	$7,2 millones (2008)
Wifredo Lam (Cuba)	*Ídolo (Oya/Divinité de l'air et de la mort)*	$4,5 millones (2015)
Fernando Botero (Colombia)	*Los músicos*	$2,6 millones (2006)

*Caltrava recibió esta cantidad por su diseño. El costo total del proyecto fue casi ocho mil millones de dólares.

14-32 Identifica. Identifica la información según **Panoramas**.

1. algunos ejemplos de artes visuales

2. el nombre de un arquitecto español que ha diseñado edificios en EE. UU.

3. un pintor catalán-español cuyas obras son sumamente valiosas

4. un pintor surrealista chileno

5. un pintor uruguayo que reprodujo escenas de Nueva York

6. una pintora mexicana que fue reconocida después de su muerte

7. un artista español surrealista cuyas obras muchas veces representan animales

14-33 Investigación: Una pieza de arte. Las obras mencionadas en **Panoramas** representan solo algunas de las más valiosas en el mundo del arte. Selecciona una obra u otra que te interese y busca más información sobre ella en Internet. Escribe un párrafo describiéndola (los colores y el estilo y tu opinión de la obra) y preséntasela a la clase.

> **Busca:** Pablo Picasso; Santiago Calatrava; Joan Miró; Rufino Tamayo; Frida Kahlo; Fernando Botero; Wifredo Lam; Roberto Matta; María Izquierdo

MODELO: *Encontré una pintura del artista mexicano, Rufino Tamayo. Tiene tres figuras...*

Páginas

14.8 Draw a mental picture while you read

"La música" (Eduardo Galeano, Uruguay)

Estrategia para leer

Draw a mental picture while you read. Some stories encourage you to draw a mental picture while you read. You create the characters and scenes, and react to them emotionally and intellectually. You not only comprehend the words and plot, but you also retain the story to relate it to new situations.

Eduardo Galeano

ANTES DE LEER

14-34 Un dibujo mental. Eduardo Galeano era un maestro en contar. Dijo una vez, "Salgo a la calle cada día con mis oídos y ojos bien limpios para oír las voces secretas y descubrir los colores escondidos. Soy un cazador (*pursuer*) de historias, un escuchador de voces". En este cuento, vas a dibujar mentalmente los personajes, la escena y la acción. Lee el primer párrafo e imagina el aspecto físico y personal del músico: su edad, su ropa, su cara, sus manos; su personalidad: alegre, triste, amable, desinteresado, etc.

AL LEER

 14-35 La escena y la acción. Sigue leyendo el cuento e imagina la escena y la acción.

Imagina la escena:

- ¿Es una ciudad, el campo, la montaña, la playa?
- ¿Qué colores predominan?

Imagina la acción:

- ¿Cómo son los otros personajes: su ropa, sus edades, sus caras, sus personalidades?
- ¿Cómo reaccionas a sus acciones: con alegría, repugnancia, tristeza?

La música

Era un mago[1] del arpa. En los llanos[2] de Colombia, no había fiesta sin él. Para que la fiesta fuera fiesta, Mesé Figueredo tenía que estar allí, con sus dedos bailaderos que alegraban los aires y alborotaban[3] las piernas.

Una noche, en algún sendero[4] perdido, lo asaltaron los ladrones. Iba Mesé Figueredo camino de una boda, a lomo de mula, en una mula él, en la otra el arpa, cuando unos ladrones se le echaron encima y lo molieron a golpes[5].

Al día siguiente, alguien lo encontró. Estaba tirado en el camino, un trapo[6] sucio de barro[7] y sangre[8], más muerto que vivo. Y entonces aquella piltrafa[9] dijo, con un resto de voz:

—Se llevaron las mulas.

Y dijo:

—Y se llevaron el arpa.

Y tomó aliento[10] y se rió:

—Pero no se llevaron la música.

Los llanos de Colombia

[1]*wizard* [2]*plains*

[3]*shook*
[4]*path*

[5]*pummeled him*

[6]*rag (fig. exhausted)*
[7]*mud* [8]*blood*
[9]*wretched soul*

[10]*breath*

DESPUÉS DE LEER

14-36 La acción. Selecciona la respuesta más lógica para completar las oraciones.

1. El músico regresaba de...
   a. una boda.
   b. un funeral.
   c. un partido.

2. Montaba...
   a. en bicicleta.
   b. a caballo.
   c. en una mula.

3. Algunos hombres lo...
   a. contrataron para una boda.
   b. asaltaron.
   c. invitaron a su casa.

4. Perdió su...
   a. bicicleta.
   b. arpa.
   c. caballo.

5. No perdió su...
   a. buen ánimo.
   b. dinero.
   c. tristeza.

14-37 Continuemos la historia. Imagínense que ustedes representan a los/las policías que investigan el caso el día siguiente.

Paso 1 En parejas, preparen preguntas para entrevistar y darle consejos a Mesé Figueredo. A continuación hay algunas sugerencias.

Mesé Figueredo, ...

- ¿nos podría decir...?
- en el futuro, usted debería...
- ¿hay alguien que...?
- ¿tiene usted dónde...?
- ¿necesita usted...?
- ¿...?

Paso 2 Túrnense para hacer el papel de policía y entrevistar a otra pareja de la clase. Tomen nota de las respuestas del otro grupo y escriban un resumen de la entrevista.

MODELO: *Mesé Figueredo dijo que era de noche cuando...*

14-38 Más allá del cuento. Entre los temas que aparecen en las obras de Galeano se incluyen la ecología, la política internacional, la historia, el fútbol, el lugar de la mujer, los derechos humanos y el amor. En parejas, conversen sobre el tema detrás de las líneas de este cuento. En su opinión, ¿tiene un mensaje universal?

Taller

14.9 Use words to paint a picture

Pintar un personaje con palabras

Estrategia para escribir

Use words to paint a picture. Have you ever tried to describe someone by their actions and words, and the reactions of others? This requires using the verb *to be* less frequently and instead choosing other verbs to illustrate the characters. The result can be much richer for the reader.

14-39 Crear un personaje. En este taller, vas a crear un personaje por medio de sus acciones y las reacciones de otras personas. Trata de usar verbos que pinten al personaje, en lugar de simplemente describirlo. Como referencia, vuelve a leer "La música" donde el autor retrata al personaje principal.

ANTES DE ESCRIBIR

- **El personaje.** Piensa en un personaje que quieras pintar. Haz una lista de sus características físicas y personales, y las acciones que las ilustren.

  MODELO:
  Es una mujer vieja. → *Tiene canas* (gray hair). *Viste a la moda de los años 50. Camina lentamente y usa bastón* (cane), *etc.*
  Es altruista. → *Siempre saluda a sus vecinos. Prepara dulces para los niños del barrio. Aunque no tiene mucho dinero, trata de ayudar a las personas necesitadas, etc.*
  Es muy querida. → *Sus vecinos la respetan y le piden consejos. La invitan a sus fiestas familiares, etc.*

AL ESCRIBIR

- **Una descripción.** Escribe dos o tres párrafos pintando a tu personaje. Incluye sus acciones, sus palabras y las reacciones de los demás. Trata de incluir una variedad de verbos y la expresión **hace... que**.

  MODELO: *Hace diez años que soy vecina de la señora Echevarría. Vive en una casa pequeña al final de la calle, la misma casa en que vivía con su querido esposo hasta que él murió hace cinco años. Antes de la muerte de su esposo, ella nunca había pasado un día sin él. Ahora sola, todos los días sale con su bastón en una mano y un ramo de flores de su jardín en la otra. Se dirige al cementerio donde limpia la tumba de su esposo y le pone sus flores. Si ve una persona sin hogar* (homeless), *le ofrece una de las pocas monedas que lleva en su bolso…*

DESPUÉS DE ESCRIBIR

- **Revisar.** Revisa tu descripción para verificar los siguientes puntos:
  - ☐ el uso del pluscuamperfecto del indicativo (**Había creído que...**)
  - ☐ el uso de **hace... que...** (**Hace una hora que no habla.**)
  - ☐ la concordancia y la ortografía

- **Intercambiar.** Intercambia tu descripción con la de un/a compañero/a para hacer correcciones y sugerencias y reaccionar a lo que ha escrito.

- **Entregar.** Pon tu descripción en limpio, incorporando las sugerencias de tu compañero/a. Después, entrégasela a tu profesor/a.

En este capítulo...

))) Vocabulario

Primera parte

La ópera, la música clásica y el jazz	Opera, classical music, and jazz
la audición	audition
el bailarín / la bailarina	dancer
la comedia musical	musical comedy
el/la compositor/a	composer
el/la coreógrafo/a	choreographer
el/la director/a	conductor, director
el escenario	stage
el/la músico/a	musician
la ópera	opera
la ovación de pie	standing ovation
la pieza (musical / de baile)	(musical/dance) piece
el público	audience
la sinfonía	symphony
el/la solista	soloist
talentoso/a	talented
la voz	voice

Verbos	Verbs
aplaudir	to clap, applaud
cantar	to sing
componer	to compose
improvisar	to improvise

Los grupos musicales	Musical groups
la banda	band
el conjunto	musical group
el cuarteto	quartet
la orquesta sinfónica	symphony orchestra

Los instrumentos musicales	Musical instruments
el arpa	harp
la batería	drums
el chelo	cello
el clarinete	clarinet
el contrabajo	bass
la corneta	cornet, horn
la flauta	flute
la guitarra	guitar
las maracas	maracas
la marimba	marimba
el piano	piano
el saxofón	saxophone
el tambor	drum
el trombón	trombone
la trompeta	trumpet
el violín	violin

Algunos bailes	Some dances
el baile de salón	ballroom dancing
el ballet	ballet
la danza moderna	modern dance
el flamenco	flamenco

Segunda parte

La moda	Style
la alta costura	high fashion
el conjunto	outfit
el desfile de moda	fashion show
el/la diseñador/a	designer
el disfraz	costume, disguise
el esmoquin	tuxedo
el estilo	style
el/la modelo	model
el modo (de vestir)	way, manner (of dressing)
la novedad	latest fashion
la prenda	garment
la sencillez	simplicity
el traje de noche	evening gown

Telas y materiales	Fabrics and materials
el elástico	elastic
las lentejuelas	sequins
el nilón	nylon
la paja	straw
la pana	corduroy
la piel	leather, fur
el poliéster	polyester
el rayón	rayon
el terciopelo	velvet
el tul	tulle (silk or nylon net)

Otras palabras y expresiones	Other words and expressions
encantador/a	enchanting, delightful
bien hecho/a	well made

Repaso	
el algodón	
el cuero	
la lana	
la seda	
estar de moda	

Hacer in time expressions   *See page 450.*

¿Te gusta la política?

«Por agarrar una silla, el político promete villas y Castilla».

Códice Fejérváry-Mayer, de origen azteca. The ancient Aztecs created colorful pictogram codices to chronicle events and depict norms of behavior and rites of passage. This is one of the rare pre-Hispanic manuscripts to survive the conquest of Mexico.

Fuente: Werner Forman Archive / Liverpool Museum, Liverpool

Learning Objectives

15.1 Discuss world problems and possible solutions

15.2 Provide additional information about ideas, events, and situations

15.3 Discuss politics, and learn about a popular border band

15.4 Express political points of view, and identify types of government

15.5 Talk about unexpected events, and make excuses

In this Chapter

ENFOQUE CULTURAL: GUINEA ECUATORIAL
Club cultura: Introducción a Guinea Ecuatorial

Video

Indica con **C (Cierto)** o **F (Falso)** si escuchas/ves o no esta información en el video.

1. _____ dónde se sitúa Guinea Ecuatorial

2. _____ su población

3. _____ cuándo se independizó de España

4. _____ la comida

5. _____ la economía

15.1 Primera parte

Vocabulario

15.1 Discuss world problems and possible solutions

Las crisis políticas y económicas

 **La paz es el derecho de todos. Lograr la paz** y defender **los derechos humanos** es el deber de todos. Cada **ciudadano** elige cómo va a **promover la justicia** para **abolir la pobreza** y **los conflictos**. Algunos prefieren efectuar el cambio a través de una elección; otros prefieren **protestar** contra el gobierno.

Los activistas apoyan los derechos humanos y protestan contra **la guerra**.

ACTIVISTA 1: ¡Lo que queremos es **el desarme** universal!

ACTIVISTA 2: ¡Eliminemos la guerra!

ACTIVISTA 3: ¡Ciudadanos! ¡**Unámonos** a la causa de la paz **duradera**!

¿Comprendes? Indicate whether each concept or condition is positive (**P**) or negative (**N**).

1. _____ la paz duradera

2. _____ la pobreza

3. _____ el conflicto

4. _____ la justicia

Respuestas: 1. P; 2. N; 3. N; 4. P

))) Vocabulario

Cuestiones	Issues
la bomba (nuclear)	(nuclear) bomb
el conflicto	conflict
el derecho (humano)	(human) right
el desarme	disarmament
el desastre natural	natural disaster
la deuda pública	public debt
el esfuerzo	effort
el golpe de estado	coup d'état
la guerra	war
la huelga	strike
la inmigración	immigration
la (in)justicia	(in)justice
el mercado global	global market
el país en vías de desarrollo	developing country
la paz (mundial, duradera)	(world, lasting) peace
la pobreza	poverty
el poder	power
el terrorismo	terrorism

Los personajes	People
el/la activista	activist
el/la ciudadano/a	citizen
el/la ejército	army
el/la pacifista	pacifist
el/la político/a	politician
el/la soldado	soldier

Verbos	Verbs
abolir	to abolish
apoyar	to support
firmar (un acuerdo, un tratado)	to sign (an accord, a treaty)
lograr	to achieve
protestar	to protest
promover (ue)	to promote
unirse (a)	to join forces
violar	to violate

Variaciones

- **La bomba** occurs in numerous contexts outside of violence. In the Andes, **la bomba** is a *gas station*. In Chile, **la bomba** can be a fire truck, fire station, or even fire department! In Argentina, **ser una bomba** is *to be gorgeous*. In Spain, **pasarlo bomba** means to *have a great time*.
- In Latin America, **la huelga** is commonly **el paro**. In Spain, however, **el paro** means *unemployment*.

Aplicación

15-1 La política mundial. Selecciona el significado o ejemplo de cada expresión.

1. _____ el/la ciudadano/a
2. _____ el desarme
3. _____ el ejército
4. _____ en vías de desarrollo
5. _____ la pobreza
6. _____ el/la activista
7. _____ el/la pacifista
8. _____ el conflicto
9. _____ el golpe de estado
10. _____ la deuda pública

a. una fuerza armada
b. lucha vigorosamente por una causa en la que cree
c. trabaja por la paz
d. la acción de desarmar a una nación
e. puede resultar en una guerra si no se resuelve
f. no tener lo suficiente para vivir
g. el estado de un país que intenta mejorar su situación económica
h. es miembro del país en que nació
i. las obligaciones financieras del gobierno
j. una rebelión contra el gobierno en el poder

15-2 Una fundación impactante. Es importante reconocer la gran labor que hacen algunos para mejorar la condición humana.

Paso 1 Escucha el reportaje sobre el fundador de una organización importante y su misión. Selecciona la opción que mejor completa cada oración.

1. Óscar Arias es… (a) el expresidente de Costa Rica. (b) el embajador a EE. UU. (c) el jefe ejecutivo de una empresa multinacional.

2. Ganó el premio Nobel de la Paz por sus esfuerzos para conseguir una paz duradera en… (a) Colombia. (b) Venezuela. (c) Centroamérica.

3. El propósito de la Fundación incluye… (a) la eliminación del hambre. (b) la reconstrucción después de un desastre natural. (c) la protección de los derechos humanos.

4. Tuvo éxito en… (a) la desmilitarización de Panamá y Haití. (b) la eliminación de la pobreza en su país. (c) la reducción de la deuda pública en Guatemala.

5. En algunos países, el ejército sirve para… (a) torturar a sus ciudadanos. (b) mantener la estabilidad política. (c) organizar un golpe de estado.

6. La Fundación espera controlar… (a) la inmigración de indocumentados. (b) la compra de armas. (c) el tráfico de personas.

Paso 2 Busca información en línea sobre otra organización que tenga influencia en Latinoamérica. Escribe un párrafo sobre la organización, sus metas y sus éxitos.

📍 **Busca:** fundación humanitaria latinoamericana

15-3 ¿Por ejemplo? Muchos países del mundo han experimentado períodos de conflicto o de progreso durante el último siglo. Den ejemplos de las siguientes situaciones.

MODELO: un gobierno democrático
En los años 60, había un gobierno militar en El Salvador, pero ahora tiene un gobierno democrático.

la inmigración	un desastre natural	la opresión de un grupo minoritario
un golpe de estado	una paz duradera	un conflicto

15-4 Las aspiraciones de Óscar Arias. Estas bellas palabras del Dr. Óscar Arias son parte de su discurso al aceptar el premio Nobel de la Paz. Léanlas y conversen sobre su filosofía. ¿Es realista, o un sueño imposible? Expliquen.

«Porque mi tierra es de maestros, cerramos los cuarteles, y nuestros niños marchan con libros bajo el brazo, y no con fusiles sobre el hombro. Creemos en el diálogo, en la transacción, en la búsqueda del consenso. Repudiamos la violencia.»

—Dr. Óscar Arias

15-5 ¿Qué harían ustedes? Decidan qué harían para aliviar un conflicto mundial actual o reciente. Pueden incluir la intervención militar, económica, diplomática, etcétera.

MODELO: un conflicto militar
ESTUDIANTE 1: *Le diría al Secretario de Estado que hablara con los jefes de estado de los dos países.*
ESTUDIANTE 2: *Mandaría fuerzas militares…*

1. el tráfico de armas ilegales
2. el tráfico de personas
3. el asesinato de un/a político/a
4. un ataque contra una embajada (*embassy*)
5. una huelga de trabajadores agrícolas

Presencia hispana

The League of United Latin American Citizens (LULAC), founded in 1929, is the oldest and most widely respected Hispanic civil rights organization. Its mission is "to advance the economic condition, educational attainment, political influence, housing, health, and civil rights of the Hispanic population of the United States." The organization aims to empower its members to create and develop opportunities where they are needed most. What other organizations are important in protecting civil rights in the U.S. or Canada?

Piden justicia.

Estructuras

15.2 Provide additional information about ideas, events, and situations

The relative pronouns *que*, *quien*, and *lo que*

Relative pronouns join two sentences that have a noun or a pronoun in common.

> ¡Este es, papá! ¡Este es el coche que quiero!

La Fundación escribió el código. El código prohíbe la venta de armas a ciertos países.	The Foundation wrote the code. The code prohibits the sale of arms to certain countries.
La Fundación escribió el código **que** prohíbe la venta de armas a ciertos países.	The Foundation wrote the code that prohibits the sale of arms to certain countries.

- Use the relative pronoun **que**, meaning *that, which, who*, and *whom*, for both people and objects.

El folleto **que** te di está en la mesa.	The brochure (that) I gave you is on the table.
La chica **que** está con Jorge es activista.	The girl who is with Jorge is an activist.

- Use the relative pronoun **quien(es)** to refer to persons only when the phrase is set off by commas or introduced by a preposition (Note that sentences in Spanish never end with a preposition.)

Juan Manuel Santos, **quien** era presidente de Colombia, ganó el premio Nobel de la Paz en 2016.	Juan Manuel Santos, who was president of Colombia, won the Nobel Peace prize in 2016.
Esa es la pacifista **con quien** te vi.	That's the pacifist with whom I saw you (whom I saw you with).

- When the relative pronoun refers to an abstract idea, event, or situation, use **lo que**, meaning *what* or *that which*.

> Lo que no comprendo es cómo construyeron la pirámide sin máquinas modernas.

Lo que quiero es la paz y la libertad en mi país.	What I want is peace and liberty in my country.
No me gustó **lo que** hiciste.	I didn't like what you did.

- In Spanish, the use of the relative pronoun **que** is never optional.

Busco el contrato **que** firmaste.	I'm looking for the contract (that) you signed.

¿Comprendes? Complete the sentences with the correct relative pronouns: **que, quién(es), lo que**.

El disidente, (1) _____ fue acusado de poner una bomba, fue declarado inocente. (2) _____ no entiendo es el terrorismo (3) _____ se dirige contra gente inocente.

Respuestas: 1. quien; 2. Lo que; 3. que

Aplicación

15-6 La herencia indígena. Hasta hoy, algunas mujeres de herencia inca producen textiles que imitan los de sus antepasados (*ancestors*).

Paso 1 Lee acerca de los tejidos (*weavings*) de los incas y selecciona el pronombre relativo lógico.

Los pocos tejidos de los antiguos incas (1) quienes/que todavía se conservan, usaron la lana de alpaca. Ellos los usaban para hacer la ropa (2) lo que/que los protegía del frío del altiplano, en sus decoraciones y también en sus ceremonias religiosas. Las figuras (3) que/quienes tejían representaban dioses, animales y otros elementos naturales. Las personas (4) quienes/que tejían eran maestros (5) que/lo que luego pasaban su conocimiento a las generaciones siguientes para preservar su arte. Las personas para (6) que/quienes tejían eran, por lo general, gente de la nobleza. Se sabe esto porque se han encontrado piezas muy finas en las tumbas de los incas nobles. (7) Lo que/Que sí es un misterio es cómo estos bellos tejidos han podido sobrevivir por tantos siglos sin perder sus vívidos colores.

Paso 2 Vuelve a leer el párrafo y contesta las preguntas.

1. ¿Cuál era uno de los talentos artísticos de los incas?
2. ¿Qué material usaban?
3. ¿Qué figuras se ven en sus piezas?
4. ¿Quiénes las usaban?
5. ¿Dónde las han encontrado?

15-7 El Comité del premio Nobel de la Paz. Completa la conversación con los pronombres relativos apropiados: **que, quien/es** o **lo que**.

MIEMBRO 1: ¿Dónde están las cartas (1) _____ recibimos del comité del año pasado? Vamos a considerar a las personas (2) _____ fueron nominadas.

MIEMBRO 2: El secretario con (3) _____ hablé ayer me dijo que había dejado copias en su escritorio. Los candidatos, (4) _____ son excelentes, han hecho una gran labor para promover la paz mundial.

MIEMBRO 3: (5) _____ más me preocupa es la seguridad de este proceso. Temo que la prensa se entere de nuestras deliberaciones.

MIEMBRO 1: No se preocupe. El oficial de seguridad, a (6) _____ consulté ayer, me aseguró que tenía todo bajo control. No es posible que la prensa sepa (7) _____ está pasando en este salón.

MIEMBRO 2: Pero, ¿por qué hay un micrófono en la lámpara (8) _____ hay en la mesa?

15-8 El Banco Mundial. El Banco Mundial promueve proyectos para mejorar la situación económica de países en vías de desarrollo. Túrnense para darse consejos sobre algunos de sus proyectos.

MODELO: ESTUDIANTE 1: *Perú ha experimentado una crisis humana por las inundaciones.*

ESTUDIANTE 2: *Lo que debemos / tenemos que / hay que hacer es darle un préstamo (loan) para reconstruir sus casas.*

Los proyectos

1. Un grupo de mujeres chilenas crea artesanías que se podrían vender por todo el mundo.

2. Los agricultores bolivianos quieren cambiar el cultivo de coca en sus terrenos por el cultivo de quinua.

3. El gobierno panameño quiere proteger sus costas de inundaciones causadas por el cambio climático.

4. Un grupo de activistas quiere abolir la práctica de la dote (*dowry*) en India.

5. El gobierno salvadoreño quiere mejorar los medios de comunicación en las zonas rurales.

6. Un grupo de mujeres espera información del gobierno argentino sobre sus hijos desaparecidos.

Algunos consejos

- apoyar el Acuerdo de París para reducir las emisiones y combatir el cambio climático

- ayudarles a crear un sitio web para promover sus productos

- darles equipos de radio y teléfono por vía satélite

- enseñarles a cultivar algodón u otro producto viable

- insistir en que un tribunal investigue los casos

- promover la posición de la mujer en la sociedad

¡Conversemos!

Primero, pregúntate si puedes llevar a cabo las siguientes funciones comunicativas. Después, júntate con dos o tres compañeros/as de clase para presentar las situaciones. Hagan y respondan a por lo menos cuatro preguntas en cada situación.

✓ CAN YOU. . .

☐ talk about world problems and possible solutions?

☐ provide additional information to a discussion about ideas, events, and situations?

WITH YOUR CLASSMATE(S). . .

Situación: Una organización benéfica.

Ustedes quieren ser voluntarios/as en una organización que ayuda a víctimas de alguna crisis política o desastre natural. Hablen de la organización, cómo sirve a la gente y lo que ustedes pueden contribuir a la organización.

Para empezar: *La organización Médicos sin Fronteras ayuda a... Yo puedo / quiero / voy a...*

Situación: Una causa social.

Hagan planes para organizar una campaña para una causa social o política. Piensen en temas como la pobreza, la deuda pública y otros que se presentaron en el capítulo. Incluyan sus metas y sus estrategias. Usen los pronombres relativos **que**, **quien** y **lo que**.

Para empezar: *Nuestra meta es mejorar las condiciones de los niños que... Estos inocentes, quienes no tienen... Lo que nos preocupa es que...*

Perfiles

15.3 **Discuss politics, and learn about a popular border band**

Mi experiencia

LA POLÍTICA Y LOS HISPANOS

15-9 **Para ti.** ¿Cuáles son los temas políticos más importantes para ti? ¿Por qué? Cuando tienes una opinión fuerte sobre algún tema político, ¿qué haces? Lee sobre las experiencias de Marisela Ramos como activista.

Hola, soy Marisela Ramos y soy chicana. Nací en Phoenix, Arizona, y ahora soy estudiante en la Universidad de Arizona, donde estudio relaciones internacionales. También, participo en un grupo de acción política de estudiantes latinos. Una de nuestras metas es organizar el voto latino para que tengamos mayor voz en las próximas elecciones. En las del 2016, el 11 por ciento del voto total era latino, y esperamos que sea aún más grande en las próximas elecciones. Es interesante, pues según una encuesta que les hicieron a los latinos que votaron, los temas más importantes para los votantes eran la economía, la reforma del sistema de salud y la inmigración. El comentarista de Univisión Jorge Ramos, en su libro *Tierra de todos*, declara que el voto latino será "la fuerza política del siglo" y estoy totalmente de acuerdo con él. Para mí, no tengo más remedio que participar activamente en esa fuerza si quiero que consigamos esa estabilidad política, económica y social que pide nuestra comunidad latina. Cuando termine mis estudios, pienso presentarme como candidata a la legislatura de Arizona, y después, ¿quién sabe? Ya tenemos una jueza en el Tribunal Supremo y también a Susana Martínez, gobernadora de Nuevo México. ¡Tal vez algún día sea yo la primera latina en la Casa Blanca! (Por cierto, hay un montón de corridos sobre el tema de los inmigrantes. El grupo más popular es los Tigres del Norte. ¡Búsquenlos en Internet!)

15-10 **En su opinión.** En parejas, comparen sus experiencias con las de Marisela Ramos.

1. ¿Cuál es la meta del grupo de latinos en que ella participa? ¿Participan ustedes en un grupo semejante? ¿Por qué?

2. ¿Cuáles eran los temas más importantes para los votantes latinos? ¿Cuáles son los temas más importantes para ustedes?

3. ¿Cuál es la opinión de Jorge Ramos sobre la influencia latina? ¿Y la de ustedes?

4. ¿A qué aspira Marisela después de terminar sus estudios? ¿Creen que es una aspiración alcanzable (*achievable*)? ¿Por qué?

Mi música

"DE PAISANO A PAISANO" (LOS TIGRES DEL NORTE, MÉXICO/EE. UU.)

Este es un conjunto de música norteña mexicana (por haberse originado en el norte de México). Cantan principalmente corridos (canciones que cuentan una historia), los cuales han sido censurados en varias ocasiones, incluso en su propio país. Es uno de los grupos más reconocidos del género, debido a su larga historia y éxitos a nivel mundial.

ANTES DE VER Y ESCUCHAR

15-11 El paisano. Un **paisano** es una persona compatriota (de la misma patria) que comparte la misma historia, cultura y tradiciones. Escribe una lista de cosas y personas que echarías de menos (*you would miss*) si tuvieras que dejar tu patria e irte a otro país. ¿Cuáles serían algunos de los problemas que tendrías si no hablaras la lengua del nuevo país?

MODELO: *Si tuviera que dejar mi patria, echaría de menos a mis amigos...*

PARA VER Y ESCUCHAR

15-12 La canción. Observa el video, "De paisano a paisano" en que se mencionan algunos de los problemas que tienen los inmigrantes. Mientras escuchas la canción, selecciona la expresión que mejor completa cada frase.

Los inmigrantes...

1. _____ vuelan como…   a. bandera.
2. _____ desafían…   b. el extranjero.
3. _____ defienden…   c. el honor.
4. _____ exploran…   d. fronteras.
5. _____ no quieren morir en…   e. otras tierras.
6. _____ solo buscan…   f. pago.
7. _____ muchas veces no reciben… g. trabajo.
8. _____ preferirían vivir bajo una sola… h. un águila (*eagle*).

> ⚲ **Busca:** Tigres Paisano video oficial; Tigres Paisano letra

DESPUÉS DE VER Y ESCUCHAR

15-13 Consejos para un inmigrante. Sabiendo las dificultades que tienen los inmigrantes, escribe cinco consejos que les darías si estuvieras en su situación.

MODELO: *Es muy importante que...*

15.2 Segunda parte

Vocabulario

15.4 Express political points of view, and identify types of government

Cargos políticos y tipos de gobierno

Julián Pérez
Gobernador

Hon. Juana Hernández
Jueza Municipal

Dr. Jorge Roldán
Ministro de Economía

¡Voten por mí! Este año hay varios **candidatos** a la presidencia de España. Aquí tienes parte del último **discurso** que pronunció Julián Pérez, **gobernador** del Banco Comercial de Bilbao, en su **campaña** electoral.

Compañeros y amigos:

Como ustedes saben, nuestro país **afronta** problemas muy serios. Se nos ha perdido el camino, y dudo que el gobierno de mis **contrincantes** pueda encontrarlo. Es importante que todos nos unamos y que ustedes **voten por** mí. Si gano las elecciones, les aseguro que **cumpliré con** las siguientes promesas:

- Generaré más oportunidades de empleo y reduciré la deuda pública.
- Bajaré **los impuestos**.
- Y para **combatir** la pobreza, invertiré mil millones de euros en programas sociales.

Recuerden mi **lema**: "¡Soy el que lo puede hacer! ¡Voten por mí!" Muchas gracias.

¿Comprendes? Select the correct word to complete the sentences: **campaña, gobernador, voten**.

El (1) _____ Pérez monta una (2) _____ para la presidencia del país. Espera que todos (3) _____ por él.

Respuestas: 1. gobernador; 2. campaña; 3. voten

Vocabulario

Cargos políticos	Political posts
el/la alcalde/alcaldesa	*mayor*
el/la dictador/a	*dictator*
el/la gobernador/a	*governor*
el/la juez/a	*judge*
el/la ministro/a	*minister*
el/la presidente/a	*president*
el/la representante	*representative*
el/la rey/reina	*king/queen*
el/la senador/a	*senator*

Tipos de gobierno	Types of government
la democracia	*democracy*
la dictadura	*dictatorship*
la monarquía	*monarchy*
la república	*republic*

Verbos	Verbs
afrontar	*to face*
aumentar	*to increase*
combatir	*to fight, to combat*
controlar	*to control*
cumplir (con)	*to make good, to fulfill (a promise)*
debatir	*to debate*
elegir (i, i)	*to elect*
eliminar	*to end*
mantener (ie)[1]	*to support (a family, etc.)*
mejorar	*to improve*
resolver (ue)	*to solve*
votar (por)	*to vote (for)*

La política y otros temas actuales	Politics and other current topics
el/la asesor/a	*consultant, advisor*
la campaña (política)	*(political) campaign*
el/la candidato/a	*candidate*
el/la contrincante	*opponent*
la corrupción	*corruption*
el deber	*duty*
el discurso	*speech*
la drogadicción	*drug addiction*
el fraude (electoral)	*(electoral) fraud*
la honradez, honestidad	*honesty*
los impuestos	*taxes*
la inflación	*inflation*
el lema	*motto*
la ley	*law*
los programas sociales	*social welfare programs*
el pueblo	*the people, the masses*
la tasa (de desempleo)	*rate (of unemployment)*
el tribunal	*court*

Variaciones

In the Río de la Plata region (Argentina and Uruguay), **el/la alcalde/alcaldesa** is more commonly **el/la intendente**.

 Letras y sonidos

Linking and rhythm

In Spanish, words often are connected or linked together, giving the impression that a phrase is one long word. One case of obligatory linking concerns a consonant followed by a vowel. A consonant at the end of a word always links to the initial vowel of a following word:

> mi**s** + **a**-mi-gas → mi-**sa**-mi-gas   ta**n** + **a**-ma-ble → ta-**na**-ma-ble

Other cases of linking affect adjacent vowels. In fast speech, two identical, adjacent vowels may be pronounced as one long vowel (where a colon designates a long vowel):

> l**a** + **a**-bue-la → l**a:**-bue-la   l**e** + **e**n-vió + flo-res → l**e:**n-vió-flo-res   m**i** + (h)**i**-jo → m**i:**-jo

Additionally, two non-identical vowels may be linked together, creating a diphthong (if one of the vowels is **i** or **u**) or two reduced vowels (if both vowels are from the set **a**, **e**, **o**).

> m**i** + **a**-mi-ga → m**ia**-mi-ga   s**u** + (h)**e**r-ma-no → s**ue**r-ma-no   m**e** + **a**-ma → m**ea**-ma

Linking directly affects the rhythm of Spanish. When speaking Spanish, make sure to give equal time to each syllable and follow a steady rhythm.

---

[1]like **tener**: *mantengo, mantienes…*

Aplicación

15-14 En otras palabras. Selecciona la definición o el ejemplo que mejor explica cada expresión.

1. _____ los impuestos
2. _____ la alcaldesa
3. _____ el juez
4. _____ la inflación
5. _____ los contrincantes
6. _____ el deber
7. _____ los programas sociales
8. _____ la dictadura

a. dirige el gobierno municipal
b. compiten en las elecciones
c. programas para las personas necesitadas
d. se los pagamos al gobierno
e. la concentración del poder en un solo individuo sin permitir oposición política
f. preside un tribunal
g. el aumento de precios y depreciación monetaria
h. una obligación ética

15-15 ¿Quién es Julián Pérez? Contesta las siguientes preguntas basadas en la plataforma de Julián Pérez en **Vocabulario**.

1. ¿Para qué posición se presenta Julián Pérez?
2. ¿Cuáles son sus promesas económicas?
3. ¿Hay alguna contradicción en lo que promete?
4. ¿Votarías por él? ¿Por qué?

15-16 Voten por Maldonado. Escucha el discurso de Pepe Maldonado, otro candidato. Indica con **Sí** o **No** sus cualificaciones y su plataforma política.

1. _____ Está casado.
2. _____ Tiene hijos.
3. _____ Es rico.
4. _____ Es trabajador.
5. _____ Va a darles una casa a todos los ciudadanos.
6. _____ Va a reducir la inflación.
7. _____ Va a aumentar la tasa de empleo.
8. _____ Va a apoyar la educación.
9. _____ Va a proteger el medio ambiente.
10. _____ Va a resolver el problema de los políticos deshonestos.

15-17 Una campaña política. Sigan los pasos para completar esta actividad.

Paso 1 En parejas, hagan el papel de candidato/a y asesor/a para planear una campaña política. Identifiquen el cargo político (presidente/a, alcalde/alcaldesa, etc.). Después, usen los verbos de la lista para construir su plataforma y su lema.

afrontar	combatir	cumplir	mejorar
ayudar	controlar	eliminar	resolver

MODELO: CANDIDATO/A: *Quiero montar una campaña para ser senador/a. Creo que puedo aumentar… y mejorar…*
ASESOR/A: *En mi opinión, es mejor controlar… y eliminar…*

Paso 2 Presenten su plataforma al resto de la clase. Sus compañeros decidirán si votarán por el/la candidato/a que presenten.

Presencia hispana

Although Hispanics make up about 17% of the U.S. population, they are still not well represented in the U.S. Congress or in the courts. In the House of Representatives, states with the highest number of members who are of Hispanic descent include California, Texas, and Florida. Moreover, according to a Michigan State University survey, Hispanics hold only 3% of federal judgeships. What factors contribute to political participation among any group?

15-18A ¡Necesito información! Eres candidato/a en las próximas elecciones municipales y tu compañero/a es reportero/a. Como buen/a político/a, no quieres dar mucha información pero quieres saber la opinión de los demás. Aquí tienes algunas respuestas y preguntas tuyas para el/la reportero/a. **Estudiante B**: por favor, ve al **Apéndice 1**, página A-17.

Estudiante A: Candidato/a

- Porque soy la persona con las mejores ideas. ¿Conoce a alguien que entienda mejor a su pueblo?

- Tengo muchos expertos económicos, pero realmente depende de ustedes los consumidores. ¿Cuál es su opinión?

- En este momento no tengo respuesta. Pero creo que es una buena idea trabajar hasta los ochenta años de edad. ¿Cuál es su opinión?

- No sé todavía. ¿Conoce usted a alguien que pueda hacerlo?

- Mi contrincante no entiende la situación. Mi plan es usar pesticidas para erradicar el cultivo de la planta de la coca. ¿Tiene usted una idea mejor?

Estructuras

15.5 Talk about unexpected events, and make excuses

Se for unplanned occurrences

Sometimes the unexpected happens, and no one wants to take the blame. In Spanish you can shift the blame from a person to an inanimate object.

- In English we say a person forgets (breaks, loses, drops, etc.) something. In Spanish, the thing forgets (breaks, loses, drops, etc.) "on" the person. Notice the thing(s) is (are) the subject of the verb, and the person is an indirect object of the verb. The construction is similar to verbs like **gustar**:

Se me perdió el discurso.

se + ind. obj. + 3rd-person verb + subject

Se te cayeron los platos.
You dropped the plates.
(Lit. *The plates dropped themselves "on" you.*)

- As always, you can clarify or emphasize the indirect object with a prepositional phrase **a (mí, ti, usted, etc.)**:

  En el accidente, **a Ramón** se **le**   *In the accident, Ramón's jeans were*
  rompieron los jeans, y **a ti** se **te**   *torn, and your t-shirt was torn.*
  rompió la camiseta.

- Use the definite article to show possession, since the indirect object pronoun indicates who is involved. Add the preposition **a** + *noun or pronoun* for clarity or emphasis.

  Al senador se le perdieron **los**   *The senator lost his papers.*
  papeles.

- Here are some common verbs that use **se** for unplanned occurrences:

acabarse	*to run out (of)*	**perderse**	*to get lost*
caerse	*to fall down, to drop*	**quedarse**	*to get left behind*
dañarse	*to get damaged*	**romperse**	*to get broken/torn*
olvidarse	*to forget*		

¿Comprendes? Complete the sentence with the correct form of the logical verb: **caerse**, **romperse**.

¡Pobre de ti! (1) _____ los vasos de la mesa y (2) _____ en el piso.

Respuestas: 1. Se te cayeron; 2. se te rompieron

Aplicación

15-19 Todo le fue mal a Alejandro. Alejandro, el asesor de campaña de uno de los candidatos en las elecciones para la presidencia de Colombia, no dirigió una buena campaña.

Paso 1   Lee lo que le pasó y selecciona el verbo lógico para completar las oraciones.

En las últimas elecciones, todo le fue mal a Alejandro, el asesor de uno de los candidatos para la presidencia. En el primer debate, por ejemplo, (1) se le perdieron/se le rompieron las instrucciones de dónde iba a tener lugar, y por eso, el candidato llegó tarde. Después, a Alejandro (2) se le cayó/se le quedó el discurso del candidato en casa y, por eso, la presentación pareció muy desorganizada. Además, a Alejandro (3) se le olvidó/se le perdió recoger a la esposa del candidato, y ella se puso furiosa. En el debate, a Alejandro (4) se le cayeron/se le dañaron los apuntes y cuando fue a recogerlos, colisionó con el candidato. (5) Se le quedaron/Se le cayeron los lentes al candidato y (6) se le rompieron/se le quedaron y no pudo leer sus apuntes. Después del debate, cuando Alejandro lo llevaba a casa, los detuvo un policía. Entonces Alejandro se dio cuenta que (7) se le había dañado/se le había quedado la licencia de conducir en casa. El policía lo llevó a la cárcel y…

Paso 2   Ahora contesta las preguntas siguientes.

1. ¿Qué cargo tenía Alejandro?
2. ¿Por qué llegó tarde al debate el candidato?
3. ¿Por qué se molestó la esposa del candidato?
4. ¿Por qué pareció desorganizada la presentación del candidato?
5. ¿Por qué el candidato no pudo leer sus apuntes?
6. ¿Qué le pasó a Alejandro cuando llevaba al candidato a su casa? ¿Y al día siguiente?

Paso 3   En parejas, túrnense para contar la historia de Alejandro como si fueras él.

MODELO: A Alejandro se le quedó el discurso en casa.
Alejandro dice: *Ay, ¡se me quedó el discurso en casa!*

15-20 Sucesos inesperados. En parejas, túrnense para explicarse qué pasó inesperadamente en una reunión. Combinen elementos de cada columna para describir seis acciones diferentes que ocurrieron. Inventen por lo menos dos oraciones originales.

MODELO: al candidato / caerse / los papeles
Al candidato se le cayeron los papeles.

al presidente	perderse	la fecha de la reunión
a la congresista	caerse	el informe en casa
a mí / a ti	quedarse	los apuntes para la reunión
a nosotros	olvidarse	el portátil
a la jueza	romperse	los carteles políticos
a los senadores	acabarse	la presentación para la reunión
a los activistas		la crema para el café
¿a ...?	¿...?	¿...?

Madres de la Plaza de Mayo

Cultura en vivo

During the 1980s, many Argentine political prisoners disappeared at the hands of the military dictatorship. However, in 2010, the Argentine courts brought some of the perpetrators to justice, finally bringing a degree of closure to some of the many families who lost loved ones, known as **los desaparecidos**. The group **Madres de la Plaza de Mayo** was instrumental in keeping the names of their "disappeared" children in public view. What other women's groups have been successful in keeping human rights issues in the public eye?

 15-21 Excusas. Túrnense para representar las situaciones a continuación. Dense excusas para disculparse.

MODELO: PROFESOR/A: ¿Dónde está la tarea?
        ESTUDIANTE: *¡Ay! ¡Se me quedó en casa esta mañana!*

se me cayó/cayeron	se me olvidó/olvidaron	se me quedó/quedaron
se me dañó/dañaron	se me perdió/perdieron	se me rompió/rompieron

1. PROFESOR/A: ¿Por qué no tiene el libro abierto en el Capítulo 15?
   ESTUDIANTE:

2. BIBLIOTECARIO/A: Tiene que devolvernos los tres libros que le prestamos o nos los tiene que pagar.
   CLIENTE/A:

3. DUEÑO/A DEL APARTAMENTO: No recibí su alquiler (*rent*) este mes.
   INQUILINO/A:

4. POLICÍA: Se prohíbe estacionar (*park*) el carro aquí.
   CONDUCTOR/A:

5. CAMARERO/A: Aquí tiene la cuenta. ¿Cómo prefiere pagar?
   CLIENTE/A:

6. JUEZ/A: ¿Por qué estaba usted en la calle a las tres de la mañana?
   ACUSADO/A:

7. AMIGO/A: ¿Dónde está el suéter que te presté (*lent*) ayer?
   AMIGO/A:

8. SUPERVISOR/A: No entiendo por qué esta lámpara no funciona.
   DEPENDIENTE/A:

15-22 Fue sin querer (*I didn't mean to*). En parejas, túrnense para preguntarse sobre lo que les ha ocurrido sin querer en el pasado.

MODELO: ¿Se te quedaron las llaves en el carro alguna vez?
Sí, se me quedaron las llaves en el carro ayer y tuve que caminar a casa.

1. ¿Se te olvidó algo hoy?
2. ¿Se te ha roto algún objeto últimamente?
3. ¿Se te han perdido algunas cosas en estos días?
4. ¿Se te quedó la licencia de conducir en casa alguna vez?
5. ¿Se te caían objetos de las manos cuando eras pequeño/a?
6. ¿Se te ha dañado la computadora alguna vez? ¿Se te perdió mucha información?

¡Conversemos!

Primero, pregúntate si puedes llevar a cabo las siguientes funciones comunicativas. Después, júntate con dos o tres compañeros/as de clase para presentar las situaciones. Hagan y respondan a por lo menos cuatro preguntas en cada situación.

✓ CAN YOU...

☐ express political points of view and identify types of government?

☐ describe unplanned events and make excuses?

WITH YOUR CLASSMATE(S)...

Situación: Una discusión política.

Ustedes quieren examinar las ventajas y desventajas de diferentes tipos de gobiernos. Cada uno/a apoya y defiende solo uno.

Para empezar: *Para algunos países, la única forma de gobierno posible es... En mi opinión,...*

Situación: Pedir disculpas.

Uno/a de ustedes ha llegado tarde hoy al trabajo. Explica lo que pasó y por qué no fue culpa tuya. La otra persona no quiere aceptar las excusas. Usen expresiones con el **se** inesperado para defender su punto de vista.

Para empezar: *Perdone, jefe/a. No llegué tarde porque quería, es que se me quedaron las llaves en el carro y...*

Club cultura

15.6 **Monitor your viewing strategies**

Civilizaciones antiguas de Bolivia

Estrategia para ver

Monitor your viewing strategies. As you watch, take note of the strategies you use. Do you think about what you know about a topic and try to confirm it? Do you listen/watch for the main idea, or for details? Do you stop and try to summarize what you have seen? Being aware of what strategies work best for you will help you employ them purposefully in the future.

ANTES DE VER EL VIDEO

15-23 ¿Qué intuyes de Bolivia? Sigue los pasos para completar esta actividad.

Paso 1 Usa un proceso de eliminación para intuir y seleccionar la mejor opción.

1. La civilización más antigua de Bolivia es la de los (tiwanakotas / aztecas / mayas).

2. Los incas construyeron un sendero que extendía 39.900 kilómetros entre (Arizona y Cartagena / México y Panamá / Colombia y Argentina).

3. Bolivia es una nación multiétnica y multilingüe. Esto implica que tiene más de (una capital / una lengua oficial / un jefe de estado).

Paso 2 ¿Cuáles de estas estrategias para comprender usas con regularidad?

_____ think about what you know about   _____ stop and try to summarize
       a topic and try to confirm it   _____ ask questions about the content
_____ listen/watch for the main idea   _____ connect the images with what
_____ listen/watch for details   you hear

AL VER EL VIDEO

15-24 Tu conocimiento y tus estrategias. Ve el video para verificar tu conocimiento sobre las antiguas civilizaciones de Bolivia y las estrategias que usaste para comprender. ¿Cuáles están en tu lista inicial? ¿Cuáles usaste que no están allí?

DESPUÉS DE VER EL VIDEO

15-25 ¿Comprendiste? Selecciona la opción que mejor completa cada oración.

1. Se podría decir que Bolivia es una nación (bilingüe / pluricultural / oprimida).

2. Existen dos calendarios, uno lineal y el otro (circular / religioso / festivo).

3. Para los aimaras, (la alpaca es una diosa / el pasado se sitúa enfrente de ellos / no hay futuro, solo pasado).

4. La Pachamama representa (el dios de la lluvia / el sol y la luna / la madre tierra).

15-26 Para saber más. Busca más información en Internet sobre uno de los aspectos que viste en el video. Escribe un párrafo explicando tu estrategia para encontrar más información, lo que aprendiste y por qué te interesa.

   MODELO: *Quería saber más sobre la cosmovisión* (worldview) *inca. Busqué...*

15.3 Nuestro mundo

Panoramas

15.7 **Identify and research indigenous heritage in Hispano-American culture**

La herencia indígena

Los pueblos indígenas han cwontribuido mucho a la cultura que ahora llamamos hispanoamericana. Representan una variedad de culturas que todavía conservan aspectos de su herencia lingüística, artística, agrícola y arqueológica.

Los antiguos mayas desarrollaron el concepto del "cero". Conocían los movimientos de los astros. Mantenían un calendario ritual, y otro agrícola para predecir cuándo plantar y cosechar sus productos.

Antes de la llegada de los colonizadores, los indígenas sabían confeccionar bellas piezas de oro y de plata. Usaban piedras preciosas y semipreciosas: esmeraldas, jade y ópalos en su joyería, y también en decoraciones dentales. Los chibchas de Colombia tenían la costumbre de pintar de oro a un cacique (jefe) nuevo.

Los indígenas americanos cultivaban muchas plantas para comer (el tomate, el cacao, la papa, la calabaza, el chile, el maíz y el frijol, entre muchas) y para uso medicinal y religioso (la menta, la yerba mate y la quinina). Esta mujer tuesta semillas de cacao, que se consideraba un don (*gift*) de los dioses.

Los incas y las culturas de Mesoamérica sabían construir enormes templos y pirámides sin usar ruedas (*wheels*) ni herramientas (*tools*) modernas de metal. Un ejemplo es la fortaleza de Sacsahuamán, Cuzco, Perú.

Las lenguas indígenas han contribuido muchas expresiones al léxico español: **la canoa**, **la hamaca**, **la iguana**, **el manatí**, **el jaguar**, **el huracán** y los nombres de muchas plantas y comidas. Esta canoa, que navega el río Amazonas de Ecuador, fue fabricada del tronco de un solo árbol.

Aportes[1] de indígenas de las Américas	
Museo del Oro de Bogotá:	Más de 10.000 artefactos de oro
Deporte mesoamericano:	Juego de pelota
Lenguas indígenas actuales:	749
Países multilingües:	Bolivia, Guatemala, México, Paraguay, Perú

[1]*Contributions*

15-27 Identifica. Identifica la información según **Panoramas**.

1. algunas comidas y medicinas de origen americano
2. el número de lenguas indígenas que aún se hablan en Latinoamérica
3. algunos logros de los mayas
4. cómo los incas construyeron la fortaleza de Sacsahuamán
5. un museo conocido por su colección de artefactos de oro
6. un deporte popular entre los mesoamericanos

15-28 Desafío. En parejas, túrnense para identificar los países y o las regiones de estas civilizaciones. Si no recuerdan, busquen la información en Internet.

1. los aztecas
2. los aimara
3. los chibchas
4. los guaraníes
5. los incas
6. los mayas

15-29 Investigación: Civilizaciones indígenas. Los aportes de las civilizaciones indígenas mencionados en **Panoramas** representan solo algunos de los más impactantes. Selecciona una civilización que te interese y busca más información sobre ella en Internet. Escribe un párrafo describiendo otros de sus aportes, creencias o costumbres. Luego, presenta tu informe a la clase.

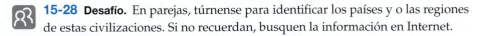

Busca: guaraní; tiwanakota; aimara; azteca; inca; maya; olmeca, chibcha, *etc.*

MODELO: *La civilización olmeca fue la primera en desarrollar un sistema de escritura jeroglífica…*

Páginas

15.8 Divide the task into chunks

"En solidaridad" (fragmento) (Francisco Jiménez, México/EE. UU.)

Estrategia para leer

Divide the task into chunks. Longer readings may seem harder to tackle. But don't get discouraged; instead of reading straight through, divide the reading into manageable chunks and summarize each chunk in ten words or less after reading it.

Francisco Jiménez

ANTES DE LEER

15-30 El primer trozo (chunk). Lee el comienzo de "En solidaridad" (párrafos 1 a 5) para identificar el conflicto entre el autor y su madre. Resúmelo en diez palabras o menos.

AL LEER

15-31 Divide la lectura en trozos. Sigue leyendo para identificar los trozos en la historia. Resume cada trozo brevemente en tus propias palabras y escribe un título original para el último trozo, la resolución.

1. (el conflicto entre madre e hijo)
2. un evento decisivo
3. la decisión de tomar acción
4. las consecuencias académicas de su decisión
5. la larga marcha
6. el discurso del organizador
7. la llegada a Sacramento
8. ¿…?

"En Solidaridad"

Al comienzo del tercer trimestre de mi último año, yo tomé una decisión a la cual mi mamá se opuso fuertemente y que afectó mis notas parciales en mi clase de ética: decidí apoyar la lucha de César Chávez para sindicalizar a los trabajadores agrícolas.

—Vamos a perder nuestros empleos; nos correrán[1] si hacemos huelga, mijo[2] —me dijo mi mamá—.

—¿Quién va a alimentar a nuestra familia cuando estemos sin trabajo?

Yo le expliqué a ella que al hacer los trabajadores huelga y afiliarse a la Asociación Nacional de Trabajadores Agrícolas, los dueños[3] de las granjas[4] se verían forzados a darnos a nosotros y a otros trabajadores agrícolas un seguro contra el desempleo, mejores condiciones de trabajo, y a garantizar un salario mínimo.

—¡Ay, mijo, piénsalo bien! Los granjeros[5] tienen todo el poder. Los trabajadores agrícolas pobres, como nosotros, no tenemos ninguna posibilidad de ganarles—. Dejé de discutir[6] con ella por respeto. Además, yo comprendía sus temores[7].

Me afiancé[8] en la convicción de que había tomado la decisión correcta después de asistir a un foro sobre el tema de los trabajadores agrícolas que tuvo lugar al mediodía del 4 de abril frente al edificio de la Unión de Estudiantes.

El Padre Tenant Wright, un joven y dinámico sacerdote[9] jesuita que organizó el evento, se paró en medio de un grupito de estudiantes y preguntó:

—¿Es necesario formar un sindicato[10] para representar a los trabajadores agrícolas?

Él miró en derredor[11] y gritó la misma pregunta, instando[12] a los estudiantes que pasaban por ahí[13] a unirse a la creciente[14] multitud. A medida que crecía la

[1]*they will fire* [2]mijo = mi hijo

[3]*owners* [4]*farms*

[5]*farmers*

[6]*arguing* [7]*fears*
[8]*I became strengthened*

[9]*priest*

[10]*(labor) union*
[11]*around* [12]*urging*
[13]*allí* [14]*growing*

concentración, yo vi a Laura a unos cuantos pies de distancia. Me abrí paso a codazos[15] entre el gentío hasta el lugar donde se encontraba ella y me paré a su lado. Me alegraba que ella estuviera ahí.

El Padre Wright explicó el propósito de aquel foro. Dijo que la huelga de uvas en Delano había empezado siete meses antes, cuando los trabajadores agrícolas de Delano se retiraron de las granjas viñeras de uvas de mesa, exigiendo[16] salarios que estuviesen[17] al nivel del salario mínimo federal. La huelga estaba siendo dirigida por César Chávez y Dolores Huerta, de la Asociación Nacional de Trabajadores Agrícolas. Ellos les estaban pidiendo a los trabajadores agrícolas que se unieran a su sindicato.

—Una vez más: ¿es esto necesario? —preguntó el Padre Wright—. Para ayudarnos a responder a esta pregunta, he invitado a dos personas a hablar sobre este asunto[18].

El Padre Wright presentó entonces a Frank Bergon, el hijo de un granjero, que expuso[19] la posición de los granjeros, y a Les Grube, un distribuidor de huevos y activista de larga trayectoria en programas católicos de asistencia social, quien defendía el punto de vista de la NFWA. Bergon dispuso[20] que los trabajadores agrícolas estaban ya bien pagados y que el número de huelguistas era pequeño.

—¿Cómo puede él decir eso? —Puse los ojos en blanco[21] y sacudí la cabeza. A los jornaleros[22] agrícolas se les pagaba ochenta y cinco centavos la hora y a veces menos.

—¿Por qué no dices tú algo? —dijo Laura.

Sentí el corazón latiéndome aceleradamente[23] y un fuego en el estómago, pero yo aún era demasiado tímido para hablar ante un público numeroso. Supe que la había defraudado[24] y deseé no haber estado con ella en ese momento. Ella se disculpó por retirarse[25] y se fue a su clase.

Cogí un volante[26] que me dio un representante de la Asociación Nacional de Trabajadores Agrícolas y me apresuré[27] en regresar a mi cuarto con el fin de prepararme para mi clase de ética esa tarde. Yo completé la tarea de lectura en nuestro libro de texto titulado *Right and Reason* (Derecho y razón) y luego leí el volante. Era una invitación abierta de César Chávez para unirse a él en una marcha hacia Sacramento. Puse el volante sobre mi escritorio y me puse a caminar en el cuarto de un lado a otro, pensando en si yo debería unirme o no a la marcha. Había aprendido en Sodality[28], así como en mis clases de religión y filosofía, que era una obligación moral el luchar por la justicia social. Recordaba al Padre Shanks diciéndome que los líderes deben tener un fuerte sentido de la responsabilidad personal, y dar algo de ellos mismos para impulsar[29] el cambio positivo en la sociedad. Una ola[30] de tristeza y de coraje[31] se apoderó[32] de mí. Yo tenía que unirme a la peregrinación a Sacramento.

Al concluir mi clase de ética, le dije al Padre Charles McQuillan, el instructor, que yo faltaría a[33] la clase el jueves porque había decidido unirme a la marcha a Sacramento. Él me recordó que ese día teníamos examen.

—Supongo que pensaste bien esto y estás al tanto de las consecuencias, —dijo, ajustándose su cuello romano[34].

—Sí, pero esperaba que usted me permitiera hacer el examen en otra ocasión.

—Sabes que yo no hago exámenes especiales.

—Sí, lo sé, pero…

—Así que, ¿vale la pena[35] sacrificar tu calificación por ir a la marcha? —preguntó él, clavándome la vista en los ojos[36].

—Sí —dije sin vacilación.

—Entonces, anda. Algunas veces tenemos que hacer sacrificios por lo que creemos. —Él sonrió y me estrechó[37] la mano.

---

[15]Me… codazos *I elbowed my way*

[16]*demanding*   [17]estuvieran

[18]*matter*

[19]explicó

[20]dijo

[21]Puse… en blanco: *I rolled my eyes*
[22]*day laborers*

[23]Sentí… aceleradamente: *I felt my heart racing*
[24]desilusionado
[25]*to leave*
[26]*flier*
[27]*I hurried*

[28]una organización religiosa de la universidad

[29]promover
[30]*wave*   [31]enojo   [32]*took hold*

[33]estaría ausente de

[34]*Roman collar*

[35]vale… pena: *is it worthwhile*
[36]clavándome… ojos: *staring at me*

[37]*he shook*

Tres días antes de Pascuas, la mañana del Jueves Santo, el siete de abril a las cinco de la mañana, Jerry McGrath nos llevó a cuatro estudiantes y a mí en un microbús de ocho pasajeros en un viaje de hora y media, hasta que encontramos la cola de la manifestación.

Delante de mí, a unos cuantos pasos de distancia, marchaba César Chávez. El caminaba flanqueado por trabajadores agrícolas que portaban[38] la bandera americana, la bandera de México, la bandera de las Filipinas y un pendón[39] de la Virgen de Guadalupe.

El candente[40] sol brillaba en el cielo azul pálido. Podía sentir el asfalto calcinante[41] en las plantas[42] de mis cansados pies, mientras seguíamos caminando a lo largo de centenares de acres de campos verdes que se extendían por muchas millas a ambos lados de la Autopista 99. Mi familia había recorrido este mismo camino un año tras otro, durante nueve años, buscando trabajo durante las épocas de cosecha[43] de uvas y algodón.

Cuando los conductores[44] hacían sonar el claxon[45] de sus autos y saludaban con la mano, yo les sonreía y levantaba la bandera. El conductor de una camioneta *pick up* hizo una señal[46] grosera con el dedo del medio y nos gritó por la ventana: —¡Regresen a México!

¡Qué idiota!, pensé, mientras ardía de[47] coraje. A lo largo del camino[48], los simpatizantes locales se nos unían por un rato, mientras otros nos ofrecían tacos de arroz con frijoles y agua para el almuerzo.

Esa noche nos congregamos como un grupo en las afueras de Galt, un pueblito donde los organizadores habían planeado un programa para nosotros.

—¡Viva la causa! ¡Viva la huelga! —gritamos todos. Sentí una ola de energía que no había experimentado nunca antes. Cuando César Chávez subió al estrado[49], nosotros nos aquietamos[50]. Él nos agradeció nuestro apoyo y dijo:

—Si ustedes están indignados por las condiciones prevalecientes[51], entonces ustedes no podrán ser libres ni felices hasta que dediquen todo su tiempo a cambiarlas y no hagan nada más que eso. Luchar por la justicia social, me parece, es uno de las más profundas formas en que hombres y mujeres podemos decirle sí a la dignidad humana, y eso significa realmente sacrificio. La mejor fuente[52] de poder, la mejor fuente de esperanza, emana directamente de ustedes, el pueblo. El boicot no es solo un asunto de uvas y lechugas. El boicot es básicamente el pueblo, es básicamente la preocupación del pueblo por el pueblo…

El domingo de Pascua, miles de nosotros entramos en Sacramento. Nos apoderamos de las gradas[53] del Capitolio, donde César Chávez anunció que Schenley[54] había aceptado reconocer al sindicato. Todos aplaudimos y gritamos con alegría ¡Sí se puede! durante varios minutos. Después de agradecer a los sindicatos, la iglesia y a todos los estudiantes y trabajadores que defendían los derechos sociales y que nos habían ayudado a ganar esta victoria, César Chávez nos dijo en español:

—Es bueno recordar que debe haber valor, pero también que, en la victoria, debe haber humildad…

Mientras él continuaba hablando, yo miraba el estandarte[55] de la Virgen de Guadalupe y sentía profundamente el sufrimiento y el dolor de los trabajadores migrantes.

—¿Qué puedo y debo hacer en mi vida para ayudarles? —me pregunté. Aún no tenía la respuesta.

[38]llevaban

[39]*banner*

[40]muy caliente [41]quemando

[42]*soles*

[43]*harvest*

[44]*drivers* [45]*horn*

[46]*signal*

[47]*burned with* [48]*A… camino: Along the way*

[49]plataforma

[50]*we calmed down*

[51]*prevailing*

[52]*source*

[53]Nos… gradas: *We took over the bleachers* [54]una empresa que fabrica vino

[55]la bandera

DESPUÉS DE LEER

15-32 ¿Ocurrió o no ocurrió? Indica si las siguientes afirmaciones son ciertas (**C**) o falsas (**F**) según lo que leyeron en el cuento "En solidaridad". Explica las falsas.

1. _____ En este relato, el narrador estudiaba en su tercer año de la universidad.

2. _____ Una de las clases que cursaba era la de ética.

3. _____ El profesor de su curso insistió en que presentara su examen parcial con el resto de la clase.

4. _____ Los padres del joven estaban a favor de su decisión de apoyar la huelga.

5. _____ Los sindicalistas organizaron un boicot de las uvas.

6. _____ Las acciones del sindicato tuvieron éxito.

7. _____ Según la ley, el gobierno federal todavía no garantiza el sueldo de los trabajadores migrantes.

8. _____ Para el narrador, le fue fácil decidir qué tenía que hacer en el futuro para ayudar a los trabajadores migrantes.

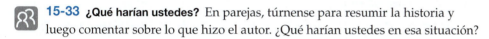 **15-33 ¿Qué harían ustedes?** En parejas, túrnense para resumir la historia y luego comentar sobre lo que hizo el autor. ¿Qué harían ustedes en esa situación?

15-34 César Chávez. El activista fue importante en organizar el sindicato de trabajadores agrícolas. Busca más información sobre él y sus esfuerzos para mejorar la condición de los trabajadores migrantes. Incluye esta información en un párrafo.

- el lema del sindicato y cómo inspiró a los miembros
- lo que fue el Programa Bracero y por qué se opuso a él Chávez
- cuándo y cómo se celebra el Día de César Chávez

15-35 La polémica sobre la inmigración. Hay mucha controversia sobre la situación de los inmigrantes indocumentados que vienen a EE. UU. en busca de trabajo. En parejas, conversen sobre las causas y las consecuencias de algunas de las siguientes propuestas.

> MODELO: El gobierno federal debe abrirles la frontera a los trabajadores migrantes.
>> ESTUDIANTE 1: *Es verdad que pocos estadounidenses quieren hacer el trabajo duro que hacen los trabajadores migrantes.*
>> ESTUDIANTE 2: *Pero en esta economía, no es justo darles el trabajo a los indocumentados y negárselo a los que sí son legales.*

1. Los agricultores deben mejorar las condiciones de vivienda y salud de todos los trabajadores migrantes.

2. No se les debe dar servicios sociales a los inmigrantes indocumentados.

3. Si todos ganan un sueldo mínimo, el costo de la vida va a subir.

4. Se debe vigilar para que no se explote a los menores de edad, obligándolos a trabajar.

5. Hay que proteger mejor la frontera para impedir que entren los indocumentados.

César Chávez

Presencia hispana

The United Farm Workers of America (UFWA) was founded by Philip Vera Cruz, Dolores Huerta, and César Chávez. In 1965, the organization launched a boycott of table grapes that, after five years of struggle, resulted in a contract with the major grape growers in California. Among the goals of the strike was the elimination of five of the most toxic chemicals plaguing farm workers and their families. What other labor unions have been instrumental in improving conditions and wages for workers?

Taller

15.9 **Use dictionaries wisely**

Un recuerdo

Estrategia para escribir

Use dictionaries wisely. Dictionaries are good tools if used wisely. Make sure that you get the right part of speech (noun, verb, adjective, etc.). Note how the word is used in context: does it fit into your context grammatically and meaningfully? Check the Spanish definition and synonyms of the expression. Reverse translate: take the Spanish term and translate it to English. Is that still the expression you want?

15-36 **Un recuerdo.** "En solidaridad" es un recuerdo de una experiencia que tuvo Francisco Jiménez. En este taller, vas a escribir un recuerdo tuyo de una experiencia que te haya impresionado mucho (un viaje, una persona memorable, un lugar especial, una decisión ética).

> **MODELO:** *Cuando tenía diez años, mi familia se mudó de Nueva Jersey a Texas. El cambio fue muy difícil para mí hasta que conocí a…*

ANTES DE ESCRIBIR

- **Ideas.** Piensa en una experiencia que tuviste alguna vez que te impresionó mucho.

AL ESCRIBIR

- **Usa el diccionario con cuidado.** Sigue la estrategia para escribir cada vez que uses un diccionario.
- **Presentación.** Escribe una o dos oraciones para presentar el tema y para explicar por qué te impresionó.
- **Tu punto de vista.** Presenta tu punto de vista y da por lo menos tres razones que lo apoyen.
- **Las consecuencias.** Explica las consecuencias del incidente y cómo se resolvió o no se resolvió.
- **Conclusión.** Termina tu recuerdo e incluye lo que aprendiste o cómo te ha afectado el futuro.

DESPUÉS DE ESCRIBIR

- **Revisar.** Revisa tu recuerdo para verificar los siguientes puntos:
  - ☐ el uso de los pronombres relativos **que**, **quien** y **lo que**, por ejemplo: **Lo que más me gustaba…**
  - ☐ el uso del **se** inesperado, por ejemplo: **…y luego en el restaurante, mi amigo me dijo que ¡se le había olvidado el dinero!**
  - ☐ la concordancia y la ortografía
- **Intercambiar.** Intercambia tu recuerdo con un/a compañero/a para hacer correcciones y sugerencias y comentar el texto.
- **Entregar.** Pon tu recuerdo en limpio, incorporando las sugerencias de tu compañero/a. Después, entrégaselo a tu profesor/a.

En este capítulo...

))) Vocabulario

Primera parte

Cuestiones	Issues
la bomba (nuclear)	(nuclear) bomb
el conflicto	conflict
el derecho (humano)	(human) right
el desarme	disarmament
el desastre natural	natural disaster
la deuda pública	public debt
el esfuerzo	effort
el golpe de estado	coup d'état
la guerra	war
la huelga	strike
la inmigración	immigration
la (in)justicia	(in)justice
el mercado global	global market
el país en vías de desarrollo	developing country
la paz (mundial, duradera)	(world, lasting) peace
la pobreza	poverty
el poder	power
el terrorismo	terrorism

Los personajes	People
el/la activista	activist
el/la ciudadano/a	citizen
el/la ejército	army
el/la pacifista	pacifist
el/la político/a	politician
el/la soldado	soldier

Verbos	Verbs
abolir	to abolish
apoyar	to support
firmar (un acuerdo, un tratado)	to sign (an accord, a treaty)
lograr	to achieve
protestar	to protest
promover (ue)	to promote
unirse (a)	to join forces
violar	to violate

Segunda parte

Cargos políticos	Political posts
el/la alcalde/alcaldesa	mayor
el/la dictador/a	dictator
el/la gobernador/a	governor
el/la juez/a	judge
el/la ministro/a	minister
el/la presidente/a	president
el/la representante	representative
el/la rey/reina	king/queen
el/la senador/a	senator

Tipos de gobierno	Types of government
la democracia	democracy
la dictadura	dictatorship
la monarquía	monarchy
la república	republic

Verbos	Verbs
afrontar	to face
aumentar	to increase
combatir	to fight, to combat
controlar	to control
cumplir (con)	to make good, to fulfill (a promise)
debatir	to debate
elegir (i, i)	to elect
eliminar	to end
mantener (ie)	to support (a family, etc.)
mejorar	to improve
resolver (ue)	to solve
votar (por)	to vote (for)

La política y otros temas actuales	Politics and other current topics
el/la asesor/a	consultant, advisor
la campaña (política)	(political) campaign
el/la candidato/a	candidate
el/la contrincante	opponent
la corrupción	corruption
el deber	duty
el discurso	speech
la drogadicción	drug addiction
el fraude (electoral)	(electoral) fraud
la honradez, honestidad	honesty
los impuestos	taxes
la inflación	inflation
el lema	motto
la ley	law
los programas sociales	social welfare programs
el pueblo	the people, the masses
la tasa (de desempleo)	rate (of unemployment)
el tribunal	court

Verbs that use *se* for unplanned occurrences   *See page 485.*

Appendix 1
Estudiante B

CAPÍTULO 1

1-14B **¡Necesito información!** In pairs, take turns telling each other how many people are in different places to see if you agree.

MODELO: ESTUDIANTE A: (15 estudiantes en clase)
Hay (There are) 15 estudiantes en clase.
ESTUDIANTE B: (14 estudiantes en clase)
No es cierto. Hay catorce.

Estudiante B:

65 estudiantes en la cafetería	77 profesoras en la universidad
29 universidades en Miami	98 profesores en la universidad
100 clases en la lista	

Return to Activity **1-14A**.

1-29B **¡Necesito información!** You are a student worker in the bookstore. A departmental worker calls you to give a supply order over the phone. Below is a list of items you have. Respond whether you have enough, and mark the items the caller would be able to purchase. When you finish, compare your lists.

MODELO: ESTUDIANTE A: *¿Hay cinco calculadoras?*
ESTUDIANTE B: *Sí, tengo diez. / No, solo (only) hay cuatro.*

Estudiante B:

Hay...	Necesita...	Hay...	Necesita...	Hay...	Necesita...
2 relojes	_____	14 tabletas	_____	15 diccionarios	_____
11 sillas	_____	79 bolígrafos	_____	95 cajas (*boxes*) de marcadores	_____
96 mapas	_____	30 lápices	_____	90 cajas de papel	_____
22 libros	_____	1 mesa	_____		

Return to Activity **1-29A**.

1-34B **¡Necesito información!** Take turns asking each other questions to fill in the missing days, dates, and months on each of your grids.

> MODELO: ESTUDIANTE A: (You need) *¿Un mes de otoño?*
> ESTUDIANTE B: (Your partner needs) *octubre*

Estudiante B:

You need . . .	My partner gives me . . .	Your partner needs . . .
		octubre
1. un mes de primavera		miércoles
2. el primer día de la semana		el 4 de julio
3. un mes con veintiocho o veintinueve días		el domingo
4. el Día de San Valentín		septiembre
5. un mes con cinco letras		agosto

Return to Activity **1-34A**.

CAPÍTULO 2

 2-13B **¡Necesito información!** Complete your calendar by asking your partner when events with missing times take place. To ask your partner to repeat something, remember to say: **Repite, por favor**.

> MODELO: la clase de inglés (09:30)
> ESTUDIANTE A: *¿A qué hora es la clase de inglés?*
> ESTUDIANTE B: *Es a las nueve y media de la mañana.*

Estudiante B:

Hora	Actividad
(09:30)	la clase de inglés
_____	la clase de historia
10:30	la clase de arte
_____	la clase de español
16:30	el examen
_____	el partido[1] de fútbol
20:00	el programa de televisión *Juego de tronos*
_____	el programa de noticias en la televisión
24:00	el concierto

[1]*match*

Return to Activity **2-13A**.

2-19B ¡Necesito información! Each of you will assume a new identity, and then ask your partner questions to learn what you have in common.

Paso 1   Choose the identity of one of the people outlined below and read the information.

Estudiante B:

Identidad masculina	Identidad femenina

Juan López García	María Jiménez Cruz
España	México
alto, guapo y muy activo	alta, simpática y muy activa
Universidad Complutense de Madrid	Universidad de Salamanca
arte	sociología
muy interesante	fantástica
el profesor Sánchez	la profesora Alvarado
25 estudiantes en la clase	50 estudiantes en la clase

Paso 2   Use the prompts below to find out what you have in common.

> **MODELO:**   ESTUDIANTE A: (Where studying?) ¿*Dónde* estudias?
> ESTUDIANTE B: *Estudio en la Universidad Complutense. ¿Y tú? ¿Dónde estudias?*

1. (Name?) ¿_____ te llamas?
2. (From?) ¿De _____ eres?
3. (Description?) ¿_____ eres?
4. (Favorite class?) ¿_____ es tu clase favorita?
5. (What is class like?) ¿_____ es la clase?
6. (How many students?) ¿_____ estudiantes hay en la clase?

Return to Activity **2-19A**.

 2-36B ¡Necesito información! In pairs, ask each other questions to share information about daily activities. Add one original question. Do you have any responses in common?

> **MODELO:**   ESTUDIANTE A: *¿A qué hora llegas a clase?*
> ESTUDIANTE B: *Llego a la una y media de la tarde.*
> ESTUDIANTE A: *Pues, yo llego a la una.*

Estudiante B:

1. ¿Dónde estudias?
2. ¿Qué estudias en clase?
3. ¿Qué música escuchas?

4. ¿Qué comes en un restaurante?
5. ¿Qué programa miras en la televisión?
6. ¿…?

Return to Activity **2-36A**.

CAPÍTULO 3

3-7B ¡Necesito información! You and your classmate are compiling end-of-year inventory figures in a bookstore. Each of you has missing data. Take turns asking each other questions to fill in the missing information on your grids. Then, check all your figures by calling out each item and quantity. **¡Ojo!** (*Watch out!*) Make sure you use the correct form of **un/a**, when necessary.

MODELO: ESTUDIANTE A: *Necesito escritorios. ¿Cuántos tienes?*
          ESTUDIANTE B: *Tengo cinco mil dos (5.002) escritorios.*

Estudiante B:

5.002 escritorios	_____ calculadoras
_____ pizarras	672 computadoras
_____ cuadernos	_____ diccionarios
185 mapas	_____ libros de texto
101 sillas	2.700.000 bolígrafos

Return to Activity **3-7A**.

3-26B ¡Necesito información! In pairs, take turns asking and answering questions in order to complete the missing information on your class schedules. Use the verb **ser** in all of your questions and responses.

MODELO: ESTUDIANTE A: *¿A qué hora es la clase de cálculo?*
          ESTUDIANTE B: *Es a las 8:30. ¿Dónde es la clase de cálculo?*

Estudiante B:

Hora	Clase	Lugar	Profesor/a
8:30	cálculo	Facultad de Informática	María Gómez García
9:00			Ramón Sánchez Guillón
10:00	biología	Facultad de Medicina	
	educación física	gimnasio	
1:55		Facultad de Ingeniería	Carlos Santos Pérez

Return to Activity **3-26A**.

CAPÍTULO 4

4-12B ¡Necesito información! Each of you has a separate set of questions for a pair of newlyweds. First, form the verbs according to their subject. Then, ask each other your questions and respond logically.

MODELO: ESTUDIANTE A: ¿Quién *quiere* (querer) ir a una fiesta?
          ESTUDIANTE B: Mi primo Juan siempre quiere ir. Le gusta mucho bailar.

Estudiante B:

Mis preguntas	Mis respuestas
1. ¿Quiénes en tu familia _____ (jugar) al tenis?	Sueño con viajar por Centroamérica.
2. Los domingos, ¿quién prepara y _____ (servir) la comida?	Almorzamos todos los días en casa.
3. ¿_____ (Pensar) ustedes vivir en El Salvador?	Porque tiene sueño después de almorzar.
4. ¿Cuándo _____ (empezar: ustedes) su luna de miel (*honeymoon*)?	Mis padres siempre recuerdan la fecha.

Return to Activity **4-12A**.

4-16B **¡Necesito información!** *Diario Latino* is an independent newspaper in El Salvador. You are reporters who are preparing to interview Fernando Llort, the famous Salvadoran artist who designed the renovated façade for the Catedral Metropolitana. Ask each other questions and respond logically.

MODELO: ESTUDIANTE A: *¿Tienes tu cámara?*
ESTUDIANTE B: *Sí, la tengo.*

Estudiante B:

Mis preguntas	Mis respuestas a las preguntas de mi compañero/a
1. ¿Vas a llamar al artista antes de ir?	Sí, lo habla perfectamente bien.
2. ¿Quiere el artista ver el artículo antes de su publicación?	Lo van a visitar en junio.
3. ¿Quiere su esposa leer la entrevista también?	Sí, la tiene.
4. ¿El señor Llort juega al fútbol, verdad?	Sí, la tengo.

Return to Activity **4-16A**.

4-26B **¡Necesito información!** You are friends who would like to make plans to hang out together. Talk about what you would like to do, following the guide.

Estudiante B:

1. Your partner is bored. Invite him/her to do something that he/she might enjoy.
2. If he/she declines, keep offering other ideas for things to do.
3. Once you agree on an activity, arrange the details together.

MODELO: ESTUDIANTE A: *Estoy aburrido/a.*
ESTUDIANTE B: *¿Quieres ir a bailar? (¿Te gustaría…?; ¿Prefieres…?)*
ESTUDIANTE A: *Me encantaría. ¡Vamos! / Gracias, pero no puedo. No tengo dinero.*

Algunas actividades:

poner una película...	conocer el nuevo café en...	salir a tomar un café
jugar al...	ver una película	traer comida y cenar juntos/as
organizar una fiesta	pasear por el centro	almorzar conmigo

Return to Activity **4-26A**.

Chela, ¿tienes planes para esta noche?

Pues, debo estudiar para el examen de sociología…

Yo también, pero hay una fiesta en mi casa, y…

¿A qué hora?

¿Quiénes van? ¿Van a tener música?

¡Todos van! ¿Te animas?[1]

[1]*Are you in?*

4-31B **¡Necesito información!** Each of you has a separate set of questions with demonstratives. First, choose the correct form of the demonstrative for your questions. Then, ask each other your questions and respond logically.

MODELO: ¿De quién es (esto/este) lápiz?
ESTUDIANTE A: *¿De quién es este lápiz?*
ESTUDIANTE B: *Ese lápiz es de la profesora.*

Estudiante B:

Mis preguntas	Mis respuestas
1. ¿De quién es (aquel/aquello) bolígrafo?	Aquellos son muy trabajadores.
2. ¿De quiénes son (esta/estas) entradas para el cine?	Esas son mis amigas.
3. ¿Cómo es (aquel/aquella) profesora?	Esas son de los estudiantes.
4. ¿Qué es (eso/esa)?	Esta es muy buena.

Return to Activity **4-31A**.

CAPÍTULO 5

5-26B ¡Necesito información! Se acaban de mudar (*You have just moved*) a una nueva casa y todo está muy desordenado. Ustedes tienen que encontrar los muebles y ponerlos en su lugar. Trabajen juntos/as para encontrarlos y decir dónde deben ponerlos. Al final, comparen los planos (*floor plans*) de la casa.

MODELO: ESTUDIANTE A: *¿Dónde está la bicicleta?*
ESTUDIANTE B: *Está en el dormitorio. Debemos ponerla en el garaje.*

Estudiante B busca: la cama, la plancha, la lavadora y la secadora, el sillón, el estante

Vuelve a la Actividad **5-26A**.

CAPÍTULO 6

6-6B ¡Necesito información! Hagan el papel de mesero/a (estudiante A) y cliente/a (estudiante B) en un restaurante de buena calidad. Utilicen expresiones del **Vocabulario** y otras para representar la situación.

MODELO: MESERO/A: *Buenas tardes y bienvenido/a al restaurante…*
¿Qué desea tomar?
CLIENTE/A: *¿Cuál es la especialidad de la casa?*

Estudiante B: Cliente/a

2. Debes preguntarle la especialidad de la casa.

4. No quieres la especialidad de la casa porque (tienes alergias, prefieres otro plato, es muy cara, etc.). Pide otro plato.

6. La comida está fría.

8. Tienes mucha prisa, pero el/la mesero/a está muy lento/a.

10. Explica por qué quieres un descuento o quieres hablar con el/la gerente.

Vuelve a la Actividad **6-6A**.

6-25B **¡Necesito información!** La mesa de tu compañero/a tiene cuatro objetos que tú necesitas. Tú tienes cuatro objetos que necesita tu compañero/a. Túrnense para describir sus mesas y así identificar y colocar (*place*) los objetos que faltan. Usen frases como **a la derecha de**, **al lado de**, **a la izquierda de**, **arriba de** (*on top of*) y **debajo de**.

MODELO: ESTUDIANTE A: *Hay una ensalada arriba de…*
ESTUDIANTE B: *Correcto. Y hay una cuchara y un tenedor grande al lado…*
ESTUDIANTE A: *¡Ah! Falta…*

Vuelve a la Actividad **6-25A**.

CAPÍTULO 7

7-3B **¡Necesito información!** Cada uno/a de ustedes tiene una escena con pequeñas diferencias. Túrnense para describir la escena y descubrir las diferencias. ¿Cuántas diferencias hay? Usen expresiones de la lista de **Vocabulario**.

MODELO: ESTUDIANTE A: *Hay dos mujeres en la playa.*
ESTUDIANTE B: *Correcto. Las dos mujeres llevan* (are wearing)…

Estudiante B:

Vuelve a la Actividad **7-3A**.

7-9B **¡Necesito información!** Tú y tu compañero/a publicaron en sus páginas de Facebook unos estados (*status updates*) sobre una fiesta que hubo anoche. Cada uno/a tiene parte de la información sobre la fiesta. Háganse preguntas para saber qué pasó.

Estudiante B:

La información que necesito:

1. ¿Quién dio la fiesta?
2. ¿Quiénes estuvieron en la fiesta?
3. ¿Qué sirvieron?
4. ¿Quiénes no fueron? ¿Por qué?
5. ¿Cómo lo pasaron?

Tu estado con tu versión de la fiesta:

Chelsea Cooper
Hoy a las 12:30 PM
Luisita recibió muchos regalos: una entrada para un concierto de Pitbull de Carlos y su novia, entradas para un partido de fútbol de Ramón. Y de mí, una novela cubana. Tocamos música de salsa. Ramón salió temprano porque tuvo que ir a trabajar. Luisita estuvo muy sorprendida y feliz.

A 2 personas les gusta esto.   1 Comentarios

Me gusta   Comentar   Compartir

Vuelve a la Actividad **7-9A**.

7-33B **¡Necesito información!** Ustedes son entrenadores/as que están preparándose para un partido en otra ciudad. Túrnense para preguntarse si tienen los objetos que necesitan y si pueden dárselos, o si no, buscárselos. Luego, hagan una lista de las cosas que tienen que buscar.

MODELO: ESTUDIANTE A: (la bolsa) *¿Tienes la bolsa?*
            ESTUDIANTE B: *Sí, la tengo. Te la doy. / No, no la tengo. Te la busco.*

Estudiante B:

Necesitas	Tienes
el bate de aluminio	el guante
la heladera	los lentes de sol
las toallas	las pelotas

Vuelve a la Actividad **7-33A**.

CAPÍTULO 8

8-3B **¡Necesito información!** ¿Qué compró Carmen para su viaje a Machu Picchu? Túrnense para completar la información que falta en su recibo. Usen estas preguntas guía: **¿Qué compró por…? ¿De qué talla es/son…? ¿Cuánto costó/costaron…?** Después, confirmen las compras que hizo y cuánto gastó.

> **MODELO:** ESTUDIANTE A: *¿Qué compró Carmen por veinte soles?*
> ESTUDIANTE B: *Compró una camiseta de algodón. ¿De qué talla es?*
> ESTUDIANTE A: *Es de la talla cuarenta.*

Vuelve a la Actividad **8-3A**.

8-7B **¡Necesito información!** Cada uno/a de ustedes tiene una versión diferente del dibujo que muestra lo que pasaba ayer en el almacén. Usen el imperfecto para describir lo que ven y así encontrar seis diferencias en cada versión.

> **MODELO:** ESTUDIANTE A: *Una mujer se probaba zapatos.*
> ESTUDIANTE B: *Es cierto. Una mujer se probaba zapatos.*

DOCUMENTO DE VENTA

OUFDSYEVW9NGOLWI9TOD2OJ

Vendedor	T.T	EmpCent	Operac.	Fecha	Hora	EdPIZN	T
51106219	9	001006	0367886	12/12/2018	19:16	0100000	00

Descripción	Talla	PRECIO (SOLES)
camiseta de algodón	40	S/ 20
blusa de manga corta	36	_____
_____	40	S/ 75
suéter de lana	_____	S/ 80
_____	42	S/ 200
zapatos de tacón alto	39	S/ 39
_____	50	S/ 100

TOTAL COMPRA S/ _____

Gracias por su compra.
Visítenos en www.falabella.com

Estudiante B:

Vuelve a la Actividad **8-7A**.

8-11B ¡Necesito información! Cada uno/a de ustedes tiene una parte del directorio del almacén. Túrnense para pedir información sobre dónde comprar productos o realizar (*carry out*) alguna tarea (*task*). Añadan más información cuando sea posible.

saga falabella.

1.er piso	Ropa de hombre Calzado (zapatos, botas, sandalias)	**6.° piso**	
2.° piso	Ropa de mujer (trajes, vestidos, ropa informal)	**7.° piso**	Ropa formal (trajes de noche, vestidos de noche) Trajes de novia
3.er piso		**8.° piso**	Restaurante
4.° piso	Equipo deportivo (ropa, pelotas, bates)	**9.° piso**	
5.° piso		**10.° piso**	Oficinas de empleo Cambio de moneda

MODELO: una blusa para tu mamá

ESTUDIANTE A: *Quiero comprar una blusa para mi mamá porque es su cumpleaños.*

ESTUDIANTE B: *La puede buscar en el segundo piso, en Ropa de mujer.*

ESTUDIANTE A: *Muchas gracias.*

Estudiante B:

1. platos y vasos
2. una camisa barata
3. un televisor grande
4. una botella de aceite de oliva
5. dónde pagar la cuenta
6. un suéter para tu sobrino que tiene dos años

Vuelve a la Actividad **8-11A**.

CAPÍTULO 9

9-5B ¡Necesito información! En parejas, hagan el papel de agente (estudiante A) y viajero/a (estudiante B) en el mostrador del aeropuerto de la aerolínea colombiana Avianca. Tengan una conversación siguiendo la guía.

MODELO: AGENTE: Saluda al / a la viajero/a.

Buenas tardes. ¿En qué puedo servirle?

VIAJERO/A: Saluda al / a la agente; Dile (*Tell him/her*) adónde viajas hoy.

Buenas tardes. Viajo a (Bogotá/Cartagena/Medellín, etc.).

Estudiante B: El/La viajero/a

2. Saluda al / a la agente. Dile adónde viajas hoy.

4. Repite la información del agente sobre el vuelo para confirmar. Quieres facturar _____ maletas.

6. En la maleta de mano, llevas _____ botellas grandes de champú y _____ de acondicionador.

8. Quieres sentarte en… (un asiento de ventanilla / un asiento de pasillo / clase ejecutiva / clase turista).

10. Si te parece bien el precio, paga (con tarjeta de crédito / en efectivo). Además, quieres una comida especial porque eres (vegetariano/a; alérgico/a a.., etc.)

12. Si te parece bien, dile "adiós". Si no, dile que quieres hablar con su supervisor.

Vuelve a la Actividad **9-5A**.

9-10B **¡Necesito información!** En parejas, conversen sobre los viajes que van a hacer en la primavera. Cada uno/a debe usar la información de su itinerario y las preguntas guía. Luego, deben intentar convencer (*try to convince*) a la otra persona de viajar juntos/as al destino que cada uno/a eligió.

MODELO: ESTUDIANTE A: *¿Adónde vas para las vacaciones de primavera?*
ESTUDIANTE B: *Voy a… Y tú, ¿adónde vas para las vacaciones?*

Estudiante B:

	Mi viaje	El viaje de mi compañero/a
Destino:	Isla de Margarita, Venezuela	
Propósito:	tomar el sol, divertirme, hacer windsurf	
Transporte:	barco, taxi	
Ruta:	Houston, Caracas, Isla de Margarita	
Duración del viaje:	cinco días	
Fecha de llegada:	el 2 de marzo	

Preguntas:

1. ¿Adónde vas?
2. ¿Por qué ruta vas a viajar?
3. ¿Cómo vas a viajar, por tren, por carro, por...?
4. ¿Cuándo es el viaje?
5. ¿Por cuánto tiempo vas?
6. ¿Para qué vas?

Al final, para convencer a tu compañero/a:

7. ¿Por qué no vienes conmigo? Creo que mi viaje va a ser...

Vuelve a la Actividad **9-10A**.

9-13B **¡Necesito información!** En el aeropuerto, antes de su vuelo a la Isla de Margarita, ustedes están observando lo que está pasando. Túrnense para hacerse preguntas y describir la escena. Contesten cada pregunta con un adverbio que termina en **-mente**.

MODELO: El inspector de seguridad está revisando una maleta (**especial**) misteriosa.
ESTUDIANTE A: *¿Qué hace el inspector de seguridad?*
ESTUDIANTE B: *Él está revisando una maleta especialmente misteriosa.*

Estudiante B:

Preguntas para mi compañero/a	Respuestas para mi compañero/a
1. ¿Tienes pasaje en clase turista?	• Sí, (**desafortunado**) hay una demora de una hora.
2. ¿Dónde está el asistente de vuelo?	• Está esperando (**impaciente**) la llegada de su copiloto.
3. ¿Qué pasa en el reclamo de equipaje?	• Revisa las bolsas de una señora (**particular**) nerviosa.
4. ¿Hay personas esperando a los pasajeros que están llegando?	• Están sentados (**tranquilo**) en la sala de espera.

Vuelve a la Actividad **9-13A**.

CAPÍTULO 10

10-5B ¡Necesito información! Hagan el papel de doctor/a (estudiante A) y paciente (estudiante B). Sigan la guía y tengan una conversación de sus síntomas, un diagnóstico lógico y recomendaciones para mejorarse.

> **MODELO:** DOCTOR/A: *Buenos días. ¿Cómo se siente? ¿Cuáles son sus síntomas?*
> PACIENTE: *Buenos días, doctor/a. Me siento muy mal…*

Estudiante B: Paciente

2. Explícale que te duele(n) (la garganta, el estómago, las piernas, los pies, los pulmones…).

4. Dile qué tomas regularmente (aspirina, antibióticos, calmantes, vitaminas, no tomas nada).

6. Dile qué ejercicio haces todos los días (corres, vas al gimnasio, haces yoga, caminas, no haces ejercicio).

8. Dile cuánto fumas (mucho, poco, no fumas).

10. Dile "gracias" y que vas a (seguir sus consejos, buscar otro médico, buscar un remedio en Internet…).

Vuelve a la Actividad **10-5A.**

10-9B ¡Necesito información! Ustedes trabajan en la sala de urgencias y tienen que decidir qué hacer en situaciones de emergencia. Túrnense presentando las situaciones y respondiendo con mandatos formales lógicos de su lista. Incluyan una situación original.

> **MODELO:** ESTUDIANTE A: *El niño tiene gripe.*
> ESTUDIANTE B: *Dele muchos líquidos como jugo o agua.*

Estudiante B:

Situaciones urgentes	Acciones
1. La paciente se rompió una pierna.	darle un antiácido
2. El señor viejo está muy ansioso.	buscar un tanque de oxígeno
3. La niña tiene resfriado.	ponerle una inyección de penicilina
4. La señora tiene dolor de cabeza.	tomarle la temperatura
5. Al joven le duele una muela.	darle un jarabe para controlar la tos
6. ¿…?	¿…?

Vuelve a la Actividad **10-9A.**

10-14B **¡Necesito información!** Hagan el papel de paciente (estudiante A) y doctor/a (estudiante B) en el consultorio médico. El/La paciente explica sus síntomas y el/la doctor/a reacciona y da consejos. Usen expresiones de emoción con el subjuntivo o el infinitivo según el contexto.

> **MODELO:** PACIENTE: *Doctor/a, temo tener una enfermedad muy rara.*
> DOCTOR/A: *Es mejor que me diga todos sus síntomas.*

Estudiante B: Doctor/a

2. Es sorprendente que (poder caminar, poder verme, poder hablarme).

4. Es ilógico que no (querer quitarse el sombrero, sentarse en la silla, mostrarme el brazo).

6. Siento que (no poder seguir mis consejos, no querer ir al hospital, querer buscar otro médico).

Vuelve a la Actividad **10-14A**.

10-28B **¡Necesito información!** El Spa-Hotel tiene un centro naturista donde los clientes pueden recibir consejos de un/a naturista y comprar todo tipo de productos naturales. Hagan los papeles de naturista (estudiante A) y cliente/a (estudiante B) en la tienda.

> **MODELO:** NATURISTA: *Buenos días, (señor/señora/señorita). ¿En que puedo servirle?*
> CLIENTE/A: *Buenos días. Necesito algo para…*

Estudiante B: Cliente/a

2. Saluda al / a la naturista y explícale que necesitas algo para (el dolor de cabeza, la fatiga, las náuseas, la enfermedad de altura…).

4. Explícale que (no puedes dormir/comer, tienes miedo de salir de tu cuarto, te sientes muy estresado/a…). Es que…

6. Pregúntale cuánto tiempo va a tomar el remedio.

8. Dile que tienes prisa y que (quieres suficiente del producto para un mes, necesitas pagar con tarjeta de crédito, vas a buscar un mejor remedio en otro lugar).

10. Dile "adiós" y que esperas que (tenga un buen día, encuentre otro trabajo, sirva mejor a otros clientes…).

Vuelve a la Actividad **10-28A**.

CAPÍTULO 11

11-8B **¡Necesito información!** Ustedes son el/la ayudante administrativo/a (estudiante A) y el/la organizador/a de eventos (estudiante B) en una empresa donde hoy va a haber una reunión importante, y tienen que resolver situaciones urgentes. Respondan de una manera apropiada a las urgencias que se presentan.

> **MODELO:** AYUDANTE ADMINISTRATIVO/A: *La reunión es ahora, pero no hay café.*
> ORGANIZADOR/A DE EVENTOS: ¡(Llamar) al restaurante ahora mismo!
> *¡Llama al restaurante ahora mismo!*

Estudiante B: Organizador/a de eventos

Situaciones urgentes	Posibles soluciones para el/la ayudante administrativo/a
1. El gerente quiere la lista de invitados.	• ¡(Mandarles) todos los documentos por correo electrónico!
2. El ayudante administrativo dice que va a empezar sus vacaciones hoy y no puede asistir a la reunión.	• ¡(Llamar) al técnico en computadoras!
3. Hay agua por todas partes en el baño.	• ¡(No dársela) nunca!
4. La contadora dice que hay una gran discrepancia en la cuenta.	• ¡(Decirle) que no puede trabajar en el salón ahora!
5. Los invitados de China dicen que no entienden bien el español.	• ¡(Pedirle) a la enfermera que venga enseguida!

Vuelve a la Actividad **11-8A**.

11-26B **¡Necesito información!** Hagan los papeles de jefe/a de personal (estudiante A) y de aspirante (estudiante B) para dramatizar una entrevista de trabajo.

> **MODELO:** JEFE/A DE PERSONAL: *Bienvenido/a. Soy…. Siéntese, por favor.*
> ASPIRANTE: *Gracias. Soy y quiero…*

Estudiante B: Aspirante

2. Saluda al / a la jefe/a de personal y dile tu nombre. Explícale por qué estás aquí.

4. Dile que (tienes experiencia trabajando en… / no tienes experiencia, pero eres muy entusiasta).

6. Dile que (tu padre es jefe ejecutivo de… / tu madre es _____, una actriz famosa / tu hermana es esposa del presidente).

8. Responde que (no importa / tú le vas a pagar a la empresa por la experiencia / quieres _____ dólares por mes).

10. Dile (gracias por su tiempo / que tienes otra oferta / que prefieres continuar tu estudios).

Vuelve a la Actividad **11-26A**.

11-29B **¡Necesito información!** Hagan los papeles de emprendedor/a (estudiante A) y ayudante adminstrativo/a (estudiante B) en una empresa incipiente (*startup*) multinacional. Háganse y contesten preguntas sobre lo que necesitan para su empresa.

> **MODELO:** Dile que necesitan empleados que (**tener**) experiencia.
> EMPRENDEDOR/A: *Necesitamos empleados que tengan experiencia.*
> AYUDANTE ADMINISTRATIVO/A: *Tengo muchas solicitudes de personas que tienen experiencia.*

Estudiante B: Ayudante administrativo/a

2. Dile que no, pero que hay muchas vacantes que (**necesitar**) analistas de sistemas. Pregúntale si busca una persona que (**tener**) mucha experiencia.

4. Dile que sí, hay una buena candidata que también (**saber**) francés. Pregúntale si no hay nadie que le (**gustar**).

6. Dile que sí, que hay muchas personas que (**tener**) la formación y la experiencia necesaria.

8. Dile que vas a llamar a…, la persona que (**ser**) la mejor calificada.

Vuelve a la Actividad **11-29A**.

CAPÍTULO 12

12-26B ¡**Necesito información!** Vean las situaciones y túrnense para hacer conjeturas (*guesses*) sobre por qué serán. Respondan de una manera lógica para cada situación.

> **MODELO:** Recibes una llamada por teléfono a las siete de la mañana.
> ESTUDIANTE A: *Será algo urgente de mi jefa.*
> ESTUDIANTE B: *Tendrás que salir para la oficina ahora mismo.*

Estudiante B:

Situaciones	Conjeturas
2. Hay un programa para conservar agua.	• (ser) un programa de reforestación
4. Ha fallado el servidor principal.	• (instalar) paneles solares
6. Hay un derrame serio de petróleo en Nebraska.	• alguien (estar) fumando o cocinando algo
8. La planta nuclear está cerrada.	• (haber) una inundación

Vuelve a la Actividad **12-26A**.

12-29B ¡**Necesito información!** Hagan los papeles de periodista investigador/a (estudiante A) y jefe/a ejecutivo/a de una planta nuclear (estudiante B). Individualmente, preparen sus preguntas y sus respuestas para la entrevista.

> **MODELO:** **reciclar** los desechos de la planta nuclear
> PERIODISTA INVESTIGADOR/A: *Usted dijo que reciclaría los desechos de la planta nuclear.*
> JEFE/A EJECUTIVO/A: *Tiene razón. Pero también dije que este proyecto tomaría su tiempo.*

Estudiante B: Jefe/a ejecutivo/a

(Posiblemente, pero…; No es verdad…; Usted no tiene razón…; Con todo respeto…; ¡Yo no dije eso!, etc.) Dije que…

- **hacerlo** en colaboración con el estado
- **implementar** todos los cambios para el año 2025
- **necesitar** la ayuda de la comunidad
- **poder** filmar en cualquier momento
- **ser** difícil hacerlo en menos de un año
- **tener** que conseguir nueva maquinaria

Vuelve a la Actividad **12-29A**.

CAPÍTULO 13

 13-9B ¡**Necesito información!** Túrnense para preguntarse cómo se sentían en estas situaciones en el pasado.

MODELO: ESTUDIANTE A: *De joven, ¿qué querías que hicieran tus amigos?*
ESTUDIANTE B: invitarme a su casa a jugar videojuegos
Quería que me invitaran a su casa a jugar videojuegos.

Estudiante B:

Mis preguntas	Posibles respuestas a las preguntas de mi compañero/a
2. En el restaurante, ¿qué esperabas que hiciera el camarero?	• (nosotros/as) pasarlo bien
4. En el trabajo, ¿qué temías que hiciera tu jefe/a?	• darnos una prueba cuando no estaba preparado/a
6. En un examen, ¿qué temías que pasara?	• haber un final feliz
8. En el periódico, ¿qué dudabas que pasara?	• permitirme salir con mis amigos durante la semana

Vuelve a la Actividad **13-9A**.

13-32B ¡**Necesito información!** Túrnense para reflexionar sobre lo que harían en estas situaciones hipotéticas.

MODELO: subir los precios de las entradas del cine
ESTUDIANTE A: *¿Qué harías si subieran los precios de las entradas del cine?*
ESTUDIANTE B: *Pues, iría menos...*

Estudiante B:

Mis preguntas	Posibles respuestas a las preguntas de mi compañero/a
¿Qué harías si...?	
2. (yo) no **tener** dinero para ir a un concierto	• **consultar** a un/a amigo/a que sabe mucho sobre aparatos electrónicos
4. (tú) **comprar** dos entradas para el teatro	• **ir**, sin duda
6. un director **darte** la oportunidad de participar como extra en una película	• **pedirle** su autógrafo
8. **llamarte** una estrella de cine	• **invitar** a todos mis amigos a cenar
10. alguien **ofrecerte** un millón de dólares por una novela que escribiste	• **visitar** el Teatro Chino *Grauman*

Vuelve a la Actividad **13-32A**.

CAPÍTULO 14

14-8B ¡Necesito información! A continuación tienen información sobre dos famosos artistas. Háganse y contesten preguntas sobre cuánto tiempo hace que participan en su arte o sobre actividades o eventos que les ocurrieron en el pasado.

> **MODELO:** Miguel Zenón toca jazz desde (*since*) 1995
> ESTUDIANTE A: *¿Cuánto tiempo hace que Miguel Zenón toca jazz?*
> ESTUDIANTE B: *Hace... años que lo toca. Empezó en 1995.*

Estudiante B:

Preguntas sobre Dafnis Prieto

2. ¿Cuántos años hace que nació? ¿Dónde nació?
4. ¿Cuántos años hace que salió de su patria?
6. ¿Cuántos años hace que recibió el MacArthur Fellowship Award?
8. ¿Cuántos años hace que fue nominado al Grammy Latino?
10. ¿Cuántos años hace que da clases en Miami?

Perfil de Miguel Zenón

- lugar y fecha de nacimiento: Puerto Rico, 1976
- hizo una gira por África: 2003
- fue nombrado el mejor artista de jazz por la revista *JazzTimes* en 2006
- recibió el Guggenheim Fellowship Award en 2008; el MacArthur Fellowship Award en 2008
- fue nominado al Grammy en 2014

Vuelve a la Actividad **14-8A**.

CAPÍTULO 15

15-18B ¡Necesito información! Eres reportero/a y tu compañero/a es candidato/a en las próximas elecciones municipales. Trata de conseguir toda la información posible a la vez que contestas sus preguntas.

Estudiante B: Reportero/a

1. ¿Por qué quiere ser usted candidato/a?
2. ¿Cómo piensa usted resolver el problema de la economía de su distrito?
3. ¿Nos puede explicar su posición sobre el seguro social?
4. ¿Quién será responsable de administrar las donaciones a su campaña?
5. ¿Cómo va a resolver el tráfico de drogas en esta ciudad?

Vuelve a la Actividad **15-18A**.

Appendix 2
Verb Charts

Regular Verbs: Simple Tenses

Infinitive / Present Participle / Past Participle	Indicative					Subjunctive		Imperative
	Present	Imperfect	Preterit	Future	Conditional	Present	Imperfect	Commands
hablar / hablando / hablado	hablo	hablaba	hablé	hablaré	hablaría	hable	hablara	
	hablas	hablabas	hablaste	hablarás	hablarías	hables	hablaras	habla (tú), no hables
	habla	hablaba	habló	hablará	hablaría	hable	hablara	hable (usted)
	hablamos	hablábamos	hablamos	hablaremos	hablaríamos	hablemos	habláramos	hablemos
	habláis	hablabais	hablasteis	hablaréis	hablaríais	habléis	hablarais	hablad (vosotros), no habléis
	hablan	hablaban	hablaron	hablarán	hablarían	hablen	hablaran	hablen (Uds.)
comer / comiendo / comido	como	comía	comí	comeré	comería	coma	comiera	
	comes	comías	comiste	comerás	comerías	comas	comieras	come (tú), no comas
	come	comía	comió	comerá	comería	coma	comiera	coma (usted)
	comemos	comíamos	comimos	comeremos	comeríamos	comamos	comiéramos	comamos
	coméis	comíais	comisteis	comeréis	comeríais	comáis	comierais	comed (vosotros), no comáis
	comen	comían	comieron	comerán	comerían	coman	comieran	coman (Uds.)
vivir / viviendo / vivido	vivo	vivía	viví	viviré	viviría	viva	viviera	
	vives	vivías	viviste	vivirás	vivirías	vivas	vivieras	vive (tú), no vivas
	vive	vivía	vivió	vivirá	viviría	viva	viviera	viva (usted)
	vivimos	vivíamos	vivimos	viviremos	viviríamos	vivamos	viviéramos	vivamos
	vivís	vivíais	vivisteis	viviréis	viviríais	viváis	vivierais	vivid (vosotros), no viváis
	viven	vivían	vivieron	vivirán	vivirían	vivan	vivieran	vivan (Uds.)

Regular Verbs: Perfect Tenses

Indicative								Subjunctive			
Present Perfect		Past Perfect		Future Perfect		Conditional Perfect		Present Perfect		Past Perfect	
he	hablado	había	hablado	habré	hablado	habría	hablado	haya	hablado	hubiera	hablado
has	comido	habías	comido	habrás	comido	habrías	comido	hayas	comido	hubieras	comido
ha	vivido	había	vivido	habrá	vivido	habría	vivido	haya	vivido	hubiera	vivido
hemos		habíamos		habremos		habríamos		hayamos		hubiéramos	
habéis		habíais		habréis		habríais		hayáis		hubierais	
han		habían		habrán		habrían		hayan		hubieran	

Irregular Verbs

Infinitive / Present Participle / Past Participle	Indicative					Subjunctive		Imperative
	Present	Imperfect	Preterit	Future	Conditional	Present	Imperfect	Commands
andar andando andado	ando andas anda andamos andáis andan	andaba andabas andaba andábamos andabais andaban	anduve anduviste anduvo anduvimos anduvisteis anduvieron	andaré andarás andará andaremos andaréis andarán	andaría andarías andaría andaríamos andaríais andarían	ande andes ande andemos andéis anden	anduviera anduvieras anduviera anduviéramos anduvierais anduvieran	anda (tú), no andes ande (usted) andemos andad (vosotros), no andéis anden (Uds.)
caer cayendo caído	caigo caes cae caemos caéis caen	caía caías caía caíamos caíais caían	caí caíste cayó caímos caísteis cayeron	caeré caerás caerá caeremos caeréis caerán	caería caerías caería caeríamos caeríais caerían	caiga caigas caiga caigamos caigáis caigan	cayera cayeras cayera cayéramos cayerais cayeran	cae (tú), no caigas caiga (usted) caigamos caed (vosotros), no caigáis caigan (Uds.)
dar dando dado	doy das da damos dais dan	daba dabas daba dábamos dabais daban	di diste dio dimos disteis dieron	daré darás dará daremos daréis darán	daría darías daría daríamos daríais darían	dé des dé demos deis den	diera dieras diera diéramos dierais dieran	da (tú), no des dé (usted) demos dad (vosotros), no deis den (Uds.)
decir diciendo dicho	digo dices dice decimos decís dicen	decía decías decía decíamos decíais decían	dije dijiste dijo dijimos dijisteis dijeron	diré dirás dirá diremos diréis dirán	diría dirías diría diríamos diríais dirían	diga digas diga digamos digáis digan	dijera dijeras dijera dijéramos dijerais dijeran	di (tú), no digas diga (usted) digamos decid (vosotros), no digáis digan (Uds.)

Irregular Verbs (continued)

Infinitive / Present Participle / Past Participle	Indicative Present	Imperfect	Preterit	Future	Conditional	Subjunctive Present	Imperfect	Imperative Commands
estar / estando / estado	estoy / estás / está / estamos / estáis / están	estaba / estabas / estaba / estábamos / estabais / estaban	estuve / estuviste / estuvo / estuvimos / estuvisteis / estuvieron	estaré / estarás / estará / estaremos / estaréis / estarán	estaría / estarías / estaría / estaríamos / estaríais / estarían	esté / estés / esté / estemos / estéis / estén	estuviera / estuvieras / estuviera / estuviéramos / estuvierais / estuvieran	está (tú), no estés / esté (usted) / estemos / estad (vosotros), no estéis / estén (Uds.)
haber / habiendo / habido	he / has / ha / hemos / habéis / han	había / habías / había / habíamos / habíais / habían	hube / hubiste / hubo / hubimos / hubisteis / hubieron	habré / habrás / habrá / habremos / habréis / habrán	habría / habrías / habría / habríamos / habríais / habrían	haya / hayas / haya / hayamos / hayáis / hayan	hubiera / hubieras / hubiera / hubiéramos / hubierais / hubieran	N/A
hacer / haciendo / hecho	hago / haces / hace / hacemos / hacéis / hacen	hacía / hacías / hacía / hacíamos / hacíais / hacían	hice / hiciste / hizo / hicimos / hicisteis / hicieron	haré / harás / hará / haremos / haréis / harán	haría / harías / haría / haríamos / haríais / harían	haga / hagas / haga / hagamos / hagáis / hagan	hiciera / hicieras / hiciera / hiciéramos / hicierais / hicieran	haz (tú), no hagas / haga (usted) / hagamos / haced (vosotros), no hagáis / hagan (Uds.)
ir / yendo / ido	voy / vas / va / vamos / vais / van	iba / ibas / iba / íbamos / ibais / iban	fui / fuiste / fue / fuimos / fuisteis / fueron	iré / irás / irá / iremos / iréis / irán	iría / irías / iría / iríamos / iríais / irían	vaya / vayas / vaya / vayamos / vayáis / vayan	fuera / fueras / fuera / fuéramos / fuerais / fueran	ve (tú), no vayas / vaya (usted) / vamos, no vayamos / id (vosotros), no vayáis / vayan (Uds.)
oír / oyendo / oído	oigo / oyes / oye / oímos / oís / oyen	oía / oías / oía / oíamos / oíais / oían	oí / oíste / oyó / oímos / oísteis / oyeron	oiré / oirás / oirá / oiremos / oiréis / oirán	oiría / oirías / oiría / oiríamos / oiríais / oirían	oiga / oigas / oiga / oigamos / oigáis / oigan	oyera / oyeras / oyera / oyéramos / oyerais / oyeran	oye (tú), no oigas / oiga (usted) / oigamos / oíd (vosotros), no oigáis / oigan (Uds.)

Irregular Verbs (continued)

Infinitive / Present Participle / Past Participle	Indicative					Subjunctive		Imperative
	Present	Imperfect	Preterit	Future	Conditional	Present	Imperfect	Commands
poder pudiendo podido	puedo puedes puede podemos podéis pueden	podía podías podía podíamos podíais podían	pude pudiste pudo pudimos pudisteis pudieron	podré podrás podrá podremos podréis podrán	podría podrías podría podríamos podríais podrían	pueda puedas pueda podamos podáis puedan	pudiera pudieras pudiera pudiéramos pudierais pudieran	N/A
poner poniendo puesto	pongo pones pone ponemos ponéis ponen	ponía ponías ponía poníamos poníais ponían	puse pusiste puso pusimos pusisteis pusieron	pondré pondrás pondrá pondremos pondréis pondrán	pondría pondrías pondría pondríamos pondríais pondrían	ponga pongas ponga pongamos pongáis pongan	pusiera pusieras pusiera pusiéramos pusierais pusieran	pon (tú), no pongas ponga (usted) pongamos poned (vosotros), no pongáis pongan (Uds.)
querer queriendo querido	quiero quieres quiere queremos queréis quieren	quería querías quería queríamos queríais querían	quise quisiste quiso quisimos quisisteis quisieron	querré querrás querrá querremos querréis querrán	querría querrías querría querríamos querríais querrían	quiera quieras quiera queramos queráis quieran	quisiera quisieras quisiera quisiéramos quisierais quisieran	quiere (tú), no quieras quiera (usted) queramos quered (vosotros), no queráis quieran (Uds.)
saber sabiendo sabido	sé sabes sabe sabemos sabéis saben	sabía sabías sabía sabíamos sabíais sabían	supe supiste supo supimos supisteis supieron	sabré sabrás sabrá sabremos sabréis sabrán	sabría sabrías sabría sabríamos sabríais sabrían	sepa sepas sepa sepamos sepáis sepan	supiera supieras supiera supiéramos supierais supieran	sabe (tú), no sepas sepa (usted) sepamos sabed (vosotros), no sepáis sepan (Uds.)
salir saliendo salido	salgo sales sale salimos salís salen	salía salías salía salíamos salíais salían	salí saliste salió salimos salisteis salieron	saldré saldrás saldrá saldremos saldréis saldrán	saldría saldrías saldría saldríamos saldríais saldrían	salga salgas salga salgamos salgáis salgan	saliera salieras saliera saliéramos salierais salieran	sal (tú), no salgas salga (usted) salgamos salid (vosotros), no salgáis salgan (Uds.)

Irregular Verbs (continued)

Infinitive / Present Participle / Past Participle	Indicative Present	Imperfect	Preterit	Future	Conditional	Subjunctive Present	Imperfect	Imperative Commands
ser / siendo / sido	soy	era	fui	seré	sería	sea	fuera	sé (tú), no seas
	eres	eras	fuiste	serás	serías	seas	fueras	sea (usted)
	es	era	fue	será	sería	sea	fuera	seamos
	somos	éramos	fuimos	seremos	seríamos	seamos	fuéramos	sed (vosotros), no seáis
	sois	erais	fuisteis	seréis	seríais	seáis	fuerais	sean (Uds.)
	son	eran	fueron	serán	serían	sean	fueran	
tener / teniendo / tenido	tengo	tenía	tuve	tendré	tendría	tenga	tuviera	ten (tú), no tengas
	tienes	tenías	tuviste	tendrás	tendrías	tengas	tuvieras	tenga (usted)
	tiene	tenía	tuvo	tendrá	tendría	tenga	tuviera	tengamos
	tenemos	teníamos	tuvimos	tendremos	tendríamos	tengamos	tuviéramos	tened (vosotros), no tengáis
	tenéis	teníais	tuvisteis	tendréis	tendríais	tengáis	tuvierais	tengan (Uds.)
	tienen	tenían	tuvieron	tendrán	tendrían	tengan	tuvieran	
traer / trayendo / traído	traigo	traía	traje	traeré	traería	traiga	trajera	trae (tú), no traigas
	traes	traías	trajiste	traerás	traerías	traigas	trajeras	traiga (usted)
	trae	traía	trajo	traerá	traería	traiga	trajera	traigamos
	traemos	traíamos	trajimos	traeremos	traeríamos	traigamos	trajéramos	traed (vosotros), no traigáis
	traéis	traíais	trajisteis	traeréis	traeríais	traigáis	trajerais	traigan (Uds.)
	traen	traían	trajeron	traerán	traerían	traigan	trajeran	
venir / viniendo / venido	vengo	venía	vine	vendré	vendría	venga	viniera	ven (tú), no vengas
	vienes	venías	viniste	vendrás	vendrías	vengas	vinieras	venga (usted)
	viene	venía	vino	vendrá	vendría	venga	viniera	vengamos
	venimos	veníamos	vinimos	vendremos	vendríamos	vengamos	viniéramos	venid (vosotros), no vengáis
	venís	veníais	vinisteis	vendréis	vendríais	vengáis	vinierais	vengan (Uds.)
	vienen	venían	vinieron	vendrán	vendrían	vengan	vinieran	
ver / viendo / visto	veo	veía	vi	veré	vería	vea	viera	ve (tú), no veas
	ves	veías	viste	verás	verías	veas	vieras	vea (usted)
	ve	veía	vio	verá	vería	vea	viera	veamos
	vemos	veíamos	vimos	veremos	veríamos	veamos	viéramos	ved (vosotros), no veáis
	veis	veíais	visteis	veréis	veríais	veáis	vierais	vean (Uds.)
	ven	veían	vieron	verán	verían	vean	vieran	

Stem-Changing and Orthographic-Changing Verbs

Infinitive / Present Participle / Past Participle	Indicative					Subjunctive		Imperative
	Present	Imperfect	Preterit	Future	Conditional	Present	Imperfect	Commands
almorzar (ue) (c) almorzando almorzado	almuerzo almuerzas almuerza almorzamos almorzáis almuerzan	almorzaba almorzabas almorzaba almorzábamos almorzabais almorzaban	almorcé almorzaste almorzó almorzamos almorzasteis almorzaron	almorzaré almorzarás almorzará almorzaremos almorzaréis almorzarán	almorzaría almorzarías almorzaría almorzaríamos almorzaríais almorzarían	almuerce almuerces almuerce almorcemos almorcéis almuercen	almorzara almorzaras almorzara almorzáramos almorzarais almorzaran	almuerza (tú), no almuerces almuerce (usted) almorcemos almorzad (vosotros), no almorcéis almuercen (Uds.)
buscar (qu) buscando buscado	busco buscas busca buscamos buscáis buscan	buscaba buscabas buscaba buscábamos buscabais buscaban	busqué buscaste buscó buscamos buscasteis buscaron	buscaré buscarás buscará buscaremos buscaréis buscarán	buscaría buscarías buscaría buscaríamos buscaríais buscarían	busque busques busque busquemos busquéis busquen	buscara buscaras buscara buscáramos buscarais buscaran	busca (tú) no busques busque (usted) busquemos buscad (vosotros), no busquéis busquen (Uds.)
corregir (i, i) (j) corrigiendo corregido	corrijo corriges corrige corregimos corregís corrigen	corregía corregías corregía corregíamos corregíais corregían	corregí corregiste corrigió corregimos corregisteis corrigieron	corregiré corregirás corregirá corregiremos corregiréis corregirán	corregiría corregirías corregiría corregiríamos corregiríais corregirían	corrija corrijas corrija corrijamos corrijáis corrijan	corrigiera corrigieras corrigiera corrigiéramos corrigierais corrigieran	corrige (tú), no corrijas corrija (usted) corrijamos corregid (vosotros), no corrijáis corrijan (Uds.)
dormir (ue, u) durmiendo dormido	duermo duermes duerme dormimos dormís duermen	dormía dormías dormía dormíamos dormíais dormían	dormí dormiste durmió dormimos dormisteis durmieron	dormiré dormirás dormirá dormiremos dormiréis dormirán	dormiría dormirías dormiría dormiríamos dormiríais dormirían	duerma duermas duerma durmamos durmáis duerman	durmiera durmieras durmiera durmiéramos durmierais durmieran	duerme (tú), no duermas duerma (usted) durmamos dormid (vosotros), no durmáis duerman (Uds.)
incluir (y) incluyendo incluido	incluyo incluyes incluye incluimos incluís incluyen	incluía incluías incluía incluíamos incluíais incluían	incluí incluiste incluyó incluimos incluisteis incluyeron	incluiré incluirás incluirá incluiremos incluiréis incluirán	incluiría incluirías incluiría incluiríamos incluiríais incluirían	incluya incluyas incluya incluyamos incluyáis incluyan	incluyera incluyeras incluyera incluyéramos incluyerais incluyeran	incluye (tú), no incluyas incluya (usted) incluyamos incluid (vosotros), no incluyáis incluyan (Uds.)

Stem-Changing and Orthographic-Changing Verbs (continued)

Infinitive Present Participle Past Participle	Indicative Present	Indicative Imperfect	Indicative Preterit	Indicative Future	Conditional	Subjunctive Present	Subjunctive Imperfect	Imperative Commands
llegar (gu) llegando llegado	llego llegas llega llegamos llegáis llegan	llegaba llegabas llegaba llegábamos llegabais llegaban	llegué llegaste llegó llegamos llegasteis llegaron	llegaré llegarás llegará llegaremos llegaréis llegarán	llegaría llegarías llegaría llegaríamos llegaríais llegarían	llegue llegues llegue lleguemos lleguéis lleguen	llegara llegaras llegara llegáramos llegarais llegaran	llega (tú), no llegues llegue (usted) lleguemos llegad (vosotros), no lleguéis lleguen (Uds.)
pedir (i, i) pidiendo pedido	pido pides pide pedimos pedís piden	pedía pedías pedía pedíamos pedíais pedían	pedí pediste pidió pedimos pedisteis pidieron	pediré pedirás pedirá pediremos pediréis pedirán	pediría pedirías pediría pediríamos pediríais pedirían	pida pidas pida pidamos pidáis pidan	pidiera pidieras pidiera pidiéramos pidierais pidieran	pide (tú), no pidas pida (usted) pidamos pedid (vosotros), no pidáis pidan (Uds.)
pensar (ie) pensando pensado	pienso piensas piensa pensamos pensáis piensan	pensaba pensabas pensaba pensábamos pensabais pensaban	pensé pensaste pensó pensamos pensasteis pensaron	pensaré pensarás pensará pensaremos pensaréis pensarán	pensaría pensarías pensaría pensaríamos pensaríais pensarían	piense pienses piense pensemos penséis piensen	pensara pensaras pensara pensáramos pensarais pensaran	piensa (tú), no pienses piense (usted) pensemos pensad (vosotros), no penséis piensen (Uds.)
producir (zc) (j) produciendo producido	produzco produces produce producimos producís producen	producía producías producía producíamos producíais producían	produje produjiste produjo produjimos produjisteis produjeron	produciré producirás producirá produciremos produciréis producirán	produciría producirías produciría produciríamos produciríais producirían	produzca produzcas produzca produzcamos produzcáis produzcan	produjera produjeras produjera produjéramos produjerais produjeran	produce (tú), no produzcas produzca (usted) produzcamos producid (vosotros), no produzcáis produzcan (Uds.)
reír (i, i) riendo reído	río ríes ríe reímos reís ríen	reía reías reía reíamos reíais reían	reí reíste rio reímos reísteis rieron	reiré reirás reirá reiremos reiréis reirán	reiría reirías reiría reiríamos reiríais reirían	ría rías ría riamos riáis rían	riera rieras riera riéramos rierais rieran	ríe (tú), no rías ría (usted) riamos reíd (vosotros), no riáis rían (Uds.)

Stem-Changing and Orthographic-Changing Verbs (continued)

Infinitive Present Participle Past Participle	Indicative					Subjunctive		Imperative
	Present	Imperfect	Preterit	Future	Conditional	Present	Imperfect	Commands
seguir (i, i) (ga) siguiendo seguido	sigo sigues sigue seguimos seguís siguen	seguía seguías seguía seguíamos seguíais seguían	seguí seguiste siguió seguimos seguisteis siguieron	seguiré seguirás seguirá seguiremos seguiréis seguirán	seguiría seguirías seguiría seguiríamos seguiríais seguirían	siga sigas siga sigamos sigáis sigan	siguiera siguieras siguiera siguiéramos siguierais siguieran	sigue (tú), no sigas siga (usted) sigamos seguid (vosotros), no sigáis sigan (Uds.)
sentir (ie, i) sintiendo sentido	siento sientes siente sentimos sentís sienten	sentía sentías sentía sentíamos sentíais sentían	sentí sentiste sintió sentimos sentisteis sintieron	sentiré sentirás sentirá sentiremos sentiréis sentirán	sentiría sentirías sentiría sentiríamos sentiríais sentirían	sienta sientas sienta sintamos sintáis sientan	sintiera sintieras sintiera sintiéramos sintierais sintieran	siente (tú), no sientas sienta (usted) sintamos sentid (vosotros), no sintáis sientan (Uds.)
volver (ue) volviendo vuelto	vuelvo vuelves vuelve volvemos volvéis vuelven	volvía volvías volvía volvíamos volvíais volvían	volví volviste volvió volvimos volvisteis volvieron	volveré volverás volverá volveremos volveréis volverán	volvería volverías volvería volveríamos volveríais volverían	vuelva vuelvas vuelva volvamos volváis vuelvan	volviera volvieras volviera volviéramos volvierais volvieran	vuelve (tú), no vuelvas vuelva (usted) volvamos volved (vosotros), no volváis vuelvan (Uds.)

Appendix 3
Spanish-English Vocabulary

A

a favor (de) in favor (of)
a la parrilla grilled **6**
a la(s)... at . . . o'clock **2**
a lo largo de along
a pie by/on foot
¿A qué hora? At what time? **2**
a veces sometimes **5**
abandonar to abandon
abarcar to extend
abogado/a, el/la lawyer **11**
abogar to advocate
abolir to abolish **15**
abordar to board **9**
abrazar to embrace
abrazo, el hug; embrace
Abre (Abran) el libro. Open your book(s). **1**
abrigo, el coat **8**
abril April **1**
abrir to open **2**
abstenerse (ie) to abstain
abuelita, la grandma (*diminutive*)
abuelo/a, el/la grandfather/ grandmother **4**
abundar to abound
aburrido/a bored **2**; boring **1**
aburrir to bore; to tire
abuso, el abuse
acabar (de) (+ *inf*.) to finish; to have just (done something)
académico/a academic
acampar to camp
acantilado, el cliff
acceder to accede; to access **12**
accesorio, el accessory **5, 8**
accidente, el accident

acción, la action
aceite (de oliva), el (olive) oil **6**
aceituna, la olive
acelerar to accelerate
aceptar to accept **4**
acerca de about
acertado/a accurate; correct
ácimo/a unleavened
acomodar to accommodate
acompañante, el/la escort; companion
acompañar to accompany; to go with
acondicionador, el conditioner **5, 8**
aconsejar to advise
acontecimiento, el event
acordeón, el accordion
acostar (ue) to put to bed
acostarse (ue) to go to bed **5**
acostumbrar to accustom
acostumbrarse a to become accustomed to
actividad, la activity **5, 7**
activista, el/la activist **15**
activo/a active **2**
actor, el actor
actriz, la actress
actual current **15**
actualidad, la current events; present day
actualizar (un programa) to update (a program) **12**
actualmente now, currently
actuar to act **13**
acuático/a aquatic
acudir to attend, to resort (to)
acueducto, el aqueduct
acuerdo, el accord **15**
acupuntura, la acupuncture **10**

adaptador eléctrico, el electrical adaptor
adecuado/a adequate
adelgazar to lose weight **10**
ademán, el gesture
además in addition
Adiós. Good-bye. **1**
adivinar to guess
adivino/a, el/la fortune-teller
administración, la administration
administración de empresas, la business administration **3**
administrativo/a administrative **11**
admiración, la admiration
admirador/a, el/la admirer
admitir to admit
¿Adónde...? To where . . . ? **2**
adoptivo/a adoptive
adoquín, el cobblestone
adorar to adore
adornado/a adorned
adornar to adorn
adquirir (ie, i) to acquire
aduana, la customs **9**
aduanero/a, el/la customs officer
adverbio, el adverb **1**
advertir (ie, i) to warn
aeróbico/a aerobic **10**
aerolínea, la airline **9**
aeropuerto, el airport **9**
afectar to affect
afectuoso/a affectionate
afectuosamente affectionately
afeitarse to shave **5**
afianzar (c) to strengthen; to fortify
aficionado/a, el/la fan **7**

a fin de que in order that
afirmación, la statement
afirmar to affirm
afrodisíaco, el aphrodisiac
afrontar to face **15**
afueras, las outskirts
agarrar to grab
agencia de viajes, la travel agency
agente, el/la agent **9**
agente de viajes, el/la travel agent
agosto August **1**
agradable agreeable
agradecer (zc) to thank
agregar to add
agrícola agricultural
agua (mineral), el (*fem.*) (mineral) water **6**
aguacate, el avocado
águila, el (*fem.*) eagle
ahora (mismo) (right) now
ahorrar to save
aire acondicionado, el air conditioning
aire libre, al outside; open-air **8**
ajo, el garlic **6**
ajustar to adjust
al escribir while writing
al extranjero abroad **9**
al horno baked **6**
al leer while reading
al mismo tiempo at the same time
alabanza, la praise
albergar to house
alborotar to shake
álbum, el album
alcalde/alcaldesa, el/la mayor **15**
alcanzable achievable; reachable

alcanzar to reach

alcoba, la bedroom

alegrarse (de) to become happy 5; to be glad 5

alegremente happily

aliento, el breath

alejarse to go away

alemán, el German (language)

alemán/alemana German 2

Alemania Germany 2

alergia, la allergy

alérgico/a allergic 10

alerta, la alert 12

alfombra, la carpet

álgebra, el (*fem.*) algebra

algo something 7; anything 7

algodón, el cotton 8, 14

alguien someone 7

algún día someday

alguno/a(s) some 7, 10

alimentación, la nutrition

alimentar to nourish

alimentos, los foods

aliviado/a alleviated

aliviar to alleviate

allá there

alma, el (*fem.*) soul

almacén, el department store 8

almacenar (en la nube) to store (in the cloud) 12

almorzar (ue) to eat lunch 4, 6

almuerzo, el lunch

alpinismo, el mountain climbing 7

alquilar to rent

alquiler, el rent

alrededor about; around

alta costura, la high fashion 14

alta velocidad, la high speed

altavoz, el speaker

alternar(se) to alternate

alternativo/a alternative 12

altiplano, el high plateau

alto/a tall 2

altura, la altitude

aluminio, el aluminum 12

ama de casa, el (*fem.*) housewife

amado/a beloved

amanecer, el dawn

amante, el/la lover

amar to love

amarillo/a yellow 1

amargo/a bitter

amasar to knead, to mix

ambiental environmental

ambiente, el atmosphere

ambigüedad, la ambiguity

ambulancia, la ambulance

ambulante walking

a menos (de) que unless

amenaza, la threat 12

americana, la blazer (*Spain*)

amigo/a, el/la friend 2

amor, el love

amoroso/a amorous

ampliar to expand

amplio/a wide; extensive

amueblado/a furnished

análisis, el analysis

analista (financiero/a, de sistemas), el/la (financial/ systems) analyst 11

anaranjado/a orange (*color*) 1

ancho/a wide; **el ancho de la banda** bandwidth

anciano/a, el/la elderly person

andino/a Andean

anécdota, la anecdote

anfitrión/anfitriona, el/la host/hostess

angosto/a narrow

anillo (de oro), el (gold) ring 8

animadamente enthusiastically

animado/a animated

animal, el animal

animar to encourage; to cheer

animarse to be interested

aniversario, el anniversary

anoche last night

anotar to note; to write down

ansioso/a anxious

ante before

anteayer day before yesterday

antena parabólica, la satellite dish 12

antepasado/a, el/la ancestor

antes (de) before

antes de escribir pre-writing

antes de leer pre-reading

antes (de) que before

antes de ver y escuchar pre-viewing and listening

antiácido, el antacid 10

antibiótico, el antibiotic 10

anticipación, la anticipation

anticipar to anticipate

antiguo/a ancient

antioxidantes, los antioxidants 10

antropología, la anthropology

anual yearly 11

anualmente yearly

anudado/a knotted

anunciar to announce

anuncio, el advertisement

anuncio de venta, el sales ad

anuncios clasificados, los classified ads

añadir to add

año, el year

años, tener (ie)... to be . . . years old

apagar to turn off 12; **apagar (fuegos/ incendios)** to put out; to extinguish (fires)

aparato, el appliance

aparato doméstico, el household appliance 5

aparatos electrónicos, los electronic devices 12

aparecer (zc) to appear

apariencia, la appearance

aparente apparent

aparentemente apparently

apartamento, el apartment

apasionar to impassion

apellido, el surname; **apellido materno** maternal surname; **apellido paterno** paternal surname

apenas barely

aprender to learn

aperitivo, el appetizer

apetecer (zc) to feel like; to appeal to

aplaudir to applaud 14; to clap 14

aplicación, la app 12

apoderarse to take hold

apodo, el nickname

aporte, el contribution

apoyar to support 15

apoyo, el support

apreciado/a appreciated

apreciar to appreciate

aprender (a + *inf.*) to learn (to do something) 2

aprendizaje a distancia, el distance learning 12

aprobar to pass (a test)

apropriado/a appropriate

aprovechar to take advantage of

aproximadamente approximately

apunte, el note

aquel/la that (over there); that one (over there)

aquello that (*neuter*) (over there)

aquellos/as those (over there)

aquí here 1

aquietar to calm down

árabe, el Arab; Arabic

araña, la spider

árbitro/a, el/la referee 7

árbol, el tree

archipiélago, el archipelago

arco, el bow

arder to burn

ardilla, la squirrel

área, el (*fem.*) space; area

arena, la sand

arenisca, la sandstone

aretes (de diamantes), los (diamond) earrings (posts) 8

argentino/a Argentine 2

argumento, el argument; plot

aria, el (*fem.*) aria

arma, el (*fem.*) weapon

armado/a armed
armar to assemble; to furnish
arpa, el (*fem.*) harp 14
arqueólogo/a, el/la archeologist
arquitecto/a, el/la architect 11
arquitectura, la architecture 3
arrancar to yank out
arreglo, el arrangement
arrepentido/a repentant
arribada, la arrival
arriba de above
arrojar to throw
arroz, el rice 6; **el arroz con leche** rice pudding
arte, el art 3
artefacto, el artifact
artesanía, la handicraft
artesano/a, el/la artisan
artículo, el article 13
artículos de uso personal, los personal care items 5
artículos indefinidos, los indefinite articles
artritis, la arthritis
arzobispo, el archbishop
asado/a roasted 6
ascendencia, la ancestry
ascendente ascending
ascender (ie) to promote 11; to move up
asco, el disgust 6
asegurar to ensure 12
asesinato, el murder
asesor/a, el/la consultant; advisor 15
asiento (de ventanilla/de pasillo), el (window/aisle) seat 9
asistente, el/la assistant
asistente de vuelo, el/la flight attendant 9
asistir (a) to attend 2
asma, el (*fem.*) asthma
asociación, la association
asociar to associate
aspa del molino, el windmill blade
aspecto, el aspect
aspiración, la aspiration

aspiradora, la vacuum cleaner 5
aspirante, el/la job candidate 11
aspirina, la aspirin 10
asunto, el matter
atacar to attack
ataque, el attack
atención al cliente, la customer service
aterrizar to land 9
a tiempo on time
atleta, el/la athlete 7
atletismo, el track and field 7
atmósfera, la atmosphere
atracción, la attraction 9
atracción natural, la natural attraction 9
atracción turística, la tourist attraction 9
atractivo, el attraction
atractivo/a attractive
atraer to attract
atrapar to trap
atrás behind
a través de along
atrevido/a sassy; daring
atribuir to attribute
audición, la audition
audio parlantes, los speakers
auditorio, el auditorium 3
aumentar to increase 15
aumento, el raise 11; increase
aún even
aunque although 7; even though 7
auriculares, los earbuds 12; headphones 12
ausente absent
auténtico/a authentic
auto, el car
autobiográfico/a autobiographical
autobús, el (intercity) bus 9
autógrafo, el autograph
autónomo/a autonomous
autor/a, el/la author
autoridad, la authority
autorretrato, el self-portrait
avanzado/a advanced
ave, el (*fem.*) bird
avenida, la avenue

aventura, la adventure
avergonzado/a ashamed
avión, el plane 9
aviso, el notice; announcement
avisos clasificados, los classified ads 11
ayer yesterday
ayuda, la help
ayudante (administrativo, clínico/a), el/la (administrative/clinical) assistant 11
ayudar to help 2
azúcar, el sugar 10
azucena, la lily
azul blue 1

B

bailable danceable
bailar to dance 2
bailarín/a, el/la dancer 14
baile, el dance 14
baile de salón, el ballroom dancing 14
bajar to decrease; to download 12; to lower
bajar de peso to lose weight 10
bajarse (de) to get off (of) 9; to get down (from) 9
bajo, el bass
bajo/a short (in stature) 2
balada, la ballad
balboa, el Panamanian currency
ballet, el ballet 14
balón, el (soccer, basket) ball 7
banana, la banana 6
banco, el bank; bench
banda, la band 14
banquete, el banquet
bañarse to take a bath 5
baño, el bathroom 5
bar, el bar
barato/a cheap; inexpensive 1
barbaridad, la outrage
barco, el boat 9; ship 9
barítono, el baritone
barrio, el neighborhood
barro, el earth; mud
basado/a based

básquetbol, el basketball 7
bastante quite; fairly
bastar to be enough
bastón, el cane
basura, la garbage 5
basurero, el garbage can 5
batalla, la battle
bate, el bat 7
batería, la drums 14
batir to beat
beber to drink
bebida, la beverage 6; drink
bebidas alcohólicas, las alcoholic beverages 10
béisbol, el baseball 7
beisbolista, el/la baseball player
belleza, la beauty
bellísimo/a gorgeous; really beautiful
bello/a beautiful
beneficio, el benefit 10, 11
benéfico/a charitable
berenjena, la eggplant
beso, el kiss
biblioteca, la library 3
bibliotecario/a, el/la librarian
bicicleta, la bicycle 7
bien well 1
bien, el good
bien hecho/a well made/done 14
bienes, los goods
bienes raíces, los real estate
bienestar, el well-being
bienvenida, la welcome
bilingüe bilingual
billetera, la wallet 8
biografía, la biography
biología, la biology 3
biológico/a biological
biosfera, la biosphere
bistec, el steak 6
blanco/a white 1
bloque, el block
blusa, la blouse 8
bobo de patas azules, el blue-footed booby
boca, la mouth 10
bocadillo, el sandwich

boda, la wedding

boicot, el boycott

boleto (electrónico), el (e-)ticket **9**

bolígrafo, el pen **1**

bolívar, el Venezuelan currency

bolsa, la (big) bag **7**

bolso, el bag; purse

bomba (nuclear), la (nuclear) bomb **15**

bomba, la fire truck; fire station (*Chile*); gas station (*Andes*)

bomba, ser una to be gorgeous

bombero/a, el/la firefighter

bondad, la goodness

bonificación anual, la yearly bonus **11**

bonito/a pretty; cute **2**

bordar to embroider

bordo, a aboard

borrar to erase **12**

bosque, el forest **9, 12**

bosque nublado, el cloud forest

bosque (pluvial), el (rain) forest **12**

botas, las boots **8**

bota pantanera, la tall rubber boot

botella, la bottle

Brasil Brazil **2**

brasileño/a Brazilian **2**

brazo, el arm **10**

breve brief

brillante brilliant

brillar to shine

brillo de labios, el lip gloss **5**

broma, la joke

bucear to scuba dive **9**; to snorkel **9**

buche, el belly

budista Buddhist

Buenas noches. Good evening. **1**; Good night.

Buenas tardes. Good afternoon. **1**

¿Bueno? Hello? (*on the phone*)

bueno... well . . .

bueno/a good **1**

Buenos días. Good morning. **1**

¡Buen provecho! Enjoy (your meal)! **6**

buen tiempo, el good weather **7**

buscador, el search engine **13**

buscar to look for **2**

búsqueda, la search **11**

búsqueda de empleo, la job search **11**

C

caballo, el horse

cabeza, la head **10**

cacique, el chief

cada each

cadáver, el cadaver

cadena, la network **13**

cadena (de plata), la (silver) chain **8**

caerse to fall down

café (al aire libre), el (outdoor) café **4**

café (con leche), el coffee (with hot milk) **6**

cafeína, la caffeine

cafetera, la coffee maker **6**

cafetería, la cafeteria **3**

caída, la fall

caimaneada, la alligator hunting

caja, la box; cash register **8**

cajero automático, el ATM (automatic teller machine) **9**

calabaza, la gourd (*Argentina*); pumpkin; squash

calamar, el squid

calavera, la skull

calcetines, los socks **8**

calcio, el calcium

calculadora, la calculator **1**

calcular to calculate

cálculo, el calculus **3**

calentamiento, el warm-up

calentamiento global, el global warming

calentar (ie) to heat **6**

calidad, la quality

caliente hot **6**

calle, la street

calmante, el tranquilizer, **10**; painkiller **10**

calor, hace (mucho) it's (very) hot **7**

calor, tener (ie) to be hot

caloría, la calorie

calzado, el footwear

calzar to wear a shoe size **8**

cama, la bed **5**

cámara, la camera

cámara de video, la video camera

cámara digital, la digital camera

camarero/a, el/la waiter/waitress **6**; cleaning staff **9**

camarones, los shrimp **6**

cambiar to change

cambio, el change; exchange

cambio climático, el climate change **12**

camiche, el poodle

caminar to walk **2**

caminata, la trek; long walk

camino, el path; road

Camino Inca, el Inca Trail

camión, el pickup truck; van; truck; bus (*Mexico*)

camioneta, la pickup truck; van

camisa, la shirt **5, 8**

camiseta (sin mangas), la t-shirt (tank top) **8**

campamento, el camp

campaña, la campaign **15**

campeón/campeona, el/la champion **7**; winner **7**

campesino, el peasant; farmer

campo, el country **9**

campo abierto, el cross-country

cana, la gray hair

Canadá Canada

canadiense Canadian **2**

canal, el canal; channel **13**

canas, tener (ie) to be gray-haired

cancelar to cancel

cáncer, el cancer **10**

cancha (de tenis), la (tennis) court **3**

canción, la song

candidato/a, el/la candidate **15**

cansado/a tired **2**

cansancio, el fatigue

cansar to tire; **cansarse** to get tired

cantante, el/la singer

cantar to sing **14**

cantautor/a, el/la singer-songwriter

cantidad, la quantity

caña, la small beer; reed; cane

capacidad, la capacity

capaz capable **11**

capilla, la chapel

capital, la capital city **2**

capucha, la hood **8**

cara, la face **5**

carácter, el character

característica, la characteristic

carbohidratos, los carbohydrates **10**

carbón, el coal **12**

cárcel, la jail

cardiólogo/a, el/la cardiologist

cardo, el thistle

cargador, el charger

cargo, el position **11**

cargo político, el political post **15**

caricatura política, la political cartoon **13**

caries, la (tooth) cavity

cariño, con with affection

caritativo/a charitable

carnaval, el Mardi Gras

carne, la meat **6**

carne de res, la beef

carnero, el mutton

carnicería, la butcher (shop) **8**

caro/a expensive **1**

carpintero/a, el/la carpenter **11**

carrera, la career; field; major **3**; race **7**; **carrera académica, la** degree course of study

carretera, la highway

carro, el car **9**; cart (*Spain*)

carta comercial, la business letter

carta de presentación, la cover letter **11**

carta de recomendación, la letter of recommendation **11**

cartel, el poster

cartelera, la entertainment section **13**

cartero/a, el/la mail carrier

casa, la home **5**; house **5**

casa de cambio, la currency exchange **9**

casado/a (con) married (to) **2, 4**

casar to marry

casarse to get married

cascadas, las cascades, waterfalls

casco, el helmet

casi almost; **casi nunca llueve** it almost never rains

caso, hacer to pay attention

castaño/a brown **2**; brunette

castañuelas, las castanets

castigar to punish

castigo, el punishment; retribution

castillo, el castle

catarata, la waterfall **9**

catedral, la cathedral **9**

católico/a Catholic

causa, la cause

causar to cause

caza, la hunting

cazador, el pursuer; hunter

cazar to hunt

cazuela, la stewpot **6**; casserole dish **6**; saucepan **6**; stew (*Chile*)

cebolla, la onion **6**

cebolleta, la shallot

celebración, la celebration

celebrar to celebrate

celebridad, la celebrity

celofán, el cellophane

celos, los jealousy

celos, tener (ie) to be jealous

celoso/a jealous

celta Celtic

celular, el cell phone **8**

cementerio, el cemetery

cena, la dinner

cenar to eat dinner **6**

cenizas, las ashes

censo, el census

censura, la censorship

censurar to censure

centenares, los hundreds

centenario, el centennial

centro, el downtown **4**

centro comercial, el shopping center **8**; mall **8**

centro estudiantil, el student union **3**

centro histórico, el historical center **9**

cepillarse to brush **5**

cepillo (de dientes), el (tooth) brush **5, 8**

cerámica, la ceramic

cerca (de) near(by); close (to) **3**

cercano/a nearby

cerdo, el pork

ceremonia, la ceremony

cerrado/a closed

cerrar (ie) to close

cerro, el hill **9**

cerveza, la beer **6**

cesta, la basket

¡Chaito! So long!

champán, el champagne

champú, el shampoo **5**

chancla, la flip-flop **8**

¡Chao! Good-bye!

chaqueta, la jacket **8**; windbreaker **8**

charada, la charade

charango, el guitar-like instrument

charqui, el jerky

chatear to chat **7**

chelista, el/la cellist

chelo, el cello **14**

chévere super

chicano/a Mexican-American

chicharrón, el crackling (fried pork skin)

chico/a, el/la boy / girl **3**

chileno/a Chilean **2**

chimichurri, la sauce popular in Argentina

chinchilla, la chinchilla

China China **2**

chino, el Chinese (language)

chino/a Chinese **2**

chismoso/a gossipy

chispa, la spark

chocolate, el chocolate

chofer, el chauffeur

chorizo, el sausage

chubasco, el heavy rain; shower

ciclismo, el cycling **7**

cielo, el heaven; sky

ciencia, la science

ciencia ficción, la science fiction

ciencias políticas, las political science **3**

ciencias sociales, las social science **3**

científico/a, el/la scientist **11**

cien(to) hundred

Cierra (Cierren) el libro. Close your book(s). **1**

cierto/a certain; true

cigarra, la cricket

cigüeña, la stork

cima plana, la flat top

cine, el movie theater **4**

cinematografía, la cinematography

cinematógrafo/a, el/la cinematographer

circulación, la circulation

cita, la appointment **10**

ciudad, la city **2, 9**

ciudadanía, la citizenship

ciudadano/a, el/la citizen **15**

civil civil **11**

civilización, la civilization

clarinete, el clarinet **14**

claro of course **4**

claro, el clearing

claro/a clear; light (color)

clase, la class **1**

clase ejecutiva, la business class **9**

clase turista, la coach class **9**

clásico/a classic **14**; classical

clasificar to qualify

cláusula, la clause

clavadismo, el diving

clavar to drive; to thrust; to nail

clave, la key

claxon, el horn

cliente/a, el/la client; customer **8**

clima, el climate

clínica, la clinic

clínico/a clinical **11**

cobardía, la cowardice

cobrar to charge

cobre, el copper

coche, el car

cochinillo, el suckling pig

cocina, la cuisine; kitchen **5, 6**

cocinar to cook **6**

cocinero/a, el/la chef **11**; cook **11**

coco, el coconut

cocodrilo, el crocodile

codazo, el elbow jab

codicia, la greed

código, el code

codo, el elbow

coincidir to coincide

cola, hacer to stand in line **9**

cola, la line **9**; **en la cola** standing in line

colaborar to collaborate **12**

colección, la collection

colega, el/la colleague

cólera, el cholera

colesterol, el cholesterol **10**

colgar (ue) to hang

collar, el necklace **8**

colocar to place

colombiano/a Colombian **2**

colonia, la colony;
cologne 8

colonizador/a, el/la
colonizer

color café, el brown 1

colorido/a brightly colored;
coloring

comal, el hot plate

combatiente, el/la
combatant

combatir to combat 15; to
fight 15

combinación, la
combination

combustible fósil, el fossil
fuel 12

comedia (musical), la
(musical) comedy 13, 14

comedor, el dining room 5

comentar to comment

comentario, el commentary

comentarista, el/la
newscaster;
commentator 13

comentarista deportivo/a,
el/la sportscaster 13

comenzar (ie) to begin

comer to eat 2, 10

comerciar to trade

comercio, el commerce

comestibles, los
provisions; groceries

cometer to commit

cómico/a comic

comida, la food; meal 4, 6

comida basura, la junk
food

comida chatarra, la junk
food 10

comienzo, el beginning

comisión, la fee;
commission

comité, el committee

cómo how; what

como since; as

¿Cómo...? How . . . ?;
What . . . ? 2

cómoda, la dresser 5

comodidad, la comfort

cómodo/a comfortable

¿Cómo estás? How are
you? (inf.) 1

¿Cómo está usted? How
are you? (for.) 1

¿Cómo se dice...? How do
you say . . . ? 1

¿Cómo se llama usted?
What's your name?
(for.) 1

¿Cómo se escribe...? How
do you write . . . ? 1

¿Cómo te llamas (tú)?
What's your name?
(inf.) 1

compañero/a de clase, el/la
classmate

compañero/a de reparto,
el/la co-star

compañía, la company;
firm

comparación, la
comparison

comparar to compare

compartimento superior,
el overhead bin 9

compartir to post/share
online 12

compatriota, el/la
compatriot

competencia, la
competition 7

competir (i, i) to compete 7

complacer (zc) to please

complejo/a complex 10

complementar to
complement

completo/a complete

complicado/a complicated

complicar to complicate

componer to compose 14

composición, la
composition

compositor/a, el/la
composer 14

comprar to buy 2, 9

compras, ir de to go
shopping

comprender to
understand 2

comprensión, la
comprehension

comprobar (ue) to prove

compromiso, el
commitment; obligation

computación, la computer
science 3

computadora, la
computer 1

computadora portátil, la
laptop computer 1

común common

comunicaciones, las
communications 3

comunidad, la community;
comunidad virtual, la
online community 12

con with

con cariño with affection

concepto, el concept

concienciar al público
to raise public
consciousness

concierto, el concert 4

concha, la shell

concordancia, la agreement

concreto/a concrete

concursante, el/la
contestant 13

concurso, el contest; game
show 13; pageant 13

condenado/a condemned

condenar to condemn

condición, la condition 10

condimentos, los
condiments 6

cóndor, el condor

conducir (zc) to drive

conductora, el/la conductor

conectar to connect

conexión, la connection

confeccionar to make up

conferencia, la lecture

conferencia de prensa, la
press conference

confianza, la trust;
confidence

confiar to trust

conflicto, el conflict 15

confundir to confuse

congelador, el freezer

congestionado/a congested

congregar to gather

congresista, el/la
congressman/woman

congreso, el congress

conjetura, la conjecture

conjunto, el outfit 14;
group 14

conmemorar to
commemorate

conmigo with me 4

conmovedor/a moving

conocedor, el/la connoisseur

conocer (zc) to know
(someone); to be familiar
with (something) 4; to
meet

conocido/a known

conocimiento, el
knowledge

conquista, la conquest

consecuencias, las
consequences

conseguir (i, i) to get 11; to
obtain 11

consejero/a, el/la counselor

consejo, el advice 10

consenso, el consensus

conservador/a conservative

conservar to conserve 12;
to preserve 12

considerado/a considered;
considerate

considerar to consider

construcción, la
construction 11

construir to construct

consultar to consult

consultorio, el doctor's
office 10

consultorio sentimental, el
advice column 13

consumidor/a, el/la
consumer

consumir to consume 12

consumo, el consumption

contabilidad, la
accounting 3

contactar to contact

contador/a, el/la
accountant 11

con tal (de) que provided
(that)

contaminación, la
pollution 12; smog

contaminar to contaminate
12; to pollute 12

contar (ue) to tell (a story);
contarse (ue) to tell each
other

contemporáneo/a
contemporaneous

contenedor, el container

contener (ie) to contain

contenido, el content

contento/a happy 2, 5

Contesta (Contesten) en español. Answer in Spanish. **1**

contestar to answer

contigo with you **4**

continuación, a following

continuar to continue

contra, (en) against

contrabajo, el bass **14**

contrario, por lo on the contrary

contraste, el contrast

contratar to contract; to hire **11**

contrato, el contract **11**

contribuir to contribute

contrincante, el/la opponent **15**

controlar to control **15**

control de seguridad, el security checkpoint **9**

convencer (z) to convince

convencional conventional

convenio, el agreement

conversación, la conversation

conversar to converse

convertir (ie, i) to convert

convicción, la conviction

cooperar to cooperate

coordinador/a, el/la coordinator

copado/a cool (*Argentina*)

copia, la copy

corazón, el heart **10**

corbata, la tie **8**

cordero, el lamb

Cordialmente… Cordially yours…

Corea Korea **2**

coreano, el Korean (language)

coreano/a Korean **2**

coreografiar to choreograph

coreógrafo/a, el/la choreographer **14**

corneta, la cornet **14**; horn **14**

corredor, el corridor

corregir (i, i) to correct

correo, el mail; **correo electrónico, el** e-mail **3**

correr to run **7**; to fire someone (*Mexico*)

corresponsal, el/la correspondent

corrida de toros, la bullfighting

corriente, la electric current

corrupción, la corruption **15**

cortar to cut **6**

cosa, la thing

cosecha, la harvest

cosmopolita cosmopolitan

cosmovisión, la worldview

cosquillas (a), hacerle to tickle

costa, la coast

costar (ue) to cost **4**

costarricense Costa Rican

costo, el cost

costoso/a costly; expensive

costumbre, la custom

creador/a, el/la creator

crear to create

creatividad, la creativity

creciendo growing

creciente growing

creencia, la belief

creer to believe **2**

crema (hidratante/ de afeitar), la (facial shaving) cream **5, 8**

cresta de las olas, la crest of the waves

cría, la raising; chick; hatchling

criadero, el hatchery

criar to raise

criarse to grow up

crimen, el crime

criollo/a creole

cristalino/a clear; crystalline

cristianizar to christianize

cristiano/a Christian

crítico/a, el/la critic **13**

crónico/a chronic

cronología, la chronology

crucero, el cruise **9**

cruzar to cross

cuaderno, el notebook **1**

cuadra, la block

cuadrado/a square

cuadro, el picture; painting **5**

cuadros, de plaid **8**

¿Cuál(es)...? What . . . ?; Which (one/ones) . . . ? **2**

cualidad, la quality

cualificaciones, las qualifications **11**

cualquier/a any; anyone

cuando when

¿Cuándo...? When . . . ? **2**

¿Cuándo es? When is it? **3**

¿Cuánto/a(s)...? How much (many) . . . ? **2**

cuarteto, el quartet **14**

cuarto, el bedroom **5**; room **5**

cuarto/a fourth; quarter **2**

cuarto doble, el double room **9**

cuarto individual, el single room **9**

cuate, el/la buddy; pal (*Mexico*)

cubano/a Cuban **2**

cubeta, la bucket

cubierto/a covered; enclosed

cubrir to cover

cuchara, la spoon **6**

cucharada, la tablespoon

cucharadita, la teaspoon

cuchillo, el knife **6**

cuello, el neck; collar

cuenca, la basin

cuenta, la account; bill **6**

cuenta, por su on one's own

cuentista, el/la storyteller

cuento, el story

cuerda, la cord; string

cuero, el leather **8, 14**

cuerpo, el body **10**

cuestión, la issue **15**

cuestionario, el questionnaire

cueva, la cave

cuidado, tener (ie) to be careful

cuidadoso/a careful

cuidar(se) to take care (of oneself) **10**

culebra, la snake

culinario/a culinary

culto/a cultured

cultura, la culture

cumpleaños, el birthday

cumplir to complete

cumplir (con) to make good (on a promise) **15**; to fulfill (a promise) **15**

cuñado/a, el/la brother-in-law/sister-in-law **4**

curandero/a, el/la healer

curar to cure

curioso/a curious

currículum vitae, el curriculum vitae (vita) **11**

curso, el course

curvado/a curved

cuy, el guinea pig

cuyo/a(s) whose

D

danza (moderna), la (modern) dance **14**

dañarse to break down

daño, el damage; harm

dar to give

dar igual to be the same

dar la vuelta to turn

dar una mirada rápida to skim through

dar un paseo to go out **7**; to take a walk **7**

dar vuelta to turn over

dato, el data; information

de acuerdo fine with me **4**; okay **4**; in agreement; agreed

de hecho in fact

de película fantastic; awesome

debate, el debate

debatir to debate **15**

deber (+ *inf.*) to owe (to ought to do something) **2**

deber, el duty **15**; obligation

débil weak

debut, el debut

debutar to debut

década, la decade

decidir to decide **2**

décimo/a tenth

decir (i) to say; to tell

declaración, la declaration

decoración, la decoration

dedicado/a dedicated

dedicar to dedicate

dedo (del pie), el finger (toe) **10**

¿De dónde...? From where . . . ? **2**

defecto, el defect

defender (ie) to defend

defensa propia, la self-defense

definir to define

deforestación, la deforestation **12**

defraudar to disillusion

dejar (de) to leave (behind); to quit/stop (doing something) **10, 11**

delante (de) in front (of) **3**

delgado/a slender **2**

delicia, la delight

delicioso/a delicious

demás, los the rest

demasiado too (much)

democracia, la democracy **15**

democratización, la democratization

demográfico/a demographic

demora, la delay **9**

De nada. You're welcome. **1**

dentista, el/la dentist **11**

dentro de within; inside of

denunciar to denounce

departamento, el apartment; department

dependiente/a, el/la sales clerk **8**

deporte, el sport

deportiva, la sección sports section **13**

deportivo/a sporting **7**

depósito, el deposit

depresión, la depression **10**

¿De qué color es? What color is it? **1**

¿De quién(es)...? Whose . . . ? **2**

derecha (de), a la to/on the right (of) **3**

derecho, el law **3**; right **15**

derecho humano, el human right **15**

de repente suddenly

derivar to derive

derrame cerebral, el stroke

derrame (de petróleo), el (oil) spill **12**

derredor, en around

desafiante defiant

desafiarse to challenge one another

desafío, el challenge

desanimado/a discouraged; lifeless

desaparecer (zc) to disappear

desarmar to disarm

desarme, el disarmament **15**

desarrollar to develop

desarrollo, el development **12**

desastre (natural), el (natural) disaster **15**

desayunar to eat breakfast **6**

desayuno, el breakfast **6**

descafeinado/a decaffeinated

descansar to rest **2**

descanso, el rest

descender (ie) to descend

descendiente, el/la descendant

desconocido/a unknown

describir to depict; to describe

descripción, la description **8**

descubierto/a discovered

descubrimiento, el discovery

descubrir to discover

descuento, el discount **8**

desde from; since

¿Desea(n) algo de tomar/ comer? Would you like something to drink/ eat? **6**

desear to desire; to wish **2**

desechos, los waste **12**

desempleo, el unemployment **11, 15**

desengaño, el disillusionment

desenlace, el conclusion

desenterrar (ie) to dig up

deseo, el desire

Deseo tomar... I'd like to have . . . **6**

desertor/a, el/la dropout

desfile, el parade

desfile de moda, el fashion show **14**

desgarrarse un músculo to tear a muscle

desgraciadamente unfortunately

deshonesto/a dishonest

deshonrar to dishonor

desierto, el desert

desierto/a deserted

desilusionar to disillusion

desinstalar to uninstall **12**

deslizamiento de tierra, el mudslide

desocupar to vacate

desodorante, el deodorant **8**

desorden, el disorder

desordenado/a disorganized **5**

desorientado/a disoriented

despacho, el office

despacio slowly

despedida, la closing; farewell **1**

despedir (i, i) to fire **11**

despedirse (i, i) to say good-bye

despegar to take off **9**

despejado/a clear

desperdiciar to waste

despertarse (ie) to wake up **5**

despoblación, la depopulation

despojar to strip

desprender to loosen; to detach; to omit

después (de) (que) after

después de escribir post-writing

después de leer post-reading

después de ver y escuchar post-viewing and listening

destacado/a outstanding

destacar to stand out

destinatario/a, el/la addressee

destino, el destination **9**

destruir to destroy

desventaja, la disadvantage **11**

detalle, el detail

detener (ie) to arrest; to detain

deteriorar to deteriorate

detestar to detest

detrás (de) behind **3**

deuda (pública), la (public) debt **15**

¿De verdad? Really? **1**

de vez en cuando once in a while

devolver (ue) to return (something) **8**

día, el day

Día de Acción de Gracias, el Thanksgiving Day

Día de Año Nuevo, el New Year's Day

Día de los Muertos, el Day of the Dead

día festivo, el holiday

diabetes, la diabetes **10**

diagnóstico, el diagnosis **10**

diamante, el diamond

diamantes, de (made of) diamond **8**

diario/a daily **5**

dibujar to draw

dibujo, el drawing

diccionario, el dictionary **1**

diciembre December **1**

dictador/a, el/la dictator **15**

dictadura, la dictatorship **15**

dientes, los teeth **5**; cloves (of garlic)

diestro/a skilled; skillful

dieta, estar a to be on a diet **10**

dieta, la diet **10**

dieta, seguir (i, i) una to follow a diet **10**

diferente different

difícil difficult **2**

dificultar to make difficult

¿Diga? Hello? (*on the phone*)

¿Dígame? Hello? (*on the phone*)
dignidad, la dignity
dignificar to dignify
Dile... Tell him/her . . .
dilema, el dilemma
dinámico/a dynamic
dineral, el lots of money
dinero, el money
dios, el god
dirección equivocada, la wrong address
directamente directly
director/a, el/la director 11, 14; conductor 14; editor-in-chief 13
director/a de escena, el/la stage manager
dirigido/a directed
dirigir to conduct; to direct
discapacitado/a, el/la disabled person
disco compacto, el compact disc (CD)
disco duro (externo), el (external) hard drive
discoteca, ir a una to go to a nightclub
discreto/a discreet
disculparse to apologize
discurso, el speech 15
discusión, la argument; discussion
diseñado/a designed
diseñador/a, el/la designer 14
diseñar to design 11
diseño, el design
disfraz, el disguise 14; costume 14
disfrutar (de) to enjoy
disminuir to decrease; to diminish; to lessen
disparar to shoot
disponible available
dispuesto/a willing; ready; disposed
disputar to dispute
distancia, la distance
distinto/a different
diva, la diva
diversidad, la diversity
divertido/a fun

divertirse (ie, i) to enjoy oneself; to have fun 5
divorciado/a divorced 2, 4
doble double 9
docencia, la teaching
doctor/a, el/la doctor
doctorado, el doctorate
documental, el documentary 13
documento, el document 12
dólar, el dollar
doler (ue) to hurt 10
dolor, el pain; ache
dolor de cabeza, el headache
doméstico/a domestic
dominar to dominate
domingo, el Sunday
dominicano/a Dominican 2
don, el gift
donar to donate
donde where
¿Dónde...? Where . . . ? 2
¿Dónde está? Where is it? 3
dormir (ue, u) to sleep 4, 5
dormirse (ue, u) to fall asleep 5
dormitorio, el bedroom 5
dote, la dowry
drama, el drama 13
dramático/a dramatic
dramatizar to dramatize
droga, la drug
drogadicción, la drug addiction 15
ducha, la shower
ducharse to take a shower 5
duda, la doubt
dudar to doubt
dudoso/a doubtful
dueño/a, el/la owner
dulces, los sweets 10
durabilidad, la durability
duradero/a lasting 15
durante during
durar to last
durazno, el peach
DVD, el DVD

E

echar to add 6; to throw in 6; **echar de menos** to miss

ecológico/a ecological
economía, la economy; economics 3
económico/a economic; economical 9
ecoturismo, el ecotourism
eco voluntariado, el eco-volunteering
ecuatoriano/a Ecuadorian 2
edad, la age; **edad cuando murió, la** age at death
edición, la edition
edificio, el building 3
editar to edit
editor/a, el/la editor
editorial, el editorial (section) 13
educación, la education
educación física, la physical education 3
educar to educate
EE. UU. United States
efectivo, en in cash 8
efectivo/a effective
efectuar to bring into effect
eficiente efficient
ejecución, la execution
ejecutivo/a, el/la executive
ejemplo, el example
ejercer (z) to exercise
ejercicio, hacer to exercise
ejercicios aeróbicos, los aerobics 10
ejército, el army 15
él he
el the
elaboración, la elaboration
elaborado/a elaborated
elaborar to elaborate
elástico, el elastic 14
elección, la election
electo/a elected
electoral electoral 15
electricidad, la electricity
electricista, el/la electrician
eléctrico/a electrical 3, 11
electrizante electrifying
electrónico/a electronic 12
elegir (i, i) to elect 15; to choose
eliminación, la elimination
eliminar to end 15
ella she
ellos/as they

emanar to emanate
embajada, la embassy
embajador/a, el/la ambassador
embalse, el dam
emisora, la radio station (business entity)
emoción, la emotion 5
emocional emotional; exciting
emocionante exciting
empanada (empanadilla), la turnover
empaquetado/a packaged
emparejar to pair
empatar to tie (the score) 7
empezar (ie) to begin 4
empleado/a, el/la employee 11
empleo, el employment 11
emprendedor/a, el/la entrepreneur 11
empresa, la company 11; firm 11
empresario/a, el/la businessman/woman; impresario
en in; on 3
enamorado/a (de) in love (with) 2
enamorarse (de) to fall in love (with) 5
encabezar to head
encajar to fit
Encantado/a. Delighted.; Pleased to meet you. 1
encantador/a enchanting 14; delightful 14
encantar to delight; to be extremely pleasing
encanto, el charm; delight
encargar to take on
encargarse de to be responsible for; to take responsibility
encargo, el request
en caso de que in case
en contra against
encender (ie) to light; to turn on 12
encenderse to set fire
encerrar (ie) to enclose 12
encierro, el running of the bulls

encoger (j) to draw up

encontrar (ue) to find **4, 5**

encontrarse (ue) con to meet up with someone **5**

en cuanto as soon as

en forma in shape **10**

en Internet on the Internet **12**

en parejas in pairs

en paro out of work

en punto on the dot **2**

¿En qué puedo servirle(s)? How can I help you? **8**

encuentro, el encounter

encuesta, la survey; poll

enemigo/a, el/la enemy

energía (alternativa/solar/ verde), la (alternative/ solar/green) energy **12**

enero January **1**

enfermar to make sick

enfermarse to become sick **5**

enfermedad, la illness **10**

enfermero/a, el/la nurse **11**

enfermo/a sick **2**

enfrentar to confront; to face

enfrente in front

enfrente (de) facing; across (from) **3**

engañar to deceive

engaño, el deceit

engordar to gain weight **10**

enlace, el hyperlink

enojado/a angry **2**

enojar to anger

enojarse (con) to become/ get angry (with) **5**

enojo, el anger

enorme enormous

ensalada, la salad

ensayar to rehearse **13**

ensayo, el rehearsal **13**

enseguida right away

enseñar to teach **2**

entender (ie) to understand **4**

enterarse (de) to become aware; to find out **11**

enterrar (ie) to bury

entonación, la intonation

entonces then **7**

entrada, la appetizer; (admission) ticket **4**

entre between **3**

entregar to deliver; to turn in

entrenador/a, el/la trainer **7**; coach **7**

entrenamiento, el training **11**

entrenar(se) to train

entre sí among themselves

entretener (ie) to entertain

entretenimiento, el entertainment

entrevista, la interview **11**

entrevistador/a, el/la interviewer

entusiasta enthusiastic **11**

envase, el container **12**

enviar to send **12**; to post online

en vías de desarrollo developing **15**

en voz alta aloud

envío, el shipment

envuelto/a wrapped

época, la epoch; **época de examen, la** exam time

equidad, la equity

equilibrado/a balanced **10**

equipaje (permitido), el baggage **9**; luggage (policy) **9**

equipo, el team **7**; equipment **7**

equivocado/a mistaken

equivocarse to make a mistake

Érase una vez... Once upon a time . . .

erradicar to eradicate

erupción, la eruption

es un día perfecto para... It's a perfect day for . . . **7**

escala, la stopover **9**

escalar to climb

escalera, la ladder

escalofrío, el chill

escalón, el step

escándalo, el scandal

escáner, el scanner **12**

escaparse to escape

escasez, la shortage **12**; scarcity

escaso/a scarce

escena, la scene

escenario, el stage **14**

esclavo/a, el/la slave

escoger (j) to choose

escolar scholastic

Escribe (Escriban) en la pizarra. Write on the board. **1**

escribir to write **2**

escritor/a, el/la writer

escritorio, el desk

Escucha (Escuchen). Listen. 1

escuchar to listen **2**; **escuchar música** to listen to music **7**

escuela, la school

escultor/a, el/la sculptor

escultura, la sculpture

ese/a that; that one

esencial essential

esfuerzo, el effort **15**

esmeralda, la emerald

esmoquin, el tuxedo **14**

esos/as those

espaguetis, los spaghetti

espalda, la back **10**

España Spain

español, el Spanish (language)

español/a Spanish **2**

español/a, el/la Spaniard

espátula, la spatula

especial special

especialidad de la casa, la house specialty **6**

especializarse (en) to specialize (in)

especialmente especially

especie, la species **12**

especies en peligro de extinción, las endangered species **12**

espectacular spectacular

espectáculo, el show business; show

espectador/a, el/la spectator **13**

espejo, el mirror **5**

esperanza, la hope

esperar to expect; to hope (for) **9**; to wait (for) **9**

espiar to spy

espíritu, el spirit

esposo/a, el/la husband; wife **4**

esquí, el skiing

esquiar (en el agua) to (water) ski **7**

esquina, la corner

¿Está...? Is . . . ?

está nublado it's cloudy **7**

establecer (zc) to establish

estación, la season **1**; station

estacionar to park

estación de radio, la radio station

estaciones del año, las seasons of the year

estadía, la stay **9**

estadio, el stadium **3**

estadísticas, las statistics

estado, el state; status

estado libre asociado, el commonwealth

estadounidense American (from the US) **2**

estancia, la ranch

estandarte, el banner

estante, el bookcase **5**

estar to be

estar a dieta to be on a diet **10**

estar de acuerdo to agree

estar de moda to be in style **14**

estar en rebaja/liquidación to be on sale/clearance **8**

estar seguro/a (de) to be sure of

estar sin trabajo to be out of work **11**

estatua, la statue **9**

estatura, la height

esta vez this time

este... uhh . . .

este/a this; this one

estereotipo, el stereotype

estilo, el style **14**

estimado/a esteemed

estimularse to stimulate

estímulo, el stimulus

estirar to stretch

Estocolmo Stockholm

estofado, el stew

estómago, el stomach 10
estornudar to sneeze
estos/as these; these ones
Estoy muy ocupado/a. I'm very busy. 4
estratégico/a strategic
estrechar (la mano) to shake (someone's hand); to extend (one's hand)
estrecho/a narrow; tight (clothing)
estrella, la star
estrenar to debut
estrés, el stress 10
estricto/a strict
Estudia (Estudien). Study. 1
estudiante, el/la student 1; **estudiante de intercambio, el/la** exchange student
estudiantil student (*adj.*)
estudiar (lenguas) to study (languages) 2
estudio, el studio 13; study
estufa, la stove 6
estupendo/a terrific
etapa, la stage
eterno/a eternal
ética, la ethics
etnia, la ethnicity
étnico/a ethnic
eusquera, el Basque language
evento, el event 11
evitar to avoid 10
evolución, la evolution
exagerar to exaggerate
examen, el exam
examen físico, el (medical) checkup 10
excelente excellent
excepcional exceptional
excesivo/a excessive
excursión, ir de to go on an excursion; to tour 9
excursión, la excursion 9
excusa, la excuse
exhausto/a exhausted
exhibir to exhibit
exigente challenging; demanding 3
existir to exist

éxito, el success
éxito, tener (ie) to be successful
exitoso/a successful
exótico/a exotic
expectativa (de educación formal), la (school life) expectancy
expediente, el dossier
experiencia, la experience
experimentar to experience
explicar to explain
explícito/a explicit
explotación, la exploitation
explotar to exploit
exponer to explain
exportar to export
exposición, la exposition; show
expresar to express
expresarse to express oneself
expresión, la expression 11
extender (ie) to extend
extenso/a extensive
extinción, la extinction
extranjero/a foreign
extranjero/a, el/la foreigner
extraño/a strange
extraordinario/a extraordinary
extremo/a extreme
extrovertido/a outgoing

F

fábrica, la factory 12
fabricante, el manufacturer
fabricar to make; to fabricate; to manufacture
fábula, la fable
fabuloso/a fabulous; great 7
fácil easy 2
facilidad, la facility
facilitar to facilitate
fácilmente easily
factible doable
factor, el factor
facturar el equipaje to check luggage 9
Facultad de Arte, la School of Art 3
Facultad de Ciencias, la School of Sciences 3

Facultad de Derecho, la School of Law 3
Facultad de Filosofía y Letras, la School of Humanities 3
Facultad de Ingeniería, la School of Engineering 3
Facultad de Matemáticas, la School of Mathematics 3
Facultad de Medicina, la School of Medicine 3
Facultad de Pedagogía, la School of Education 3
falda, la skirt 8; slope
fallar to break down 12
falso/a false
falta, la lack
faltar to be missing; to be lacking
familia, la family 4
familia política, la in-laws
familiarizarse to familiarize oneself
fanático/a, el/la fanatic
fantasía, la fantasy
fantástico/a fantastic
farmacia, la pharmacy 8
fascinante fascinating
fascinar to be fascinating
fatiga, la fatigue
favor de, a in favor of
febrero February 1
fecha, la date
fecha de vencimiento, la expiration date
felicidad, la happiness
feliz happy
femenino/a feminine
feminidad, la femininity
feo/a ugly 2
feria, la fair
feroz ferocious
feto, el fetus
fibra, la fiber 10
ficción, la fiction
fiebre, la fever 10
fiesta, la party; celebration; **Fiesta de la Vendimia, la** Grape Harvest Feast
figura, la figure
figurar to represent
fijarse to notice
filarmónico/a philharmonic

filmación, la filming
filmar to film 13
filme negro, el film noir
filosofía, la philosophy 3
fin, el end
fin de semana, el weekend 3
final, al finally, at the end
final, el end 13
financiera, la sección business section 13
financiero/a financial 11
finanzas, las finance
fingir (j) to pretend
firma, la signature
firmar to sign 15
física, la physics 3
físico/a physical
flaco/a skinny
flamenco, el flamingo; flamenco (dance) 14
flamenco/a flamenco
flan, el custard dessert 6
flanquear to flank
flauta, la flute 14
flecha, la arrow
flor, la flower
florecer (zc) to flourish
florería, la flower shop 8
folleto, el brochure
fondo, el bottom; background
fondo fiduciario, el trust fund
fondos, los funds
footing, hacer to go jogging
forma, en in shape 10
formación, la education 11
formar to form
fórmula, la formula
formular to formulate
formulario, el form 11
foro, el forum
fortalecer (zc) to strengthen; to fortify
fortaleza, la fortress
foto, la photograph
fotocopiadora, la photocopier
fotocopiar to photocopy
fotógrafo/a, el/la photographer
fragmento, el fragment

francés, el French (language)

francés/francesa French 2

Francia France 2

frase, la phrase

fraude (electoral), el (electoral) fraud 15; **fraude electrónico, el** phishing 12

frecuencia, con frequently

frecuente frequent

frecuentemente frequently

freír (i, i) to fry 6

frenar to slow down; to brake

fresa, la strawberry 6

fresco, hace it's cool 7

fresco/a fresh

frigorífico, el refrigerator

frijoles, los beans 6; legumes 6

frío, hace (mucho) it's (very) cold 7

frío, tener (ie) to be cold

frío/a cold

frito/a fried 6

frontera, la frontier; border

frotar to rub

frutas, las fruits 6

fruto, el fruit; benefit; profit

fue he/she was

fuego, el fire; **fuego lento, el** low heat

fuegos artificiales, los fireworks

fuente, la source

fuera outside

fuerte strong 2; **fuerte abrazo, un** a big hug

fuerte, el fortress

fuerza, la force

fumar to smoke 10

función, la show 4; function; event

funcionar to function 12; to work 12

fundación, la founding; foundation

fundado/a founded

fundar to found

fundir to melt

furgoneta, la van

furia, la fury

furibundo/a raging

furioso/a angry 5

fusión, la fusion

fusionar to fuse

fútbol (americano), el soccer (football) 7

futuro, el future

G

gabardina, la gabardine (lightweight wool)

gabinete, el cabinet

gafas, las glasses

gaita, la bagpipe

galán, el leading man 13

galápago, el tortoise

galleta María, la Marie biscuit

galletas, las cookies 6

ganado, el cattle

ganador/a, el/la winner 7

ganar to earn 4; to win 7

ganas de, tener (ie) + inf. to be eager (to); to feel like (doing something)

ganga, la bargain 8; good deal 8

garaje, el garage 5

garantizado/a guaranteed

garantizar to guarantee

garganta, la throat 10

garza, la heron

gasolina, la gasoline

gastado/a worn out; spent

gastar to spend 8

gasto, el expense

gato/a, el/la cat

gaucho, el Argentine cowboy

gemelo/a, el/la twin

genealógico/a genealogical

generación, la generation

generalizar to generalize

generalmente generally

generar to generate

género, el genre

generoso/a generous

genético/a genetic

gente, la people 13

geografía, la geography 3

geología, la geology 3

gerente, el/la manager 9

gesto, el gesture

gimnasia deportiva, la gymnastics 7

gimnasio, el gymnasium 3

gira, la tour 9

gitano/a, el/la gypsy

glaciar, el glacier 9

global global 15

globalización, la globalization

gloria, la glory

gobernador/a, el/la governor 15

gobierno, el government 15

gol, el goal

golf, el golf 7

golpe, de suddenly

golpear to thump

golpe de estado, el coup d'état 15

gordo/a chubby; fat 2

gorra, la cap 8

gorro, el winter cap

gozar (de) to enjoy

grabación, la recording

grabado/a recorded

grabadora de DVD, la DVD recorder

grabar to record 12

Gracias. Thank you. 1

Gracias, pero no puedo... Thanks, but I can't . . . 4

gracioso/a funny

gradas, las bleachers

grado, el degree

gramática, la grammar

grande big 1

Gran Depresión, la Great Depression

granja, la farm

granjero/a, el/la farmer

grano, el grain

grasa, la fat 10

grasas monoinsaturadas (poliinsaturadas), las monounsaturated (polyunsaturated) fats 10

grasas saturadas (trans), las saturated (trans) fats 10

grasoso/a fatty

gratis free

grave serious

gripa, la flu (*Mexico*)

gripe, la flu 10

gripe porcina, la swine flu

gris gray 1

gritar to yell

grito, el cry; shout

grosero/a crude; rough

gruñón/gruñona grumpy

grupo, el group 14; **grupo meta, el** target group

guacamayo, el macaw

guanábana, la soursop

guante, el glove 7

guapo/a good-looking 2

guaraní, el Guarani

guardar to save 6, 12; to keep 6; to put away 6

guardar cama to stay in bed (due to sickness) 10

guardar un documento to save a document 12

guardar la línea, la to stay trim 10; to watch one's figure 10

guardería, la nursery; daycare center 11

guardia, el/la guard

guay super (*Spain*)

guayaba, la guava

guayabera, la men's shirt typical of the Caribbean

gubernamental governmental

guerra, la war 15

Guerra Civil, la Civil War

guerrero/a, el/la warrior

guía, el/la (tour) guide 9

guiar to guide

guía turística, la guidebook 9

guion, el script 13

guionista, el/la script writer

guitarra, la guitar 14

gustar to like

gusto, el taste; pleasure

H

haber (*auxiliary verb*) to have 12

Había una vez... There once was . . .

habilidad, la ability

habitación, la room

habitante, el/la inhabitant
habitar to inhabit; to live
hábito, el habit
hablar to speak **2**; to talk **2**
hace... it's . . . **7**
hace (*in time expressions*) ago; since
hacendado/a, el/la rancher; landowner
hacer to do **3, 7**; to make **3**
hacer (la maleta) to pack (the suitcase) **9**
hacer clic to click on **12**
hacer cola to stand in line **9**
hacer ejercicio to exercise
hacer escala to make a stopover **9**
hacer el papel to play the role
hacer juego (con) to match **8**; to go well with **8**
hacer la cama to make the bed **5**
hacer las compras to go grocery shopping **5**
hacer planes to make plans **7**
hacerse daño to hurt oneself (*Spain*)
hacer una cita to make an appointment **10**
hacer una gira to take a tour **9**
hacer un crucero to take a cruise **9**
hacer un pícnic to have a picnic **7**
hacer yoga to do yoga **7**
hacia toward
hamaca, la hammock
hambre, tener (ie) to be hungry
hamburguesa, la hamburger
harina, la flour
hasta until
Hasta luego. See you later. **1**
Hasta mañana. See you tomorrow. **1**
Hasta pronto. See you soon. **1**
hasta que until
hay there is/are **1**

hay que one must
haz do; make (*inf. command*)
heladera, la cooler **7**
heladería, la ice cream shop **8**
helado, el ice cream **6**
helicóptero, el helicopter
heno, el hay
herbal herbal **10**
herencia, la heritage
hermanastro/a, el/la stepbrother/stepsister **4**
hermano/a, el/la brother/ sister **4**
hermoso/a beautiful
héroe, el hero **9**
herramienta, la tool
híbrido/a hybrid
hielo, el ice **7**
hierro, el iron
hijo/a, el/la son/daughter **4**
hijos, los children
hipermercado, el hypermarket, superstore
hipervínculo, el hyperlink **12**
hipótesis, la hypothesis
hipotético/a hypothetical
hispano/a Hispanic
historia, la history **3**
histórico/a historical
hockey, el hockey **7**
hogar, el home
hoja, la leaf
hoja electrónica, la spreadsheet
hojear to leaf through
Hola. Hello; Hi. **1**
holandés/holandesa Dutch
hombre, el man **1**
hombre de Estado, el statesman
hombre de negocios, el businessman **11**
hombre/mujer del tiempo, el/la meteorologist
hombreras, las shoulder pads
hombro, el shoulder
homeopatía, la homeopathy
honestidad, la honesty **15**
honesto/a honest **11**
honradez, la honesty **15**

honrado/a honest **11**; honored
horario (de clases), el (class) schedule **3**
hornear to bake **6**; to roast **6**
horno, el oven **6**; **al horno** baked **6**
horóscopo, el horoscope **13**
horrorizado/a horrified
hospital, el hospital
hostal, el hostel **9**
hotel (de lujo), el (luxury) hotel **9**
hoy today **1**
hoy en día nowadays
huaso, el horseman (*Chile*)
hubo there was/were
huelga, la strike **15**
huelguista, el/la striker
huella, la trace
hueso, el bone **10**
huésped, el/la guest
huevo, el egg **6**
huir to flee
humanidad, la humanity
humanista humanist
humano/a human **10**
humedad, hace (mucha) it's (very) humid **7**
humildad, la humility
humilde humble
humo, el smoke **12**
humorístico/a humorous
huracán, el hurricane

I

ibérico/a Iberian
ibero/a Iberian
ida y vuelta roundtrip **9**
ideal ideal
idealista idealistic
identidad, la identity
identificar to identify
ideología, la ideology
idioma, el language
iglesia, la church
igualdad, la equality
igual de equally
Igualmente. Likewise. **1**
ilegalidad, la illegality
ilógico/a illogical
iluminar to illuminate
ilusión, la illusion

ilustrar to illustrate
imagen, la image
imaginar to imagine
impaciente impatient
impactante stunning
imparable, el hit (*baseball*)
imperio, el empire
implementar to implement
importante importante
importar to import
imposible impossible
impresionante impressive
impresionar to impress
impresora, la printer **12**
imprimir to print **12**
improvisar to improvise **14**
impuestos, los taxes **15**
impulsar to push; to promote
inacabado/a unfinished
inalámbrico/a wireless **12**
inaugurar to inaugurate
inca Inca
incendio, el fire
incentivo, el incentive
incipiente startup
incluir to include
incluso even; including
incógnito/a unknown
incómodo/a uncomfortable
incorporar incorporate
incorporarse to join
increíble incredible
indefinido/a indefinite
indicar to indicate
índice, el index
índice de natalidad, el birthrate
indiferente indifferent
indígena indigenous
indispensable crucial
individual single **9**
industria, la industry
inesperado/a unexpected; without warning
infantil childish
infección, la infection **10**
inflación, la inflation **15**
influencia, la influence
influido/a influenced
influir to influence
influyente influential
informar to inform; to report **13**

informática, la computer science **3**
informe, el report
ingeniería (eléctrica), la (electrical) engineering **3**
ingeniero/a, el/la engineer **11**
Inglaterra England **2**
inglés, el English (language)
inglés, inglesa English **2**
ingrediente, el ingredient
iniciado/a initiated
iniciar to begin; to initiate
iniciativa, la initiative
inicio, el beginning; home (*website*) **13**
injusticia, la injustice **15**
inmediatamente immediately
inmediato/a immediate
inmenso/a immense
inmigración, la immigration **9, 15**
inmoralidad, la immorality
inmunología, la immunology
innecesario/a unnecessary
innovador/a innovative
inolvidable unforgettable
insertar to insert
insistir (en) to insist (on)
insólito/a unusual
insoportable unbearable
inspeccionar to inspect
inspector/a de aduanas, el/la customs inspector **9**
inspiración, la inspiration
inspirador/a inspiring
instalar to install **12**
instar to urge
instrumento, el instrument **14**
intacto/a intact
integración, la integration
inteligente intelligent
intendente, el/la mayor
intenso/a intense
intercambiar to exchange
intercambio, el exchange
interés, el interest
interesante interesting
interesar to be interesting

internacional international
internado, el internship
Internet, en on the Internet **12**
interpretar to perform (*Spain*)
intérprete, el/la interpreter **11**
intervención, la intervention
íntimo/a intimate
intriga, la intrigue
introvertido/a introverted
inundación, la flood **12**
invasión, la invasion
inventar to invent
inversión, la investment
invertir (ie, i) to invest
investigación, la research; investigation
investigador/a, el/la researcher
investigar to investigate; to research
invierno, el winter **1**
invitación, la invitation **4**
invitado/a, el/la guest
invitar to invite **4**
involucrar to involve
inyección, la shot **10**
ir (a) to go **3, 5**
ir a pie to walk
ir a un club nocturno to go to a nightclub **7**
ir a un concierto to go to a concert **7**
ir a un festival to go to a festival **7**
ir de excursión to go on an excursion **9**; to tour
irlandés/irlandesa Irish
irónico/a ironic
irse to go away; to leave **5**
isla, la island **9**
italiano, el Italian (language)
italiano/a Italian **2**
Italia Italy **2**
itinerario, el itinerary
izquierda (de), a la to/on the left (of) **3**

J

jabalí, el wild pig
jabón, el soap **5**

jaguar, el jaguar
jalea, la jelly
jamás never
jamón, el ham **6**
Japón Japan **2**
japonés, el Japanese (language)
japonés/japonesa Japanese **2**
jarabe, el cough syrup **10**
jardín, el garden **5**
jazz, el jazz **14**
jeans, los jeans
jefe/a, el/la boss **11**
jefe/a ejecutivo/a, el/la CEO **11**
jesuita, el Jesuit
jeroglífico, el hieroglyphic
jogging, el jogging **7**
jornalero/a, el/la day laborer
joven young **2**
joven, el/la youth
joya, la jewel
joyería, la jewelry store **8**
jubilado/a, el/la retiree
jubilarse to retire
judías verdes, las green beans **6**; string beans **6**
judío/a Jewish
judío/a, el/la Jew
juego electrónico, el computer (electronic) game **12**
Juegos Olímpicos, los Olympic Games
jueguitos de consola, los console games
jueves, el Thursday
juez/a, el/la judge **15**
jugador/a, el/la player
jugar (ue) a to play **4, 7**
jugo, el juice **6**
julio July **1**
junio June **1**
junta directiva, la board of directors
juntarse to get together
juntos/as together
jurado, el jury
justicia, la justice **15**
justificar to justify
justo/a just; fair **11**

juvenil juvenile
juventud, la youth

K

kilo, el kilogram

L

la/s the
labio, el lip **5**
laboral work (related)
laboratorio, el laboratory **3**
lácteo/a dairy
lado (de), al next to **3**
lado, el side
lago, el lake **9**
lágrima, la tear
lamentable regrettable
lamentar to regret
lámpara, la lamp **5**
lana, la wool **8, 14**
lanza, la lance
lanzar to launch
lápida, la tombstone
lápiz, el pencil **1**; **lápiz labial, el** lipstick
largo/a long
lástima, la shame
lastimado/a injured
lastimarse to hurt oneself **10**
latir to beat
lavadora, la washing machine **5**
lavaplatos, el dishwasher **5**
lavar to wash **5**
lavar la ropa to wash clothes **5**
lavar los platos to wash dishes **5**
lavarse to wash (oneself) **5**
le to/for him/her (*masc./fem.*); to/for you (*for.*) (*masc./fem.*)
lección, la lesson; moral
leche, la milk **6**
lechuga, la lettuce **6**
lector/a, el/la reader **13**
lector de CD/DVD, el CD/DVD player
lector de libros electrónicos, el eBook reader **12**
lectura, la reading
Lee (Lean) el diálogo. Read the dialogue. **1**

leer to read **2, 7**
legumbre, la vegetable
lejano/a faraway
lejos (de) far (from) **3**
lema (publicitario), el motto; slogan **15**
lengua, la language **2**; tongue **10**
lentamente slowly
lentejuelas, las sequins **14**
lentes, los glasses
lentes de natación, los swim goggles **7**
lentes de sol, los sunglasses **7**
lento/a slow
les to/for them (*masc./fem.*); to/for you (*for. pl.*)
lesión, la injury
letra, la letter; lyrics
letrero, el sign
letrina, la latrine
levantar to lift **7**
levantarse to get up **5**; to stand up **5**; **levantarse con el pie izquierdo** to get up on the wrong side of the bed
léxico, el lexicon
ley, la law **15**
ley del más fuerte, la survival of the fittest
leyenda, la legend
liberar to liberate
libra, la pound
libre free
librería, la bookstore **3**
libro, el book **1**
licencia por enfermedad/ maternidad, la sick/ maternity leave **11**
licenciatura, la (bachelor's) degree
licuadora, la blender
líder, el/la leader
liderazgo, el leadership
limitar to limit
límite, el limit
limón, el lemon
limonada, la lemonade
limosina, la limousine
limpiar (la casa) to clean (the house) **5**
limpio/a clean **5**

lindo/a pretty
línea, la line; figure **10**
línea ecuatorial, la equator
lingüístico/a linguistic
liquidación, en on clearance **8**
listo/a clever; ready **2**
literatura, la literature
litio, el lithium
llama, la flame
llamar to call **5**
llamarse to be called **5**
llanos, los plains
llave, la key
llegada, la arrival **9**
llegar to arrive **2**
llenar (el lavaplatos) to fill (the dishwasher) **5**
llevar to take; to wear **8**; to spend time; to carry
llevar a cabo to carry out
llorar to cry
lloroso/a teary
llover (ue) to rain **7**
lluvia, la rain
lluvioso/a rainy
lobo, el wolf
lobo marino, el sea lion
loción de afeitar, la shaving lotion
loco/a crazy
locutor/a, el/la announcer
lodo, el mud
lógico/a logical
logotipo, el emblem
lograr to achieve **15**
logro, el achievement
lomo de cerdo, el pork loin
lo/la you (*for.*); him/her it (*masc./fem.*)
lo que what; that which
lo que pasó what happened
loro, el parrot
Lo siento. I'm sorry. **1**
Lo siento, tengo que... I'm sorry, I have to . . . **4**
los/las you (*for. pl.*); them (*masc./fem.*)
Lo(s)/La(s) saluda atentamente,... Very truly yours, . . .
lucha, la struggle
lucha libre, la wrestling

luchador/a, el/la wrestler
lucir (zc) to look; to shine
luego later
luego que as soon as
lugar, el place; setting
lujo, de luxury **9**
lujoso/a luxurious
luna, la moon
luna de miel, la honeymoon
lunes, el Monday
luto, el mourning
luz, la light

M

machacar to crush; to mash
madera, la wood
madrastra, la stepmother **4**
madre, la mother **4**
madrugada, la dawn
maduro/a mature
maestro/a, el/la master/ mistress; teacher
magia, la magic
magnífico/a great; wonderful
mago, el wizard
maíz, el corn **6**
mal bad (*adv.*) **1**; ill
mal tiempo, el bad weather **7**
maleducado/a rude
maleta, la suitcase **9**
maletas, (hacer) las (to pack) the suitcases **9**
maletín, el briefcase
mallas, las leggings
malo/a bad **1**
maloca, la small hut
mamá, la mom
mami, la mommy
manantial, el spring
mandar (mensajes de texto) to send (text messages) **2**
mandato, el command
manera, la way
manga, la sleeve **8**
manga, sin sleeveless
manga corta/larga, de short-/long-sleeved **8**
manifestación, la protest
mano, a by hand
mano, la hand **5**

¡Manos a la obra! Let's get to work! **11**
mantener (ie) to maintain; to support (a family, etc.) **15**
mantenerse (ie) en forma to stay in shape **10**
mantequilla, la butter **6**
manzana, la apple **6**; block (*Spain*)
mañana, la morning **2**; tomorrow **1**
mapa, el map **1**
maquiladora, la assembly plant
maquillaje, el makeup **5**
maquillarse to put makeup on **5**
máquina, la machine
máquina de afeitar, la electric shaver **5**
mar, el ocean **7**; sea **9**
maracas, las maracas **14**
maracuyá, la passionfruit
maratón, el marathon
maravillado/a surprised
maravillosamente marvelously
maravilloso/a marvelous
marca, la brand **12**
marcador, el marker **1**
marcar to mark
marcharse to go away
marco, el framework
marea, la tide
margen, el margin
mariachi, el mariachi musician (*Mexico*)
marimba, la marimba **14**
marino/a marine
mariscos, los seafood **6**; shellfish **6**
marrón brown **1**
Marte Mars (*planet*)
martes, el Tuesday
marzo March **1**
más more
más... que more . . . than
masa, la dough
mascota, la pet
masivo/a massive
Más o menos. So-so; More or less. **1**
masticar to chew

matar to kill
matemáticas, las mathematics 3
materia, la academic subject; course 3
material, el material 8, 14
matrícula, la tuition
matrimonio, el matrimony
mayo May 1
mayor older 4, 5
mayúscula uppercase; capital letter
me me
mecánico/a mechanical 11
mecánico/a, el/la mechanic 11
mecánicos, los jeans (*Cuba*)
Me da igual. It's all the same to me. 7
medianoche, la midnight
mediante through; by way of
medicamento herbal, el herbal medicine 10
medicina, la medicine 3
médico/a medical 10
médico/a, el/la doctor 10
medida, la measurement; measure
medio/a half 2
medio ambiente, el environment 12
medio de transporte, el mode of transportation
mediodía, el noon
medios, los means; media 13; **medios digitales, los** digital media 12
medir (i, i) to measure 6
Me encantaría. I would love to. 4
Me gusta/n… I like… 2
Me gustaría… I would like . . . 8
mejor better 5
mejorar to improve 15
mejorarse to get better 10; to get well 10
Me llamo… My name is . . . 1
Me queda(n) bien / estrecho/a(s) / grande(s). It fits/They fit fine/ small/large. 8

melocotón, el peach
memoria, la memory
memoria USB, la flash drive
memorizar to memorize
mencionar to mention
menor younger 4, 5
menos less
Menos mal. Thank goodness.
menos, por lo at least
menos... que less . . . than
mensaje, el message 2
mente, en in mind
mentiroso/a lying; deceitful
menú, el menu 6
menú de degustación, el tasting menu
menudo, a often
mercado (al aire libre/ global), el (open-air/ global) market 8, 15
mercado callejero, el flea market
mercado global, el global market 15
merecer (zc) to deserve
merendar (ie) to eat a snack 6
merengue, el merengue (*dance*)
merienda, la (afternoon) snack 6
mérito, el merit
mes, el month
mesa, la table 1, 6
mesa de noche, la nightstand 5
mesero/a, el/la waiter/ waitress 6
meses del año, los months of the year
mestizo/a of mixed race
meta, la finish line; goal 11
meteorólogo/a, el/la meteorologist 13
meterse to get involved in
metro, el meter
mexicano/a Mexican 2
mezcla, la mixture
mezclar to mix 6
mezclilla, de mixed fibers
mí me

mi/s my
micrófono, el microphone
microondas, el microwave 6
microscopio, el microscope
miedo, tener (ie) to be afraid
miembro, el member 4
mientras while
mientras que as long as
miércoles, el Wednesday
migración, la migration
migrante migrant
migraña, la migraine
milenio, el millennium
militar military
milla, la mile
millón/millones, el/los million/s
mineral, el mineral 10
minifalda, la miniskirt 8
mínimo, el minimum
mínimo/a minimum 11
ministro/a, el/la minister 15
Mi nombre es... My name is . . . 1
minoría, la minority
minúscula lowercase
minuto, el minute
mío/a(s) mine; my; (of) mine
mirada, la glance
mirar to look at 2; to watch
misa, la Mass
miseria, la misery
mismo/a same
misterio, el mystery
misterioso/a mysterious
mito, el myth
mochila, la backpack 1
moda, de in style 8, 14
moda, la fashion; style 14
modelo, el/la model 14
moderación, la moderation 10
moderno/a modern
modo (de vestir), el way/ manner (of dressing) 14
mola, la Panamanian reverse appliqué
moler (ue) to grind; **moler (ue) a golpes** to pummel

molestar to bother; to annoy
molesto/a annoyed 5
monarquía, la monarchy 15
moneda, la coin
monótono/a monotonous
montaña, la mountain 9
montañoso/a mountainous
montar to mount; to ride
montar a caballo to go horseback riding 9
montar en bicicleta to go bike riding 7, 9
montón, el pile
monumento, el monument 9
morado/a purple 1
moraleja, la moral (of the story)
moralidad, la morality
moreno/a dark (skin/hair) 2
morir (ue, u) to die
moro/a, el/la Moor (Arab)
mostrador, el counter 9
mostrar (ue) to show
motivar to motivate
motivo, el motive
movilidad, la mobility
movimiento, el movement
muchacho/a, el/la boy/girl 2
Mucho gusto. Pleased to meet you. 1
mudanza, la move
mudarse to move
muebles, los furniture 5
muela, la molar 10
muerte, la death
muestra, la sample
mujer, la woman 1
mujer de Estado, la stateswoman
mujer de negocios, la businesswoman 11
multa, la fine
multar to fine 12
multinacional multinational
mundial world (*adj.*) 15
mundialmente worldwide
mundo, el world 12
muralista, el/la muralist
muralla, la wall

murciélago, el bat
muro, el wall
músculo, el muscle
musculoso/a muscular
museo, el museum 3
música, la music 14
música clásica, la classical music 14
musical musical 14
músico/a, el/la musician 14
musulmán/musulmana Muslim
mutuo/a mutual
muy very 1

N

nacer (zc) to be born
nacimiento, el birth
nación, la nation
nacionalidad, la nationality 2
Naciones Unidas, las United Nations
nada nothing 7
nadar to swim 7
nadie no one; nobody 7
naranja, la orange 6
nariz, la nose
narración, la narration
narrador/a, el/la narrator
natación, la swimming 7
naturaleza, la nature 12
naturaleza muerta, la still life
náuseas, las nausea 10
navaja de afeitar, la razor (blade) 5
nave, la ship
navegable navigable
navegante, el/la navigator
navegar (a vela) to sail
Navidad, la Christmas
necesario/a necessary
necesitado/a in need
necesitar to need 1
necio/a, el/la fool
negar (ie) to deny
negativo/a negative
negocio, el business
negro/a black 1
neoyorquino/a New Yorker
nervioso/a nervous 2
nevar (ie) to snow 7
nevera, la refrigerator

ni nor 7
ni... ni neither . . . nor 7
nido, el nest
niebla, la fog
nieto/a, el/la grandson/ granddaughter 4
nilón, el nylon 14
ninguna vez never
ningún, ninguno/a(s) none, not any 7
niño/a, el/la child 4
niños/as, los/las children
nivel, el level
nobleza, la nobility
noche, la night 2
Noche de Brujas, la Halloween
Nochevieja, la New Year's Eve
noción, la notion
nocivo/a harmful
No comprendo. I don't understand. 1
no creer to not believe
no estar seguro/a (de) to not be sure of
nombrar to name
nombre, el name
nominación, la nomination
no pensar (ie) to not think
normalmente normally
norteamericano/a American (US)
nos us 4, 6
Nos vemos. See you. 1
No sé. I don't know. 1
nosotros/as we
nota, la grade
No te preocupes. Don't worry.
noticias, las news 7, 13
noticias en línea, las news online 13
noticiero, el newscast 13
notificar to notify
novedad, la latest fashion 14; novelty
novedoso/a new
novela, la novel
novelista, el/la novelist
noveno/a ninth
noviembre November 1

novio/a, el/la boyfriend/ girlfriend; groom/ bride 4
nube, la cloud 12
nublado/a cloudy 7
nuclear nuclear 12, 15
núcleo, el nucleus
nudo, el knot
nuera, la daughter-in-law 4
nuestro/a(s) our; (of) ours
nuevas séptimas maravillas del mundo, las New Seven Wonders of the World
nuevo/a new 2
número, el number; size
nunca never 7

O

o or 7
o... o either . . . or 7
objeto, el object 1
obligación, la obligation
obligar to oblige
obligatorio/a obligatory; required
obra (de arte), la play (theater) 13; work (of art)
obra maestra, la masterpiece
obrero/a, el/la worker 11
obrero/a de construcción, el/la construction worker 11
observar to observe
observatorio, el observatory 3
obtener (ie) to obtain
océano, el ocean
ocio, el leisure time 4
octavo/a eighth
octubre October 1
ocupado/a busy 2
ocupar to occupy
ocurrir to occur
odio, el hatred
oferta, la offer
oficial official
oficina, la office
oficina de turismo, la tourist office 9
oficio, el trade; occupation 11
ofrecer (zc) to offer

oído, el inner ear 10
oír to hear
Ojalá I hope; God willing 9
ojo, el eye 5
¡Ojo! Watch out!
ola, la wave
oleoducto, el (oil) pipeline 12
olor, el odor; smell
olvidar(se) (de) to forget
ONU, la UN
ópera, la opera 14
opinar to express an opinion
opinión, la opinion
oportunidad, la opportunity
oportuno/a opportune
opresión, la oppression
oprimido/a oppressed
optimista optimistic
opulencia, la opulence
oración, la sentence
¡Órale! Wow! (Mexico)
orden, el order
ordenar la casa to clean/ straighten up the house 5
oreja, la outer ear 10
orgánico/a organic
organización, la organization
organizador/a (de eventos), el/la (events) organizer 11
orgulloso/a proud
orientación, la orientation
origen, el origin
originalidad, la originality
orilla, la bank; edge; shore
orinar to urinate
ornamento, el ornament
oro, de (made of) gold 8
oro, el gold
orquesta (sinfónica), la (symphony) orchestra 4, 14
ortiga, la nettle (a stinging plant)
ortografía, la spelling
os you (inf. fam. Spain)
oscuro/a dark
oso, el bear

otoño, el fall; autumn **1**

otorgar to be granted

otra vez again **5**

Otra vez, por favor. Again, please. **1**

otro/a other; another

ovación de pie, la standing ovation **14**

oveja, la sheep

oxígeno, el oxygen

Oye. Listen. (*command*)

oyente de podcast, el/la podcast listener **13**

oyeres whatever you hear

P

paciente patient

paciente, el/la patient **10**

pacifista, el/la pacifist **15**

padecer (zc) (de) to suffer (from) **10**

padrastro, el stepfather **4**

padre awesome (*Mexico*)

padre, el father **4**

padres, los parents **2**

pagar (en efectivo) to pay (in cash) **8**

página, la page

página web, la web page **12**

pago, el payment

país (en vías de desarrollo), el (developing) country **2**, **15**

paisaje, el landscape

paisano/a, el/la countryman/woman

paja, la straw **14**

pájaro, el bird

palabra, la word

palacio, el palace

palmada, la clap

palos, los stilts

pampas, las plains (of Argentina)

pan, el bread **6**

pana, la corduroy **14**

panadería, la bakery **8**

panameño/a Panamanian **2**

pandereta, la tambourine

panqueques, los pancakes

pantalla, la screen **12**

pantalones (cortos), los pants (shorts) **8**

pantalones de mezclilla, los jeans (*Mexico*)

pañuelo, el bandana

papá, el dad

papalote, el kite **7**

papas, las potatoes **6**

papas fritas, las potato chips; French fries

papel, el paper **1**; role (play, movie, or television) **13**

papelería, la stationery shop **8**

papel maché, el papier mâché

papi, el daddy

paquete de viaje, el travel package **9**

para for; in order to

para colmo to make matters worse; to top it all

para concluir in conclusion

para empezar getting started; to begin

para mí for me

para ti for you

para ver y escuchar while viewing and listening

paraíso, el paradise

parapente, el hang gliding; **parapente, hacer** to hang glide

paravelismo, el parasailing

para que in order that; so that

pararse to stand up

parcial biased

pardo/a brown

parecer (zc) to appear; to seem

pareja, la couple; partner

pariente, el/la relative (family)

parlamento, el parliament

paro, el strike (*Latin America*); unemployment (*Spain*)

parodia, la parody **13**

parque, el park **4**

parque de atracciones, el amusement park **9**

párrafo, el paragraph

parrilla, la grill **6**; **a la parrilla** grilled **6**

parrillada, la grill; barbecue

parte, la part **10**

participante, el/la participant

participar to participate

particularmente particularly

partidario/a partisan

partidario/a, el/la supporter

partido, (ir a un) (to go to a) game

partido, el (sports) game **4**; match

partir to split; to divide

pasa, la raisin

pasado, el past

pasado/a last

pasaje (de ida y vuelta), el (roundtrip) fare **9**; ticket **9**

pasajero/a, el/la passenger **9**

pasante, el/la intern

pasantía, la internship

pasaporte, el passport **9**

pasar to happen; to spend (time) **4**

pasar la aspiradora to vacuum **5**

pasarlo bien/mal/de maravilla to have a good/bad/wonderful time **7**, **9**

pasarlo bomba to have a great time **15**

pasar por ... to pass through . . . **9**

pasar tiempo con amigos to spend time with friends **7**

pasatiempo, el pastime **7**

paseador/a de perros, el/la dog walker

pasear to take a walk **4**

paseo, dar un to take a walk **7**

paseo, el stroll; walk

pasillo, el hallway **5**; aisle **9**

pasión, la passion

paso, el step

Paso por ti. I'll come by for you. **4**; I'll pick you up. **4**

pasta de dientes, la toothpaste **8**

pastel, el cake; pie **6**

pastelería, la pastry shop **8**

pastilla, la pill **10**; lozenge **10**

pata, la leg (*animal*)

patear to kick

patín/patines, el/los skate(s) **7**

patinaje, el skating

patinar to skate **7**

patio, el backyard **5**; patio **5**

pato, el duck

patrimonio, el heritage; **Patrimonio de la Humanidad, el** World Heritage Site

patrocinador/a, el/la sponsor

patrocinar to sponsor

patronato, el board of trustees

pavo, el turkey **6**

paz, la peace **15**

pecho, el chest **10**

pedagogía, la education; teaching **3**

pedazo, el piece

pedicura, la pedicure

pedido, el order; request

pedir (i, i) to ask; to ask for **4**; to request **4**

pedir (i, i) prestado to borrow

peinarse to comb (one's hair) **5**

peine, el comb **5**

pelar to peel **6**

pelea, la fight

peli, la movie; film

película, la movie **4**; film; **de película** fantastic; awesome

película, poner una to show a movie **4**

peligro, el danger

peligroso/a dangerous

pelo, el hair 5

pelota, la baseball 7

peluquero/a, el/la hairdresser 11

pena, la pity; sorrow

penalización, la punishment

pendientes, los earrings (pendants) 8

pendón, el banner

penicilina, la penicillin

península, la peninsula

pensador/a, el/la thinker

pensamiento, el thought

pensar (ie) to think

pensar (ie) (en) to think about 4

pensar (ie) (+ *inf*.) to plan to do something 4

peor worse 5

pequeño/a small 1

percusión, la percussion

percusionista, el/la percussionist

perder (ie) to lose 4, 7; to miss (someone)

pérdida, la loss

perdido/a lost

Perdone. Excuse me. 1

peregrino/a, el/la pilgrim

perejil, el parsley

perezoso/a lazy 1

perfeccionar to perfect

perfecto/a perfect

perfil, el profile

perfume, el perfume 8

perfumería, la perfume shop 8

periódico, el newspaper

periódico digital, el online newspaper 13

periodista, el/la journalist 11

perjudicar to damage; to harm 12

perla, la pearl

perlas, de (made of) pearl 8

permancer (zc) to remain

permanente permanent

permiso, el permit

permitir to permit

pero but

perro/a, el/la dog 4

perseverancia, la perseverance

persona, la person 1

personaje, el character 13; person 15

personal, el personnel

personalidad, la personality

pertenecer (zc) a to belong to

pertenencias, las belongings

peruano/a Peruvian 2

perversidad, la perversity

pesado/a heavy

pesas, las weights 7

pesas, levantar to lift weights 7

pescado, el fish 6

pescador/a, el/la fisherman/woman

pescar to fish 9

pesimista pessimistic

peso, el weight 10

pesquero/a fishing

pesticidas, los pesticides 12

petróleo, el oil 12

piano, el piano 14

PIB (Producto Interno Bruto), el GDP (Gross Domestic Product)

picadura, la (insect) bite

picante spicy 6

picar to chop 6

pícnic, hacer un to have a picnic 7

pico, el beak

pie, el foot 10

piedra, la rock; stone

piel, la skin; leather 14; fur 14

pierna, la leg 10

pieza (musical), la (musical) piece 14; item

pijama, la pajamas

pila, la battery

piloto, el/la pilot 9

piltrafa, la wretch

pimentón rojo, el red pepper

pimienta, la pepper 6

pimiento verde, el green pepper

pincho, el bar snack (*Spain*); morsel; **pinchos**

de tortilla, los slices of Spanish omelet

pingüino, el penguin

pino, el pine nut

pintado/a painted

pintalabios, el lipstick

pintor/a, el/la painter

pintura, la painting

pirámide, la pyramid

pirata, el/la pirate

piratear to pirate

piropo, el compliment

pisar to crush; to step on

piscina, la pool; swimming pool 7

pisco, el brandy (*Peru*)

piso, el apartment; floor 5

pizarra, la chalkboard 1

pizzara interactiva, la interactive whiteboard 1

pizca, la pinch 6

placer, el pleasure

plancha, la iron; metal sheet

planchar to iron 5

plan de retiro, el retirement plan 11

planear to plan

plano, el floor plan

plano de la ciudad, el city map 9

planta nuclear, la nuclear plant 12

plantar to plant

plástico, el plastic 12

plata, de (made of) silver 8

plataforma, la platform 15

plátano, el banana

platería, la silver

plato, el plate 6

platos, los dishes 5

playa, la beach 7

plaza central, la town square 9

pleno/a long form

plomero/a, el/la plumber 11

plumaje, el plumage

plural de los sustantivos, el plural forms of nouns

pluscuamperfecto, el pluperfect

población, la population

pobre poor 2

pobreza, la poverty 15

poder (ue) to be able; can 4

poder, el power 15

poeta, el/la poet

polémica, la controversy

policía, la police

poliéster, el polyester 14

política, la politics 15

político/a, el/la politician 15

político/a political 15

pollo, el chicken 6

poner to put 4; to place 4

poner la mesa to set the table 5

poner los ojos en blanco to roll one's eyes

poner una película to show a movie 4

ponerse to become 5; to get 5

ponerse en forma to get in shape 10

pongo... I put . . . 4

por for; through; during; by

por ahora for now

por aquí around here

por casualidad by chance; coincidentally

por Dios for heaven's (*lit.* God's) sake

por ejemplo for example

por eso that's why 7; therefore

por favor please

por fin finally; at last

por lo general in general

por mi cuenta on my own

porque because

¿Por qué...? Why . . . ? 2

¿Por qué será? How could it be?

porquerías, las junk food

por supuesto of course

portada, la front page

portar to carry

portátil, la computadora laptop computer 1

Portugal Portugal 2

portugués, el Portuguese (language)

portugués/portuguesa
Portuguese 2
por último finally
posar to perch
posible possible
postre, el dessert 6
pozo de petróleo, el oil well
practicar (un deporte) to
practice (a sport) 2, 7; to
play (a sport) 2
precio, el price 8
precioso/a precious
preciso/a essential; precise
precolombino/a
pre-Columbian
predecesor/a, el/la
predecessor
predecible predictable
predecir (i) to predict
predominante
predominant
predominar to
predominate
preferencia, la preference
preferir (ie, i) to prefer 4
pregunta, la question
preguntar to ask
prehispánico/a prehispanic
prehistórico/a prehistoric
premiar to reward
premio, el prize 7, 13
prenda, la garment 14
prensa, la press 13
preocupación, la
preoccupation
preocupado/a worried 2
preocuparse to worry
preparación, la
preparation 6
preparar to prepare 2
presenciar to witness
presentación, la
introduction 1
presentador/a, el/la
announcer 13; host/
hostess (on television,
radio) 13; moderator
presidencia, la presidency
presidente/a, el/la
president 15
presidir to preside
presión, la blood
pressure 10
prestación, la service

préstamo, el loan
prestar to lend
presupuesto, el budget
prevaleciente prevalent
prevenible preventable
previo/a previous
primavera, la spring 1
primera actriz, la leading
lady 13
primera plana, la front
page 13
primer/o/a first
primo/a, el/la cousin 4
princesa, la princess
príncipe, el prince
principio, al at first
principio, el beginning 13
prioridad, la priority
prisa, tener (ie) to be in a
hurry
prístino/a pristine
privacidad, la privacy
privado/a private
probablemente probably
probador, el fitting room 8
probar (ue) to try
probarse (ue) to try on 8
problema, el problem 10
procesión, la procession
proceso, el process
producir (zc) to produce
producto, el product
productor/a, el/la
producer 13
productos lácteos, los
dairy products
profesión, la profession 11
profesional de la salud, el/
la healthcare worker 11
profesor/a, el/la professor 1
profundamente deeply 10;
profoundly
profundo/a deep; profound
programa, el program
12, 13
programación, la
programming
programador/a, el/la
programmer
programar to program 12
programas sociales,
los social welfare
programs 15
progreso, el progress

prohibido/a prohibited
prohibir to prohibit
prolífico/a prolific
promedio, el average
promesa, la promise
prometer to promise
prominente prominent
promoción, la promotion
promocionar to promote
promover (ue) to
promote 15
pronóstico, el forecast
pronto soon
pronunciar to pronounce
propiedad, la property
propina, la tip
(monetary) 6
propio/a own
proponer to propose
proporcionar to
proportion; to provide
propósito, el goal;
objective
protagonista, el/la
protagonist 13; star 13
protección, la protection
proteger (j) to protect 12
protegido/a protected
proteínas, las proteins 10
protestar to protest 15
provenir (ie) to orginate; to
arise from
provocar to provoke
próximo/a nearby; close;
next
proyecto, el project
prueba, la quiz 1; test; trial;
sample
psicología, la psychology 3
psicólogo/a, el/la
psychologist 11
púas, las barbs
publicar to publish
publicidad, la publicity
publicista, el/la publicist
publicitario/a publicity
público, el public;
audience 13
público/a public
pueblo, el people 15; town;
masses 15
puente colgante, el
hanging bridge
puerta, la door 1

puerta de embarque, la
boarding gate 9
puertorriqueño/a Puerto
Rican 2
pues well; because; **pues,**
mira well, look
puesto, el place; stall;
stand; position 11; job 11
pulir to polish
pulmón, el lung 10
pulpa, la wood pulp
pulsera, la bracelet 8
puntiagudo/a sharp
punto (de vista), el point
(of view)
punto, en on the dot 2
puntualmente punctually
pureza, la purity
puro/a pure

Q

que that; which; who;
whom
qué what
¿Qué...? What . . . ? 2
¡Qué asco! How
revolting! 6
¡Qué barbaridad! What
nonsense!
¡Qué bárbaro! How terrific!
qué dirán, el what people
will say
¿Qué es? What is it?
¿Qué tal? What's up? (*inf.*) 1
¿Qué tal le queda(n)? How
does it/do they fit? 8
¿Qué te apetece (comer)?
What do you feel like
(eating)?
quedar to be left; to be
remaining; to fit
quedarse to stay
(somewhere) 9; to remain
¡Qué estudiantes! What
students!
¡Que gane el mejor! May
the best win!
quehaceres (domésticos),
los (household) chores 5
¿Qué haces? What do you
do (are you doing)? 2
¿Qué haces cuando...?
What do you do
when . . . ?

¿Qué hora es? What time is it?

¿Qué húbole? What's up? (*Venezuela*)

quejar(se) to complain

quena, la Andean flute

¿Qué número calza? What size shoe do you wear? 8

¿Qué onda? What's up?

¡Qué padre! How awesome! (*Mexico*)

¿Qué pasa? What's happening?; What's up? (*inf.*) 1

¿Qué sabes? What do you know?

¡Qué rico/a! How delicious! 6

¡Qué sabroso/a! How delicious! 6

¿Qué tal si...? What if . . . ? 7

querer (ie) to want 4; to love 4

querido/a dear

quesadilla, la melted cheese tortilla

quesería, la cheese shop 8

queso, el cheese 6

¿Qué se hace en...? What do people do in . . . ?

¿Qué significa...? What does . . . mean? 1

¡Qué suerte! What luck! 2

¿Qué tal sí... ? How about (if) . . . ? 4

¿Qué talla usa? What size do you wear? 8

¿Qué te gusta hacer? What do you like to do? 2

¿Qué tiempo hace? What is the weather like? 7

¡Qué vergüenza! How embarrassing!

¡Que vivan los novios! Long live the bride and groom!

quien who; whom

¿Quién(es)...? Who . . . ? 2

¿Quién es? Who is it?

¿Quién soy yo? Who am I?

¿Quieres ir a...? Do you want to go to . . . ? 4

Quiero... I want . . . 8

química, la chemistry 3

quinto/a fifth

quipu, el knotted string (*Inca*)

quiropráctico/a, el/la chiropractor

quitar to remove 5

quitar la mesa to clear the table 5

quitarse to take off (clothing) 5

quizás perhaps

R

radio, la radio 13

radioactividad, la radioactivity 12

radiografía, la X-ray 10

radio por satélite, la satellite radio

radioyente, el/la radio listener 13

raíz, la root

rama, la branch

ramo, el bouquet

rápidamente rapidly

rápido/a rapid

raqueta, la racket 7

raro/a strange; uncommon

rascacielos, el skyscraper

rato, el short time; a little while

ratón (inalámbrico), el (wireless) mouse 12

rayas, de striped 8

rayo, el ray

rayón, el rayon 14

razón, la reason

razón, tener (ie) to have a point; to be right

razonable reasonable

reacción, la reaction

reaccionar to react 6

real royal

realeza, la royalty

realista realistic

realizar to achieve; to carry out

realmente really

rebaja, en on sale 8

rebaja, la sale 8

rebelión, la rebellion

recámara, la bedroom

recargable rechargeable

recaudar fondos to raise funds

recepción, la reception desk 9

recepcionista, el/la receptionist

receptor, el receiver

receta (médica), la (medical) prescription; recipe 6

rechazar to reject 4

recibir to receive 2

recibo, el receipt 8

reciclaje, el recycling 12

reciclar to recycle 12

recién casados, los newlyweds

recientemente recently

recíproco/a reciprocal

reclamo de equipaje, el baggage claim 9

recoger (j) to pick up 5

recolección, la gathering

recolectar to harvest

recomendar (ie) to recommend

recompensa, la compensation

reconocido/a recognized

recordar (ue) to remember 4

recorrer to travel around 9; to tour 9

recorrido, el trip

recortar to clip

rectificar to rectify

recto, todo straight ahead

rectoría, la president's office 3

recuerdo, el souvenir; memory 9

recuperar to recuperate

recurso (natural), el (natural) resource 12

recursos humanos, los human resources

red, la network

red social, la social network

redacción, la editing

redondo/a round

reducir (zc) to reduce

reencarnar to reincarnate

referir (ie, i) to refer

reflejar to reflect

reforestación, la reforestation 12

refresco, el refreshment; soda 6; soft drink 4, 6

refrigerador, el refrigerator 6

refugio, el refuge

regalar to give (as a gift)

regalo, el gift

regatear to bargain 8; to haggle over 8

regateo, el haggling

régimen, el diet; regime

registrar to register

región, la region

regla, la rule

regresar to return 2

regreso, el return

reina, la queen 15

reinar to reign

reino, el kingdom

reírse (i, i) to laugh

relación, la relation; relationship

relajamiento, el relaxation

relámpago, el lightning flash

relatar to relate

relativo/a relative

religioso/a religious

rellenar to fill completely 11; to fill out 11

relleno, el filling

relleno/a filled

reloj, el clock; watch 1

reloj inteligente/de pulsera, el smart watch/ wristwatch 8

remediar to remedy

remedio, el remedy 10

remesa, la remittance; payment 4

remolino, el whirlwind

remoto/a remote

remover (ue) to remove

remunerado/a paid

rendir (i, i) to defeat; **rendirse (i, i)** to give up

renombre, el renown

renovable renewable

renunciar to renounce

reparar to repair 11

repartir to deliver 11; to distribute 11

repaso, el review

repente, de suddenly

repertorio, el repertoire

repetir (i, i) to repeat 4; to have a second helping 4

Repita, por favor. Repeat, please. 1

Repite (Repitan). Repeat. 1

repoblación, la repopulation

reponer to restock

reportaje, el feature 13

reportar report

reportero/a, el/la (television) reporter 13

represa, la dam

representante, el/la representative 15

representar to perform 13; to represent

representativo/a representative

reproducir (zc) to reproduce

reproductor de mp3, el mp3 player

república, la republic 15

requisito, el requirement

res, la beef

resaltar to feature

rescate, el rescue

reseña, la review 13

reserva, la reservation 9

reservación, la reservation 9

resfriado, el cold 10

residencia, la residence

resolver (ue) to solve 15

respaldar to support

respetar to respect

respeto, el respect

respetuoso/a respectful

respirar to breathe 10

respiratorio/a respiratory

responder to respond

responsabilidades, las responsibilities

responsable responsible

respuesta, la answer; response 1

restaurante, el restaurant 6

resto, el rest

restos, los remains; leftovers

resultado, el result

resumen, el summary

resumir to summarize

retar to challenge; **retarse** to challenge each other

retirado/a distant; retired

retirarse to excuse oneself; **retirarse (de)** to retire (from) 11

retrasar to detain; to be behind

reunión, la meeting; get-together

reunirse to meet with someone

revelar to reveal

reventar un vaso sanguíneo to break a blood vessel

revisar to inspect 9; to check 13; to review

revista (del corazón), la (celebrity) magazine 7, 13

revolución, la revolution 9

revolucionado/a revolutionized

revolucionar to revolutionize

revólver, el revolver

rey, el king 15

rico/a rich 2, 10; delicious

ridículo/a ridiculous

riego, el irrigation

riesgo, el risk 10

rígido/a rigid

río, el river

riqueza, la wealth; richness

risa, la laughter

ritmo, el rhythm

robo, el robbery

roca, la rock

rodaje, el filming

rodar (ue) to film

rodeado/a surrounded

rodear to surround

rodilla, la knee 10

rojo/a red 1

romano/a Roman

romántico/a romantic

romper to break

romperse (un hueso) to break (a bone) 10;

romperse un cartílago to rupture/tear cartilage; **romperse un ligamento** to rupture/tear a ligament

ropa, la clothing 8

roquero/a, el/la rocker (*music*)

rosado/a pink 1

roto/a broken

rubio/a blond (fair) 2

rueda, la wheel

ruina, la ruin

rumbo a toward

Rusia Russia

ruso, el Russian

rústico/a rustic

ruta, la route

rutina, la routine

S

sábado, el Saturday

sabelotodo, el/la know-it-all

saber to know (something) 4

saber (+ *inf*.) to know (how to do something) 4

sabor, el flavor

sabroso/a delicious; tasty 6

Saca (Saquen) la tarea. Take out your homework. 1

sacar to take (out) 1, 5; to take off

sacar fotos to take pictures 9

sacar la voz to speak out

saco, el blazer

sacudir to shake; to dust

sagrado/a sacred

sal, la salt 6

sala, la living room 5

sala de espera, la waiting room 9

sala de reclamación, de equipaje baggage claim area

sala de urgencias, la emergency room 10

salario, el salary

salchicha, la sausage

salida, la departure 9

salir to leave 4; to go out 4

salir a comer to go out to eat 7

salir bien to end well

salón, el room

salón de clase, el classroom 1

salpicado/a dotted; spattered

salsa, la sauce 6

salsero/a, el/la salsa performer

saltar to leap

salto (de agua), el waterfall 9

salto de longitud, el long jump

salto en bungee, hacer to bungee jump

salud, la health 10

saludable healthy

saludo/s, el/los greeting/s; salutation/s 1

salvadoreño/a Salvadorian 2

salvaje wild

salvar to save

sandalias, las sandals 8

sándwich, el sandwich 6

sanfermines, los San Fermín festival

sangre, la blood

sanidad, la sanitation; public health

sapo, el toad

sartén, la skillet 6; frying pan

satisfacción, la satisfaction

satisfactorio/a satisfactory

satisfecho/a satisfied

saturado/a saturated 10

saxofón, el saxophone 14

se himself; herself; yourself; itself; themselves 5

secado rápido, el quick-drying

secador, el hair dryer 5

secadora, la clothes dryer 5

secarse to dry yourself off 5

sección, la section

sección deportiva, la sports section 13

sección financiera, la financial section 13

seco/a dry
secretario/a, el/la secretary
secreto, el secret
secuestrar to kidnap
sed, la thirst
sed, tener (ie) to be thirsty
seda, la silk 8, 14
sede, la head office; headquarters; seat of government
seguidor/a, el/la follower
seguir (i, i) to follow 4, 10
según according to
segunda mano, de secondhand
segundo/a second
seguramente surely
seguridad, la security 9
seguro/a sure 2; certain
seguro médico, el health insurance 11
selección, la selection
seleccionar to select
selva, la jungle 12
semana, la week
Semana Santa, la Holy Week
semejante similar
semestre, el semester 3
senador/a, el/la senator 15
sencillez, la simplicity 14
sencillo/a simple 10
senda peatonal, la walking path
sendero, el path
sensación, la sensation
sensacionalista sensationalist
sentarse (ie) to sit 5
sentido de seguridad, el feeling safe
sentimental sentimental
sentir (ie, i) to regret
sentirse (ie, i) to feel 5
señal, la signal
señalar to point out
señor, el (Sr.) Mr. 1
señora, la (Sra.) Mrs., Ms. 1
señorita, la (Srta.) Miss 1
septiembre September 1
séptimo/a seventh
sepulcro, el grave
sequía, la drought 12
ser to be 1

ser humano, el human being
serie, la series
serio/a serious
serpiente, la snake
servicio, el service
servicio de limpieza, el cleaning service
servidor, el server 12
servilleta, la napkin 6
servir (i, i) to serve 4
severo/a severe
sexto/a sixth
Sí, claro. Yes, of course. 4
siempre always
siglas, las call letters
siglo, el century
significado, el meaning
significante significant
significar to mean
significativo/a significant
siguiente following
silla, la chair 1
sillón, el armchair 5; overstuffed chair 5
simbolizar to symbolize
simpático/a kind; nice; amusing 1
simpatizante, el/la sympathizer
simpatizar to sympathize
sindicalizar to unionize
sindicato, el union
sin duda without a doubt
sin embargo however; nevertheless
sinfonía, la symphony 14
sino (que) but; (but) rather
sin (que) without
sin fines de lucro nonprofit
sin querer unintentionally
síntesis, la synthesis
sintético/a synthetic
síntoma, el symptom 10
sin trabajo, estar to be out of work 11
sirviente/a, el/la servant
sistema, el system 11
sitio, el place
sitio social, el a social media site 12
sitio web, el website 9, 12

situación, la situation
situado/a situated
sobre about; on
sobreconsumo, el overconsumption
sobrenatural supernatural
sobrepeso, el excess weight 10; obesity
sobrepoblación, la overpopulation
sobrevivencia, la survival
sobrevivir to survive
sobrino/a, el/la nephew/niece 4
socialista, el/la socialist
sociología, la sociology
socorro, el help
sofá, el sofa 5; couch 5
sol, hace (mucho) it's (very) sunny 7
sol, tomar el to sunbathe
solamente only
solar solar 12
soldado, el/la soldier 15
solemne solemn
solicitar to apply for
solicitud de empleo, la job application 11
sólido/a solid
solista, el/la soloist 14
solitario/a solitary
solo only
solo/a alone
soltar (ue) to let go
soltero/a single 4; unmarried 4
sombrilla, la umbrella 7
sondear to survey 13
sonreír (i, i) to smile
sonriendo smiling
soñador/a, el/la dreamer
soñar (ue) (con) to dream about) 4
sopa, la soup 6
soplar to blow
sorprendente surprising
sorprender(se) to surprise
sorpresa, la surprise
sospecha, la suspicion
sostén deportivo, el sports bra
sostenible sustainable 12
su/sus his/her/your/their

subempleo, el underemployment
subir to raise; to go up; to climb 9; to upload 12
subir de peso to gain weight 10
subrayar to underscore
subvencionar to subsidize
sucio/a dirty 5
sudadera (con capucha), la (hooded) sweatshirt 8
sudor, el sweat
suegro/a, el/la father-in-law/mother-in-law 4
sueldo (mínimo), el (minimum) wage 11
sueño, el dream; sleep
sueño, tener (ie) to be sleepy
suerte, la luck
suéter, el sweater 8
sufrimiento, el suffering
sufrir (de) to suffer (from)
sugerencia, la advice 10; suggestion
sugerir (ie, i) to suggest
sumamente very
sumario, el summary
superación, la overcoming
superar to overcome
superventas, el bestseller 13
supervisión, la supervision
supervisor/a, el/la supervisor 11
sur, el south
sureño/a southern
surfear to surf 7
surgir to emerge
suspender to suspend
suspensivo/a suspenseful
sustancia, la substance
sustantivo, el noun 1
suyo/a(s) your (*for. pl.*) (of) yours; his/her (of) his/hers (of) its; their

T

tabla, la board; surfboard; table
tableta, la tablet 1, 12
tacaño/a stingy
tacógrafo, el tachograph
tacón, el heel 8

táctica, la tactic
talco, el talcum powder 8
talentoso/a talented 14
talla, la clothing size 8;
   size 8
tallado, el carving
tallado/a carved
taller, el workshop
tal vez perhaps
tamaño, el size
también also; too
tambor, el drum 14
tampoco neither; (not)
   either 7
tan... como as . . . as
tan pronto como as soon as
tanque, el tank
tanto/a so much
tantos/as so many
tanto/a(s)... como as
   many/much . . . as
tapado/a stuffy
tapas, las appetizers
taquilla, la box office
tardar to take (time)
tarde late
tarde, la afternoon 2
tarea, la homework 1; task
tarifa, la fee; commission
tarjeta, la card
tarjeta de crédito, la credit
   card 8
tarjeta de embarque, la
   boarding pass 9
tarjeta de memoria, la
   memory card
tarjeta postal, la postcard 9
tarjeta prepaga, la gift card
tarta, la pie
tasa (de desempleo), la rate
   (of unemployment) 15
taxista, el/la taxi driver
taza, la cup 6; mug
tazón (de cristal), el (glass)
   bowl 6
te you (*inf.*)
té (caliente), el (hot) tea 6
¿Te animas? Are you in?;
   Are you interested?
teatro, el theater 13
techo, el roof; place to live
   (*fig.*)
teclado, el keyboard 12
técnica, la technique

tecnología, la technology
tecnológico/a technological
Te gusta/n… You
   like . . . 2
¿Te gustaría (+ *inf.*)?
   Would you like (+ *inf.*)? 4
¡Te invito! (It's) My
   treat! 4
te toca a ti it's your turn
tejanos, los jeans (*Spain*)
tejer to weave
tejido, el weaving
tela, la cloth; fabric 14
tele, la television
teléfono celular/
   inteligente, el smart
   phone 1
telenovela, la soap
   opera 13
televidente, el/la television
   viewer 13
televisión (en directo/
   en vivo), la (live)
   television 13
televisión (por cable), la
   cable television 13
televisión (por satélite), la
   satellite television 13
televisor de alta
   definición, el high-
   definition television
tema, el theme; topic 15
temer to fear
temor, el fear
temperatura, la
   temperature 10
tempestad, la storm
templado/a temperate
templo, el temple
temporada, la season 7
temporal temporary
temprano/a early
tender (ie) a to tend to
tenedor, el fork 6
tener (ie) to have 1; **tener**
   (ie) que to have to
tener (ie) en cuenta to keep
   in mind
tener (ie) éxito to be
   successful 13
tener (ie) un derrame
   cerebral to have a stroke
tenis, el tennis 7
tenista, el/la tennis player

tensión, la tension,
   pressure
tenso/a tense
tentación, la temptation
teoría, la theory
tercer/o/a third
terciopelo, el velvet 14
termal thermal
terminar to end; to finish
términos, los terms 11
terrateniente, el landowner
terraza, la terrace
terremoto, el earthquake
terreno, el land; terrain
terrestre terrestrial
terrorismo, el terrorism 15
tesoro, el treasure
testigo, el/la witness
ti you (*inf.*)
tibio/a lukewarm
tiburón, el shark
tiempo, el time; weather 7
tiempo completo,
   trabajar a to work full-
   time 11
tiempo parcial, trabajar a
   to work part-time 11
tienda, la store 8; shop 8
tienda especializada, la
   speciality store
tierra, la earth; land
tímido/a shy; timid
tinta, la ink
tinto red (wine) 6
tío/a, el/la uncle/aunt 4
típico/a typical
tipo, el type 15
tira cómica, la comic strip
tirar to throw (away/
   out) 12
titular to title
titular, el headline 13
título, el degree;
   title 1
tiza, la chalk
toalla, la towel 7
tobillo, el ankle
tocar (un instrumento/
   música) to play (an
   instrument/music) 4;
   to touch
todavía still
todo/a(s) all; every;
   everyone

Todo bien. All's well. 1
todoterreno, el ATV 9; off-
   road/four-wheel-drive
   vehicle
tomar to drink 2, 10; to
   take 2
tomar la presión to take
   blood pressure (*Latin
   America*) 10
tomar la temperatura to
   take temperature 10
tomar la tensión to
   take blood pressure
   (*Spain*)
tomate, el tomato 6
tonto/a stupid
topografía, la topography
torcer(se) (ue) to
   twist 10
torneo, el tournament 7
torno a, en pertaining to
toro, el bull
toronja, la grapefruit 6
torta, la cake 6
torta de chocolate, la
   chocolate cake
tortilla, la Spanish omelet
tortuga, la turtle
torturar to torture
tos, la cough 10
toser to cough 10
tostadora, la toaster 6
tostar (ue) to toast 6
trabajador/a
   hardworking 1
trabajador/a, el/la
   worker
trabajar to work 2, 11
trabajar (a comisión) to
   work (on commission)
trabajo, el work 11
trabajo, estar sin to be out
   of work 11
tradición, la tradition
traducir (zc) to translate
traer to bring
traficar to traffic
tráfico, el traffic
tragedia, la tragedy 13
traje, el suit 8
traje de baño, el
   swimsuit 7
traje de noche, el evening
   gown 14

tranquilamente calmly
transferir (ie, i) to transfer
transformar to transform
transición, la transition
transmitir to transmit 13
transportar to transport
transporte (terrestre), el transportation; (ground) transport
trapo, el rag
tras behind
tratado, el treaty 15
tratamiento, el treatment 10
tratar to try
trayectoria, la trajectory
trekking, el hike
tremendo/a tremendous
tren, el train 9
tribu, la tribe
tribunal, el court 15
triste sad 2
triunfo, el triumph
trol, el/la Internet troll 12
trombón, el trombone 14
trompeta, la trumpet 14
tu/tus your (inf.)
tú you (inf.)
tuit, el tweet 12
tuitear to tweet 12
tul, el tulle (silk or nylon net) 14
tumba, la tomb
turismo, el tourism
turista, el/la tourist
turístico/a touristy 9
turnarse to take turns
turno, el shift; turn
tuyo/a(s) your (inf.) (of) yours

U

ubicación, la location
ubicado/a located
ufano/a conceited
úlcera, la ulcer
últimamente lately
último/a last; latest; recent
última hora, de latest 13
una vez one time 5; once 5
único/a only; unique

unidad, la unity
unido/a close 4; close-knit 4
uniforme, el uniform
unirse (a) to join 12; to join forces 15
universidad, la university 1
un/o/a a; one 1
urgente urgent
usando using
usar to use
usted/es you (for.) (masc./ fem.)
usualmente usually
utensilio, el utensil
útil useful
utilizar to use
uvas, las grapes 6

V

vaca, la cow
vacaciones, las vacation
vacante, la vacancy 11
vaciar to empty 5
vacuna, la vaccine
vainilla, la vanilla 6
valer to be worth; to cost
valioso/a useful
valle, el valley 9
valor, el value
vamos let's go; we go; we're going
¿Vamos a...? Should we go . . . ? 4
vaqueros, los jeans (Spain) 8
variar to vary
variedad, la variety
varios/as several; various
vaso, el glass 6
vaso sanguíneo, el blood vessel
Ve (Vayan) a la pizarra. Go to the board. 1
veces, a sometimes; at times 5
vecino/a, el/la neighbor
vegetariano/a vegetarian
vegetariano/a, el/la vegetarian
velocidad, la speed
vencer (zc) to conquer
vendedor/a ambulante, el/ la street vendor

vender to sell 2
venezolano/a Venezuelan 2
venganza, la revenge
venir (ie) to come 4
venta, en on sale
venta, la sale
ventaja, la advantage 11
ventana, la window
ventanilla, la window (airplane) 9
ver (la televisión/una película) to see; to watch (television/a movie) 2
verano, el summer 1
verbo, el verb 1
verdad, la truth
verdaderamente truly
verdadero/a true
verde green 1, 12
verduras, las vegetables 6
verificar to verify
versátil versatile
versión, la version
vestido, el dress 8
vestimenta, la clothing
vestir (i, i) to dress 14
vestirse (i, i) to get dressed 5
vestuario, el locker room
veterano/a veteran
veterinaria, la veterinary science
veterinario/a, el/la veterinarian 11
vez, la time; instance 5
vez en cuando, de once in a while 5
vía, la lane; way
vía de agua, la waterway
viajante, el/la traveling salesperson
viajar to travel 2, 9
viaje, el trip 9
viajero/a, el/la traveler 9
vías de desarrollo, en developing 15
víctima, la victim
vida, la life
videoconferencia, la videoconference 12
videograbadora, la VCR

videojuegos, los videogames 7
vidrio, el glass 12
viejo/a old 2
viejo/a, el/la elderly person
viento, el wind
viento, hace (mucho) it's (very) windy 7
vieres whatever you see
viernes, el Friday
vigente current (adj.)
vigilar to watch
vigoroso/a vigorous
vinagre, el vinegar 6
vino (tinto/blanco), el (red/white) wine 6
viña, la vineyard
viola, la viola
violar to violate 15
violencia, la violence
violento/a violent
violín, el violin 14
virreinato, el viceroyalty
visa, la visa
visado, el visa (Spain)
visita, la guest; visit
visitante, el/la visitor
visitar to visit 2
vista, la view 9
vistoso/a showy
vitamina, la vitamin 10
vitrina, la display case
viudo/a, el/la widower, widow
vivienda, la housing
vivir to live 2
vivo/a alive
volante, el flyer
volar (ue) to fly 7
volcán, el volcano 9
voleibol, el volleyball 7
voluntad, la will
voluntario/a voluntary
voluntario/a, el/la volunteer
voluptuoso/a voluptuous
volver (ue) to return 4
vosotros/as you (inf. pl.) (Spain)
votante, el/la voter
votar (por) to vote (for) 15
voto, el vote
voz, la voice 14

vuelo, el flight **9**
vuestro/a(s) your; yours
  (*inf. pl.*); (of) yours

Y

y and
¿Y tú? And you? **1**
ya already
yacimiento, el deposit
yapa, la add-on (*Quechua*)
yerno, el son-in-law **4**
yo I
yogur, el yogurt **6**

Z

zampoña, la panpipe
zanahoria, la carrot **6**
zapatería, la shoe store **8**
zapatilla de deporte, la
  athletic shoe; running
  shoe **8**; sneaker **8**
zapatos (de tacón
  alto), los (high-heeled)
  shoes **8**
zoológico, el zoo
zorro, el fox
zumo, el juice (*Spain*)

Appendix 4
English-Spanish Vocabulary

A

a un/o/a
abandon abandonar
ability la habilidad
aboard a bordo
abolish abolir **15**
abound abundar
about sobre
above arriba de
abroad al extranjero **9**
absent ausente
abstain abstenerse (ie)
abuse el abuso
academic académico/a
academic subject la materia **3**
accede acceder
accelerate acelerar
accept aceptar **4**
access acceder **12**
accessory el accessorio **5**; la prenda
accident el accidente
accommodate acomodar
accompany acompañar
accord el acuerdo **15**
according to según
accordion el acordeón
account la cuenta
accountant el/la contador/a **11**
accounting la contabilidad **3**
accustom acostumbrar
accurate acertado/a
ache el dolor
achievable alcanzable
achieve lograr **15**; realizar
achievement el logro
acquire adquirir (ie, i)
across (from) enfrente (de) **3**
act actuar **13**
action la acción
active activo/a **2**
activist el/la activista **15**

activity la actividad **5, 7**
actor el actor
actress la actriz
acupuncture la acupuntura **10**
ad el anuncio
add añadir; **add (in)** echar **6**; agregar
add-on la yapa (*Quechua*)
addressee el/la destinatario/a
adequate adecuado/a
adjust ajustar
administration la administración
administrative administrativo/a **11**
admiration la admiración
admirer el/la admirador/a
admission ticket la entrada **4**
admit admitir
adoptive adoptivo/a
adore adorar
adorn adornar
adorned adornado/a
advanced avanzado/a
advantage la ventaja **11**
adventure la aventura
adverb el adverbio
advice el consejo **10**; la sugerencia **10**
advice column el consultorio sentimental **13**
advise aconsejar
advisor el/la asesor/a **15**
advocate abogar
aerobic aeróbico/a **10**
aerobics ejercicios aeróbicos **10**
affect afectar
affection el cariño
affectionate afectuoso/a
affectionately afectuosamente

affirm afirmar
after después (de) (que)
afternoon la tarde **2**
afternoon snack la merienda **6**
again otra vez
Again, please. Otra vez, por favor. **1**
against (en) contra
age la edad **4**
age at death la edad cuando murió
agent el/la agente **9**
agree estar de acuerdo
agreeable agradable
agreed de acuerdo
agreement el convenio; la concordancia
agricultural agrícola
air conditioning el aire acondicionado
airline la aerolínea **9**
airplane el avión
airport el aeropuerto **9**
aisle el pasillo **9**
album el álbum
alcoholic beverages las bebidas alcohólicas **10**
algebra el álgebra (*fem.*)
alive vivo/a **3**
all todo/a(s)
All's well. Todo bien. **1**
allergic alérgico/a **10**
allergy la alergia
alert la alerta **12**
alleviate aliviar
alleviated aliviado/a
alligator hunting la caimaneada
almost casi
along a lo largo de; a través de
aloud en voz alta
already ya

also también
alternate alternar(se)
alternative alternativo/a **12**
although aunque **7**
altitude la altura
aluminum el aluminio **12**
always siempre
ambassador el/la embajador/a
ambiguity la ambigüedad
ambulance la ambulancia
American (from the US) estadounidense **2**
among themselves entre sí
amorous amoroso/a
ample amplio/a
amusement park el parque de atracciones **9**
amusing simpático/a **1**
analysis el análisis
analyst el/la analista **11**
ancestor el/la antepasado/a
ancestry la ascendencia
ancient antiguo/a
and y
And you? ¿Y tú? **1**
Andean andino/a
Andean flute la quena
anecdote la anécdota
anger el enojo; enojar
angry enojado/a **2**; furioso/a **5**
animal el animal
animated animado/a
ankle el tobillo
anniversary el aniversario
announce anunciar
announcement el aviso
announcer el/la locutor/a
annoy molestar
annoyed molesto/a **5**
another otro/a
answer contestar; la respuesta

Answer in Spanish.
Contesta (Contesten)
en español. 1
antacid el antiácido 10
anthropology la
antropología
antibiotic el antibiótico 10
anticipate anticipar
anticipation la anticipación
antioxidants los
antioxidantes 10
anxious ansioso/a
any cualquier(a)
anyone cualquier/a
anything algo 7
apartment el apartamento;
el departamento; el piso
aphrodisiac el afrodisíaco
apologize disculparse
app la aplicación 12
apparent aparente
apparently aparentemente
appeal to apetecer (zc)
appear aparecer (zc)
appearance la apariencia
appetizer el aperitivo; la
entrada; las tapas
applaud aplaudir 14
apple la manzana 6
appliance el aparato
applicant el/la
aspirante 11
application la solicitud 11
apply for solicitar
appointment la cita 10
appreciate apreciar
appreciated apreciado/a
appropriate apropiado/a
approximately
aproximadamente
April abril 1
aquatic acuático/a
aqueduct el acueducto
Arab el/la árabe
Arabic el árabe
archbishop el arzobispo
archeologist el/la
arqueólogo/a
archipelago el archipiélago
architect el/la arquitecto/a
11
architecture la arquitectura 3
Are you in/interested? ¿Te
animas?

area el área (*fem.*)
Argentine argentino/a 2
Argentine cowboy
el gaucho
argument el/la argumento;
la discusión
aria el aria (*fem.*)
arise from provenir (ie)
arm el brazo 10
armchair el sillón 5
armed armado/a
army el ejército 15
around alrededor de
around here por aquí
arrangement el arreglo
arrest detener (ie)
arrival la arribada; la
llegada 9
arrive llegar 2
arrow la flecha
art el arte 3
arthritis la artritis
article el artículo 13
artifact el artefacto
artisan el/la artesano/a
as como
ascending ascendente
ashamed avergonzado/a
ashes las cenizas
ask preguntar
ask for pedir (i, i) 4
aspect el aspecto
aspiration la aspiración
aspirin la aspirina 10
assemble armar
assembly plant la
maquiladora
assistant el/la asistente;
el/la ayudante 11
associate asociar
association la asociación
as soon as en cuanto;
luego que; tan pronto
como
asthma el asma (*fem.*)
at first al principio
at last por fin
at least por lo menos
athlete el/la atleta 7
athletic shoe la zapatilla de
deporte
ATM (automatic teller
machine) el cajero
automático 9

atmosphere el ambiente; la
atmósfera
attack atacar; el ataque
attend asistir (a) 2; acudir
at . . . o'clock a la(s)... 2
at the same time al mismo
tiempo
at times a veces 5
At what time? ¿A qué
hora? 2
attract atraer
attraction la atracción 9;
el atractivo
attractive atractivo/a
attribute atribuir
ATV (all-terrain vehicle) el
todoterreno 9
audience el público 13, 14
audition la audición 14
auditorium el auditorio 3
August agosto 1
aunt la tía 4
authentic auténtico/a
author el/la autor/a
authority la autoridad
autobiographical
autobiográfico/a
autograph el autógrafo
autonomous autónomo/a
autumn el otoño 1
available disponible
avenue la avenida
average el promedio
avocado el aguacate
avoid evitar 10
awesome de película;
padre (*Mexico*)

B

bachelor's degree la
licenciatura
back la espalda 10
background el fondo
backpack la mochila 1
backyard el patio 5
bad mal (*adv.*) 1; malo/a 1
bad weather el mal tiempo 7
bag el bolso; la bolsa 7
baggage el equipaje 9
baggage claim el reclamo
de equipaje 9; la sala
de reclamación de
equipaje 9
bagpipe la gaita

bake hornear 6
baked al horno 6
bakery la panadería 8
balanced equilibrado/a 10
ball (soccer, basketball)
el balón 7
ballad la balada
ballet el ballet 14
ballroom dancing el baile
de salón 14
banana el plátano; la
banana 6
band la banda 14
bandana el pañuelo
bandwidth el ancho de
la banda
bank el banco; la orilla
banner el pendón, el
estandarte
banquet el banquete
bar el bar
barbs las púas
barely apenas
bargain la ganga 8;
regatear 8
baritone el barítono
baseball el béisbol 7;
la pelota 7
baseball player el/la
beisbolista
based basado/a
basin la cuenca
basket la cesta
basketball el básquetbol 7
Basque el eusquera
bass el bajo; el contrabajo 14
bat el bate 7; el murciélago
bathe bañarse 5
bathroom el baño 5
battery la pila
battle la batalla
be estar; ser
be . . . years old tener... años
be able poder (ue)
beach la playa 7
beak el pico
beans los frijoles 6
bear el oso
beat batir; latir
beautiful bello/a;
hermoso/a
beauty la belleza
beauty supply shop la
perfumería 8

be behind retrasar

be born nacer (zc)

be called llamarse **5**

because porque; pues

become (+ *adj.*) ponerse (+ *adj.*) **5**

become accustomed to acostumbrarse a

become angry enojarse

become aware enterarse

become happy alegrarse (de) **5**

become sick enfermarse **5**

bed la cama **5**

bedroom la alcoba; el cuarto **5**; el dormitorio **5**; la recámara

be enough bastar

beef la (carne de) res

beer la cerveza **6**

be extremely pleasing encantar

be familiar with (something) conocer (zc) **4**

be fascinating fascinar

before antes (de) (que)

begin comenzar (ie); empezar (ie) **4**; iniciar; **to begin** para empezar

beginning el comienzo; el inicio; el principio **13**

be glad alegrarse (de) **5**

behind atrás; detrás (de) **3**; tras

be interested animarse

be interesting interesar

belief la creencia

believe creer **2**

belly el buche

belong to pertenecer (zc) a

belongings las pertenencias

beloved amado/a

below debajo (de)

be missing faltar

bench el banco

benefit el beneficio **10**, **11**

be on sale/clearance estar en rebaja/liquidación **8**

be on a diet estar a dieta **10**

be out of work estar sin trabajo **11**

beside al lado (de) **3**

bestseller el superventas **13**

be successful tener éxito **13**

better mejor **5**

between entre **3**

beverage la bebida **6**

be worth valer

biased parcial

bicycle la bicicleta

big grande **1**

big hug un fuerte abrazo

bilingual bilingüe

bill la cuenta **6**

biography la biografía

biological biológico/a

biology la biología **3**

biosphere la biosfera

bird el pájaro; el ave (*fem.*)

birth el nacimiento

birthday el cumpleaños

birthrate el índice de natalidad; la natalidad

bite (insect) la picadura

bitter amargo/a

black negro/a **1**

blazer el saco; la americana (*Spain*)

bleachers las gradas

blender la licuadora

block el bloque; la cuadra; la manzana (*Spain*)

blond rubio/a **2**

blood la sangre

blood pressure la presión (arterial) **10**

blood vessel el vaso sanguíneo

blouse la blusa **8**

blow soplar

blue azul **1**

blue-footed booby el bobo de patas azules

board abordar **9**; la tabla

boarding gate la puerta de embarque **9**

boarding pass la tarjeta de embarque **9**

board of directors la junta directiva

board of trustees el patronato

boat el barco **9**

body el cuerpo **10**

bomb la bomba **15**

bone el hueso **10**

bonus la bonificación **11**

book el libro **1**

bookcase el estante **5**

bookstore la librería **3**

boot (tall rubber) la bota pantanera

boots las botas **8**

border la frontera

bore aburrir

bored aburrido/a **2**

boring aburrido/a **1**

borrow pedir (i, i) prestado

boss el/la jefe/a **11**

bother molestar

bottle la botella

bottom el fondo

bow el arco

bowl el tazón **6**

box la caja

box office la taquilla

boy el chico **3**; el muchacho **2**

boycott el boicot

boyfriend el novio **4**

bracelet la pulsera **8**

branch el ramo; la rama

brand la marca **12**

brandy el pisco (Peru)

Brazil Brasil **2**

Brazilian brasileño/a **2**

bread el pan **6**

break romper

break (a bone) romperse (un hueso) **10**

break a blood vessel reventar un vaso sanguíneo

break down dañarse; fallar **12**

breakfast el desayuno **6**

breath el aliento

breathe respirar **10**

bride la novia **4**

brief breve

briefcase el maletín

brightly colored colorido/a

brillant brillante

bring traer

broadcast transmitir **13**

brochure el folleto

broken roto/a

brother-in-law el cuñado **4**

brother el hermano **4**

brown castaño/a; color café **1**; marrón **1**; pardo/a

brunette castaño/a; moreno/a

brush el cepillo **5**; cepillarse **5**

bucket la cubeta

Buddhist budista

buddy el/la cuate (*Mexico*)

budget el presupuesto

building el edificio **3**

bull el toro

bullfighting la corrida de toros

bungee jump hacer salto en bungee

burn arder

bury enterrar (ie)

bus el autobús **9**; el camión (*Mexico*)

business el negocio

business administration la administración de empresas **3**

business class la clase ejecutiva **9**

business letter la carta comercial

business section la sección financiera **13**

businessman el empresario; el hombre de negocios **11**

businesswoman la empresaria; la mujer de negocios **11**

busy ocupado/a **2**

but pero; sino (que)

but rather sino (que)

butcher (shop) la carnicería **8**

butter la mantequilla **6**

buy comprar **2, 9**

by por

by chance por casualidad

by foot a pie

by way of mediante

C

cabinet el gabinete

cable television la televisión por cable **13**

cadaver el cadáver

café el café **4**
cafeteria la cafetería **3**
caffeine la cafeína
cake el pastel; la torta **6**
calcium el calcio
calculate calcular
calculator la calculadora **1**
calculus el cálculo **3**
call llamar **5**
call letters las siglas
calm down aquietar
calmly tranquilamente
calorie la caloría
camera la cámara
camp acampar; el
  campamento
campaign la campaña **15**
can poder (ue) **4**
Canada Canadá
Canadian canadiense **2**
canal el canal
cancel cancelar
cancer el cáncer **10**
candidate el/la
  candidato/a **15**
cane el bastón; la caña
cap la gorra **8**
capable capaz **11**
capacity la capacidad
capital city la capital **2**
capital letter la mayúscula
car el auto; el carro **9**;
  el coche
carbohydrates los
  carbohidratos **10**
card la tarjeta
cardiologist el/la
  cardiólogo/a
career la carrera **3**
careful cuidadoso/a
careful, to be tener
  cuidado
carpenter el/la
  carpintero/a **11**
carpet la alfombra
carrot la zanahoria **6**
carry llevar, portar
carry out llevar a cabo;
  realizar
cart el carro (*Spain*)
carved tallado/a
carving el tallado
cascades las cascadas
cash register la caja **8**

casserole dish la cazuela **6**
castanets las castañuelas
castle el castillo
cat el/la gato/a
cathedral la catedral **9**
Catholic católico/a
cattle el ganado
cause causar; la causa
cave la cueva
cavity (tooth) la caries
CD player el lector de CD
celebrate celebrar
celebration la celebración;
  la fiesta
celebrity la celebridad
celebrity magazine la
  revista del corazón **13**
cellist el/la chelista
cello el chelo **14**
cellophane el celofán
cell phone el teléfono
  celular/móvil **8**
Celtic celta
cemetery el cementerio
censorship la censura
censure censurar
census el censo
centennial el centenario
century el siglo
CEO el/la jefe/a
  ejecutivo/a **11**
ceramic la cerámica
ceremony la ceremonia
certain cierto/a; seguro/a
chain la cadena **8**
chair la silla **1**
chalk la tiza
chalkboard la pizarra **1**
challenge el desafío; el
  reto; challenge each
  other desafiarse; retarse
challenging exigente **3**
champagne el champán
champion el/la campeón/
  campeona **7**
change cambiar; el cambio
channel el canal **13**
chapel la capilla
character el carácter; el
  personaje **13**
characteristic la
  característica
charade la charada
charge cobrar

charger el cargador
charitable benéfico/a;
  caritativo/a
charm el encanto
chat chatear **7**
chauffeur el chofer
cheap barato/a **1**
check revisar **13**
check baggage facturar el
  equipaje **9**
checkup el examen físico **10**
cheer animar
cheese el queso **6**
chef el/la cocinero/a **11**
chemistry la química **3**
chest el pecho **10**
chew masticar
chick la cría
chicken el pollo **6**
chief el cacique
childish infantil
children los hijos; los/las
  niños/as
Chilean chileno/a **2**
chill el escalofrío
China China **2**
chinchilla la chinchilla
Chinese el chino
  (*language*); chino/a **2**
chiropractor el/la
  quiropráctico/a
chocolate el chocolate;
  chocolate cake la torta
  de chocolate
cholera el cólera
cholesterol el colesterol **10**
choose elegir (i, i);
  escoger (j)
chop picar **6**
choreograph coreografiar
choreographer el/la
  coreógrafo/a **14**
chores los quehaceres **5**
Christian cristiano/a
christianize cristianizar
Christmas la Navidad
chronic crónico/a
chronology la cronología
chubby gordo/a
church la iglesia
cinematographer el/la
  cinematógrafo/a
cinematography la
  cinematografía

circulation la circulación
citizen el/la
  ciudadano/a **15**
citizenship la ciudadanía
city la ciudad **2, 9**
city map el plano de la
  ciudad **9**
civil civil **11**
civilization la civilización
Civil War la Guerra Civil
clap la palmada; aplaudir **14**
clarinet el clarinete **14**
class la clase **1**
classic clásico/a
classical clásico/a
classical music la música
  clásica **14**
classified ads los avisos
  clasificados **11**; los
  anuncios clasificados
classmate el/la
  compañero/a de clase
classroom el salón de clase **1**
clause la cláusula
clean limpio/a **5**
clean (the house) limpiar,
  ordenar (la casa) **5**
cleaning service el
  servicio de limpieza
cleaning staff el/la
  camarero/a **9**
clear claro/a; cristalino/a;
  despejado/a; quitar **5**
clearance sale la
  liquidación **8**
clear the table quitar la
  mesa **5**
clearing el claro
clever listo/a
client el/la cliente/a
click on hacer clic (en) **12**
cliff el acantilado
climate el clima
climate change el cambio
  climático **12**
climb escalar; subir **9**
clinic la clínica
clinical clínico/a **11**
clip recortar
clock el reloj **1**
close cerrar (ie);
close (to) cerca (de) **3**;
  próximo/a; unido/a **4**
closed cerrado/a

close-knit unido/a **4**
closing la despedida
cloth la tela
clothes dryer la secadora **5**
clothing la ropa **8**; la vestimenta
clothing size la talla **8**
cloud la nube **12**
cloudy nublado/a **7**
coach el/la entrenador/a **7**
coach class la clase turista **9**
coal el carbón **12**
coast la costa
coat el abrigo **8**
cobblestone el adoquín
coconut el coco
code el código
coffee el café **6**; **coffee with (hot) milk** el café con leche **6**
coffee maker la cafetera **6**
coin la moneda
coincide coincidir
coincidentally por casualidad
cold el resfriado **10**; el frío; frío/a
cold, it's (very) hace (mucho) frío **7**
collaborate colaborar **12**
collar el cuello
colleague el/la colega
collect recoger **5**
collection la colección
cologne la colonia **8**
Colombian colombiano/a **2**
colonizer el/la colonizador/a
colony la colonia
coloring colorido/a
comb el peine **5**
combat combatir **15**
combatant el/la combatiente
combination la combinación
comb (one's hair) peinarse **5**
come venir (ie) **4**
comedy la comedia **13, 14**
comfort la comodidad
comfortable cómodo/a
comforts las comodidades

comic cómico/a
comic strip la tira cómica
command el mandato
commemorate conmemorar
comment comentar
commentary el comentario
commentator el/la comentarista **13**
commerce el comercio
commission la comisión; la tarifa
commit cometer
commitment el compromiso
committee el comité
common común
commonwealth el estado libre asociado
communications las comunicaciones **3**
community la comunidad **12**
compact disc (CD) el disco compacto
companion el/la acompañante
company la compañía; la empresa **11**
compare comparar
comparison la comparación
compatriot el/la compatriota
compensation la recompensa
compete competir (i, i) **7**
competition la competencia **7**
complain quejarse
complement complementar
complete completo/a; cumplir
complex complejo/a **10**
complicate complicar
complicated complicado/a **3**
compliment el piropo
compose componer **14**
composer el/la compositor/a **14**
composition la composición
comprehension la comprensión

computer la computadora **1**
computer game el juego electrónico **12**
computer science la computación **3**; la informática **3**
conceited ufano/a
concept el concepto
concert el concierto **4**
conclusion el desenlace
concrete concreto/a
condemn condenar
condemned condenado/a
condiment el condimento **6**
condition la condición **10**
conditioner el acondicionador **5, 8**
condor el cóndor
conduct dirigir
conductor el/la conductora; el/la director/a **14**
confidence la confianza
conflict el conflicto **15**
confront enfrentar
confuse confundir
congested congestionado/a
congress el congreso
congressman/woman el/la congresista
conjecture la conjetura
connect conectar
connection la conexión
connoisseur el/la conocedor/a
conquer vencer
conquest la conquista
consensus el consenso
consequence la consecuencia
conservative conservador/a
conserve conservar **12**
consider considerar
considerate considerado/a
considered considerado/a
console games los jueguitos de consola
construct construir
construction la construcción

construction worker el/la obrero/a de construcción **11**
consult consultar
consultant el/la asesor/a **15**
consume consumir **12**
consumer el/la consumidor/a
consumption el consumo
contact contactar
contain contener (ie)
container el contenedor; el envase **12**
contaminate contaminar **12**
contemporaneous contemporáneo/a
content el contenido
contest el concurso **13**
contestant el/la concursante **13**
continue continuar
contract contratar; el contrato **11**
contrast el contraste
contribute contribuir
contribution el aporte
control controlar **15**
controversy la polémica
conventional convencional
conversation la conversación
converse conversar
convert convertir (ie, i)
conviction la convicción
convince convencer (z)
cook cocinar **6**; el/la cocinero/a **11**
cookies las galletas **6**
cool copado/a (*Argentina*)
cool, it's hace fresco **7**
cooler la heladera **7**
cooperate cooperar
coordinator el/la coordinador/a
copper el cobre
copy la copia
cord la cuerda
Cordially yours . . . Cordialmente…
corduroy la pana **14**
corn el maíz **6**
corner la esquina
cornet la corneta **14**

correct acertado/a; corregir (i, i)
correspondent el/la corresponsal
corridor el corredor
corruption la corrupción
cosmopolitan cosmopolita
cost costar (ue) **4**; valer; el costo
co-star el/la compañero/a de reparto
Costa Rican costarricense
costly costoso/a
costume el disfraz **14**
cotton el algodón **8, 14**
couch el sofá **5**
cough la tos **10**; toser **10**
cough syrup el jarabe **10**
counselor el/la consejero/a
counter el mostrador **9**
country el campo; el país **2, 15**
countryman el paisano
countryside el campo **9**
countrywoman la paisana
coup d'état el golpe de estado **15**
couple la pareja
course el curso; la materia **3**; **course, of** claro **4**
court el tribunal **15**; la cancha **3**
cousin el/la primo/a **4**
cover cubrir
covered cubierto/a
cover letter la carta de presentación **11**
cow la vaca
cowardice la cobardía
crackling el chicharrón
crazy loco/a
cream la crema **5**
create crear
creativity la creatividad
creator el/la creador/a
credit card la tarjeta de crédito **8**
creole criollo/a
crest of the waves la cresta de las olas
cricket la cigarra
crime el crimen
critic el/la crítico/a **13**
crocodile el cocodrilo

cross cruzar
cross-country el campo abierto
crucial indispensable
crude grosero/a
cruise el crucero **9**
crush machacar; pisar
cry el grito; llorar
crystalline cristalino/a
Cuban cubano/a **2**
cuisine la cocina
culinary culinario/a
culture la cultura
cultured culto/a
cup la taza **6**
cure curar
curious curioso/a
currency exchange la casa de cambio **9**
current actual **15**; vigente
current events la actualidad
currently actualmente
curriculum vitae (vita) el currículum vitae **11**
curved curvado/a
custard dessert el flan **6**
custom la costumbre
customer el/la cliente/a **8**
customer service la atención al cliente
customs la aduana **9**
customs inspector el/la inspector/a de aduanas **9**
customs officer el/la aduanero/a
cut cortar **6**
cute bonito/a **2**
cycling el ciclismo **7**

D

dad el papá
daddy el papi
daily diario/a **5**
dairy lácteo/a
dairy products los productos lácteos
dam el embalse; la represa
damage dañar; el daño; perjudicar
dance bailar **2**; el baile **14**; la danza **14**
danceable bailable

dancer el/la bailarín/ bailarina **14**
danger el peligro
dangerous peligroso/a
daring atrevido/a
dark oscuro/a
dark (skin, hair) moreno/a **2**
data los datos
date la fecha
daughter la hija **4**
daughter-in-law la nuera **4**
dawn el amanecer; la madrugada
day el día
day before yesterday anteayer
daycare center la guardería **11**
day laborer el/la jornalero/a
Day of the Dead el Día de los Muertos
days of the week los días de la semana
dear querido/a
death la muerte
debate debatir **15**; el debate
debt la deuda **15**
debut debutar; el debut; estrenar
decade la década
decaffeinated descafeinado/a
deceit el engaño
deceive engañar
December diciembre **1**
decide decidir **2**
declaration la declaración
decoration la decoración
decrease bajar; disminuir
dedicate dedicar
dedicated dedicado/a
deep profundo/a
deeply profundamente **10**
defeat rendir (i, i)
defect el defecto
defend defender (ie)
defiant desafiante
define definir
deforestation la deforestación **12**

degree el grado; el título; la licenciatura
degree course of study la carrera académica
delay la demora **9**
delicious delicioso/a; rico/a **6**; sabroso/a **6**
delight el encanto; encantar **6**; la delicia
Delighted. Encantado/a.
delightful encantador/a **14**
deliver entregar; repartir **11**
demanding exigente **3**
democracy la democracia **15**
democratization la democratización
demographic demográfico/a
denounce denunciar
dentist el/la dentista **11**
deny negar (ie)
deodorant el desodorante **8**
department el departamento
department store el almacén **8**
departure la salida **9**
depict describir
depopulation la despoblación
deposit el depósito; el yacimiento
depression la depresión **10**
derive derivar
descend descender (ie)
descendant el/la descendiente
describe describir
description la descripción **8**
desert el desierto
deserted desierto/a
deserve merecer (zc)
design diseñar **11**; el diseño
designed diseñado/a
designer el/la diseñador/a **14**
desire desear; el deseo
desk el escritorio
dessert el postre **6**
destination el destino **9**
destroy destruir
detach desprender

detail el detalle
detain detener (ie); retrasar
deteriorate deteriorar
detest detestar
develop desarrollar
developing en vías de desarrollo **15**
development el desarrollo **12**
device el aparato **12**
diabetes la diabetes **10**
diagnosis el diagnóstico **10**
diamond de diamantes **8**; el diamante
dictator el/la dictador/a **15**
dictatorship la dictadura **15**
dictionary el diccionario **1**
die morir (ue, u)
diet la dieta **10**; el régimen
different diferente; distinto/a
difficult difícil **2**
dig up desenterrar (ie)
digital camera la cámara digital
digital media los medios digitales **12**
dignify dignificar
dignity la dignidad
dilemma el dilema
diminish disminuir
dining room el comedor **5**
dinner la cena **6**
direct dirigir
directed dirigido/a
directly directamente
director el/la director/a **11, 14**
dirty sucio/a **5**
disabled person el/la discapacitado/a
disadvantage la desventaja **11**
disappear desaparecer (zc)
disarm desarmar
disarmament el desarme **15**
disaster el desastre **15**
discount el descuento **8**
discouraged desanimado/a
discover descubrir
discovered descubierto/a

discovery el descubrimiento
discreet discreto/a
discussion la discusión
disguise el disfraz **14**
disgust el asco **6**
dishes los platos **5**
dishonest deshonesto/a
dishonor deshonrar
dishwasher el lavaplatos **5**
disillusion defraudar; desilusionar
disillusionment el desengaño
disorder el desorden
disorganized desordenado/a **5**
disoriented desorientado/a
display case la vitrina
disposed dispuesto/a
dispute disputar
distance la distancia
distance learning el aprendizaje a distancia **12**
distant retirado/a
distribute repartir **11**
diva la diva
diversity la diversidad
divide partir, dividir
diving el clavadismo
divorced divorciado/a **2**
do hacer **3, 7**
do aerobics hacer ejercicios aeróbicos **10**
do yoga hacer yoga **7**
doable factible
doctor el/la doctor/a; el/la médico/a **10**
doctorate el doctorado
doctor's office el consultorio **10**
document el documento **12**
documentary el documental **13**
dog el/la perro/a **4**
dog walker el/la paseador/a de perros
dollar el dólar
domestic doméstico/a
dominate dominar
Dominican dominicano/a **2**

donate donar
Don't worry. No te preocupes.
door la puerta **1**
dossier el expediente
dot, on the en punto **2**
dotted salpicado/a
double doble **9**
double room el cuarto doble **9**
doubt dudar; la duda
doubtful dudoso/a
dough la masa
download bajar **12**
downtown el centro **4**
dowry la dote
Do you want go to . . . ? ¿Quieres ir a...? **4**
drama el drama **13**
dramatic dramático/a
dramatize dramatizar
draw dibujar
drawing el dibujo
draw up encoger (j)
dream el sueño
dream (about) soñar (ue) (con) **4**
dreamer el/la soñador/a
dress el vestido **8**; vestir (i, i) **14**
dresser la cómoda **5**
drink la bebida; beber; tomar **2, 6, 10**
drive conducir (zc); manejar
dropout el/la desertor/a
drought la sequía **12**
drug la droga
drug addiction la drogadicción **15**
drum el tambor **14**
drums la batería **14**
dry seco/a
dry (yourself) off secarse **5**
dryer la secadora **5**
duck el pato
durability la durabilidad
during durante; por
dust sacudir
Dutch holandés, holandesa
duty el deber **15**
DVD el DVD

DVD player la grabadora de DVD
dynamic dinámico/a

E

each cada
eager, to be tener ganas
eagle el águila (*fem.*)
ear (inner) el oído **10**; **ear (outer)** la oreja **10**
earbuds los auriculares **12**
early temprano/a
earn ganar **4**
earrings (pendants) los pendientes **8**; **(posts)** los aretes **8**
earth el barro; la tierra
earthquake el terremoto
easily fácilmente
easy fácil **2**
eat comer **2, 6, 10**
eat a snack merendar (ie) **6**
eat breakfast desayunar **6**
eat dinner cenar **6**
eat lunch almorzar (ue) **6**
eBook reader el lector de libros electrónicos **12**
ecological ecológico/a
economic económico/a
economical económico/a **9**
economics la economía **3**
economy la economía
ecotourism el ecoturismo
eco-volunteering el eco voluntariado
Ecuadorian ecuatoriano/a **2**
edge la orilla
edit editar
editing la redacción
edition la edición
editor el/la editor/a
editorial (section) el editorial **13**
editor-in-chief el/la director/a **13**
educate educar
education la educación; la formación **11**; la pedagogía **3**
effective efectivo/a
efficient eficiente
effort el esfuerzo **15**
egg el huevo **6**
eggplant la berenjena

eighth octavo/a

either tampoco **7**

either . . . or o... o **7**

elaborate elaborar

elaborated elaborado/a

elaboration la elaboración

elastic el elástico **14**

elbow el codo

elbow jab el codazo

elderly person el/la anciano/a; el/la viejo/a

elect elegir (i, i) **15**

elected electo/a

election la elección

electoral electoral **15**

electrical eléctrico/a **11**

electrical adaptor el adaptador eléctrico

electrical engineering la ingeniería eléctrica **3**

electric current la corriente

electrician el/la electricista

electricity la electricidad

electric shaver la máquina de afeitar **5**

electrifying electrizante

electronic electrónico/a **12**

electronic devices los aparatos electrónicos **12**

electronic game el juego electrónico **12**

elimination la eliminación

e-mail el correo electrónico **3**

emanate emanar

embassy la embajada

emblem el logotipo

embrace abrazar; el abrazo

embroider bordar

emerald la esmeralda

emerge surgir

emergency room la sala de urgencias **10**

emotion la emoción **5**

emotional emocional

empire el imperio

employee el/la empleado/a **11**

employment el empleo **11**

employment application la solicitud de empleo **11**

empty vaciar **5**

enchanting encantador/a **14**

enclose encerrar (ie)

enclosed cubierto/a

encounter el encuentro

encourage animar

end el fin; el final; eliminar **15**; terminar

endangered species las especies en peligro de extinción **12**

end well salir bien

enemy el/la enemigo/a

energy la energía **12**

engineer el/la ingeniero/a **11**

engineering la ingeniería **3**

England Inglaterra **2**

English el inglés (*language*); inglés, inglesa **2**

enjoy disfrutar (de); gozar (de)

enjoy oneself divertirse (ie, i)

Enjoy (your meal)! ¡Buen provecho! **6**

enormous enorme

ensure asegurar **12**

entertain entretener (ie)

entertainment el entretenimiento

entertainment section la cartelera **13**

enthusiastic entusiasta **11**

enthusiastically animadamente

entrepreneur el/la emprendedor/a **11**

environment el medio ambiente **12**

environmental ambiental

epoch la época

equality la igualdad

equally igual de

equator la línea ecuatorial

equipment el equipo **7**

equity la equidad

eradicate erradicar

erase borrar **12**

eruption la erupción

escape escapar(se)

escort el/la acompañante

especially especialmente

essential esencial; preciso/a

establish establecer (zc)

esteemed estimado/a

eternal eterno/a

ethics la ética

ethnic étnico/a

ethnicity la etnia

e-ticket el boleto electrónico **9**

even aún; incluso

even though aunque **7**

evening la noche

evening gown el traje de noche **14**

event el acontecimiento; el evento **11**; la función

events organizer el/la organizador/a de eventos **11**

even though aunque **7**

every todo/a(s)

everyone todo/a(s)

evolution la evolución

exaggerate exagerar

exam el examen; **exam time** la época del examen

example el ejemplo; **for example** por ejemplo

excellent excelente

exceptional excepcional

excessive excesivo/a

excess weight el sobrepeso **10**

exchange el cambio; el intercambio; intercambiar

exchange student el/la estudiante de intercambio

exciting emocional; emocionante

excursion la excursión **9**

excuse la excusa

Excuse me. Perdone. **1**

excuse oneself retirarse

execution la ejecución

executive el/la ejecutivo/a

exercise el ejercicio; ejercer (z) **15**; hacer ejercicio

exhausted exhausto/a

exhibit exhibir

exist existir

exotic exótico/a

expand ampliar

expect esperar

expectation la expectativa

expense el gasto

expensive caro/a **1**; costoso/a

experience experimentar; la experiencia

expiration date la fecha de vencimiento

explain explicar; exponer

explicit explícito/a

exploit explotar

exploitation la explotación

export exportar

exposition la exposición

express expresar

express an opinion opinar

express oneself expresarse

expression la expresión **1, 11**

extend extender (ie)

extensive extenso/a

extinction la extinción

extinguish (fires) apagar (fuegos/incendios)

extraordinary extraordinario/a

extreme extremo/a

eye el ojo **5**

F

fable la fábula

fabric la tela **14**

fabricate fabricar

fabulous fabuloso/a **7**

face afrontar **15**; enfrentar; la cara **5**

facial cream la cream hidratante **8**

facilitate facilitar

facility la facilidad

facing enfrente (de) **3**

factor el factor

factory la fábrica **12**

fail (computer disk) fallar

fair justo/a **11**; la feria

fairly bastante

fall la caída; el otoño **1**

fall down caerse

fall asleep dormirse (ue, u) **5**

fall in love (with) enamorarse (de) **5**

falls las cataratas, el salto de agua
false falso/a
familiarize oneself familiarizarse
family la familia **4**
fan el/la aficionado/a
fanatic el/la fanático/a
fantastic de película; fantástico/a
fantasy la fantasía
far (from) lejos (de) **3**
faraway lejano/a
fare el pasaje **9**
farewell la despedida **1**
farm la granja
farmer el/la campesino/a; el/la granjero/a
fascinating fascinante
fashion la moda **14**
fashion show el desfile de moda **14**
fat gordo/a **2**; la grasa **10**
father el padre **4**
father-in-law el suegro **4**
fatigue el cansancio; la fatiga
fatty grasoso/a
favor of, in a favor de
fear el temor; temer; tener (ie) miedo
feature el reportaje **13**; resaltar
February febrero **1**
fee la comisión; la tarifa
feel sentirse (ie, i) **5**
feel like tener (ie) ganas
feeling safe el sentido de seguridad
feminine femenino/a
femininity la feminidad
ferocious feroz
fetus el feto
fever la fiebre **10**
fiber la fibra **10**
fiction la ficción
field la carrera **3**
fifth quinto/a
fight la pelea; combatir **15**
figure la figura; la línea **10**
file archivar
fill out (completely) rellenar **11**
filled relleno/a

filling el relleno
fill (the dishwasher) llenar (el lavaplatos) **5**
film la peli; la película **4**; filmar **13**; rodar (ue)
filming el rodaje; la filmación
film noir el filme negro
finally al final; por fin; por último
finance las finanzas
financial financiero/a **11**
financial section la sección financiera **13**
find encontrar (ue) **4, 5**
find out (about) enterarse de **11**
fine la multa; multar **12**
fine with me de acuerdo **4**
finger el dedo **10**
finish acabar; terminar
finish line la meta
fire despedir (i, i) **11**; el fuego; el incendio
fire truck la bomba **15**
firefighter el/la bombero/a
fireworks los fuegos artificiales
firm la compañía; la empresa **11**
first primer/o/a
fish el pescado **6**; pescar **9**
fisherman/woman el/la pescador/a
fishing pesquero/a
fit encajar; quedar
fitting room el probador **8**
flame la llama
flamenco el flamenco **14**; flamenco/a
flamingo el flamenco
flank flanquear
flash drive la memoria USB
flat top la cima plana
flavor el sabor
flea market el mercado callejero
flee huir
flyer el volante
flight el vuelo **9**
flight attendant el/la asistente de vuelo **9**
flip-flop la chancla **8**
flood la inundación **12**

floor el piso **5**
floor plan el plano
flour la harina
flourish florecer (zc)
flower la flor
flower shop la florería **8**
flu la gripa (*Mexico*); la gripe **10**
flute la flauta **14**
fly volar (ue) **7**
fog la niebla
follow seguir (i, i) **4, 10**
follower el/la seguidor/a
following a continuación; siguiente
food la comida
foods los alimentos
fool el/la necio/a
foot el pie **10**
football el fútbol americano **7**
footwear el calzado
for para; por
for example por ejemplo
for me para mí
for you para ti
force la fuerza
forecast el pronóstico
foreign extranjero/a
foreigner el/la extranjero/a
forest el bosque **9, 12**
forget olvidar(se) (de) **5**
fork el tenedor **6**
form el formulario **11**; formar
formula la fórmula
formulate formular
fortify afianzar; fortalecer (zc)
fortress la fortaleza; el fuerte
fortune teller el/la adivino/a
forum el foro
fossil fuel el combustible fósil **12**
found fundar
foundation la fundación
founded fundado/a
founding la fundación
fourth cuarto/a
four-wheel-drive vehicle el todoterreno

fox el zorro
fragment el fragmento
framework el marco
France Francia **2**
fraud el fraude **15**
free gratis; libre
freezer el congelador
French el francés (*language*); francés/ francesa **2**
French fries las papas fritas
frequent frecuente
frequently con frecuencia; frecuentemente
fresh fresco/a
Friday el viernes
fried frito/a **6**
friend el/la amigo/a **2**
from desde
front, in enfrente
frontier la frontera
front of, in delante de
front page la portada; la primera plana **13**
fruit el fruto; las frutas **6**
fry freír (i, i) **6**
frying pan la sartén **6**
fulfill cumplir (con) **15**
full-time a tiempo completo **11**
fun divertido/a
function funcionar **12**; la función
funds los fondos
funny gracioso/a
fur la piel **14**
furnish armar
furnished amueblado/a
furniture los muebles **5**
fury la furia
fuse fusionar
fusion la fusión
future el futuro

G

gabardine (lightweight wool) la gabardina
gain weight engordar **10**; subir de peso **10**
game (sports) el partido **4**
game show el concurso **13**
garage el garaje **5**

garbage la basura **5**
garbage can el basurero
garden el jardín **5**
garlic el ajo **6**
garment la prenda **14**
gasoline la gasolina
gather congregar
gathering la recolección
GDP (Gross Domestic Product) el PIB (Producto Interno Bruto)
genealogical genealógico/a
general, in por lo general
generalize generalizar
generally generalmente
generate generar
generation la generación
generous generoso/a
genetic genético/a
genre el género
geography la geografía **3**
geology la geología **3**
German el alemán (*language*); alemán/alemana **2**
Germany Alemania **2**
gesture el ademán; el gesto
get conseguir (i, i) **11**; **get (+ *adj.*)** ponerse (+ *adj.*) **5**
get angry (with) enojarse (con) **5**
get better mejorarse **10**
get down (from) bajarse (de) **9**
get dressed vestirse (i, i) **5**
get in shape ponerse en forma **10**
get involved in meterse
get married casarse
get off (of) bajarse (de) **9**
get tired cansarse
get together juntarse
get-together la reunión
get up levantarse **5**; **get up on the wrong side of the bed** levantarse con el pie izquierdo
get well mejorarse **10**
getting started para empezar
gift el don; el regalo
gift card la tarjeta prepaga
girl la chica **3**; la muchacha **2**
girlfriend la novia **4**

give dar
give (as a gift) regalar
give up rendirse (i, i)
glacier el glaciar **9**
glance la mirada
glass el vaso **6**; el vidrio **12**
glass bowl el tazón de cristal **6**
glasses las gafas; los lentes
globalization la globalización
global market el mercado global **15**
global warming el calentamiento global
glory la gloria
glove el guante **7**
go ir (a) **3, 5**
go bike riding montar en bicicleta **7**
go by boat ir en barco **9**
go horseback riding montar a caballo **9**
go to a concert ir a un concierto **7**
go to a festival ir a un festival **7**
goal el gol; el propósito; la meta **11**
go to a nightclub ir a un club nocturno **7**
go away alejarse; irse **5**; marcharse
go to bed acostarse (ue) **5**
Go to the board. Ve (Vayan) a la pizarra. **1**
go bike riding montar en bicicleta **7**
go grocery shopping hacer las compras **5**
god el dios
God willing Ojalá **9**
gold de oro **8**; el oro
gold ring el anillo de oro
golf el golf **7**
good bueno/a **1**; el bien
Good afternoon. Buenas tardes. **1**
Good-bye. Adiós. **1**; ¡Chao!
good deal la ganga **8**
Good evening. Buenas noches. **1**
good-looking guapo/a **2**

Good morning. Buenos días. **1**
Good night. Buenas noches.
good weather el buen tiempo **7**
goodness la bondad
goods los bienes
gorgeous bellísimo/a
go on an outing ir de excursión **9**
go out dar un paseo **7**; salir **4**; **go out to eat** salir a comer **7**
go round recorrer **9**
go through (security) pasar por (seguridad) **9**
go shopping ir de compras
gossipy chismoso/a
go up subir
gourd la calabaza (*Argentina*)
government el gobierno **15**
governmental gubernamental
governor el/la gobernador/a **15**
go well (with) hacer juego (con) **8**
go with acompañar
grab agarrar
grade la nota
grain el grano
grammar la gramática
granddaughter la nieta **4**
grandfather el abuelo **4**
grandma la abuelita (*diminutive*)
grandmother la abuela **4**
grandson el nieto **4**
grant conceder; otorgar
grapefruit la toronja **6**
grapes las uvas **6**; **Grape Harvest Feast** la Fiesta de la Vendimia
grave el sepulcro
gray gris **1**
gray hair la cana
great fabuloso/a **7**; magnífico/a
Great Depression la Gran Depresión
greed la codicia
green verde **1, 12**

green beans las judías verdes **6**
green pepper el pimiento verde
greeting/s el/los saludo/s **1**
grill la parrilla; la parrillada
grilled a la parrilla **6**
grind moler (ue)
groceries los comestibles
groom el novio **4**
ground transport el transporte terrestre
group el conjunto **14**; el grupo **14**
growing creciendo; creciente
grow up criarse
grumpy gruñón/gruñona
Guarani language el guaraní
guarantee garantizar
guaranteed garantizado/a
guard el/la guardia
guava la guayaba
guess la conjetura; adivinar
guest el/la huésped/a; el/la invitado/a
guest la visita
guide el guía; guiar
guidebook la guía turística **9**
guinea pig el cuy
guitar la guitarra **14**
guitar-like instrument el charango
gymnasium el gimnasio **3**
gymnastics la gimnasia **7**
gypsy el/la gitano/a

H

habit el hábito
haggle over regatear **8**
haggling el regateo
hair el pelo **5**
hairdresser el/la peluquero/a **11**
hair dryer el secador **5**
hairstylist el/la peluquero/a
half medio/a **2**
Halloween la Noche de Brujas
hallway el pasillo **5**

ham el jamón **6**

hamburger la hamburguesa

hammock la hamaca

hand la mano **5; by hand** a mano

handicraft la artesanía

hang colgar (ue)

hanging bridge el puente colgante

hang glide hacer parapente

hang gliding el parapente

happen pasar

happily alegremente

happiness la felicidad

happy contento/a **2, 5;** feliz

hard drive el disco duro

hardworking trabajador/a **1**

harm el daño; perjudicar **12**

harmful nocivo/a

harp el arpa (*fem.*) **14**

harvest la cosecha; recolectar

hatchery el criadero

hatchling la cría

hatred el odio

have tener (ie) **1**

have a good/bad/ wonderful time pasarlo bien/mal/de maravilla **7, 9**

have a great time pasarlo bomba

have a picnic hacer un pícnic **7**

have a point tener (ie) razón

have a second helping repetir (i, i) **4**

have a stroke tener (ie) un derrame cerebral

have fun divertirse (ie, i) **5**

have lunch (with me/ with you) almorzar (ue) (conmigo/contigo) **4**

have just (done something) acabar de (+ *inf.*)

have to tener (ie) que

hay el heno

he él

he was fue

head encabezar; la cabeza **10**

headache el dolor de cabeza **10**

headline el titular **13**

headphones los auriculares **12**

headquarters la sede

head office la sede

healer el/la curandero/a

health la salud **10**

health care worker el/la profesional de la salud **11**

health insurance el seguro médico **11**

healthy saludable

hear oír

heart el corazón **10**

heat calentar (ie) **6**

heaven el cielo

heaven's (*lit.* God's) sake, for por Dios

heavy pesado/a

heavy rain el chubasco

heel el tacón **8**

height la estatura

helicopter el helicóptero

Hello Hola. **1**

Hello? (*on the phone*) ¿Bueno?; ¿Diga?; ¿Dígame?

helmet el casco

help ayudar **2;** el socorro; la ayuda

her su/sus

herbal medicine el medicamento herbal **10**

here aquí **1**

heritage el patrimonio; la herencia

hero el héroe **9**

heron la garza

Hi. Hola. **1**

hieroglyphic el jeroglífico

high-definition television el televisor de alta definición

high fashion la alta costura **14**

high-heeled shoes los zapatos de tacón alto **8**

high plateau el altiplano

high speed la alta velocidad

highway la carretera

hike el trekking

hill el cerro **9**

hire contratar **11**

his su/sus

Hispanic hispano/a

historical histórico/a

historical center el centro histórico **9**

history la historia **3**

hit (*baseball*) el imparable

hockey el hockey **7**

holiday el día festivo

Holy Week la Semana Santa

home la casa **5;** el hogar

home (*web site*) el inicio **13**

homeopathy la homeopatía

homework la tarea **1**

honest honesto/a **11;** honrado/a **11**

honesty la honestidad **15;** la honradez **15**

honeymoon la luna de miel

honored honrado/a

hood la capucha **8**

hope la esperanza; **hope for** esperar **9**

horn el claxon, la corneta **14**

horoscope el horóscopo **13**

horrified horrorizado/a

horse el caballo

horseman el huaso (*Chile*)

hospital el hospital

hostel el hostal **9**

host/hostess el/la anfitrión/anfitriona; (*on television, radio*) el/la presentador/a **13**

hot caliente **6;** picante (*spicy*) **6**

hot, it's (very) hace (mucho) calor **7**

hot plate el comal

hot, to be tener (ie) calor

hotel el hotel **9**

house albergar; la casa **5**

house specialty la especialidad de la casa **6**

household appliance el aparato doméstico

household chores los quehaceres domésticos **5**

housing la vivienda

housewife el ama de casa (*fem.*)

how cómo

How . . . ? ¿Cómo...? **2**

How about . . . ? ¿Qué tal si...? **4**

How are you? (*for.*) ¿Cómo está usted? **1**

How are you? (*inf.*) ¿Cómo estás? **1**

How awesome! ¡Qué padre! (*Mexico*)

How can I help you? ¿En qué puedo servirle(s)? **8**

How could it be? ¿Por qué será?

How delicious! ¡Qué rico/a, sabroso/a! **6**

How do you say . . . ? ¿Cómo se dice...? **1**

How do you write . . . ? ¿Cómo se escribe...? **1**

How does it / do they fit? ¿Qué tal le queda(n)? **8**

How embarrassing! ¡Qué vergüenza!

How lucky! ¡Qué suerte! **2**

How much/many . . . ? Cuánto/a(s)...? **2**

How revolting! ¡Qué asco! **6**

How terrific! ¡Qué bárbaro!

however sin embargo

hug el a abrazo; a **big hug** un fuerte abrazo

human humano/a **10**

human being el ser humano

humanist humanista

humanity la humanidad

human resources los recursos humanos

human right el derecho humano **15**

humble humilde

humid, it's (very) hace (mucha) humedad **7**

humidity la humedad

humility la humildad

humorous humorístico/a

hundred cien(to)

hundreds los centenares
hunger el hambre
hunt cazar
hunting la caza
hurricane el huracán
hurry tener (ie) prisa
hurt doler (ue) **10**
hurt oneself hacerse daño (*Spain*); lastimarse **10**
husband el esposo **4**
hut (small) la maloca
hybrid híbrido/a
hyperlink el enlace; el hipervínculo **12**
hypothesis la hipótesis
hypothetical hipotético/a

I

I yo
Iberian ibero/a, ibérico/a
ice el hielo **7**
ice cream el helado **6**
ice cream shop la heladería **8**
I'd like to have . . . Deseo tomar... **6**
ideal el ideal
idealistic idealista
identify identificar
identity la identidad
ideology la ideología
I don't know. No sé. **1**
I don't understand. No comprendo. **1**
I hope Ojalá **9**; Espero
I like . . . Me gusta/n... **2**
I would like . . . Me gustaría... **8**
I'll come by for you. Paso por ti. **4**
I'll pick you up. Paso por ti. **4**
illegality la ilegalidad
illness la enfermedad **10**
illogical ilógico/a
illuminate iluminar
illusion la ilusión
illustrate ilustrar
image la imagen
imagine imaginar
immediate inmediato/a
immediately inmediatamente
immense inmenso/a

immigration la inmigración **9, 15**
immorality la inmoralidad
immunology la inmunología
impassion apasionar
impatient impaciente
implement implementar
import importar
important importante
impossible imposible
impresario el empresario
impress impresionar
impressive impresionante
improve mejorar **15**
improvise improvisar **14**
I'm sorry. Lo siento. **1; I'm sorry, I have to . . .** Lo siento, tengo que... **4**
I'm very busy. Estoy muy ocupado/a. **4**
in en **3**
in addition además
in agreement de acuerdo
inaugurate inaugurar
Inca inca; **Inca Trail** el Camino Inca
in case en caso de que
in cash en efectivo **8**
in conclusion para concluir
in fact de hecho
in favor a favor
in front (of) delante (de) **3**
in love (with) enamorado/a (de) **2**
incentive el incentivo
include incluir
including incluso
incorporate incorporar
increase aumentar **15**; el aumento
incredible increíble
indefinite indefinido/a
indefinite articles los artículos indefinidos
index el índice
indicate indicar
indifferent indiferente
indigenous indígena
industry la industria
inexpensive barato/a **1**
infection la infección **10**

inflation la inflación **15**
influence influir; la influencia
influenced influido/a
influential influyente
inform informar
information el dato
ingredient el ingrediente
inhabit habitar
inhabitant el/la habitante
iniciate iniciar
initiated iniciado/a
initiative la iniciativa
injured lastimado/a
injury la lesión
injustice la injusticia **15**
ink la tinta
in-laws la familia política
inn el hostal
in need necesitado/a
inner ear el oído **10**
innovative innovador/a
in order that a fin de que; para que
in order to para
in pairs en parejas
insert insertar
inside of dentro de
insist (on) insistir (en)
inspect inspeccionar; revisar **9**
inspiration la inspiración
inspiring inspirador/a
install instalar **12**
instance la vez **5**
instrument el instrumento **14**
in style de moda **8, 14**
intact intacto/a
integration la integración
intelligent inteligente
intense intenso/a
interactive whiteboard la pizarra interactiva **1**
intercity bus el autobús
interest el interés
interesting interesante
intern el/la pasante
international internacional
Internet, on the en Internet **12**
Internet troll el/la trol **12**

internship el internado; la pasantía
interpreter el/la intérprete **11**
intervention la intervención
interview la entrevista **11**
interviewer el/la entrevistador/a
intimate íntimo/a
intonation la entonación
intrigue la intriga
introduction la presentación **1, 11**
introverted introvertido/a
invasion la invasión
invent inventar
invest invertir (ie, i)
investigate investigar
investigation la investigación
investment la inversion
invitation la invitación **4**
invite invitar
involve involucrar
Irish irlandés/irlandesa
iron el hierro; la plancha; planchar **5**
ironic irónico/a
irrigation el riego
Is . . . ? ¿Está...?
island la isla **9**
issue la cuestión **15**
it lo/la
it almost never rains casi nunca llueve
It fits fine/small/large. Me queda bien/estrecho(a)/ grande. **8**
Italian italiano/a **2**; el italiano (*language*)
Italy Italia **2**
item la pieza
itinerary el itinerario
it's . . . hace... **7**
It's a perfect day for . . . Es un día perfecto para... **7**
It's all the same to me. Me da igual. **7**
it's cloudy está nublado **7**
It's my treat! ¡Te invito! **4**
it's your turn te toca a ti
I would love to. Me encantaría. **4**

J

jacket la chaqueta 8
jaguar el jaguar
jail la cárcel
January enero 1
Japan Japón 2
Japanese japonés/a 2; el japonés (*language*)
jazz el jazz 14
jealous celoso/a
jealousy los celos
jeans los jeans; los mecánicos (*Cuba*); los pantalones de mezclilla (*Mexico*); los tejanos (*Spain*); los vaqueros (*Spain*) 8
jelly la jalea
jerky el charqui
Jesuit el jesuita
Jew el/la judío/a
jewel la joya
jewelry store la joyería 8
Jewish judío/a
job el puesto 11
job application la solicitud de empleo
job candidate el/la aspirante
job search la búsqueda de empleo 11
jog hacer footing; hacer jogging
jogging el jogging 7
join incorporarse
join (a social media site) unirse (a un sitio social) 12
join forces unirse (a) 15
joke la broma
journalist el/la periodista 11
judge el/la juez/a 15
juice el jugo 6; el zumo (*Spain*)
July julio 1
June junio 1
jungle la selva 12
junk food la comida basura; la comida chatarra 10; la porquería
jury el jurado
just justo/a

justice la justicia 15
justify justificar
juvenile juvenil

K

keep guardar 6
keep in mind tener (ie) en cuenta
key la clave; la llave
keyboard el teclado 12
kick patear
kidnap secuestrar
kill matar
kilogram el kilo
kind simpático/a
king el rey 15
kingdom el reino
kiss el beso
kitchen la cocina 5, 6
kite el papalote 7
knead amasar
knee la rodilla 10
knife el cuchillo 6
knot el nudo
knotted anudado/a
know (someone) conocer (zc) 4; **know (something)** saber 4
know how to do something saber (+ *inf.*) 4
know-it-all el/la sabelotodo
knowledge el conocimiento
known conocido/a
Korea Corea 2
Korean el coreano (*language*); coreano/a 2

L

laboratory el laboratorio 3
lack faltar; la falta
ladder la escalera
lake el lago 9
lamb el cordero
lamp la lámpara 5
lance la lanza
land aterrizar 9; el terreno; la tierra
landowner el hacendado; el terrateniente
landscape el paisaje
lane la vía

language el idioma; la lengua 2
laptop computer la computadora portátil 1
last durar; pasado/a; último/a
lasting duradero/a 15
last night anoche
late tarde
lately últimamente
later luego
latest último/a; de última hora 13
latest fashion la novedad 14
latrine la letrina
laugh reírse (i, i)
laughter la risa
launch lanzar
law el derecho 3; la ley 15
lawyer el/la abogado/a 11
lazy perezoso/a 1
leader el/la líder
leadership el liderazgo
leading lady la primera actriz 13
leading man el galán 13
leaf la hoja
leaf through hojear
leap saltar
learn (to do something) aprender (a + *inf.*) 2
leather el cuero 8, 14; la piel 14
leave licencia 11; irse 5; salir 4; **leave behind** dejar
lecture la conferencia
left (of), to the a la izquierda (de) 3
leftovers los restos
leg la pierna 10; **leg (animal)** la pata
legend la leyenda
leggings las mallas
legumes los frijoles 6
leisure time el ocio 4
lemon el limón
lemonade la limonada
lend prestar
less menos
less . . . than menos... que

lessen disminuir
lesson la lección
let go soltar (ue)
Let's get to work! ¡Manos a la obra! 11
let's go vamos
letter la letra
letter of introduction/ recommendation la carta de presentación/ recomendación 11
lettuce la lechuga 6
level el nivel
lexicon el léxico
liberate liberar
librarian el/la bibliotecario/a
library la biblioteca 3
life la vida
lifeless desanimado/a
lift levantar
lift weights levantar pesas 7
light (color; *adj.*) claro/a
light (*noun*) la luz; (*verb*) encender (ie)
lightning flash el relámpago
like gustar
likewise igualmente 1
lily la azucena
limit el límite; limitar
limousine la limusina
line la cola 9; la línea
linguistic lingüístico/a
lip el labio 5
lip gloss el brillo de labios 5
lipstick el lápiz labial; el pintalabios
listen escuchar 2
Listen. Escucha (Escuchen). 1; Oye. (*command*)
listen to music escuchar música 7
listener el/la radioyente 13
literature la literatura
lithium el litio
live habitar; vivir 2
live television la televisión en vivo y en directo 13
living room la sala 5

loan el préstamo
located ubicado/a
location la ubicación
locker room el vestuario
logical lógico/a
long largo/a
long as, as mientras que
long form pleno/a
long jump el salto de longitud
Long live the bride and groom! ¡Que vivan los novios!
long-sleeved de manga larga 8
long walk la caminata
look lucir (zc)
look for buscar 2
look at mirar 2
loosen desprender
lose perder (ie) 4, 7
lose weight adelgazar 10; bajar de peso 10
loss la pérdida
lost perdido/a
lots of money el dineral
love amar; el amor; querer (ie) 4
lover el/la amante
low heat el fuego lento
lower bajar
lowercase minúscula
lozenge la pastilla 10
luck la suerte
luggage (policy) el equipaje (permitido) 9
lukewarm tibio/a
lunch el almuerzo 6
lung el pulmón 10
luxurious lujoso/a
luxury de lujo 9
lying mentiroso/a
lyrics (of a song) la letra

M

macaw el guacamayo
machine la máquina
magazine la revista 7, 13
magic la magia
mail el correo
mail carrier el/la cartero/a
maintain mantener (ie)
major (Univ.) la carrera 3
make fabricar; hacer 3

make a mistake equivocarse
make a stopover hacer escala 9
make an appointment hacer una cita 10
make difficult dificultar
make good cumplir (con) 15
make matters worse, to para colmo
make plans hacer planes 7
make sick enfermar
make the bed hacer la cama 5
makeup el maquillaje 5
mall el centro comercial 8
mama la mamá
man el hombre 1
manager el/la gerente 9
manner el modo 14
manufacture fabricar
manufacturer el fabricante
many . . . as, as tantos/as... como
map el mapa 1
maracas las maracas 14
marathon el maratón
March marzo 1
Mardi Gras el carnaval
margin el margen
Marie biscuit la galleta María
marimba la marimba 14
marine marino/a
mark marcar
marker el marcador 1
market el mercado 8, 15
married (to) casado/a (con) 2, 4
marry casar
Mars (planet) Marte
marvelous maravilloso/a
marvelously maravillosamente
mash machacar
Mass la misa
masses, the el pueblo 15
massive masivo/a
master/mistress el/la maestro/a
masterpiece la obra maestra

match el partido; match with hacer juego con 8
material el material 8, 14
maternal surname el apellido materno
maternity leave la licencia por maternidad 11
mathematics las matemáticas 3
matrimony el matrimonio
matter el asunto
mature maduro/a
May mayo 1
May the best win! ¡Que gane el mejor!
mayor el/la alcalde/ alcaldesa 15; el/la intendente
me me 4; mí; with conmigo 4
meal la comida 4, 6
mean significar
meaning el significado
means los medios
measure la medida; medir (i, i) 6
measurement la medida
meat la carne 6
mechanic el/la mecánico/a 11
mechanical mecánico/a 11
media los medios 13
medical médico/a 10
medical checkup el examen físico 10
medicine la medicina 3
meet conocer (zc)
meeting la reunión
meet up with someone encontrarse (ue) con 5
meet with someone reunirse
melt fundir
melted cheese tortilla la quesadilla
member el miembro 4
memorize memorizar
memory el recuerdo; la memoria
memory card la tarjeta de memoria
men's shirt typical of the Caribbean la guayabera
mention mencionar

menu el menú 6
merengue el merengue (dance)
merit el mérito
message el mensaje 2
messy desordenado/a 5
metal sheet la plancha
meteorologist el/la meteorólogo/a 13
meter el metro
Mexican mexicano/a 2
Mexican-American chicano/a
microphone el micrófono
microscope el microscopio
microwave el microondas 6
midnight la medianoche
migraine la migraña
migrant migrante
migration la migración
mile la milla
military militar
milk la leche 6
millennium el milenio
million el millón
mind, in en mente
mine mío/a(s)
mineral el mineral 10
mineral water el agua mineral 6
minimum mínimo/a 11; el mínimo
minimum wage el sueldo mínimo 11
miniskirt la minifalda 8
minister el/la ministro/a 15
minority la minoría
minute el minuto
mirror el espejo 5
misery la miseria
Miss la señorita (Srta.) 1
miss perder (ie); (ie); miss someone extrañar; echar de menos
mistaken equivocado/a
mix amasar; mezclar 6
mixed fibers de mezclilla
mixed race, of mestizo/a
mixture la mezcla
mobility la movilidad
model el/la modelo 14
mode of transportation el medio de transporte

moderation la moderación **10**
moderator el/la presentador/a
modern moderno/a
modern dance la danza moderna **14**
molar la muela **10**
mom la mamá
mommy la mami
monarchy la monarquía **15**
Monday el lunes
money el dinero
monotonous monótono/a
monounsaturated fats las grasas monoinsaturadas **10**
month el mes
months of the year los meses del año
monument el monumento **9**
moon la luna
Moor (Arab) el/la moro/a
moral la lección; la moraleja
morality la moralidad
more más
more . . . than más... que
More or less. Más o menos.
morning la mañana **2**
mother la madre **4**
mother-in-law la suegra **4**
motivate motivar
motive el motivo
motto el lema (publicitario) **15**
mount montar
mountain la montaña **9**
mountain climbing el alpinismo **7**
mountainous montañoso/a
mourning el luto
mouse el ratón **12**
mouth la boca **10**
move la mudanza; mudarse
movement el movimiento
move up ascender (ie)
movie la peli; la película **4**
movie theater el cine **4**
moving conmovedor/a

mp3 player el reproductor de mp3
Mr. el señor (Sr.) **1**
Mrs. la señora (Sra.) **1**
Ms. la señora (Sra.) **1**
mud el barro, el lodo
mudslide el deslizamiento de tierra
multinational multinacional
muralist el/la muralista
murder el asesinato
muscle el músculo
muscular musculoso/a
museum el museo **3**
music la música **14**
musical musical **14**
musical group el conjunto **14**; el grupo musical **14**
musician el/la músico/a **14**
Muslim musulmán/ musulmana
mutton el carnero
mutual mutuo/a
my mi/mis
My name is . . . Me llamo... **1**; Mi nombre es... **1**
My treat! ¡Te invito! **4**
mysterious misterioso/a
mystery el misterio
myth el mito

N

name el nombre; nombrar
napkin la servilleta **6**
narration la narración
narrator el/la narrador/a
narrow angosto/a; estrecho/a
nation la nación
nationality la nacionalidad **2**
natural attractions las atracciones naturales **9**
natural disaster el desastre natural **15**
natural resource el recurso natural **12**
nature la naturaleza **12**
nausea las náuseas **10**
navigable navegable
navigator el/la navegante
near cerca

nearby cerca (de); cercano/a; próximo/a
necessary necesario/a
neck el cuello
necklace el collar **8**
need necesitar **1**
negative negativo/a
neighbor el/la vecino/a
neighborhood el barrio
neither tampoco **7**
neither . . . nor ni... ni **7**
nephew el sobrino **4**
nervous nervioso/a **2**
nest el nido
nettle (a stinging plant) la ortiga
network la cadena **13**; la red
never jamás; ninguna vez; nunca
nevertheless sin embargo
new novedoso/a; nuevo/a **2**
New Seven Wonders of the World las nuevas séptimas maravillas del mundo
newlyweds los recién casados
news las noticias **7, 13**
newscast el noticiero **13**
newscaster el/la comentarista **13**
news online las noticias en línea **13**
newspaper el periódico
New Year's Day el Día de Año Nuevo
New Year's Eve la Nochevieja
New Yorker neoyorquino/a
next próximo/a
next to al lado (de) **3**
nice simpático/a **1**
Nice to meet you. Mucho gusto. **1**
nickname el apodo
niece la sobrina **4**
night la noche **2**
nightstand la mesa de noche **5**
ninth noveno/a
nobility la nobleza

nobody nadie **7**
nomination la nominación
none ningún, ninguno/a(s) **7**
nonprofit sin fines de lucro
noon el mediodía
no one nadie; ninguno/a **7**
nor ni **7**
normally normalmente
nose la nariz
not believe no creer
not be sure of no estar seguro/a (de)
note anotar; el apunte
notebook el cuaderno **1**
not either tampoco
nothing nada
notice el aviso; fijarse
notify notificar
notion la noción
not think no pensar (ie)
noun el sustantivo **1**
nourish alimentar
novel la novela
novelist el/la novelista
November noviembre **1**
now actualmente; ahora; **for now** por ahora
nowadays hoy en día
nuclear bomb la bomba nuclear **15**
nuclear plant la planta nuclear **12**
nuclear waste los desechos nucleares **12**
nucleus el núcleo
number el número
nurse el/la enfermero/a **11**
nursery la guardería **11**
nutrition la alimentación
nylon el nilón **14**

O

obesity el sobrepeso, la obesidad
object el objeto **1**
objective el propósito
obligation el compromiso; el deber; la obligación
oblige obligar
observatory el observatorio **3**
observe observar

obtain conseguir (i, i) **11**; obtener (ie)

occupation el oficio **11**

occupy ocupar

occur ocurrir

ocean el mar **7**; el océano

October octubre **1**

odor el olor

of course por supuesto

offer la oferta; ofrecer (zc)

office el despacho; la oficina

official oficial

off-road vehicle el todoterreno

often a menudo

oil el aceite **6**; el petróleo

oil pipeline el oleoducto **12**

oil spill el derrame de petróleo **12**

oil well el pozo de petróleo

okay de acuerdo **4**

old antiguo/a; viejo/a **2**

older mayor **4, 5**

olive la aceituna; **olive oil** el aceite de oliva **6**

Olympic Games los Juegos Olímpicos

omelet la tortilla (*Spain*)

omit desprender

on en **3**; sobre

on foot a pie

on the dot en punto **2**

on the Internet en Internet **12**

on my own por mi cuenta

once una vez **5**

once in a while de vez en cuando **5**

Once upon a time . . . Érase una vez...

one un/o/a

one must hay que

one time una vez **5**

onion la cebolla **6**

online community la comunidad virtual **12**

online dictionary el diccionario en línea **1**

online news las noticias en línea **13**

online newspaper el periódico digital **13**

only solamente; solo; único/a

on one's own por su cuenta

on sale en rebaja **8**; en venta

on the contrary por lo contrario

on time a tiempo

on top of arriba de

open abrir **2**

open-air al aire libre **8**

Open your book(s). Abre (Abran) el libro. **1**

opera la ópera **14**

opinion la opinión

opponent el/la contrincante **15**

opportune oportuno/a

opportunity la oportunidad

oppressed oprimido/a

oppression la opresión

optimistic optimista

opulence la opulencia

or o **7**

orange anaranjado/a (*color*) **1**; la naranja **6**

orchestra la orquesta **4, 14**

order el orden; el pedido

organic orgánico/a

organization la organización

organizer el/la organizador/a **11**

orginate from provenir (ie)

orientation la orientación

origin el origen

originality la originalidad

ornament el ornamento

other otro/a; **others** los demás

ought to do something deber (+ *inf.*) **2**

our/s nuestro/a(s)

outdoor café el café al aire libre **4**

outer ear la oreja **10**

outfit el conjunto **14**

outgoing extrovertido/a

outrage la barbaridad

outside al aire libre **4**; fuera

outskirts las afueras

outstanding destacado/a

ovation, standing la ovación de pie **14**

oven el horno **6**

overcome superar

overcoming la superación

overconsumption el sobreconsumo

overhead bin el compartimento superior **9**

overpopulation la sobrepoblación

overstuffed chair el sillón **5**

owe deber **2**

own propio/a

owner el/la dueño/a

oxygen el oxígeno

P

pacifist el/la pacifista **15**

pack (the suitcase) hacer (la maleta) **9**

packaged empaquetado/a

page la página

pageant el concurso **13**

paid remunerado/a

pain el dolor

painkiller el calmante **10**

painted pintado/a

painter el/la pintor/a

painting el cuadro **5**; la pintura

pair emparejar

pajamas la pijama

pal el/la cuate (*Mexico*)

palace el palacio

Panamanian panameño/a **2**

Panamanian currency el balboa

Panamanian reverse appliqué la mola

pancakes los panqueques

panpipe la zampoña

pants los pantalones **8**

paper el papel **1**

papier mâché el papel maché

parade el desfile

paradise el paraíso

paragraph el párrafo

parasailing el paravelismo

parents los padres **2**

park el parque **4**; estacionar

parliament el parlamento

parody la parodia

parrot el loro

parsley el perejil

part la parte **10**

participant el/la participante

participate participar

particularly particularmente

partisan partidario/a

partner la pareja

part-time a tiempo parcial **11**

party la fiesta

pass (a test) aprobar (un examen)

passenger el/la pasajero/a **9**

passion la pasión

passionfruit la maracuyá

passport el pasaporte **9**

pass through (. . .) pasar por (...) **9**

past el pasado

pastime el pasatiempo **7**

pastry shop la pastelería **8**

paternal surname el apellido paterno

path el camino; el sendero

patient el/la paciente **10**; paciente (*adj.*)

patio el patio **5**

pay (in cash) pagar (en efectivo) **8**

pay attention hacer caso

payment el pago; la remesa

peace la paz **15**

peach el durazno; el melocotón

pearl de perlas **8**; la perla

peasant el/la campesino/a

pedicure la pedicura

peel pelar **6**

pen el bolígrafo **1**

pencil el lápiz **1**

penguin el pingüino

penicillin la penicilina

peninsula la península

people, the el pueblo **15**; la gente **13**; los personajes **15**

pepper la pimienta **6**; **red pepper** el pimentón

rojo; **green pepper** el pimiento verde

perch posar

percussion la percusión

percussionist el/la percusionista

perfect perfeccionar; perfecto/a

perform interpretar (*Spain*); representar 13

perfume el perfume 8

perfume shop la perfumería 8

perhaps quizás; tal vez

permanent permanente

permit el permiso; permitir

perseverance la perseverancia

person la persona 1, 2; el personaje 15

personal care item el artículo de uso personal 5

personality la personalidad

personnel el personal

pertaining to en torno a

Peruvian peruano/a 2

perversity la perversidad

pessimistic pesimista

pesticides los pesticidas 12

pet la mascota

pharmacy la farmacia 8

philharmonic filarmónico/a

philosophy la filosofía 3

phishing el fraude electrónico 12

phone el teléfono 1

photocopier la fotocopiadora

photocopy fotocopiar

photograph la foto

photographer el/la fotógrafo/a

phrase la frase

physical físico/a

physical characteristics las características físicas 2

physical education la educación física 3

physics la física 3

piano el piano 14

pick up recoger (j) 5

pickup truck el camión; la camioneta

picture el cuadro 5

pie el pastel 6; la tarta

piece el pedazo; la pieza 14

pile el montón

pilgrim el/la peregrino/a

pill la pastilla 10

pilot el/la piloto 9

pinch la pizca 6

pine nut el pino

pink rosado/a 1

pirate el/la pirata; piratear

pity la pena

place el lugar 2; el sitio; colocar; poner 4

place to live (*fig.*) el techo

plaid de cuadros 8

plains los llanos; plains **(of Argentina)** las pampas

plan el plan 11; planear; **plan (to do something)** pensar (ie) (+ *inf.*) 4

plane el avión 9

plant plantar

plastic el plástico 12

plate el plato 6

platform la plataforma

play (a sport, videogames, etc.) jugar (ue) a (un deporte, videojuegos, etc.) 4, 7; practicar (un deporte) 2

play (an instrument/ music) tocar (un instrumento/música) 4

play the role hacer el papel

play (theater) la obra 13

player el/la jugador/a

please complacer; por favor

Pleased to meet you. Encantado/a. 1; Mucho gusto.

pleasure el gusto; el placer

plot el argumento

plumage el plumaje

plumber el/la plomero/a 11

pluperfect el pluscuamperfecto

plural forms of nouns el plural de los sustantivos

podcast listener el/la oyente de podcast 13

poet el/la poeta

point of view el punto de vista

point out señalar

police la policía; el/la policía

polish pulir

political político/a 15

political cartoon la caricatura política 13

political post el cargo político 15

political science las ciencias políticas 3

politician el/la político/a 15

politics la política 15

poll la encuesta

pollute contaminar 12

pollution la contaminación 12

polyester el poliéster 14

polyunsaturated fats las grasas poliinsaturadas

poodle el camiche

pool la piscina

poor pobre 2

population la población

pork el cerdo; **pork loin** el lomo de cerdo

Portugal Portugal 2

Portuguese el portugués (*language*); portugués/ portuguesa 2

position el cargo 11; el puesto

possible posible

post el cargo 15

postcard la tarjeta postal 9

poster el cartel

post online compartir 12

post-reading después de leer

post-viewing and listening después de ver y escuchar

post-writing después de escribir

potato chips las papas fritas

potatoes las papas 6

pound la libra

poverty la pobreza 15

power el poder 15

practice (a sport) practicar (un deporte) 2

praise la alabanza

precious precioso/a

pre-Columbian precolombino/a

predecessor el/la predecesor/a

predict predecir (i)

predictable predecible

predominant predominante

predominate predominar

prefer preferir (ie, i) 4

preference la preferencia

prehispanic prehispánico/a

prehistoric prehistórico/a

preoccupation la preocupación

preparation la preparación 6

prepare preparar 2

pre-reading antes de leer

prescription (medical) la receta (médica) 10

present day la actualidad

present oneself presentarse

preserve conservar 12

preside presidir

presidency la presidencia

president el/la presidente/a 15

president's office (Univ.) la rectoría 3

press la prensa 13

press conference la conferencia de prensa

pretend fingir (j)

pretty bonito/a 2; lindo/a

prevalent prevaleciente

preventable prevenible

pre-viewing and listening antes de ver y escuchar

previous previo/a

pre-writing antes de escribir

price el precio 8

prickly plant la ortiga

prince el príncipe

princess la princesa

print imprimir 12

printer la impresora **12**
priority la prioridad
pristine prístino/a
privacy la privacidad
private privado/a
prize el premio **7, 13**
probably probablemente
problem el problema **10**
process el proceso
procession la procesión
produce producir (zc)
producer el/la
productor/a **13**
product el producto
profession la profesión **11**
professor el/la
profesor/a **1**
profile el perfil
profit el fruto (*fig.*); el
beneficio
profound profundo/a
profoundly
profundamente
program el programa **12,
13**; programar **12**
programmer el/la
programador/a
programming la
programación
progress el progreso
prohibit prohibir
prohibited prohibido/a
project el proyecto
prolific prolífico/a
prominent prominente
promise la promesa;
prometer
promote ascender (ie) **11**;
impulsar; promocionar;
promover (ue) **15**
promotion la promoción
pronounce pronunciar
property la propiedad
proportion proporcionar
propose proponer
protagonist el/la
protagonista **13**
protect proteger (j) **12**
protected protegido/a
protection la protección
proteins las proteínas **10**
protest la manifestación;
protestar **15**
proud orgulloso/a

prove comprobar (ue)
provide proporcionar
provided (that) con tal
(de) que
provisions los comestibles
provoke provocar
psychologist el/la
psicológico/a **11**
psychology la
psicología **3**
public el público;
público/a
public debt la deuda
pública **15**
public health la sanidad
publicist el/la publicista
publicity publicitario/a; la
publicidad
publish publicar
Puerto Rican
puertorriqueño/a **2**
pummel moler (ue) a
golpes
pumpkin la calabaza
punctually puntualmente
punish castigar
punishment el castigo, la
penalización
pure puro/a
purity la pureza
purple morado/a **1**
purse el bolso
pursuer el/la cazador/a
push impulsar
put poner; **put away**
guardar **6**
put to bed acostar (ue)
put makeup on
maquillarse **5**
put out (fires) apagar
(fuegos/incendios)
pyramid la pirámide

Q

qualifications las
cualificaciones **11**
qualify clasificar
quality la calidad; la
cualidad
quantity la cantidad
quarter cuarto/a **2**
quartet el cuarteto **14**
queen la reina **15**
question la pregunta

questionnaire el
cuestionario
quick-drying el secado
rápido
quit (doing something)
dejar (de) + *inf.* **10**
quite bastante
quiz la prueba **1**

R

race la carrera **7**; la raza
racket la raqueta **7**
radio la radio **13**
radioactivity la
radioactividad **12**
radio listener el/la
radioyente **13**
radio station la estación
de radio
**radio station (business
entity)** la emisora
rag el trapo
raging furibundo/a
rain la lluvia; llover (ue) **7**
rain forest el bosque
pluvial **12**
rainy lluvioso/a
raise criar; subir; el
aumento **11**
raise funds recaudar fondos
raise public consciousness
concienciar al público
raisin la pasa
raising la cría
ranch la estancia
rancher el/la hacendado/a
rapid rápido/a
rapidly rápidamente
rate (of unemployment) la
tasa (de desempleo) **15**
rather sino que
rayon el rayón **14**
razor la navaja de afeitar **5**
reach alcanzar
reachable alcanzable
react reaccionar **6**
reaction la reacción
read leer **2**
reader el/la lector/a **13**
reading la lectura
ready dispuesto/a;
listo/a **2**
real estate los bienes raíces
realistic realista

Really? ¿De verdad? **1**
really realmente
really beautiful
bellísimo/a
reason la razón
reasonable razonable
rebellion la rebelión
receipt el recibo **8**
receive recibir **2**
receiver el receptor
recent último/a
recently recientemente
reception desk la
recepción **9**
receptionist el/la
recepcionista
rechargeable recargable
recipe la receta **6**
reciprocal recíproco/a
recognized reconocido/a
recommend
recomendar (ie)
recommendation la
recomendación **11**
record grabar **12**
recorded grabado/a
recording la grabación
rectify rectificar
recuperate recuperar
recycle reciclar **12**
recycling el reciclaje **12**
red rojo/a **1**; **red wine** vino
tinto **6**
red pepper el pimentón
rojo
reduce reducir (zc)
reed la caña
refer referir (ie, i)
referee el/la árbitro **7**
reflect reflejar
reforestation la
reforestación **12**
refreshment el refresco
refrigerator el frigorífico; el
refrigerador **6**; la nevera
refuge el refugio
region la región
register la caja; registrar
regret lamentar; sentir (ie, i)
regrettable lamentable
rehearsal el ensayo **13**
rehearse ensayar **13**
reign reinar
reincarnate reencarnar

reject rechazar **4**
relate relatar
relation la relación
relationship la relación
relative relativo/a
relative (family) el/la pariente
relaxation el relajamiento
religious religioso/a
remain permanecer (zc); quedar; quedarse
remains los restos
remedy el remedio **10**; remediar
remember recordar (ue) **4**
remittance la remesa
remote remoto/a
remove quitar **5**; remover (ue)
renewable renovable
renounce renunciar
renown el renombre
rent alquilar; el alquiler
repair reparar **11**
repeat repetir (i, i) **4**
Repeat. Repite (Repitan). **1**
Repeat, please. Repita por favor. **1**
repentant arrepentido/a
repertoire el repertorio
repopulation la repoblación
report el informe; informar **13**; reportar
reporter el/la reportero/a **13**
represent figurar; representar
representative el/la representante **15**; representativo/a
reproduce reproducir (zc)
republic la república **15**
request el encargo; el pedido; pedir (i, i) **4**
requirement el requisito
rescue el rescate
research investigar; la investigación
researcher el/la investigador/a
reservation la reserva **9**; reservación **9**
residence la residencia

resort (to) acudir
resource el recurso **12**
respect el respeto; respetar
respectful respetuoso/a
respect to, with acerca de
respiratory respiratorio/a
respond responder
response la respuesta **1**
responsibilities las responsabilidades
responsible responsable
rest descansar **2**; el descanso; **the rest** los demás; el resto
restaurant el restaurante **6**
restock reponer
result el resultado
retire jubilarse; retirarse **11**
retiree el/la jubilado/a
retirement plan el plan de retiro **11**
retribution el castigo
return regresar **2**; volver (ue) **4**; el regreso
return (something) devolver (ue) **8**
reveal revelar
revenge la venganza
review el repaso; la reseña **13**; revisar
revolution la revolución **9**
revolutionize revolucionar
revolutionized revolucionado/a
revolver el revólver
reward premiar
rhythm el ritmo
rice el arroz **6**; **rice pudding** el arroz con leche
rich rico/a **2, 10**
richness la riqueza
ride montar
ridiculous ridículo/a
right el derecho **15**
right, to be tener (ie) razón
right away enseguida
right now ahora mismo
right (of), to the a la derecha (de) **3**
rigid rígido/a
ring el anillo **8**
risk el riesgo **10**
river el río

road el camino
roast hornear **6**
roasted asado/a **6**
robbery el robo
rock la piedra; la roca
rocker (music) el/la roquero/a
role el papel **13**
roll one's eyes poner los ojos en blanco
Roman romano/a
romantic romántico/a
roof el techo
room el cuarto **5, 9**; el salón; la habitación
root la raíz
rough grosero/a
round redondo/a
roundtrip el viaje de ida y vuelta **9**
route la ruta
routine la rutina
royal real
royalty la realeza
rub frotar
rude maleducado/a
ruin la ruina
rule la regla
run correr **7**
running of the bulls el encierro
running shoes las zapatillas de deporte **8**
rupture cartilage romperse un cartílago
rupture a ligament romperse un ligamento
Russia Rusia
Russian el ruso; el/la ruso/a
rustic rústico/a

S

sacred sagrado/a
sad triste **2**
sail navegar (a vela)
salad la ensalada
salary el salario; el sueldo **11**
sale la rebaja **8**; la venta
sales ad el anuncio de venta
sales clerk el/la dependiente/a **8**

salsa performer el/la salsero/a
salt la sal **6**
salutation/s el/los saludo/s
Salvadoran salvadoreño/a **2**
same igual; mismo/a
sample la muestra; la prueba
sand la arena
sandals las sandalias **8**
sandstone la arenisca
sandwich el bocadillo; el sándwich **6**; la torta
San Fermín festival los sanfermines
sanitation la sanidad
sassy atrevido/a
satellite dish la antena parabólica **12**
satellite radio la radio por satélite
satellite television la televisión por satélite **13**
satisfaction la satisfacción
satisfactory satisfactorio/a
satisfied satisfecho/a
saturated saturado/a **10**
saturated (trans) fats las grasas saturadas (trans) **10**
Saturday el sábado
sauce la salsa **6**
saucepan la cazuela **6**
sausage el chorizo; la salchicha
save ahorrar; guardar **6**; salvar; **save (a document)** guardar (un documento) **12**
saxophone el saxofón **14**
say decir (i)
say good-bye despedirse (i, i)
scandal el escándalo
scanner el escáner **12**
scarce escaso/a; **scarcity** la escasez
scene la escena
schedule el horario **3**
scholastic escolar
school la escuela; **school life expectancy** la

expectativa de educación formal

School of Art la Facultad de Arte **3**

School of Education la Facultad de Pedagogía **3**

School of Engineering la Facultad de Ingeniería **3**

School of Humanities la Facultad de Filosofía y Letras **3**

School of Law la Facultad de Derecho **3**

School of Mathematics la Facultad de Matemáticas **3**

School of Medicine la Facultad de Medicina **3**

School of Sciences la Facultad de Ciencias **3**

science la ciencia

science fiction la ciencia ficción

scientist el/la científico/a **11**

screen la pantalla **12**

script el guion **13**

script writer el/la guionista

scuba dive bucear **9**

sculptor el/la escultor/a

sculpture la escultura

sea el mar **9**

seafood los mariscos **6**

sea lion el lobo marino

search la búsqueda

search engine el buscador **13**

season la estación **1**; la temporada **7**

seasons of the year las estaciones del año

seat el asiento **9**; la sede

seat of government la sede

second segundo/a

secondhand de segunda mano

secret el secreto

secretary el/la secretario/a

section la sección

security la seguridad **9**

security checkpoint el control de seguridad **9**

see ver **2**

seem parecer (zc)

See you. Nos vemos. **1**

See you later. Hasta luego. **1**

See you soon. Hasta pronto. **1**

See you tomorrow. Hasta mañana. **1**

select seleccionar

selection la selección

self-defense la defensa propia

self-portrait el autorretrato

sell vender **2**

semester el semestre **3**

senator el/la senador/a **15**

send enviar **12**; **send (text messages)** mandar (mensajes de texto) **2**

sensation la sensación

sensationalist sensacionalista

sentence la oración

sentimental sentimental

September septiembre **1**

sequins las lentejuelas **14**

series la serie

serious grave; serio/a

servant el/la sirviente/a

serve servir (i, i) **4**

server el servidor **12**

service el servicio; la prestación

set fire encenderse (ie)

set the table poner la mesa **5**

setting el lugar

seventh séptimo/a

several varios/as

severe severo/a

shake alborotar; sacudir; **shake (someone's hand)** estrechar (la mano)

shallot la cebolleta

shame la lástima

shampoo el champú **5**

shape, in en forma **10**

share (online) compartir **12**

shark el tiburón

sharp puntiagudo/a

shave afeitarse **5**

shaving cream la crema de afeitar **5, 8**

shaving lotion la loción de afeitar

she ella

sheep la oveja

shell la concha

shellfish los mariscos **6**

shift el turno

shine brillar; lucir (zc)

ship el barco **9**; la nave

shipment el envío

shirt la camisa **5, 8**

shoes los zapatos **8**

shoe store la zapatería **8**

shoot disparar

shop la tienda **8**

shopping center el centro comercial **8**

shore la orilla

short (in stature) bajo/a **2**

shortage la escasez **12**

short-sleeved de manga corta **8**

short time el rato

shorts los pantalones cortos **8**

shot la inyección **10**

shoulder el hombro

shoulder pads las hombreras

Should we go . . . ? ¿Vamos (a)...? **4**

shout el grito

show la exposición; la función **4**; mostrar (ue); **show (business)** el espectáculo

show a movie poner una película **4**

shower ducharse **5**; la ducha

showy vistoso/a

shrimp los camarones **6**

shy tímido/a

sick enfermo/a **2**

sick leave la licencia por enfermedad **11**

side el lado

sign el letrero; firmar **15**

signal la señal

signature la firma

significant significante; significativo/a

silk la seda **8, 14**

silver de plata **8**; la plata; la platería

similar semejante

simple sencillo/a **10**

simplicity la sencillez **14**

since desde; hace

sing cantar **14**

singer el/la cantante

singer-songwriter el/la cantautor/a

single soltero/a **4**

single room el cuarto individual **9**

sister la hermana **4**

sister-in-law la cuñada **4**

sit (down) sentarse (ie) **5**

situated situado/a

situation la situación

sixth sexto/a

size el número; la talla **8**; el tamaño

skate el patín **7**; patinar **7**

skating el patinaje

ski esquiar **7**

skiing el esquí

skilled diestro/a

skillet la sartén **6**

skillful diestro/a

skim through dar una mirada rápida

skin la piel

skinny flaco/a

skirt la falda **8**

skull la calavera

sky el cielo

skyscraper el rascacielos

slave el/la esclavo/a

sleep dormir (ue, u) **4, 5**; el sueño

sleeve la manga **8**

sleeveless sin manga

slender delgado **2**

slice (of Spanish omelet) el pincho (de tortilla)

slogan el lema publicitario

slope la falda

slow lento/a

slow down frenar

slowly despacio; lentamente

small pequeño/a **1**

small beer la caña

smart phone el teléfono inteligente **1**

smart watch el reloj inteligente **8**

smell el olor

smile sonreír (i, i)

smiling sonriendo

smog contaminación

smoke el humo **12**; fumar **10**

snack la merienda **6**

snake la culebra; la serpiente

sneakers las zapatillas de deporte **8**

sneeze estornudar

snorkel bucear

snow nevar (ie) **7**

so many tantos/as

so much tanto/a

soap el jabón **5**

soap opera la telenovela **13**

soccer el fútbol **7**

social media site el sitio social **12**

social network la red social

socialist el/la socialista

social science las ciencias sociales **3**

social welfare programs los programas sociales **15**

sociology la sociología

socks los calcetines **8**

soda el refresco **6**

sofa el sofá **5**

soft drink el refresco **4**

solar solar **12**

soldier el/la soldado **15**

solemn solemne

solid sólido/a

solitary solitario/a

soloist el/la solista **14**

solve resolver (ue) **15**

some alguno/a(s) **7, 10**

someday algún día

someone alguien **7**

something algo **7**

sometimes a veces **5**

son el hijo **4**

song la canción

son-in-law el yerno **4**

soon pronto

sorrow la pena

So-so. Más o menos. **1**

so that para que

soul el alma (*fem.*)

soup la sopa **6**

soursop la guanábana

source la fuente

south el sur

southern sureño/a

souvenir el recuerdo **9**

spaghetti los espaguetis

Spain España

Spaniard el/la español/a

Spanish español/a **2**; el español (*language*)

spark la chispa

spattered salpicado/a

spatula la espátula

speak hablar **2**; **speak out** sacar la voz

speaker el altavoz

speakers los audio parlantes

special especial

speciality store la tienda especializada

specialize (in) especializarse (en)

species la especie **12**

spectacular espectacular

spectator el/la espectador/a **13**

speech el discurso **15**

speed la velocidad

spelling la ortografía

spend gastar **8**

spend (time) pasar **4**; **spend time in** llevar; **spend time with friends** pasar tiempo con amigos **7**

spent gastado/a

spicy picante **6**

spider la araña

spill el derrame **12**

spirit el espíritu

split partir

sponsor el/la patrocinador/a; patrocinar

spoof la parodia **13**

spoon la cuchara **6**

sport el deporte **7**

sporting deportivo/a **7**

sportscaster el/la comentarista deportivo/a **13**

sports bra el sostén deportivo

sports section la sección deportiva **13**

sports teams los equipos deportivos

spreadsheet la hoja electrónica

spring el manantial; la primavera **1**

spy espiar

square cuadrado/a

squash la calabaza

squid el calamar

squirrel la ardilla

stadium el estadio **3**

stage el escenario **14**; la etapa

stage manager el/la director/a de escena

stall el puesto

stand el puesto

standing in line en la cola

standing ovation la ovación de pie **14**

stand in line hacer cola **9**

stand out destacar

stand up levantarse **5**; pararse

star el/la protagonista **13**; la estrella

startup incipiente

state el estado

statement la afirmación

statesman el hombre de Estado

stateswoman la mujer de Estado

station la estación

stationery shop la papelería **8**

statistics las estadísticas

statue la estatua **9**

status el estado

stay la estadía **9**; quedarse **9**

stay in bed (due to sickness) guardar cama **10**

stay in shape mantenerse (ie) en forma **10**

stay trim guardar la línea **10**

steak el bistec **6**

step el escalón; el paso; **step on** pisar

stepbrother el hermanastro **4**

stepfather el padrastro **4**

stepmother la madrastra **4**

stepsister la hermanastra **4**

stereotype el estereotipo

stew el estofado; la cazuela (*Chile*)

stewpot la cazuela **6**

still todavía

still life la naturaleza muerta

stilts los palos

stimulate estimular

stimulus el estímulo

stingy tacaño/a

Stockholm Estocolmo

stomach el estómago **10**

stone la piedra

stop (doing something) dejar de **11**

stopover la escala **9**

store la tienda **8**; **store (in the cloud)** almacenar (en la nube) **12**

stork la cigüeña

storm la tempestad

story el cuento

storyteller el/la cuentista

stove la estufa **6**

straight ahead todo recto; derecho

straighten up (the house) ordenar (la casa) **5**

strange extraño/a **10**; raro/a

strategic estratégico/a

straw la paja **14**

strawberry la fresa **6**

street la calle

street vendor el/la vendedor/a ambulante

strengthen afianzar; fortalecer (zc)

stress el estrés **10**

stretch estirar

strict estricto/a

strike el paro (*Latin America*); la huelga **15**

striker el/la huelguista
string la cuerda
string beans las judías verdes 6
strip despojar
striped de rayas 8
stroll el paseo
strong fuerte
struggle la lucha
student el/la estudiante 1; estudiantil
student union el centro estudiantil 3
student teacher el/la pasante
studio el estudio 13
study el estudio; estudiar 2
Study. Estudia (Estudien). 1
stuffy tapado/a
stunning impactante
stupid tonto/a; estúpido/a
style el estilo 14; la moda 14
subject la materia 3
substance la sustancia
subsidize subvencionar
success el éxito
successful exitoso/a
suckling pig el cochinillo
suddenly de golpe; de repente
suffer (from) padecer (zc) (de) 10; sufrir (de)
suffering el sufrimiento
sugar el azúcar 6, 10
suggest sugerir (ie, i)
suggestion la sugerencia
suit el traje 8
suitcase la maleta 9
summarize resumir
summary el resumen; el sumario
summer el verano 1
sunbathe tomar el sol
Sunday el domingo
sunglasses los lentes de sol 7
sunny, it's (very) hace (mucho) sol 7
super chévere; guay (*Spain*)
superstore el hipermercado
supernatural sobrenatural
supervision la supervisión

supervisor el/la supervisor/a 11
support apoyar 15; mantener (ie) 15; respaldar; el apoyo
supporter el/la partidario/a
sure seguro/a 2
surely seguramente
surf surfear 7
surfboard la tabla
surname el apellido
surprise la sorpresa; sorprender(se)
surprised maravillado/a
surprising sorprendente
surround rodear
surrounded rodeado/a
survey la encuesta; sondear 13
survival la sobrevivencia
survival of the fittest la ley del más fuerte
survive sobrevivir
suspend suspender
suspenseful suspensivo/a
suspicion la sospecha
sustainable sostenible 12
sweat el sudor
sweater el suéter 8
sweatshirt la sudadera 8
sweets los dulces 10
swim nadar 7
swim goggles los lentes de natación 7
swimming la natación 7
swimming pool la piscina 7
swimsuit el traje de baño 7
swine flu la gripe porcina
symbolize simbolizar
sympathize simpatizar
sympathizer el/la simpatizante
symphony la sinfonía 14
symphony orchestra la orquesta sinfónica 14
symptom el síntoma 10
synthesis la síntesis
synthetic sintético/a
systems de sistemas 11

T

table la mesa 1, 5; la tabla
tablespoon la cucharada

tablet la tableta 1, 12
tachograph el tacógrafo
tactic la táctica
take llevar; sacar; tomar 2; **take (time)** tardar
take a bath bañarse 5
take a cruise hacer un crucero 9
take advantage aprovechar
take a shower ducharse 5
take a tour hacer una gira 9
take a walk dar un paseo 7; pasear 4
take blood pressure tomar la tensión (*Spain*); tomar la presión (*Latin America*) 10
take care (of oneself) cuidar(se) 10
take hold apoderarse
take off sacar; **take off (airplane)** despegar 9; **take off (clothing)** quitarse 5
take on encargar
take temperature tomar la temperatura 10
take out (the garbage) sacar (la basura) 5
Take out your homework. Saca (Saquen) la tarea. 1
take pictures sacar fotos 9
take responsibility encargarse
take turns turnarse
talcum powder el talco 8
talented talentoso/a 14
talk hablar 2
tall alto/a 2
tall rubber boot la bota pantanera
tambourine la pandereta
tank el tanque
tank top la camiseta sin mangas 8
target group el grupo meta
task la tarea
taste el gusto
tasting menu el menú de degustación
tasty sabroso/a 6
taxes los impuestos 15
taxi driver el/la taxista

tea el té 6
teach enseñar 2
teacher el/la maestro/a
teaching la docencia; la pedagogía 3
team el equipo 7
tear la lágrima
tear cartilage romperse un cartílago
tear a ligament romperse un ligamento
tear a muscle desgarrarse un músculo
teary lloroso/a
teaspoon la cucharadita
technique la técnica
technological tecnológico/a
technology la tecnología
teeth los dientes 5
television la tele; la televisión 13
television viewer el/la televidente 13
tell decir (i); **tell (each other)** contarse (ue)
tell (a story) contar (ue)
Tell him/her. Dile.
temperate templado/a
temperature la temperatura 10
temple el templo
temporary temporal
temptation la tentación
tend to tender (ie) a
tennis el tenis 7
tennis court la cancha de tenis 3
tennis player el/la tenista
tense tenso/a
tension la presión
tenth décimo/a
term el término 11
terrace la terraza
terrain el terreno
terrestrial terrestre
terrific estupendo/a
terrorism el terrorismo 15
test la prueba
thank agradecer (zc)
Thank goodness. Menos mal.
Thank you. Gracias. 1

Thanks, but I can't . . . Gracias, pero no puedo... 4

Thanksgiving Day el Día de Acción de Gracias

that ese/a; eso; que 15

that (over there) aquel/ aquella; aquello

that one ese/a

that one (over there) aquel/aquella

that's why por eso 7

that which lo que

the el; la; los; las

theater el teatro 3, 13

their suyo/a(s)

theme el tema

then entonces 7

theory la teoría

there allí; allá

therefore por eso

there is/are hay 1; **there was/were** hubo

There once was . . . Había una vez...

thermal termal

these estos/as

these ones estos/as

they ellos/as

They fit fine/small/large. Me quedan bien/ estrechos(as)/grandes. 8

thin delgado/a

thing la cosa

think (about) pensar (ie) (en) 4

third tercer/o/a

thirst la sed

thirsty, to be tener (ie) sed

this este/a

this one este/a

this time esta vez

thistle el cardo

those esos/as

those (over there) aquellos/as

thought el pensamiento

threat la amenaza 12

throat la garganta 10

through mediante; por

throw arrojar; **throw (in)** echar 6; **throw (away/ out)** tirar 12

thrust clavar

thump golpear

Thursday el jueves

ticket el boleto 9; la entrada 4; el pasaje 9

tickle hacerle cosquillas (a)

tide la marea

tie la corbata 8

tie (the score) empatar

tight (clothing) estrecho/a

tiled enlozado/a

time el tiempo; la vez 5

timid tímido/a

tip (monetary) la propina 6

tire aburrir 6; cansar

tired cansado/a 2

title el título 1; titular

to begin para empezar

toad el sapo

toast tostar (ue) 6

toaster la tostadora 6

today hoy 1

toe el dedo del pie 10

together juntos/as

tomato el tomate 6

tomb la tumba

tombstone la lápida

tomorrow la mañana 1

tongue la lengua 10

too también

too (much) demasiado

tool la herramienta

toothbrush el cepillo de dientes 5, 8

toothpaste la pasta de dientes 8

top it all, to para colmo

topic el tema 15

topography la topografía

tortoise, giant el galápago

torture torturar; la tortura

touch tocar

tour ir de excursión 9; recorrer 9; la gira 9

tour guide el/la guía 9

tourism el turismo

tourist el/la turista

tourist attractions las attraciones turísticas 9

tourist office la oficina de turismo 9

touristy turístico/a 9

tournament el torneo 7

toward hacia; rumbo a

towel la toalla 7

town el pueblo

town square la plaza central 9

trace la huella

track and field el atletismo 7

trade comerciar; el oficio

tradition la tradición

traffic el tráfico; traficar

tragedy la tragedia 13

train el tren 9; entrenar(se) 6

trainer el/la entrenador/a 7

training el entrenamiento 11

trajectory la trayectoria

tranquilizer el calmante 10

transfer transferir (ie, i)

transform transformar

transition la transición

translate traducir (zc)

transmit transmitir

transport transportar

transportation el transporte

trap atrapar

travel viajar 2, 9

travel agency la agencia de viajes 9

travel agent el/la agente de viajes

travel around recorrer 9

travel package el paquete de viaje 9

travel through/across recorrer 9

traveler el/la viajero/a 9

traveling salesperson el/la viajante

treasure el tesoro

treatment el tratamiento 10

treaty el tratado 15

tree el árbol

trek la caminata

tremendous tremendo/a

trial la prueba

tribe la tribu

trip el recorrido; el viaje

triumph el triunfo

trombone el trombón 14

truck el camión

true cierto/a; verdadero/a

truly verdaderamente

trumpet la trompeta 14

trust la confianza; confiar

trust fund el fondo fiduciario

truth la verdad

try tratar

try (on) probar(se) (ue) 8

t-shirt la camiseta 8

Tuesday el martes

tuition la matrícula

tulle el tul 14

turkey el pavo 6

turn dar la vuelta; el turno

turn in entregar

turn off apagar 12

turn on encender (ie) 12

turn over dar vuelta

turnover la empanada (la empanadilla)

turtle la tortuga

tuxedo el esmoquin 14

tweet el tuit 12; tuitear 12

twin el/la gemelo/a

twist torcer(se) (ue) 10

type el tipo 15

typical típico/a

U

ugly feo/a 2

uhh . . . este...

ulcer la úlcera

umbrella la sombrilla 7

UN la ONU

unbearable insoportable

uncle el tío 4

uncomfortable incómodo/a

uncommon raro/a

under debajo (de)

underemployment el subempleo

underscore subrayar 5

understand comprender 2; entender (ie) 4

unemployment el desempleo 11, 15; el paro (*Spain*)

unexpected inesperado/a

unfinished inacabado/a

unforgettable inolvidable

unfortunately desgraciadamente

uniform el uniforme

uninstall desinstalar **12**
unintentionally sin querer
union el sindicato
unionize sindicalizar
unique único/a
United Nations las Naciones Unidas
United States EE. UU.
unity la unidad
university la universidad **1**
unknown desconocido/a; incógnito/a
unleavened ácimo/a
unless a menos (de) que
unmarried soltero/a **4**
unnecessary innecesario/a
until hasta; hasta que
unusual insólito/a
update (a program) actualizar (un programa) **12**
upload subir **12**
uppercase mayúscula
urge instar
urgent urgente
urinate orinar
us nos
use usar; utilizar
useful útil; valioso/a
using usando
usually usualmente
utensil el utensilio

V

vacancy la vacante **11**
vacate desocupar
vacation las vacaciones
vaccine la vacuna
vacuum pasar la aspiradora **5**
vacuum cleaner la aspiradora **5**
valley el valle **9**
value el valor
van el camión; la camioneta; la furgoneta
vanilla la vainilla **6**
variety la variedad
various varios/as
vary variar
VCR la videograbadora
vegetable la legumbre
vegetables las verduras **6**

vegetarian vegetariano/a; el/la vegetariano/a
velvet el terciopelo **14**
Venezuelan venezolano/a **2**
Venezuelan currency el bolívar
verify verificar
versatile versátil
version la versión
very muy **1**; sumamente
Very truly yours . . . Lo(s)/La(s) saluda atentamente...
veteran el/la veterano/a
veterinarian el/la veterinario/a **11**
veterinary science la veterinaria
viceroyalty el virreinato
victim la víctima
video camera la cámara de video
videoconference la videoconferencia **12**
videogames los videojuegos **7**
view la vista **9**
vigorous vigoroso/a
vinegar el vinagre **6**
vineyard la viña
viola la viola
violate violar **15**
violence la violencia
violent violento/a
violin el violín **14**
visa el visado (*Spain*); la visa
visit la visita; visitar **2**
visitor el/la visitante
vitamin la vitamina **10**
voice la voz **14**
volcano el volcán **9**
volleyball el voleibol **7**
voluntary voluntario/a
volunteer el/la voluntario/a
voluptuous voluptuoso/a
vote el voto
vote (for) votar (por) **15**
voter el/la votante

W

wage el sueldo **11**

wait (for) esperar **9**
waiter/waitress el/la camarero/a; el/la mesero/a **6**
waiting room la sala de espera **9**
wake up despertarse (ie) **5**
walk caminar **2**; ir a pie; el paseo **7**
walking ambulante
walking path la senda peatonal
wall la muralla; el muro
wallet la billetera **8**
want querer (ie) **4**; **want to** tener (ie) ganas de
war la guerra **15**
warm-up el calentamiento
warn advertir (ie, i)
warrior el/la guerrero/a
wash lavar **5**; **wash oneself** lavarse **5**
wash clothes lavar la ropa **5**
wash dishes lavar los platos **5**
washing machine la lavadora **5**
waste los desechos **12**; desperdiciar
watch el reloj **1**; mirar **2**; vigilar
watch (television/a movie) ver (la televisión/una película) **2**
watch one's figure guardar la línea **10**
Watch out! ¡Ojo!
water el agua (*fem.*) **6**
waterfall el salto de agua **9**; la catarata **9**
waterski esquiar en el agua **7**
waterway la vía de agua
wave la ola
way la manera; el modo **14**; la vía
we nosotros/as
we go vamos
weak débil
wealth la riqueza
weapon el arma (*fem.*)
wear llevar **8**
wear a shoe size calzar **8**

weather el tiempo
weatherman/woman el/la meteorólogo/a
weave tejer
weaving el tejido
web page la página web **12**
website el sitio web **12**
wedding la boda
Wednesday el miércoles
week la semana
weekend el fin de semana **3**
weight el peso **10**
weights las pesas
welcome la bienvenida
well bien **1**; **well . . .** bueno...; pues
well-being el bienestar
well, look pues, mira
well done bien hecho/a
well made bien hecho/a **14**
we're going vamos
what lo que
What . . . ? ¿Cómo...? **2**; ¿Qué...? **2**; ¿Cuál...?
What are they like in . . . ? ¿Cómo son en …?
What color is it? ¿De qué color es? **1**
What do people do in . . . ? ¿Qué se hace en…?
What do you do when . . . ? ¿Qué haces cuando...?
What do you feel like (eating)? ¿Qué te apetece (comer)? **6**
What do you know? ¿Qué sabes?
What do you like do? ¿Qué te gusta hacer? **2**
What do you do (are you doing)? ¿Qué haces? **2**
What does . . . mean? ¿Qué significa...? **1**
What if . . . ? ¿Qué tal si? **7**
What is it? ¿Qué es?
what happened lo que pasó
What luck! ¡Qué suerte! **2**
What nonsense! ¡Qué barbaridad!
What is the weather like? ¿Qué tiempo hace? **7**

what people will say el qué dirán
What size do you wear? ¿Qué talla usa? **8**
What size shoe do you wear? ¿Qué número calza? **8**
What's happening? ¿Qué pasa? **1**
What students! ¡Qué estudiantes!
What's up? ¿Qué onda?; ¿Qué pasa? **1**; ¿Qué tal? **1**; (*Venezuela*) ¿Qué húbole?
What's your name? (*for.*) ¿Cómo se llama usted? **1**; (*inf.*) ¿Cómo te llamas (tú)? **1**
What time is it? ¿Qué hora es?
whatever you hear oyeres
whatever you see vieres
wheel la rueda
when cuando
When . . . ? ¿Cuándo...? **2**
When is it? ¿Cuándo es? **3**
Where . . . ? ¿Dónde...? **2**; **From where . . . ?** ¿De dónde...? **2**; **To where . . . ?** ¿Adónde...? **2**
Where is it? ¿Dónde está? **3**
Which (one/ones) . . . ? ¿Cuál/Cuáles...? **2**
while el rato; mientras
while reading al leer
while viewing and listening para ver y escuchar
while writing al escribir
whirlwind el remolino
white blanco/a **1**

who que; quien
Who . . . ? ¿Quién(es)...? **2**
Who am I? ¿Quién soy yo?
Who is it? ¿Quién es?
whom que; quien
whose cuyo/a(s)
Whose . . . ? ¿De quién(es)...? **2**
Why . . . ? ¿Por qué...? **2**
wide amplio/a; ancho/a
widow/widower el/la viudo/a
wife la esposa **4**
wild salvaje
wild pig el jabalí
will la voluntad
willing dispuesto/a
win ganar **7**
winner el/la ganador/a
wind el viento **7**
window la ventana; la ventanilla (*airplane*) **9**
windy, it's (very) hace (mucho) viento **7**
wine (red/white) el vino (tinto/blanco) **6**
winner el/la campeón/ campeona **7**; el/la ganador/a **7**
winter el invierno **1**
winter cap el gorro
wireless inalámbrico/a **12**
wish desear **2**; el deseo
with con
with affection con cariño
within dentro de
with me conmigo **4**
without sin (que)
without a doubt sin duda
without warning inesperado
with you contigo **4**

witness el/la testigo; presenciar
wizard el mago
wolf el lobo
woman la mujer **1**
wonderful magnífico/a
wood la madera; **wood pulp** la pulpa
wool la lana **8, 14**
word la palabra
work el trabajo **11**; **work (of art)** la obra (de arte); funcionar **12**; trabajar **2**; **work-related** laboral
work (on commission) trabajar (a comisión)
worker el/la obrero/a **11**; el/la trabajador/a
workshop el taller
world el mundo **12**; mundial **15**
World Heritage Site el Patrimonio de la Humanidad
worldview la cosmovisión
worldwide mundialmente
worn out gastado/a
worried preocupado/a **2**
worry preocuparse
worse peor **5**
Would you like (+ *inf.*) . . . ? ¿Te gustaría (+ *inf.*)...? **4**
Would you like something to drink/ eat? ¿Desea(n) algo de tomar/comer? **6**
Wow! ¡Órale! (*Mexico*)
wrapped envuelto/a
wrestler el/la luchador/a
wrestling la lucha libre
wretch la piltrafa
wristwatch el reloj de pulsera **8**

write escribir **2**
write down anotar
writer el/la escritor/a
wrong address la dirección equivocada

X
X-ray la radiografía **10**

Y
yank out arrancar
yard el patio **5**
year el año
yearly anualmente
yearly bonus la bonificación anual **11**
yell gritar
yellow amarillo/a **1**
Yes, of course. Sí, claro. **4**
yesterday ayer
yogurt el yogur **6**
you tú (*inf.*); usted/es (*for.*); vosotros/as (*inf. pl. Spain*); **with you** contigo **4**
You like . . . Te gusta/n... **2**
you put . . . pones... **4**
young joven **2**
young person el/la joven
younger menor **4, 5**
You're welcome. De nada. **1**
your/s su/s (*for.*); suyo/a(s) (*for.*); tu/tus (*inf.*); tuyo/a(s) (*inf.*); vuestro/a(s) (*inf. pl. Spain*)
youth el/la joven; la juventud

Z
zoo el zoológico

Credits

Text Credits

p. 279: Alegría, Ciro. *Fábulas y leyendas americanas*. Espasa-Calpe: Madrid, 1982. Print.

p. 469: Courtesy Eduardo Galeano, en *Patas arriba*, Ediciones Akal S.A. (XXI CENTURY EDITORS SPAIN). Print.

p. 476: "Óscar Arias Sánchez - Only Peace Can Write the New History". Nobelprize.org. Nobel Media AB 2014. Web. 23 Oct 2017. http://www.nobelprize.org/nobel_prizes/peace/laureates/1987/arias-lecture-sp.html

p. 479: El Banco Mundial. Mission Statement. World Bank/UNESCO. May 10, 2012.

pp. 492–494: Jiménez, Francisco. *Más allá de mí*. Graphia: New York, 2009.

Photo Credits

Photos in the **Club cultura** sections are stills from the *Club cultura* video to accompany *¡Arriba!, Comunicación y cultura*, 7th edition © 2019.

Cover (Full): Anna Gorin/Getty Images; **Cover (Brief):** Anna Gorin/Getty Images; **p. EP1:** rawpixel/123RF; **p. 9:** Susan M. Bacon; **p. 10:** Susan M. Bacon; **p. 11, R:** Mayabuns/Shutterstock; **p. 11, BL:** Susan M. Bacon; **p. 13:** sassenfeld/Fotolia; **p. 14, T:** Bettman/Getty Images; **p. 14, B:** Bettman/Getty Images; **p. 16:** Chris Clinton/Getty Images; **p. 17:** Steven Lawton/Getty Images; **p. 21:** Susan M. Bacon; **p. 23:** AGCuesta/Fotolia; **p. 24:** Jupiter Images/Getty Images; **p. 27:** Susan M. Bacon; **p. 29:** ocon10/Fotolia; **p. 32, TL:** Mik Man/Fotolia; **p. 32, ML:** pytyczech/123RF; **p. 32, MR:** Tifonimages/Fotolia; **p. 32, BL:** Richard Cummins/Getty Images; **p. 32, BR:** Danita Delimont/Alamy; **p. 34:** Susan M. Bacon; **p. 35:** Susan M. Bacon; **p. 36:** Hero Images Inc./Alamy; **p. 38:** ImageZebra/Fotolia; **p. 42:** Graficart.net/Alamy; **p. 43, L:** Rune Hellestad/Getty Images; **p. 43, M:** Frederick M. Brown/Getty Images; **p. 43, R:** Ed Zurga/Getty Images; **p. 44:** *Club cultura*/Pearson; **p. 46, T:** Judy Eddy/Newscom; **p. 46, B:** Konstantin Kalishko/Alamy; **p. 50:** Shutterstock; **p. 52:** José Jordan/Getty Images; **p. 53:** sedat saatcioglu/Fotolia; **p. 56:** Jupiterimages/Getty Images; **p. 57:** Robert Marquardt/Getty Images; **p. 61:** Santiago Silver/Fotolia; **p. 64:** Susan M. Bacon; **p. 66:** Jean-Pierre Lescourret/Getty Images; **p. 70, TL:** Teresa Esteban/Getty Images; **p. 70, TR:** Scott R Larsen/Getty Images; **p. 70, ML:** Susan M. Bacon; **p. 70, MR:** Andrea Pistolesi/Getty Images; **p. 70, B:** Loza-Koza/Shutterstock; **p. 72, L:** Fresnel6/Fotolia; **p. 72, TR:** face_reader_img/Fotolia; **p. 72, TMR:** natalielb/Fotolia; **p. 72, MR:** ajr_images/Fotolia; **p. 72, BMR:** Andy Dean/Fotolia; **p. 72, BR:** Gino Santa María/Fotolia; **p. 73:** Eduardo Zayas-Bazán; **p. 74:** Carlos Álvarez/Getty Images; **p. 76:** Courtesy the Instituto Nacional de Antropología e Historia; **p. 84:** pkchai/Fotolia; **p. 87:** JC Olivera/Getty Images; **p. 88:** Taylor Hill/Getty Images; **p. 90:** Stephen Coburn/Fotolia; **p. 91:** Alberto E. Tamargo/Newscom; **p. 96:** Associated Press; **p. 98:** Jeremy Woodhouse/Holly Wilmeth/Getty Images; **p. 99:** Peter Macdiarmid/Staff/Getty Images; **p. 100:** Tec de Monterrey; **p. 102, M:** Susan M. Bacon; **p. 102, TL:** Susan M. Bacon; **p. 102, TR:** Susan M. Bacon; **p. 102: BL:** Aneese/Fotolia; **p. 102, BR:** Ben Pipe/Alamy; **p. 104, L:** David R. Frazier Photolibrary, Inc.; **p. 104, M:** Erich Lessing/Art Resource, NY; **p. 104, R:** Susan M. Bacon; **p. 105:** Deposit Photos/Glow Images; **p. 108:** Courtesy Fernando Llort; **p. 112:** Joana Lopes/123RF; **p. 116, T:** JOHAN ORDÓÑEZ/Getty Images; **p. 117:** Image Source/Getty Images; **p. 118:** WavebreakMediaMicro/Fotolia; **p. 121:** John Crux Photography/Getty Images; **p. 122, T:** Susan M. Bacon; **p. 122, B:** Paulo Alfonso/Shutterstock; **p. 124:** Jack Hollingsworth/Getty Images; **p. 125:** Courtesy of Glenn Flores;

Index

Mar Caribe

OCÉANO
ATLÁNTICO

Barranquilla
Cartagena
Maracaibo
Caracas
Barquisimeto
VENEZUELA
Georgetown
Paramaribo
Medellín
Río Orinoco
GUYANA
Cayenne
Manizales
Salto
Ángel
SURINAM
GUAYANA
FRANCESA
(Francia)
Bogotá
COLOMBIA
Cali
Quito
ECUADOR
Ecuador
Guayaquil
Cuenca
Iquitos
Manaus
Río Amazonas
Belém
*Islas
Galápagos
(Ec.)*
Fortaleza
Cajamarca
Río Madeira
Trujillo
Río Branco
B R A S I L
Recife
PERÚ
Machu
Picchu
Lima
Ayacucho
Cuzco
BOLIVIA
Lago
Titicaca
La Paz
Salvador
Brasília
Arequipa
Cochabamba
Santa Cruz
Arica
Sucre
Belo
Horizonte
Iquique
Potosí
PARAGUAY
Antofagasta
São Paulo
Río de Janeiro
Trópico de Capricornio
Salta
Asunción
Santos
Salto
Iguazú
CHILE
San Miguel
de Tucumán
ARGENTINA
Pòrto Alegre
Coquimbo
Córdoba
Rivera
Río Paraná
Río Uruguay
Valparaíso
Rosario
URUGUAY
Santiago
Mendoza
Buenos Aires
La Plata
Montevideo
OCÉANO
ATLÁNTICO
Concepción
Bahía Blanca
Río de la Plata

Puerto Montt

OCÉANO
PACÍFICO

Estrecho de
Magallanes
*Islas
Malvinas
(G.B.)*
Punta Arenas
TIERRA DEL FUEGO
Cabo de Hornos

Desierto de Atacama

CORDILLERA DE LOS ANDES

CORDILLERA DE LOS ANDES

OCÉANO
PACÍFICO

I. Pinta
I. Fernandina ▲ *I. Marchena*
I. San Salvador
Santa Cruz
I. Isabela ▲ *I. Santa Cruz*
Puerto
Ayora *I. San
Cristóbal*
Puerto
Villamil
Puerto
Baquerizo
Moreno

**ISLAS GALÁPAGOS
(ECUADOR)**

OCÉANO
PACÍFICO

Cabo Norte
*Volcán
Katiki*
Hanga Roa ▲ *Cabo
Cumming*
Mataveri

**ISLA DE PASCUA
(CHILE)**

⊛ Capital
• Otra ciudad
▲ Volcán
♣ Ruinas

América del Sur